THE POEMS OF

WILLIAM COWPER

THE POEMS OF
William Cowper

Volume I: 1748 – 1782

∿vol. II to be pub.

EDITED BY

JOHN D. BAIRD

AND

CHARLES RYSKAMP

OXFORD

AT THE CLARENDON PRESS

1980

Oxford University Press, Walton Street, Oxford OX2 6DP

OXFORD LONDON GLASGOW
NEW YORK TORONTO MELBOURNE WELLINGTON
KUALA LUMPUR SINGAPORE HONG KONG TOKYO
DELHI BOMBAY CALCUTTA MADRAS KARACHI
NAIROBI DAR ES SALAAM CAPE TOWN

Published in the United States by
Oxford University Press, New York

© *Oxford University Press 1980*

British Library Cataloguing in Publication Data
Cowper, William
  The poems of William Cowper
  Vol. 1: 1748–1782. – (Oxford English texts)
  I. Title II. Baird, John D
  III. Ryskamp, Charles
  821'.6   PR3380   78–40749
  ISBN 0–19–811875–9

Printed in Great Britain
at the University Press, Oxford
by Eric Buckley
Printer to the University

ACKNOWLEDGEMENTS

This edition of Cowper's poetry stands in place of that which the late Kenneth Povey undertook nearly twenty years ago and did not live to complete. At the time of his sudden death, in 1965, he was the doyen of Cowperian scholars. In a long series of learned articles he had unravelled tangled issues in the biography of the poet; he had been the friend and adviser of younger scholars; his edition would have been the culmination of many years of distinguished study. The present editors hoped at first to present what he had done as he had left it. This has not been possible: recent discoveries of manuscripts and other materials have made a fresh start necessary. Nevertheless, his notes have been a constant source of assistance; in particular, his meticulous bibliographical investigations have been unfailingly helpful. With respect and gratitude, this edition is dedicated to his memory.

Special mention must be made of the *Bibliography of William Cowper to 1837* by Norma Russell (now Lady Dalrymple-Champneys). Her devoted work of scholarship has shortened our labours by many years.

Professor James King of McMaster University, who is editing Cowper's letters, has frequently assisted us with information and encouragement.

The editors are grateful to those who have permitted them to study and to publish from manuscripts in their possession: the Misses C. and A. Cowper Johnson; Miss C. M. Bull; the Marquess of Salisbury; Mr. Arthur A. Houghton, Jr.; Mr. Robert H. Taylor; Sir Robert Throckmorton, Bt.; the British Library; the William Andrews Clark Library; the Cowper and Newton Museum; the Fitzwilliam Museum; the Harvard University Library; the Henry E. Huntington Library; the Pierpont Morgan Library; the Berg Collection, New York Public Library; the Princeton University Library; the John Rylands Library; the Victoria and Albert Museum.

This volume has been prepared almost entirely in the Princeton University Library, not only the home of the Hannay and Povey Collections of William Cowper but also the hospitable environment of every kind of literary research. Thanks are due as well to the E. J. Pratt Library of Victoria University, Toronto, and to the John P.

Robarts Research Library and Thomas Fisher Rare Book Library of the University of Toronto.

John Baird has been assisted by two research grants and a leave fellowship from the Canada Council. A generous research fellowship from the American Council of Learned Societies made possible the completion of this volume.

For advice and help of various kinds we wish to thank: Professor J. R. deJ. Jackson; Mr. Verlyn Klinkenborg; Professor A. Walton Litz; Professor James McCaughey; Professor Michael Millgate; Dr. Stephen Parks; Professor James H. Tatum; Professor Richard Wendorf.

Finally, we must mention what we cannot adequately express, our gratitude to Eileen Coumont Baird, wife, friend, and fellow scholar. She has contributed more than she knows, more than we can guess.

JOHN D. BAIRD
CHARLES RYSKAMP

CONTENTS

CONTENTS

COWPER AND HIS POETRY
1731–1782

WILLIAM COWPER was born on 15 November 1731 O.S., the eldest son to survive of the Revd. John Cowper, rector of Berkhamsted. His family, staunch Whigs, had been associated for generations with politics and the law, as well as the Church; his grandfather, Spencer Cowper, was a puisne Justice of the Common Pleas, and his great-uncle, William, first Earl Cowper, had been twice Lord Chancellor. His mother, Ann Cowper, likewise belonged to an ancient and honourable family, the Donnes of Norfolk, although she was not, as her son William liked to fancy her, a descendant of the great poet and Dean of St. Paul's. She died in 1737, a few days after giving birth to another son, John. Of her seven children, only these two boys lived beyond infancy. The loss of his mother made a deep impression on William, as his heartfelt lines on being given her portrait more than half a century later abundantly testify, but he seems generally to have had a happy childhood. Certainly he returned regularly to the rectory until his father died in 1756, and it was in the quiet Berkshire countryside that he learned to love the world of nature.

William was educated first by a neighbouring clergyman in the village of Aldbury, then at the establishment of the Revd. William Pittman in Markyate Street, Bedfordshire. When he was about eight, he suffered from 'specks' on his eyes (their precise nature remains obscure), and was domiciled for two years with a Mrs. Disney, an eminent oculist. At the age of 10, in April 1742, he entered Westminster School, where he was to spend the best part of the next six years. It was a natural choice; his father, his father's father, one of his uncles, and two of his cousins had preceded him there.

Westminster School stands in the shadow of Westminster Abbey, a stone's throw from the Houses of Parliament, and a few minutes' walk from Westminster Hall, where in the eighteenth century the Law Courts sat. Its situation symbolizes its importance at that period, as a first step on the way to eminence in the Church, government, or the law. Many of the boys contemporary with Cowper made their mark in later life; for example: Warren Hastings; Frederick Hervey,

Bishop of Cloyne and of Derry and fourth Earl of Bristol; the Honourable Thomas Harley, Lord Mayor of London; George Hobart, third Earl of Buckinghamshire and Ambassador to St. Petersburg. These are but four who happen to fall under the letter H, but they indicate the scope of Westminster's importance in the public life of that time. Their education was of course exclusively classical and literary. It was also thoroughly traditional, for it still followed the lines laid down by Renaissance taste. Cowper, like most of his contemporaries, had learned the elements of Latin from Lyly's grammar, for two centuries the standard introduction. The curriculum would have been familiar enough to a Westminster boy of Queen Elizabeth's time. German scholarship had not yet proclaimed a scientific philology, nor had the Arnoldian quest for a higher truth and a higher seriousness yet changed the direction of literary studies. Instead, there was considerable emphasis on composition, especially in Latin; the teachers tried to impart a sound knowledge of grammar, and especially of prosody; the epigram was a literary form in good repute; and the boys, labouring to render English verse into elegiac couplets, were urged to take as their model the frivolous Ovid. Narrow and impractical as this programme might appear, it was understood and appreciated in Cowper's day. His fifth-form master, Vincent Bourne (1695–1747), had been offered preferment in the Church on the strength of his *Poematia* (1734, enlarged in 1743 and later editions), a collection of Latin versions of familiar English poems, together with original Latin verses notable for gentle wit and a delight in living creatures—qualities which endeared them so lastingly to Cowper.

Cowper's first composition, now lost, was a translation of one of the elegies of Tibullus which he made at the age of 14. Westminster had equipped him and no doubt encouraged him to translate a Latin poet, but his choice of Tibullus, poet of the Italian countryside, reflects his own enduring joy in the natural world. 'No bard could please me but whose lyre was tuned / To Nature's praises', he wrote, many years later, in *The Task*, describing his youthful reading; his own earliest poetry, 'the first-born efforts of my youthful muse', he describes with one epithet, 'rural'. The same passage (IV. 691–730) names three poets who appealed to this passion: Virgil in his pastoral poetry; Milton, whose excellence first struck the young Cowper at the age of 14; and Cowley, himself once a Westminster boy, in retirement in his garden at Chertsey. Looking back over nearly forty years, Cowper speaks of himself as having been reclaimed from the 'erroneous taste' which led him to admire Cowley, but this redemption seems to have taken place some time after his schooldays were over. Cowley's influence is plain in the surviving verse of his late adolescence.

Cowper's juvenile verses have all been lost. As it happens, the earliest work of his which has come down to us was written at Bath in 1748, no doubt during the interval of several months between his leaving Westminster School and beginning the world in earnest.

THE EARLY POETRY, 1748–1763

Cowper's family destined him for the law; since he was a gentleman, for a barrister. It was then the custom to place a would-be barrister as a clerk in the office of an attorney or solicitor, where he could learn the essentials of litigation and the distinctions between law and equity. Cowper was placed in the office of a Mr. Chapman, an attorney and solicitor of some reputation, and lived for three years in Chapman's house in Greville Street, Holborn. Another such pupil in the office was Edward Thurlow (1732–1806), recently sent down from Caius College, Cambridge, for insolence, a quality which was to distinguish his later long tenure as Lord Chancellor. Whatever Cowper may have gained in legal acumen in Chapman's office was offset by the distaste for his profession which he acquired there. Lady Hesketh recalled that 'the Tricks and illiberal Conduct of his fellow Clerks did I doubt not give him a disgust to the whole business, which did not leave him, even when placed (where he shou'd have been at *first*) at the Temple'.[1] Cowper had been admitted to the Honourable Society of the Middle Temple on 29 April 1748, but he did not secure chambers there until November 1753. Having been a member of the Society for the requisite length of time, and having evaded the assigned legal exercises by payment of fines, Cowper was called to the bar in June 1754. In November 1757 he migrated to the more fashionable Inner Temple. His legal studies seem to have been at best fitful, his attention to business wavering. It is doubtful whether he ever made very much money by practising law, except his income as a Commissioner of Bankrupts (appointed 1759), and that was only £60 a year. By the early 1760s he had spent most of his patrimony and was approaching the end of his means.

The uncongenial atmosphere of Mr. Chapman's office was probably rendered the more oppressive by loneliness. Many of Cowper's

[1] Lady Hesketh to William Hayley, 1 July 1801 (B.L. Add. MS. 30803A, fo. 142).

friends had gone up to the universities. Some of his letters to one of these, Chase Price (1731–77), who had moved on to Christ Church, Oxford, have survived, as has Price's Commonplace Book. Poetry was often an ingredient of these letters, and Price copied a good deal of his friend's verse into his Commonplace Book. These poems show Cowper in 1750 writing in the burlesque mode adumbrated in his 1748 verses on finding a shoe-heel in Bath. Cowley's influence is still apparent. His early songs, written about 1751, are experiments in the vein of another Old Westminster, Matthew Prior. His first attempt at Milton's manner, a paraphrase of Job 14, was written in 1752. During the four years since he had left school, Cowper had trained himself in a variety of styles. His apprenticeship in verse was far from complete, but he had laid the foundations for what was to follow.

Cowper could take refuge from the 'illiberal' aspects of legal life at the near-by home of his uncle, Ashley Cowper (1701–88), holder of a lucrative and powerful sinecure, the Clerkship of the Parliaments. Ashley had three daughters: Harriot (1733–1807), who about 1754 married a wealthy Lancashire landowner, Thomas Hesketh (1727–78), created a baronet in 1761; Theodora (1734?–1824), who never married; Elizabeth Charlotte (d. 1805), who married a baronet, Sir Archer Croft, in 1759. With his cousins at their home in Southampton Row, Cowper later recalled, he was 'constantly employed from Morning to Night in giggling and making giggle instead of studying the Law'.[1]

Then in 1752, apparently while they were both on holiday with relatives of his mother in Norfolk, William fell in love with his cousin Theodora, and she with him. Immediately he began to address poems to her, giving her the name 'Delia' in his verses. The earliest pieces in this series, dating from that summer holiday of 1752, are slight, but cheerful, expressing an absolute confidence in their mutual affection. There follows a group of longer and more substantial poems, written later in 1752 and in 1753, some perhaps as late as 1754, which tell of the pains of temporary separation and the joys of meeting again. But Ashley Cowper would not sanction his daughter's marriage unless William could provide adequately for her—perhaps he hoped for a more glorious match altogether—and Theodora would not marry in defiance of her father's wishes. Finally, in 1755, the two young people were forbidden to meet. The last

---

[1] To Lady Hesketh, 17 Apr. 1786.

poems to Delia express Cowper's misery and his continued, his undying love.

The details of Cowper's life during the next seven years are obscure. His friendships with Thurlow and another young lawyer, a protégé of Ashley Cowper's named Joseph Hill (1733–1811), continued. Hill was the only friend of this period who never lost touch with Cowper throughout the rest of his life. We know that after 1754 Cowper spent a good deal of his time studying Homer, comparing the original to Pope's translation. Only two original poems survive from the years 1755 to 1763, but we should not too readily assume that the break with Theadora stultified his imagination. The poignant lines on the death of his friend Sir William Russell in 1757, and his answer to Mrs. Greville's 'Prayer for Indifference', have been preserved only by accident; much else may have vanished without a trace. We have his own recollection that while he lived in the Temple he 'produced several halfpenny ballads, 2 or three of which had the honor to be popular'.[1] These were ballads on current political events designed to be sung in the streets, strongly Whiggish in sentiment. And Southey saw, though he was not allowed to print, 'a burlesque cantata on Spencer Madan's fiddling', which, since it was composed jointly with Frederick Madan, who was born in 1742, can hardly have been earlier than the late 1750s.

As the decade wore on, a number of Cowper's Westminster friends returned to London from the universities. By 1760 they formed a notable group of young writers. They met as a club, the Nonsense Club, where they sang songs of their own composition and read mock-serious papers to each other. Among the members were George Colman (1732–94), playwright and theatre manager; Bonnell Thornton (1725–68), co-editor with Colman of the *Connoisseur*, 1754–6, to which Cowper contributed some papers; Robert Lloyd (1733–64), son of one of the Westminster masters, who tried and failed to make a living by the pen, and died worn out in the Fleet prison. Associated with them was Charles Churchill (1732–64), who began his brief but notable career as a satirist with the *Rosciad* in 1761. These, with some others of lesser note, were spoken of as 'the Geniuses'.

With the possible exception of one ballad in the Price Commonplace Book, whatever verse Cowper wrote for the amusement of these talented friends has been lost, and apart from the two shorter

[1] To John Newton, 4 Dec. 1781.

pieces mentioned above, the only poetical works of the late 1750s and early 1760s which have come down to us are translations. Joseph Hill told Hayley that Cowper used to undertake such work for friends. His versions of two satires by Horace were published in 1759 by old friends of his father's family, William Duncombe (1690–1769) and his son John (1729–86). Cowper furnished his brother with a translation of four books of Voltaire's *Henriade* for the English Voltaire edited by Tobias Smollett and Thomas Francklin; this was published in 1762.

In 1763 Cowper's career as a barrister with literary and social preoccupations came to an end. He accepted from Ashley Cowper the Clerkship of the Journals in the House of Lords, a position which would have suited his temperament and brought him a respectable income. Unhappily, just at this time his uncle's conduct as Clerk of the Parliaments came under hostile scrutiny by the Lords, and Cowper was required to be examined at the Bar of the House to establish his qualifications. The strain of preparing for that ordeal (he had a lifelong dread of public appearances), together with other personal conflicts which can only be guessed at, proved too much for him. After making several attempts to take his own life, he suffered a complete mental and physical breakdown. In the last days of 1763 he was removed to St. Albans and placed in the care of Dr. Nathaniel Cotton, a well-known physician who specialized in the treatment of lunatics. It was a watershed in his life. When Cowper passed into Dr. Cotton's asylum he left the Temple, the Geniuses, and the smart life of London behind him for ever.

THE OLNEY HYMNS, 1764–1772

In his *Memoir* Cowper records the moment of his conversion, when, in the summer of 1764, he came on Romans 3: 25. 'In a moment I believed, and received the gospel.' That moment shaped the rest of his life. It brought an instant transformation from blackest despair to overwhelming joy; it also confirmed his separation from his former life, and all but a few of his family and friends. For the faith which was granted to him was of the kind known as Evangelical—Calvinistic in its theology, severe in its morality, often bitter in its controversy. And in the 1760s the Evangelicals were very far from being the power in the Church of England they were to become sixty years later. They were few, and without the support of such patrons as

Cowper's former schoolfellow, the second Earl of Dartmouth, they would have had great difficulty in establishing themselves as a recognizable party in the Church of England. Indeed, so rare were clergymen of an evangelical stamp that it was not until Cowper accompanied his cousin Martin Madan on a preaching tour in 1766 that he heard a true 'gospel sermon'. Cowper's letters to Lady Hesketh following his conversion are defensive; those to another cousin, Mrs. Cowper, show him hesitating to correspond with her on religious topics for fear that she might reprobate his views. Cowper's isolation during the next twenty years was largely self-imposed, and in part the consequence of poverty, but it was also a tacit recognition that to many of his former associates in that less tolerant age deliberate adoption of Evangelical Christianity seemed almost a worse lunacy than trying to hang oneself with a pair of garters.

In June 1765, strengthened in his new faith by a further year in the care of the sympathetic Dr. Cotton, Cowper left St. Albans to settle in Huntingdon, chosen as an attractive town within easy riding distance of his brother, a fellow of Corpus Christi College, Cambridge. He brought with him from Dr. Cotton's a servant, Sam Roberts, and a seven-year-old boy, Dick Coleman, whom Cowper had rescued from a drunken father. Both were to remain with him for thirty years. Five months later he gave up housekeeping on his own and became resident in the family of the Revd. Morley Unwin, a retired schoolmaster. From his first meeting with them he found them delightful, especially Mrs. Unwin, who quickly became like a mother to him, although she was only seven years his senior. The Unwins had two children: William (1744–86), who became curate of Comberton, Cambridgeshire, in 1769, and rector of Stock, in Essex, in 1778; and Susanna (1746–1835), who married the Revd. Matthew Powley in 1774.

For the next eighteen months Cowper devoted himself largely to religion, to prayer, theological reading, and to conversation upon 'serious subjects'. Mrs. Unwin, once a lively figure in Huntingdon society, ceased to pay visits and became his constant companion in these studies. The younger Unwins were drawn toward a livelier faith; only their father, a clergyman of the old school, appears to have remained untouched by the efflorescence of piety. There was but little edification, therefore, to be received from his death in July 1767, when he was thrown from his horse. It was decided immediately that Cowper would continue to reside with Mrs. Unwin, and that they would take the opportunity to move to some place where they might enjoy the ministrations of a truly Evangelical divine. By chance, a few days after Morley Unwin died, the Revd. John Newton called on Cowper and Mrs. Unwin on the recommendation of friends. He undertook to help them choose a suitable place. After considering various possibilities, they decided on Newton's own parish of Olney in Buckinghamshire, whither they removed in September 1767. A house known as Orchard Side, fronting on the market square and accessible to the vicarage through the garden at the back, was to be their home for nineteen years.

John Newton (1725–1807), after starting life as a slave-trader, had left the sea and discovered a vocation to the priesthood. In the face of great difficulty he educated himself in theology, and in 1764 found a bishop willing to ordain him despite his evangelical views. He immediately became curate of Olney, under the Earl of Dartmouth's patronage. His force of character, his boldness, and his ready pen quickly made him a leader of the Evangelical party, a position which he retained for more than thirty years. Cowper, so close in faith, so different in nature, became his devoted friend. Newton, for his part, was deeply attached to Cowper, but many have doubted whether he gave adequate consideration to Cowper's sensitivities. He persuaded Cowper, always fearful of public appearances, to take part in large prayer meetings and religious discussions. He urged Cowper to compose hymns for their joint collection. Lady Hesketh, for one, believed that the rigours of his regime were responsible for her cousin's second lapse into insanity; Newton's

unguarded proposal of composing Hymns from ev'ry Text of Scripture they cou'd Collect, did infinite injury to our friend! certain it is that he was well and in health when this idea was started. That he had been well for several years but he pursued the proposed Task with such eagerness and avidity that it heated his brain, Sunk his Spirits and brought on that dreadful depression, which rendered him Miserable during the Space of 7 years!— only imagine a man of his Genius dwelling incessantly on this one Subject! walking for Hours by himself in that great rambling Church at Olney, composing these Hymns! he has told me that the idea never quitted him night or day, but kept him in a *constant fever*; add to that when he left the Church, it was to attend their prayer meetings, and all the enthusiastic conversation which these meetings were sure to occasion.[1]

---

[1] Lady Hesketh to William Hayley, 30 Aug. 1801 (B.L. Add. MS. 30803A, fo. 156).

Though highly coloured, this account probably reflects accurately enough Cowper's perception of his situation in 1771 or 1772. However, it would be an error to suppose that all of his hymns were written under such conditions.

Between the time of his conversion and his relapse into insanity in 1773 Cowper composed hymns to the exclusion of all other forms of verse. This restriction was not so narrow as it may now appear. Johnson, for example, defines 'hymn' as 'an encomiastic song, or song of adoration to some superior being', a definition which covers Cowper's 'Song of Mercy and Judgment' as well as the two hymns written at St. Albans (*Olney Hymns*, nos. 46 and 47). The modern sense of the word 'hymn' may be seriously misleading if it suggests that Cowper composed his hymns primarily for congregational singing in church. To him, a justified sinner, a hymn was in the first place a vivid effusion of the heart, the record of some episode of God's dealings unto salvation with an individual soul. The verses might later serve to edify other souls, who could find therein some echo of their own experience and fresh grounds for praise, but they had come into being to express the feelings of a grateful spirit. This quality in Cowper's hymns was recognized by the Revd. Samuel Greatheed, a friend of the poet's later years; they describe, he wrote, 'both the general tenor of his thoughts and their occasional wanderings, with a force of expression dictated by the liveliness of his feelings'.[1]

Hymns were rarely, if ever, sung in church in Cowper's day. There was a widespread feeling that the word of God alone should be used in public worship, which meant in effect that only the Psalms might be sung. Paradoxically, this did not mean that the Psalms, translated into English prose, were chanted by the congregation, as is now commonly done in Anglican churches. Rather, when the time came for the Psalms in Morning and Evening Prayer, the congregation sang them in one of the metrical versions, most frequently that of Sternhold and Hopkins. The parish clerk gave out the words two lines at a time and led the singing.[2] Chanting, and musical refinements generally, were left to cathedral churches.

The chief public use for Cowper's hymns was at the meetings for prayer and religious instruction held on Tuesday and Sunday

[1] *A Practical Improvement of the Divine Counsel*, Newport Pagnell, 1800, p. 17.
[2] The procedure is clearly illustrated by Richardson in *Pamela*, in the description of the service held in Mr. B's chapel on the Sunday before his wedding.

evenings in a large room in the so-called Great House, a mansion in Olney conveniently close to both vicarage and church.[1] The room could hold 130 people, and the meetings were well attended; 'thronged exceedingly', Newton reported to a friend in January 1772. Here Newton and like-minded parishioners could relinquish the set forms of Anglican worship in favour of more evangelical exercises. Extemporary prayer was offered by lay persons, of whom Cowper was sometimes one; Newton spoke on some passage of scripture, or expounded one of his hymns, as he did on 6 December 1772, and they sang a hymn.[2]

For these, and for other similar gatherings conducted by Newton, Cowper composed hymns which arose not from personal religious experience but from the exigencies of public occasions—most of his contributions to Book II of *Olney Hymns* obviously belong to this second category. But in default of external evidence, most of the hymns resist classification under these heads. Cowper himself has left no account of his collaboration with Newton, and Newton's description of the origin of *Olney Hymns* is couched in general terms:

A desire of promoting the faith and comfort of sincere christians, though the principal, was not the only motive to this undertaking. It was likewise intended as a monument, to perpetuate the remembrance of an intimate and endeared friendship. With this pleasing view I entered upon my part, which would have been smaller than it is, and the book would have appeared much sooner, and in a very different form, if the wise, though mysterious providence of GOD, had not seen fit to cross my wishes. We had not proceeded far upon our proposed plan, before my dear friend was prevented, by a long and affecting indisposition, from affording me any further assistance. My grief and disappointment were great; I hung my harp upon the willows, and for some time thought myself determined to proceed no farther without him. Yet my mind was afterwards led to resume the service.[3]

What the plan was, and when it was proposed, Newton does not specify, and indeed the passage of time may have affected his recollection of it. We should not assume that it is reflected in the arrangement of *Olney Hymns* as published in 1779.

The collection as Newton published it is strikingly deficient in any concession to the singing of hymns. Cowper and Mrs. Unwin, indeed, sang hymns at home,[4] but Newton presumably preferred

[1] See Commentary on *Olney Hymns*, no. 26.
[2] Josiah Bull, *John Newton*, 1868, pp. 179, 183.
[3] *Olney Hymns*, 1779, sig. a.   [4] Cowper to M. F. C. Cowper, 20 Oct. 1766.

to expound them. There is no trace of music in *Olney Hymns*; no tunes, no names of tunes, not even the indications of long metre, short metre, and so on, which appear in contemporary collections and which would help an accompanist to choose a suitable tune. Newton had in mind a manual of evangelical devotion rather than a hymn-book in the modern sense. It was to encourage piety, not hymnody, that his patron John Thornton bought up a thousand copies, half the first edition, for presentation to worthy souls.[1]

The interposition of providence to which Newton refers in his Preface to *Olney Hymns* was, of course, the terrible attack of insanity which seized Cowper in 1773. Its origins are obscure, but it is known that he had been increasingly depressed, and concerned about his religious state, in the later months of 1772. The precipitating factor may well have been the proposal that he should marry Mrs. Unwin. Even while Morley Unwin was alive there had been unpleasant gossip about his wife and his lodger, and it may safely be assumed that the townsfolk of Olney who absented themselves from prayer meetings at the Great House did not lag behind the people of Huntingdon in vile imaginings. In 1772 the prospective marriage of Susanna Unwin to a Yorkshire clergyman—which would deprive Cowper and Mrs. Unwin of whatever respectability her chaperonage could bestow —would provide an occasion for their friends to urge them to marry. Cowper probably felt, or was persuaded to feel, that it was his duty to marry Mrs. Unwin;[2] on the other hand, he had always thought of her as a mother rather than as a potential wife. And he had pledged lifelong fidelity to Theadora. This conflict of moral imperatives at a time when his religious sensibilities were seriously disturbed proved too much for him. Early in the morning of 2 January 1773 Newton and his wife were summoned from the vicarage to Orchard Side to assist Mrs. Unwin in dealing with 'a very alarming turn'. Cowper's second breakdown had begun.

THE RETURN TO POETRY, 1774-1782

Cowper had been depressed in the later months of 1772, and it seems that at first the 'alarming turn' was regarded by Newton and others

---

[1] One of these copies is described by Russell, p. 21.

[2] Twenty years later Hayley gave great offence to Mrs. Unwin by complimenting her on the chastity or rather the hallow'd intemperance of her attachment' (B.L. Add. MS. 30803B, fo. 160).

as an episode in the course of an attack of melancholy which would pass in time. Great as were his afflictions, Cowper himself remained confident that they were sent by God to try him, to temper the steel of his saving faith. Then on 24 January he had the dream which changed everything. A voice spoke the words 'Actum est de te, periisti'—'it is all up with you, you have perished.'[1] This he interpreted to mean that God had cast him away utterly, that his soul was condemned to extinction, that it was God's will that he should make away with himself at the first opportunity. In vain did his friends point out that the elect could not be thus disqualified; Cowper was convinced he was the unique instance of the contrary. He believed he had committed the unforgivable sin, and nothing Newton could say would shake him. His general religious beliefs remained exactly as they had been, but his view of his own relationship to God was transformed. Other people ought still to go to church, and say their prayers; a lively faith still brought with it the confident hope of a glorious salvation to any soul—but his. From that day forth Cowper never entered a church, never attended a prayer meeting, never said a prayer, never so much as said grace at his table, for in God's eyes, so he thought, he had already ceased to exist.

The oblique language of Newton's diary, and the proper reserve of his letters to others, make it difficult to trace the course of Cowper's malady with precision. In April 1773 he was moved to the vicarage so that he would not be disturbed by the annual fair; he was reluctant to leave Orchard Side, but once installed under Newton's roof he stayed for thirteen months. We know he was prescribed for by Dr. Cotton, who, after the manner of the day, did not examine the patient, relying instead on an apothecary's report of a blood sample; but this treatment did little for Cowper. In the autumn of 1773 he attempted to kill himself. In his letter to Lady Hesketh of 16 January 1786 he describes symptoms strikingly reminiscent of those recorded of Virginia Woolf in 1915. Improvement was very slow, and there were many bitter setbacks. But gradually the terrible cloud of melancholia began to lift. The gift of three leverets, later known to the world as Bess, Tiney, and Puss, was one of the earliest interests which diverted him from his gloomy reflections. Gardening, too, could absorb his entire attention. Household carpentry was another helpful avocation, especially the construction of cages for a variety of

[1] Characteristically, the words were recalled from a book Cowper almost certainly studied at Westminster School: Terence, *Eunuchus*, 54-5.

animals and birds. He tried his hand at drawing, under the instruction of a self-taught local sculptor.

After a lapse of more than two years Cowper began to write again to his old friend Joseph Hill. The tone of these letters of the mid-1770s reveals the magnitude of the transformation which the crisis of 1773 had worked in him. Gone, of course, are the solemn professions and the religious language of the late 1760s. Instead, there are references to the garden, to current literature, and current events. Abandoned by God, Cowper was beginning to take an interest in the world again.

The return to poetry was slow, however. After a last despairing glance backward to Theodora, in the lines 'Heu quam remotus vescor ab omnibus', dated 'die ultimo 1774', he seems to have written no verse, except possibly some translations from Horace and Vincent Bourne, for about four years. Then, perhaps as early as 1778, certainly by 1779, he started once more to compose. The first piece which can be dated is the Latin version of Prior's 'Chloe and Euphelia' of 1 May 1779, which may serve as an indicator of the change which had come over Cowper. It is in no sense a personal utterance; it is a translation of a poem which he had carried in his memory for twenty years and more, as he tells Unwin in the letter which contains it. Prior had been one of the models of his youth, and in turning Prior's well-groomed lines into iambic pentameters he was performing a typical Westminster School exercise such as Vincent Bourne would have approved.

As a young man in the Temple Cowper had written political ballads, and now once again a lively interest in politics informs his verse. He celebrates one of Rodney's victories, he takes Keppel's side in the row between Admirals Keppel and Palliser, and then defends Palliser against his detractors; he launches a bitter attack on the Queen of France; he urges Sir Joshua Reynolds to draw a political cartoon. These pieces, like the lines on the Gordon Riots of 1780, evince a sovereign contempt for the French and an estimate of England's prospects that proved more patriotic than prophetic. They mark another reversion to the mood of twenty years before, to the spirit of 1759 and the glorious victories sponsored by the elder Pitt.

Not all of Cowper's poetry in 1779 and early 1780 was political; there are fables, reflective pieces, epigrams, even an account of a labourer who preferred to die rather than blaspheme. These are linked to the political poems, however, by one quality: their topicality. Almost all of them turn out, on examination, to arise out of some recent experience or observation. In general, therefore, Cowper's poetry of this period shows him responding vigorously, often combatively, to his world; both to immediate, personal experience of an everyday sort, and to the vicarious experience offered by the newspapers—politics, war, the atrocities of the London mob.

Verse-writing thus became one of Cowper's favourite occupations. He refers to it frequently in his letters of the early 1780s as an 'amusement'—a term which covers both distraction from the miserable contemplation of his religious terrors, and the proper pastime of a gentleman living in retirement. In his letter to William Unwin of 11 July 1780 he explains that he cannot compose to order; the lines come to him and he sets them down. Once they have been submitted to a friend's judgement he ceases to take any trouble with them. He may here exaggerate his indifference to his own productions (although Lady Hesketh and John Johnson were later to be shocked by his carelessness about his poetical manuscripts), but the passage clearly shows that as late as the summer of 1780 Cowper was far from undertaking any sustained poetical endeavour.

The stimulus which transformed Cowper into a poet came in the first place from a contemporary event involving persons to whom he was attached by ties of blood and friendship. In February of 1780 John Newton, then recently removed to London as rector of St. Mary Woolnoth, informed Cowper that the Revd. Martin Madan was preparing to publish a treatise on female ruin. Madan (1725-90) was Cowper's first cousin, and had shown him great kindness, especially at the time of his breakdown in 1763. Madan was also a notable preacher and a leader of the Evangelical party. As Chaplain of the Lock Hospital, an institution for the medical care of fallen women, he became convinced that the only remedy for the crying evil of prostitution was a return to what he held to be the institution of marriage as divinely appointed and set down in the Pentateuch. Since the consequence would have been a form of polygamy, Newton and other evangelical clergymen tried earnestly to persuade Madan to withhold his book. He refused, and his book, entitled *Thelyphthora*, was published at the end of May 1780. A long and bitter public controversy followed. During the spring and summer of 1780 Cowper produced a sheaf of squibs against his cousin's book. These were intended for private circulation only, but when in November he saw a review by Samuel Badcock which seemed to refute Madan's arguments, he celebrated this victory by writing the narrative *Antithelyphthora*, the longest original poem he had ever composed up to that time. He was emboldened to permit Newton to show it to his publisher, Joseph Johnson, who agreed to publish it anonymously. It appeared within two months of its completion, but the impetus of its composition had already carried Cowper into further and even longer works, 'The Progress of Error' and 'Truth'. In the first of these, as it was originally written, Madan plays a major role as an example of error run riot, but he is by no means the only such character; in the final version his importance is reduced, and he appears as one of a gallery of misguided souls. It matters little that Cowper had not read his cousin's book (he got through the second volume a few months later, but never attempted the first); the idea of a clergyman recommending polygamy was potent enough; Madan's relationship to Cowper, and the memory of many past kindnesses no doubt added to his symbolic power in Cowper's imagination. He and his book are long forgotten, but they have their memorial; without them, Cowper might have remained merely a gentleman dabbling in verse.

Scarcely had a fair copy of *Antithelyphthora* been dispatched to Newton when Cowper embarked upon a further assault on his cousin. This poem was longer, discursive rather than narrative, the first of the so-called 'moral satires'. Its title, 'The Progress of Error', has sometimes been misunderstood. Cowper's original intention, perhaps somewhat obscured by his later revisions, was to exhibit various current forms of error, especially among those (like Madan) who owe the world a better example; the 'progress' of error is its spreading through society. Before the end of December 1780, Cowper had begun another long poem. Its title, 'Truth', should be understood to mean 'religious truth'. It sets forth in many examples the contrast of error and truth; indifference or hostility to what Newton, in his Preface to the 1782 *Poems*, calls 'experimental religion' is shown as the way that leads to hell. Indeed, Cowper was later moved to request the preface from Newton precisely by his fear that this poem offered so plain a presentment of the evangelical creed that only a soothing foreword would render it acceptable to the worldly reader. 'Truth' was completed on or soon after 21 January 1781, and its author turned immediately to a new subject.

Having set out in 'The Progress of Error' and in 'Truth' the negative and positive poles of his moral universe, Cowper went on to compose a third of these 'moral satires', named 'Table Talk'. This he designed to stand as an introduction to its predecessors, and in so doing marked a slight but significant change of direction. In November 1780 he had written essentially for his own satisfaction; early in February 1781 we find him in his letters to Newton beginning to consider the needs of a potential readership that extended beyond his closest friends. Before that month was out he had embarked on a fourth long poem, 'Expostulation', in which he reflects bitterly on the national life of England. Here he assumes the mantle of a Hebrew prophet to denounce God's judgement on a backsliding people, and thus commits himself fully to public utterance as a poet.

Newton and Joseph Johnson consulted together, and it was agreed that these four poems, with a selection of the shorter pieces written during the past two or three years, should form a volume of poems, scheduled originally for publication in the spring of 1781. At Johnson's request, Cowper reluctantly assented to putting his name to his book. On 1 May 1781 he broke the news of the impending publication to William Unwin, who, as Cowper had expected, felt slighted at having been left out of the secret. Unwin's sensibilities were fairly easily soothed, however; a far greater difficulty arose from Johnson's slowness in having the book printed. About the middle of May it became apparent that the volume would not be ready for the spring season, and publication was deferred to avoid the slack sales period of the summer. Then there were further delays, as if Johnson, having secured a postponement, had lost interest in the project, and publication seemed at times to disappear into a remote future. The lull freed Cowper to write more poems, at first with the idea of saving them for a second collection; then, as the weeks went by and the expected proof sheets failed to arrive, they became supplements to the volume already supposed to be 'in the press'. 'Hope', 'Charity', 'Conversation', and 'Retirement' were completed between May and October 1781. The pace was slower, for his first great surge of psychic energy had passed, and Cowper was now more restrained in his language and imagery, more critical of his own writing. These poems, too, move away from the sharp opposition between author and audience which had characterized 'Expostulation' towards a closer and more harmonious relationship in which the poet's revelation of himself establishes a common ground of experience linking him to his readers. The didactic element remains, but it seeks to operate by persuasion rather than by threats. It is, of course, a movement towards the matter and the manner of *The Task*. But Cowper's masterpiece lay still two years and more in the future. As 1781 ended his creative energies seemed to dwindle, and he wrote no verse in the first months of the new year. Indeed, he had reason to rest on his laurels. On 1 March 1782 he stepped before the public with *Poems by William Cowper, of the Inner Temple, Esq.* He was just fifty years old.

TEXTUAL INTRODUCTION

THIS is an edition of all Cowper's original poems and translations, with two exceptions: his translation of Homer, first published in 1791, and his joint translation with William Hayley of Andreini's *Adamo*. No apology is required for the omission of the *Adamo*, which, as we have it, is certainly more Hayley's than Cowper's. The translation of Homer, however, was Cowper's most ambitious and extended poetical undertaking, and its absence distorts the impression of Cowper's career given by these volumes. It has been passed over on grounds of expediency. Cowper took great pains with the translation, and his friends, aware of its importance, preserved many of his manuscript drafts. In his last years he revised his work so thoroughly that the posthumous edition of 1802 amounts to a new version. There are in existence, besides the printed texts of 1791 and 1802: complete proof sheets of the 1791 edition, with revisions and rewritings; one intermediate manuscript version of the *Iliad*, and two intermediate manuscript versions of the *Odyssey*, together with numerous other manuscript fragments. To edit this material properly would be a vast labour; to publish the result would be prohibitively expensive.

We have been able to add to the canon a number of poems which have not hitherto appeared in collected editions, most notably the new poems found in 1968 in a manuscript commonplace book at Hatfield House, and the translation of four cantos of Voltaire's *Henriade*. On the other hand, we have omitted many scraps of verse in his letters which have appeared in earlier editions; these are best regarded as integral parts of the letters in which they are found. Poems wrongly or doubtfully attributed to Cowper are described in an Appendix. Another Appendix gives the texts of certain rather obscure poems which Cowper translated.

i. PRINCIPAL SOURCES OF THE TEXT

The Early Poetry, 1748–1763

Only one of the early poems is now known to exist in Cowper's holograph: an early version of the 'Ode on Reading Mr. Richardson's History of Sir Charles Grandison'.

The two principal sources for the text of Cowper's poems of this period are:

T   Chase Price's Commonplace Book, volume I, pp. 1–51; described, and the new poems printed, by Charles Ryskamp, 'New Poems by William Cowper', *Book Collector*, xxii (1973), 443–78;

Croft Poems, the *Early Productions of William Cowper; Now First Published from the Originals in the Possession of James Croft* (London: Baldwin, Cradock, and Joy, 1825); described by Russell, pp. 106–7 (no. 144).

Chase Price (1731–77) was a friend of Cowper's at Westminster School; when he became an undergraduate at Christ Church, Oxford, they corresponded; there is no documentary record of their friendship after the mid-1750s. Allusions in Cowper's letter to Price of 1 April 1752 show that the first fifteen of Cowper's poems in *T* must have been copied by Price himself about that time (he was convalescing after an attack of rheumatic fever). The remaining twenty-five were copied, again by Price himself, two or three years afterward, probably late in 1754 or early in 1755. His examplar on the latter occasion seems to have been Cowper's record book of his poems, in which Cowper wrote down his compositions at or about the time of their inditing. Price was a hasty and sometimes a careless copyist; his capitalization and punctuation are erratic, and in transcribing the second group of poems he omitted punctuation almost entirely. *T* is therefore unreliable as a record of Cowper's accidentals. It is, however, the unique source of twenty-three poems.

James Croft, Theodora Cowper's great-nephew, was by his own admission a man little skilled in literature. In 1824 he inherited from his great-aunt her collection of Cowper's poems, a manuscript or manuscripts written in the poet's own hand. This manuscript collection has disappeared, but references in Theodora's correspondence establish that Croft did not print its entire contents. He omitted poems which had already been printed; he omitted passages and perhaps even whole poems which he, or his advisers, considered below Cowper's standard. The twenty-seven poems which he printed are styled according to the typographical conventions of 1825, but the punctuation and some of the misreadings in the text suggest strongly that Croft gave Cowper's manuscript to the printers for their copy. His book is the unique source of ten poems.

Thus *T* and *Croft* are alike at one remove from Cowperian manuscript; but not from the same manuscript. Most of the 'Delia' poems appear in both collections, most of them in the same order in both collections; where there are substantive variants which may be ascribed to the author, the readings of *Croft* invariably appear to be revisions. We deduce that Cowper, about the time of his enforced break with Theadora in 1755, went through his record book and copied out appropriate poems in a memento collection later given to Theadora, revising the poems from time to time as he did so. *Croft* thus represents the author's later intentions, and is here chosen for copy-text for all but one of the poems which appear both in *T* and in *Croft* (the exception, 'On the Green Margin of a Brook', is defective and somewhat garbled in *Croft*).

Three poems are known only as they appear in Hayley's *Life of Cowper*, and a fourth only as it appears in John Johnson's supplementary volume of Cowper's *Posthumous Poetry* (1815). The translations of two of Horace's satires and of four cantos of Voltaire's *Henriade* were first published in 1759 and 1762 respectively; in both cases only the first edition has authority.

The Olney Hymns, 1764–1772

The principal source for the poems of this period is

1779 *Olney Hymns in Three Books* (London: W. Oliver, 1779); described by Russell, p. 21 (no. 21).

The sixty-six hymns by Cowper which John Newton printed in *Olney Hymns* comprise almost all the verse he is known to have written between 1764 and 1772. Four of the hymns survive in Cowper's autograph: nos. 1, 31, 53, 61. Five (nos. 1, 35, 36, 46, 47) are found in the Maitland–Madan Commonplace Book in the Bodleian Library, of which nos. 35, 46, 47 came to Mrs. Madan in copies by Newton. Four hymns (nos. 1, 10, 35, 36) are known in copies in M. F. C. Cowper's Commonplace Book in the Cowper Museum; the provenance of three is uncertain, but no. 10 was transcribed from a letter (or a copy of a letter) from Newton. Fifty-three of the hymns are known only as they appear in *Olney Hymns*, for which copy was prepared by Newton alone. Eight or perhaps nine of the hymns were printed in periodicals or collections before 1779 (nos. 1, 4, 7, 15, 18, 35, 36?, 41, 43); it is likely that most if not all of these found their way into print through Newton's extensive correspondence. So far as one can judge, Newton copied Cowper's hymns faithfully

—though without particular care as to accidentals—for private circulation, but he seems to have made some revisions for publication (cf. nos. 7, 35) or for congregational use (cf. no. 53). In preparing copy for *Olney Hymns* he added footnote references to the Bible.

The early editions of *Olney Hymns* are badly printed. In the case of the first (*1779*), the compositor may have had difficulty in reading Newton's manuscript, but this cannot explain all the errors. The punctuation is poor throughout; the quotation marks in particular are so irregularly used, and so often misrepresent scriptural passages that they are unlikely to be Newton's work. It is hard to believe that Newton (or anybody else) read proof for this edition. The second edition (*1781*) is almost worse; such gross errors as 'Chrsit' reappear in the company of many new mistakes. None the less, the attempts in this and the third edition (*1783*) to correct the attribution of the tenth hymn in Book III (see Commentary on no. 33) show that Newton was trying to improve matters, but it seems unlikely that he did more than tell the printer of errors which had chanced to come to his attention.

The first edition (*1779*) is here taken as copy-text for all of the hymns save nos. 1, 31, 53, 61, which are printed from Cowper's holograph, and nos. 35, 46, 47, which are printed from the Maitland–Madan Commonplace Book. The obvious misprints of *1779* have been corrected silently; a few readings which might be genuine variants rather than errors are recorded in the apparatus. Readings of the second (*1781*) and third (*1783*) editions which appear to be corrections are adopted into the text and duly noted in the apparatus.

The fact of first publication before 1779 is recorded where it occurs, but variants found in printings before 1779 are given only where they seem to have some possible value in witnessing to Cowper's own intentions. Contrary to the usual practice of this edition, all the known printings before 1779 are listed in the Commentary.

The 'Song of Mercy and Judgment', a song of praise too personal to be included in *Olney Hymns*, survives in Cowper's holograph among the Ash MSS. The fragment of a hymn, 'To Jesus the Crown of My Hope', was found in a manuscript discovered after Cowper's death by his servant, Sam Roberts. The manuscript has since been lost, but it appears to have included also two pieces, 'Heu quam remotus vescor ab omnibus' and 'Hatred and Vengeance My Eternal Portion' which were written after the breakdown of 1773.

The Return to Poetry, 1774–1782

Two sets of Latin verses, 'Tales et nostri viguissent' and 'Cæsa est nostra Columba', survive in Cowper's autograph; they date from 1774, and plainly reflect the wretchedness of that year. For at least three years from the beginning of 1775 he wrote no poetry (with the possible exception of some translations from Horace and Vincent Bourne), so that the return to poetry which culminated in the publication of *Poems by William Cowper, of the Inner Temple, Esq.* in 1782 begins, in effect, in 1778 or 1779.

There are three important manuscript sources for the poems of this period:

U the series of letters addressed to William Unwin, 1778–86, now in the British Library;
A the Ash collection of poetical manuscripts and letters, also in the British Library;
H Cowper's record book of his poems, now in the Huntington Library.

Cowper corresponded regularly with William Unwin from 1778, when Unwin moved to Stock in Essex. He frequently included poems in his letters, which thus help to establish dates of composition. However, when Cowper had the advantage of a franked cover, he would sometimes enclose a poem written on a separate sheet. Such sheets cannot always be linked to a specific letter; they are now bound together at the end of the collection of dated letters. Altogether, sixteen poems of the years 1779–82 are found in Cowper's letters to Unwin.

The Ash manuscripts, which are now bound in a single volume, bear the name of their owner, E. P. Ash, who had inherited them from his aunt, to whom they had been given or bequeathed by Joseph Hill's widow. Fos. 1–18 contain, with other material, the texts of sixteen poems or parts of poems of this period, a number of them being early drafts.

Cowper's record book of his poems in the Huntington Library (H) is a collection of forty-eight poems written throughout in the poet's own hand. They are contained in a volume of 124 small quarto leaves, the versos of which are usually blank, but which occasionally record additions or revisions. Three vertical lines are visible on the right-hand side of the rectos, suggesting that the book was designed for the keeping of accounts. The lower edges of the leaves have been severely cropped by the binder. Forty-one of the poems can be dated at least approximately by independent evidence, and fall between the autumn of 1779 and the spring of 1781; most of the remaining seven probably belong to the same period. Cowper appears to have begun writing poems in the book about the end of May 1780, and at first entered only his new pieces, as they were composed; then, about the middle of June, he began to enter poems written months or even years before, presumably as he came across copies of them among his papers. The earliest statement of his intentions comes in his letter to William Unwin of 6 August 1780, where he asks Unwin to send him his translations from Vincent Bourne, 'for I am making a Collection, not for the Public, but for Myself'. (Unwin was dilatory, and the translations were never entered in the book; they do, however, appear in *Poems*, 1782.) Cowper continued to enter new poems as they were composed and old ones as they came to hand through the summer and early autumn of 1780. There is no indication that he made any attempt to order his collection either by subject or by date of composition.

Towards the end of 1780 the book began to fill more quickly. References in Cowper's letters to Newton establish that *Antithelyphthora* was entered as soon as it was finished, on or just before 27 November; the new lines mentioned in his letter of 2 December appear as later additions in *H*. 'The Progress of Error' and 'Truth' follow, both apparently entered upon completion; that is, about 21 December 1780 and about 21 January 1781 respectively. Three short poems follow: two pieces addressed to Newton, 'On His Return from Ramsgate' and 'An Invitation into the Country', and 'Boadicea. An Ode'. 'Table Talk' is next, entered presumably when it was completed, about 4 February 1781. The book was now almost full, and 'Expostulation', the next of the long poems, could not be included, but there was room for the short piece 'To the Reverend W. C. Unwin', which was composed late in March or early in April 1781. About that time Cowper was preparing copy for the press, and this led him to revise and extend the three 'moral satires' in *H*. To make room for new material, he frequently removed the original pages from the book, and substituted new ones of a different paper stock. Many passages of the original versions have thus been lost, and one can only guess how much of them is preserved in the revised versions.

Having filled up his record book, Cowper seems not to have bothered to obtain a fresh book. The labour of transcription was always tedious to him, and he seems to have decided not to bother with it. The prospect of seeing his work in print may well have contributed to this decision. At any rate, no manuscript copies of 'Expostulation' or of the four later 'moral satires' are now known to exist.

Of the printed sources for the poetry of this period, the two volumes which Cowper published require notice here. The first, *Antithelyphthora*, was published by Joseph Johnson at the beginning of January 1781. (Described by Russell, pp. 36–7 (no. 67).) All the arrangements for publication were made by Newton. Cowper did not see any proofs. Primarily for this reason we have chosen *H* for our copy-text; a more detailed discussion will be found in the Commentary.

Cowper's next publication was:

1782 Poems by William Cowper, of the Inner Temple, Esq. (London: J. Johnson, 1782); described by Russell, pp. 48–52 (no. 68).

This volume has a longer and more complex publishing history. Joseph Johnson must have been favourably impressed by *Antithelyphthora*, for he was willing to read 'The Progress of Error' as soon as Newton received a copy from Cowper—or so Newton's letter to Cowper of 22 January 1781 seems to imply. Cowper's descriptions of 'Table Talk', which he began about that date, suggest that it was from the first conceived as an introduction to the other long poems, an introduction addressed to the common reader of poetry. Johnson must have expressed a tentative interest in publishing more of Cowper's verse quite soon after the appearance of *Antithelyphthora*. Publication had been decided on by 5 March, on which date Cowper wrote to Newton authorizing—not without reluctance—the use of his name, but insisting that he must rewrite parts of 'The Progress of Error' to eliminate all direct reference to Martin Madan. On 8 April he sent to Newton a package containing 'my Works complete, bound in brown paper, and numbered according to the Series in which I would have them publish'd', and suggested that Newton should attempt to soften the painful truthfulness of 'Truth' by writing a preface to the volume. Despite the earlier reference, in Cowper's letter to Newton of 18 March, to his 'bookfull' of shorter poems which might fill out a volume, the 'Works' of 8 April consisted of four long poems only: 'Table Talk', 'The Progress of Error', 'Truth', and 'Expostulation'. On 23 April he wrote to Newton that he had thought of sending some shorter pieces, but found them insufficiently serious. Two days later, however, he wrote again to Newton, who had clearly passed on a message from Johnson that more material was required to make up a respectable volume, that he could supply a number of minor poems which, with the addition of translations from Vincent Bourne, would amount to roughly 1,000 lines. Johnson appears to have agreed finally to publish the volume in this form (four long poems and a miscellany of shorter pieces) about the end of April, and to have announced it as forthcoming a few days later.[1]

Johnson had originally intended to publish the volume in the spring of 1781, but before long it became clear that the book would not be ready before the London season was over and its potential purchasers were dispersed. On 21 May Cowper wrote to Newton agreeing to a delay until the autumn—cheerfully, since this would enable him to correct the proofs himself. (In fact, Newton corrected the first sheet of 'Table Talk' a few days later,[2] but thereafter proofs were sent to Cowper.) The middle of May also saw the return of Cowper's creative urge; he began work on 'Hope', to be followed by 'Charity', which he completed by 12 July.

The latter part of July and the beginning of August were occupied with the writing of 'Conversation', which Cowper, no doubt still expecting his volume to appear within a month or two, designed as the opening work in a new collection of poems. Johnson preferred to add 'Conversation' to the volume already in hand, together with 'Retirement', begun towards the end of August and completed in October. By the middle of October, the proof sheets had still not reached the end of 'Hope'. These delays, however frustrating, gave Cowper opportunity to change his mind about some things. Early in November he sent Joseph Johnson a 'new Edition' of the title-page he proposed for his volume—a matter of some importance, since advance copies of the title-page were used to advertise books. Later in the same month he began to have qualms about lines 390–413 of 'Expostulation'. Was this attack on Roman Catholicism perhaps open to the charge of bigotry; could it even be construed as an incitement to a renewal of the Gordon Riots? Newton approved of his

---

[1] To William Unwin, 1 May 1781; to Joseph Hill, 9 May 1781.
[2] To John Newton, and to William Unwin, 28 May 1781. Cowper later saw proof of this first sheet.

scruples, and Cowper wrote immediately to Johnson asking if a fresh passage could be substituted. On 4 December he sent to Newton twenty-four lines to replace the offending passage. This change would necessitate a cancel (sig. I6, pp. 123–4). At the same time Cowper instructed Newton to make changes in the miscellany of shorter poems, which had not yet been set in type: 'A Present for the Queen of France' and 'To Sir Joshua Reynolds', rendered obsolete by the collapse of British military power in America following Cornwallis's surrender at Yorktown, were to be deleted, and replaced by 'Heroism' and a new poem in stanzas, not yet finished (clearly 'Friendship'). A few days later (the covering letter is not dated) Cowper sent 'Friendship' to Johnson, asking that it be placed first of the shorter pieces, and 'Heroism' placed last. On 21 December Cowper proposed the inclusion of another new poem, 'The Flatting Mill', suggesting to Newton that it would make a good introduction to the whole volume. These late additions met with little favour: Johnson disliked 'Friendship', and Newton thought 'The Flatting Mill' no more than a repetition of the motto from Caraccioli already printed on the title-page. In his letter to Newton of 31 December Cowper assents to these adverse judgments.[1] He also mentions that he has received proofs to the middle of 'The Mahometan Hog', that is, 'The Love of the World Reproved', but that Newton's lines are not inserted. Clearly Cowper had received sig. X, taking him down to p. 320. Since Newton's lines are ll. 9–14 of the published text, which appear (together with a footnote probably also by Newton) on p. 320, it is clear that this page must have been reset to accommodate the addition.[2]

In the middle of February Cowper received the last two sheets of proofs, together with all the previously corrected sheets. He returned the whole book to Johnson with his letter of 17 February, enclosing a list of errata, and noting that the bad rhyme on p. 60 (i.e. 'The Progress of Error', ll. 373–4) had not been corrected; apparently Newton had not followed Cowper's instructions in his letter of 7 July 1781. Sig. E6 had to be cancelled to permit the insertion of the revised couplet. Cowper also points out that he has not seen proof of the substituted passage in 'Expostulation'. It appears, therefore, that Johnson had not yet prepared the cancel leaf I6, and

---

[1] Johnson rejected the first version of 'Friendship', now lost.

[2] Cowper did not receive any more proof sheets until late January; cf. his letters to Newton, 13 Jan. and 2 Feb. 1782, and to Johnson, 31 Jan. 1782.

that both cancels were printed at the end of February after some copies had already been made up containing the cancellanda.

Johnson had a reputation for being dilatory, and these last-minute changes, together with the eleventh-hour cancellation of Newton's Preface, have usually been laid at his door. However, it is at least as likely that Newton was to blame in all three cases. It was to him that Cowper had sent the corrected couplet in 'The Progress of Error' and the new lines for 'Expostulation'. And his Preface, which Cowper had accepted on 18 September 1781, is dated 18 February 1782. That does not prove conclusively that Johnson had seen it before then, but since within a day or two he was writing to Cowper for permission to cancel it, it is a reasonable inference that he had hitherto been unaware of its tone and content. Johnson thought the Preface too pious for the majority of potential readers, and about 23 February obtained Cowper's permission to suppress it if Newton would agree. The Preface had already been printed (probably Johnson sent it straight to the printer without reading it first), but Newton did agree, with reluctance, to the omission. Some copies exist which contain the Preface, but they represent a sop to Newton's feelings; the copy which Johnson sent to the Earl of Dartmouth on Cowper's behalf does not contain it.[1] Newton's Preface was included in the fifth edition of Cowper's poems (1793), which Johnson published for Cowper's benefit, and in subsequent editions.

The volume was supposed to appear on 1 March 1782, but it seems to have been a few days late; Cowper wrote to William Unwin on 7 March that he had not yet received a copy.

Following the success of *The Task* in 1785, Johnson reprinted both volumes in 1786 as *Poems by William Cowper, of the Inner Temple, Esq. In Two Volumes*, of which the contents of *1782* formed volume I. The volumes were reprinted by Johnson several times in Cowper's lifetime (1787, 1788, 1793, 1794–5, 1798, 1799), but there is no evidence that Cowper read proof for any edition after the first, or that any of the changes in the text were made by him.[2] The only authority for the text of Cowper's 'first volume' is *1782* itself.

---

[1] Russell, p. 52. Cowper presented to the Revd. William Bull a copy which includes the Preface (ibid., p. 51), but this was surely a tribute to Bull's friendship with Newton.

[2] The many variations of punctuation and of spelling in the first five editions were carefully tabulated by Kenneth Povey; his tables confirm that these alterations were made in the printing-house. It has sometimes been suggested that the fairly numerous verbal changes in *1787* were made by Cowper. They are with few exceptions merely changes of pronouns ('who' for 'that', etc.), and altogether suggest a compositor with strict notions of grammar.

Some characteristics of Cowper's poetical manuscripts should be mentioned here. Cowper's hand is neat and legible, and there is seldom any difficulty in deciding what he wrote, save that some of his capital and lower-case letters are hard to distinguish: his *A* and his *a*, for example. The digraphs Æ/æ and Œ/œ are especially ambiguous (they were both phonetic equivalents of *ē*), but fortunately they occur only rarely. The known manuscripts run from 1754 to 1800, and show that he tended to capitalize fewer nouns as he grew older. His spelling of *-or/-our* endings was always variable. He was equally inconsistent in preterite and past participle endings, writing sometimes *-ed*, sometimes *-'d*, and occasionally *-d* without the apostrophe. Despite the remarks in his letter to Lady Hesketh of 3 April 1786, no pattern is discernible in these variations. Cowper's punctuation is usually light but adequate. In his couplet verse he has a tendency to put a comma at the end of every line, whether appropriate or not, until he reaches the end of the sentence. There is no evidence that he objected to the re-punctuation of his verse by the printer; the strictures on the danger of presumptuous intermeddling in the printing-house, in his letter to Unwin of 23 May 1781, refer to verbal alterations only.

The most vexatious problem in editing Cowper's poems is the question of how much authority to attribute to early printings in periodicals. Some of these are known to have originated from Cowper himself, but most of them did not; the difficulty lies in deciding which are which. In the eighteenth century the law of copyright (8 Anne c. 19) covered only books, and not periodicals. Magazines and newspapers therefore could and did reprint material freely from their contemporaries. An item which appeared in a magazine might be reprinted in a newspaper a few days later, and in another magazine two months, or two years, after that.[1] In consequence, one can seldom be quite sure whether any given publication of a poem by Cowper in a periodical is a first publication, or just a reprint. Secondly, whereas in the twentieth century poems are printed in journals because their authors submit them, in the eighteenth century the reverse was more commonly the case, especially when the author was, like Cowper, of gentle birth. To admire a friend's poem enough to send it to a magazine was to pay a gracious compliment.[2] Furthermore,

---

[1] Magazines even reprinted material from books, apparently with impunity; John Wesley printed copious extracts from *1782* in the *Arminian Magazine* in 1787–8; several of the shorter poems in *1782* were printed in the *European Magazine* about the same time.

[2] A good example is given by Anna Seward, *Memoirs of the Life of Dr. Darwin*, 1804,

Cowper's contemporaries thought highly of poetry; they learned it and remembered it for years, and they circulated poems that they liked in letters to their friends. A poem might be known all over England without ever having appeared in print, and any one of scores of copies might find its way into a periodical.[1] Accordingly, while we have searched in newspapers and magazines from the 1740s to the end of the century for early printings of Cowper's poems, we have generally ignored them in the constitution of the text, unless some external evidence suggests that a particular poem was submitted by Cowper, or by one of his friends who might reasonably be supposed to have access to an authoritative manuscript.

ii. ARRANGEMENT AND METHOD

The arrangement of Cowper's poetry has always presented difficulties. He himself prepared no comprehensive collected edition. The two volumes of 1782 and 1785, which had been augmented by Joseph Johnson even before Cowper's death, and the supplementary volume of 1815, formed the basis of almost all the nineteenth-century editions. Various distinctions thus arose which merely confuse the reader—that between poems published during the author's lifetime and poems published posthumously, for instance. In 1832 the Revd. J. S. Memes edited Cowper's works, and rearranged the poetry, placing the long poems at the beginning of the book, then the shorter original pieces, then the religious poems; an example unhappily followed by Milford in his long-current edition, first published in 1905. (Memes's commentary, the first on Cowper's poetry, is a fountain of error from which many of his successors have drunk unwarily.) We have preferred to follow the lead of Bailey (1905) in adopting a general chronological framework within which the published collections retain their identities. There are inevitably some anomalies, but it is hoped that this arrangement will give a sense of Cowper's career as a whole, while permitting the reader, if he so chooses, to come to know Cowper as contemporary readers of poetry knew him.

pp. 130–3. Darwin sent lines she had written to the *Gentleman's Magazine*, having made some alterations in them without her approval.

[1] In 1767 a General Fitzwilliam told a friend that from her copy of Mrs. Greville's 'Prayer for Indifference' he himself had taken and given forty copies (Anne Raine Ellis, ed., *The Early Diary of Frances Burney*, 1768–1778, 1907, i. 26).

In choosing copy-text for the poems, our object has been to select that text which most faithfully records Cowper's latest intentions. Often there is no choice to be made, for roughly half the poems in this volume are known only from a single source; two-thirds of the early poems, almost all of the *Olney Hymns*, and five of the 'moral satires' of *1782* fall into this category. Elsewhere, we have generally preferred a manuscript in Cowper's hand (or in the hand of Mrs. Unwin or John Johnson, writing under Cowper's supervision), to a printed source. In the case of *Poems*, 1782, however, we have taken the printed text for copy-text, since Cowper read and approved the proofs of that volume. There are, of course, a number of poems which present special problems; these are discussed in the Commentary as they arise.

We have attempted to reproduce copy-text accurately. Changes of substantives and accidentals, whether to adopt the readings of other texts, or to incorporate editorial corrections, are recorded in the textual apparatus. However, certain features of the text have been altered silently throughout. Contractions are expanded and superscript letters lowered without notice. Omitted apostrophes in preterite and past participle -*'d* endings are silently inserted, as are missing apostrophes in possessive endings. Misplaced apostrophes are corrected silently. Certain typographical features, such as reference marks for footnotes, have been adjusted in conformity with modern practice; the long *s* has likewise been modernized throughout.

In writing out his poems Cowper customarily marked stanza divisions by means of a horizontal stroke, and the end of a poem by several such strokes; these devices, and the braces which indicate triplets in couplet verse, are not reproduced here. Stanza numbers are likewise omitted. Line-numberings are given to all poems at intervals of five lines.

The apparatus records, as stated, all changes in the substantives and accidentals of the copy-text, except those mentioned above which are made silently throughout. When a reading of MS. *B* is substituted for that of the copy-text *A* (for example), it is recorded in this form: cat] *B*; dog *A*. An editorial correction is recorded thus: cat] cant *A*. Deleted substantive variants in the copy-text are noted in the apparatus. Obvious graphic errors in manuscripts, and obvious typographical errors in printed texts are ignored.

The apparatus records variant readings in all known manuscripts in Cowper's hand, together with those prepared under his supervision by Mrs. Unwin and John Johnson. Other manuscripts are collated when there is reason to believe they have some degree of authority. Printed texts are collated only when they seem to have some authority independent of known manuscripts. The many but minor alterations of the text in Joseph Johnson's editions of 1786 and later are not recorded, for there is no evidence that Cowper ever revised the texts of these volumes after their first publication. No notice is taken of alterations made by Hayley and later editors, unless they are accepted as corrections by the present editors. Exceptions are noted in the Commentary.

SYMBOLS, SHORT TITLES
AND ABBREVIATIONS

i. MANUSCRIPTS

The manuscripts most frequently referred to in this volume are:

A   Ash MSS., miscellaneous poems in Cowper's hand, containing sixteen poems or parts of poems included in this volume;

H   Cowper's record book of his poems, containing forty-eight poems of 1779–81, all in his own hand;

T   Chase Price's Commonplace Book, containing forty poems by Cowper, *c.* 1750–5, and two which have been ascribed to him; all in Price's hand;

U   Cowper's letters to William Unwin, containing twenty-four poems included in this volume, all in Cowper's hand save one in Mrs. Unwin's.

A   Ash MSS., British Library Add. MS. 37059

B   collection of the British Library

C   collection of the Cowper and Newton Museum, Olney, Bucks.

E   Cowper's Entry Book of his poems, Henry E. Huntington Library, San Marino, California (MS. HM 12587)

F   collection of the Fitzwilliam Museum, Cambridge

G   Throckmorton MSS., Coughton Court, Warwickshire

H   Cowper's record book of his poems, Henry E. Huntington Library, San Marino, California (MS. HM 12588)

J   collection of the Misses C. and A. Cowper Johnson

K   collection of Harvard University Library

L   collection of the William Andrews Clark Library, University of California, Los Angeles

M   collection of The Pierpont Morgan Library, New York

N   collection of Miss C. M. Bull

P   collection of Princeton University Library (the Hannay and Povey Collections of William Cowper)

Q   collection of the Victoria and Albert Museum

R   collection of Mr. Robert H. Taylor

S   MSS. presented by John Johnson to Bishop Manners Sutton (Hannay Collection, Princeton University Library)

T   Chase Price's Commonplace Book, property of the Marquess of Salisbury

U	Cowper's letters to William Unwin, British Library Add. MSS. 24154-5
V	collection of Charles Ryskamp
W	formerly owned by Arthur A. Houghton, Jr.
X	The Berg Collection, New York Public Library
Y	collection of the John Rylands Library, Manchester

ii. PRINTED BOOKS, ETC.

The printed books containing poems by Cowper most frequently referred to in this volume are:

Croft	*Poems, the Early Productions of William Cowper* (1825); containing twenty-seven poems, *c.* 1752–5, mostly addressed to Theodora Cowper (Russell, no. 144);
1779	*Olney Hymns, in Three Books* (1779); containing hymns by Cowper and John Newton, sixty-six of them by Cowper; prepared for publication by Newton alone (Russell, no. 21);
1782	*Poems by William Cowper, of the Inner Temple, Esq.* (1782); containing forty-three poems (Russell, no. 68).
Bailey	J. C. Bailey, ed., *The Poems of William Cowper*, 1905
Benham	William Benham, ed., *The Poetical Works of William Cowper*, 1870
BNYPL	*Bulletin of the New York Public Library*
Bruce	John Bruce, ed., *Poetical Works of William Cowper*, 3 vols., 1865
Bull, 1801	*Poems, Translated from the French of Madame de la Mothe Guion, by the late William Cowper, Esq. To which are added some original poems of Mr. Cowper, not inserted in his works*, Newport Pagnell, 1801
Croft	*Poems, the Early Productions of William Cowper, Now First Published from the Originals in the Possession of James Croft*, 1825
DNB	*The Dictionary of National Biography*
Hayley	William Hayley, *The Life, and Posthumous Writings, William Cowper, Esqr.*, 3 vols., 1803–4
Johnson	Samuel Johnson, *A Dictionary of the English Language*, 2 vols., 1755
Johnson, 1815	*Poems, by William Cowper, of the Inner Temple, Esq. in Three Volumes. Vol. III. Containing his posthumous poetry, and a sketch of his life. By his kinsman, John Johnson, LL.D.*, 1815

Milford   H. S. Milford, ed., *The Poetical Works of William Cowper*, 4th ed., 1937

Milford–Russell   *Cowper. Poetical Works*, edited by H. S. Milford. Fourth edition with corrections and additions by Norma Russell, 1971

MLR   *Modern Language Review*

N & Q   *Notes and Queries*

OED   *The Oxford English Dictionary*

Povey   unpublished notes of the late Kenneth Povey

RES   *Review of English Studies*

Russell   Norma Russell, *A Bibliography of William Cowper to 1837*, Oxford, 1963

Ryskamp   Charles Ryskamp, *William Cowper of the Inner Temple, Esq. A study of his life and works to the year 1768*, Cambridge, 1959

Ryskamp, *BC*   Charles Ryskamp, 'New Poems by William Cowper', *The Book Collector*, xxii, 1973, 443–78

Southey   *The Works of William Cowper, Esq. Comprising his correspondence, and translations. With a life of the author, by the editor, Robert Southey, Esq. LL.D.*, 15 vols., 1835–7

Spiller   *Cowper. Poetry and Prose. Selected by Brian Spiller. 1968*

EARLY POEMS
1748–1763

HARDY COMMON

VERSES WRITTEN AT BATH, IN 1748, ON FINDING THE HEEL OF A SHOE

Fortune! I thank thee: gentle Goddess! thanks!
Not that my Muse, tho' bashful, shall deny,
She would have thank'd thee rather, hadst thou cast
A treasure in her way; for neither meed
Of early breakfast to dispell the fumes,   5
And bowel-racking pains of emptiness,
Nor noon-tide feast, nor evening's cool repast
Hopes she from this, presumptuous, tho' perhaps
The Cobler, leather-carving artist! might.
Nathless she thanks thee, and accepts thy boon   10
Whatever, not as erst the fabled Cock,
Vainglorious fool! unknowing what he found,
Spurn'd the rich gem, thou gav'st him. Wherefore ah!
Why not on me that favour, (worthier sure!)
Conferr'dst thou, Goddess! Thou art blind, thou say'st: 15
Enough!—Thy blindness shall excuse the deed.

   Nor does my Muse no benefit exhale
From this thy scant indulgence!—even here
Hints, worthy sage philosophy, are found;
Illustrious hints to moralize my song!   20
This pond'rous Heel of perforated hide
Compact, with pegs indented, many a row,
Haply (for such its massy form bespeaks)
The weighty tread of some rude peasant clown
Upbore: on this supported oft, he stretch'd,   25
With uncouth strides, along the furrow'd glebe,
Flatt'ning the stubborn clod, 'till cruel time,
(What will not cruel time?) on a wry step
Sever'd the strict cohesion: when, alas!
He, who could erst, with even, equal pace,   30
Pursue his destin'd way with symetry,
And some proportion form'd, now, on one side,

COPY-TEXT: Hayley, 1803, i. 21–3 (first printing).

Curtail'd and maim'd, the sport of vagrant boys,
Cursing his frail supporter, treacherous prop!
With toilsome steps, and difficult, moves on.   35
Thus fares it oft with other, than the feet
Of humble villager—the statesman thus,
Up the steep road, where proud ambition leads,
Aspiring first, uninterrupted winds
His prosp'rous way; nor fears miscarriage foul,   40
While policy prevails, and friends prove true:
But that support soon failing, by him left,
On whom he most depended, basely left,
Betray'd, deserted, from his airy height
Head-long he falls; and thro' the rest of life,   45
Drags the dull load of disappointment on.

A LETTER TO CHASE PRICE

Dear Toby,
   I am heartily sorry for poor Arthington. Remember him? ay, or my Memory
must be very Treacherous Indeed. But however no more upon this melan
choly Subject.

          No, rather in the silent Tomb,
          Death's dismal dark Capacious Womb,
       Be the Remembrance with the Body laid,
          Than let vain Sorrow discompose
          Our Minds with unavailing Woes;   5
       Perhaps our Tears but persecute the Dead,
       Tears against Heav'n's Decrees Impertinently Shed.

   If I my Friend should drop before you,
          Think the Joyful Prize is mine,
   A whole Eternity of Glory,   10
          While poor Mortality is thine.
   Then if one silent Tear should fall,
   One Sigh escape, let that be all,

Composed June 1750 (?).
COPY-TEXT: *T*, whence first printed by Ryskamp, *BC*, pp. 467–9. (Punctuation supplied.)

Lest bitter Envy claim a part
In thy Friendly faithfull Heart;   15
Death's the best Blessing Heaven can give:
We live to Dye, but dye to Live.

Well said, good Mistress Clio! I ask your pardon for Invoking you at the
wrong End of a Poem, but better so than not at all—

    Come Heavenly Muse, who Cowley's Bosom fired,
His Judgment Strengthen'd and his Wit inspired,
Explore the Secrets of my Mind; Expell
All Sin-born Counsels, all the just reveal.
    Hail Happy Freedom of the Mind!   5
Guiltless, Generous, Unconfin'd,
Wisdom's Sister, Bane of Lust,
Sweet Companion of the Just,
Scorning Censure's keenest Edge,
Virtue's Choicest Privilege.   10
Virtue, the plant so seldom found
In British or in Foreign Ground,
Buds in the Morning, blows at Noon,
And Ripens with the Setting Sun;
Gracefull alike in Every Stage   15
Of Life—Youth, Manhood and Old Age—
Intended e'er Mankind began
The lasting Ornament of Man;
Cherish the Plant and it shall be
A Lasting Ornament to thee.   20

If you must botch, my Friend, let your botches be your own. Clio is good-
natur'd; Give her good Words and She is always ready to assist, Especially
in the Country—

    The Muses are Romantick Jades,
And only Frisk it in the Shades,
Love-Tinkling Rills and Cooling Streams,
Harmonious Groves And airy Dreams,
But fly the City with Disdain,   5
Where ceaseless Hubbub stuns the Brain.
Thus sung old Horace, and thus sings

Each Bard that mounts on Fancy's Wings.
You then may safely dare to rise,
Stride Pegasus and reach the Skys,   10
Whether you climb the threat'ning Steep,
Or in the lowly Valley creep,
(The Hill whence, many a Rood between,
Fair Oxford's Glittering Spires are Seen,
The Vale where Simple Shepherds dwell   15
In Cottage clean or Mossy Cell),
Or if within the Dusky Grove
All pensive you delight to rove,
Where Woodbine creeps the Trees among;
All aid the Gentle Poet's Song.   20
Sing, Gentle Poet, then with Chyme
Of Jingling Ear-bewitching Rhyme.

Just what you please, any thing you know by way of Botch. Now Methinks
I hear you Cry—

            Curse, Curse,
     On the Prose and the Verse,
     This Jingling is worse
     Than the Noise of a Herse,
     Or another Man's Purse.   5
          Neither here nor there,
          Like a Sow with one Ear,
          Or a Pie-bald Mare,
          Or a Baited Bear
          Who has lost Half his Hair   10
          At a Wake or a Fair
          In a Damnable War
          With Killbuck and Star.
               Ding Dong!
     For an end to the Song   15
     Of this Villain e'er long,
     Or we'll cut out his Tongue,
     Or give him a Dose,
     A Hogshead of Physick,

1–2]   Curse Curse the
          On the Prose and Verse *T* (see *Commentary*

Some Kicks and some Blows,   20
For having made me Sick.

I am, Dear Toby, yours Sincerely,

              William Cowper.

'WHY THOU SCURVY CURMUDGEON'

Why thou Scurvy Curmudgeon,
   Thus to take it in Dudgeon
That I write not—what mean you?—have at ye!
   Thou Slubberdegullian,
     Thou may'st chatter and Bully on,   5
Till you Stun both yourself and poor *Watty*—

But hold, my Muse—Sublimer let me Soar.
Where Billinsgate extends her Fishy Shore,
There let me search around with curious Eye,
If any Nymph expose the scaly Fry,   10
Whose Lungs each Morn successfully declare
The Price, the Size, the Freshness of her Ware,
Nor can the City Clamours drown her Voice,
The rumbling Drays' or rattling Coaches' Noise;
But if unwarily the Deaf draw near,   15
The Screaming Nymph the very Deaf shall hear,
And curse her Throat and stop his tortur'd Ear—
If such a Damsel on the Shore there be,
Bring her, ye Swains of Billinsgate, to me;
A Theme I have shall exercise her Lungs,   20
And could She boast a thousand different Tongues,
A thousand! slightly would revenge my wrongs.

Let Heavenly Gin, Nectareous Juice, prepare
Her Bosom panting to the dreadful War,
Glow on her Cheeks and Sparkle in her Eyes: 25
And bid the Fame-besmearing Tiwey rise,
Till the base Mob extend their opening Jaws

COPY-TEXT: *T*, whence first printed by Ryskamp, *BC*, pp. 470–1. (Punctuation supplied.)

3] *see Commentary*   10 expose] expect *T*   11 Morn] Morts *T*   successfully]
succesfuly *T*

And loud proclaim or silent stare Applause.
So when Alecta's Trumpet rous'd the Swains
That wander'd peaceful o'er the Latian plains,   30
Sudden in smaller Bounds collected Stood
At the first blast th'attentive Multitude,
Till all at length their dismal Faces shew,
And rude Amazement sits on ev'ry Brow.

TO MISS HALFORD,
UPON HER STEALING A BOOK OUT OF MY POCKET,
AND THEN REPROACHING ME WITH
CARELESSNESS

Say, Was it fair, thou generous Maid,
    Consult your own good Sense,
First to disarm me, then upbraid
    For making no Defence.

Easy to Rob, when at your Feet   5
    The wretch submissive lies;
The Prize you gain'd when first we met
    Made this an easy Prize,

And render'd that which would have been,
    Against so fair a Foe,   10
An unavailing Caution then,
    Impracticable now.

UPON MISS HALFORD,
SINGING AND PLAYING UPON THE HARPSICORD

If Truth alone, so Boileau writ,
    And Boileau was no Fool,
Affords us to decide of wit
    A Sure unerring Rule,

30 wander'd] wandred T   33 length] lenght H
COPY-TEXT: T, whence first printed by Ryskamp, BC, p. 471. (Punctuation supplied.)
COPY-TEXT: T, whence first printed by Ryskamp, BC, p. 472. (Punctuation supplied.)

Then all that ever Cowley sung   5
  And Twenty Bards as wise,
Of Chloe with a Syren's Tongue,
  Or Seraphs in Disguise,

May, and this Instant let them be,
  With one decisive Dash,   10
Struck from the List of Poetry,
  Convicted Errant Trash.

Pity the Sov'reigns of all verse
  Should be at length disgrac'd;
Not in themselves the Fault appears,   15
  But in the Nymphs they prais'd.

Then that each Thought may fairly pass
  For genuine and compleat,
Let Halford stand in Chloe's place,
  And I pronounce it wit.   20

'WHEREFORE DID I LEAVE THE FAIR'

Wherefore did I leave the Fair
In rural Fields to range?
Silly Swain! to Town repair,
Thou hast left thy Treasure there,
Delia's Breath for Country Air,   5
Silly Strephon to Exchange!

For when e'er abroad I stray,
In the Garden, or the Grove,
Every Object I survey,
Like my Delia trim and gay,   10
Cannot chace my Grief away,
While I fly from her Love.

COPY-TEXT: *T*, whence first printed by Ryskamp, *BC*, pp. 448–9.
4 hast] has *T*

What avail these empty Shews,
That adorn each bright Parterre,
What are all these painted Rows,   15
Of the Dappled Pink, and Rose,
What is every Flow'r that Blows,
When alas! compar'd with her.

Did not Delia's kiss exceed
All these Shining Toys, that fill   20
Pansied Lawn, or painted Mead,
E'er they hang the drooping Head,
Were they in their Native Bed
Sweet as is my Delia's Smile.

Yet such Trifles would not ease   25
Pains that in the Bosom dwell,
But what more Substantial Bliss,
Delia, I expect than this,
Than a Smile, or than a Kiss,
Cannot ev'ry Lover tell.   30

'VARIOUS BEAUTYS BY POSSESSING'

Various Beautys by possessing,
  Various Pleasures we enjoy,
All afford a different Blessing,
  And a diff'rent Taste Employ.

This has Language so endearing,   5
  And has that bewitching Art,
While it captivates our Hearing,
  Steals a Passage to the Heart.

This by Nature was intended,
  To Engage the Lover's Eye,   10
This by something recommended,
  Makes us Love we know not why.

23 Bed] Bed, *T*   25 ease] ease, *T*   28 Delia,] Delia *T*

COPY-TEXT: *T*, whence first printed by Ryskamp, *BC*, pp. 449–50.
7 While] Which *deleted T*

Why then should we by confineing,
    Strive to make our Pleasures less,
Nature many Means designing,   15
    Many Appetites to please.

Thus who chuse their Garlands well,
    With the Fragrant mix the gay,
This for Sight, and that for Smell,
    Each is pleasing in it's Way.   20

A SONG

Come sorrowful Chloe now prithee discover,
    Why thus at this terrible rate,
You Sigh, and you sob for the loss of a Lover,
    Whom once you pretended to Hate;

No manner of Reason or cause can I see,   5
    Why you should his absence bemoan,
Who had he been formerly favour'd by thee,
    Had ne'er been in haste to be gone.

When present you cruelly bid him despair
    And fly from the cause of his Pain,   10
And these Sighs which he certainly never can hear,
    Say how should they bring him again?

But Women from hence a good Lesson may learn,
    To banish all manner of Art,
And at once in their Looks let their Lovers discern   15
    The Meaning and Truth of the Heart.

For whether they sweetly dissemble their Hate,
    Or Love when they seem to detest,
They little can gain by the former deceit,
    And Surely will lose by the last.   20

COPY-TEXT: *T*, whence first printed by Ryskamp, *BC*, pp. 451–2.

'IF OUGHT MIGHT REACH THE GIRL I LOVE'

If ought might reach the Girl I Love,
Or Tears could melt, or Sighs could move,
   My Sorrows should exceed
The Blasts that Fan the waving Woods,
The Rains that fill the swelling Floods,   5
   And drown the level Mead.

But since some Dæmon does Impart
Such Idle Fancys to her Heart,
   Of Love refin'd and pure;
E'en let the Simple Maid Enjoy   10
That Trifling, useless, Senseless Toy,
   Her Chastity secure.

Yet if in Wedlock there were Sin,
Repentance might a Pardon Win,
   And purge the guilty Stain;   15
But all the Tears by Virgins Shed,
When Beauty, Youth, and Bloom are fled,
   Are Impotent and Vain.

Repentants of each other kind,
In Heav'n some Mercy surely find,   20
   To Heal this inward Wound:
For Maids alone who weep too late
The Sorrows of a Single State
   No Remedy is found.

Come then dear Girl be wise at last,   25
Nor fear those harmless Joys to Tast,
   You never can Repent;
Rather than let that Folly Stain
Your Youth, which surely but in vain
   In Age you will lament.   30

copy-text: *T*, whence first printed by Ryskamp, *BC*, pp. 452–3.

3 exceed] exceed, *T*   10 Enjoy] Enjoy, *T*   23 State] State; *T*   28 Stain]
Stain, *T*

'WHAT! NOT ONE LOOK, ONE GRACIOUS SMILE'

What! not one Look, one gracious Smile,
   My Fair one e'er we part,
The tedious Absence to beguile,
   And ease my throbbing Heart;

Think what a Life the Wretch endures,   5
   Who feels that dreadful Pain
Which but thy Favour nothing cures,
   Yet suffers thy Disdain.

Which tho' it cancel'd all my Joys,
   Yet left one Hope behind,   10
But this that Idle Hope destroys
   That thou will e'er be kind.

Didst thou with pity hear my Pain?
   Where is that pity now!
Or didst thou Sooth my Sorrow then,   15
   But to torment me now?

So sweet the Syren lured along
   The Stranger to her Shore,
But whilst She tun'd her pleasing Song,
   Meant only to devour.   20

A SONG

The sparkling eye, the mantling cheek,
The polish'd front, the snowy neck,
   How seldom we behold in one!
Glossy locks, and brow serene,
Venus' smiles, Diana's mien,   5
   All meet in you, and you alone.

COPY-TEXT: *T*, whence first printed by Ryskamp, *BC*, p. 453.
16 now?] now. *T*

COPY-TEXT: Croft, 1825, pp. 45–6 (first printing). Collated: *T*.
4 Glossy] *T*; Glassy *Croft*

Beauty, like other pow'rs, maintains
Her empire, and by *union* reigns;
  Each single feature faintly warms:
But where at once we view display'd   10
Unblemish'd grace, the perfect maid
  Our eyes, our ears, our heart alarms.

So when on earth the God of day
Obliquely sheds his temper'd ray,
  Through convex orb the beams transmit;   15
The beams that gently warm'd before,
Collected, gently warm no more,
  But glow with more prevailing heat.

'ON THE GREEN MARGIN OF A BROOK'

On the green Margin of a Brook,
  Despairing Phyllida reclin'd,
Whilst every Sigh, and every Look,
  Declar'd the Sorrows of her Mind;
Her Damon's Crook beside her lay;   5
His Crook, the Shepherd cast away,
  And left the Nymph behind;

Am I less lovely then? she crys,
  And in the Waves her form survey'd,
O yes! I see my languid Eyes,   10
  My faded Cheek, my Colour fled!
These Eyes no more like Lightning pierc'd,
These Cheeks grew pale, when Damon first
  His Phyllida betray'd.

12 heart] Hearts *T*

15 orb] *T*; orbs *Croft*   transmit;] transmit, *Croft*

COPY-TEXT: *T*. First printed by Croft, 1825, pp. 46–7.

Title] A Song. *Croft*; *untitled in T*   1 of a] of the *Croft*   4 Sorrows] anguish
Croft   5–7 *not in Croft*   5 lay;] lay *T*   8 then? she crys,] then, she
crys? *T*

The Rose he in his Bosom wore,   15
    How oft upon my Breast was seen,
And when I kiss'd the drooping flower,
    Behold, he cry'd, it blooms again;
The Wreaths that bound my braided Hair,
Himself next Day was proud to wear   20
    At Church, or on the Green.

While thus sad Phyllida lamented,
    Chance brought unlucky Thyrsis on:
Unwillingly the Nymph consented,
    But Damon first the Cheat begun;   25
She wiped the falling Tears away,
Then Sigh'd, and blush'd as who should say,
    Ah Thyrsis I am won!

TO A YOUNG LADY WITH HER BREAST KNOT

        Henceforth let not ev'ry Fair
        Green and White presume to wear,
        Celia wisely can reduce
        Colours to a real Use,
        In this Mystic Knot I find   5
        A true Emblem of her Mind,
        By the Virgin White is seen,
        Bord'ring on the lively Green,
        Spotless Virtue, pure as Snow!
        Such as Heav'nly Spirits know,   10
        By the smiling Brow confest,
        Not in Frowns demurely drest,
        Ever cheerful, ever gay,
        Charming ev'ry Care away,
        But the first, and best of Cares,   15
        How to Shun the gilded Snares,

18 Behold, he cry'd,] Behold he cry'd *T*   26 She wiped the falling] He wiped the fallen *Croft*   27 say,] say *T*

COPY-TEXT: *T*, whence first printed by Ryskamp, *BC*, pp. 450-1.

1, 3, 5] *commas at the ends of these lines have been omitted*   9 as] a *T*

Which the giddy Maid entice
To the flat'ring paths of Vice;
Henceforth let not ev'ry Fair
Green and White presume to wear.   20
But when ev'ry Fair can boast
A Mind by no rude passion toss'd,
Easy, Sensible, and Free,
Happy Celia, likest thee!
Safely then may ev'ry Fair   25
Green, and White presume to wear.

A CHARACTER

William was once a bashfull Youth,
    His Modesty was such,
That one might say (to say the Truth)
    He rather had too much;

Some said that it was want of Sense,   5
    And others want of Spirit,
(So blest a thing is Impudence)
    While others could not bear it;

But some a different Notion had,
    And at each other winking,   10
Observ'd that tho' he little said
    He paid it off with thinking;

Howe'er it was, by Slow degrees
    He mended and grew perter,
In Company was more at ease,   15
    And Dress'd a little Smarter;

Nay now and then would look quite gay
    As other People do,
And often said or try'd to say
    A witty thing or so;   20

17, 19, 21, 25] *commas at the ends of these lines have been omitted*

COPY-TEXT: *T*, whence ll. 29–56 first printed by Ryskamp, *BC*, p. 454; ll. 1–28 first printed
by Croft, 1825 (see below, 'Of Himself').

He eyed the Women and made free
    To comment on their Shapes,
So that there was or seem'd to be
    No fear of a Relapse;

The Women said, who thought him rough   25
    Yet did not think him Foolish,
The Creature may do well enough,
    But wants a little Polish.

And prithee Friend what think you now,
    Had wrought this mighty change?   30
You'll hardly credit it I know
    'Tis so exceeding Strange!

Once having found his Celia's knot
    Fit Subject for a Sonnet,
He took the Hint and fairly wrote   35
    A Set of Rhymes upon it;

Thus having bid adieu to Prose,
    And ventur'd to discover
What Sense he had you may Suppose
    He soon commenc'd a Lover;   4c

And next would he succeed with her
    He found 'twas necessary,
That his Behaviour should appear
    More cheerful and more Airy;

Therefore so upright and erect   45
    He grew you'd scarce have known him,
Such a most wonderful Effect
    This Trifle had upon him;

And lately what with Business, Time
    And Absence altogether,   50
Lovers he finds howe'er Sublime
    Are fickle as the Weather;

30 change?] change *T*   40 commenc'd] comenc'd *T*

Yet tho' his Passion he forgets,
  And all the Pain it gave him,
Since by that means he found his Wits,   55
  'Tis well and so we leave him.

'BEHOLD! THE CHARMING CELIA CRY'D'

Behold! the Charming Celia cry'd,
  As Laura pass'd along,
Strephon, behold her Sexes Pride,
  The Gentle, Fair, and Young;

But all the while, as well she knew,   5
  That Laura was a Scold,
And if her Senses told her true
  Was Ugly, Brown, and Old;

Say whence this Goodness you derive,
  Dear Charitable Maid,   10
Bloom to a wither'd Face to give,
  And Youth to the Decay'd;

Could ev'ry Female Learn like you,
  By your Example taught,
Her Fav'rite Scandal to forego,   15
  And Pity where She ought;

Ye Gods how happy were the Change!
  What mighty Wars would cease,
When ev'ry Batter'd Belle might range
  The Pitying World in Peace;   20

But now so Insolent at best,
  So very Pert they're grown;
That to Disturb each other's Rest,
  They sacrifice their own.

COPY-TEXT: *T*, whence first printed by Ryskamp, *BC*, p. 455.
3 Strephon, ... Pride,] Strephon ... Pride *T*   5 while,] while *T*

SONG

No more shall hapless Celia's ears
   Be flatter'd with the cries
Of lovers drown'd in floods of tears,
   Or murder'd by her eyes;
No serenades to break her rest,   5
Nor songs her slumbers to molest,
     With my fa, la, la.

The fragrant flowers that once would bloom
   And flourish in her hair,
Since she no longer breathes perfume   10
   Their odours to repair,
Must fade, alas! and wither now,
As placed on any common brow,
     With my fa, la, la.

Her lip, so winning and so meek,   15
   No longer has its charms;
As well she might by whistling seek
   To lure us to her arms;
Affected once, 'tis real now,
As her forsaken gums may show,   20
     With my fa, la, la.

The down that on her chin so smooth
   So lovely once appear'd,
That, too, has left her with her youth,
   Or sprouts into a beard;   25
As fields, so green when newly sown,
With stubble stiff are overgrown,
     With my fa, la, la.

Then, Celia, leave your apish tricks,
   And change your girlish airs,   30
For ombre, snuff, and politics,
   Those joys that suit your years;

COPY-TEXT: Croft, 1825, pp. 8–10 (first printing).
3 Of] *Southey*; And *Croft*

No patches can lost youth recal,
Nor whitewash prop a tumbling wall,
    With my fa, la, la.   35

TO C. P., ILL WITH THE RHEUMATISM

Could Mine, my Friend, like Orpheus' pleasing Strain,
Charm the keen Anguish of Tormenting Pain,
Could I the sharp Rheumatick Grief Asswage,
And bid the Raging Humour, cease to Rage,
Strait should my Lines the wish'd-for Ease Impart   5
And the kind Poet, play the Doctor's part.

And wherefore, Phœbus, since to thee Mankind
Have the two precious Attributes assign'd,
Med'cine to Heal, and Musick to delight,
Why not in one these glorious Ends unite?   10
Why not on Verse the various Powers bestow,
That please our Ear, and mitigate our Woe?
So should the Sick some well wrote page Survey,
Smile while He reads and bless the saving Lay!
So should smooth Verse o'er ev'ry Pang prevail   15
And Pope succeed, where haply Mead might fail.
'If Rising Vapours fill your Aching Head,
Trust me, let Swift's, or Butler's page be read,
Wouldst thou Confirm the Cure, my Friend, at least
Five Acts of Shakespear take, Probatum est!   20
If sleepless Nights your wand'ring Thoughts confound,
In Blackmore's Page much Opiate may be found;
E'en Garth tho' dead shall thy Physician be,
And still more wondrous! cure without a Fee!'
Methinks I see your heavy Eye-lids close,   25
Lo! for a while my Friend forgets his Woes,

Composed about March 1752.

COPY-TEXT: *T*, whence first printed in full by Ryskamp, *BC*, pp. 458–9. Lines 39–46 first printed by Croft, 1825, p. 4.

5 wish'd-for] wish'd for *T*   7 wherefore, Phoebus,] wherefore Phoebus *T*   Mankind] makind *T*   12 That] The *T*   18 me,] me *T*   19 Cure,] Cure *T*   least] least, *T*

Tho' Phebus does the healing Art deny
To Tuneful Bards, and tho' no Bard am I,
Yet may this Verse thy tort'ring Grief Allay,
Benumb thy Sense, and charm the Pain away;   30
Oh were I sure that glorious End to gain,
Torpedo-like to free thy Limbs from pain!
Plenteous my Numbers should for ever flow,
Nor Peace my Brain, nor Rest my Fingers know,
Then shouldst thou Yawning their soft Influence own,   35
And let the purpose for the Faults Attone;
Then shouldst thou drop the Leaf, forget thy Pain,
And Doze, and Wake, and Read, and Doze again.

Grant me the Muse, ye Gods! whose humble flight
Seeks not the Mountain-top's pernicious Height!   40
Who can the tall Parnassian Cliff forsake,
To Visit oft the Still Lethæan Lake,
Now her slow Pinions brush the silent Shore,
Now gently Skim the unwrinkled Waters o'er,
There dips her downy Plumes, then upward fly's   45
And Sheds soft Slumbers in her Vot'ry's Eyes:
My Pray'rs are heard; I feel the Lulling Power
O'erload my Brain, my Lazy Sense obscure—
Adieu my Friend! may Slumbers mild as these,
The Raging Anguish of thy Limbs appease,   50
Success attend my Pray'rs, be thine prefer'd
To the same Pow'r, and share the same Reward.

27 deny] deny, *T*   31 gain,] gain *T*   32 Torpedo-like] Torpedo like *T*
Limbs from pain!] Limbs pain! *T*   33 Plenteous] *marginal correction for* Endless *T*
39–46] *entitled in Croft* In a Letter to C. P. Esq./ Ill with the Rheumatism   39 Muse,]
Croft; Muse *T*   40 Height] heights *Croft*   43 Shore,] *Croft*; Shore *T*
45 Plumes] *Croft*; Plume *T*   then] there *Croft*   46 Slumbers in] *Croft*; Slumber
o'er *T*   47 heard;] heard *T*   Power] Power, *T*   48 obscure—] obscure *T*
52 Reward] *altered from* Regard *T*

IN A LETTER TO C. P. ESQUIRE
In Imitation of Shakespeare

Trust me, the Meed of Praise dealt thriftily
From the Nice Scale of Judgment, Honours more,
Than does the lavish and o'erbearing Tide
Of profuse Courtesy—not all the Gems
Of India's richest Soil at random spread   5
O'er the gay Vesture of some glittering Dame,
Give such alluring Vantage to the person,
As the scant Lustre of a few, with choice
And Comely guise of Ornament disposed.

'O! ASK NOT WHERE CONTENTMENT MAY ABIDE'

O! ask not where Contentment may abide
    In whose still Mansion those true Joys abound
    That pour sweet Balm o'er Fortune's fest'ring Wound,
Whether she chuse sequester'd to reside
In the lone Hamlet on some Mountain wide,   5
    Whose rough top with brown Oaks or Pine Trees crown'd,
    Casts a dim Shade, a settled gloom around:—
Or whether She amidst the glittering Tide
    Of Courtiers, pouring from the thick-throng'd Gate
Of Majesty, be seen: She nor assumes   10
    The high-swol'n Pomp of haughty-miened State,
Nor constant to the low-roof'd Cottage comes:
    On Honest Minds alone she deigns to wait.
There closes still her downy-feather'd Plumes;
    Nor wand'ring thence shifts her serene Abode,   15
    Pleas'd to possess the *Noblest Work of God.*

Composed 1 April 1752.

copy-text: letter to Chase Price, 1 Apr. 1752 (*R*). Collated: Croft, 1825, p. 5 (first printing).
Title] Croft, *reading* to C. P. Esquire *for* to the Same; *no title in R*   4 —not] —[See(?)
deleted] not *R*   7 alluring Vantage] *Croft*; bewitching Graces *R*   9 disposed]
Croft; bestow'd *R*

Composed late March 1752.

copy-text: letter to Chase Price, 1 Apr. 1752 (*R*). First printed, from a sale catalogue, by
    Ryskamp, pp. 182–3.
7 Shade,] Shade *R*   16 *God.*] *God R*

'CUM TOT SUSTINEANT REGES ET TANTA, NEQUE ULLA'

Cum tot sustineant Reges et tanta, neque ullâ
  Parte, Voluptati Deliciisque Vacent:
Cum varios Capiti affigat Diadema Dolores,
  Bellorumque premant Sollicitentque Minæ:
Cur queritur Populus? cur cæco Murmure mussat?   5
  Inque suum Insane Vim meditatur Herum?
Qui Vigil Excubias agit usque, et sustinet usque
  Imperii, Populus ne quà Laboret, Onus.
Hoc Satanæ scelus est, nec Dæmone dignius ull[um]
  Nam primum in Satanæ pectore, Crime[n erat]   10
Præmia quin date digna Viro, verusque sequatur
  Collata in gentem commoda, Gentis Amor.
Illum Iure colant Populi, tueantur, Amante[s,]
  Ille colit Populos, ille tuetur, Amat.
Tu vero (si talis erit) quicunque verendum   15
  Execrare caput Principis, Eia! Tace;
Nec quia rara, fides Regi fert præmia, Demens
  Immeritum Regem quem Venerere, putes;
Ipse tibi plaudas, quæ Laus est Optima, Laudem
  Externam Ingenuis est meruisse Satis—   20

JOB CHAPTER FOURTEENTH

Short is thy Race, O Man! the Goal is Death,
Not distant far, nor without many a Rub
Attainable, tho' near: Man, as a Flower,
Even as a tender Flower, to day smells sweet,
With shining Leaves adorn'd, to morrow withers,   5
And as an Airy Shadow flits away
Unpermanent; withdraw then mighty God!

COPY-TEXT: letter to Chase Price, of uncertain date (L). First printed by Thomas Wright, *William Cowper*, 1895 (pamphlet), then published in his *Unpublished and Uncollected Poems of William Cowper*, 1900, pp. 14–15. The bracketed portions were supplied by Wright.

COPY-TEXT: *T*, whence first printed by Ryskamp, *BC*, pp. 457–9.

1 Race,] Race *T*

Withdraw thy Vengeance! nor on Man so low,
So vile a Creature, pour thy Wrath; shall he
The slightest Search of thy Dread Judgment stand,   10
Unblameable, and shall Cleaness, from Uncleaness spring,
Pure from Impure, then rather let him rest,
(If rest he can) Unsentenc'd, unexplored;
Till as the wearied Hireling, he shall leave
His Task accomplish'd, and with inward Joy   15
Behold his Setting Sun, and bless the Ray,
The parting Ray, sure Harbinger of rest
To his unquiet Soul: if the Sharp Ax
From it's deep Root sever the groaning Oak,
Still shall the Genial Moisture unrestrain'd   20
Shoot upward, and with Vegetable Life
Supply the spreading Branches; But if Man
With grinding Care, and Misery oppress'd
Lay down his Marrowless Bones in the cold Grave,
Sapless, and dry, who shall again bid flow   25
The Circulating Juices? who restore
Light to the Sightless Eye-balls? Hide me then
In some deep Cavern! Hide me where the Sun
Sends not his glorious Beams! but underneath
Night-shade, or Hemlock, or the pois'nous Leaf   30
Of Aconite, with pestilential Vapour fed,
Sprouts horrible; here hide me till thy Wrath
Be past, here let me dwell with thickest Night
Surrounded; Night more pleasing far than Day
Lowring with Wrath to come; Yet will I wait   35
With Patience, wait my Doom, till thou shalt call—
For thou wilt call, and into Joy receive
Thy Creature, Joy eternal, as beseems
Thy Goodness—then with Spirit elate obey
Thy Summons, upwards towering to the Realms   40
Of Bliss Celestial, unallay'd by time:
The mouldring Rocks into the fluid Air
Annihilated pass, and with the light
Etherial particles their Substance mix
Invisible; or while beneath their Roots   45

20 unrestrain'd] unrestrain'd, *T*   36 Patience,] Patience *T*   call—] call *T*
39 Goodness—] Goodness, *T*

Gently the slow corroding Waters glide,
Nod o'er the Plain Impendent, then with vast
And ruinous Dissolution, downwards born
Come shadowing, and o'er the plain beneath
Spread Distant Desolation! Thus frail Man!   50
While proud Imagination swells thy Heart,
With Airy Hopes of Princedom, and Domain
Imperial, thou fall'st; then Palaces,
Or prisons to thy Progeny bequeath'st,
Dismal Inheritance! But neither Joy   55
Their Glory, nor Anxiety their Shame,
Worketh in thee, Unintellectual Clay.

PSALM CXXXVII

To Babylon's proud waters brought,
    In bondage where we lay,
With tears on Sion's Hill we thought,
    And sigh'd our hours away;
Neglected on the willows hung   5
Our useless harps, while ev'ry tongue
    Bewail'd the fatal day.

Then did the base insulting foe
    Some joyous notes demand,
Such as in Sion used to flow   10
    From Judah's happy band—
Alas! what joyous notes have we
Our country spoil'd, no longer free,
    And in a foreign land?

Oh! Solyma! if e'er thy praise   15
    Be silent in my song,
Rude and unpleasing be the lays,
    And artless be my tongue!
Thy name my fancy still employs;
To thee, great fountain of my joys,   20
    My sweetest airs belong.

57 thee,] thee *T*

COPY-TEXT: Croft, 1825, pp. 6–8 (first printing).

Remember, Lord! that hostile sound,
  When Edom's children cry'd,
Razed be her turrets to the ground,
  And humbled be her pride;   25
Remember, Lord! and let the foe
The terror of thy vengeance know—
  The vengeance they defied.

Thou too, great Babylon, shall fall
  A victim to our God;   30
Thy monstrous crimes already call
  For Heaven's chastising rod.
Happy who shall thy little ones
Relentless dash against the stones,
  And spread their limbs abroad.   35

'MORTALS, AROUND YOUR DESTIN'D HEADS'

Mortals, around your destin'd heads
  Thick fly the Shafts of Death,
And lo! the Savage spoiler spreads
  A thousand Toils beneath.

In Vain we trifle with our fate,   5
  Try ev'ry Art in Vain,
At best we but prolong the date,
  And lengthen out our Pain.

Fondly we think all danger fled,
  For Death is ever Nigh,   10
Out-strips our Unavailing speed,
  Or Meets us as we flie.

Thus the Wreck'd Mariner may strive
  Some Desart Shore to gain,
Secure of Life, if he survive   15
  The fury of the Main.

COPY-TEXT: ll. 1–20, copy in Theadora Cowper's hand, B.L. Add. MS. 30803A, fo. 199 (*B*); ll. 21–4, Croft, 1825, pp. 34–5 (first printing). Also collated: *T*.
Title] *none in B, Croft*; A Meditation *T*   2 Thick] Which *Croft*

But there, to Famine doom'd a prey,
    Finds the mistaken Wretch,
He but escaped the troubled Sea,
    To perish on the Beach.   20

Since then in vain we strive to guard
    Our frailty from the foe;
Lord, let me live not unprepared
    To meet the fatal blow!

'ANXIOUS AS SAD OFFENDERS ARE'

Anxious as sad Offenders are,
    Whose troubled days are spent
'Twixt Hope of Pardon, and the Fear
    Of Final Punishment,

Is the poor Wretch whose Vital Heat   5
    Diseases daily chill;
Whom Hopes of Life uncertain yet,
    And Fears of Death assail.

O save me Lord! dispell my Fears!
    Let this O God suffice,   10
Confound not thus my growing Years,
    With Age's Miserys.

For ah, I feel and long have felt
    What grief the Sick-Man knows,
In secret sorrowing for the Guilt,   15
    From whence those Griefs arose.

21–4] *not in B*

Composed spring 1752?

COPY-TEXT: *T*, whence first printed by Ryskamp, *BC*, pp. 459–60.

1 are,] are *T*   2 spent] spent, *T*   4 Punishment,] Punishment. *T*   5 Heat] Heat, *T*   9 Lord!] Lord. *T*   10 Let this] *altered from* Thus much *T*   13 ah,] ah *T*

When Health supply'd each steady Nerve,
 And Vigour fill'd my Frame,
The Being I forgot to serve
 From whom that Vigour came.   20

In Health tho' I despis'd the Fear,
 The Thought of future Pain,
In Sickness let me not despair
 To know that Health again.

Yes I will hope, for thou hast said,   25
 Come to me ye distressed,
All ye that Labour, and are sad;
 And I will give you rest.

O then my God I will repent,
 Thy Burthen is but light,   30
Absence from thee is Banishment
 And Heav'n is in thy Sight.

AN APOLOGY
FOR NOT SHOWING HER WHAT I HAD WROTE

Did not my muse (what can she less)
Perceive her own unworthiness,
Could she by some well chosen theme,
But hope to merit your esteem,
She would not thus conceal her lays,   5
Ambitious to deserve your praise.
But should my Delia take offence,
And frown on her impertinence,
In silence, sorrowing and forlorn,
Would the despairing trifler mourn;   10
Curse her ill-tuned, unpleasing lute,
Then sigh and sit for ever mute.

23 despair] despair, *T*   25 hope,] hope *T*

Composed July 1752.

COPY-TEXT: Croft, 1825, pp. 12–13 (first printing).

In secret, therefore, let her play,
Squand'ring her idle notes away;
In secret as she chants along,   15
Cheerful and careless in her song;
Nor heeds she whether harsh or clear,
Free from each terror, ev'ry fear,
From that, of all most dreaded, free,
The terror of offending *Thee*.   20

'DELIA, TH'UNKINDEST GIRL ON EARTH'

Delia, th'unkindest girl on earth,
    When I besought the fair,
That favour of intrinsic worth,
    A ringlet of her hair,—

Refused that instant to comply   5
    With my absurd request,
For reasons she could specify,
    Some twenty score at least.

Trust me, my dear, however odd
    It may appear to say,   10
I sought it merely to defraud
    Thy spoiler of his prey.

Yet when its sister locks shall fade,
    As quickly fade they must,
When all their beauties are decay'd,   15
    Their gloss, their colour, lost,—

Ah then! if haply to my share
    Some slender pittance fall,
If I but gain one single hair,
    Nor age usurp them all;—   20

Composed summer 1752.

COPY-TEXT: Croft, 1825, pp. 14–15 (first printing).

When you behold it still as sleek,
  As lovely to the view,
As when it left thy snowy neck—
  That Eden where it grew—

Then shall my Delia's self declare,   25
  That I profess'd the truth,
And have preserved my little share
  In everlasting youth.

'THIS EVENING, DELIA, YOU AND I'

This evening, Delia, you and I
Have managed most delightfully,
  For with a frown we parted;
Having contrived some trifle that
We both may be much troubled at,   5
  And sadly disconcerted.

Yet well as each perform'd their part,
We might perceive it was but art;
  And that we both intended
To sacrifice a little ease;   10
For all such petty flaws as these
  Are made but to be mended.

You knew, Dissembler! all the while,
How sweet it was to reconcile
  After this heavy pelt;   15
That we should gain by this allay
When next we met, and laugh away
  The care we never felt.

Composed summer 1752.

COPY-TEXT: Croft, 1825, pp. 16–17 (first printing). Collated: T.

1 Delia, you] little The: T   2 most] so T   3 For] That T   5 much troubled]
uneasy T   7–8]   Yet tho' we never did agree
                        Upon this Quarrel you might see T
9 And that we both] We mutually T   11 all] why T   13 You]She T
14 was] were T   17 laugh] kiss T

Happy! when we but seem t'endure
A little pain, then find a cure   20
  By double joy requited;
For friendship, like a sever'd bone,
Improves and gains a stronger tone
  When aptly reunited.

'IN A FOND HOUR MY DELIA SWORE'

In a fond Hour my Delia swore,
  And kiss'd me while she spoke,
She did despise, detest, abhor,
  And Loath my very Look.

When, straining the Dissembling Maid   5
  Still closer to my Side,
Half hesitating, half afraid,
  Yet Eager I reply'd:

Howe'er thy Words may seem severe,
  While their Effects are such,   10
Believe me, Delia, when I Swear,
  Nor think I swear to much:

Rather, much rather would I be—
  Be thus thy Scorn express'd—
Detested and despis'd by thee,   15
  Than by the World caress'd.

19 seem] *T*; seek *Croft*   23 gains] *T*; joins *Croft*

Composed summer 1752.

copy-text: *T*, whence first printed by Ryskamp, *BC*, p. 462. Punctuation supplied.

OF HIMSELF

William was once a bashful youth,
  His modesty was such,
That one might say (to say the truth)
  He rather had too much.

Some said that it was want of sense,   5
  And others, want of spirit,
(So blest a thing is impudence)
  While others could not bear it.

But some a different notion had,
  And at each other winking,   10
Observed that though he little said,
  He paid it off with thinking.

Howe'er, it happen'd, by degrees,
  He mended and grew perter,
In company was more at ease,   15
  And dress'd a little smarter.

Nay now and then would look quite gay,
  As other people do;
And sometimes said, or try'd to say
  A witty thing or so.   20

He eyed the women, and made free
  To comment on their shapes,
So that there was, or seem'd to be,
  No fear of a relapse.

The women said, who thought him rough,   25
  But now no longer foolish,
The creature may do well enough,
  But wants a deal of polish.

COPY-TEXT: Croft, 1825, pp. 1–3 (first printing). See above, 'A Character'.

At length improved from head to heel,
    'Twere scarce too much to say,   30
No dancing bear was so genteel,
    Or half so dégagé.

Now that a miracle so strange
    May not in vain be shown,
Let the dear maid who wrought the change   35
    E'en claim him for her own.

'BID ADIEU, MY SAD HEART, BID ADIEU TO THY PEACE'

Bid adieu, my sad heart, bid adieu to thy peace,
Thy pleasure is past, and thy sorrows increase;
See the shadows of evening how far they extend,
And a long night is coming, that never may end;
For the sun is now set that enliven'd the scene,   5
And an age must be past e'er it rises again.

Already deprived of its splendour and heat,
I feel thee more slowly, more heavily beat;
Perhaps overstrain'd with the quick pulse of pleasure,
Thou art glad of this respite to beat at thy leisure;   10
But the sigh of distress shall now weary thee more
Than the flutter and tumult of passion before.

The heart of a lover is never at rest,
With joy overwhelm'd, or with sorrow oppress'd:
When Delia is near, all is ecstasy then,   15
And I even forget I must lose her again:
When absent, as wretched, as happy before,
Despairing I cry, I shall see her no more.

36 E'en] *conj. Bruce*; E'er *Croft*

Composed October 1752.

COPY-TEXT: Croft, 1825, pp. 17–18. (first printing). Collated: *T*. *Title*] *none in Croft*;
Upon hearing She was just going to Lancashire *T*   3] Thy Day is far spent, see
the shadows extend, *T*   6 And an age must] And Age may *T*   10 beat]
be *T*

WRITTEN AFTER LEAVING HER AT NEW BARNS

How quick the change from joy to woe,
How chequer'd is our lot below!
Seldom we view the prospect fair,
Dark clouds of sorrow, pain, and care,
(Some pleasing intervals between)   5
Scowl over more than half the scene.
Last week with Delia, gentle maid!
Far hence in happier fields I stray'd,
While on her dear enchanting tongue
Soft sounds of grateful welcome hung,   10
For absence had withheld it long.
Welcome my long-lost love, she said,
E'er since our adverse fates decreed
That we must part, and I must mourn
'Till once more blest by thy return,   15
Love, on whose influence I relied
For all the transports I enjoy'd,
Has play'd the cruel tyrant's part,
And turn'd tormentor to my heart;
But let me hold thee to my breast,   20
Dear partner of my joy and rest,
And not a pain, and not a fear,
Or anxious doubt, shall enter there.—
Happy thought I, the favour'd youth,
Blest with such undissembled truth!—   25

Five suns successive rose and sat,
And saw no monarch in his state,
Wrapt in the blaze of majesty,
So free from every care as I.—
Next day the scene was overcast,   30
Such day till then I never pass'd,—

Composed summer or early autumn 1754?

COPY-TEXT: Croft, 1825, pp. 19–21 (first printing). Collated: *T*.

Title] After our Meeting at New Barns *T*   Barns] Burns *Croft*
7–8]   Last week on Delia's Bosom laid
    These Eyes beheld the tender Maid *T*
11 it] us *T*   25, 37] *spaces following these lines from T; not in Croft*

For on that day, relentless fate!
Delia and I must separate.
Yet e'er we look'd our last farewell,
From her dear lips this comfort fell:—   35
'Fear not that time, where'er we rove,
Or absence, shall abate my love.'

And can I doubt, my charming maid!
As unsincere what you have said?
Banish'd from thee to what I hate,   40
Dull neighbours and insipid chat,
No joy to cheer me, none in view,
But the dear hope of meeting you;—
And that through passion's optic seen,
With ages interposed between,—   45
Blest with the kind support you give,
'Tis by your promised truth I live;
How deep my woes, how fierce my flame,
You best may tell, who feel the same.

ON HER ENDEAVOURING TO CONCEAL
HER GRIEF AT PARTING

Ah! wherefore should my weeping maid suppress
Those gentle signs of undissembled woe?
When from soft love proceeds the deep distress,
Ah! why forbid the willing tears to flow?

Since for my sake each dear translucent drop   5
Breaks forth, best witness of thy truth sincere,
My lips should drink the precious moisture up,
And, e'er it falls, receive the trembling tear.

32 fate] fate! *Croft*   43 meeting] seeing *T*
46–7]   Did not thy Words some Comfort give
         Could I my Delia could I live *T*
49 may] can *replacing* may *deleted T*

COPY-TEXT: Croft, 1825, pp. 22–3 (first printing). Collated: *T*.

4 to] that *T*   7 should] shall *T*   moisture] *T*; mixture *Croft*

Trust me, these symptoms of thy faithful heart,
In absence shall my dearest hope sustain,   10
Delia! since such thy sorrow that we part,
Such when we meet thy joy shall be again.

Hard is that heart and unsubdued by love
That feels no pain, nor ever heaves a sigh,
Such hearts the fiercest passions only prove,   15
Or freeze in cold insensibility.

Oh! then indulge thy grief, nor fear to tell
The gentle source from whence thy sorrows flow!
Nor think it weakness when we love to feel,
Nor think it weakness what we feel to show.   20

THE SYMPTOMS OF LOVE

Would my Delia know if I love, let her take
My last thought at night, and the first when I wake;
With my prayers and best wishes preferr'd for her sake.

Let her guess what I muse on, when rambling alone
I stride o'er the stubble each day with my gun,   5
Never ready to shoot till the covey is flown.

Let her think what odd whimsies I have in my brain,
When I read one page over and over again
And discover at last that I read it in vain.

Let her say why so fix'd and so steady my look,   10
Without ever regarding the person who spoke,
Still affecting to laugh, without hearing the joke.

9 faithful] trembling *T*   10 absence] absence, *Croft*   12] Such shall thy Joy
be when we meet again *T*

COPY-TEXT: Croft, 1825, pp. 23–4, except ll. 13–15, from *T*. First printed by Croft, 1825,
except ll. 13–15, by Ryskamp, p. 232.

1 if] how *T*   10 so steady] stedfast *T*   12 Still] With *T*   the] a *T*

Why when I would see how the dull minutes pass,
I apply to my watch with a serious face,
And return it again just as wise as I was.   15

Or why when with pleasure her praises I hear,
(That sweetest of melody sure to my ear,)
I attend, and at once inattentive appear.

And lastly, when summon'd to drink to my flame,
Let her guess why I never once mention her name,   20
Though herself and the woman I love are *the same.*

AN ATTEMPT AT THE MANNER OF WALLER

Did not thy reason and thy sense,
With most persuasive eloquence,
Convince me that obedience due
None may so justly claim as you,
By right of beauty you would be   5
Mistress o'er my heart and me.

Then fear not I should e'er rebel
My gentle love! I might as well
A forward peevishness put on,
And quarrel with the mid-day sun;   10
Or question who gave him a right
To be so fiery and so bright.

Nay, this were less absurd and vain
Than disobedience to thy reign:
His beams are often too severe;   15
But thou art mild, as thou art fair;
First from necessity we own your sway,
Then scorn our freedom, and by choice obey.

13–15] T, *punctuation supplied*   18 inattentive] Unattentive T

Composed March 1753.

copy-text: Croft, 1825, pp. 25–6 (first printing). Collated: *T. Title] not in T*   5 you
would] thou wouldst T   9 forward] Froward T   12] To shine insufferably
bright. T

HORTI AD FLORAM DEDICATIO. 1753

Quæ tibi Sacros (ubi vel pruinis
Albicant Agri vel tibi ipse torrens
Arbiter Cæli Canis urit arva)
   Protegis Hortos,

Flora, Odorata redimita Vitta   5
Aureum Crinem, mea rura præsens
Sint licet parvo decorata Sumptu,
   Diva, tuere;

Textili si nec Violæ sub umbra
Rore gaudentes pluviaque desint,   10
Quæque candori nivium recenteum
   Lilia certent,

Da sinus Soli patulos tumentes
Explicent Gemmæ, radiosque et almos
Hauriant Imbres, neque Cochlearum   15
   Præda tabescant;

Nec sinas olim mea pervicaces
Septa deturbent Satyri, Coronam
Dum mea dignam juvat otiose
   Affingere Nympha.   20

Sic ubi gressum Deacunque tendis
Ventus aspiret tibi nullus, oro,
Nullus aspiret nisi blandientis
   Aura Favoni.

COPY-TEXT: *T*, whence first printed by Ryskamp, *BC*, pp. 466–7. (Punctuation supplied.)

1 (ubi] Cubi *T*   3 arva)] arva *T*   15 Cochlearum] Cocklearum *T*   19
otiose] otiosum *T*   20 Nympha] Numpha *T*

WRITTEN IN A QUARREL,

The delivery of it prevented by a reconciliation

Think, Delia, with what cruel haste
  Our fleeting pleasures move,
Nor heedless thus in sorrow waste
  The moments due to love.

Be wise, my fair, and gently treat   5
  These few that are our friends;
Think, thus abused, what sad regret
  Their speedy flight attends!

Sure in those eyes I loved so well,
  And wish'd so long to see,   10
Anger I thought could never dwell,
  Or anger aim'd at me.

No bold offence of mine I knew
  Should e'er provoke your hate;
And early taught to think you true,   15
  Still hoped a gentler fate.

With kindness bless the present hour,
  Or oh! we meet in vain!
What can we do in absence more
  Than suffer and complain?   20

Fated to ills beyond redress,
  We must endure our woe;
The days allow'd us to possess,
  'Tis madness to forego.

Composed early 1754?

COPY-TEXT: Croft, 1825, pp. 10–12 (first printing).

5 treat] treat, *Croft*   7 Think,] Think *Croft*

'HOPE, LIKE THE SHORT-LIVED RAY THAT GLEAMS AWHILE'

Hope, like the short-lived ray that gleams awhile
   Through wintry skies upon the frozen waste,
Cheers e'en the face of misery to a smile;
   But soon the momentary pleasure's past!

How oft, my Delia! since our last farewell,   5
   (Years that have roll'd since that distressful hour,)
Grieved I have said, when most our hopes prevail,
   Our promised happiness is least secure.

Oft I have thought the scene of troubles closed,
   And hoped once more to gaze upon your charms;   10
As oft some dire mischance has interposed,
   And snatch'd th'expected blessing from my arms.

The seaman thus, his shatter'd vessel lost,
   Still vainly strives to shun the threat'ning death;
And while he thinks to gain the friendly coast,   15
   And drops his feet, and feels the sands beneath,

Borne by the wave, steep-sloping from the shore,
   Back to th'inclement deep, again he beats
The surge aside, and seems to tread secure;
   And now the refluent wave his baffled toil defeats.   20

Had you, my love, forbade me to pursue
   My fond attempt, disdainfully retired,
And with proud scorn compell'd me to subdue
   Th'ill-fated passion by yourself inspired;

Composed 1755?

COPY-TEXT: Croft, 1825, pp. 26–8 (first printing). Collated: *T* (second and fourth lines not indented).

Title] *none in Croft*; Often Expecting to meet her and Disappointed *T*   1 ray] ray, *Croft*
2 skies] skies, *Croft*   3 to a smile] to Smile *T*   7 Grieved I have said] Then I
have found *T*   8] Least is our promis'd Happiness secure. *T*   9 I have] have I *T*
troubles] Trouble *T*   10 gaze upon your] dwell upon thy *T*   16 beneath,] beneath:
Croft   18 deep,] deep *Croft*   19 and] now *T*   21 Had you] Hadst thou *T*

Then haply to some distant spot removed,   25
   Hopeless to gain, unwilling to molest
With fond entreaties whom I dearly loved,
   Despair or absence had redeem'd my rest.

But now, sole partner in my Delia's heart,
   Yet doom'd far off in exile to complain,   30
Eternal absence cannot ease my smart,
   And hope subsists but to prolong my pain.

Oh then! kind heaven, be this my latest breath;
   Here end my life, or make it worth my care;
Absence from whom we love is worse than death,   35
   And frustrate hope severer than despair.

1755

All-worshipp'd gold! thou mighty mystery!
Say by what name shall I address thee rather,
Our blessing, or our bane? without thy aid,
The gen'rous pangs of pity but distress
The human heart, that fain would feel the bliss   5
Of blessing others; and, enslaved by thee,
Far from relieving woes which others feel,
Misers oppress themselves. Our blessing then
With virtue when possess'd; without, our bane!
If in my bosom unperceived there lurk   10

26 unwilling] nor willing *T*   29 in] of *T*   34] Or let me live, if I must
live, With her; *T*

COPY-TEXT: Croft, 1825, pp. 30–1 (first printing). Collated: *T*.

Title 1755] R.S.S. Croft (*see Commentary*); Love the Noblest Passion and Most Conducive
to Virtue *T*   1]   Thanks to the God of Nature Who endued
                         My Soul With Nobler passions than the Thirst
                         Of all subduing Gold Mysterious Power *T*
5 that fain would feel] Which fain would taste *T*
between 9 *and* 10 *T has*:
                         The Tinsel Splendor of a Pageant Show
                         Those gaudy Trifles that surprize the Vulgar
                         And set the staring Multitude agape
                         Ne'er could Extort one Anxious Wish from me
                         Mine is an humbler yet a Nobler Aim

The deep-sown seeds of av'rice or ambition,
Blame me, ye great ones, (for I scorn your censure)
But let the gen'rous and the good commend me;
That to my Delia I direct them all,
The worthiest object of a virtuous love.   15
Oh! to some distant scene, a willing exile
From the wild uproar of this busy world,
Were it my fate with Delia to retire;
With her to wander through the sylvan shade
Each morn, or o'er the moss-imbrowned turf,   20
Where, blest as the prime parents of mankind
In their own Eden, we would envy none;
But, greatly pitying whom the world calls happy,
Gently spin out the silken thread of life;
While from her lips attentive I receive   25
The tend'rest dictates of the purest flame,
And from her eyes (where soft complacence sits
Illumined with the radiant beams of sense)
Tranquillity beyond a monarch's reach!

Forgive me, heav'n! this only avarice   30
My soul indulges; I confess the crime,
(If to esteem, to covet such perfection
Be criminal,) Oh grant me Delia! grant me wealth!
Wealth to alleviate, not increase my wants,
And grant me virtue, without which nor wealth   35
Nor Delia can avail to make me blest.

---

12 your] the *T*   14 my Delia] one Object *T*   19 shade] shade; *Croft*
28] Not unenliven'd with becoming Lustre *T*   29 a monarch's] the Sage's *T*   *space
following* 29 *from T; not in Croft*   30 heav'n] *T*; heaven *Croft*   avarice] *T*; av'rice
Croft   33 me Delia!] me, Delia! *Croft*   grant me wealth!] give me Wealth *T*
35 grant] give *T*

WRITTEN IN A FIT OF ILLNESS
1755

In these sad hours, a prey to ceaseless pain,
While feverish pulses leap in ev'ry vein,
When each faint breath the last short effort seems
Of life just parting from my feeble limbs;
How wild soe'er my wand'ring thoughts may be,   5
Still, gentle Delia! still they turn on thee!
At length if, slumbering to a short repose,
A sweet oblivion frees me from my woes,
Thy form appears, thy footsteps I pursue,
Through springy vales, and meadows wash'd in dew;   10
Thy arm supports me to the fountain's brink,
Where, by some secret pow'r forbid to drink,
Gasping with thirst, I view the tempting flood
That flies my touch, or thickens into mud,
Till thine own hand immerged the goblet dips,   15
And bears it streaming to my burning lips;
Then borne aloft on fancy's wing we fly,
Like souls embodied to their native sky;
Now ev'ry rock, each mountain, disappears;
And the round earth an even surface wears;   20
When lo! the force of some resistless weight
Bears me straight down from that pernicious height;
Parting, in vain our struggling arms we close;
Abhorred forms, dire phantoms interpose;
With trembling voice on thy loved name I call,   25
And gulphs yawn ready to receive my fall;
From these fallacious visions of distress
I wake; nor are my real sorrows less.
Thy absence, Delia! heightens every ill,

COPY-TEXT: Croft, 1825, pp. 32–4 (first printing). Collated: *T*.

Title Written in] Wrote during *T*   1755] R.S.S. *Croft* (*see Commentary*); *not in T*
2 leap] beat *T*   4 feeble] Languid *T*   11 fountain's] Fountain *T*   17 Then]
There *Croft*
17–18]   Thence light as Air tho' Wingless thro' the Sky
              Wrapt in each other's Arms aloft we fly *T*
22 Bears me straight] Bears strait *T*   25 trembling] feeble *T*   *between* 28 *and* 29 *T*
has:
              Sickness and Pain the Evils I endure
              Evils indeed but not Without a Cure

And gives e'en trivial pains the power to kill.   30
Oh! wert thou near me; yet that wish forbear!
'Twere vain, my love—'twere vain to wish thee near,
Thy tender heart would heave with anguish too;
And by partaking, but increase my woe.
Alone I'll grieve, till, gloomy sorrow past,   35
Health, like the cheerful day-spring, comes at last—
Comes fraught with bliss to banish ev'ry pain,
Hope, joy, and peace, and Delia in her train!

'SEE WHERE THE THAMES, THE PUREST STREAM'

See where the Thames, the purest stream
That wavers to the noon-day beam,
    Divides the vale below:
While like a vein of liquid ore
His waves enrich the happy shore,   5
    Still shining as they flow.

Nor yet, my Delia! to the main
Runs the sweet tide without a stain,
    Unsullied as it seems:
The nymphs of many a sable flood   10
Deform with streaks of oozy mud
    The bosom of the Thames.

Some idle rivulets, that feed
And sucker ev'ry noisome weed,
    A sandy bottom boast: 15
For ever bright, for ever clear,
The trifling shallow rills appear
    In their own channels lost.

30 e'en] ev'n *T*   33 heave with anguish too] feel What I sustain *T*   34 my woe]
my Pain *T*
35–8]   Oh spare me then nor let my Cares impart
                       One pang one Thought of Sorrow to thy Heart
                       While 'tis my own I can endure my Woe
                       But cannot if it wounds my Delia too *T*

COPY-TEXT: Croft, 1825, pp. 36–8 (first printing). Collated: *T*.

8 sweet] clear *T*   11 Deform] *T*; Deform'd *Croft*   14 sucker] *T*; suckle *Croft*
18 channels] *T*; channel *Croft*

Thus fares it with the human soul,
Where copious floods of passion roll,   20
  By genuine love supply'd:
Fair in itself the current shows,
But ah! a thousand anxious woes
  Pollute the noble tide.

These are emotions known to few;   25
For where at most a vap'ry dew
  Surrounds the tranquil heart,
There as the triflers never prove
The glad excess of real love,
  They never prove the smart.   30

Oh! then my life, at last relent,
Though cruel the reproach I sent,
  My sorrow was unfeign'd:
Your passion, had I loved you not,
You might have scorn'd, renounced, forgot,   35
  And I had ne'er complain'd.

While you indulge a groundless fear,
Th'imaginary woes you bear
  Are real woes to me:
But thou art kind, and good thou art,   40
Nor wilt, by wronging thine own heart,
  Unjustly punish me.

'HOW BLEST THE YOUTH WHOM FATE ORDAINS'

How blest the youth whom Fate ordains
A kind relief from all his pains,
  In some admired fair;
Whose tend'rest wishes find express'd
Their own resemblance in her breast   5
  Exactly copied there.

20 floods] Tides *T*   28 There] *T*; Then *Croft*   38 woes you bear] Ills you hear *T*
39 woes] Ills *T*   40 kind, and good] good, and kind *T*   41 wilt] will *T*   thine] your *T*

COPY-TEXT: Croft, 1825, pp. 38–40 (first printing). Collated: *T*.

Title. none in Croft; Her Love the best Protection from Sorrow *T*   1 the] this *T*
2 from] for *T*   4 find] *T*; finds *Croft*

What good soe'er the Gods dispense,
Th'enjoyment of its influence
    Still on her love depends;
Her love the shield that guards his heart,   10
Or wards the blow, or blunts the dart,
    That peevish Fortune sends.

Thus, Delia, while thy love endures
The flame my happy breast secures
    From Fortune's fickle pow'r;   15
Change as she list, she may increase,
But not abate my happiness,
    Confirm'd by thee before.

Thus while I share her smiles with thee,
Welcome, my love, shall ever be   20
    The favours she bestows;
Yet not on those I found my bliss,
But on the noble ecstacies
    The faithful bosom knows.

And when she prunes her wings for flight,   25
And flutters nimbly from my sight,
    Contented I resign
Whate'er she gave; thy love alone
I can securely call my own,
    Happy while that is mine.   30

UPON A VENERABLE RIVAL

Full thirty frosts since thou wert young
    Have chill'd the wither'd grove,
Thou wretch! and hast thou lived so long,
    Nor yet forgot to love?

16 list] will *T*   21 favours] Favour *T*   23 on] *T*; in *Croft*   noble] nobler *T*
29 can] may *T*

COPY-TEXT: Croft, 1825, pp. 40–1 (first printing).

Ye Sages! spite of your pretences 5
    To wisdom, you must own
Your folly frequently commences
    When you acknowledge none.

Not that I deem it weak to love,
    Or folly to admire, 10
But ah! the pangs we lovers prove
    Far other years require.

Unheeded on the youthful brow
    The beams of Phœbus play,
But unsupported Age stoops low 15
    Beneath the sultry ray.

For once, then, if untutor'd youth,
    Youth unapprov'd by years,
May chance to deviate into truth,
    When your experience errs; 20

For once attempt not to despise
    What I esteem a rule:
Who early loves, though young, is wise—
    Who old, though grey, a fool.

TO DELIA

1755

Me to whatever state the Gods assign,
Believe, my love, whatever state be mine,
Ne'er shall my breast one anxious sorrow know,
Ne'er shall my heart confess a real woe;
If to thy share heaven's choicest blessings fall, 5
As thou hast virtue to deserve them all:
Yet vain, alas! that idle hope would be
That builds on happiness remote from thee.
Oh! may thy charms, whate'er our fate decrees,
Please, as they must, but let them only please— 10

COPY-TEXT: Croft, 1825, pp. 48-50 (first printing).

Not like the sun with equal influence shine,
Nor warm with transport any heart but mine.
Ye who from wealth th'ill-grounded title boast
To claim whatever beauty charms you most;
Ye sons of fortune, who consult alone   15
Her parents' will, regardless of her own,
Know that a love like ours, a gen'rous flame,
No wealth can purchase, and no pow'r reclaim.
The soul's affection can be only given
Free, unextorted, as the grace of heaven.   20
   Is there whose faithful bosom can endure
Pangs fierce as mine, nor ever hope a cure?
Who sighs in absence of the dear-loved maid,
Nor summons once indiff'rence to his aid?
Who can, like me, the nice resentment prove,   25
The thousand soft disquietudes of love;
The trivial strifes that cause a real pain;
The real bliss when reconciled again?
Let him alone dispute the real prize,
And read his sentence in my Delia's eyes;   30
There shall he read all gentleness and truth,
But not himself, the dear distinguish'd youth;
Pity for him perhaps they may express—
Pity, that will but heighten his distress.
But, wretched rival! he must sigh to see   35
The sprightlier rays of love directed all to me.
   And thou, dear antidote of ev'ry pain
Which fortune can inflict, or love ordain,
Since early love has taught thee to despise
What the world's worthless vot'ry's only prize,   40
Believe, my love! no less the gen'rous God
Rules in my breast, his ever blest abode;
There has he driven each gross desire away,
Directing ev'ry wish and ev'ry thought to thee!
Then can I ever leave my Delia's arms,   45
A slave, devoted to inferior charms?
Can e'er my soul her reason so disgrace?
For what blest minister of heavenly race
Would quit that heaven to find a happier place?

28 again?] again. *Croft*   38 ordain,] ordain *Croft*   49 place?] place. *Croft*

ODE.
SUPPOSED TO BE WRITTEN ON THE MARRIAGE OF A FRIEND

Thou magic lyre, whose fascinating sound
  Seduced the savage monsters from their cave;
Drew rocks and trees, and forms uncouth around,
  And bade wild Hebrus hush his list'ning wave;
No more thy undulating warbles flow   5
O'er Thracian wilds of everlasting snow!

Awake to sweeter sounds, thou magic lyre,
  And paint a lover's bliss—a lover's pain—
Far nobler triumphs now thy notes inspire,—
  For see, Euridice attends thy strain;   10
Her smile, a prize beyond the conjuror's aim—
Superior to the cancell'd breath of fame.

From her sweet brow to chase the gloom of care,
  To check that tear that dims the beaming eye,
To bid her heart the rising sigh forbear,   15
  And flush her orient cheek with brighter joy,
In that dear breast soft sympathy to move,
And touch the springs of rapture and of love.

Ah me! how long bewilder'd and astray,
  Lost and benighted, did my footsteps rove,   20
Till, sent by heaven to cheer my pathless way,
  A star arose—the radiant star of love.
The God propitious join'd our willing hands,
And Hymen wreathed us in his rosy bands.

Yet not the beaming eye, or placid brow,   25
  Or golden tresres, hid the subtle dart;
To charms superior far than those I bow,
  And nobler worth enslaves my vanquish'd heart;
The beauty, elegance, and grace combined,
Which beam transcendant from that angel mind;   30

COPY-TEXT: Croft, 1825, pp. 51–3 (first printing).

1 Thou] *Southey*; The *Croft*   5 warbles] *Povey*; waters *Croft*; warblings *Southey*
21 way] *Southey*; ray *Croft*

While vulgar passions—meteors of a day,
  Expire before the chilling blasts of age,
Our holy flame, with pure and steady ray,
  Its glooms shall brighten, and its pangs assuage;
By Virtue (sacred vestal) fed, shall shine,   35
And warm our fainting souls with energy divine.

'HAPPY THE MAN WHOSE AMOROUS FLAME HAS FOUND'

Happy the Man whose amorous Flame has found
The Glorious Sanction of ten thousand pound,
But happier he whose Eyes securely stray
Where Thirty thousand mark the glittering way;
The brave Emotions of his Ardent Soul   5
No Parents Slacken and no Fears controul;
Smooth lies the path that leads him to his Joys,
And Envy's self shall praise the prudent Choice.
Not so the Youth shall fare whose luckless Flame
Haply shall light on some unmoney'd Dame;   10
For him shall throb the trembling Parent's Heart,
And sage Advice this Constant Truth Impart:
My Son, let me thy Principles correct:
Love may allure, but Int'rest should direct.
Venus when naked charms the Fool alone;   15
Let but the Goddess put her Armour on,
Her Golden Arms, that kindle keen Desire,
The Grave shall worship and the wise Admire.

COPY-TEXT: *T*, whence first printed by Ryskamp, *BC*, p. 473. (Punctuation supplied.)
11 For] Form *T*

A NEW BALLAD
INTITLED THE SORROWFULL HUSBAND'S GARLAND OR THE GREY MARE THE BETTER HORSE

No great Matter Where, how it happen'd, or When,
You'll not presently hear such a Frolick again;
How to kill a good Husband a Jade of a Wife
Thought proper to Counterfeit Death to the Life.

This Wife had a Title—I cannot say Which,   5
Whether Brimstone or Baggage or Vixen or each—
But lest We should wrong her as haply We shall,
If we give her but one We'll e'en give her them all.

Our Couple agreed then their Lodging to take
At a Distance, for peace and good Neighbourhood sake,   10
Since for Banging and Bruising they car'd not a Rush,
And never could part till they'd had t'other Brush.

Yet both Were so Manfull and both were so Stout
That the Nicest of Judges have still been in doubt
Whose Talons could draw the most Blood at a Scratch,   15
So it must be confest 'twas an Excellent Match.

And now to my Story: this Wife, as I Said,
Must needs have her Husband inform'd she was dead,
Most craftily thinking, as well it may seem,
The Excess of his Transport might rid her of him.   20

But unlucky for her he perceiv'd the Design,
(How he did it you know is no Business of Mine)
So he let a great Sigh and he thump'd at his Breast,
Being sorry to find it was only a Jest.

Yet thought he to himself, being cunning, Suppose   25
I make a right use of this Matter, Who knows
But having once fairly confess'd she is dead,
I may lawfully take a new Wife in her Stead.

COPY-TEXT: *T*, whence first printed by Ryskamp, *BC*, pp. 464–6. (Punctuation supplied.)
8 her them all] them her all *T*   23 So he let] So let *T*   25 himself] himsel *T*

Nor Would he have ventur'd again had he thought
That 'for better for Worse' could have stuck in his Throat; 30
But should he take another this follow'd of course,
He might take her for better but hardly for Worse.

The Business thus settled he cheers up his Sp'rites,
And sorrowful Letter most Merrily Writes,
That his Grief at her Illness no Mortal could tell,   35
Nor how glad he should be could he hear she was Well.

But Whether from Pity, or Whether from Spite,
Whether thinking 'twere cruel to kill him outright,
Or Whether resolving to drub him again
Much rather than so put him out of his Pain,   40

In her very next Letter this Shrew of a Wife
Declar'd she was never so Well in her Life.
She die, no indeed—she should Cudgell the Knave,
And dance a brisk Hornpipe or two on his grave.

You may guess how he look'd when he saw in the Letter 45
Wrote in her own hand that she never was better;
His Condition was certainly just the reverse,
And for his part poor Devil he never was Worse.

And now for the Moral: the Moral is this,
And sure a most Excellent Moral it is,   50
If there lives such another unfortunate Man,
He must bear his Misfortune as well as he can.

AN ODE ON READING MR. RICHARDSON'S
HISTORY OF SIR CHARLES GRANDISON

Say, Ye Apostate and Profane,
Wretches! who blush not to disdain
  Allegiance to your God,
Did e'er your idly-boasted Love
Of Virtue for Her sake, remove   5
  And Lift you from the Crowd?

Would you the Race of Glory run,
Know the Devout, and They alone,
  Are Equal to the Task,
The Labours of th'Illustrious Course   10
Far other than th'unaided force
  Of Human Vigour ask.

To Arm against repeated Ill
The Patient Heart, too brave to feel
  The Tortures of Despair,   15
Nor suffer yet high-crested Pride
When Wealth flows in with ev'ry Tide
  To gain Admittance there:

To Rescue from the Tyrant's Sword
Th'Oppress'd; Unseen and unimplor'd   20
  To cheer the Face of Woe;
From Lawless Insult to Defend
An Orphan's Right, a fallen Friend,
  And a Forgiven Foe.

These, These distinguish from the Crowd 25
(And These alone) the Great and Good,
  The Guardians of Mankind!

Composed late February or early March 1754.

COPY-TEXT: lines 1–36, holograph in the Victoria and Albert Museum (*Q*); lines 37–42, Croft, 1825, pp. 42-4. Also collated: *T*; copy in John Johnson's hand, Berg Collection (*X*). Lines 19–42 first printed by Hayley, 1803, i. 20–1; lines 1–18 by Croft.

Title] *T*, *X* (*omits* Mr.), *Croft*; An Ode Occasion'd by Reading the History of Sir Charles Grandison *Q*   2 blush] scorn *X*   4 idly-boasted] idly-wasted *Croft*
10 Course] Course, *Q*   16 suffer] safer *Croft*   17] *T*, *X*, *Croft*; (Apt from ourselves, ourselves to hide) *Q*   23 a fallen] *T*, *X*, *Croft*; an Injur'd *Q*

Whose Bosoms with these Virtues heave,
Oh! with what Matchless Speed they leave
   The Multitude behind!   30

Then ask Ye from what Source on *Earth*
Virtues like These derive their Birth?—
   Deriv'd from *Heav'n* alone
Full on that favour'd Breast they shine,
Where Faith and Resignation Join   35
   To call the Blessing down.

Such is that Heart—but while the Muse
Thy Theme, O Richardson, pursues,
   Her feebler Spirits faint,
She cannot reach, and shall not wrong   40
That Subject for an Angel's song,
   The Hero and the Saint.

AN EPISTLE TO ROBERT LLOYD, ESQR. 1754

'Tis not that I design to rob
Thee of thy birth-right, gentle Bob,
For thou art born sole heir, and single,
Of dear Mat Prior's easy jingle;
Nor that I mean, while thus I knit   5
My thread-bare sentiments together,

32 derive] derived *Croft* above, *nothing deleted* T Heart to Shine   33 Deriv'd from] Derive, 'tis *then* Indulgent *added later*   34 on that] *X*, *Croft*; on the *Q*; *T has* Directs them on that

37–42] *Q has*   Such is that Happy, blameless Heart—
But hold—a Grandison's Desert
   Makes all Description faint;
Nor let the Muse attempt to Sing
A Theme too lofty for her Wing,
   The Hero and the Saint

so T, *except* 38 Grandison's] Richardson's
37 *Such is that Heart*] *italics only in Croft*   40 shall] would *X*

COPY-TEXT: Hayley, 1803, first edition, i. 15–18 (first printing). Collated: ll. 1–2 copied from her MS. collection by Theodora Cowper, as reported in letter from John Johnson to Hayley, 13 Apr. 1814 (*F*).
1 design] intend *F*

To shew my genius, or my wit,
When God and you know, I have neither;
Or such, as might be better shewn
By letting Poetry alone.   10
'Tis not with either of these views,
That I presume to address the Muse;
But to divert a fierce banditti,
(Sworn foes to every thing that's witty!)
That, with a black, infernal train,   15
Make cruel inroads in my brain,
And daily threaten to drive thence
My little garrison of sense:
The fierce banditti, which I mean,
Are gloomy thoughts, led on by spleen.   20
Then there's another reason yet,
Which is, that I may fairly quit
The debt, which justly became due
The moment, when I heard from you:
And you might grumble, crony mine,   25
If paid in any other coin;
Since twenty sheets of lead, God knows
(I would say twenty sheets of prose)
Can ne'er be deem'd worth half so much
As one of gold, and yours was such.   30
Thus, the preliminaries settled,
I fairly find myself *pitch-kettled*;
And cannot see, tho' few see better,
How I shall hammer out a letter.

    First, for a thought—since all agree—   35
A thought—I have it—let me see—
'Tis gone again—Plague on't! I thought
I had it—but I have it not.
Dame Gurton thus, and Hodge her son,
That useful thing, her needle, gone;   40
Rake well the cinders;—sweep the floor,
And sift the dust behind the door;
While eager Hodge beholds the prize
In old Grimalkin's glaring eyes;
And Gammer finds it on her knees   45

In every shining straw she sees.
This simile were apt enough;
But I've another critic-proof!
The Virtuoso thus, at noon
Broiling beneath a July sun,   50
The gilded Butterfly pursues,
O'er hedge and ditch, thro' gaps and mews;
And after many a vain essay
To captivate the tempting prey,
Gives him at length the lucky pat,   55
And has him safe, beneath his hat:
Then lifts it gently from the ground;
But ah! 'tis lost, as soon as found;
Culprit his liberty regains;
Flits out of sight, and mocks his pains.   60
The sense was dark; 'twas therefore fit
With simile t'illustrate it;
But as too much obscures the sight,
As often as too little light,
We have our similies cut short,   65
For matters of more grave import.
That Matthew's numbers run with ease,
Each man of common sense agrees;
All men of common sense allow,
That Robert's lines are easy too: 70
Where then the preference shall we place?
Or how do justice in this case?
Matthew (says Fame) with endless pains
Smooth'd, and refin'd, the meanest strains;
Nor suffer'd one ill chosen rhyme   75
T'escape him, at the idlest time;
And thus o'er all a lustre cast,
That, while the language lives, shall last.
An't please your Ladyship (quoth I)
For 'tis my business to reply;   80
Sure so much labour, so much toil,
Bespeak at least a stubborn soil:
Theirs be the laurel-wreath decreed,
Who both write well, and write full speed!

46 straw] straw, *1803*

Who throw their Helicon about 85
As freely, as a conduit spout!
Friend Robert, thus like *chien sçavant*,
Lets fall a poem *en passant*,
Nor needs his genuine ore refine;
'Tis ready polish'd from the mine. 90

A LETTER IN VERSE TO JOSEPH HILL

Mr. Hill—
  If I write not to you
  As I gladly would do
To a Man of your Mettle and Sense,
  'Tis a Fault I must own
  For which I'll attone 5
When I take my Departure from hence.

  To tell you the Truth,
  I'm a queer kind of Youth
And I care not if all the World knows it;
  Whether Sloven, or Beau, 10
  In Square, Alley, or Row,
At Whitehall in the Court, or the Closet.

  Having written thus much
  In Honest high Dutch,
I must now take a Nobler Stile up: 15
  Give my Fancy, a prick,
  My Invention, a Kick,
And my Genius a pretty smart Fillip.

  For the Bus'ness in hand
  You are to Understand, 20
Is indeed neither trifling nor small:

88 Lets] *1803 2nd ed.*; Let's *1st ed.*

10 October 1755.

COPY-TEXT: autograph letter in the Cowper Johnson collection (*J*), whence first printed by
Milford, 1905, pp. 624–5.
Title supplied by Milford   6 hence.] hence *J*

But which you may transact
      If your Scull is not crackt
As well as the best of them all.

   And so may your *Dear Wife*   25
      Be the Joy of your Life,
And of all our brave Troops the Commandress,
      As you shall convey
      What herein I say
To the very fair Lady, my Laundress.   30

   That to Town I shall Trot
      (No I Lie, I shall not,
For to Town I shall Jog in the Stage)
      On October the Twentieth,
      For my Father consenteth   35
To make me the Flower of the Age.

   So bid her prepare
      Every Table and Chair,
And Warm well my Bed by the Fire,
      And if this be not done   40
      I shall break her Back bone
As sure as I ever come nigh her.

   I am Jovial and Merry,
      Have writ till I'm weary,
Am become, with a great deal of Talking, horse   45
      So farewell—Sweet Lad!
      Is all I shall add,
Except—

                           Your Obedient *Stalking Horse*
                              W Cowper.

THE SHADE OF HOMER: AN ODE
From the French of Houdar de la Motte

O thou, whose Numbers with true Genius fir'd
Great Phœbus prompted and the Nine inspir'd,
Thou, in whose sacred Lays divinely great
On thy own Gods Immortal Honours wait,
    Homer, envy'd happy Shade,   5
    Leave the Regions of the Dead;
A moment rise, review thy kindred Sky
Sway'd by the gentle Force of Magick Harmony.

Nor would I ask, with Appion's learned Pride,
What Years elaps'd and Ancient Ages hide: 10
    From what Æra right to date
    Hapless Illium's fallen State;
Or whether the rich Mæonia best may boast
Thee for her Son, or Io's happier Coast;
    Whatever State that Honour claim,   15
      Where'er thy Genius Sprung,
    For ever secret be the Name,
      And by the Muse unsung.

Far Nobler Fires my panting Bosom warm,
No Dangers Scare me nor no Fears alarm,   20
Resolv'd to bid thy ancient Song revive,
On other Strings, in other Numbers live.
Thou, if thy Glorys ought thy Soul engage,
    Wondrous Bard, arise, attend,
    All thy Aid, thy Influence lend,   25
Teach me to trace thee thro' thy Godlike Page,
Govern my Force and regulate my Rage.

    Strange Effect of Musick's Power,
      See the Radiant Shade arise;
    Lo! he leaves the Stygian Shore,   30
      Splendor beaming from his Eyes.

Composed about 1755.

COPY-TEXT: *T*, whence first printed by Ryskamp, *BC*, pp. 473–6. (Punctuation supplied.)
Title] *supplied*; Translation Ode De la Motte L'Ombre d' Homere *T*

Illustrious Homer, point the Way,
　　Speak thy Laws and I obey.
Repress thy Fears, the Sage replys, withdraw
This Faith Implicit and this Humble Awe.   35
Wouldst thou, my Son, my dang'rous Steps pursue,
Let Judgment guide and Wisdom lead thee through;
Dare to Dislike and venture to condemn
What bigots Worship, and what Fools esteem.

Of Human Race, to Human Errors prone,   40
Wrong'd by the Partial Multitude alone,
Some Faults I claim; those latent Faults explore
And from the Dross refine the Virgin Ore.
Weigh well each Line, each gen'rous Thought Sustain,
Tho' bold yet Just, tho' lively yet not vain;   45
Then onward tend, be these thy Arts profess'd;
These once obtain'd, I'll furnish all the rest.
But still whatever Pains, whatever Care it cost,
Let not Attention, tir'd in tedious Tales, be lost.

Rul'd by Caprice, by Factious Passions led,   50
Such were the Deitys our Age ador'd;
Heroes and Kings with Rev'rence we survey'd,
Tho' Pride their Bosom fill'd and Av'rice swell'd their Hoard.
Forth from thy Work these vicious Errors cast;
Be every Line with perfect Beauty grac'd;   55
Regard the Moderns, let their Taste be thine
Who, tho' like us from Virtue they decline,
Better her Sacred Form, her Excellence define.

'Tis not enough thy Similes are like,
Some Artful Beautys should the Fancy Strike;   60
Nor be those graceful Periods once forgot
Which erst in Grecian Souls such mighty Transports wrought.
Still be thou Faithful to th'Heroick stile,
Still eager to produce with ceaseless Toil
Those slow Effects of Labour and of Time,   65
The Nervous Diction and the Sense sublime.
Thy Happy Tast let solid Reason Frame;
Mine was the Power to please, be thine the same,
Or from thy self believe th'unpleasing Error came.

Boldly suppose the Fates for once agree   70
To bate the Rigour of their Stern Decree,
Kindly for once permit the Stygian Oar
To bear me up to bless'd Britannia's Shore.
There were I plac'd, believe me, were my Lays
Dress'd in their decent unaffected Phrase,   75
Sooner my Fav'rite Chiefs should win the Day,
Nor long Narrations Interrupt the Fray,
Then should my Heroes worthy their Renown
With Force Resistless bear whole Armys down,
But leave that Task to Fame, to make their Praises known.   80

Then should my work from Monstrous Tales be clear,
Nor groundless Fiction find Admittance there,
Deriv'd from Truth should ev'ry Thought be found,
Nor gods themselves Transgress the sacred Bound.
Vulcan, his Art too exquisitely fine,   85
Should to the Tenour of this Rule Resign;
No animated Sculpture grace the Shield
With breathing Life and Active Vigour fill'd:
Nature some easier Image might bestow
To prompt Achilles forth with Vengeance on the Foe.   90

Pluto forbids me more. With this the Shade
Sunk from my Sight and mingled with the Dead.
Within my Breast I feel the Rising Flame,
And Gods and Heroes shall adorn my Theme.
  Nature's Bosom I'll explore,   95
  Rifle all her Beautys o'er,
  There a Matchless Treasure find,
  Pleasing, Usefull and Refin'd.
  To me great Homer does impart
  The full Perfection of his Art;   100
Be but my Force then equal to my Fire,
Like him I'll sing, like him to deathless Fame Aspire.

ON THE PICTURE OF A SLEEPING CHILD
From the Latin of Vincent Bourne

Sweet Babe! Whose Image here express'd,
    Does thy peaceful slumbers shew,
Guilt or fear to break thy rest,
    Never did thy spirits know.

Soothing Slumbers, soft repose,   5
    Such as mock the Painter's skill,
Such as Innocence bestows,
    Harmless Infant! lull thee still!

'DOOM'D, AS I AM, IN SOLITUDE TO WASTE'

Doom'd, as I am, in solitude to waste
The present moments, and regret the past;
Depriv'd of every joy, I valued most,
My Friend torn from me, and my Mistress lost;
Call not this gloom, I wear, this anxious mien,   5
The dull effect of humour, or of spleen!
Still, still, I mourn, with each returning day,
Him snatch'd by Fate, in early youth, away.
And Her—thro' tedious years of doubt and pain,
Fix'd in her choice, and faithful—but in vain!   10
O prone to pity, generous, and sincere,
Whose eye ne'er yet refus'd the wretch a tear;
Whose heart the real claim of friendship knows,
Nor thinks a lover's are but fancied woes;
See me—ere yet my destin'd course half done,   15
Cast forth a wand'rer on a wild unknown!
See me neglected on the world's rude coast,
Each dear companion of my voyage lost!

COPY-TEXT: copy in Theodora Cowper's hand, B.L. Add. MS. 30803A, fo. 200. First printed by Croft, 1825, p. 29.

4 spirits] spirit *Croft*

Composed after 21 September 1757.

COPY-TEXT: Hayley, 1803, first edition, i. 12–13 (first printing).

Nor ask why clouds of sorrow shade my brow!
And ready tears wait only leave to flow!   20
Why all, that sooths a heart, from anguish free,
All that delights the happy—palls with me!

TRANSLATIONS FROM THE SATIRES OF HORACE

THE FIFTH SATIRE OF THE FIRST BOOK
By William Cowper, Esq.

*A humorous Description of the Author's Journey
from* Rome *to* Brundusium

'Twas a long Journey lay before us,
When I and honest *Heliodorus*,
(Who far in Point of Rhetoric
Surpasses every living *Greek*),
Each leaving our respective Home,   5
Together sally'd forth from *Rome*.
   First at *Aricia* we alight,
And there refresh, and pass the Night.
Our Entertainment? rather coarse
Than sumptuous, but I've met with worse.   10
   Thence o'er the Causeway, soft and fair,
To *Appii-forum* we repair.
But as this Road is well supply'd
(Temptation strong!) on either Side
With Inns commodious, snug and warm,   15
We split the Journey, and perform
In two Days time, what's often done
By brisker Travellers in one.
   Here rather chusing not to sup
Than with bad Water mix my Cup,   20
After a warm Debate, in spite
Of a provoking Appetite,

Composed about 1758.

COPY-TEXT: *The Works of Horace in English Verse. By Several Hands. Collected and Published by Mr. Duncombe*, ii (1759), 107–16 (first printing).

Title. The . . . Book] *supplied*

I sturdily resolve at last
To balk it, and pronounce a Fast;
And, in a moody Humour, wait   25
While my less dainty Comrades bait.
   Now o'er the spangled Hemisphere
Diffus'd, the starry Train appear,
When there arose a desperate Brawl;
The Slaves and Bargemen, one and all,   30
Rending their Throats (have Mercy on us!)
As if they were resolv'd to stun us.
'Steer the Barge this Way to the Shore!
I tell you, we'll admit no more—
Plague! will you never be content!'   35
Thus a whole Hour at least is spent,
While they receive the several Fares,
And kick the Mule into his Gears.
Happy! these Difficulties past,
Could we have fall'n asleep at last;   40
But, what with humming, croaking, biting,
Gnats, Frogs, and all their Plagues uniting,
These tuneful Natives of the Lake
Conspir'd to keep us broad awake.
Besides, to make the Concert full,   45
Two maudlin Wights, exceeding dull,
The Bargeman and a Passenger,
Each in his Turn essay'd an Air
In Honour of his absent Fair.
At length, the Passenger, opprest   50
With Wine, left off, and snor'd the rest.
The weary Bargeman too gave o'er,
And, hearing his Companion snore,
Seiz'd the Occasion, fix'd the Barge,
Turn'd out his Mule to graze at large,   55
And slept, forgetful of his Charge.
   And now the Sun, o'er Eastern Hill,
Discover'd that our Barge stood still;
When one, whose Anger vex'd him sore,
With Malice fraught, leaps quick on Shore;   60
Plucks up a Stake; with many a Thwack
Assails the Mule and Driver's Back.

Then, slowly moving on, with Pain,
At ten, *Feronia*'s Stream we gain,
And in her pure and glassy Wave   65
Our Hands and Faces gladly lave.
Climbing three Miles, fair *Anxur*'s Height
We reach, with stony Quarries white.
  While here, as was agreed, we wait,
'Till, charg'd with Business of the State,   70
Mæcenas and *Cocceius* come,
(The Messengers of Peace) from *Rome*;
My Eyes, by watry Humours blear
And sore, I with black Balsam smear.
At length they join us, and with them   75
Our worthy Friend *Fonteius* came;
A Man of such complete Desert,
Antony lov'd him at his Heart.
  At *Fundi* we refus'd to bait,
And laugh'd at vain *Aufidius*' State;   80
A *Prætor* now (a Scribe before)
The purple-border'd Robe he wore;
His Slave the smoking Censer bore.
  Tir'd, at *Muræna*'s we repose
At *Formia*; sup at *Capito*'s.   85
  With Smiles the rising Morn we greet;
At *Sinuessa* pleas'd to meet
With *Plotius*, *Varius*, and the Bard,
Whom *Mantua* first with Wonder heard.
The World no purer Spirits knows,   90
For none my Heart more warmly glows.
O what Embraces we bestow'd,
And with what Joy our Breasts o'erflow'd!
Sure, while my Sense is sound and clear,
Long as I live, I shall prefer   95
A gay, good-natur'd, easy Friend
To every Blessing Heaven can send!
  At a small Village, the next Night,
Near the *Vulturnus* we alight;
Where, as employ'd on State Affairs,   100
We were supply'd by the Purvey'rs
Frankly at once, and without Hire,

With Food for Man and Horse, and Fire.
  Capua, next Day, betimes we reach,
Where *Virgil* and myself, who each   105
Labour'd with different Maladies,
His such a Stomach, mine such Eyes,
As would not bear strong Exercise,
In drowsy Mood to Sleep resort;
Mæcenas to the Tennis-court.   110
   Next at *Cocceius'* Farm we're treated,
Above the *Caudian* Tavern seated;
His kind and hospitable Board
With Choice of wholesome Fare was stor'd.
   Now, O ye Nine, inspire my Lays;   115
To nobler Themes my Fancy raise!
Two Combatants, who scorn to yield
The noisy Tongue-disputed Field,
Sarmentus and *Cicirrus*, claim
A Poet's Tribute to their Fame.   120
Cicirrus, of true *Oscian* Breed;
Sarmentus, who was never freed,
But ran away; we don't defame him;
His Lady lives, and still may claim him.
Thus dignify'd, in hardy Fray   125
These Champions their keen Wit display;
And first *Sarmentus* led the Way:
'Thy Locks, quoth he, so rough and coarse,
Look like the Mane of some wild Horse.'
We laugh.—*Cicirrus*, undismay'd,   130
'Have at you,' cries; and shakes his Head.—
' 'Tis well, *Sarmentus* says, you've lost
That Horn, your Forehead once could boast,
Since, maim'd and mangled as you are,
You seem to butt.'—A hideous Scar   135
Improv'd, 'tis true, with double Grace
The native Horrors of his Face.
Well, after much jocosely said
Of his grim Front, so fiery red,
For Carbuncles had blotch'd it o'er,   140
As usual on *Campania's* Shore;
'Give us, he cry'd, since you're so big,

A Sample of the *Cyclops'* Jig;
Your Shanks, methinks, no Buskins ask,
Nor does your Phyz require a Mask.'   145
To this *Cicirrus*: 'In return,
Of you, Sir, now I fain would learn
When 'twas (no longer deem'd a Slave)
Your Chains you to the *Lares* gave?
For though a Scrivener's Right you claim,   150
Your Lady's Title is the same.
But what could make you run away,
Since, Pygmy as you are, each Day
A single Pound of Bread would quite
O'erpower your puny Appetite.'   155
    Thus jok'd the Champions, while we laugh'd,
And many a chearful Bumper quaff'd.
    To *Beneventum* next we steer,
Where our good Host, by over-care
In roasting Thrushes, lean as Mice,   160
Had almost fall'n a Sacrifice.
The Kitchen soon was all on Fire,
And to the Roof the Flames aspire.
There might you see each Man and Master
Striving, amidst this sad Disaster,   165
To save the Supper—then they came
With Speed enough to quench the Flame.
    From hence we first at Distance see
Th'*Apulian* Hills, well known to Me,
Parch'd by the sultry Western Blast,   170
And which we never should have past,
Had not *Trivicus*, by the Way,
Receiv'd us at the Close of Day:
But each was forc'd, at entering here,
To pay the Tribute of a Tear;   175
For more of Smoke than Fire was seen,
The Hearth was pil'd with Logs so green.
    From hence in Chaises we were carry'd
Miles twenty-four, and gladly tarry'd
At a small Town, whose Name my Verse   180
(So barbarous is it!) can't rehearse.
Know it you may by many a Sign;

Water is dearer far than Wine;
Their Bread is deem'd such dainty Fare,
That every prudent Traveller   185
His Wallet loads with many a Crust;
For, at *Canusium*, you might just
As well attempt to gnaw a Stone,
As think to get one Morsel down.
That too with scanty Streams is fed: 190
Its Founder was brave *Diomed*.
Good *Varius* (ah! that Friends must part!)
Here left us all with aching Heart.
    At *Rubi* we arriv'd that Day,
Well jaded by the Length of Way;   195
And sure poor Mortals ne'er were wetter.
Next Day, no Weather could be better,
No Roads so bad; we scarce could crawl
Along to fishy *Barium*'s Wall.
    Th'*Egnatians* next, who, by the Rules   200
Of Common-sense, are Knaves or Fools,
Made all our Sides with Laughter heave;
Since we with them must needs believe
That Incense in their Temples burns,
And, without Fire, to Ashes turns.   205
To Circumcision's Bigots tell
Such Tales. For Me, I know full well
That in high Heaven, unmov'd by Care,
The Gods eternal Quiet share;
Nor can I deem their Spleen the Cause   210
Why fickle Nature breaks her Laws.
    Brundusium last we reach, and there
Stop short the Muse and Traveller.

TRANSLATIONS FROM THE SATIRES OF HORACE

THE NINTH SATIRE OF THE FIRST BOOK
Adapted to the present Times
By W. C. Esquire

The Description of an Impertinent

Saunt'ring along the Street, one Day,
On Trifles musing by the Way,
Up steps a free familiar Wight,
(I scarcely knew the Man by Sight)
'*Carlos* (he cry'd) your Hand, my Dear—   5
Gad! I rejoice to meet you here;
Pray Heaven I see you well!'—So, so,
E'en well enough, as Times now go;
The same good Wishes, Sir, to you.
Finding he still pursu'd me close—   10
Sir, you have Business, I suppose:—
'My Business, Sir, is quickly done,
'Tis but to make my Merit known;—
Sir, I have read'—O learned Sir!
You, and your Reading, I revere—   15
Then, sweating with Anxiety,
And sadly longing to get free,
Gods! how I scamper'd, scuffled for't,
Ran, halted, ran again—stopp'd short—
Beckon'd my Boy, and pull'd him near,   20
And whisper'd—nothing in his Ear.
    Teaz'd with his loose unjointed Chat—
'What Street is this? Whose House is that?'
O *Harlow!* how I envy'd thee
Thy unabash'd Effrontery,   25
Who dar'st a Foe with Freedom blame,
And call a Coxcomb by his Name.

Composed about 1758.

COPY-TEXT: *The Works of Horace in English Verse. By Several Hands. Collected and Published by Mr. Duncombe*, ii (1759), 147–54 (first printing).

Title. The . . . Book] *supplied*   *Adapted* . . . Esquire] Modernized by William Cowper Esquire *2nd ed. 1767*

When I return'd him Answer none,
Obligingly the Fool ran on—
'I see you're dismally distress'd,   30
Would give the World to be releas'd,
But, by your Leave, Sir! I shall still
Stick to your Skirts, do what you will—
Pray which Way does your Journey tend?'
O! 'tis a tedious Way, my Friend—   35
Across the *Thames*, the Lord knows where,
I would not trouble *you* so far.
'Well, I'm at Leisure to attend you'—
Are you? (thought I) the De'el befriend you!—
    No Ass with double Panniers rack'd,   40
Oppress'd, o'erladen, broken-back'd,
E'er look'd a thousandth Part so dull
As I, nor half so like a Fool.
'Sir, I know little of myself,
(Proceeds the pert conceited Elf)   45
If *Gray* or *Mason* you will deem
Than Me, more worthy your Esteem.
Poems I write by *Folios*,
As fast as other Men write Prose.
Then can I sing so loud, so clear!   50
That *Beard* cannot with Me compare;
In Dancing too I all surpass,
Not *Cooke* can move with such a Grace'—
    Here I made shift, with much ado,
To interpose a Word or two—   55
Have you no Parents, Sir? no Friends,
Whose Welfare on your own depends?—
'Parents, Relations, say you?—No—
They're all dispos'd of, long ago'—
    Happy! to be no more perplex'd—   60
My Fate too threatens; I go next.
Dispatch me, Sir! 'tis now too late,
Alas! to struggle with my Fate:
Well! I'm convinc'd my Time is come;
When young, a Gipsy told my Doom;   65

53 Grace'—] Grace— *1759*   60 Happy] 'Happy *1759*

The Beldam shook her palsy'd Head,
As she perus'd my Palm, and said—
'Of Poisons, Pestilence, or War,
Gout, Stone, Defluxion, or Catarrh,
You have no Reason to beware.   70
Beware the Coxcomb's idle Prate,
Chiefly, my Son, beware of that;
Be sure, when you behold him, fly
Out of all Ear-shot, or you die.'
     To *Rufus'* Hall we now drew near,   75
Where he was summon'd to appear,
Refute the Charge the Plaintiff brought,
Or suffer Judgment by Default.
'For Heaven's sake, if you love me, wait
One Moment, I'll attend you strait'—   80
     Glad of a plausible Pretence—
Sir! I must beg you to dispense
With my Attendance in the Court;
My Legs will surely suffer for't—
     'Nay, pr'ythee *Carlos*, stop awhile'—   85
Faith, Sir, in Law I have no Skill;
Besides, I have no Time to spare,
I must be going you know where—
'Well, I protest, I'm doubtful now,
Whether to leave my Suit, or you'—   90
Me, without Scruple—I reply—
Me, by all means, Sir!— 'No! not I—
Allons, Monsieur!'—'Twere vain, you know,
To strive with a victorious Foe;
So I reluctantly obey,   95
And follow where he leads the Way.
     'You and *Newcastle* are so close,
Still Hand and Glove, Sir, I suppose'—
Newcastle, let me tell you, Sir,
Has not his Equal every-where—   100
'Well! there indeed your Fortune's made;
Faith, Sir, you understand your Trade.
Would you but give me your good Word,
Just introduce me to my Lord—

97, 99 *Newcastle*] *2nd ed. 1767*; N——— *1759*

I should serve charmingly, by way   105
Of *second Fiddle*, as they say—
What think you, Sir?—'twere a good Jest;
'Slife! we should quickly scout the rest.'
Sir, you mistake the Matter far—
We have no *second Fiddles* there—   110
Richer than I, some Folks may be;
More learned; but it hurts not Me;
Friends though he has of different kind,
Each has his proper Place assign'd—
    'Strange Matters these alledg'd by you!'   115
Strange they may be, but they are true.
'Well! then I vow 'tis mighty clever;
Now I long ten times more than ever
To be advanc'd extremely near
One of his shining Character.'   120
Have but the Will, there wants no more;
'Tis plain enough you have the Power.
His easy Temper (that's the worst)
He knows, and so is shy at first;
But such a Cavalier as you!   125
Lord, Sir! you'll quickly bring him to—
    'Well—if I fail in my Design,
Sir, it shall be no Fault of mine;
If by the saucy servile Tribe
Deny'd, what think you of a Bribe?   130
Shut out To-day, not die with Sorrow,
But try my Luck again To-morrow—
Never attempt to visit him,
But at the most convenient Time;
Attend him on each *Levée* Day,   135
And there my humble Duty pay.
Labour, like this, our Want supplies;
And they must stoop, who mean to rise.'
    While thus he wittily harrangu'd,
(For which you'll guess I wish'd him hang'd)   140
Campley, a Friend of mine, came by,
Who knew his Humour more than I—
We stop, salute:—'And, why so fast,
Friend *Carlos?*—whither all this Haste?'

Fir'd at the Thoughts of a Reprieve,   145
I pinch him, pull him, twitch his Sleeve,
Nod, beckon, bite my Lips, wink, pout,
Do every thing, but speak plain out—
While he, sad Dog! from the Beginning
Determin'd to mistake my Meaning,   150
Instead of pitying my Curse,
By jeering made it ten times worse—
   Campley, what Secret, pray, was that,
You wanted to communicate?—
'I recollect, but 'tis no matter;   155
Carlos! we'll talk of that herea'ter—
E'en let the Secret rest; 'twill tell
Another Time, Sir, just as well.'—
   Was ever such a dismal Day!
Unlucky Cur! he steals away,   160
And leaves me, half bereft of Life,
At Mercy of the Butcher's Knife—
   When, sudden, shouting from afar
See his Antagonist appear!
The Bailiff seiz'd him, quick as Thought,   165
'Ho! Mr. Scoundrel, are you caught!
Sir! you are Witness to th'Arrest.'—
Aye! marry, Sir, I'll do my best.—
The Mob huzzas—away they trudge,
Culprit and all, before the Judge;   170
Mean-while I, luckily enough,
(Thanks to *Apollo*) got clear off.

153 *Campley*] '*Campley 1759*   154 You . . . communicate?—] 'You . . . communicate?'—*1759*   168 Aye . . . best.—] 'Aye . . . best.'— *175.*

ADDRESSED TO MISS ——
ON READING THE PRAYER FOR
INDIFFERENCE

And dwells there in a female heart,
   By bounteous heav'n design'd
The choicest raptures to impart,
   To feel the most refin'd—

Dwells there a wish in such a breast   5
   Its nature to forego,
To smother in ignoble rest
   At once both bliss and woe!

Far be the thought, and far the strain,
   Which breathes the low desire,   10
How sweet soe'er the verse complain,
   Tho' Phœbus string the lyre.

Come then, fair maid (in nature wise)
   Who, knowing them, can tell
From gen'rous sympathy what joys   15
   The glowing bosom swell.

In justice to the various pow'rs
   Of pleasing, which you share,
Join me, amid your silent hours,
   To form the better pray'r.   20

With lenient balm, may *Ob'ron* hence
   To fairy-land be driv'n;
With ev'ry herb that blunts the sense
   Mankind receiv'd from heav'n.

'Oh! if my Sov'reign Author please,   25
   Far be it from my fate,
To live, unblest, in torpid ease,
   And slumber on in state.

Composed about 1760.
COPY-TEXT: Johnson, 1815, pp. 32-8 (first printing).

Each tender tie of life defied
    Whence social pleasures spring,   30
Unmov'd with all the world beside,
    A solitary thing—'

Some Alpine mountain, wrapt in snow,
    Thus braves the whirling blast,
Eternal winter doom'd to know,   35
    No genial spring to taste.

In vain warm suns their influence shed,
    The zephyrs sport in vain,
He rears unchang'd his barren head,
    Whilst beauty decks the plain.   40

What tho' in scaly armour drest,
    Indifference may repel
The shafts of woe—in such a breast
    No joy can ever dwell.

'Tis woven in the world's great plan,   45
    And fix'd by Heav'n's decree,
That all the true delights of man
    Should spring from *Sympathy*.

'Tis nature bids, and whilst the laws
    Of nature we retain,   50
Our self-approving bosom draws
    A pleasure from its pain.

Thus grief itself has comforts dear,
    The sordid never know;
And ecstasy attends the tear,   55
    When virtue bids it flow.

For, when it streams from that pure source,
    No bribes the heart can win,
To check, or alter from its course
    The luxury within.   60

Peace to the phlegm of sullen elves,
    Who, if from labour eas'd,
Extend no care beyond themselves,
    Unpleasing and unpleas'd.

'Let no low thought suggest the pray'r,   65
    Oh! grant, kind Heav'n, to me,
Long as I draw ethereal air
    Sweet Sensibility.'

Where'er the heav'nly nymph is seen,
    With lustre-beaming eye,   70
A train, attendant on their Queen,
    (Her rosy chorus) fly.

The jocund Loves in Hymen's band,
    With torches ever bright,
And gen'rous Friendship hand in hand,   75
    With Pity's wat'ry sight.

The gentler virtues too are join'd,
    In youth immortal warm,
The soft relations, which, combin'd,
    Give life her ev'ry charm.   80

The Arts come smiling in the close,
    And lend celestial fire,
The marble breathes, the canvas glows,
    The Muses sweep the lyre.

'Still may my melting bosom cleave   85
    To suff'rings not my own,
And still the sigh responsive heave,
    Where'er is heard a groan.

So Pity shall take Virtue's part,
    Her natural ally,   90
And fashioning my soften'd heart,
    Prepare it for the sky.'

65–8 'Let . . . Sensibility.'] Let . . . Sensibility. *Johnson*

This artless vow may heav'n receive,
  And you, fond maid, approve:
So may your guiding angel give   95
  Whate'er you wish or love.

So may the rosy-finger'd hours
  Lead on the various year,
And ev'ry joy, which now is yours,
  Extend a larger sphere.   100

And suns to come, as round they wheel,
  Your golden moments bless,
With all a tender heart can feel,
  Or lively fancy guess.

TRANSLATION OF FOUR CANTOS OF VOLTAIRE'S *LA HENRIADE*

THE

HENRIADE

CANTO THE FIFTH

THE ARGUMENT

The besieged are very sharply pressed. Discord persuades Clement *to go to* Paris *and assassinate the king. He is conducted by Fanaticism, whom Discord calls for that purpose from the infernal regions. Sacrifice of the Leaguers to the spirits of darkness.* Henry III. *is assassinated. Sentiments of* Henry IV. *upon the occasion. He is acknowledged king of* France *by the army.*

Now marching on, those dread machines appear'd,
Which death attended, and the rebels fear'd.
A hundred mouths pour'd forth the rapid balls,
And iron tempests rattl'd on the walls.
Now was employ'd, and exercis'd in vain   5
The zeal of party, and the wiles of May'ne.
The guards of Paris, and the noisy crowd,
The prating doctors insolent, and loud,
Tried, but in vain, our hero to subdue,
Beneath whose feet victorious laurels grew.   10
By Rome, and Philip were the thunders hurl'd,
But Rome diffus'd no terrors through the world.
His native sloth the old Iberian shew'd,
And all his succours were too late bestow'd.

Composed 1762.

COPY-TEXT: *The Works of Voltaire*, ed T. Smollett and T. Francklin, xxiv (1762), 103–200 (first printing).

Title] *supplied*

Through Gallia's realms the plund'ring troops enjoy'd   15
The spoils of cities which their arms destroy'd.
An easy conquest o'er opprest allies
Was first, and fairest in the traitor's eyes.
The falling League but waited to receive
Whate'er the pride of tyranny could give,   20
When fate, that governs with supreme command,
Appear'd suspended by a zealot's hand.

  Forgive, ye citizens, whose peaceful days
Are calm, and bright'ned by serener rays,
Forgive the bard who paints the horrid crimes   25
That stain'd the annals of preceding times.
Yourselves unsullied may the lays approve,
Whose hearts are warm with loyalty, and love.

  In ev'ry age, some venerable seer
For heav'ns pure joys has shed the pious tear;   30
Some rigid anchorets with vows divine
Have heap'd their incense on religion's shrine:
Lost to the world, to each idea lost
That friendship loves, or charity can boast.
Their gloomy shades, and cloisters ever rude   35
The beams of fair humanity exclude.
Others in flowing periods have display'd
Religion's truths by learning's pow'rful aid.
In these ambition has produc'd desires
Mean, and unworthy virtue's sacred fires.   40
Oft' have their schemes extended far, and wide,
And all their piety been sunk in pride.
Thus by perverse, untoward abuses still
The highest good becomes the greatest ill.
Those, who the life of Dominic embrac'd,   45
In Spain with wreaths of glory have been grac'd.
From mean employments have with lustre shone,
Like painted insects glitt'ring round the throne.
In France they flourish'd in the days of yore,
With equal zeal, but far unequal pow'r.   50
The kindly patronage, from kings deriv'd,
Might still attend them, had not Clement liv'd.

The soul of Clement, gloomy, and austere,
Was form'd to virtues rigid, and severe.
Soon as the torrent of rebellion flow'd,   55
The tide he follow'd, and pronounc'd it good.
Fell Discord rising had profusely shed
Infernal poisons o'er his youthful head.
The long-drawn isle, and venerable shrine
Witness what pray'rs fatigued the pow'rs divine.   60
This was their form, before the throne of grace,
While dust, and ashes sanctifi'd his face.

  Almighty being, whose avenging arm
Protects religion, and her sons from harm,
How long shall justice sleep, or tyrants live,   65
The perjur'd flourish, and oppression thrive?
Let us, O God, thy gracious mercies tell,
Thy fiery scourges let the sinner feel.
Dispel death's horrid gloom, assist the brave,
And crush the tyrant, whom thy fury gave.   70
Send thy destroying angel from above,
Descend in flames, and let thy thunders move.
Descend, and quell the sacrilegious host,
Defeat their triumphs, and confound their boast.
Let ruin seize, great sov'reign lord of all,   75
Kings, chiefs, and armies in one common fall.
As gath'ring storms the leaves of Autumn bear
O'er hills, and vallies through the fields of air.
The League shall praise thy name with holy tongue,
Whilst blood, and murder elevate the song.   80

  Discord, attentive, heard his hideous cries,
And swift to Pluto's dreary regions flies.
From those dark realms the worst of tyrants came,
Fanatic Dæmon is his horrid name.
Religion's son, but rebel in her cause,   85
He tears her bosom, and disdains her laws.
'Twas him that guided Ammon's frantic race,
Where silver Arnon winds his liquid maze.
When weeping mothers, with mad zeal possest,
Slew their fond infants clinging to the breast.   90

Through him, rash Jeptha vow'd, the fiend imbrued
The father's dagger in the daughter's blood.
By him the impious Chalchas was inspir'd,
And tender Iphigenia's death requir'd.
Thy forests, France, the cruel pow'r approv'd;   95
There smoak'd the incense which Teutates lov'd.
Thy shades have seen the human victims bleed,
Whilst hoary druids authoriz'd the deed.
From Rome's proud capitol he gave the word,
When christians shudder'd at the pagan sword.   100
When Rome submitted to the son of God,
High o'er the church he wav'd his iron rod.
Christians, once doom'd to feel the tort'ring flame,
Were deaf to mercy, and unmov'd by shame.
On Thames's banks the seeds of faction grew,   105
Whose bloody arm the feeble monarch slew.
The same fierce genius fans the annual fire
At Lisbon, or Madrid, when Jews expire:
Unwilling to desert the cause of heav'n,
Or quit the faith their ancestors have giv'n.   110

    Like some high priest his part the dæmon play'd,
In the pure vest of innocence array'd.
Now, from the wardrobe of eternal night
For other crimes equipp'd, he sprung to light.
Deceit, for ever plausible, and fair,   115
Dress'd him like Guise in person, height, and air.
The haughty Guise, whose artifice alone
Enchain'd the listless monarch on his throne,
Whose pow'r still working, like some fatal star,
Foreboded ruin, and inspir'd to war.   120
The dreaded helmet glitter'd on his head;
The sword, prepar'd for ev'ry murd'rous deed,
Flam'd in his hand;—and many a wound could tell
How once at Blois the factious hero fell.
For vengeance calling loud, the crimson tide   125
Fast flow'd in copious streams adown his side.
Clad in this mournful garb, when night had shed
Her peaceful slumbers over Clement's head,

v. 96 Teutates] Tentates *1762*

In that still hour, when horrid spectres meet,
He sought the zealot in his calm retreat.   130
Cabal, and superstition, nurse of sin,
Unbarr'd the doors, and let the chieftain in.

Thy pray'rs, he cried the pow'rs of heav'n receive,
But more than tears, or pray'rs should Clement give.
The Leaguer's god will other off'rings claim;   135
More fit, more worthy of his holy name.
Far other incense must adorn his shrine;
Off'rings more pure, and worship more divine.
Had Judith only wept with plaintive sighs,
A female's grief, and unavailing cries,   140
Had life been dearer than her country's call,
Judith had seen Bethulia's levell'd wall.
These exploits copy, these oblations bring,
Derive thy currents from that sacred spring.
I see thee blush;—go, fly at my command,   145
Let royal blood now consecrate thy hand.
Set wretched Paris from her tyrant free,
Revenging Rome, the universe, and me.
Go, murder Valois, as he murder'd Guise,
Nor deem it faulty in religion's eyes.   150
Who guards the church, and vindicates her laws,
Is bravely acting in fair virtue's cause.
When heav'n commands, then ev'ry deed is good,
Attend her accents, and prepare for blood.
Thrice happy, could'st thou join the tyrant's death 155
To Bourbon's fall, and gain a nobler wreath!
Oh could thy citizens!—but fate denies
Thy hand the honors of that happy prize.
Yet, should thy fame with rays inferior shine,
Scorn not the gift, but finish heaven's design.   160

Thus spoke the phantom, and unsheath'd the blade,
By hatred once in Stygian waters laid.
To Clement's hand he gave the fatal steel,
Then swiftly fled, and downward sunk to hell.
The young recluse, too easily deceiv'd,   165
Himself th' almighty's delegate believ'd:

Embrac'd the gift with reverential love,
And begg'd assistance from the pow'rs above.
The fiend no superstitious influence spar'd,
But all his soul for parricide prepar'd.   170
How apt is error to mislead mankind!
And reason's piercing eye how often blind!
The raging Clement, happy, and at ease,
Happy as those whom truth and virtue please;
With down-cast looks, and virtue's clouded brow,   175
To heav'n address'd the sacrilegious vow.
On as he march'd, his penitential veil
Conceal'd from view the parricidal steel.
The fairest flow'rs each conscious friend bestow'd,
And balmy odors to perfume the road.   180
These guides, in counsel, or in praises join'd
To add new fervor to his zealous mind.
The holy calendar receiv'd his name,
Equal to saints in virtue, and in fame.
Now hail'd as patron, now ador'd as God,   185
And fed with incense by the kneeling crowd.
Transports less warm, less moving raptures fir'd
The christian heroes, and their souls inspir'd,
When pious brethren were consign'd to death,
Firm, and intrepid to their latest breath.   190
They kissed each footstep, thought each torture gain,
And wish'd to feel the agonizing pain.
Fanatics thus religion's ensigns bear,
Like worthies triumph, and like saints appear.
The same desire the good, and impious draws,   195
Unnumber'd martyrs fall in error's cause.

    May'ne's piercing eyes beheld the future blow,
And more was known, than what he seem'd to know.
Intending wisely, when the blood was spilt,
To reap the profits, but avoid the guilt.   200
Sedition's sons were left to guide the whole,
And steel with rage the impious zealot's soul.
To Paris' gates they lead the traitor on;
Whilst the Sixteen with fond impatience run
To arts infernal, and devoutly pray   205

That heav'n her secret counsels would display.
This science once distinguish'd Cath'rine's reign,
Tho' always criminal, and often vain.
The servile people, that for ever love
Each courtly vice, and what the great approve,   210
Fond of whate'er is marvellous, or new,
The same impieties with zeal pursue.

    When night's still shades conceal'd the bands impure,
Silence conducts them to a vault obscure.
By the pale torch, which faintly pierc'd the gloom,   215
They raise an altar on the mould'ring tomb.
There both the royal images appear,
Alike the objects of their rage, and fear.
There to almighty pow'r their vows are paid,
And hellish dæmons summon'd to their aid.   220
High on the walls, a hundred lances stood,
Mysterious, awful terrors! plung'd in blood.
Their priest was one of that unhappy race
Proscrib'd on earth, and sentenc'd to disgrace.
Slaves long inur'd to superstition's lore,   225
Whose crimes, and sorrows spread from shore to shore.
The Leaguers next the sacrifice begin
With horrid cries, and bacchanalian din:
Now bathe their arms within the crimson tide;
Now on the altar strike at Valois' side.   230
Now with more rage, the terror to compleat,
See Henry's image trod beneath their feet.
Death, as they thought, would aid the impious blow,
And send the heroes to the shades below.

    The Hebrew tried by blasphemy to move   235
The depths beneath, and all the pow'rs above.
Invok'd the spirits that in æther dwell,
Swift light'nings, thunders, and the flames of hell.
Endor's fam'd priestess erst such off'rings made,
And rais'd by dire inchantments Samuel's shade,   240
Thus in Samaria once 'gainst Judah hung
The lying accent on the prophet's tongue.

v. 225 inur'd] inrur'd *1762*

And thus inflexibly Ateius rose
The high designs of Crassus to oppose.

The League's mad ruler waited to receive   245
To charms, and spells what answer heav'n would give.
Convinc'd that vows, thus offer'd, wing their way
To the pure regions of eternal day.
Heav'n heard the magic sounds, which only drew
From thence the vengeance to their errors due.   250
For them were stopt the laws which nature gave,
And plaintive murmurs fill'd the silent cave.
Successive light'nings in the depth of night
Flash'd all around, and gleam'd with horrid light.
Great Henry shone amidst the lambent flames,   255
Encircl'd round with glory's golden beams.
High on the car of triumph as he rode,
Grace on his brow the laurel wreath bestow'd,
The royal sceptre glitter'd in his hand,
Emblem of pow'r, and ensign of command.   260
Loud rolling thunders gave the fatal sign,
And op'ning earth receiv'd the flaming shrine.
The priest, and Leaguers shudder'd at the sight,
And veil'd their crimes beneath the shades of night.
The rolling thunders, and the fiery blaze   265
Declar'd that God had number'd Valois' days.
Grim death rejoic'd; and, such th' almighty's will,
Crimes were allow'd his sentence to fulfil.

Now Clement to the royal tent drew near.
And begg'd admission undismay'd by fear.   270
For heav'n, he said, had sent him to bestow
Reviving honors on the monarch's brow;
And secrets to unfold, which might appear
Worthy reception from his sovereign's ear.
All mark his looks, and many a question ask   275
Least his attire some bad design should mask.
He undisturb'd, with calm, and simple air
Returns them answers plausible, and fair.
Each accent seems from innocence to spring.
The guards attend, and lead him to their king.   280

Calm as before, he bent the suppliant knee;
Unruffl'd, and unaw'd by majesty:
Mark'd where to strike, and thus, by falsehood's aid,
With treach'rous lies his feign'd addresses paid.

Pardon, dread sovereign, him who trembling brings   285
Submissive praises to the king of kings.
Oh let me thank kind heav'n, whose gracious aid
Has showr'd down blessings on thy sacred head.
Potier the good, and Villerois the sage
Have faithful prov'd in this rebellious age.   290
Harlay the great, whose brave, intrepid zeal
Was ever active in the public weal,
Immur'd in prison, still thy cause defends,
Confounds the League, and animates thy friends.

That mighty being, whose all-piercing eyes   295
Defeat the counsels of the great, and wise:
Whose will no human knowledge can withstand,
Whose works are finish'd by the weakest hand:
To Harlay guided thy devoted slave,
That loyal subject ever good, and brave.   300
His sage advice, and sentiments refin'd
Diffus'd a radiance o'er my clouded mind.
To bring these lines with eagerness I flew,
By Harlay counsell'd, and to Valois true.

The king receiv'd the letters with surprize,   305
And tears of holy rapture fill'd his eyes.
Oh when, he cried, shall Valois' hand supply
Rewards proportion'd to thy loyalty?
Thus spoke the monarch with affection warm,
Love undissembl'd, and extended arm.   310
Each motion well the monstrous traitor eyed,
And fiercely plung'd the dagger in his side.
Soon as they saw the crimson torrents flow,
A thousand hands reveng'd the fatal blow.
The zealot wish'd not for a happier time,   315
But stood unmov'd, and triumph'd in his crime.

Through op'ning skies he saw the heav'nly dome,
And endless glories in the world to come.
Claim'd the bright wreath of martyrdom from God,
And falling, bless'd the hand that shed his blood.   320
Oh dread illusion terrible, and blind,
Worthy the hate, and pity of mankind.
Infectious preachers more deserv'd the blame,
From whom the madness, and the poison came.

   The hour arriv'd when Valois' darken'd sight   325
Faintly beheld the parting, glimm'ring light.
Surrounding slaves with many a falling tear
Express'd their griefs dissembl'd, or sincere.
For some there were, whose sorrows soon expir'd,
With pleasing hopes of future greatness fir'd.   330
Others, whose safety with the king was fled,
Themselves lamented, not the royal dead.
Amidst the various sounds of plaintive cries
Tears unaffected flow'd from Henry's eyes.
Thy foe, great Bourbon, fell; but souls like thine   335
In such dread moments ev'ry thought resign,
Save those which friendship, and compassion claim:
Self-love destroys not the cælestial flame.
The gen'rous chief forgot his own renown,
Tho' to himself devolv'd the regal crown.   340
To raise his eyes the dying monarch strove,
And clasp'd his hand with tenderness, and love.

   Bourbon, he cried, thy gen'rous tears refrain,
Let others weep whose conduct I disdain.
Fly thou to vengeance, spread the dire alarm,   345
Go reign, and triumph with victorious arm.
I leave thee struggling on the stormy coast
Where shipwreck'd Valois was for ever lost.
My throne awaits thee, take it as thy due,
Its sole protection was deriv'd from you.   350
Eternal thunders threaten Gallia's kings,
Then fear the pow'r from whom the glory springs.
By thee, from impious tenets undeceiv'd,
Be all the honours of his shrine reviv'd.

Farewell, brave prince, and reign by all ador'd,   355
Guarded by heav'n from each assassin's sword.
You know the League, with us begins the blow,
Nor stays it's fury, but would end with you.
In future days perchance some barb'rous hand,
Obedient slave to faction's dread command,   360
Some arm——but oh! ye Guardian angels, spare
Virtues so pure, so exquisite, and rare.
Permit——no more he said; departing breath
Consign'd the monarch to the arms of death.

Now was all Paris fill'd with joyful cries,   365
And odious songs of triumph rent the skies.
The fanes are open'd wide at Valois' death,
And ev'ry Leaguer wears the flow'ry wreath.
All labour ends whilst faction blith, and gay,
To mirth, and feasting consecrates the day.   370
Bourbon appear'd the object of their sport,
And glorious valour seem'd his sole support.
Say, could he rise, and e'er resist again
The strengthen'd League, the angry church, and Spain:
The Roman thunders with such fury hurl'd,   375
And the bright treasures of the western world!

Some warlike few, who little understood
What most contributes to the public good,
Affecting scruples foolish, and refin'd,
Calvin's defence already had resign'd.   380
Redoubl'd ardour in the royal cause
The rest inflam'd, and rul'd by other laws.
These gen'rous soldiers, well approv'd in war,
Who long had rode on triumph's radiant car,
To Bourbon give unsettl'd Gallia's throne,   385
And all proclaim him worthy of the crown.
Those valiant knights, the Givris, and Daumonts,
The Montmorencis, Sancis, and Crillons,
Swear to remain inviolable friends,
And guard his person to earth's utmost ends.   390
True to their laws, and faithful to their God,
They boldly march where honour points the road.

From you, my friends, cried Bourbon, is deriv'd
That lot which kindred heroes have receiv'd.
No peers have authorized our high command,   395
No holy oil, or consecrating hand.
All due allegiance, in the days of yore,
Your brave forefathers on their buckler swore.
To vict'rys laurell'd field your hands confin'd
From thence send forth the monarchs of mankind.   400
Thus spoke the chief, and, marching first, prepar'd
By martial deeds to merit his reward.

v. 393 Bourbon,] Bourbon *1762*

THE

HENRIADE

CANTO THE SIXTH

THE ARGUMENT

After the death of Henry III. *the Leaguers assemble in* Paris *to elect a king. In the midst of their debates,* Henry IV. *storms the city. The assembly is dismissed. The members that composed it repair to the ramparts. Description of the ensuing battle.*

In France an ancient custom we retain,
When death's rude stroke has closed the monarch's reign,
When destiny cuts short the smooth descent,
And all the royal pedigree is spent,
The people to their former rights restor'd,   5
May change the laws or chuse their future lord.
The states in council represent the whole,
Elect the king, and limit his controul;
Thus our renown'd forefathers did ordain
That Capet should succeed to Charlemagne.   10

The League with vain presumption arrogates
This right, and hastens to convene the states.
They thought the murder of the king bestow'd
That pow'r perhaps, on those who shed his blood,
Thought that the semblance of a throne would shroud   15
Their dark designs, and captivate the croud,
Would help their jarring counsels to unite,
And give their foul pretence an air of right;
That from what source soe'er his claim may spring,
Just or unjust, a king is still a king,   20
And worthy or unworthy of the sway,
A Frenchman must have something to obey.

Swift to the Louvre with imperious air
And fierce demeanour the proud chiefs repair;
Thither whom Spain embassador had sent,   25
And Rome, with many a priestly bigot went,
To speed th' election with tumultuous haste.
An insult on the kings of ages past,
And in the splendor of their trains, expence
Was seen, the child of public indigence.   30
No princely potentate or high-born peer
Sprung from our old nobility, was there,
Their grandeur now a shadowy form alone,
Though lawgivers by birth and kinsmen of the throne.
No sage assertors of the public claim   35
Strenuous and hardy, from the commons came,
No lilies as of old the court array'd,
But foreign pomp and pageant in their stead.
There sumptuous o'er the throne for May'ne prepar'd,
A canopy of royal state was rear'd,   40
And on the front with rich embroid'ry graced,
Oh dire indignity! these lines were traced.
'Kings of the earth, and judges of mankind,
Who deaf to mercy, by no laws confin'd,
Lay nature waste beneath your fierce domain,   45
Let Valois' fate instruct you how to reign.'

Forthwith contentious rage with jarring sound,
And clam'rous strife discordant eccho round.
Slave to the smiles of Rome, obsequious here
A venal flatt'rer soothes the legate's ear;   50
'Tis time, he cries, the lily should bow down
Her head, obedient to the triple crown,
Time that the church should lift her chast'ning hand,
And from her high tribunal scourge the land.*
Cruel tribunal! scene of monkish pow'r,   55
Which ev'n the realms that suffer it, abhor;
Whose fiery priests by bigotry prepar'd,
Torture and death without remorse award,
Disgraceful to the sacred cause they guard.
As if mankind were, as of old, possess'd   60

* The dukes of Guise wanted to establish the inquisition in France.

With pagan blindness, when the lying priest
T'appease the wrath of heav'n with vengeance fir'd,
The sacrifice of human blood requir'd.

Some for Iberian gold betray the state,
And sell it to the Spaniard whom they hate.   65
But mightier than the rest, their pow'r was shewn,
Who destin'd May'ne already to the throne.
The splendour of a crown was wanting yet,
To make the fullness of his fame complete;
To that bright goal his daring wish he sends,   70
Nor heeds the danger that on kings attends.

Then Potier rose; plain, nervous and untaught
His eloquence, the language of his thought.
No blemish of the times had touch'd the sage,
Rever'd for virtue in a vicious age;   75
Oft had he check'd, with courage uncontroul'd,
The tide of faction headlong as it roll'd,
Asserted hardily the laws he loved,
Nor ever fear'd reproof, or was reprov'd.
He raised his voice; struck silent at the sound   80
The croud was hush'd, and list'ning gather'd round.
So when at sea the winds have ceas'd to roar,
And the loud sailor's cries are heard no more,
No sound survives, but of the dashing prow
That cleaves with prosp'rous course th' obedient wave below. 85
Such Potier seem'd; no rude disturbance broke
Th' attentive calm, while freely thus he spoke.

'May'ne, I perceive then, has the gen'ral voice,
And though I praise not, can excuse your choice;
His virtues I esteem not less than you,   90
And were I free to chuse, might chuse him too.
But if the laws ambitious he pervert,
His claim of empire cancels his desert.'

Thus far the sage; when lo! that instant May'ne
Himself appear'd, with all a monarch's train.   95

'Prince! he pursued, and spoke it boldly forth,
I dare oppose you, for I know your worth;

Dare step between your merit and the throne,
Warm in the cause of France, and in our own.
Vain your election were, your right unsound,   100
While yet in France a Bourbon may be found;
Heav'n in its wisdom placed you near the throne,
That you might guard but not usurp the crown;
His ashes sprinkled with a monarch's gore
The shade of injured Guise can ask no more;   105
Point not your vengeance then at Henry's head,
Nor charge him with the blood he never shed.
Heav'ns influence on you both too largely flows,
And 'tis your rival virtue makes you foes.
But hark! the clamour of the common herd   110
Ascends the skies, and heretick's the word;
And see the priesthood ranged in dark array,
To deeds of blood insatiate urge their way!
Barbarians hold—what custom yet unknown,
What law, or rather frenzy of your own,   115
Can cancel your allegiance to the throne.
Comes he, this Henry, savage and unjust,
To'erthrow your shrines, and mix them with the dust?
He, to those shrines in search of truth he flies,
And loves the sacred laws yourselves despise;   120
Virtue alone, whatever form she wears,
Whatever sect she graces he reveres;
Nor like yourselves, weak, arrogant and blind,
Dares do the work of God, and judge mankind;
More righteous, and more christian far than you,   125
He comes to rule, but to forgive you too.
And shall you judge your master, and shall he,
The friend of freedom, not himself be free?
Not such, alas! nor sullied with your crimes,
Were the true christian race of elder times;   130
They tho' all heathen errors they abhorred,
Serv'd without murmuring their heathen lord,
The doom of death without a groan obey'd,
And bless'd the cruel hand by which they bled:
Such are the christians whom true faith assures,   135
They died to serve their kings, you murder yours,
And God, whom you describe for ever prone

To wrath, if he delights to show'r it down
On guilty heads, shall aim it at your own.'

He closed his bold harrangue, confusion scar'd   140
Their conscious souls, none answer'd him, or dar'd;
In vain they would have shaken from their hearts,
The dread which truth to guiltiness imparts,
With fear and rage their troubled thoughts were toss'd,
When sudden a loud shout from all their host   145
Was heard, to arms, to arms or we are lost.

Dark clouds of dust in floating volumes rise
Wide o'er the champian, and obscure the skies;
The clarion and the drum with horrid sound,
Dread harbingers of slaughter eccho round.   150
So from his gloomy chambers in the north,
When the fierce spirit of the storm breaks forth,
His dusky pinions shroud the noon-day light,
And thunder and sharp winds attend his dreary flight.

'Twas Henry's host came shouting from afar,   155
Disdaining ease, and eager for the war;
O'er the wide plain they stretch'd their bright array,
And to the ramparts urged their furious way.

These hours the chief vouchsaf'd not to consume
In empty rites perform'd at Valois' tomb,   160
Unprofitable tribute! fondly paid
By the proud living to th' unconscious dead;
No lofty dome, or monumental pile,
On the waste shore he rais'd with fruitless toil,
Vain arts! to rescue the departed great,   165
From the rough tooth of time and rage of fate;
A nobler meed on Valois' shade below,
And worthier gifts he hasten'd to bestow,
T'avenge his murder, make rebellion cease,
And rule the subjugated land in peace.   170

The din of battle gath'ring at their gates,
Dissolv'd their council, and dispers'd the states.

Swift from the walls to view th' advancing host
The gen'ral flew, the soldier to his post,
With shouts th' approaching hero they incense,   175
And all is ripe for onset and defence.

Tho' pleasure now, and peace securely reign
In all her courts, not such was Paris then,
But girt with massy walls, and unexpos'd,
An hundred forts the narrower town inclos'd;   180
The suburbs now defenceless and unbarr'd,
The gentle hand of peace their only guard,
Adorn'd with all the pomp that wealth supplies,
Proud spires and palaces that pierce the skies,
Were then a cluster of rude huts alone,   185
A rampart all around of earth was thrown,
With a deep foss to part them from the town.
From th'east the mighty chief his march began,
And death with hasty strides came foremost in his van.
Wing'd with red flames impetuous from on high   190
And from below, the show'ry bullets fly,
The rattling storm resistless thickens round,
And tumbles tow'r and bastion to the ground;
Gor'd and defaced the gay battalions bleed,
And on the plain their shatter'd limbs are spread.   195

   In earlier times, unaided and untaught,
His fate by simpler means the soldier wrought;
Strength against strength oppos'd the contest tried,
And on their swords alone the combatants relied;
More cruel wars their children learn'd to wage,   200
Nor less than light'ning satisfied their rage.
Then first was heard the thunder-bearing bomb,
Imprison'd mischief struggling in it's womb,
Swift on the destin'd mark the pond'rous shell
Came down, and spread destruction where it fell.   205

   Next, dire improvement on the barb'rous trade,
In hollow vaults the secret mine was laid;
In vain the warrior trusting in his might,
Speeds his bold march, and seeks the promis'd fight,
A sudden blast divides the yawning earth,   210

And the black vapour kindles into birth,
Smote by strange thunder sinks th'astonish'd host,
Deep in the dark abyss for ever lost.
These dangers Bourbon unappall'd defies,
Impatient for the strife, a throne the prize.   215
Where'er his hardy bands the hero leads,
'Tis hell beneath, and tempest o'er their heads,
His glorious steps undaunted they pursue,
Fir'd by his deeds still bright'ning in their view.

    Grave in the midst the valiant Mornay went,   220
Though slow his march, intrepid his intent;
Rage he alike disdain'd and slavish dread,
Nor heard the thunders bursting round his head;
War was heav'n's scourge on man, he wisely thought,
Nor lov'd the task, but took it as his lot;   225
Ev'n for the wonders of his sword he griev'd,
And loath'd it for the glories it atchiev'd.

    Now pour'd their legions down the dreadful way,
Where smear'd with blood the sloping Glacis lay;
More fierce as more in danger, with the slain   230
They choke the foss, and lift it to the plain,
Then born upon the supple numbers, reach
The ramparts, and rush headlong to the breach.
Waving his bloody fauchion, Henry led
The way, and enter'd furious at their head.   235
Already fixt by his victorious hand
High on the walls his glitt'ring banners stand:
Awe-struck the Leaguers seem'd, as they implor'd
The conqu'ror's mercy, and confess'd their lord;
But May'ne recalls them to their guilty part,   240
And drives the dawning grace from ev'ry heart,
'Till crowded in close Phalanx, they beset
Their king, whose eye their hardiest fear'd to meet.
Fierce on the battlements, and bathed in blood
Of thousands slain, the fury Discord stood;   245
There best her horrid mandates they obey,
And join'd in closer fight more surely slay.

vi. 218 undaunted] undunated *1762*

Sudden the deep-mouth'd engines cease to roar,
And the loud thunder of the war is o'er:
At once an universal silence round,   250
With awful pause, succeeds the deaf'ning sound;
Now thro' his foes the soldier cleaves his way,
And on the sword alone depends the day;
Alternate the contending leaders boast
The bloody ramparts won, and yield them lost: 255
Still victory the doubtful balance sway'd,
And join'd in air the mingling banners play'd,
'Till oft triumphant, and as oft subdued,
Fled the pale League, and Henry swift pursued.
'Tis thus the restless billows wash the shore,   260
By turns o'erwhelm it, and by turns restore.

Then most in that tremendous hour was shewn,
The might of Bourbon's rival, and his own;
'Twas then each hero's warlike soul was prov'd,
That in the shock of charging hosts unmov'd,   265
Amidst confusion, horror and despair,
Ranged the dread scene and ruled the doubtful war.

Mean while renown'd for many a martial deed,
A gallant English band brave Essex led,
In Gallia's cause with wonder they advance,   270
And scarcely can believe they fight for France.
On the same ramparts where the conquer'd Seine
Saw in old time their great forefathers reign,
For England's sake they wage the mortal strife,
Proud to enhance her fame, and prodigal of life.   275
Impetuous Essex first the breach ascends,
Where fierce D'Aumale the crowded pass defends,
To fight like fabled demi-gods they came,
Their age, their ardour, and their force the same;
French, English, Lorronese in combat close,   280
And in one stream the mingled slaughter flows.

Oh thou! the genius of that fatal day,
Soul of the strife, destroying angel, say,

vi. 272 Seine] Seine, *1762*

Whose was the triumph then, which hero's host
Yourself assisted, and heav'n favour'd most.   285
Long time the chiefs with rival glory crown'd,
Dealt equal slaughter thro' the legions round;
At length, by factious rage in vain assail'd,
The righteous cause and Henry's arms prevail'd;
Worn with disastrous toil and long fatigue,   290
Exhausted, hopeless, fled the vanquish'd League.
As on Pyrene's ever-clouded brow,
When swelling torrents threat the vale below,
A while with solid banks and lofty mounds,
They stay the foaming deluge in it's bounds;   295
But soon, the barrier broke, the rushing tide
Roars unresisted down the mountain's side,
Unroots the forest oaks, and bears away,
Flocks, folds and herds, an undistinguish'd prey:
So from the smoaking walls with matchless force,   300
Victorious Bourbon urged his rapid course,
Such havock where the royal warrior pass'd,
Deform'd the ranks and lay'd the battle waste.
At length the friendly gates, by May'ne's command
Flung wide, receiv'd the desolated band.   305
The victor host around the suburbs fly
Incensed, and hurl the blazing torch on high,
Their temp'rate valour kindles into rage,
And spoil and plunder are the war they wage.
Henry perceiv'd it not; with eager flight   310
He chaced the foe, dispers'd before his sight;
Spurr'd by his courage, with success elate
And ardent joy, he reach'd the hostile gate,
Thence on his scatter'd pow'r aloud he calls,
'Haste, fly my friends, and scale the haughty walls.'   315

When sudden in a rolling cloud enshrin'd,
A beauteous form came floating on the wind,
With gracious mien and awful to the view,
Tow'rds Henry the descending vision flew,
His brow was with immortal splendor grac'd,   320
And horror mixt with love his radiant eyes express'd.

vi. 316 enshrin'd] enshin'd *1762*

Hold hapless conqu'ror of your native land!
The phantom cried, and stay your vengeful hand;
This fair dominion you with war deface,
Is yours of old, the birthright of your race;   325
These lives you seek, are vassals of your throne,
This wealth you give to plunder, is your own;
Spare your own heritage, nor seek to reign
A solitary monarch o'er the slain.
Amaz'd the soldier heard the solemn sound,   330
And dropp'd his spoils, and prostrate kiss'd the ground.
Then Henry, rage still boiling in his breast,
Like seas hoarse—murm'ring while they sink to rest,
Say bright inhabitant of heav'n, what means
Your hallow'd form amidst these horrid scenes?   335
Mild as the breeze, at summer's ev'ning tide
Serene, the visionary shape replied.
Behold the sainted king whom France adores,
Protector of the Bourbon race, and yours,
That Louis, who like you once urged the fight,   340
Whose shrines you heed not, and whose faith you slight;
Know when the destin'd days their course have run,
Heav'n shall itself conduct you to the throne;
Thine is the vict'ry, but that great reward,
Is for thy mercy, not thy might, prepar'd.   345

   He spoke, the list'ning chief with rapture hears,
And down his cheek fast flow the joyful tears;
Peace sooth'd his tranquil heart, he dropp'd his sword,
And on his knees devout the shade ador'd.
Then twice around his neck his arms he flung,   350
And thrice deceiv'd on vain embraces hung;
Light as an empty dream at break of day,
Or as a blast of wind, he rush'd away.

   Mean while in haste to guard th'invested town,
The swarming multitude the ramparts crown,   355
Thick from above a fiery flood they pour,
And at the monarch aim the fatal show'r,
But heav'n's bright influence, round his temples shed,
Diverts the storm, and guards his sacred head.

'Twas then he saw, protected as he stood,   360
What thanks to his paternal saint he ow'd;
Tow'rds Paris his sad eye in sorrow thrown,
Ye French! he cried, and thou ill-fated town,
Ye citizens, a blind deluded herd,
How long will you withstand your lawful lord!   365
Nor more; but as the star that brings the day,
At eve declining in his western way,
More mildly shoots his horizontal fires,
And seems an ampler globe as he retires,
Such from the walls the parting hero turn'd,   370
While all his kindred saint within his bosom burn'd.
Vincennes he sought, where Louis whilom spoke
His righteous laws beneath an aged oak.
Vincennes, alas! no more a calm retreat,*
How art thou chang'd, thou once delightful seat!   375
Thy rural charms, thy peaceful smiles are fled,
And blank despair possesses thee instead.
'Tis there the great, their hapless labours done,
And all the short-liv'd race of glory run,
The fickle changes of their various lot   380
Conclude, and die neglected and forgot.

  Now night o'er heav'n pursued her dusty way,
And hid in shades the horrours of the day.

* It is well known how many illustrious prisoners the cardinals Richelieu and Mazarin
confin'd at Vincennes.

THE

HENRIADE

CANTO THE SEVENTH

THE ARGUMENT

Henry IV. is transported in a vision by St. Louis *to heaven, and the infernal regions. He arrives at the palace of the Destinies; where he has an opportunity of seeing his posterity, and the great men hereafter to be produc'd in* France.

The great, the boundless clemency of God,
To sooth the ills of life's perplexing road,
Sweet sleep, and hope, two friendly beings gave,
Which earth's dark, gloomy confines never leave.
When man, fatigued by labours of the day,   5
Has toiled his spirits, and his strength away,
That, nature's friend, restores her pow'rs again,
And brings the blest forgetfulness of pain.
This, oft deceitful, but for ever kind,
Diffuses warmth and transport through the mind.   10
From her the few, whom heaven approves, may learn
The pleasing issue of each high concern.
Pure as her author in the realms above
To them she brings the tidings of his love.

Immortal Louis bid the faithful pair   15
Expand their downy wings, and soften Henry's care.
Still sleep repairs to Vincenne's shady ground;
The winds subside, and silence reigns around.
Hope's blooming offspring, happy dreams succeed,
And give the pleasing, though ideal meed.   20
The verdant olive, and the laurel bough,
Entwined with poppies, grace the hero's brow.

On Bourbon's temples Louis plac'd the crown
Whose radiant honours once adorn'd his own.
Go, reign, he cried, and triumph o'er thy foes;   25
No other hope the race of Louis knows.
Yet think diviner presents to receive,
Far more, my son, than royalty I give.
What boots renown in arms, should heav'n withhold
Her light more precious than the purest gold?   30
These wordly honours are a barren good;
Rewards uncertain on the brave bestow'd:
A transient greatness, and a fading wreath
Blasted by troubles, and destroy'd by death.
Empire more durable, for thee designed,   35
I come to shew thee, and inform thy mind.
Attend my steps through paths thou ne'er hast trod,
And fly to meet the bosom of thy God.

Thus spoke the saint; they mount the car of light,
And swiftly traverse the ætherial height.   40
Thus midnight light'nings flash, while thunders rowl,
And cleave the ambient air from pole, to pole.
Thus rose Elijah on the fiery cloud;
The radiant æther with effulgence glow'd:
To purer worlds, array'd in glories bright,   45
The prophet fled, and vanish'd from the sight.

Amidst those orbs which move by certain laws
Known to each sage whom love of science draws,
The sun revolving round his axle turns,
Shines undiminish'd, and for ever burns,   50
Thence spring those golden torrents, which bestow
All vital warmth, and vigor as they flow.
From thence the welcome day, and year proceeds;
Through various worlds his genial influence spreads.
The rolling planets beam with borrowed rays,   55
And all around reflect the solar blaze;
Attract each other, and each other shun:
And end their courses where they first begun.
Far in the void unnumber'd worlds arise,
And suns unnumber'd light the azure skies.   60

Far beyond all the God of heav'n resides,
Marks ev'ry orbit, ev'ry motion guides.

Thither the hero, and the saint repair;
Myriads of spirits are created there,
Which amply people all the globe, and fill   65
The human body; such th'Almighty's will.
There, with immortal spirits at his feet,
The judge incorruptible holds his seat.
The God eternal, in all climes ador'd
By diff'rent names, Jehova, Jove, or Lord.   70
Before his throne our plaintive sorrows rise;
Our errors he beholds with pitying eyes:
Those senseless portraits, figur'd by mankind,
To paint his image, and omniscient mind.
All who on earth's inferior confines breathe,   75
Attend his summons through the gates of death.
The eastern sage, with holy wisdom fraught,
The sons of science, whom Confucius taught;
Those, who succeed in Zoroaster's cause,
And blindly yield submission to his laws: 80
The pale inhabitants of Zembla's coast,
That dreary region of eternal frost;
Canadia's sons, with fatal error blind,
Where truth illumines not the savage mind.
The gazing Dervis looks in vain around   85
At God's right hand no prophet to be found.
The Bonze, with gloomy, penitential brow,
Derives no comfort from his rigid vow.

At once enlight'ned, all the dead await
To hear their sentence, and approaching fate.   90
That mighty Being, whose extended view,
And boundless knowledge looks all nature through,
The past, the present, and the future times,
Rewards their love, or punishes their crimes.
The prince approach'd not, in those realms of light,   95
The throne invisible to human sight;
Whence issues forth the terrible decree
Which man presumes too fondly to foresee.

Is God, said Henry to himself, unjust,
On whom the world's created beings trust? 100
Will the Almighty not vouchsafe to save
For want of knowledge which he never gave?
Expect religion where it never shone;
And judge the universe by laws unknown?
His hand created all, and all will find 105
That heaven's high king is merciful, and kind.
His voice informs the whole, and ev'ry part;
Fair nature's laws are stamp'd on ev'ry heart.
Nature, the same through each inferior clime,
Pure, and unspotted to the end of time, 110
By this the pagan's sentence will proceed,
And pagan virtue is religion's deed.

While thus, with reason narrow, and confin'd,
On truths mysterious he employ'd his mind,
A solemn, awful voice was heard around; 115
All heav'n, all nature shudder'd at the sound.
Such were the thunders, which from Sinai's brow,
Diffus'd a horror through the plains below.
Each seraph glow'd with adoration's fire,
And silence reign'd through all the cherub choir. 120
The rolling spheres the sacred accents caught,
And truths divine to other planets taught.
Distrust thy mental pow'rs, nor blindly stray
As pride, or feebler reason points the way,
The high invisible who rules above, 125
Escapes thy knowledge, but demands thy love.
His pow'r, and justice punish, and controul
Each wilful error of the stubborn soul.
To pure devotion be thy heart consign'd,
Truth's radiant orb illumine all thy mind. 130
These were the sounds, when, through the fields of light,
A rapid whirlwind from the ætherial height
Convey'd the prince to dark, and dreary climes,
Like those where Chaos reign'd in elder times.
No solar influence, like it's author mild, 135
Diffuses comfort through the savage wild.

Angels abhor the desolated waste,
Which life's fair, fruitful blossom never grac'd.
Confusion, death, each terror of despair,
Fix'd on his throne, presides a tyrant there.   140
O heav'ns! what shrieks of woe, what piteous cries,
What sulph'rous smoaks, what horrid flames arise!
What fiends, cried Bourbon, to these climes retreat!
What gulphs, what torrents burst beneath our feet!
See here, the saint return'd, the gates of hell,   145
Which justice form'd, where impious spirits dwell.
Come, view the dismal regions of distress;
These paths are always easy of access.
There squint-eyed Envy lay, whose pois'nous breath
Consumes the verdure of each laurel wreath: 150
In night's impenetrable darkness bred,
She hates the living, but applauds the dead.
Her sparkling eyes, which shun the orb of day,
Perceiving Henry, Envy turn'd away.
Near her, self-loving, self-admiring pride,   155
And down-cast weakness, ever pale, reside.
Weakness, which yields to each persuasive crime,
And crops the flow'r of virtue in it's prime.
Ambition there with head-strong fury raves,
With thrones surrounded, sepulchres, and slaves.   160
Submissive, meek Hypocrisy was nigh,
Hell in her heart, all heav'n in her eye.
There Int'rest, father of all crimes, appear'd,
And blinded Zeal by cruelty rever'd.
These wild, tyrannic rulers of mankind,   165
When Henry came, their savage air resign'd.
Their impious troop ne'er reach'd his purer soul,
Such virtue yields not to their mad controul.
Who comes, they cried, to break the peaceful rest
Of night eternal, and these shades molest?   170

Our hero view'd the subterraneous scene,
And slowly travell'd through the ranks obscene.
Louis led on.—Oh heav'n! is that the hand,
Which murder'd Valois at the League's command?
Is that the monster? yes, I know him well,   175

His arm still holds the parricidal steel.
While barb'rous priests proclaim the wretch divine,
And place his portrait on the hallow'd shrine,
Though Rome, and faction celebrate his name,
To hymns, and praises hell denies his claim.   180

    Princes, and kings, the honour'd saint replied,
Meet in these realms the punishment of pride.
Behold those tyrants, once ador'd by all,
Whose height but serv'd to aggrandize their fall.
God pours his vengeance on the scepter'd crowd,   185
For vice committed, and for crimes allow'd.
Death, from on high commission'd to destroy,
Cut short the transport of each wayward joy.
No pomp of greatness could the victim save;
Their beams of glory set within the grave.   190
Now is no civil, sly deceiver near,
To whisper error in the sovreign's ear.
Once injur'd truth the sword of terror draws;
Displays each crime, and indicates her cause.
Behold yon heroes tremble at her nod,   195
Esteem'd as tyrants in the eyes of God.
Now on their heads descend those thunders dire,
Form'd by themselves to set the world on fire.
Close by their side, the weakest of mankind,
Each listless, feeble monarch is reclin'd;   200
Whose indolence disgrac'd the subject land,
Meer airy forms, meer nothings in command.
Sinister counsellors on these await,
Once their imperious ministers of state.
Proud, avaritious, of immoral lives,   205
Who sold what honours Mars, or Themis gives:
Sold what our fathers purchas'd by their blood,
And all that's precious to the great, and good.

    Tell me, said Henry, O ye sons of ease,
Must tender spirits dwell in climes like these?   210
You, who, on flow'ry couches, pass away
The tranquil moments of life's useless day.

vii. 179 name,] name *1762*

Shall virtue's friends in fiery torments roll?
Whose faults have risen from expanse of soul.
Shall one mistaken, momentary joy   215
Maturer Wisdom's plenteous fruits destroy?
This, cried the prince, the lot of human race?
Condemn'd for endless ages to distress!
If all mankind one common hell devours,
Eternal tortures close our transient hours,   220
Who was not more in non-existence blest?
Who would not perish at his mother's breast?
Far happier man! had God's creative hand
Form'd him less free, in innocence to stand:
Had God, thus awfully severe, bestow'd   225
The sole capacity of doing good.

   Think not, the saint replied, that sinners feel
Vengeance too heavy, or deserve not hell.
Think not the great creator of mankind
To these his works is cruel, or unkind.   230
Lord of all beings, he presides above
With mercy infinite, and boundless love.
Though mortals see the tyrant in their God,
Parental tenderness directs his rod.
Let not these horrid scenes thy soul alarm;   235
Compassion checks the fury of his arm:
Nor endless punishments inflicts on those
Whose faults from human imperfection rose:
Whose pleasures, follow'd by remorse, have been
The transient cause of momentary sin.   240
Such were his accents—to the realms of light
Both are convey'd with instantaneous flight.
Infernal darkness shuns those flow'ry plains
Where spotless innocence for ever reigns.
There, in the floods of purest æther play   245
The beams refulgent of eternal day.
Each blooming scene seraphick joys bestow'd;
And Henry's soul with unknown raptures glow'd.
There tranquil pleasure spreads her ev'ry charm
Which thought can fancy, or which heav'n can form.   250
No cares sollicit, and no passions move;

But all is govern'd by angelic love.
Far other love, than that of wild desires,
Which grosser sense, and luxury inspires.
The bright, the sacred flame on earth unknown,   255
Which burns in heav'n, and heav'nly minds alone.
Its chaste endearments all their hours employ,
And endless wishes meet with endless joy.
There dwell true heroes; there each pious sage,
And monarchs once the glory of their age.   260
Thence Charlemagne, and Clovis turn their eyes
On Gallia's empire from the azure skies:
On golden thrones for ever plac'd sublime,
And clad in honours unimpair'd by time.
There, fiercest foes the happy union prove   265
Of pure affection, and a brother's love.
Louis the wise,* amidst the royal band,
Tall as a cedar, issues his command.
Louis, of France the glory, and the pride,
Who rul'd our realms with justice by his side.   270
Oft' would he pardon, oft' relief supply;
And wipe the falling tear from ev'ry eye.
D'Amboise is still commission'd to attend;
His faithful minister, and warmest friend.
To him alone was Gallia's honour dear: 275
To him alone her homage was sincere.
His gentler hands were sullied not with blood;
His ev'ry wish was center'd in her good.

 Oh spotless manners! bright, and halcyon days!
Worthy eternal memory, and praise.   280
Then wholesome laws adorn'd, and bless'd the state;
Subjects were happy, and the monarch great.
Return, ye halcyon days, with golden wing:
And equal blessings, equal honours bring.
Virtue, descend, another Louis frame   285
As rich in merit, and as great in fame.

 Farther remote, those worthy heroes stood,
Careless of life, and prodigal of blood,

     * Louis XII.

Who died with transport for the public weal;
Led on by duty, not enrag'd by zeal.   290
Brave Montmorency,* Tremouille,† de Foix,‡
Who fought their passage to those fields of joy.
There Guesclin§ drinks of pleasures purer springs:
Guesclin, th'avenger, and the dread of kings.
There too appear'd the Amazonian dame,‖   295
The tott'ring throne's support, and England's shame.

These, cried the saint, who now possess the skies,
Like thee with glory dazzled Europe's eyes.
Virtue alone their simpler minds could move:
The church was nourish'd by their filial love.   300
Like me they honour'd truth's diviner name:
Our worship uniform, our church the same.
Say, why does Bourbon follow other laws,
Or why defend religion's weaker cause?

Time, with incessant flight prepar'd to roam,   305
Quits, and revisits this terrific dome:
And pours with plenteous hand on all mankind
The good, and evil for each race design'd.
An altar high of massy iron bears
The fatal annals of succeeding years.   310
Where God's own hand has mark'd, nor mark'd in vain
Each transient pleasure, each severer pain.
There liberty, that haughty slave, is bound,

* *Montmorency.*] It would fill a volume, should we specify the services done to the state by this family.

† *Tremouille.*] Amongst many great men of this name, Guy de la Tremouille is particularly alluded to. He was surnamed *the Valiant*; carried the royal standard : and refus'd the high constable's sword in the reign of Charles VI.

‡ *de Foix.*] Gaston de Foix, duke of Nemours, and nephew to Louis XII. He was slain at the famous battle of Ravenna; having received fourteen wounds, and defeated the enemy.

§ *Guesclin.*] France owed her preservation to this great man, in the reign of Charles V. He conquered Castile, placed Henry de Transtamare upon the throne of Peter the cruel, and was constable of France, and Castile.

‖ *Amazonian Dame.*] Joan d'Arc (known by the name of the Maid of Orleans). She was servant-maid at an inn; and born at the village of Domremy upon the Meuse: being superior to her sex in strength of body, and bravery of mind, she was employed by the count de Dunois to retrieve the affairs of Charles VII. taken prisoner in a sally at Compiegne in the year 1430, conducted to Rouen, tried as a sorceress in an ecclesiastical court, and burnt by the English.

With chains invisible encircled round.
Beneath the yoke she bends her stubborn head,   315
Still unconstrain'd, unconscious of the deed.
This suppliant turn that hidden chain supplies
Wisely conceal'd for ever from her eyes.
The fates appear her sentence to fulfill:
Each action seems the product of free-will.   320

From thence, cried Louis, on the human race
Descends the influence of heav'nly grace.
In future times its pow'r thy tongue shall tell:
Its purer radiance all thy heart shall feel.
Those precious moments God alone bestows;   325
No mortal hastens, and no being knows.
But Oh how slowly comes that period on
When God shall love, and own thee for his son!
Too long shall weakness hide thy brighter rays;
And lead thy steps through error's slipp'ry ways.   330
Teach him, kind heav'n, the happier, better road;
Shorten the days which part him from his God.

But see what crowds in long succession press
Through the vast region of unbounded space.
These sacred mansions to thy view display   335
The unborn offspring of some future day.
All times, and places are for ever nigh,
All beings present to Jehova's eye.
Here fate has mark'd their destin'd hour of birth,
Their rise, their grandeur, and their fall on earth.   340
The various changes of each life to come,
Their vices, virtues, and their final doom.
Draw near, for heav'n allows us to foresee
What kings, and heroes shall descend from thee.
That graceful personage is Bourbon's son,   345
Form'd to support the glory of the crown.
The warlike leader shall his triumphs boast
O'er Belgia's plains, and proud Iberia's coast.
To deeds more noble shall his son aspire;
And wreaths more splendid first adorn his sire.   350

On beds of lillies, near a tow'ring throne,
Two radiant forms before our hero shone.
Monarchs they seem'd, of high, imperious pride,
And Roman purple flow'd adown their side.
A subject nation couch'd beneath their feet,   355
And guards unnumber'd form'd the train complete.
These, said the saint, are doom'd to endless fame:
In all things sov'reigns, save the royal name.
Richelieu, and Mazarin, design'd by fate
Immortal ministers of Gallia's state.   360
To them shall policy consign her aid;
And fortune raise them from the altar's shade.
Rul'd by despotic pow'r, shall France confess
Great Richelieu's genius, Mazarin's address.
One flies* with art before the rising storm: 365
One braves all danger in it's fiercest form.
Both to the princes of our royal blood
With hate relentless enemies avow'd.
With high ambition, and with pride inspir'd,
By all dislik'd and yet by all admir'd.   370
Their artful schemes, and industry shall bring
Plagues on their country, glory on their king.

O thou, great Colbert,† whose enlighten'd mind
Schemes less extensive for our good design'd!
No lustre equals, none excells thy own,   375
Save that which gilds, and decorates the crown.
Nurs'd by thy genius, heav'n-born plenty reigns,
And pours her treasures over Gallia's plains.
Colbert by gen'rous deeds to glory rose:
His only vengeance was to bless his foes.   380
Thus were dispens'd the gifts of heav'nly grace,
By God's own confident on Israel's race.
That race, whose blasphemy could ne'er remove,
Or quench the beams of mercy, and of love.

* *One flies*.] Cardinal Mazarin was oblig'd to leave the kingdom in the year 1651; notwithstanding he had the entire government of the queen Regent. Cardinal Richelieu on the contrary always maintain'd his situation in spite of his enemies, and the king, who was disgusted at his behaviour.

† Colbert was detested by the people. That blind, and savage monster would have dug his body out of the ground; but the approbation of men of sense, which at length prevailed, has rendered his name for ever dear, and respectable.

What troops of slaves before that monarch* stand!   385
What numbers tremble at his high command!
No king did Gallia ever yet obey
With such profound submission to his sway.
Though less belov'd, more dreaded in her eyes,
Like thee he claims fair glory's richest prize.   390
Firm in all danger, in success too warm
When fortune smiles, and conquest meets his arm.
Himself shall crush, superior to intrigue,
Full twenty nations join'd in pow'rful league.
Praise shall attend him to his latest breath,   395
Great in his life, but greater in his death.
Thrice happy age! when nature's lavish hand
With all her graces shall adorn the land.
Thrice happy age! when ev'ry art refin'd
Spreads her fair polish o'er the ruder mind.   400
The muse for ever our retreats shall love
More than the shades of Aganippe's grove.
From sculptur'd stone the seeming accent flows;
With animated tints the canvass glows.
What sons of science in that period rise,   405
Measure the universe, and read the skies!
The purer ray of philosophic light
Reveals all nature, and dispells the night.
Presumptuous error from their view retreats;
Truth crowns their labours, and their joy compleats.   410
Thy accents too sweet music, strike mine ear,
Music, descended from the heav'nly sphere.
'Tis thine to sooth, to soften, and controul
Each wayward passion of the ruffled soul.
Unpolish'd Greece, and Italy have own'd   415
The strong inchantments of thy magic sound.
The subjects rul'd by Gallia's pow'rful king
Shall bravely conquer, and as sweetly sing.
Shall join the poet's to the warrior's praise,
And twine Bellona's with Apollo's bays.   420
E'en now I see this second age of gold
Produce a people of heroic mould.
Here num'rous armies skim before my sight;

* *That monarch.*] Louis XIV.

There fly the Bourbons eager for the fight.
At once his master's terror, and support,   425
Great Condé* makes the flames of war his sport.
Turenne more calmly meets the hostile pow'r,
In arms his equal, and in wisdom more.
Assemblage rare! in Catinat† are seen
The hero's talents, and the sage's mien.   430
Known by his compass Vauban‡ from the tow'r
Smiles at the tumult, and the cannon's roar.
England shall tell of Luxembourg's§ renown,
In war invincible, at court unknown.
Onward I see the martial Villars‖ move   435

---

* *Condé.*] Louis de Bourbon, generally called the great Condé; and Henry viscount de Turenne, have been look'd upon as the greatest generals of their time. They have both gained very important victories, and acquired glory even in their defeats. The prince of Condé's genius seemed, as it was said, more proper for a day of battle, and that of Mr. de Turenne for a whole campaign. It is certain at least, that Mr. de Turenne gained considerable advantages over the Great Condé at Gien, Etampes, Paris, Arras, and the battle of Dunes. We shall not however attempt to determine which was the greatest man.

† *Catinat.*] The marshal de Catinat, born in 1637; he gained the battle of Staffarde, and Marse Iles: and obeyed without reluctance, or murmuring the marshal de Villerois, who sent him orders without consulting him. He resigned his command with the utmost composure; never complained of any person's treatment, asked nothing of the king, and died like a true philosopher at his country-seat at St. Gratien. He never augmented or diminished his estate, and never for a moment acted unworthy his character as a man of temperance, and moderation.

‡ *Vauban.*] The Marshal de Vauban, born in 1633, the greatest engineer that ever lived. He repaired upon a new plan of his own no less than 300 old fortifications, and built 33. He conducted 53 seiges, and was present at 140 actions. He left behind him at his death 12 manuscript volumes full of designs for the good of the state: none of which have ever yet been executed. He was a member of the academy of sciences, and did more honour to it than any other person, by rendering mathematics subservient to the advantage of his country.

§ *Luxembourg.*] Francis Henry de Montmorency, who took the name of Luxembourg; marshal of France, and both duke, and peer of the realm. He gained the battle of Cassel, under the direction of Monsieur, the brother of Louis XIV. and won the celebrated victories of Mons, Fleurus, Steinkerke, and Nerwinde, where he acted as commanding officer. He was confined to the Bastile, and exceedingly ill treated by the ministry.

‖ *Villars.*] It was the author's original design to mention no living character through the whole poem: and the rule proposed has only been deviated from in favour of the marshal duke de Villars. He gained the battle of Fredelingue, and that of the first Hocstet. It is remarkable that in this engagement he posted himself on the same spot of ground which the duke of Marlborough afterwards occupied, when he won that very signal victory of the second Hocstet, so fatal to France. Upon resuming the command of the army, the marshal was afterwards engaged in the famous battle of Blangis, or Malplaquet, in which twenty thousand of the enemy were slain; and the loss of which was owing to the marshal's being wounded. In the year 1712, when the enemy threatened to proceed to Paris, and it was deliberated whether Louis XIV. should not quit Versailles, the marshal de Villars defeated prince Eugene at Denain, dislodged the enemy from their post at Marchienne, raised the seige of

To wrest the thunder from the bird of Jove.
Conquest attends to bid the battle cease,
And leaves him sov'reign arbiter of peace.
Denain shall own brave Villars to have been
The worthy rival of the great Eugene. 440

What princely youth* draws near, whose manly face
United majesty, and sweetness grace?
See how unmov'd——Oh heav'ns! what sudden shade
Conceals the beauties which his form display'd!
Death flutters round; health, beauty, all is gone: 445
He falls just ready to ascend the throne.
Heav'n form'd him all that's truly just, and good:
Descended, Bourbon, from thy royal blood.
Oh gracious God! shall fate but shew mankind
A flow'r so sweet, and virtues so refin'd! 450
What could a soul so gen'rous not obtain!
What joys would France experience from his reign!
Produc'd, and nurtur'd by his fost'ring hand
Fair peace, and plenty had enrich'd the land.
Each day some new beneficence had brought: 455
Oh how shall Gallia weep! alarming thought!
When one dark, silent sepulchre contains
The son's, the mother's, and the sire's remains.

Fall'n is the tree, and from it's ruins springs
An infant successor to Gallia's kings. 460
A tender shoot, from whose increasing shade
France may derive some salutary aid.
Conduct him, Fleury, to the throne of truth;
Wait on his years, and cultivate his youth.
Teach him self-knowledge, and, if Fleury can, 465
Teach him that Louis is no more than man.
Inspire each virtue which can life adorn;
Kings for their subjects, not themselves are born.
And thou, O France, once more arise to day;
Resume thy majesty beneath his sway. 470

Landrecy, took Douay, Quesnoy, and Bouchain at discretion, and afterwards agreed upon a peace at Radstat in the king's name, with the same prince Eugene, the emperor's plenipotentiary.

* *Princely youth.*] This poem was composed in the infancy of Louis XV.

Let ev'ry science, which retir'd before,
Crown thy fair temples, and adorn thy shore.
The azure waters with thy navies sweep:
So wills the monarch of the hoary deep.
See, from the Nile, the Euxine, and the Ind,   475
Each port by nature, or by art design'd,
Commerce aloud demands thee for her seat;
And spreads her richest treasures at thy feet.
Adieu to terrour, and adieu to war,
The peaceful olive be thy future care.   480

Pursued by envy, and distraction's crew,
A chief renown'd* advances to the view;
Easy, not weak, when glory spurs him on,
Engag'd by novelties, by trifles won.
Though luxury displays a thousand charms,   485
And smiling pleasure courts him to her arms,
Yet shall he keep all Europe in suspense
By artful politics, and manly sense.
The world shall move as Orleans shall guide;
And ev'ry science flourish at his side.   490
Empire, my son, himself shall never reach;
'Tis his the art of government to teach.

Now burst the light'ning from the op'ning skies,
And Gallia's standard wav'd before their eyes.
Iberia's troops, array'd in arms compleat,   495
The German eagle crush'd beneath their feet.
When thus the saint—no more remains the trace
Of Charles the fifth, his glory, or his race.
Each earthly being has it's final hour;
Eternal wisdom let us all adore.   500
From thence all human revolutions spring:
E'en Spain from Bourbon shall request a king.
Illustrious Philip shall receive the crown;
And sit as monarch on Iberia's throne.
Surprize was soon succeeded by delight,   505
And Henry's soul enraptur'd at the sight.

* *A chief renowned.*] A true portrait of the duke of Orleans.

Repress thy transports, cried the saint, and dread
This great event, this present to Madrid.
Say, who can fathom heav'n's conceal'd intent,
Dangers may come, and Paris may repent.   510
Oh Philip! Oh my sons! shall France, and Spain
Thus meet, and never be disjoin'd again!
How long shall fatal politics forbear
To light the flames of discord, and of war!

   Thus Louis spoke—when lo! the scene withdrew,   515
Each object vanish'd from our hero's view.
The sacred portals clos'd before his eyes,
And sudden darkness overspread the skies.
Far in the east Aurora moving on
Unlock'd the golden chambers of the sun.   520
Night's sable robe o'er other climes was spread,
Each dream retir'd, and ev'ry flitting shade.
The prince arose, with heav'nly ardor fir'd,
Unusual vigor all his soul inspir'd.
Fear, and respect, great Bourbon, now were thine: 525
Full on thy brow sat majesty divine.
Thus when before the tribes great Moses stood,
Return'd at length from Sinai, and from God,
His eyeballs flash'd intolerable light;
Each prostrate Hebrew shudder'd at the sight.   530

THE

HENRIADE

CANTO THE EIGHTH

THE ARGUMENT

The earl of Egmont *comes to assist* May'ne *and the* League. *Battle of* Ivry, *in which* May'ne *is defeated, and* Egmont *slain. Valour, and clemency of* Henry the Great.

Dejected by their loss, the states appear
Less haughty, and assume an humbler air,
Henry, such terrour in their hearts had wrought,
Their king creating schemes were all forgot;
Wav'ring and weak in counsel, and afraid   5
To crown their idol May'ne, or to degrade,
By vain decrees they labour to complete
And ratify a pow'r, not giv'n him yet.

    This self-commission'd chief,* this king uncrown'd
In chains of iron rule his faction bound;   10
His willing slaves obedient to his laws,
Resolve to fight and perish in his cause;
Thus flush'd with hope, to council he convenes
The haughty lords, on whom his fortune leans.
They came: despair, and unextinguish'd hate,   15
And malice on their faded features sate;
Some tremble in their pace, and feebly tread,
Faint with the loss of blood in battle shed,
But keen resentment prompts them to repair
Their losses, and revenge the wounds they bear.   20
Before the chief their sullen ranks they range,

* He was declared by the parliament, which continued attached to him, lieutenant-general of the state, and kingdom of France.

And grasp their shining arms, and vow revenge.
So the fierce sons of earth, as fable feigns,
Where Pelion overlooks Thessalia's plains,
With mountains piled on mountains, vainly strove,   25
To scale the everlasting throne of Jove.
When sudden on a car of radiant light
Exalted, Discord flash'd upon their sight;
Courage, she said, 'tis now the times demand
Your fixt resolves, lo! succour is at hand.   30
First ran d'Aumale, and joyful from afar
Beheld the Spanish launces gleam in air;
Then cried aloud, 'tis come; th' expected aid,
So oft demanded, and so long delay'd.

    Near to that hallow'd spot, where rest rever'd   35
The reliques of our kings, their march appear'd;
The groves of polish'd spears, the targets bound
With circling gold, the shining helms around,
Against the sun with full reflection play,
Rival his light and shed a second day.   40
To meet their march the roaring rabble went,
And hail'd the mighty chief Madrid had sent;
That chief was Egmont;* fam'd for martial fire,
Ambitious son of an unhappy sire;
At Brussels first he drew the vital air;   45
His country's weal was all his father's care,
For that, the rage of tyrants he defied,
And in the cause of freedom, bravely died.
The servile son, as base as he was proud,
Fawn'd on that hand which shed his father's blood,   50
For sordid int'rest join'd his country's foes,
And fought for France, regardless of her woes.
Philip, on May'ne the warlike youth bestow'd,
And arm'd him forth to be his guardian God;
Nor doubted May'ne, but slaughter and dismay   55
Should spread to Bourbon's tent, when Egmont led the way.
With heedless arrogance their march they drew,
And Henry's heart exulted at the view,

---

* The earl of Egmont, son of admiral Egmont, who was beheaded at Brussels together with the prince de Horn.

Gods! how his eager hopes anticipate
And meet the moment that decides his fate.   60

   Their streams where Iton and fair Eura lead,
By nature blest, a fertile plain is spread,
No wars had yet approach'd the peaceful scene,
Nor warrior's footstep press'd the flow'ry green,
The shepherds there, while civil rage destroy'd   65
The regions round, their happy hours enjoy'd,
Screen'd by their poverty, they seem'd secure
From lawless rapine and the soldier's pow'r,
Nor heard beneath their humble roofs the jar
Of arms, or clamour of the sounding war.   70

   Thither each hostile leader his array
Directs, and desolation marks their way,
A sudden horror strikes the trembling floods,
The frighted shepherds seek the shelt'ring woods,
The partners of their grief attend their flight,   75
And bear their weeping infants from the sight.

   Ye hapless natives of this sweet recess!
Charge not at least your king with your distress,
For peace he courts the combat, and his hand
Shall shed the bounteous blessing o'er the land;   80
He shares your sorrows, and shall end your woes,
Nor seeks you, but to save you from your foes.

   Along the ranks he darts his glancing eyes,
Swift as the winds his foaming courser flies,
Proud of his load, he catches with delight   85
The trumpets sound, and hopes the promis'd fight.

   Crown'd with his laurels, at their master's side,
A well distinguish'd groupe of warriors ride,
D'Aumont,* beneath five kings a chief renown'd,

* John D'Aumont, marshal of France, who did wonders at the battle of Ivry, was the son
of Peter d'Aumont and Frances de Sully, an heiress of the ancient family of Sully. He served
under Henry II. Francis II. Charles II. Henry III. and Henry IV.

Biron,* whose name bore terrour in the sound,   90
His son,† whom toil nor danger could restrain,
Who soon alas!—but he was faithful then;
Crillon and Sully by the guilty fear'd,
Chiefs whom the League detested, yet rever'd,
Turenne,‡ whose virtues and unrival'd fame,   95
Won the fair honours of the Bouillon name,
Ill-fated pow'r alas! and ill maintain'd,
Crush'd in the birth, and lost as soon as gain'd.
His crest amid the band brave Essex rears,
And like a palm beneath our skies appears,   100
Among our elms the lofty stranger shoves
His growth, as if he scorn'd the native groves.
From his bright casque with orient gems array'd
And burnish'd gold, a starry lustre play'd;
Dear, valued gifts! with which his mistress strove   105
Less to reward his courage, than his love,
Ambitious chief! the mighty bulwark grown
Of Gallia's prince, and darling of his own.
Such was the monarch's train, with stedfast air
And firm, they wait the signal of the war,   110
Glad omens from their Henry's eyes they took,
And read their conquest sure in his inspiring look.

    'Twas then, afflicted with inglorious dread,
Unhappy May'ne perceiv'd his courage fled,
Whether at length his boding heart divines   115
The wrath of heav'n on his unjust designs,
Whether the soul prophetic of our doom,
Foresees the dreary train of ills to come,
Whate'er the cause, he feels a chilling fear,
But veils it with a shew of seeming cheer,   120
Inspires his troops with ardour of renown,
And fills their hearts with hopes that dwell not in his own.

    * Henry de Contand de Biron, marshal of France, and grand master of the artillery. He
was a great warriour, commanded the corps de reserve at Ivry, and was very instrumental in
gaining the victory.
    † Charles Contand de Biron, son of the former. He conspired afterwards against Henry
IV. and was beheaded in the court of the Bastile in 1602.
    ‡ Henry de la Tour d'Oiliegues, viscount of Turenne, marshal of France. Henry the great
married him to Charlotte de la Mark, princess of Sedan, in 1591. The marshal went on the
wedding night to take Stenay by assault.

But Egmont at his side, with glory fir'd,
And the rash confidence his youth inspir'd,
Flush'd for the fight, and eager to display   125
His prowess, chides his infamous delay.
As when the Thracian courser from afar,
Hears the shrill trumpet and the sound of war,
A martial fire informs his vivid eye,
He neighs, he snorts, he bears his head on high,   130
Impatient of restraint he scorns the rein,
Springs o'er the fence and scours along the plain;
Such Egmont seem'd, with beating heart he stood,
And in his eye the rage of battle glow'd.
Ev'n now he ponders his approaching fame,   135
And looks on conquest as his rightful claim;
Alas! he dreams not that his pride shall gain
Nought but a grave, in Ivry's fatal plain.

Bourbon at length drew near, and thus inspir'd
His ardent warriors whom his presence fir'd.   140
Ye sons of France! your king is at your head,
You see your foes, then follow where I lead,
Mark well this waving plume amid the fight,
Nor let the tempest shade it from your sight,
To that alone direct your constant aim,   145
Still sure to find it in the road to fame.
Thus spoke the chief; his bands exulting hear,
And with new fury court the glorious war;
Then march'd, and as he went, his pious breast
With silent pray'rs the God of hosts address'd.   150
At once the legions rush with headlong pace
Behind their chiefs, and snatch the middle space.
So where the seas with narrow Frith divide
Contabria's coast from Afric's desert side,
If eastern storms along the channel pour,   155
Sudden the fierce conflicting oceans roar,
Earth trembles at the shock, the sheeted brine
Invades the skies, the sun forgets to shine,
The trembling Moor believes all nature hurl'd
In ruin, and expects the falling world.   160

viii. 159 Moor] moor *1762*

Now lengthen'd with the spear the musket spread
The carnage wide, and slew with double speed,
That fatal engine in Bayonne design'd,
And fram'd by Discord to lay waste mankind,
Strikes a twin death, and can at once afford   165
The worst effect of fire, and havock of the sword.
Trembled the stedfast earth beneath their feet
As sword to sword and lance to lance they met,
From rank to rank despair and horror strode,
The shame of flight and impious thirst of blood.   170
Here from his stronger son the father flies,
There by the brother's arm the brother dies,
Nature was shock'd, and Eura's conscious bank
Shrunk with abhorrence from the blood it drank.
Bourbon his path right on to glory clears   175
Through bristly forests of portended spears,
O'er many a crested helm his course he sped,
Close in his rear, serene and undismay'd
Went Mornay, thoughtful and intent alone
On Henry's life, regardless of his own.   180
So, veil'd in human shape, the poets feign
The gods engaged in arms on Phrygia's plain;
'So when an angel by divine command,
With rising tempests shakes a guilty land,
Well pleas'd th'Almighty's orders to perform,   185
He rides the whirlwind, and directs the storm.'
The royal chief his dread commands express'd,
The prudent dictates of a hero's breast,
Mornay the mighty charge attentive caught,
And bore it where the distant leaders fought,   190
The distant leaders to their troops convey
The word, their troops receive it, and obey.
They part, they join, in various forms are seen,
One soul informs and guides the vast machine.
Swift thro' the field return'd in haste he seeks   195
The prince, accosts, and guards him while he speaks.
But still the stoic warrior kept unstain'd
With human blood, his inoffensive hand,
The king alone employ'd his gen'rous thought,
For his defence th' imbattled field he sought,   200

Detested war, and singularly brave
Knew boldly to face death, but never gave.

Turenne already with resistless pow'r,
Repuls'd the shatter'd forces of Nemours;
Scarce d'Ailly fill'd the plain, with dire alarms,   205
Proud of his thirty years consum'd in arms;
Still spite of age the vet'ran chief displays
The well-strung vigour of his youthful days;
Of all his foes, one only would presume
To match his might, a hero in the bloom;   210
Now first indignant to the field he came,
And parted eager for the goal of fame.
New to the taste of Hymen, yet he fled
The chaste endearments of his bridal bed,
Disdain'd the trivial praise by beauty won,   215
And panted for a soldier's fame alone.
That cruel morn, accusing heav'n in vain,
And the curs'd League that call'd him to the plain,
His beauteous bride with trembling fingers laced
His heavy corslet on her hero's breast,   220
And cover'd with his helm of polish'd gold
Those eyes which still she languish'd to behold.

Tow'rds d'Ailly the fierce youth, despising fear,
Spurr'd his proud steed, and couch'd his quiv'ring spear,
Their headlong courses trampled, as they fled,   225
The wounded heaps, the dying and the dead;
Poachy with blood the turf and matted grass,
Sink fetlock deep beneath them as they pass.
Swift to the shock they come; their shields sustain
The blow, their spears well pointed but in vain,   230
In scatter'd splinters shine upon the plain.
So when two clouds with thunder fraught draw near,
And join their dark encounter in mid air,
Struck from their sides the light'ning quivers round,
Heav'n roars, and mortals tremble at the sound.   235
Now from their steeds with unabated rage

viii. 207 chief] chiefs *1762*

Alighting swift, a closer war they wage;
Ran Discord to the scene, and near her stood,
Death's horrid spectre, pale and smear'd with blood.
Already shine their fauchions in their hands,   240
No kind preventing pow'r their rage withstands,
The doom is past, their destiny commands.
Full at each other's heart they aim alike,
Nor knows their fury at whose heart they strike;
Their bucklers clash, thick strokes descend from high,   245
And flakes of fire from their hard helmets fly,
Blood stains their hands, but still the temper'd plate
Retards a while and disappoints their fate.
Each wond'ring at the long unfinish'd fight,
Esteems his rival, and admires his might;   250
'Till d'Ailly with a vig'rous effort found
The fatal pass, and stretch'd him on the ground.
His faded eyes for ever closed remain,
And his loose helmet rowls along the plain;
Then saw the wretched chief, too surely known,   255
The kindred features, and embraced his son.
But soon with horror and remorse oppress'd,
Revers'd the guilty steel against his breast.
That just revenge his hast'ning friends oppose;
When furious from the dreadful scene he rose;   260
Forth to the woods his cheerless journey sped,
From arms for ever and from glory fled,
And in the covert of a shaggy den,
Dwell a sad exile from the ways of men.
There when the dawning day salutes the skies,   265
And when at eve the chilling vapours rise,
His unexhausted grief still flows the same,
Still eccho sighs around his son's lamented name.
Tender alarms, and boding terrours brought
The bride enquiring to the fatal spot,   270
Uncertain of her doom, with anxious haste
And fault'ring knees between the dead she pass'd,
'Till stetch'd upon the plain her lord she spied,
Then shriek'd, and sunk expiring at his side.
The damps of death upon her temples hung,   275
And feeble sounds scarce parted from her tongue,

Once more her eyes a last farewel assay'd,
Once more her lips upon his lips she lay'd,
Within her arms the lifeless body press'd,
Then look'd, and sigh'd, and died upon his breast.   280

    Deplor'd examples of rebellious strife,
Ill-fated victims, father, son, and wife,
Oh may the sad remembrance of your woe,
Teach tears from ages yet unborn to flow,
With wholesome sorrow touch all future times,   285
And save the children from their father's crimes.

    But say what chief disperses thus abroad
The flying League, what hero, or what god?
'Tis Biron, 'tis his youthful arm o'erthrows
And drives alone the plain his scatter'd foes.   290
D'Aumale beheld, and madd'ning at the sight,
Stand fast he cried, and stay your coward flight;
Friends of the Guise and May'ne, their vengeance due
Rome and the church and France expect from you;
Return then, and your pristine force recall,   295
Conquest is theirs who fight beneath d'Aumale.
Fosseuse assisting and Beauveau sustain
Their part, and rally the disorder'd train,
Before the van d'Aumale his station took,
And the closed lines caught courage from his look.   300
The chance of war now flows a backward course,
Biron in vain withstands the driving force,
Nesle and Augenne within his sight are slain,
And Parabere and Clermont press the plain,
Himself scarce liv'd, so fast the purple tide   305
Flow'd from his wounds, and happier, had he died
A death so glorious with unfading fame
For ever had adorn'd the hero's name.

    Soon learn'd the royal chief to what distress
The youth was fall'n, courageous in excess;   310
He lov'd him, not as monarchs condescend
To love, but well, and plainly as a friend,

viii. 284 ages] ages, *1762*   viii. 297 Beauveau] Beauvean *1762*

Nor thought a subject's blood so mean a thing,
A smile alone o'erpaid it from a king.
Hail heav'n-born friendship! the delight alone   315
Of noble minds, and banish'd from the throne.
Eager he flies, the gen'rous fires that feed
His heart augment his vigour and his speed.
He came, and Biron kindling at the view,
His gather'd strength to one last effort drew,   320
Cheer'd by the well-known voice again he plies
The sword, all force before the monarch flies,
The king redeems thee from th'unequal strife;
Rash youth, be faithful and deserve thy life.

    Hark a loud peal comes thund'ring from afar,   325
'Tis Discord blows afresh the flames of war,
To thwart the monarch's virtue, with new fires
His fainting foes the beldam fiend inspires;
She winds her fatal trump, the woods around
And mountains tremble at th'infernal sound.   330
Swift to d'Aumale the baleful notes impart
Their pow'r, he feels the summons at his heart;
Bourbon alone he seeks: the boist'rous throng
Close at his heels tumultuous pour along.
So the well-scented pack, long train'd to blood,   335
Deep in the covert of a spacious wood,
Bay the fierce boar to battle, and elate
With heedless wrath rush headlong on their fate,
The shrillness of the cheering horn provokes
Their rage, and ecchoes from the distant rocks.   340
Thus stood the monarch by the croud inclosed,
An host against his single arm opposed,
No friend at hand, no welcome aid he found,
Abandon'd, and by death incompass'd round.
'Twas then his sainted sire his strength renew'd   345
With tenfold force and vigour unsubdued,
Firm as a rock, pois'd on it's base he stood,
That braves the blast, and scorns the dashing flood.
Who shall relate, alas! what heroes died
In that dread hour on Eura's purple side.   350

viii. 323 strife;] strife *1762*

Shade of the first of kings, do thou diffuse
Thy spirit o'er my song, be thou my muse.
Now from afar his gath'ring nobles came,
They died for Bourbon, and he fought for them,
When Egmont rush'd with yet unrival'd force,   355
To check the storm and thwart the monarch's course.

   Long had the chief, misled by martial pride,
Sought Henry thro' the combat far and wide,
Nor cared he, so his vent'rous arm might meet
That strife, for aught of danger or defeat.   360
Bourbon, he cried, advance; behold a foe
Prepar'd to plant fresh laurels on your brow;
Now let your arm it's utmost might display,
Ours be the strife, let us decide the day.
He spoke, and lo! portentuous from on high   365
A stream of light'ning shot along the sky,
Slow peals of mutt'ring thunder growl'd around,
Beneath the trembling soldier shook the ground.
Egmont, alas! a flatt'ring omen draws,
And dreams that heav'n shall combat in his cause,   370
That partial nature in his glory shar'd,
And by the thunder's voice his victory declar'd.
At the first onset with full force applied
His driving faulchion reach'd the monarch's side,
Fast flow'd a stream of trickling blood, tho' slight   375
The wound, and Egmont triumph'd at the sight.
But Bourbon unconcern'd receiv'd the blow,
And with redoubled ardour press'd his foe;
Pleas'd when the field of glory could afford
A conquest hardly earn'd and worthy of his sword.   380
The stinging smart serv'd only to provoke
His rage, and add new vigour to his stroke.
He springs upon the blow; the champion reels,
And the keen edge within his bosom feels,
O'erthrown beneath the trampling hoof he lies,   385
And death's dim shadow skims before his eyes,
He sees the dreary regions of the dead,
And shrinks and shudders at his father's shade.

Then first, their leader slain, th'Iberian host
Declin'd the fight, their vaunted spirit lost,   390
Like a contagion their unwarlike fear
Siez'd all the ranks and caught from van to rear.
Gen'ral and soldier felt the same dismay,
Nor longer these command, nor those obey.
Down fall the banners, routed and o'erthrown   395
And yelling with unmanly shrieks they run;
Some bend the suppliant knee, submissive join
Their hands, and to the chain their wrists resign,
Some from the fierce pursuer wildly fled,
And to the river stretch'd their utmost speed,   400
There plunged downright, amid the foaming tide
They sink, and meet the death they would avoid.
The waves incumber'd intermit their course,
And the choak'd stream recoils upon it's source.

May'ne in the tumult of this troubled scene   405
Lord of himself, afflicted yet serene,
Survey'd his lots still tranquil and sedate,
And ev'n in ruin hoped a better fate.
D'Aumale, his eye with burning rage suffus'd,
His cruel stars and dastard bands accus'd.   410
All's lost, he cried, see where the cowards fly,
Illustrious May'ne! our task then is to die.
Die! said the chief, live rather to replace
Our fortune, and sustain the cause you grace,
Live to regain the laurels we have lost,   415
Nor now desert us, when we need you most.
Fly then, and where they straggle o'er the plain,
Glean up the wreck and remnant of our train.
He hears, reluctant sobs his passion speak,
And tears of anguish trickle down his cheek,   420
A slow compliance sullenly he pays,
And frowning stern at the command, obeys.
Thus the proud lion whom the Moor has tam'd,
And from the fierceness of his race reclaim'd,
Bows down beneath his swarthy master's hand,   425
And bends his surly front at his command,

With low'ring aspect stalks behind his lord,
And grumbles while he crouches at his word.

Meanwhile in flight unhappy May'ne confides,
And close within the walls his shame he hides; 430
Prone at the monarch's feet the vanquish'd wait
From his award, the sentence of their fate;
When from the firmament's unfolded space
Appear'd the manes of the Bourbon race;
Louis in that important hour came down, 435
To gaze intent upon his godlike son,
To prove if the triumphant chief could tame
His soul to mercy, and deserve his fame.
Th'assembl'd captives by their looks besought
The monarch's grace, but trembled at their lot, 440
When thus with gentle, but determin'd look,
The suppliant crowd the mighty chief bespoke.
'Be free, and use your freedom as you may,
Free to take arms against me, or obey;
On May'ne or me let your election rest, 445
His be the sceptre who deserves it best,
Chuse your own portion, your own fate decree,
Chains from the League, or victory with me.'

Astonish'd that a king with glory crown'd,
And lord of the subjected plains around, 450
Ev'n in the lap of triumph should forego
His right of arms, and vantage o'er the foe,
His grateful captives hail him at his feet
Victorious, and rejoice in their defeat.
No longer hatred rankles in their minds, 455
His might subdued them, and his bounty binds,
Proudly they mingle with the monarch's train,
And turn their juster vengeance upon May'ne.

Now Bourbon merciful and mild had stay'd
The carnage, and the soldier's wrath allay'd; 460
No longer thro' the ranks he cleaves his way,
Fierce as the lion bearing on his prey,
But seems a bounteous deity, inclin'd

To quell the tempest, and to cheer mankind.
Peace o'er his brows had shed a milder grace,   465
And smooth'd the warlike terrours of his face;
Snatch'd from the jaws of the devouring strife,
His captives feel themselves restor'd to life,
Their dangers he repells, their wants supplies,
And views and guards them with a parent's eyes.   470

Fame, the swift messenger of false and true,
Still as she flies encreasing to the view,
O'er mountains and o'er seas, from clime to clime,
Expatiates, rapid as the flight of time.
Millions of piercing eyes to fame belong,   475
As many mouths still ply the restless tongue,
And round with list'ning ears her miscreant form is hung.
Where'er she roams, credulity is there,
And curiosity with craving ear,
And doubt, and hope, and ever-boding fear.   480
With the same speed she bears upon her wings
From far, the glory and the shame of kings,
And now unfolds them, eager to proclaim
Great Henry's deeds, and fill the nations with his name.
From Tagus swift to Po the tidings ran,   485
And eccho'd thro' the lofty vatican.
Joy to the north the spreading sounds convey,
To Spain, confusion, terrour and dismay.
Ill-fated Paris, and thou faithless League,
Ye priests, full-fraught with malice and intrigue,   490
How trembled then your temples, and what dread
Disast'rous, hung o'er ev'ry guilty head!
But see your guardian deity appears,
See May'ne returning to dispel your fears!
Tho' foil'd, not lost, not hopeless tho' o'erthrown,   495
For still rebellious Paris is his own.
With specious gloss he covers his defeat,
Calls ruin, victory, and flight, retreat,
Confirms the doubtful, and with prudent aim
Seeks by concealing, to repair his shame.   500
Transient, alas! the joy that art supplies,
For cruel truth soon scatter'd the disguise,

The veil of falsehood from their fate withdrew,
And open'd all it's horrors to their view.

Not thus the fury cried, with raging mind,   505
Shall Discord's pow'r be conquer'd, and confin'd:
'Tis not for this these wretched walls have seen
Torrents of blood, and mountains of the slain:
'Tis not for this the raging fires have shone,
That hated Bourbon might enjoy the throne.   510
Henceforth by weakness be his mind assail'd,
Weakness may triumph where the sword has fail'd.
Force is but vain; all other hopes are gone:
For Henry yields but to himself alone.
This day shall beauty's charms his bosom warm;   515
Subdue his valour, and unnerve his arm.

Thus Discord spoke; and, through the fields of air,
Drawn by fierce hatred on her blood-stained car,
Swiftly repair'd to Cytherea's grove
Assur'd of vengeance, and in search of love.   520
Clouds of thick darkness then obscur'd the day,
Nature turned pale, and horror marked her way.

OLNEY HYMNS
AND OTHER POEMS
1764–1772

A SONG OF MERCY AND JUDGMENT

Lord! I love the Habitation
  Where the Saviour's Honour dwells,
At the Sound of thy Salvation
  With Delight my Bosom swells.
Grace Divine how sweet the Sound,   5
Sweet the grace that I have found.

Me thro' Waves of deep Affliction
  Dearest Saviour! thou hast brought,
Fiery Deeps of sharp Conviction
  Hard to bear and passing Thought.   10
Sweet the Sound of Grace Divine,
Sweet the grace which makes me thine.

From the cheerful Beams of Morning
  Sad I turn'd mine Eyes away:
And the Shades of Night returning   15
  Fill'd my Soul with new Dismay.
Grace Divine how sweet the Sound,
Sweet the grace that I have found.

Food I loath'd nor ever tasted
  But by Violence constrain'd,   20
Strength decay'd and Body wasted,
  Spoke the Terrors I sustain'd.
Sweet the Sound of Grace Divine,
Sweet the grace which make me thine.

Bound and watch'd lest Life abhorring   25
  I should my own Death procure,
For to me the Pit of Roaring
  Seem'd more easy to endure.

COPY-TEXT: *A*, whence first printed by Adelaide Collyer, *Universal Review*, vii (1890), 276–7.

17–18] Grace Divine &c. *A*   22 sustain'd.] *punctuation supplied*   23–4] Sweet the Sound— *A*

Grace Divine how sweet the Sound,
Sweet the grace which I have found.   30

Fear of Thee with gloomy Sadness,
    Overwhelm'd thy guilty Worm,
'Till reduced to moping Madness,
    Reason sunk beneath the Storm.
Sweet the Sound of Grace Divine,   35
Sweet the grace which makes me thine.

Then what Soul distressing Noises
    Seem'd to reach me from below,
Visionary Scenes and Voices,
    Flames of Hell and Screams of Woe!   40
Grace Divine how sweet the Sound,
Sweet the grace which I have found.

But at length a Word of Healing
    Sweeter than an Angel's Note,
From the Saviour's Lips distilling   45
    Chas'd Despair and chang'd my Lot.
Sweet the Sound of Grace Divine,
Sweet the grace which makes me thine.

'Twas a Word well timed and suited
    To the Need of such an Hour,   50
Sweet to One like me polluted,
    Spoke in Love and seal'd with Pow'r.
Grace Divine how sweet the Sound,
Sweet the grace which I have found.

I, he said, have seen thee grieving,   55
    Lov'd thee as I pass'd thee by,
Be not faithless but Believing,
    Look, and Live, and never Die.
Sweet the Sound of Grace Divine,
Sweet the grace which makes me thine.   60

41–2] Grace Divine— *A*   47–8] Sweet the Sound— *A*   53–4] Grace
Divine— *A*

Take the Bloody Seal I give thee,
  Deep impress'd upon thy Soul,
God, thy God, will now receive thee,
  Faith hath sav'd thee, thou art Whole.
Grace Divine, how sweet the Sound,   65
Sweet the grace which I have found.

All at once my Chains were broken,
  From my Feet my Fetters fell,
And that Word in Pity spoken,
  Snatch'd me from the gates of Hell.   70
Grace Divine, how sweet the Sound,
Sweet the grace which I have found.

Since that Hour in Hope of Glory,
  With thy Foll'wers I am found,
And relate the wondrous Story   75
  To thy list'ning Saints around.
Sweet the Sound of Grace Divine,
Sweet the grace which makes me thine.

'TO JESUS, THE CROWN OF MY HOPE'

To Jesus, the Crown of my Hope,
  My soul is in haste to be gone:
O bear me, ye Cherubims, up,
  And waft me away to his throne.

My Saviour, whom absent I love,   5
  Whom not having seen I adore;
Whose Name is exalted above
  All Glory, Dominion, and Power,

71-2] Grace Divine— *A*   77-8] Sweet the Sound—*A*

COPY-TEXT: *G* (copy in George Courtenay's hand). Collated: *Υ* (copy in an unknown hand); *Memoirs*, Cox ed., *1816*, p. 92; Thomas Taylor, *Life of William Cowper*, 3rd ed., *1833*, p. 415; *Autobiography of Cowper*, *1835*, p. 51. First printed in *Baptist Magazine*, ii (Apr. 1810), 276.

Title] *untitled in* G, *Υ*, *1833*; A Fragment *1816*; Fragment *1835*   3 Cherubims *Υ*, *1816*, *1833*, *1835*   5 Saviour] Jesus *Υ*, *1816*, *1835*

Dissolve Thou the bond that detains
My soul from her portion in Thee,   10
And strike off the adamant chains,
And make me eternally free.

When that happy æra begins,
When array'd in thy beauty I shine,
Nor pierce any more by my sins   15
The bosom, on which I recline:

9–12] *not in* Υ, *1816*   15 Nor pierce any more] And pierce no more Υ, *1816*; Nor
pierce no more *1835*   by] with Υ

COWPER'S CONTRIBUTIONS TO *OLNEY HYMNS*

BOOK I

On Select Passages of Scripture

Hymn 1

[I. iii]

WALKING WITH GOD

Genesis v. 24

Oh for a closer Walk with God,
  A calm and heav'nly Frame,
A Light to shine upon the Road
  That leads me to the Lamb!

Where is the Blessedness I knew   5
  When first I saw the Lord?
Where is the Soul-refreshing View
  Of Jesus in his Word?

What peacefull Hours I then enjoy'd,
  How sweet their Mem'ry still!   10
But they have left an Aching Void
  The World can never fill.

Return, oh Holy Dove, Return,
  Sweet Messenger of Rest,
I hate the Sins that made thee mourn   15
  And drove thee from my Breast.

Composed 9 December 1767.

COPY-TEXT: letter to Mrs. Madan, 10 Dec. 1767 (*V*). First printed by R. Conyers, *A Collection of Psalms and Hymns*, 1772, pp. 198–9. Collated: *1779*, p. 4.

Title and reference in 1779 only   3–4 *set in roman in 1779*   8 Jesus in] Jesus, and *1779*   9 then] once *1779*

The dearest Idol I have known,
    Whate'ver that Idol be,
Help me to tear it from Thy Throne,
    And worship Only Thee.   20

Then shall my Walk be close with God,
    Calm and serene my Frame,
Then purer Light shall mark the Road
    That leads me to the Lamb.

Hymn 2

[I. vi]

JEHOVAH-JIREH, THE LORD WILL PROVIDE

Genesis xxii. 14

The saints should never be dismay'd,
    Nor sink in hopeless fear;
For when they least expect his aid,
    The Saviour will appear.

This Abraham found, he rais'd the knife,   5
    GOD saw, and said, 'Forbear;'
Yon ram shall yield his meaner life,
    Behold the victim there.

Once David seem'd Saul's certain prey;
    But hark! the foe's at hand;[1]   10
Saul turns his arms another way,
    To save th'invaded land.

---

[1] 1 Samuel xxiii. 27.

---

18 Whate'ver] Whate'er *1779*   21, 23 Then] So *1779*   23 Road] *V torn;*
last three letters missing

COPY-TEXT: *1779*, pp. 7–8 (first printing).

When Jonah sunk beneath the wave
 He thought to rise no more;[1]
But GOD prepar'd a fish to save,   15
 And bear him to the shore.

Blest proofs of pow'r and grace divine,
 That meet us in his word!
May ev'ry deep-felt care of mine
 Be trusted with the LORD.   20

Wait for his seasonable aid,
 And tho' it tarry wait:
The promise may be long delay'd,
 But cannot come too late.

Hymn 3

[I. xiv]

JEHOVAH-ROPHI, I AM THE LORD THAT HEALETH THEE

Exodus xv

Heal us, EMMANUEL, here we are,
 Waiting to feel thy touch;
Deep-wounded souls to thee repair,
 And, Saviour, we are such.

Our faith is feeble we confess,   5
 We faintly trust thy word;
But wilt thou pity us the less?
 Be that far from thee, LORD!

---

[1] Jonah i. 17.

23–4. See Commentary.

COPY-TEXT: *1779*, pp. 19–20 (first printing).

Remember him who once apply'd
  With trembling for relief;
'LORD, I believe, with tears he cry'd,[1]   10
  O help my unbelief.'

She too, who touch'd thee in the press,
  And healing virtue stole;
Was answer'd, 'Daughter, go in peace,[2]   15
  Thy faith hath made thee whole.'

Conceal'd amid the gath'ring throng,
  She would have shun'd thy view;
And if her faith was firm and strong,
  Had strong misgivings too.   20

Like her, with hopes and fears, we come,
  To touch thee if we may;
Oh! send us not despairing home,
  Send none unheal'd away.

Hymn 4

[I. xvii]

JEHOVAH-NISSI, THE LORD MY BANNER

Exodus xvii. 15

By whom was David taught,
  To aim the dreadful blow,
When he Goliath fought,
  And laid the Gittite low?
No sword nor spear the stripling took,   5
But chose a pebble from the brook.

---

[1] Mark ix. 24.   [2] Mark v. 34.

COPY-TEXT: *1779*, pp. 22–3. First printed by R. Conyers, *A Collection of Psalms and Hymns*, new ed., 1774, pp. 233–4.

'Twas Israel's GOD and king,
  Who sent him to the fight;
Who gave him strength to sling,
  And skill to aim aright.   10
Ye feeble saints your strength endures,
Because young David's GOD is yours.

Who ordered Gideon forth,
  To storm th'invaders' camp,[1]
With arms of little worth,   15
  A pitcher and a lamp?
The trumpets made his coming known,
And all the host was overthrown.

Oh! I have seen the day,
  When with a single word,   20
GOD helping me to say,
  My trust is in the LORD;
My soul has quell'd a thousand foes,
Fearless of all that could oppose.

But unbelief, self-will,   25
  Self-righteousness and pride,
How often do they steal,
  My weapon from my side?
Yet David's LORD, and Gideon's friend,
Will help his servant to the end.   30

---

[1] Judges vii. 20.

12 GOD] God's *1779, corrected in Errata*

Hymn 5

[I. xxii]

JEHOVAH-SHALEM, THE LORD SEND PEACE

Judges vi. 24.

Jesus, whose blood so freely stream'd
To satisfy the law's demand;
By thee from guilt and wrath redeem'd,
Before the Father's face I stand.

To reconcile offending man,   5
Make Justice drop her angry rod;
What creature could have form'd the plan,
Or who fulfil it but a God?

No drop remains of all the curse,
For wretches who deserv'd the whole;   10
No arrows dipt in wrath to pierce
The guilty, but returning soul.

Peace by such means so dearly bought,
What rebel could have hop'd to see?
Peace, by his injur'd sovereign wrought,   15
His Sov'reign fastned to the tree.

Now, Lord, thy feeble worm prepare!
For strife with earth and hell begins;
Confirm and gird me for the war,
They hate the soul that hates his sins.   20

Let them in horrid league agree!
They may assault, they may distress;
But cannot quench thy love to me,
Nor rob me of the Lord my peace.

COPY-TEXT: *1779*, p. 29 (first printing).

Hymn 6

[I. lii]

WISDOM

Proverbs viii. 22–31

Ere GOD had built the mountains,
Or rais'd the fruitful hills;
Before he fill'd the fountains
That feed the running rills;
In me, from everlasting,   5
The wonderful I AM
Found pleasures never wasting,
And Wisdom is my name.

When, like a tent to dwell in,
He spread the skies abroad;   10
And swath'd about the swelling
Of ocean's mighty flood;
He wrought by weight and measure,
And I was with him then;
Myself the Father's pleasure,   15
And mine, the sons of men.

Thus wisdom's words discover
Thy glory and thy grace,
Thou everlasting lover
Of our unworthy race!   20
Thy gracious eye survey'd us
Ere stars were seen above;
In wisdom thou hast made us,
And dy'd for us in love.

And couldst thou be delighted   25
With creatures such as we!
Who when we saw thee, slighted
And nail'd thee to a tree?

COPY-TEXT: *1779*, pp. 66–7 (first printing).

Unfathomable wonder,
And mystery divine!   30
The voice that speaks in thunder,
Says, 'Sinner I am thine!'

Hymn 7

[I. lv]

VANITY OF THE WORLD

Ecclesiastes

GOD gives his mercies to be spent;
Your hoard will do your soul no good:
Gold is a blessing only lent,
Repaid by giving others food.

The world's esteem is but a bribe,   5
To buy their peace you sell your own;
The slave of a vain-glorious tribe,
Who hate you while they make you known.

The joy that vain amusements give,
Oh! sad conclusion that it brings!   10
The honey of a crowded hive,
Defended by a thousand stings.

'Tis thus the world rewards the fools
That live upon her treach'rous smiles;
She leads them, blindfold, by her rules,   15
And ruins all whom she beguiles.

GOD knows the thousands who go down
From pleasure, into endless woe;

COPY-TEXT: *1779*, pp. 70–1. First printed by 'Omicron' [Newton], *Twenty Six Letters on Religious Subjects*, 1774, pp. 214–15.

6 you] you'll *1774*

And with a long despairing grone
Blaspheme their Maker as they go.   20

O fearful thought! be timely wise;
Delight but in a Saviour's charms;
And GOD shall take you to the skies,
Embrac'd in everlasting arms.

Hymn 8

[I. lviii]

O LORD, I WILL PRAISE THEE!

Isaiah xii

I will praise thee ev'ry day
Now thine anger's turn'd away!
Comfortable thoughts arise
From the bleeding sacrifice.

Here in the fair gospel field,   5
Wells of free salvation yield
Streams of life, a plenteous store,
And my soul shall thirst no more.

JESUS is become at length
My salvation and my strength;   10
And his praises shall prolong,
While I live, my pleasant song.

Praise ye, then, his glorious name,
Publish his exalted fame!
Still his worth your praise exceeds,   15
Excellent are all his deeds.

19–20]   They give a long despairing groan
                  And dread their Maker as they go.   *1774*

COPY-TEXT: *1779*, pp. 73–4 (first printing).

Raise again the joyful sound,
Let the nations roll it round!
Zion shout, for this is he,
God the Saviour dwells in thee.   20

Hymn 9

[I. lxiv]

THE CONTRITE HEART

Isaiah lvii. 15

The LORD will happiness divine
   On contrite hearts bestow:
Then tell me, gracious GOD, is mine
   A contrite heart, or no?

I hear, but seem to hear in vain,   5
   Insensible as steel;
If ought is felt, 'tis only pain,
   To find I cannot feel.

I sometimes think myself inclin'd
   To love thee, if I could;   10
But often feel another mind,
   Averse to all that's good.

My best desires are faint and few,
   I fain would strive for more;
But when I cry, 'My strength renew,'   15
   Seem weaker than before.

Thy saints are comforted I know
   And love thy house of pray'r;
I therefore go where others go,
   But find no comfort there.   20

COPY-TEXT: *1779*, pp. 81–2 (first printing).

O make this heart rejoice, or ach;
Decide this doubt for me;
And if it be not broken, break,
And heal it, if it be.

Hymn 10

[I. lxv]

THE FUTURE PEACE AND GLORY OF THE CHURCH

Isaiah lx. 15–20

Hear what GOD the LORD hath spoken,
O my people, weak and few;
Comfortless, afflicted, broken,
Fair abodes I build for you:
Thorns of heart-felt tribulation   5
Shall no more perplex your ways;
You shall name your walls, Salvation,
And your gates shall all be praise.

Then, like streams that feed the garden,
Pleasures, without end, shall flow;   10
For the LORD, your faith rewarding,
All his bounty shall bestow:
Still in undisturb'd possession,
Peace and righteousness shall reign;
Never shall you feel oppression,   15
Hear the voice of war again.

You no more your suns descending,
Waning moons no more shall see;
But your griefs, for ever ending,
Find eternal noon in me;   20

COPY-TEXT: *1779*, pp. 82–3 (first printing), incorporating variants in a copy of a letter from Newton of August 1773 in M. F. C. Cowper's Commonplace Book, III. 212–13 (*C*).

Title] *untitled in C*   2 weak] *C*; faint *1779*   5 Thorns] *C*, *1783*; Themes *1779*, *1781*   9 Then] *C*; there *1779*   17 You] *C*; Ye *1779*

GOD shall rise, and shining o'er you,
Change to day the gloom of night;
He, the LORD, shall be your glory,
GOD your everlasting light.

Hymn 11

[I. lxvii]

JEHOVAH OUR RIGHTEOUSNESS

Jeremiah xxiii. 6

My GOD! how perfect are thy ways!
  But mine polluted are;
Sin twines itself about my praise,
  And slides into my pray'r.

When I would speak what thou hast done   5
  To save me from my sin;
I cannot make thy mercies known
  But self-applause creeps in.

Divine desire, that holy flame
  Thy grace creates in me;   10
Alas! impatience is its name,
  When it returns to thee.

This heart, a fountain of vile thoughts,
  How does it overflow?
While self upon the surface floats   15
  Still bubbling from below.

Let others in the gaudy dress
  Of fancied merit shine;
The LORD shall be my righteousness,
  The LORD for ever mine.   20

COPY-TEXT: *1779*, pp. 84-5 (first printing).
19 righteousness,] righteousness *1779*

Hymn 12

[I. lxviii]

EPHRAIM REPENTING

Jeremiah xxxi. 18–20

My GOD! till I receiv'd thy stroke,
  How like a beast was I!
So unaccustom'd to the yoke,
  So backward to comply.

With grief my just reproach I bear,   5
  Shame fills me at the thought;
How frequent my rebellions were!
  What wickedness I wrought!

Thy merciful restraint I scorn'd
  And left the pleasant road;   10
Yet turn me, and I shall be turn'd,
  Thou art the LORD my GOD.

Is Ephraim banish'd from my thoughts,
  Or vile in my esteem?
No, saith the LORD, with all his faults,   15
  I still remember him.

Is he a dear and pleasant child?
  Yes, dear and pleasant still;
Tho' sin his foolish heart beguil'd,
  And he withstood my will.   20

My sharp rebuke has laid him low,
  He seeks my face again;
My pity kindles at his woe,
  He shall not seek in vain.

COPY-TEXT: *1779*, pp. 85–6 (first printing).

Hymn 13

[I. lxxi]

THE COVENANT

Ezekiel xxxvi. 25–8

The LORD proclaims his grace abroad!
Behold, I change your hearts of stone;
Each shall renounce his idol god,
And serve, henceforth, the LORD alone.

My grace, a flowing stream, proceeds   5
To wash your filthiness away;
Ye shall abhor your former deeds,
And learn my statutes to obey.

My truth the great design insures,
I give myself away to you;   10
You shall be mine, I will be yours,
Your GOD unalterably true.

Yet not unsought, or unimplor'd,
The plenteous grace shall I confer;[1]
No—your whole hearts shall seek the LORD,   15
I'll put a praying spirit there.

From the first breath of life divine,
Down to the last expiring hour;
The gracious work shall all be mine,
Begun and ended in my pow'r.   20

[1] Verse 37.

COPY-TEXT: *1779*, pp. 88–9 (first printing).

Hymn 14

[I. lxxii]

JEHOVAH-SHAMMAH

Ezekiel xlviii. 35

As birds their infant brood protect,[1]
And spread their wings to shelter them;
Thus saith the LORD to his elect,
'So will I guard Jerusalem.'

And what then is Jerusalem,   5
This darling object of his care?
Where is its worth in GOD's esteem?
Who built it? who inhabits there?

JEHOVAH founded it in blood,
The blood of his incarnate Son;   10
There dwell the saints, once foes to GOD,
The sinners, whom he calls his own.

There, tho' besieg'd on ev'ry side,
Yet much belov'd and guarded well;
From age to age they have defy'd,   15
The utmost force of earth and hell.

Let earth repent, and hell despair,
This city has a sure defence;
Her name is call'd, the LORD is there,
And who has pow'r to drive him thence.   20

[1] Isaiah xxxi. 5.

COPY-TEXT: *1779*, pp. 89–90 (first printing).

Hymn 15

[1. lxxix]

PRAISE FOR THE FOUNTAIN OPENED

Zechariah xiii. 1

There is a fountain fill'd with blood
    Drawn from EMMANUEL's veins;
And sinners, plung'd beneath that flood,
    Lose all their guilty stains.

The dying thief rejoic'd to see   5
    That fountain in his day;
And there have I, as vile as he,
    Wash'd all my sins away.

Dear dying Lamb, thy precious blood
    Shall never lose its pow'r;   10
Till all the ransom'd church of GOD
    Be sav'd, to sin no more.

E'er since, by faith, I saw the stream
    Thy flowing wounds supply:
Redeeming love has been my theme,   15
    And shall be till I die.

Then in a nobler sweeter song
    I'll sing thy power to save;
When this poor lisping stamm'ring tongue
    Lies silent in the grave.   20

LORD, I believe thou hast prepar'd
    (Unworthy tho' I be)
For me a blood-bought free reward,
    A golden harp for me!

COPY-TEXT: *1779*, pp. 98–9. First printed by R. Conyers, *A Collection of Psalms and Hymns*, 1772, pp. 187–8.
4 Lose] *1781*; Loose *1779*

'Tis strung, and tun'd, for endless years,   25
  And form'd by pow'r divine;
To sound, in GOD the Father's ears,
  No other name but thine.

Hymn 16

[I. lxxxv]

THE SOWER

Matthew xiii. 3

Ye sons of earth prepare the plough,
  Break up your fallow ground!
The Sower is gone forth to sow,
  And scatter blessings round.

The seed that finds a stony soil,   5
  Shoots forth a hasty blade;
But ill repays the sower's toil,
  Soon wither'd, scorch'd, and dead.

The thorny ground is sure to baulk
  All hopes of harvest there;   10
We find a tall and sickly stalk,
  But not the fruitful ear.

The beaten path and high-way side
  Receive the trust in vain;
The watchful birds the spoil divide,   15
  And pick up all the grain.

But where the LORD of grace and pow'r
  Has bless'd the happy field;
How plenteous is the golden store
  The deep-wrought furrows yield!   20

COPY-TEXT: *1779*, pp. 105–6 (first printing).

Father of mercies we have need
Of thy preparing grace;
Let the same hand that gives the seed,
Provide a fruitful place.

Hymn 17

[I. xcvi]

THE HOUSE OF PRAYER

Mark xi. 17

Thy mansion is the christian's heart,
O Lord, thy dwelling-place secure!
Bid the unruly throng depart,
And leave the consecrated door.

Devoted as it is to thee,   5
A thievish swarm frequents the place;
They steal away my joys from me,
And rob my Saviour of his praise.

There too a sharp designing trade
Sin, Satan, and the world maintain;   10
Nor cease to press me, and persuade,
To part with ease and purchase pain.

I know them, and I hate their din,
Am weary of the bustling crowd;
But while their voice is heard within,   15
I cannot serve thee as I would.

Oh! for the joy thy presence gives,
What peace shall reign when thou art here!
Thy presence makes this den of thieves,
A calm delightful house of pray'r.   20

COPY-TEXT: *1779*, pp. 119–20 (first printing).

And if thou make thy temple shine,
Yet, self-abas'd, will I adore;
The gold and silver are not mine,
I give thee what was thine before.

Hymn 18

[I. cxviii]

LOVEST THOU ME?

John xxi. 16

Hark, my soul! it is the LORD;
'Tis thy Saviour, hear his word;
JESUS speaks, and speaks to thee;
'Say, poor sinner, lov'st thou me?

I deliver'd thee when bound,   5
And, when wounded, heal'd thy wound;
Sought thee wand'ring, set thee right,
Turn'd thy darkness into light.

Can a woman's tender care
Cease, towards the child she bare?   10
Yes, she may forgetful be,
Yet will I remember thee.

Mine is an unchanging love,
Higher than the heights above;
Deeper than the depths beneath,   15
Free and faithful, strong as death.

Composed no later than 1768.

COPY-TEXT: *1779*, pp. 146–7. First printed by T. Maxfield, *A Collection of Psalms and Hymns*, 2nd ed., 1768, p. 49 (second pagination).

8–13] *punctuation of 1781; 1779 wrongly excludes 9–12 from Jesus' speech*

Thou shalt see my glory soon,
When the work of grace is done;
Partner of my throne shalt be,
Say, poor sinner, lov'st thou me?'   20

LORD, it is my chief complaint,
That my love is weak and faint;
Yet I love thee and adore,
Oh for grace to love thee more!

Hymn 19

[i. cxxxi]

CONTENTMENT

Philippians iv. 11

Fierce passions discompose the mind,
    As tempests vex the sea;
But calm content and peace we find,
    When, LORD, we turn to thee.

In vain by reason and by rule,   5
    We try to bend the will;
For none, but in the Saviour's school,
    Can learn the heav'nly skill.

Since at his feet my soul has sat,
    His gracious words to hear;   10
Contented with my present state,
    I cast, on him, my care.

'Art thou a sinner, soul? he said,
    Then how canst thou complain?
How light thy troubles here, if weigh'd   15
    With everlasting pain!

COPY-TEXT: *1779*, pp. 162–3 (first printing).

If thou of murmuring wouldst be cur'd,
  Compare thy griefs with mine;
Think what my love for thee endur'd,
  And thou wilt not repine.   20

'Tis I appoint thy daily lot,
  And I do all things well:
Thou soon shalt leave this wretched spot,
  And rise with me to dwell.

In life my grace shall strength supply,   25
  Proportion'd to thy day;
At death thou still shalt find me nigh,
  To wipe thy tears away.'

Thus I who once my wretched days,
  In vain repinings spent;   30
Taught in my Saviour's school of grace,
  Have learn'd to be content.

Hymn 20

[I. cxxxii]

OLD-TESTAMENT GOSPEL

Hebrews iv. 2

Israel in ancient days,
  Not only had a view
Of Sinai in a blaze,
  But learn'd the gospel too:
The types and figures were a glass   5
In which they saw the Saviour's face.

The paschal sacrifice,
  And blood-besprinkled door,[1]
Seen with enlightned eyes,

---

[1] Exodus xii. 13.

COPY-TEXT: *1779*, pp. 164–5 (first printing).

And once apply'd with pow'r;   10
Would teach the need of other blood,
To reconcile an angry GOD.

    The Lamb, the Dove, set forth
    His perfect innocence,[1]
    Whose blood, of matchless worth,   15
    Should be the soul's defence:
For he who can for sin atone,
Must have no failings of his own.

    The scape-goat on his head[2]
    The people's trespass bore,   20
    And to the desart led,
    Was to be seen no more:
In him, our Surety seem'd to say,
'Behold, I bear your sins away.'

    Dipt in his fellow's blood,   25
    The living bird went free,[3]
    The type, well understood,
    Express'd the sinner's plea;
Describ'd a guilty soul enlarg'd,
And by a Saviour's death discharg'd.   30

    JESUS I love to trace
    Throughout the sacred page;
    The footsteps of thy grace,
    The same in ev'ry age!
O grant that I may faithful be   35
To clearer light, vouchsaf'd to me.

[1] Leviticus xii. 6.   [2] Leviticus xvi. 21.   [3] Leviticus xiv. 51–3.

Hymn 21

[I. cxxxviii]

SARDIS

Revelation iii. 1–6

'Write to Sardis, saith the Lord,
    And write what He declares;
He whose Spirit, and whose word,
    Upholds the seven stars:
All thy works and ways I search,   5
Find thy zeal and love decay'd;
Thou art call'd a living church,
    But thou art cold and dead.

Watch, remember, seek and strive,
    Exert thy former pains;   10
Let thy timely care revive,
    And strengthen what remains:
Cleanse thine heart, thy works amend,
Former times to mind recall;
Lest my sudden stroke descend,   15
    And smite thee once for all.

Yet I number now, in thee,
    A few that are upright;
These my Father's face shall see,
    And walk with me in white: 20
When in judgment I appear,
They for mine shall be confest;
Let my faithful servants hear,
    And woe be to the rest.'

COPY-TEXT: *1779*, pp. 171–2 (first printing).
24 rest.'] *1781*; rest. *1779*

BOOK II

On Occasional Subjects. I. Seasons.
II. Ordinances. III. Providences. IV. Creation.

Hymn 22

[II. viii]

PRAYER FOR A BLESSING

Bestow, dear LORD, upon our youth
  The gift of saving grace;
And let the seed of sacred truth
  Fall in a fruitful place.

Grace is a plant, where'er it grows,   5
  Of pure and heav'nly root;
But fairest in the youngest shews,
  And yields the sweetest fruit.

Ye careless ones, O hear betimes
  The voice of sovereign love!   10
Your youth is stain'd with many crimes,
  But mercy reigns above.

True, you are young, but there's a stone
  Within the youngest breast;
Or half the crimes which you have done   15
  Would rob you of your rest.

For you the public pray'r is made,
  Oh! join the public pray'r!
For you the secret tear is shed,
  O shed yourselves a tear.   20

COPY-TEXT: *1779*, pp. 190–1 (first printing).

We pray that you may early prove
    The Spirit's power to teach;
You cannot be too young to love
    That JESUS whom we preach.

Hymn 23

[II. xi]

PLEADING FOR AND WITH YOUTH

Sin has undone our wretched race,
    But JESUS has restor'd
And brought the sinner face to face
    With his forgiving LORD.

This we repeat from year to year,   5
    And press upon our youth;
LORD, give them an attentive ear,
    LORD, save them by thy truth.

Blessings upon the rising race!
    Make this an happy hour,   10
According to thy richest grace,
    And thine almighty pow'r.

We feel for your unhappy state,
    (May you regard it too)
And would awhile ourselves forget,   15
    To pour out pray'r for you.

We see, tho' you perceive it not,
    Th'approaching, awful doom;
O tremble at the solemn thought,
    And flee the wrath to come!   20

Dear Saviour, let this new-born year
    Spread an alarm abroad;
And cry, in ev'ry careless ear,
    'Prepare to meet thy GOD!'

COPY-TEXT: *1779*, pp. 193–4 (first printing).

Hymn 24

[II. xii]

PRAYER FOR CHILDREN

Gracious LORD, our children see,
By thy mercy we are free;
But shall these, alass! remain
Subjects still of Satan's reign?
Israel's young ones, when of old   5
Pharaoh threaten'd to withhold,[1]
Then thy messenger said, 'No;
Let the children also go.'

When the angel of the LORD
Drawing forth his dreadful sword,   10
Slew, with an avenging hand,
All the first-born of the land:[2]
Then thy people's doors he pass'd,
Where the bloody sign was plac'd;
Hear us, now, upon our knees,   15
Plead the blood of CHRIST for these!

LORD we tremble, for we know
How the fierce malicious foe,
Wheeling round his watchful flight,
Keeps them ever in his sight: 20
Spread thy pinions, King of kings!
Hide them safe beneath thy wings;
Lest the rav'nous bird of prey
Stoop, and bear the brood away.

[1] Exodus x. 9.   [2] Exodus xii. 12.

COPY-TEXT: *1779*, pp. 194–5 (first printing).

Hymn 25

[II. xxxviii]

JEHOVAH-JESUS

My song shall bless the LORD of all,
My praise shall climb to his abode;
Thee, Saviour, by that name I call,
The great Supreme, the mighty GOD.

Without beginning, or decline,   5
Object of faith, and not of sense;
Eternal ages saw him shine,
He shines eternal ages hence.

As much, when in the manger laid,
Almighty ruler of the sky;   10
As when the six days works he made,
Fill'd all the morning-stars with joy.

Of all the crowns JEHOVAH bears,
Salvation is his dearest claim;
That gracious sound well-pleas'd he hears,   15
And owns EMMANUEL for his name.

A cheerful confidence I feel,
My well-plac'd hopes with joy I see;
My bosom glows with heav'nly zeal
To worship him who dy'd for me.   20

As man, he pities my complaint,
His pow'r and truth are all divine;
He will not fail, he cannot faint,
Salvation's sure, and must be mine.

COPY-TEXT: *1779*, p. 227 (first printing).

Hymn 26

[II. xliv]

ON OPENING A PLACE FOR SOCIAL PRAYER

JESUS, where'er thy people meet,
There they behold thy mercy-seat;
Where'er they seek thee thou art found,
And ev'ry place is hallow'd ground.

For thou, within no walls confin'd,   5
Inhabitest the humble mind;
Such ever bring thee, where they come,
And going, take thee to their home.

Dear Shepherd of thy chosen few!
Thy former mercies here renew;   10
Here, to our waiting hearts, proclaim
The sweetness of thy saving name.

Here may we prove the pow'r of pray'r,
To strengthen faith, and sweeten care;
To teach our faint desires to rise,   15
And bring all heav'n before our eyes.

Behold! at thy commanding word,
We stretch the curtain and the cord;[1]
Come thou, and fill this wider space,
And bless us with a large encrease.   20

LORD, we are few, but thou art near;
Nor short thine arm, nor deaf thine ear;
Oh rend the heav'ns, come quickly down,
And make a thousand hearts thine own!

[1] Isaiah liv. 2.

Composed late March or early April 1769.
COPY-TEXT: *1779*, pp. 234–5 (first printing).
1, 3 where'er, Where'er] *1781*; wheree'r, Wheree'r *1779*   20 bless] help *1779*, bless
in Errata

Hymn 27

[II. liii]

WELCOME TO THE TABLE

This is the feast of heav'nly wine,
  And GOD invites to sup;
The juices of the living vine
  Were press'd, to fill the cup.

Oh, bless the Saviour, ye that eat,   5
  With royal dainties fed;
Not heav'n affords a costlier treat,
  For JESUS is the bread!

The vile, the lost, he calls to them,
  Ye trembling souls appear!   10
The righteous, in their own esteem,
  Have no acceptance here.

Approach ye poor, nor dare refuse
  The banquet spread for you;
Dear Saviour, this is welcome news,   15
  Then I may venture too.

If guilt and sin afford a plea,
  And may obtain a place;
Surely the LORD will welcome me,
  And I shall see his face.   20

COPY-TEXT: *1779*, p. 246 (first printing).

Hymn 28

[II. lv]

JESUS HASTING TO SUFFER

The Saviour! what a noble flame
  Was kindled in his breast,
When hasting to Jerusalem
  He march'd before the rest!

Good-will to men, and zeal for GOD,   5
  His ev'ry thought engross;
He longs to be baptiz'd with blood,[1]
  He pants to reach the cross.

With all his suff'rings full in view,
  And woes, to us, unknown,   10
Forth to the task his spirit flew,
  'Twas love that urg'd him on.

LORD, we return thee what we can!
  Our hearts shall sound abroad
Salvation, to the dying Man,   15
  And to the rising GOD!

And while thy bleeding glories here
  Engage our wond'ring eyes;
We learn our lighter cross to bear,
  And hasten to the skies.   20

[1] Luke xii. 50.

COPY-TEXT: *1779*, p. 248 (first printing).

Hymn 29

[II. lx]

EXHORTATION TO PRAYER

What various hind'rances we meet
In coming to a mercy-seat!
Yet who that knows the worth of pray'r,
But wishes to be often there.

Pray'r makes the dark'ned cloud withdraw,   5
Pray'r climbs the ladder Jacob saw;
Gives exercise to faith and love,
Brings ev'ry blessing from above.

Restraining pray'r, we cease to fight;
Pray'r makes the christian's armor bright;   10
And Satan trembles, when he sees
The weakest saint upon his knees.

While Moses stood with arms spread wide,
Success was found on Israel's side;[1]
But when thro' weariness they fail'd,   15
That moment Amalek prevail'd.

Have you no words? ah, think again,
Words flow apace when you complain;
And fill your fellow-creature's ear
With the sad tale of all your care.   20

Were half the breath thus vainly spent,
To heav'n in supplication sent;
Your cheerful song would oft'ner be,
'Hear what the LORD has done for me!'

[1] Exodus xvii. 11.

COPY-TEXT: *1779*, pp. 253–4 (first printing).
2 mercy-seat!] *1781*; mercy-seat? *1779*

Hymn 30

[II. lxii]

THE LIGHT AND GLORY OF THE WORD

The Spirit breathes upon the word,
  And brings the truth to sight;
Precepts and promises afford
  A sanctifying light.

A glory gilds the sacred page,   5
  Majestic like the sun;
It gives a light to ev'ry age,
  It gives, but borrows none.

The hand that gave it, still supplies
  The gracious light and heat;   10
His truths upon the nations rise,
  They rise, but never set.

Let everlasting thanks be thine!
  For such a bright display,
As makes a world of darkness shine   15
  With beams of heav'nly day.

My soul rejoices to pursue
  The steps of him I love;
Till glory breaks upon my view
  In brighter worlds above.   20

COPY-TEXT: *1779*, pp. 255–6 (first printing).

Hymn 31

[II. lxxiii]

ON THE DEATH OF A MINISTER

His Master taken from his Head,
  Elisha saw him go,
And in desponding Accents said,
  Ah what must Isra'el do!

But he forgot the Lord who lifts,   5
  The Beggar to the Throne,
Nor knew that all Elijah's Gifts
  Should soon be made his Own.

What? when a Paul has run his Course,
  Or when Apollos dies,   10
Is Israel left without Ressource,
  And have we no Supplies?

Yes, while the dear Redeemer lives,
  We have a boundless store,
And shall be fed with what He gives,   15
  Who lives for evermore.

COPY-TEXT: *A*, fo. 10ᵛ. First printed in *1779*, pp. 269–70.
8 Should] Would *1779*

BOOK III

On the Rise, Progress, Changes, and Comforts of the Spiritual Life

Hymn 32

[III. viii]

THE SHINING LIGHT

My former hopes are fled,
My terror now begins;
I feel, alass! that I am dead
In trespasses and sins.

Ah, whither shall I fly?   5
I hear the thunder roar;
The law proclaims destruction nigh,
And vengeance at the door.

When I review my ways,
I dread impending doom;   10
But sure, a friendly whisper says,
'Flee from the wrath to come.'

I see, or think I see,
A glimm'ring from afar;
A beam of day that shines for me,   15
To save me from despair.

Fore-runner of the sun,[1]
It marks the Pilgrim's way;
I'll gaze upon it while I run,
And watch the rising day.   20

[1] Psalm cxxx. 6.

COPY-TEXT: *1779*, p. 319 (first printing).
1 fled] *1781*; dead *1779*

Hymn 33

[III. x]

THE WAITING SOUL

[This hymn, which begins 'Breathe from the gentle South, O Lord', was composed by Newton, and is therefore omitted from this edition. See Commentary.]

Hymn 34

[III. xiii]

SEEKING THE BELOVED

To those who know the LORD I speak,
    Is my beloved near?
The bridegroom of my soul I seek,
    Oh! when will he appear!

Tho' once a man of grief and shame,   5
    Yet now he fills a throne;
And bears the greatest, sweetest name,
    That earth or heav'n have known.

Grace flies before, and love attends
    His steps where'er he goes;   10
Tho' none can see him but his friends,
    And they were once his foes.

He speaks—obedient to his call
    Our warm affections move;
Did he but shine alike on all,   15
    Then all alike would love.

COPY-TEXT: *1779*, pp. 325–6 (first printing).

> Then love in ev'ry heart would reign,
> And war would cease to roar;
> And cruel, and blood-thirsty men,
> Would thirst for blood no more.   20

> Such JESUS is, and such his grace,
> Oh may he shine on you![1]
> And tell him, when you see his face,
> I long to see him too.

Hymn 35

[III. xv]

LIGHT SHINING OUT OF DARKNESS

> God moves in a mysterious way,
> His wonders to perform,
> He plants his footsteps in the Sea,
> And rides upon the Storm.

> Deep in unfathomable Mines,   5
> Of never failing Skill,
> He treasures up his bright designs,
> And works his Sovereign Will.

> Ye fearfull Saints fresh courage take,
> The clouds ye so much dread,   10
> Are big with Mercy, and shall break
> In blessings on your head.

---

[1] Solomon's Song v. 8.

Composed in the later months of 1772.

COPY-TEXT: copy in the Maitland–Madan Commonplace Book, pp. 113–14 (*O*). Collated: copy in M. F. C. Cowper's Commonplace Book, III. 204–5 (*C*); first printing by 'Omicron' [Newton], *Twenty Six Letters on Religious Subjects*, 1774, pp. 215–16; *1779*, p. 328.

Title] *C, 1774, 1779*; *untitled in O*

Judge not the Lord by feeble sense,
But trust him for his Grace,
Behind a frowning Providence   15
He hides a Smiling face.

His purposes will ripen fast,
Unfolding every hour,
The Bud may have a bitter taste,
But *wait*, to *Smell the flower*.   20

Blind unbelief is sure to err,
And scan his work in vain,
God is his own Interpreter,
And he will make it plain.

Hymn 36

[III. xvi]

WELCOME CROSS

'Tis my happiness below
Not to live without the cross;
But the Saviour's pow'r to know,
Sanctifying ev'ry loss:
Trials must and will befall;   5
But with humble faith to see
Love inscrib'd upon them all,
This is happiness to me.

GOD, in Israel, sows the seeds
Of affliction, pain, and toil;   10
These spring up, and choke the weeds
Which would else o'erspread the soil:

15 Behind] *C, 1774, 1779*; Beneath *O*   19 taste] tast *O*   20 *wait*, to *Smell
the flower*] sweet will be the flow'r *1774, 1779*   24 he] he, *O*

COPY-TEXT: *1779*, p. 329. Also collated: copy in the Maitland–Madan Commonplace Book,
p. 115 (*O*); copy in M. F. C. Cowper's Commonplace Book, III. 209–10 (*C*). First printed in
1774 (?—see Commentary).

5 Trials] Trouble *O, C*   8 to] for *C*   10 affliction] afflictions *C*

Trials make the promise sweet,
Trials give new life to pray'r;
Trials bring me to his feet,   15
Lay me low, and keep me there.

Did I meet no trials here,
No chastisement by the way;
Might I not, with reason, fear
I should prove a cast-away: 20
Bastards may escape the rod,[1]
Sunk in earthly, vain delight;
But the true-born child of GOD,
Must not, would not, if he might.

Hymn 37

[III. xvii]

AFFLICTIONS SANCTIFIED BY THE WORD

O how I love thy holy word,
Thy gracious covenant, O LORD!
It guides me in the peaceful way,
I think upon it all the day.

What are the mines of shining wealth,   5
The strength of youth, the bloom of health!
What are all joys compar'd with those
Thine everlasting word bestows!

Long unafflicted, undismay'd,
In pleasure's path secure I stray'd;   10
Thou mad'st me feel thy chastning rod,[2]
And strait I turn'd unto my GOD.

---

[1] Hebrews xii. 8.   [2] Psalm cxix. 71.

15 bring me to] Lay me at *O, C*   17 trials] Trial *O, C*

COPY-TEXT: *1779*, p. 330 (first printing).

What tho' it pierc'd my fainting heart,
I bless thine hand that caus'd the smart;
It taught my tears awhile to flow,   15
But sav'd me from eternal woe.

Oh! hadst thou left me unchastis'd,
Thy precept I had still despis'd;
And *still* the snare in secret laid,
Had my unwary feet betray'd.   20

I love thee therefore O my GOD,
And breathe towards thy dear abode;
Where in thy presence fully blest,
Thy chosen saints for ever rest.

Hymn 38

[III. xviii]

TEMPTATION

The billows swell, the winds are high,
Clouds overcast my wintry sky;
Out of the depths to thee I call,
My fears are great, my strength is small.

O LORD, the pilot's part perform,   5
And guide and guard me thro' the storm;
Defend me from each threatning ill,
Controll the waves, say, 'Peace, be still.'

Amidst the roaring of the sea,
My soul still hangs her hope on thee,   10
Thy constant love, thy faithful care,
Is all that saves me from despair.

COPY-TEXT: *1779*, p. 331 (first printing).

1 swell,] *1781*; swell *1779*

Dangers of ev'ry shape and name
Attend the follow'rs of the Lamb,
Who leave the world's deceitful shore,   15
And leave it to return no more.

Tho' tempest-toss'd and half a wreck,
My Saviour thro' the floods I seek;
Let neither winds nor stormy main,
Force back my shatter'd bark again.   20

Hymn 39

[III. xix]

LOOKING UPWARDS IN A STORM

GOD of my life, to thee I call,
Afflicted at thy feet I fall;[1]
When the great water-floods prevail,
Leave not my trembling heart to fail!

Friend of the friendless, and the faint!   5
Where should I lodge my deep complaint?
Where but with thee, whose open door
Invites the helpless and the poor!

Did ever mourner plead with thee,
And thou refuse that mourner's plea?   10
Does not the word still fix'd remain,
That none shall seek thy face in vain?

That were a grief I could not bear,
Didst thou not hear and answer pray'r;
But a pray'r-hearing, answ'ring GOD,   15
Supports me under ev'ry load.

---

[1] Psalm lxix. 15.

COPY-TEXT: *1779*, p. 332 (first printing).
1 life,] *1781*; life *1779*   7 door] *1781*; door, *1779*

Fair is the lot that's cast for me!
I have an advocate with thee;
They whom the world caresses most,
Have no such privilege to boast.   20

Poor tho' I am, despis'd, forgot,[1]
Yet GOD, my GOD, forgets me not;
And he is safe and must succeed,
For whom the LORD vouchsafes to plead.

Hymn 40

[III. xx]

THE VALLEY OF THE SHADOW OF DEATH

My soul is sad and much dismay'd;
See, LORD, what legions of my foes,
With fierce Apollyon at their head,
My heav'nly pilgrimage oppose!

See, from the ever-burning lake   5
How like a smoky cloud they rise!
With horrid blasts my soul they shake,
With storms of blasphemies and lies.

Their fiery arrows reach the mark,[2]
My throbbing heart with anguish tear;   10
Each lights upon a kindred spark,
And finds abundant fuel there.

I hate the thought that wrongs the LORD;
Oh, I would drive it from my breast,
With thy own sharp two-edged sword,   15
Far as the east is from the west.

[1] Psalm xl. 17.   [2] Ephesians vi. 16.

COPY-TEXT: *1779*, p. 333 (first printing).

5 ever-burning] *1781*; over-burning *1779*

Come then, and chase the cruel host,
Heal the deep wounds I have receiv'd!
Nor let the pow'rs of darkness boast
That I am foil'd, and thou art griev'd!   20

Hymn 41

[III. xxiii]

PEACE AFTER A STORM

When darkness long has veil'd my mind,
And smiling day once more appears;
Then, my Redeemer, then I find
The folly of my doubts and fears.

Strait I upbraid my wand'ring heart,   5
And blush that I should ever be
Thus prone to act so base a part,
Or harbour one bad thought of thee!

Oh! let me then at length be taught
What I am still so slow to learn;   10
That GOD is love, and changes not,
Nor knows the shadow of a turn.

Sweet truth, and easy to repeat!
But when my faith is sharply try'd,
I find myself a learner yet,   15
Unskilful, weak, and apt to slide.

But, O my LORD, one look from thee
Subdues the disobedient will;
Drives doubt and discontent away,
And thy rebellious worm is still.   20

COPY-TEXT: *1779*, pp. 336–7. First printed by R. Conyers, *A Collection of Psalms and Hymns*, 1772, pp. 217–18.

8 bad] *1781*; hard *1779*   12 turn.] *1781*; turn, *1779*

Thou art as ready to forgive,
As I am ready to repine;
Thou, therefore, all the praise receive,
Be shame, and self-abhorrence, mine.

Hymn 42

[III. xxiv]

MOURNING AND LONGING

The Saviour hides his face!
My spirit thirsts to prove
Renew'd supplies of pard'ning grace,
And never-fading love.

The favor'd souls who know   5
What glories shine in him,
Pant for his presence, as the roe
Pants for the living stream!

What trifles teaze me now!
They swarm like summer flies,   10
They cleave to ev'ry thing I do,
And swim before my eyes.

How dull the sabbath day,
Without the sabbath's LORD!
How toilsome then to sing and pray,   15
And wait upon the word!

Of all the truths I hear
How few delight my taste!
I glean a berry here and there,
But mourn the vintage past.   20

COPY-TEXT: *1779*, pp. 337–8 (first printing).

Yet let me (as I ought)
Still hope to be supply'd;
No pleasure else is worth a thought,
Nor shall I be deny'd.

Tho' I am but a worm,   25
Unworthy of his care;
The LORD will my desire perform,
And grant me all my pray'r.

Hymn 43

[III. xxvi]

SELF-ACQUAINTANCE

Dear LORD accept a sinful heart,
    Which of itself complains
And mourns, with much and frequent smart,
    The evil it contains.

There fiery seeds of anger lurk,   5
    Which often hurt my frame;
And wait but for the tempter's work,
    To fan them to a flame.

Legality holds out a bribe
    To purchase life from thee;   10
And discontent would fain prescribe
    How thou shalt deal with me.

While unbelief withstands thy grace,
    And puts the mercy by;
Presumption, with a brow of brass,   15
    Says, 'Give me, or I die.'

COPY-TEXT: *1779*, p. 341. First printed by 'Omicron' [Newton], *Twenty Six Letters on Religious Subjects*, 1774, p. 212.

How eager are my thoughts to roam
  In quest of what they love!
But ah! when duty calls them home,
  How heavily they move!   20

Oh, cleanse me in a Saviour's blood,
  Transform me by thy pow'r,
And make me thy belov'd abode,
  And let me rove no more.

Hymn 44

[III. xxviii]

PRAYER FOR PATIENCE

Lord, who hast suffer'd all for me,
My peace and pardon to procure;
The lighter cross I bear for thee,
Help me with patience to endure.

The storm of loud repining hush,   5
I would in humble silence mourn;
Why should th'unburnt, tho' burning bush,
Be angry as the crackling thorn?

Man should not faint at thy rebuke,
Like Joshua falling on his face,[1]   10
When the curst thing that Achan took,
Brought Israel into just disgrace.

Perhaps some golden wedge suppress'd,
Some secret sin offends my GOD;
Perhaps that Babylonish vest   15
Self-righteousness, provokes the rod.

---

[1] Joshua vii. 10, 11.

COPY-TEXT: *1779*, pp. 343–4 (first printing).

Ah! were I buffetted all day,
Mock'd, crown'd with thorns, and spit upon;
I yet should have no right to say,
My great distress is mine alone.   20

Let me not angrily declare
No pain was ever sharp like mine;
Nor murmur at the cross I bear,
But rather weep rememb'ring thine.

Hymn 45

[III. xxix]

SUBMISSION

O LORD, my best desire fulfill
    And help me to resign,
Life, health and comfort to thy will,
    And make thy pleasure mine.

Why should I shrink at thy command,   5
    Whose love forbids my fears?
Or tremble at the gracious hand
    That wipes away my tears?

No, let me rather freely yield
    What most I prize to thee;   10
Who never hast a good withheld,
    Or wilt withhold from me.

Thy favor, all my journey thro',
    Thou art engag'd to grant;
What else I want, or think I do,   15
    'Tis better still to want.

COPY-TEXT: *1779*, pp. 344–5 (first printing).

Wisdom and mercy guide my way,
  Shall I resist them both?
A poor blind creature of a day,
  And crush'd before the moth!   20

But ah! my inward spirit cries,
  Still bind me to thy sway;
Else the next cloud that vails my skies,
  Drives all these thoughts away.

Hymn 46

[III. xliv]

BEHOLD I MAKE ALL THINGS NEW

How blest thy creature is, O God!
When with a single Eye,
He views the lustre of thy Word,
The day spring from on high.

Thro' all the storms that vail the skies   5
And frown on earthly things;
The Sun of Righteousness he Eyes
With healing on his wings.

Struck by that light, the Human heart,
A barren soil no more,   10
Sends the sweet smell of Grace abroad,
Where Serpents lurk'd before.

The soul a dreary province once,
Of Satan's dark domain;
Feels a new empire form'd within,   15
And owns an heav'nly reign.

Composed 1764 or 1765

COPY-TEXT: copy in Maitland–Madan Commonplace Book, pp. 86–7 (*O*). First printed in *1779*, pp. 363–4.

Title] The Happy Change *1779*

The glorious orb whose golden beams,
The fruitful year controul
Since first obedient to thy word,
He started from the Goal;   20

Has chear'd the nations with the joys
His orient rays impart,
But Jesus, 'tis thy light alone,
Can shine upon the heart.

Hymn 47

[III. xlv]

RETIREMENT

Far from the World, O Lord I flee,
From strife, and tumult far,
From scenes, where Satan wages still
His most successful war.

The calm retreat, the silent shade,   5
With prayer, and praise agree;
And seem, by thy sweet bounty made,
For those, who follow Thee.

There, if thy Spirit touch the Soul,
And grace her mean abode;   10
O with what peace, and joy, and love,
She communes with her God!

There, like the Nightingale she pours
Her solitary lays;
Nor asks a witness of her song,   15
Nor thirsts, for human praise.

17 golden] *1779*; Silver *O*

Composed 1764 or 1765.

COPY-TEXT: copy in Maitland–Madan Commonplace Book, pp. 88–9 (*O*). First printed in *1779*, pp. 364–5.

Title] *1779*; *untitled in O*   13 pours] *1779*; pours, *O*

Author, and Guardian of my life,
Sweet fount of light divine!
And all endearing names, in *One*,
My Saviour—I am thine!   20

What thanks I owe thee, and what love,
A boundless, endless store;
Shall echo thro' the realms above,
When time shall be no more.

Hymn 48

[III. xlvii]

THE HIDDEN LIFE

To tell the Saviour all my wants,
    How pleasing is the task!
Nor less to praise him when he grants
    Beyond what I can ask.

My lab'ring spirit vainly seeks   5
    To tell but half the joy;
With how much tenderness he speaks,
    And helps me to reply.

Nor were it wise, nor should I choose
    Such secrets to declare;   10
Like precious wines their taste they lose
    Expos'd to open air.

But this with boldness I proclaim,
    Nor care if thousands hear;
Sweet is the ointment of his name,   15
    Not life is half so dear.

18 fount] source *1779*   19 endearing] harmonious *1779*   20 I am thine!]
thou art mine! *1779*

COPY-TEXT: *1779*, pp. 366–7 (first printing).

2 task!] *1781*; task? *1779*

And can you frown, my former friends,
  Who knew what once I was;
And blame the song that thus commends
  The man who bore the cross?   20

Trust me, I draw the likeness true,
  And not as fancy paints;
Such honor may he give to you,
  For such have all his saints.

Hymn 49

[III. xlviii]

JOY AND PEACE IN BELIEVING

Sometimes a light surprizes
  The christian while he sings;
It is the LORD who rises
  With healing in his wings:
When comforts are declining,   5
  He grants the soul again
A season of clear shining
  To cheer it after rain.

In holy contemplation,
  We sweetly then pursue   10
The theme of GOD's salvation,
  And find it ever new:
Set free from present sorrow,
  We cheerfully can say,
E'en let th'unknown to-morrow,[1]   15
  Bring with it what it may.

It can bring with it nothing
  But he will bear us thro';
Who gives the lilies clothing
  Will clothe his people too: 20

---

[1] Matthew vi. 34.

COPY-TEXT: *1779*, pp. 367–8 (first printing).

Beneath the spreading heavens,
    No creature but is fed;
And he who feeds the ravens,
    Will give his children bread.

Tho' vine, nor fig-tree neither,[1]   25
    Their wonted fruit should bear,
Tho' all the fields should wither,
    Nor flocks, nor herds be there:
Yet GOD the same abiding,
    His praise shall tune my voice;   30
For while in him confiding,
    I cannot but rejoice.

Hymn 50

[III. xlix]

TRUE PLEASURES

LORD my soul with pleasure springs,
    When JESUS' name I hear;
And when GOD the Spirit brings
    The word of promise near:
Beauties too, in holiness,   5
Still delighted I perceive;
Nor have words that can express
    The joys thy precepts give.

Cloth'd in sanctity and grace,
    How sweet it is to see   10
Those who love thee as they pass,
    Or when they wait on thee:

---

[1] Habakkuk iii. 17, 18.

25 Tho'] The *1779*

COPY-TEXT: *1779*, p. 369 (first printing).

Pleasant too, to sit and tell
What we owe to love divine;
Till our bosoms grateful swell,   15
    And eyes begin to shine.

Those the comforts I possess,
    Which GOD shall still increase,
All his ways are pleasantness,[1]
    And all his paths are peace: 20
Nothing JESUS did or spoke,
Henceforth let me ever slight;
For I love his easy yoke,[2]
    And find his burden light.

Hymn 51

[III. l]

THE CHRISTIAN

Honor and happiness unite
To make the christian's name a praise;
How fair the scene, how clear the light,
That fills the remnant of his days!

A kingly character he bears,   5
No change his priestly office knows;
Unfading is the crown he wears,
His joys can never reach a close.

Adorn'd with glory from on high,
Salvation shines upon his face;   10
His robe is of th'etherial dye,
His steps are dignity and grace.

---

[1] Proverbs iii. 17.   [2] Matthew xi. 30.

---

15 bosoms grateful] *1781*; grateful bosoms *1779*
COPY-TEXT: *1779*, p. 370 (first printing).

Inferior honors he disdains,
Nor stoops to take applause from earth;
The King of kings himself, maintains   15
Th'expences of his heav'nly birth.

The noblest creature seen below,
Ordain'd to fill a throne above;
GOD gives him all he can bestow,
His kingdom of eternal love!   20

My soul is ravish'd at the thought!
Methinks from earth I see him rise;
Angels congratulate his lot,
And shout him welcome to the skies!

Hymn 52

[III. li]

LIVELY HOPE, AND GRACIOUS FEAR

I was a groveling creature once,
    And basely cleav'd to earth;
I wanted spirit to renounce
    The clod that gave me birth.

But GOD has breath'd upon a worm,   5
    And sent me, from above,
Wings, such as clothe an angel's form,
    The wings of joy and love.

With these to Pisgah's top I fly,
    And there delighted stand;   10
To view, beneath a shining sky,
    The spacious promis'd land.

COPY-TEXT: *1779*, p. 371 (first printing).

The LORD of all the vast domain,
  Has promis'd it to me;
The length and breadth of all the plain,   15
  As far as faith can see.

How glorious is my privilege!
  To thee for help I call;
I stand upon a mountain's edge,
  Oh save me, lest I fall!   20

Tho' much exalted in the LORD,
  My strength is not my own;
Then let me tremble at his word,
  And none shall cast me down.

Hymn 53

[III. lvii]

FOR THE POOR

When Hagar found the Bottle spent,
  And wept o'er Ishmael,
An Angel of the Lord was sent,
  To guide her to a Well.

Should not Elijah's Cake and Cruse,   5
  Convince us at this day
A gracious God will not refuse
  Provision by the Way.

His Saints and Servants shall be fed,
  The Promise is secure,   10
Bread shall be giv'n them, he has said,
  Their Water shall be sure.

COPY-TEXT: *A*, fo. 9. First printed in *1779*, pp. 378–9.

3 An Angel of] A message from *1779*   8 Provision] Provisions *1779*

Delights far richer they shall prove
  Than all Earth's Dainties are,
'Tis sweet to taste a Savior's Love,   15
  Tho' in the meanest Fare.

To Jesus then your Troubles bring,
  Nor murmur at your Lot,
Supply is sure while He is King,
  You shall not be forgot.   20

Hymn 54

[III. lxi]

MY SOUL THIRSTETH FOR GOD

I thirst, but not as once I did,
  The vain delights of earth to share;
Thy wounds, EMMANUEL, all forbid,
  That I should seek my pleasures there.

It was the sight of thy dear cross,   5
  First wean'd my soul from earthly things;
And taught me to esteem as dross,
  The mirth of fools and pomp of kings.

I want that grace that springs from thee,
  That quickens all things where it flows; 10
And makes a wretched thorn, like me,
  Bloom as the myrtle, or the rose.

Dear fountain of delight unknown!
  No longer sink below the brim;
But overflow, and pour me down   15
  A living, and life-giving stream!

13 Delights] Repasts *1779*   17 Troubles] trouble *1779*   19] While you are
poor, and he is King, *1779*

COPY-TEXT: *1779*, p. 383 (first printing).

For sure, of all the plants that share
The notice of thy Father's eye;
None proves less grateful to his care,
Or yields him meaner fruit than I.   20

Hymn 55

[III. lxii]

LOVE CONSTRAINING TO OBEDIENCE

No strength of nature can suffice
To serve the LORD aright;
And what she has, she misapplies,
For want of clearer light.

How long beneath the law I lay   5
In bondage and distress!
I toil'd the precept to obey,
But toil'd without success.

Then to abstain from outward sin
Was more than I could do;   10
Now, if I feel its pow'r within,
I feel I hate it too.

Then all my servile works were done
A righteousness to raise;
Now, freely chosen in the Son,   15
I freely choose his ways.

What shall I do, was then the word,
That I may worthier grow?
What shall I render to the LORD?
Is my enquiry now.   20

COPY-TEXT: *1779*, p. 384 (first printing).

2 the] *1781*; *omitted in 1779*   17 do,] do *1779*

To see the Law by Christ fulfill'd,
And hear his pard'ning voice;
Changes a slave into a child,[1]
And duty into choice.

Hymn 56

[III. lxiii]

THE HEART HEALED AND CHANGED BY MERCY

Sin enslav'd me many years,
    And led me bound and blind;
Till at length a thousand fears
    Came swarming o'er my mind.
Where, I said in deep distress,   5
Will these sinful pleasures end?
How shall I secure my peace,
    And make the LORD my friend?

Friends and ministers said much
    The gospel to enforce;   10
But my blindness still was such,
    I chose a legal course:
Much I fasted, watch'd and strove,
Scarce would shew my face abroad,
Fear'd, almost, to speak or move,   15
    A stranger still to GOD.

Thus afraid to trust his grace,
    Long time did I rebel;
Till, despairing of my case,
    Down at his feet I fell: 20

---

[1] Romans iii. 31.

COPY-TEXT: *1779*, p. 385 (first printing).

Then my stubborn heart he broke,
And subdu'd me to his sway;
By a simple word he spoke,
    'Thy sins are done away.'

Hymn 57

[III. lxiv]

HATRED OF SIN

Holy LORD GOD! I love thy truth,
Nor dare thy least commandment slight;
Yet pierc'd by sin, the serpent's tooth,
I mourn the anguish of the bite.

But tho' the poison lurks within,   5
Hope bids me still with patience wait;
Till death shall set me free from sin,
Free from the only thing I hate.

Had I a throne above the rest,
Where angels and archangels dwell;   10
One sin, unslain, within my breast,
Would make that heav'n as dark as hell.

The pris'ner, sent to breathe fresh air,
And bless'd with liberty again,
Would mourn, were he condemn'd to wear   15
One link of all his former chain.

But oh! no foe invades the bliss,
When glory crowns the christian's head;
One view of JESUS as he is,
Will strike all sin for ever dead.   20

COPY-TEXT: *1779*, p. 386 (first printing).

Hymn 58

[III. lxviii]

THE NEW CONVERT

The new-born child of gospel-grace,
Like some fair tree when summer's nigh,
Beneath EMMANUEL's shining face,
Lifts up his blooming branch on high.

No fears he feels, he sees no foes,   5
No conflict yet his faith employs,
Nor has he learnt to whom he owes,
The strength and peace his soul enjoys.

But sin soon darts its cruel sting,
And, comforts sinking day by day,   10
What seem'd his own, a self-fed spring,
Proves but a brook that glides away.

When Gideon arm'd his num'rous host,
The LORD soon made his numbers less;
And said, lest Israel vainly boast,[1]   15
'My arm procur'd me this success.'

Thus will he bring our spirits down,
And draw our ebbing comforts low;
That sav'd by grace, but not our own,
We may not claim the praise we owe.   20

[1] Judges vii. 2.

COPY-TEXT: *1779*, pp. 390–1 (first printing).

10 And,] And *1779*   day,] day; *1779*   15 lest] 'lest *1779* (*see Commentary*)

Hymn 59

[III. lxix]

TRUE AND FALSE COMFORTS

O God, whose favorable eye
 The sin-sick soul revives;
Holy and heav'nly is the joy
 Thy shining presence gives.

Not such as hypocrites suppose,   5
 Who with a graceless heart,
Taste not of thee, but drink a dose
 Prepar'd by Satan's art.

Intoxicating joys are theirs,
 Who while they boast their light,   10
And seem to soar above the stars,
 Are plunging into night.

Lull'd in a soft and fatal sleep,
 They sin, and yet rejoice;
Were they indeed the Saviour's sheep,   15
 Would they not hear his voice?

Be mine the comforts, that reclaim
 The soul from Satan's pow'r;
That make me blush for what I am,
 And hate my sin the more.   20

'Tis joy enough, my All in All,
 At thy dear feet to lie;
Thou wilt not let me lower fall,
 And none can higher fly.

COPY-TEXT: *1779*, pp. 391–2 (first printing).

Hymn 60

[III. lxxi]

A LIVING AND A DEAD FAITH

The LORD receives his highest praise,
From humble minds and hearts sincere;
While all the loud professor says,
Offends the righteous Judge's ear.

To walk as children of the day   5
To mark the precepts' holy light;
To wage the warfare, watch and pray,
Shew who are pleasing in his sight.

Not words alone it cost the LORD,
To purchase pardon for his own;   10
Nor will a soul, by grace restor'd,
Return the Saviour words alone.

With golden bells, the priestly vest,[1]
And rich pomegranates border'd round,
The need of holiness express'd,   15
And call'd for fruit, as well as sound.

Easy, indeed, it were to reach
A mansion in the courts above,
If swelling words, and fluent speech
Might serve, instead of faith and love.   20

But none shall gain the blissful place,
Or GOD's unclouded glory see;
Who talks of free and sov'reign grace,
Unless that grace has made *him* free.

[1] Exodus xxviii. 33.

COPY-TEXT: *1779*, pp. 393–4 (first printing).
11 will] with *1779, 1781, 1783*; *corrected in Errata 1783*

Hymn 61

[III. lxxii]

ANTINOMIANS

Too many Lord, abuse thy grace
  In this Licentious Day,
And while they boast they see thy Face,
  They turn their Own away.

Thy Book displays a gracious Light,   5
  That can the Blind restore,
But These are dazzled by the Sight,
  And Blinded still the more.

The Pardon such presume upon,
  They do not Beg but Steal,   10
And when they plead it at thy Throne,
  Oh, where's the Gospel Seal?

Was it for This, ye Lawless Tribe,
  The dear Redeemer Bled?
Is This the grace the Saints imbibe   15
  From Christ the Living Head?

Oh Lord! we know thy Chosen Few,
  Are fed with heav'nly Fare,
But These—the wretched Husks they chew,
  Proclaim them what they are.   20

The Liberty our Hearts implore,
  Is, not to Live in Sin,
But still to wait at Wisdom's Door,
  'Till Mercy calls us in.

COPY-TEXT: *A*, fo. 10ʳ. First printed in *1779*, pp. 394–5.

Title] Abuse of the Gospel *1779*   12 Gospel] Spirit's *1779*

Hymn 62

[III. lxxiii]

THE NARROW WAY

What thousands never knew the road!
What thousands hate it when 'tis known!
None but the chosen tribes of GOD,
Will seek or choose it for their own.

A thousand ways in ruin end,   5
One, only, leads to joys on high;
By that my willing steps ascend,
Pleas'd with a journey to the sky.

No more I ask, or hope to find,
Delight or happiness below;   10
Sorrow may well possess the mind
That feeds where thorns and thistles grow.

The joy that fades is not for me,
I seek immortal joys above;
There, glory without end, shall be   15
The bright reward of faith and love.

Cleave to the world ye sordid worms,
Contented lick your native dust;
But GOD shall fight, with all his storms,
Against the idol of your trust.   20

COPY-TEXT: *1779*, pp. 395–6 (first printing).

Hymn 63

[III. lxxiv]

DEPENDANCE

To keep the lamp alive
With oil we fill the bowl;
'Tis water makes the willow thrive,
And grace that feeds the soul.

The LORD's unsparing hand   5
Supplies the living stream;
It is not at our own command,
But still deriv'd from him.

Beware of Peter's word,[1]
Nor confidently say,   10
'I never *will* deny thee, LORD,'
But grant I never *may*.

Man's wisdom is to seek
His strength in GOD alone;
And e'en an angel would be weak,   15
Who trusted in his own.

Retreat beneath his wings,
And in his grace confide;
This more exalts the King of kings[2]
Than all your works beside.   20

In JESUS is our store,
Grace issues from his throne;
Whoever says, 'I want no more,'
Confesses he has none.

---

[1] Matthew xxvi. 33.   [2] John vi. 29.

COPY-TEXT: *1779*, pp. 396–7 (first printing).

Hymn 64

[III. lxxv]

NOT OF WORKS

Grace, triumphant in the throne,
Scorns a rival, reigns alone!
Come and bow beneath her sway,
Cast your idol works away:
Works of man, when made his plea,   5
Never shall accepted be;
Fruits of pride (vain-glorious worm)
Are the best he can perform.

Self, the god his soul adores,
Influences all his pow'rs;   10
JESUS is a slighted name,
Self-advancement all his aim:
But when GOD the Judge shall come,
To pronounce the final doom;
Then for rocks and hills to hide   15
All his works and all his pride.

Still the boasting heart replies,
What! the worthy and the wise,
Friends to temperance and peace,
Have not these a righteousness?   20
Banish ev'ry vain pretence
Built on human excellence;
Perish ev'ry thing in man,
But the grace that never can.

COPY-TEXT: *1779*, pp. 397–8 (first printing).
15 hide] hide, *1779*   18 What!] What *1779*

Hymn 65

[III. lxxx]

PRAISE FOR FAITH

Of all the gifts thine hand bestows,
    Thou Giver of all good!
Not heav'n itself a richer knows,
    Than my Redeemer's blood.

Faith too, the blood-receiving grace,   5
    From the same hand we gain;
Else, sweetly as it suits our case,
    That gift had been in vain.

Till thou thy teaching pow'r apply,
    Our hearts refuse to see;   10
And weak, as a distemper'd eye,
    Shut out the view of thee.

Blind to the merits of thy Son,
    What mis'ry we endure!
Yet fly that hand, from which alone,   15
    We could expect a cure.

We praise thee, and would praise thee more,
    To thee our all we owe;
The precious Saviour, and the pow'r
    That makes him precious too.   20

COPY-TEXT: *1779*, pp. 403–4 (first printing).

Hymn 66

[III. lxxxi]

GRACE AND PROVIDENCE

Almighty King! whose wond'rous hand,
Supports the weight of sea and land;
Whose grace is such a boundless store,
No heart shall break that sighs for more.

Thy Providence supplies my food,   5
And 'tis thy blessing makes it good;
My soul is nourish'd by thy word,
Let soul and body praise the LORD.

My streams of outward comfort came
From him, who built this earthly frame;   10
Whate'er I want his bounty gives,
By whom my soul for ever lives.

Either his hand preserves from pain,
Or, if I feel it, heals again;
From Satan's malice shields my breast,   15
Or overrules it for the best.

Forgive the song that falls so low
Beneath the gratitude I owe!
It means thy praise, however poor,
An angel's song can do no more.   20

COPY-TEXT: *1779*, pp. 404–5 (first printing).

Hymn 67

[III. lxxxiii]

I WILL PRAISE THE LORD AT ALL TIMES

Winter has a joy for me,
While the Saviour's charms I read,
Lowly, meek, from blemish free,
In the snow-drop's pensive head.

Spring returns, and brings along   5
Life-invigorating suns:
Hark! the turtle's plaintive song,
Seems to speak his dying grones!

Summer has a thousand charms,
All expressive of his worth;   10
'Tis his sun that lights and warms,
His the air that cools the earth.

What! has autumn left to say
Nothing, of a Saviour's grace?
Yes, the beams of milder day   15
Tell me of his smiling face.

Light appears with early dawn;
While the sun makes haste to rise,
See his bleeding beauties, drawn
On the blushes of the skies.   20

Ev'ning, with a silent pace,
Slowly moving in the west,
Shews an emblem of his grace,
Points to an eternal rest.

COPY-TEXT: *1779*, p. 407 (first printing).

MISCELLANEOUS POEMS
1774–1780

'TALES ET NOSTRI VIGUISSENT, JESUS, AMORES'

Tales et nostri viguissent, Jesus, amores,
Haec ni Dextra suum deseruisset Opus.
Nunc Hostes mihi sunt, quot sunt, Divique Hominesque,
Heu! Qualis, Quanta, Victima, Morte cado.

Feb: 8. 1774

'CÆSA EST NOSTRA COLUMBA, ET NOSTRO CRIMINE, CUJUS'

Cæsa est nostra Columba, et nostro Crimine, cujus,
Ah! cujus, potero posthac latitare sub alis?
Nulla fuga est—nunquam tam diro tincta furore,
Nec tam devotum ferierunt Fulgura monstrum.

'HATRED AND VENGEANCE, MY ETERNAL PORTION'

Hatred and vengeance, my eternal portion,
Scare can endure delay of execution:—
Wait, with impatient readiness, to seize my
Soul in a moment.

8 March 1774.

COPY-TEXT: *C*, whence first printed in Milford–Russell, 1967, p. 635.

1774.

COPY-TEXT: *C*. Lines 1–2 first printed by [George Dyer], *Monthly Magazine*, xvi (Jan. 1804), 532; ll. 3–4 (from *C*) in Milford–Russell, 1967, p. 635.

1774?

COPY-TEXT: *Υ* (copy in an unknown hand). Collated: *G* (copy in George Courtenay's hand); *Memoirs*, Cox ed., 1816, pp. 91–2 (first printing); *Autobiography of Cowper*, 1835, pp. 49–50.

Damn'd below Judas; more abhorr'd than he was,   5
Who, for a few pence, sold his holy master.
Twice betray'd, Jesus me, the last delinquent,
     Deems the profanest.
Man disavows, and Deity disowns me.
Hell might afford my miseries a shelter;   10
Therefore hell keeps her everhungry mouths all
     Bolted against me.
Hard lot! Encompass'd with a thousand dangers,
Weary, faint, trembling with a thousand terrors,
Fall'n, and if vanquish'd, to receive a sentence   15
     Worse than Abiram's:
Him, the vindictive rod of angry justice
Sent, quick and howling, to the centre headlong;
I, fed with judgments, in a fleshly tomb, am
     Buried above ground.   20

'HEU QUAM REMOTUS VESCOR AB OMNIBUS'

Heu quam remotus vescor ab omnibus
Quibus fruebar sub Lare Patrio,
     Quam nescius jucunda quondam
     Arva, Domum, Socios reliqui!

Et praeter omnes te mihi flebilem,   5
Te cariorem luce vel artubus,
     Te vinculo nostram jugali,
     Deserui tremulam sub ense.

Sed nec ferocem me genuit Pater,
Nec vagientem nutriit ubere   10
     Leaena dumoso sub antro,
     Fata sed hoc volueri nostra.

6 sold] slew *G*   15 Fall'n, and] *G*; I'm call'd, *Y, 1816*; Fated, *1835*   16 Abiram's]
Abyron's *G*   19 judgments] judgement *1835*   fleshly] filthy *G*

31 December 1774.

copy-text: *G* (copy in George Courtenay's hand). Collated: *Autobiography of Cowper*, 1835,
p. 52 (first printing of all save ll. 5–8, which appeared in Hayley, *Memoirs*, 1823, ii. 170).
6 cariorem] chariorem *1835*   12 volueri] voluere *1835*

Et, fluctuosum ceu mare volvitur,
Dum commovebar mille timoribus,
   Coactus in fauces Averni,   15
   Totus atro perii sub amne.
             Die ultimo 1774.

THE CANTAB.

With two Spurs or one, no great matter which,
Boots bought, or Boots borrow'd, a Whip or a Switch,
Five Shillings or less the Hire of his Beast,
Part paid into Hand—you must wait for the Rest.
Thus equipped Academicus climbs up his Horse,   5
And out they both Sally for better or worse.
His Heart void of Fear and as light as a Feather,
And in Violent Haste to go—not knowing whither,
Thro' the Fields and the Towns, see, he scampers along,
And is bark'd at and Laugh'd at by old and by young.   10
Till at length overspent, and his Sides smear'd with Blood,
Down tumbles His Horse, Man and all in the Mud.
In a Waggon or Chaise shall he finish his Route,
Oh scandalous Fate! he must do it on Foot.
Young Gentleman hear, I am older than You,   15
The Advice that I give I have proved to be true,
Wherever your Journey may be, never doubt it,
The faster you Ride, you're the longer about it.

ON THE TRIAL OF ADMIRAL KEPPEL

   Keppel Returning from afar
     With Laurels on his Brow,
   Comes Home to Wage a Sharper War
     And with a fiercer Foe.

1777?
COPY-TEXT: *U*, whence first printed by Hayley, 1803, 2nd ed., ii. 377–8.
12 Horse,] Horse *U*

February 1779.
COPY-TEXT: *A*, whence first printed by A. Collyer, *Universal Review*, vii (1890), 289.

The Blow was rais'd with cruel Aim,   5
    And meant to pierce his Heart,
But Lighting on his well-earn'd Fame,
    Struck an Immortal Part.

Slander and Envy strive to tear
    His Wreath so justly won,   10
But Truth, who made his Cause her Care,
    Has bound it faster On.

The Charge that was design'd to Sound
    The Signal of Disgrace,
Has only call'd a Navy round   15
    To Praise him to his Face.

AN ADDRESS TO THE MOB ON OCCASION
OF THE LATE RIOT AT THE HOUSE OF
SIR HUGH PALLISER

And is it thus ye Base and Blind,
And fickle as the shifting Wind,
Ye treat a Warrior staunch and true,
Grown Old in combating for You?
Can One false Step, and made in Haste,   5
Thus Cancel ev'ry Service past?
And have Ye all at once forgot,
(As whose Deservings have ye not)
That Palliser like Keppel brave,
Has baffled France on yonder Wave,   10
And when his Country ask'd the Stake,
Has pledg'd his Life for England's sake?
Tho' now he Sink oppress'd with Shame,
Forgetfull of his former Fame,
Yet Keppel with deserv'd Applause,   15
Proclaims him Bold in Britain's Cause
And to his well known Courage pays
The Tribute of Heroic Praise.

February 1779.

COPY-TEXT: *A*, whence first printed by A. Collyer, *Universal Review*, vii (1890), 290–1.

Go Learn of Him whom ye adore,
Whose Name now Sets ye in a Roar,   20
Whom ye were more than half prepar'd,
To Pay with just the same Reward,
To render Praise where Praise is due,
To keep *His* former Deeds in View
Who fought, and would have Died for You.   25

TRANSLATION OF THE 16TH. ODE OF THE 2D. BOOK OF HORACE

Ease, is the weary Merchant's Pray'r,
    Who Ploughs by Night th'Ægean Flood,
When neither Moon nor Stars appear,
    Or Glimmer faintly thro' the Cloud.

For Ease, the Mede with Quiver graced,   5
    For Ease, the Thracian Hero Sighs,
Delightfull Ease All Pant to Taste,
    A Blessing which no Treasure buys.

For neither Gold can Lull to Rest,
    Nor All a Consul's Guard beat off,   10
The Tumults of a troubled Breast,
    The Cares that Haunt a Gilded Roof.

Happy the Man whose Table shews
    A few clean Ounces of Old Plate,
No Fear intrudes on his Repose,   15
    No sordid Wishes to be Great.

Poor short-lived things! what Plans we lay,
    Ah why forsake our Native Home,
To distant Climates Speed away,
    For Self cleaves fast where'er we Roam.   20

COPY-TEXT: *H*. Collated: *M* (undated MS.), whence first printed by Johnson, 1815, pp. 128–30.
Title] Book 2. Ode. 16. *M*   4 Glimmer faintly] faintly glimmer *M*   20 cleaves fast] sticks close *M*

Care follows hard, and soon o'ertakes
   The well-rigg'd Ship, the Warlike Steed,
Her destin'd Quarry ne'er Forsakes,
   Not the Wind flies with half the Speed.

From anxious Fears of future Ill   25
   Guard well the cheerfull Happy NOW,
Gild ev'n your Sorrows with a Smile,
   No Blessing is unmixt Below.

Some Die in Youth, some Halt Behind
   And With'ring Wait the slow Decree,   30
And I perhaps may be Design'd
   For Years, that Heav'n denies to Thee.

Thy Neighing Steeds and Lowing Herds,
   Thy num'rous Flocks around thee Graze,
And the best Purple Tyre affords   35
   Thy Robe Magnificent displays.

On Me Indulgent Fate bestow'd
   A Rural Mansion, Neat and Small,
This Lyre—and as for yonder Crowd,
   The Glory to Despise them All.   40

22 well-rigg'd] flying *deleted M*   27 ev'n] well *deleted H*   28–32] *not in M*
37 Fate] Heav'n *M*   40] The Happiness to Hate them All. *M*

A TALE, FOUNDED ON A FACT,
WHICH HAPPENED IN JANUARY, 1779

Where Humber pours his rich commercial Stream,
There dwelt a Wretch, who Breath'd but to Blaspheme.
In subterraneous Caves his Life he led,
Black as the Mine in which he wrought for Bread.
When on a day, Emerging from the Deep,   5
A Sabbath day—such Sabbaths thousands keep—
The Wages of his Weekly Toil he bore
To Buy a Cock, whose Blood might win him more.
As if the Noblest of the Feather'd Kind
Were but for Battle and for Death design'd,   10
As if the Consecrated Hours were meant
For Sport to Minds on Cruelty intent.
It chanced—such Chances Providence Obey—
He met a Fellow Lab'rer on the Way,
Whose Heart the same Desires had once inflam'd   15
But now the Savage Temper was reclaim'd.
Persuasion on his Lips had taken Place,
(For All Plead well who Plead the Cause of Grace).
His Iron Heart with Scripture he Assail'd,
Wooed him to hear a Sermon and prevail'd.   20
    His faithfull Bow the Mighty Preacher drew,
Swift as the Lightning Glimpse his Arrows flew:
He wept, he trembled, cast his Eyes around
To find a worse than he, but none he found,
He felt his Sins, and wonder'd he should feel,   25
Grace made the Wound, and only Grace could Heal.
    Now farewell Oaths and Blasphemies and Lies,
He quits the Sinner's for the Martyr's Prize—

1779 or 1780.

COPY-TEXT: *H* (see Commentary). Collated: *C*; *AM* (*Arminian Magazine*, vi (1783),
51–3—first printing); *SR* (*Spiritual Register*, ed. T. Wills, 2nd ed., 1784, i. 67–9);
Hayley, ii. (1803), 297–8. (α denotes *C*, *AM*, *SR*, *1803* in agreement.)
Title] *1803*; so *C*, *omitting* A *and reading* happen'd January; A True Story *H*; The following
Lines contain a plain matter of Fact, just as it was. *AM*; *untitled in SR*   1 his] her *AM*
2 Breath'd] liv'd *AM*   14 He met a Fellow Lab'rer] α; A Fellow Lab'rer met him *H*
22 his Arrows] the arrow *1803*; the arrows *AM*   23 He wept, he trembled] The
sinner trembling *AM*   24 than he] than him *AM*   26 only Grace] Grace
alone *1803*   27 Blasphemies] blasphemy *C*

That Holy Day was wash'd with many a Tear,
Gilded with Hope, yet shaded too by Fear: 30
The next, his swarthy Brethren of the Mine
Learn'd from his alter'd Speech the Change Divine;
Laugh'd where they should have Wept, and Swore the Day
Was nigh, when he would Swear as fast as They.
No, said the Penitent, such Words shall Share   35
This Breath no more, Devoted now to Pray'r.
Oh if thou seest (thine Eye the Future sees)
That I shall yet again Blaspheme like These,
Now Strike me to the Ground on which I kneel,
E'er yet this Heart relapses into Steel.   40
Now take me to that Heav'n I once defy'd,
Thy Presence, thy Embrace—He spoke, and Died.
    Short was the Race allotted him to Run,
Just Enter'd in the Lists he Gain'd the Crown,
His Pray'r scarce Ended, e'er his Praise begun.   45

THE BEE AND THE PINE APPLE

A Bee allur'd by the Perfume
Of a rich Pine Apple in Bloom,
Found it within a Frame inclosed,
And Lick'd the Glass that interposed,
Blossoms of Apricot and Peach,   5
The Flow'rs that Blow'd within his Reach,
Were arrant Drugs compar'd with That
He strove so vainly to get at.
No Rose could Yield so rare a Treat,
Nor Jessamine was half so Sweet.   10

30 by Fear] with Fear *C*   32 from] by *1803*   Speech] lips *AM*   33 where]
when *1803*   34 fast] well *C*   36 Devoted now to] henceforth employ'd in *C*,
AM, SR   39 on which] α; whereon *H*   41 defy'd] α; denied *H*   42 thy
Embrace] α; thine Embrace *H*   spoke, and] spake, he *C, AM*   43–5 *not in 1803*
43 Race] time *AM*   44 in] on *SR*   Lists] list *SR*   Gain'd] *C, AM, SR*; Seized *H*

April–September 1779.

COPY-TEXT: *H*; also collated: *A*, whence first printed by A. Collyer, *Universal Review*, vii
(1890), 291–2.

Title] *A*; The Pine Apple and the Bee *H*

The Gard'ner saw this Much Ado,
(The Gard'ner was the Master too)
And thus he said—Poor restless Bee!
I Learn Philosophy from Thee—
I Learn how Just it is and Wise,   15
To Use what Providence supplies,
To leave fine Titles, Lordships, Graces,
Rich Pensions, Dignities and Places,
Those Gifts of a Superior kind,
To those for whom they were design'd.   20
I Learn that Comfort dwells alone
In that which Heav'n has made our Own,
That Fools incur no greater Pain
Than Pleasure Coveted in vain.

ΕΠΙΝΙΚΙΟΝ

Who Pities France? her Enterprizes cross'd,
Her Hopes confounded, and her Treasures lost—
Her Eastern Empire shaken to the Ground,
Her Western, tott'ring at the Trumpet's Sound.
Aspiring, tho' not prosperous in Arms,   5
Has she not fill'd all Nations with Alarms?
Has she not taught the thankless Child, how best
To Aim a Poignard at the Parent's Breast?
Conferr'd a Grace she had not to bestow,
Tied Independence round a Rebel's Brow,   10
Helped him to Pick a Gem from England's Crown,
In Hopes one Day to fix it in her Own?
Who Pities France? So Prosper All who dare
Awaken, unprovok'd, the Flames of War,
So Prosper All, who deem Repose well sold,   15
And Blood well barter'd, in Exchange for Gold.

Autumn 1779 (?).

COPY-TEXT: *H*, whence first printed by Ryskamp, p. 237.

12 *this line has been partially cropped; the reading is fairly certain*

TO SIR JOSHUA REYNOLDS

Dear President, whose Art sublime
Gives perpetuity to time,
And bids transactions of a day
That fleeting hours would waft away,
To dark Futurity survive,   5
And in unfading beauty live,
You cannot with a grace decline
A special Mandate of the Nine,
Yourself, whatever task you chuse,
So much indebted to the Muse.   10
    Thus say the Sisterhood—We come—
Fix well your Pallet on your thumb,
Prepare the pencil and the tints,
We come to furnish you with hints.
French Disappointment, British Glory   15
Must be the Subject of the Story.
    First strike a Curve, a gracefull Bow,
Then slope it to a point below,
Your Outline easy, airy, light,
Fill'd up, becomes a paper kite.   20
Let Independence, sanguin, horrid,
Blaze like a Meteor in the forhead;
Beneath, (but lay aside your graces)
Draw *six and twenty ruefull faces*;
Each with a staring stedfast Eye   25
Fixt on his great and good Ally.
France flies the Kite—'tis on the Wing—
Britannia's Lightning cuts the string,
The Wind that rais'd it, e'er it ceases,
Just rends it into thirteen pieces,   30
Takes charge of ev'ry flutt'ring Sheet,
And lays them all at George's feet.

November–December 1779.

COPY-TEXT: *U*. Collated: *H*. First printed, from *U*, by Johnson, *Private Correspondence of William Cowper*, 1824, i. 184–6.

11 *not indented in H*   13 tints]Tintz *H*   17 *not indented in H*   22 the
it's *H*

    Iberia trembling from afar
  Renounces the confed'rate war:
  Her Efforts and her Arts o'ercome,   35
  France calls her shatter'd navies home:
  Repenting Holland learns to mourn
  The sacred Treaties she has torn:
  Astonishment and Awe profound
  Are stamp'd upon the Nations round: 40
  Without one Friend, above all Foes,
  Britannia gives the World Repose.

A PRESENT FOR THE QUEEN OF FRANCE

    The Bruiser e'er he Strikes a Blow,
  (Such is his Friendship for his Foe)
  Cordially shakes him by the Fist,
  Then Dubbs him his Antagonist,
  And Bangs him Soundly if he can,   5
  To Prove himself the better Man.
  So Queen of France in Loving Mood,
  Feeling a Thirst for British Blood,
  E'er she began her Tilting Match,
  Sent Queen of England first a Watch.   10
  As who should say, Look sharp, take care,
  Ma très Aimable et ma Chère,
  For you and I must go to War.
  The Inference is short and sweet,
  Tho' Navies Join, and Armies meet,   15
  And Thousands in the Conflict fall,
  There was no Malice in't at all.
    Now what shall England's lovely Queen,
  Whose Act is never base or mean,
  What shall our Gloriana send   20
  In Recompense to such a Friend?
  For Something at her gracious Hands

37-8 *not in* H

November–December 1779.
COPY-TEXT: *H*, whence first printed by Ryskamp, pp. 238-9.
12 très . . . Chère] trés . . . Chere *H*

E'en Charity itself demands,
To Comfort, Gratify and Sweeten
France, so unmercifully Beaten.   25
   The Muse brings forth with little Labor,
A Present for our Royal Neighbor.
   Most Christian Heroine, behold,
Beset with Eastern Gems and Gold,
Your Friends who Stiled you *Great and Good*   30
Sov'reigns of yonder Sea of Blood,
Which *Great* and *Good* with much good Will,
You have Assisted them to Spill,
In charitable Hope to Sever
Them and their only Friends for Ever.   35
Behold a Gift you must delight in,
The Congress—after so much Fighting
A little ruefull to be sure—
The Congress, Ma'am, in Miniature.
Let these your Cabinet adorn,   40
And as you View them Night and Morn,
Reflect that *Great* and *Good* belong
Not to the King that does the Wrong;
Those Titles he Asserts alone,
Who Just and Equal on his Throne,   45
Manfully Vindicates his own:
Yet will not, dares not, Use his Might
To Violate another's Right.

31 Sov'reigns of] Escapd from *deleted H*

ON THE VICTORY GAINED BY SIR GEORGE
RODNEY OVER THE SPANISH FLEET OFF
GIBRALTAR IN 1780. FOR WHICH HE
HAS SINCE BEEN REWARDED WITH
THE LIEUTENANT GENERALSHIP
OF THE MARINES.

From Shades of Tartarus and Realms of Woe
The Trojan Hero pluck'd the Golden Bough.
Of all that Rodney ever Earn'd in Fight,
His fairest Wreath was gather'd in the Night.
'Twas not indeed a Golden Branch he won,   5
But George's Bounty soon shall make it one.

A SIMILE TRANSLATED FROM *PARADISE LOST*

Quales aerii Montis de Vertice, Nubes
Cum surgunt, et jam Boreæ tumida Ora quiêrunt,
Cœlum hilares abdit spissâ Caligine Vultûs,
Nimbosumque Nives aut Imbres cogitat Æther:
Tum si jucundo tandem Sol prodeat Ore,   5
Et croceo Montes et Pascua Lumine tingat,
Gaudent Omnia, Aves implent Concentibus Agros,
Balatûque Ovium Colles Vallesque resultant.

March 1780.
COPY-TEXT: *H*, whence first printed by Ryskamp, p. 237.
Title has] was *deleted H*

Early June 1780 (?).
COPY-TEXT: *H*. Collated; *U*. First printed by Hayley, 1804, iii. 28.
7 implent] mulcent *U*

IN SEDITIONEM HORRENDAM,
CORRUPTELIS GALLICIS (UT FERTUR)
LONDINI NUPER EXORTAM

Perfida, crudelis, Victa et Lymphata Furore,
Non Armis Laurum Gallia, Fraude petit.
Venalem Pretio Plebem conducit, et Urit
Undique Privatas Patriciasque Domos.
Necquicquam conata suâ, fœdissima Sperat   5
Posse tamen Nostrâ Nos Superare Manû.
Gallia, Vana Struis—Precibus nunc utere, Vinces,
Nam mites timidis Supplicibusque sumus.

THE SAME IN ENGLISH

False, cruel, disappointed, Stung to th'Heart,
France quits the Warrior's for th'Assassin's Part.
To dirty Hands a dirty Bribe conveys,
Bids the low Street and lofty Palace Blaze.
Her Sons too Weak to Vanquish us alone,   5
She Hires the worst and basest of our own.—
Kneel France—a Suppliant conquers us with Ease,
We always Spare a Coward on his Knees.

8–18 June 1780.

COPY-TEXT: *H.* Collated: *U* (no variants). First printed by Hayley, 1804, iii. 33.

June 1780.

COPY-TEXT: *U.* Collated: *H.* First printed by Hayley, 1804, iii. 41.

Title] *H*; *no title in U*   4 And Gothic Scenes in British Rome displays. *H*

TRANSLATION OF AN EPITAPH FOR
WILLIAM NORTHCOT

Farewel! 'But not for ever,' Hope replies,
Trace but his steps and meet him in the skies!
There nothing shall renew our parting pain,
Thou shalt not wither, nor I weep again.

EPIGRAMMA CELEBRATISSIMUM
JOHANNIS DRYDEN IN EULOGIUM MILTONI
LATINE REDDITUM

Tres, tria, sed longe distantia Sæcula, Vates
Ostentant, tribus e Gentibus, eximios.
Græcia Sublimem, cum Majestate disertum
Roma tulit, felix Anglia, utrisque Parem.
Partubus ex binis Natura exhausta, coacta est   5
Tertius ut fieret, Consociare Duos.

A RIDDLE

I am just Two and Two, I am Warm, I am Cold,
And the Parent of Numbers that cannot be told.
I am Lawfull, Unlawfull, a Duty, a Fau'lt,
I am often Sold Dear, good for Nothing when Bought.

Before 2 July 1780.
COPY-TEXT: Hayley, 1804, iii. 40 (first printing).
Title] *supplied*

Early July 1780.
COPY-TEXT: *H*. Collated: *U*. First printed by Hayley, 1804, iii. 42.
Title] *no title in U*

Mid-June 1780.
COPY-TEXT: *H*. Collated: *U*; *P* (copy of letter to Newton, 30 July 1780). Lines 1-6 first
printed by Hayley, 1804, iii. 46; ll. 7-8 by Milford, 1905, p. 628.
Title] Riddle *U*; *no title in P*

An extra'ordinary Boon, and a Matter of Course,   5
And yielded with Pleasure when taken by Force.
Alike the Delight of the Poor and the Rich,
Tho' the Vulgar is apt to Present me his Breech.

TO MR. NEWTON ON HIS RETURN FROM
RAMSGATE

That Ocean you of late survey'd,
  Those Rocks I too have seen,
But I, Afflicted and dismay'd,
  You tranquil and Serene.

You from the Flood-controuling Steep   5
  Saw Stretch'd before your View,
With conscious Joy, the threat'ning Deep,
  No longer such to You.

To me, the Waves that ceaseless broke
  Upon the dang'rous Coast,   10
Hoarsely and ominously spoke
  Of all my Treasure lost.

Your Sea of Troubles you have pass'd,
  And found the peacefull Shore;
I Tempest-toss'd and wreck'd at last,   15
  Come Home to Port no more.

12–13 October 1780.

COPY-TEXT: *H*. First printed by Hayley, 1803, ii. 292.

5 Flood-controuling] *no hyphen in H*

THE YEARLY DISTRESS,
OR, TYTHING TIME AT STOCK

Come, Ponder well, for 'tis no Jest,
   To Laugh it would be Wrong,
The Troubles of a worthy Priest
   The Burthen of my Song.

This Priest he merry is and blithe   5
   Three Quarters of the Year,
But oh it cuts him like a Scythe
   When Tything Time draws near.

He then is full of Frights and Fears,
   As One at Point to Die,   10
And long before the Day appears
   He heaves up many a Sigh.

For then the Farmers come Jog, Jog,
   Along the Miry Road,
Each Heart as heavy as a Log,   15
   To make their Payments good.

In sooth, the Sorrow of such Days
   Is not to be Express'd,
When He that Takes and He that Pays
   Are both alike Distress'd.   20

Now all unwelcome at his Gates
   The clumsy Swains alight,
With ruefull Faces and bald Pates—
   He Trembles at the Sight.

Late October 1780.

COPY-TEXT: *U*. Collated: *H*. First printed in the *Public Advertiser*, 22 Aug. 1783; whence in
Gentleman's Magazine, liii (Aug. 1783), 695.

Title at Stock] *H*; at [Stock *deleted*]——*U*   1 for 'tis] it is *H*   22 alight] appear
deleted H

And well he may, for well he knows   25
    Each Bumkin of the Clan,
Instead of Paying what he Owes
    Will cheat him if he can.

So in they come, Each makes his Leg
    And Flings his Head before,   30
And looks as if he came to Beg,
    And not to quit a Score.

'And how does Miss and Madam do,
    The little Boy and all?'
All tight and well, and how do you   35
    Good Mr. Whatd'yecall?

The Dinner comes, and down they Sit,
    Was e'er such hungry Folk!
There's little Talking and no Wit,
    It is no Time to Joke.   40

One wipes his nose upon his Sleeve,
    One Spits upon the Floor,
Yet not to give Offence or grieve,
    Holds up the Cloth before.

The Punch goes round, and they are dull   45
    And Lumpish still as ever,
Like Barrels with their Bellies full
    They only Weigh the heavier.

At length the Busy Time begins,
    Come Neighbors we must Wag—   50
The Money chinks, down drop their Chins
    Each Lugging out his Bag.

One talks of Mildew and of Frost,
    And One of Storms of Hail,
And One, of Pigs that he has Lost   55
    By Maggots at the Tail.

45–8 this stanza added later in *H*   51 drop] fall *H*

Quoth One, a Rarer Man than You
    In Pulpit none shall Hear,
But yet, methinks, to tell you true,
    You Sell it plaguy dear.   60

Oh why are Farmers made so coarse,
    Or Clergy made so Fine,
A Kick that scarce would move a Horse,
    May Kill a Sound Divine.

Then let the Boobies Stay at Home,   65
    'Twould cost him, I dare say,
Less Trouble taking twice the Sum,
    Without the Clowns that Pay.

TO MISS CREUZÉ ON HER BIRTHDAY

How many between East and West,
    Disgrace their Parent Earth,
Whose Deeds constrain us to detest
    The Day that gave them Birth!

Not so, when Stella's natal Morn   5
    Revolving Months restore,
We can rejoice that *She* was Born,
    And wish *her Born, once more.*

65 Boobies] Loobies *H*

November 1780.
COPY-TEXT: *U*, whence first printed by Hayley, 1804, iii. 359–60.
Title Creuzé] Crewzé *U*

POEMS AGAINST
MADAN'S *THELYPHTHORA*
1780

LOVE ABUSED.
THE THOUGHT SUGGESTED BY
THELYPHTHORA

What is there in the Vale of Life
Half so delightfull as a Wife,
When Friendship, Love, and Peace combine
To Stamp the Marriage Bond Divine?
The Stream of pure and genuine Love   5
Derives it's Current from Above,
And Earth a Second Eden Shows
Where'er the Healing Water flows.
But Ah! if from the Dykes and Drains
Of sensual Nature's fev'rish Veins,   10
Lust like a lawless headstrong Flood
Impregnated with Ooze and Mud,
Descending fast on ev'ry Side,
Once Mingles with the Sacred Tide,
Farewell the Soul enliv'ning Scene!   15
The Banks that wore a Smiling Green
With rank Defilement overspread,
Bewail their Flow'ry Beauties dead;
The Stream polluted, dark and dull,
Diffused into a Stygian Pool,   20
Thro' Life's last melancholy Years
Is fed with everflowing Tears;
Complaints supply the Zephyr's Part,
And Sighs that Heave a Breaking Heart.

Spring 1780.
COPY-TEXT: *U*. Collated: *H*. First printed by Hayley, 1803, ii. 293.

Title] *sub-title not in H*   18 dead;] dead, *U, H*   19 dark] dead *deleted H*
22 Tears;] Tears, *U, H*

EPIGRAM ON *THELYPHTHORA*

Oh rare Device! the Wife betray'd,
The Modest, chaste, Domestic Woman,
To Save a worthless, Wanton Jade,
From being, what she would be, Common.

'IF JOHN MARRIES MARY, AND MARY ALONE'

If John marries Mary, and Mary alone,
'Tis a very good match between Mary and John.
Should John wed a score, oh! the claws and the scratches!
It can't be a match:—'tis a bundle of matches.

ANTITHELYPHTHORA,
A TALE IN VERSE

. . . Ah Miser
Quanta Laboras in Charybdi.
Hor. Lib. 1. Ode 27.

Airy del Castro was as bold a Knight
As ever Earn'd a Lady's Love in Fight.
Many he Sought, but One above the rest
His tender Heart Victoriously impress'd,

Spring 1780.

COPY-TEXT: *H*, whence first printed by Ryskamp, p. 236.

Summer (?) 1780.

COPY-TEXT: John Johnson, *Private Correspondence of William Cowper*, 1824, i. 179.
Collated: *GM* (*Gentleman's Magazine*, l (Dec. 1780), 582).

Title] *no title in 1824*; Impromptu, by a Gentleman, on reading the Chapter of Polygamy, in
Mr. Madan's Thelypthora. *GM*   3 But if John weds a score, oh! what claws and what
scratches! *GM*

Mid-November–26 November 1780.

COPY-TEXT: *H*, save for ll. 175–8, from *P* (letter to Newton, 21 Dec. 1780). Collated: *Anti-
Thelyphthora, A Tale. In Verse*, 1781 (first printing).

In Fairy Land was Born the matchless Dame,   5
The Land of Dreams, Hypothesis her Name.
There Fancy Nurs'd her in Ideal Bow'rs,
And laid her soft in Amaranthin Flow'rs,
Delighted with her Babe th'Inchantress Smiled,
And Graced with all her Gifts the Fav'rite Child.   10
Her Woo'd Sir Airy by Meand'ring Streams,
In Daily Musings, and in Nightly Dreams,
With all the Flow'rs he found, he Wove in Haste
Wreaths for her Brow, and Girdles for her Waist,
His Time, his Talents, and his ceaseless Care   15
All consecrated to Adorn the Fair,
No Pastime but with Her, he deign'd to take,
And if he Studied, Studied for her Sake.
And for Hypothesis was somewhat long,
Nor soft enough to Suit a Lover's Tongue,   20
He call'd her Posy with an am'rous Art,
And Grav'd it on a Gem, and wore it next his Heart.
    But She inconstant as the Beams that Play
On rippling Waters, in an April Day,
With many a freakish Trick deceiv'd his Pains,   25
To pathless Wilds and unfrequented Plains
Enticed him from his Oath of Knighthood far,
Forgetfull of the glorious Toils of War.
    'Tis thus the Tenderness that Love Inspires,
Too oft Betrays the Vot'ries of his Fires,   30
Born far away on elevated Wings,
Like wanton Doves they Sport in Airy Rings,
And Laws and Duties are neglected things.
    Nor He alone Address'd the wayward Fair,
Full many a Knight had been entangl'd there,   35
And still whoever woo'd her or Embraced,
On ev'ry Mind some mighty Spell she cast.
Some she would Teach (for she was wondrous Wise,
And made her Dupes see all things with her Eyes)
That Forms Material, whatsoe'er we Dream,   40
Are not at all, or Are not what they seem,

7] Fancy [(*illegible*) her *deleted*] Nurs'd her in [fair *over caret, erased*] Ideal Bow'rs, *and* There
added later at the beginning of the line H   27 Oath] oaths *1781*   32 Like wanton
Doves they Sport] They sport like wanton Doves *1781*   36 And] But *1781*

That Substances and Modes of ev'ry kind,
Are but Impressions on the passive Mind,
And He that Splits his Cranium, breaks at most,
A Fancied Head against a Fancied Post.   45
Others, that Earth, ere Sin had drown'd it all,
Was smooth and Even as an Iv'ry Ball,
That all the Various Beauties we Survey,
Hills, Valleys, Rivers, and the boundless Sea,
Are but Departures from the first Design,   50
Effects of Punishment and Wrath divine.
She Tutor'd some in Dædalus's Art,
And Promis'd they should Act his Wildgoose Part,
On Waxen Pinions Soar without a Fall,
Swift as the proudest Gander of them All.   55
    But Fate reserv'd Sir Airy to maintain
The wildest Project of her teeming Brain,
That Wedlock is not rig'rous as suppos'd,
But Man within a wider Pale inclos'd
May Rove at Will, where Appetite shall lead,   60
Free as the Lordly Bull that Ranges o'er the Mead.
That Forms and Rites are Tricks of Human Law,
As idle as the Chatt'ring of a Daw,
That lewd Incontinence and lawless Rape
Are Marriage in its true and proper Shape,   65
That Man by Faith and Truth is made a Slave,
The Ring a Bauble, and the Priest a Knave.
    Fair fall the Deed, the Knight exulting cried,
Now is the Time to make the Maid a Bride.
    'Twas on the Noon of an Autumnal Day,   70
October hight, but Mild and fair as May,
When scarlet Fruits the russet Hedge adorn,
And floating Films invelop ev'ry Thorn,
When gently as in June the Rivers Glide,
And only Miss the Flow'rs that grac'd their Side,   75
The Linnet twitter'd out his farewell Song,
With many a Chorister the Woods among,
On Southern Banks, the ruminating Sheep
Lay snug and warm, 'twas Summer's last, last Peep.

43 but] mere *deleted H*   55 Gander] Wildgoose *deleted H*   76 farewell]
parting *1781*   79 last, last] farewel *1781*

Propitious to his fond Intent there grew 80
An Arbor near at hand of thickest Yew,
With many a Boxen Bush close-clipt between,
And Philyrea of a gilded Green.
  But what old Chaucer's merry Page befits,
The chaster Muse of Modern Days, Omitts, 85
Suffice it then in decent Terms to say,
She saw, and turn'd her rosy Cheek away.
Small need of Pray'r Book or of Priest I ween,
Where Parties are agreed, retir'd the Scene,
Occasion prompt, and Appetite so keen. 90
Hypothesis (for with such Magic Pow'r
Fancy endued her in her natal Hour)
From many a steaming Lake and reeking Bog,
Bad rise in haste, a dank and drizzling Fog,
That Curtain'd round the Scene where they Repos'd, 95
And Wood and Lawn in dusky Folds inclos'd.
  Fear siez'd the trembling Sex, in ev'ry Grove
They wept the Wrongs of Honorable Love,
In vain, they cried, are Hymeneal Rites,
Vain our delusive Hope of constant Knights, 100
The Marriage Bond has lost its Pow'r to Bind,
And flutters loose the Sport of ev'ry Wind.
The Bride while yet her Bride's Attire is on,
Shall mourn her absent Lord, for He is gone
Satiate of Her, and weary of the same, 105
To distant Wilds, in quest of other Game.
Ye fair Circassians, all your Lutes employ,
Seraglios sing, and Harams dance for Joy,
For British Nymphs, whose Lords were lately true,
Nymphs quite as fair, and happier Once than You, 110
Honor, Esteem, and Confidence forgot
Feel All the Meanness of your slavish Lot.
Oh curst Hypothesis! your hellish Arts
Seduce our Husbands, and Estrange their Hearts—
Will none arise? no Knight, who still retains 115
The Blood of ancient Worthies in his Veins?
T'assert the Charter of the Chaste and Fair,

99 vain,] *1781*; *no comma in H*   102 flutters loose] flutt'ring Roves *deleted H*
109 lately] once so *deleted H*   114 Estrange] Entice *deleted H*

Find out her treach'rous Heart, and Plant a Dagger there?
 A Knight (can He that serves the Fair do less?)
Starts at the Call of Beauty in Distress;   120
And He that does not, whatsoe'er occurrs,
Is recreant, and unworthy of his Spurs.
 Full many a Champion bent on hardy Deed,
Call'd for his Arms and for his Princely Steed.
So swarm'd the Sabine youth, and grasp'd the Shield, 125
When Roman Rapine, by no Laws withheld,
Lest Rome should End with her first Founders' Lives,
Made half their Maids, sans Ceremony, Wives.
But not the Mitred few. The Soul their Charge,
They left these Bodily Concerns at Large,   130
Forms, or no Forms, Pluralities, or Pairs,
Right Reverend Sirs! was no Concern of theirs.
The rest Alert, and Active, as became
A Courteous Knighthood, caught the gen'rous Flame,
One was accoutred when the Cry began,   135
Knight of the Silver Moon, Sir Marmadan.
 Oft as his Patroness who Rules the Night,
Hangs out her Lamp in yon cærulean Height,
His Vow was, (and he well Perform'd his Vow)
Arm'd at all Points, with Terror on his Brow,   140
To Judge the Land, to Purge atrocious Crimes,
And quell the Shapeless Monsters of the Times.
For Cedars fam'd, fair Lebanon supplied
The wellpoised Lance that quiver'd at his Side:
Truth arm'd it with a Point so keen, so just,   145
No Spell or Charm was Proof against the Thrust.
He couch'd it firm upon his puissant Thigh,
And darting through his Helm an Eagle's Eye,
On all the Wings of Chivalry advanced,
To where the fond Sir Airy lay Entranced.   150
 He dreamt not of a Foe, or if his Fear
Foretold one, dreamt not of a Foe so near;
Far other Dreams his fev'rish Mind employ'd,

125–8] *added later in H* 126 withheld] witheld *H* 129 But not] All but
deleted H 133–4] *added later in H* 135 One was accoutred] [But *deleted*] One
was [mounted *deleted*] accoutred *H* 144 wellpoised] mighty *deleted H* 153 fev'rish
painfull *deleted H*

Of Rights restor'd, Variety Enjoy'd,
Of Virtue too well fenced to fear a Flaw,   155
Vice passing current by the Stamp of Law,
Large Population on a lib'ral Plan,
And Woman trembling at the Foot of Man.
How simple Wedlock Fornication Works,
And Christians marrying may convert the Turks.   160
  The Trumpet now spoke Marmadan at hand,
A Trumpet that was heard thro' all the Land,
His high-bred Steed Expands his Nostrils wide,
And Snorts aloud to cast the Mist aside,
But He the Virtues of his Lance to show,   165
Struck thrice the Point upon his Saddle Bow,
Three Sparks ensued that chaced it all away,
And set th'unseemly Pair in open Day.
'To Horse' he cried, 'or by this good Right Hand
And better Spear I smite you where you Stand.'   170
  Sir Airy not a whit dismay'd or scar'd,
Buckled his Helm, and to his Steed repair'd,
Whose Bridle, while he cropp'd the Grass below,
Hung not far off, upon a Myrtle Bough.
His Shield with Hebrew lore was scribbled round,   175
But snatching it impatient from the ground,
And slinging it revers'd upon his Arm,
He chang'd it to a Cabbalistic charm.
He mounts at once, such Confidence infus'd
Th'insidious Witch that had his Wits abus'd,   180
And She, regardless of her softer Kind,
Seiz'd fast the Saddle, and sprang up behind.
Oh Shame to Knighthood! his Assailant cried,
Oh Shame! ten thousand ecchoing Nymphs replied.
Placed with Advantage at his list'ning Ear,   185
She whisper'd still, that he had nought to fear,
That he was cased in such Enchanted Steel,
So polish'd and compact from Head to Heel,
Come Ten, Come Twenty, should an Army call

155] *added later to replace* Crack'd Reputations join'd without a Flaw, *deleted H*
156 Vice passing] [And *deleted*] Vice [made *deleted*] passing *H*   161] [But now
deleted] the Trumpet now spoke [*illegible, deleted* war *deleted*] Marmadan at hand, *H*
170] *cropped in H; punctuation supplied*   175–8] *P; not in H, 1781*

Thee to the Field, thou shouldst withstand them all.   190
  'By Dian's Beams, Sir Marmadan exclaim'd,
The Guiltiest still are ever least asham'd.
But Guard thee well, Expect no feign'd Attack,
And Guard beside, the Sorc'ress at thy Back.'
  He spoke indignant, and his Spurs applied,   195
Tho' little need, to his good Palfrey's Side,
The Barb sprang forward, and his Lord, whose Force
Was equal to the Swiftness of his Horse,
Rush'd with a Whirlwind's Fury on the Foe,
And Phineas-like, transfix'd them at a Blow.   200
  Then sang the Married and the Maiden Throng,
Love Graced the Theme, and Harmony the Song,
The Fauns and Satyrs, a lascivious Race,
Shriek'd at the Sight, and conscious, fled the Place.
And Hymen, trimming his dim Lamp anew,   205
His Snowy Mantle o'er his Shoulders threw,
He turn'd and view'd it oft on ev'ry Side,
And redd'ning with a just and gen'rous Pride,
Bless'd the glad Beams of that propitious Day,
The Spot he Loath'd so much, for Ever cleans'd away.   210

205 Lamp] torch *H*

P O E M S

by

WILLIAM COWPER,

OF THE INNER TEMPLE, ESQ.

Shut again the reflecting glass, unbidden down
Soft repeating, for feeling's purple hue,
Often reflecting her rich purple the same
Begins, some, some not into a field, with her, has, with,

So water trembling in a polish'd vase,
Reflects the beam that plays upon its face,
The sportive light, uncertain where it falls,
Now strikes the roof, now flashes on the walls

quotation lines

LONDON:

Printed for J. Johnson, No. 72, St. Paul's Church Yard.

1782.

P O E M S

B Y

WILLIAM COWPER,

Of the INNER TEMPLE, Esq.

Sicut aquæ tremulum labris ubi lumen ahenis
Sole repercuſſum, aut radiantis imagine lunæ,
Omnia pervolitat laté loca, jamque ſub auras
Erigitur, ſummique ferit laquearia tecti. VIRG. ÆN. VIII.

So water trembling in a poliſh'd vaſe,
Reflects the beam that plays upon its face,
The ſportive light, uncertain where it falls,
Now ſtiikes the roof, now flaſhes on the walls.

Nous ſommes nés pour la vérité, et nous ne pouvons ſouffrir ſon
abord. les figures, les paraboles, les emblémes, ſont toujours
des ornements néceſſaires pour qu'elle puiſſe s'annoncer. et ſoit
quon craigne qu'elle ne découvre trop bruſquement le défaut
qu'on voudroit cacher, ou qu'enfin elle n'inſtruiſe avec trop
peu de ménagement, ou veut, en la recevant, qu'elle ſoit
déguiſée.

CARACCIOLI.

L O N D O N:

Printed for J. JOHNSON, No. 72, St. Paul's Church Yard.

1782.

TABLE TALK

Si te fortè meæ gravis uret sarcina chartæ
Abjicito.— — — Hor. Lib. i. Epis. 13.

A. You told me, I remember, glory built
On selfish principles, is shame and guilt.
The deeds that men admire as half divine,
Stark naught, because corrupt in their design.
Strange doctrine this! that without scruple tears   5
The laurel that the very light'ning spares,
Brings down the warrior's trophy to the dust,
And eats into his bloody sword like rust.
   B. I grant, that men continuing what they are,
Fierce, avaricious, proud, there must be war.   10
And never meant the rule should be applied
To him that fights with justice on his side.
   Let laurels, drench'd in pure Parnassian dews,

c. 21 January–*c.* 4 February 1781.

COPY-TEXT: *1782*, pp. 1–40 (first printing). Collated: *H*; for ll. 13–28 only: *A*; *P* (letter to
Newton, 18 Mar. 1781).

Motto] *not in H*
13–28 *replace the following passage in H*:

           When Western colonies in Arms unite
           To rob their royal master of his right,
           When France embark'd in their rebellious cause
           Stands up, forsooth, for Liberty and Laws,
           When Brother Spain for kindred sake combines
           In aid of her iniquitous designs;
           When Tradesman Hans, who charitably sends
           Arms to his foes, Defiance to his friends,
           Sullen and clumsy clubs his dirty fist,
           And sighs for knavish gains that he has miss'd,
           Like a detected traytor knits his brows,
           And means to prove his Honesty by blows;
           When arm'd Neutralities in league agree,
           And send three Ships and half a Ship to Sea,
           Bold to defy us in so dark a day,
            [*one line cropped at foot of page*]
           I wish my gallant Country large redress,
           And Him that rules it Honor and Success.

Reward his mem'ry, dear to ev'ry muse,
Who, with a courage of unshaken root,   15
In honour's field advancing his firm foot,
Plants it upon the line that justice draws,
And will prevail or perish in her cause.
'Tis to the virtues of such men, man owes
His portion in the good that heav'n bestows,   20
And when recording history displays
Feats of renown, though wrought in antient days,
Tells of a few stout hearts that fought and dy'd
Where duty plac'd them, at their country's side,
The man that is not mov'd with what he reads,   25
That takes not fire at their heroic deeds,
Unworthy of the blessings of the brave,
Is base in kind, and born to be a slave.
    But let eternal infamy pursue
The wretch to nought but his ambition true,   30
Who, for the sake of filling with one blast
The post horns of all Europe, lays her waste.
Think yourself station'd on a tow'ring rock,
To see a people scatter'd like a flock,
Some royal mastiff panting at their heels,   35
With all the savage thirst a tyger feels,
Then view him self-proclaim'd in a gazette,
Chief monster that has plagu'd the nations yet,
The globe and sceptre in such hands misplac'd,
Those ensigns of dominion, how disgrac'd!   40
The glass that bids man mark the fleeting hour,
And death's own scythe would better speak his pow'r,
Then grace the boney phantom in their stead
With the king's shoulder knot and gay cockade,
Cloath the twin brethren in each other's dress,   45
The same their occupation and success.
    A. 'Tis your belief the world was made for man,
Kings do but reason on the self same plan,
Maintaining your's you cannot their's condemn,

15 of unshaken root] sound both heart and root *A* ; of the noblest root *P*   30 nought]
naught *1782, corrected in Errata*   33 a tow'ring] [some *deleted*] a tow'ring *H*
38 monster] Devil *H*   39 such] those *deleted H*   misplac'd] disgrac'd *deleted H*
44 gay] fierce *H*

Who think, or seem to think, man made for them.   50
    B. Seldom, alas! the power of logic reigns
With much sufficiency in royal brains.
Such reas'ning falls like an inverted cone,
Wanting its proper base to stand upon.
Man made for kings! those optics are but dim   55
That tell you so—say rather, they for him.
That were indeed a king-enobling thought,
Could they, or would they, reason as they ought.
The diadem with mighty projects lin'd,
To catch renown by ruining mankind,   60
Is worth, with all its gold and glitt'ring store,
Just what the toy will sell for and no more.
    Oh! bright occasions of dispensing good,
How seldom used, how little understood!
To pour in virtue's lap her just reward,   65
Keep vice restrain'd behind a double guard,
To quell the faction that affronts the throne,
By silent magnanimity alone;
To nurse with tender care the thriving arts,
Watch every beam philosophy imparts;   70
To give religion her unbridl'd scope,
Nor judge by statute a believer's hope;
With close fidelity and love unfeign'd,
To keep the matrimonial bond unstain'd;
Covetous only of a virtuous praise,   75
His life a lesson to the land he sways;
To touch the sword with conscientious awe,
Nor draw it but when duty bids him draw,
To sheath it in the peace-restoring close,
With joy, beyond what victory bestows,   80
Blest country! where these kingly glories shine,
Blest England! if this happiness be thine.
    A. Guard what you say, the patriotic tribe

---

55 kings!] kings? H   59–62] *added later in H, apparently to replace the following lines*
which are not deleted:

        How worthless is the costliest Regal crown,
        That teems with stratagems to catch Renown,
        Defective in Benevolence, the rest
        Is all mere Lapidary's ware at best.

82 this] that H

Will sneer and charge you with a bribe.—B. A bribe?
The worth of his three kingdoms I defy,   85
To lure me to the baseness of a lie.
And of all lies (be that one poet's boast)
The lie that flatters I abhor the most.
Those arts be their's that hate his gentle reign,
But he that loves him has no need to feign.   90
    A. Your smooth eulogium to one crown address'd,
Seems to imply a censure on the rest.
    B. Quevedo, as he tells his sober tale,
Ask'd, when in hell, to see the royal jail,
Approv'd their method in all other things,   95
But where, good Sir, do you confine your kings?
There—said his guide, the groupe is full in view.
Indeed? Replied the Don—there are but few.
His black interpreter the charge disdain'd—
Few, fellow? There are all that ever reign'd.   100
Wit undistinguishing is apt to strike
The guilty and not guilty, both alike.
I grant the sarcasm is too severe,
And we can readily refute it here,
While Alfred's name, the father of his age,   105
And the Sixth Edward's grace th' historic page.
    A. Kings then at last have but the lot of all,
By their own conduct they must stand or fall.
    B. True. While they live, the courtly laureat pays
His quit-rent ode, his pepper-corn of praise,   110
And many a dunce whose fingers itch to write,
Adds, as he can, his tributary mite;
A subject's faults, a subject may proclaim,
A monarch's errors are forbidden game.
Thus free from censure, over-aw'd by fear,   115
And prais'd for virtues that they scorn to wear,
The fleeting forms of majesty engage
Respect, while stalking o'er life's narrow stage,

89 Those arts be their's] Lies may save them *H*   93–6 *added later in H to replace the following deleted lines*:
       B—Quevedo, when in Hell, with curious mind
       Enquir'd, where, tell me, are your Kings confin'd?
99 His] The *H*   the charge] his [Guest *deleted*] charge *H*   101] *indented in H*
107 Kings] King's *1782*

Then leave their crimes for history to scan,
And ask with busy scorn, Was this the man?   120
  I pity kings whom worship waits upon
Obsequious, from the cradle to the throne,
Before whose infant eyes the flatt'rer bows,
And binds a wreath about their baby brows.
Whom education stiffens into state,   125
And death awakens from that dream too late.
Oh! if servility with supple knees,
Whose trade it is to smile, to crouch, to please;
If smooth dissimulation, skill'd to grace
A devil's purpose with an angel's face;   130
If smiling peeresses and simp'ring peers,
Incompassing his throne a few short years;
If the gilt carriage and the pamper'd steed,
That wants no driving and disdains the lead;
If guards, mechanically form'd in ranks,   135
Playing, at beat of drum, their martial pranks;
Should'ring and standing as if struck to stone,
While condescending majesty looks on;
If monarchy consist in such base things,
Sighing, I say again, I pity kings!   140
  To be suspected, thwarted, and withstood,
Ev'n when he labours for his country's good,
To see a band call'd patriot for no cause,
But that they catch at popular applause,
Careless of all th' anxiety he feels,   145
Hook disappointment on the public wheels,
With all their flippant fluency of tongue,
Most confident, when palpably most wrong,
If this be kingly, then farewell for me
All kingship, and may I be poor and free.   150
  To be the Table Talk of clubs up stairs,
To which th' unwash'd artificer repairs,
T' indulge his genius after long fatigue,
By diving into cabinet intrigue,
(For what kings deem a toil, as well they may,   155
To him is relaxation and mere play)

To win no praise when well-wrought plans prevail,
But to be rudely censur'd when they fail,
To doubt the love his fav'rites may pretend,
And in reality to find no friend,   160
If he indulge a cultivated taste,
His gall'ries with the works of art well grac'd,
To hear it call'd extravagance and waste,
If these attendants, and if such as these,
Must follow royalty, then welcome ease;   165
However humble and confin'd the sphere,
Happy the state that has not these to fear.
    A. Thus men whose thoughts contemplative have dwelt,
On situations that they never felt,
Start up sagacious, cover'd with the dust   170
Of dreaming study and pedantic rust,
And prate and preach about what others prove,
As if the world and they were hand and glove.
Leave kingly backs to cope with kingly cares,
They have their weight to carry, subjects their's;   175
Poets, of all men, ever least regret
Increasing taxes and the nation's debt.
Could you contrive the payment, and rehearse
The mighty plan, oracular, in verse,
No bard, howe'er majestic, old or new,   180
Should claim my fixt attention more than you.
    B. Not Brindley nor Bridgewater would essay
To turn the course of Helicon that way;
Nor would the nine consent, the sacred tide
Should purl amidst the traffic of Cheapside,   185
Or tinkle in 'Change Alley, to amuse
The leathern ears of stock-jobbers and jews.
    A. Vouchsafe, at least, to pitch the key of rhime
To themes more pertinent, if less sublime.
When ministers and ministerial arts,   190
Patriots who love good places at their hearts,
When Admirals extoll'd for standing still,
Or doing nothing with a deal of skill;
Gen'rals who will not conquer when they may,
Firm friends to peace, to pleasure, and good pay,   195

182 Bridgewater] Bridgwater *H*   191] *cropped in H*

When freedom wounded almost to despair,
Though discontent alone can find out where,
When themes like these employ the poet's tongue,
I hear as mute as if a syren sung.
Or tell me if you can, what pow'r maintains   200
A Briton's scorn of arbitrary chains?
That were a theme might animate the dead,
And move the lips of poets cast in lead.
    B. The cause, tho' worth the search, may yet elude
Conjecture and remark, however shrewd.   205
They take, perhaps, a well-directed aim,
Who seek it in his climate and his frame.
Lib'ral in all things else, yet nature here
With stern severity deals out the year.
Winter invades the spring, and often pours   210
A chilling flood on summer's drooping flow'rs,
Unwelcome vapors quench autumnal beams,
Ungenial blasts attending, curl the streams,
The peasants urge their harvest, plie the fork
With double toil, and shiver at their work,   215
Thus with a rigor, for his good design'd,
She rears her fav'rite man of all mankind.
His form robust and of elastic tone,
Proportion'd well, half muscle and half bone,
Supplies with warm activity and force   220
A mind well lodg'd, and masculine of course.
Hence liberty, sweet liberty inspires,
And keeps alive his fierce but noble fires.
Patient of constitutional controul,
He bears it with meek manliness of soul,   225
But if authority grow wanton, woe
To him that treads upon his free-born toe,
One step beyond the bound'ry of the laws
Fires him at once in freedom's glorious cause.
Thus proud prerogative, not much rever'd,   230
Is seldom felt, though sometimes seen and heard;
And in his cage, like parrot fine and gay,
Is kept to strut, look big, and talk away.
    Born in a climate softer far than our's,

199 I hear] ear *1782, corrected in Errata*   a syren] an Angel *H*   208] *indented in H*

Not form'd like us, with such Herculean pow'rs,   235
The Frenchman, easy, debonair and brisk,
Give him his lass, his fiddle and his frisk,
Is always happy, reign whoever may,
And laughs the sense of mis'ry far away.
He drinks his simple bev'rage with a gust,   240
And feasting on an onion and a crust,
We never feel th' alacrity and joy
With which he shouts and carols, *Vive le Roy*,
Fill'd with as much true merriment and glee,
As if he heard his king say—Slave be free.   245
    Thus happiness depends, as nature shews,
Less on exterior things than most suppose.
Vigilant over all that he has made,
Kind Providence attends with gracious aid,
Bids equity throughout his works prevail,   250
And weighs the nations in an even scale;
He can encourage slav'ry to a smile,
And fill with discontent a British isle.
    A. Freeman and slave then, if the case be such,
Stand on a level, and you prove too much.   255
If all men indiscriminately share,
His fost'ring pow'r and tutelary care,
As well be yok'd by despotism's hand,
As dwell at large in Britain's charter'd land.
    B. No. Freedom has a thousand charms to show,   260
That slaves, howe'er contented, never know.
The mind attains beneath her happy reign,
The growth that nature meant she should attain.
The varied fields of science, ever new,
Op'ning and wider op'ning on her view,   265
She ventures onward with a prosp'rous force,
While no base fear impedes her in her course.
Religion, richest favour of the skies,
Stands most reveal'd before the freeman's eyes;
No shades of superstition blot the day,   270
Liberty chaces all that gloom away;
The soul, emancipated, unoppress'd,
Free to prove all things and hold fast the best,

257 pow'r] hand *deleted* H

Learns much, and to a thousand list'ning minds,
Communicates with joy the good she finds.   275
Courage, in arms and ever prompt to show
His manly forehead to the fiercest foe;
Glorious in war, but for the sake of peace,
His spirits rising as his toils increase,
Guards well what arts and industry have won,   280
And freedom claims him for her first-born son.
Slaves fight for what were better cast away,
The chain that binds them, and a tyrant's sway,
But they that fight for freedom, undertake
The noblest cause mankind can have at stake,   285
Religion, virtue, truth, whate'er we call
A blessing, freedom is the pledge of all.
Oh liberty! the pris'ner's pleasing dream,
The poet's muse, his passion and his theme,
Genius is thine, and thou art fancy's nurse,   290
Lost without thee th' ennobling pow'rs of verse,
Heroic song from thy free touch acquires
Its clearest tone, the rapture it inspires;
Place me where winter breathes his keenest air,
And I will sing if liberty be there;   295
And I will sing at liberty's dear feet,
In Afric's torrid clime or India's fiercest heat.
    A. Sing where you please, in such a cause I grant
An English Poet's privilege to rant,
But is not freedom, at least is not our's   300
Too apt to play the wanton with her pow'rs,
Grow freakish, and o'er leaping ev'ry mound
Spread anarchy and terror all around?
    B. Agreed. But would you sell or slay your horse
For bounding and curvetting in his course;   305
Or if, when ridden with a careless rein,
He break away, and seek the distant plain?
No. His high mettle, under good controul,
Gives him Olympic speed, and shoots him to the goal.
    Let discipline employ her wholesome arts,   310
Let magistrates alert perform their parts,

276 Courage, in arms and] *H*; Courage in arms, and *1782*   278–9] *added later in H*
308 mettle, under] *H*; mettle under *1782*

Not skulk or put on a prudential mask,
As if their duty were a desp'rate task;
Let active laws apply the needful curb
To guard the peace that riot would disturb,   315
And liberty preserv'd from wild excess,
Shall raise no feuds for armies to suppress.
When tumult lately burst his prison door,
And set Plebeian thousands in a roar,
When he usurp'd authority's just place,   320
And dar'd to look his master in the face,
When the rude rabble's watch-word was, destroy,
And blazing London seem'd a second Troy,
Liberty blush'd and hung her drooping head,
Beheld their progress with the deepest dread,   325
Blush'd that effects like these she should produce,
Worse than the deeds of galley-slaves broke loose.
She loses in such storms her very name,
And fierce licentiousness should bear the blame.

    Incomparable gem! thy worth untold,   330
Cheap, though blood-bought, and thrown away when sold;
May no foes ravish thee, and no false friend
Betray thee, while professing to defend;
Prize it ye ministers, ye monarchs spare,
Ye patriots guard it with a miser's care.   335
    A. Patriots, alas! the few that have been found
Where most they flourish, upon English ground,
The country's need have scantily supplied,
And the last left the scene, when Chatham died.
    B. Not so—the virtue still adorns our age,   340
Though the chief actor died upon the stage.
In him, Demosthenes was heard again,
Liberty taught him her Athenian strain;
She cloath'd him with authority and awe,
Spoke from his lips, and in his looks, gave law.   345
His speech, his form, his action, full of grace,
And all his country beaming in his face,
He stood, as some inimitable hand
Would strive to make a Paul or Tully stand.
No sycophant or slave that dar'd oppose   350
Her sacred cause, but trembl'd when he rose,

And every venal stickler for the yoke,
Felt himself crush'd at the first word he spoke.
  Such men are rais'd to station and command,
When providence means mercy to a land.   355
He speaks, and they appear; to him they owe
Skill to direct, and strength to strike the blow,
To manage with address, to seize with pow'r
The crisis of a dark decisive hour.
So Gideon earn'd a vict'ry not his own,   360
Subserviency his praise, and that alone.
  Poor England! thou art a devoted deer,
Beset with ev'ry ill but that of fear.
The nations hunt; all mark thee for a prey,
They swarm around thee, and thou standst at bay.   365
Undaunted still, though wearied and perplex'd,
Once Chatham sav'd thee, but who saves thee next?
Alas! the tide of pleasure sweeps along
All that should be the boast of British song.
'Tis not the wreath that once adorn'd thy brow,   370
The prize of happier times will serve thee now.
Our ancestry, a gallant christian race,
Patterns of ev'ry virtue, ev'ry grace,
Confess'd a God, they kneel'd before they fought,
And praised him in the victories he wrought.   375
Now from the dust of antient days bring forth
Their sober zeal, integrity and worth,
Courage, ungrac'd by these, affronts the skies,
Is but the fire without the sacrifice.
The stream that feeds the well-spring of the heart   380
Not more invigorates life's noblest part,
Than virtue quickens with a warmth divine,
The pow'rs that sin has brought to a decline.
  A. Th' inestimable estimate of Brown,
Rose like a paper-kite, and charm'd the town;   385
But measures plann'd and executed well,
Shifted the wind that rais'd it, and it fell.
He trod the very self-same ground you tread,
And victory refuted all he said.
  B. And yet his judgment was not fram'd amiss,   390

Its error, if it err'd, was merely this—
He thought the dying hour already come,
And a complete recov'ry struck him dumb.
    But that effeminacy, folly, lust,
Enervate and enfeeble, and needs must,   395
And that a nation shamefully debas'd,
Will be despis'd and trampl'd on at last,
Unless sweet penitence her pow'rs renew,
Is truth, if history itself be true.
There is a time, and justice marks the date,   400
For long-forbearing clemency to wait,
That hour elaps'd, th'incurable revolt
Is punish'd, and down comes the thunder-bolt.
If mercy *then* put by the threat'ning blow,
Must she perform the same kind office *now*?   405
May she, and if offended heav'n be still
Accessible and pray'r prevail, she will.
'Tis not however insolence and noise,
The tempest of tumultuary joys,
Nor is it yet despondence and dismay,   410
Will win her visits, or engage her stay,
Pray'r only, and the penitential tear,
Can call her smiling down, and fix her here.
    But when a country, (one that I could name)
In prostitution sinks the sense of shame,   415
When infamous venality grown bold,
Writes on his bosom, *to be lett or sold*;
When perjury, that heav'n defying vice,
Sells oaths by tale, and at the lowest price,
Stamps God's own name upon a lie just made,   420
To turn a penny in the way of trade;
When av'rice starves, and never hides his face,
Two or three millions of the human race,
And not a tongue enquires, how, where, or when,
Though conscience will have twinges now and then;   425
When profanation of the sacred cause
In all its parts, times, ministry and laws,
Bespeaks a land once christian, fall'n and lost
In all that wars against that title most,
What follows next let cities of great name,   430

And regions long since desolate proclaim,
Nineveh, Babylon, and antient Rome,
Speak to the present times and times to come,
They cry aloud in ev'ry careless ear,
Stop, while ye may, suspend your mad career;   435
O learn from our example and our fate,
Learn wisdom and repentance e'er too late.
    Not only vice disposes and prepares
The mind that slumbers sweetly in her snares,
To stoop to tyranny's usurp'd command,   440
And bend her polish'd neck beneath his hand,
(A dire effect, by one of nature's laws
Unchangeably connected with its cause)
But providence himself will intervene
To throw his dark displeasure o'er the scene.   445
All are his instruments; each form of war,
What burns at home, or threatens from afar,
Nature in arms, her elements at strife,
The storms that overset the joys of life,
Are but his rods to scourge a guilty land,   450
And waste it at the bidding of his hand.
He gives the word, and mutiny soon roars
In all her gates, and shakes her distant shores,
The standards of all nations are unfurl'd,
She has one foe, and that one foe, the world.   455
And if he doom that people with a frown,
And mark them with the seal of wrath, press'd down,
Obduracy takes place; callous and tough
The reprobated race grows judgment proof:
Earth shakes beneath them, and heav'n roars above,   460
But nothing scares them from the course they love;
To the lascivious pipe and wanton song
That charm down fear, they frolic it along,
With mad rapidity and unconcern,
Down to the gulph from which is no return.   465
They trust in navies, and their navies fail,
God's curse can cast away ten thousand sail;
They trust in armies, and their courage dies,
In wisdom, wealth, in fortune, and in lies;

459 race] heart *H*

But all they trust in, withers, as it must,   470
When he commands, in whom they place no trust.
Vengeance at last pours down upon their coast,
A long despis'd, but now victorious host,
Tyranny sends the chain that must abridge
The noble sweep of all their privilege,   475
Gives liberty the last, the mortal shock,
Slips the slave's collar on, and snaps the lock.
    A. Such lofty strains embellish what you teach,
Mean you to prophecy, or but to preach?
    B. I know the mind that feels indeed the fire   480
The muse imparts, and can command the lyre,
Acts with a force, and kindles with a zeal,
Whate'er the theme, that others never feel.
If human woes her soft attention claim,
A tender sympathy pervades the frame,   485
She pours a sensibility divine
Along the nerve of ev'ry feeling line.
But if a deed not tamely to be borne,
Fire indignation and a sense of scorn,
The strings are swept with such a pow'r, so loud,   490
The storm of music shakes th' astonish'd crowd.
So when remote futurity is brought
Before the keen enquiry of her thought,
A terrible sagacity informs
The poet's heart, he looks to distant storms,   495
He hears the thunder e'er the tempest low'rs,
And arm'd with strength surpassing human pow'rs,
Seizes events as yet unknown to man,
And darts his soul into the dawning plan.
Hence, in a Roman mouth, the graceful name   500
Of prophet and of poet was the same,
Hence British poets too the priesthood shar'd,
And ev'ry hallow'd druid was a bard.
But no prophetic fires to me belong,
I play with syllables, and sport in song.   505
    A. At Westminster, where little poets strive
To set a distich upon six and five,

473 victorious] forgotten *H*   475 lock.] lock, *1782, corrected in Errata*   500 grace-
ful] sacre[d] *deleted H*   504 fires] pow'rs *H*

Where discipline helps op'ning buds of sense,
And makes his pupils proud with silver-pence,
I was a poet too—but modern taste   510
Is so refin'd and delicate and chaste,
That verse, whatever fire the fancy warms,
Without a creamy smoothness has no charms.
Thus, all success depending on an ear,
And thinking I might purchase it too dear,   515
If sentiment were sacrific'd to sound,
And truth cut short to make a period round,
I judg'd a man of sense could scarce do worse,
Than caper in the morris-dance of verse.
    B. Thus reputation is a spur to wit,   520
And some wits flag through fear of losing it.
Give me the line, that plows its stately course
Like a proud swan, conq'ring the stream by force.
That like some cottage beauty strikes the heart,
Quite unindebted to the tricks of art.   525
When labour and when dullness, club in hand,
Like the two figures at St. Dunstan's stand,
Beating alternately, in measur'd time,
The clock-work tintinabulum of rhime,
Exact and regular the sounds will be,   530
But such mere quarter-strokes are not for me.
    From him who rears a poem lank and long,
To him who strains his all into a song,
Perhaps some bonny Caledonian air,
All birks and braes, though he was never there,   535
Or having whelp'd a prologue with great pains,
Feels himself spent, and fumbles for his brains;
A prologue interdash'd with many a stroke,
An art contriv'd to advertise a joke,
So that the jest is clearly to be seen,   540
Not in the words—but in the gap between,
Manner is all in all, whate'er is writ,
The substitute for genius, sense, and wit.
    To dally much with subjects mean and low,
Proves that the mind is weak, or makes it so.   545
Neglected talents rust into decay,

538–41] *not in* H

And ev'ry effort ends in push-pin play.
The man that means success, should soar above
A soldier's feather, or a lady's glove,
Else summoning the muse to such a theme,   550
The fruit of all her labour is whipt-cream.
As if an eagle flew aloft, and then—
Stoop'd from his highest pitch to pounce a wren.
As if the poet purposing to wed,
Should carve himself a wife in gingerbread.   555
    Ages elaps'd e'er Homer's lamp appear'd,
And ages e'er the Mantuan swan was heard,
To carry nature lengths unknown before,
To give a Milton birth, ask'd ages more.
Thus genius rose and set at order'd times,   560
And shot a day-spring into distant climes,
Ennobling ev'ry region that he chose,
He sunk in Greece, in Italy he rose,
And tedious years of Gothic darkness pass'd,
Emerg'd all splendor in our isle at last.   565
Thus lovely Halcyons dive into the main,
Then show far off their shining plumes again.
    A. Is genius only found in epic lays?
Prove this, and forfeit all pretence to praise.
Make their heroic pow'rs your own at once,   570
Or candidly confess yourself a dunce.
    B. These were the chief, each interval of night
Was grac'd with many an undulating light;
In less illustrious bards his beauty shone
A meteor or a star, in these, the sun.   575
    The nightingale may claim the topmost bough,
While the poor grasshopper must chirp below.
Like him unnotic'd, I, and such as I,
Spread little wings, and rather skip than fly,
Perch'd on the meagre produce of the land,   580
An ell or two of prospect we command,
But never peep beyond the thorny bound
Or oaken fence that hems the paddock round.
    In Eden e'er yet innocence of heart

547 play.] play, *1782, corrected in Errata*   579 and] but *H*   583 paddock] *H*;
paddoc *1782*

Had faded, poetry was not an art;   585
Language above all teaching, or if taught,
Only by gratitude and glowing thought,
Elegant as simplicity, and warm
As exstasy, unmanacl'd by form,
Not prompted as in our degen'rate days,   590
By low ambition and the thirst of praise,
Was natural as is the flowing stream,
And yet magnificent, a God the theme.
That theme on earth exhausted, though above
'Tis found as everlasting as his love,   595
Man lavish'd all his thoughts on human things,
The feats of heroes and the wrath of kings,
But still while virtue kindled his delight,
The song was moral, and so far was right.
'Twas thus till luxury seduc'd the mind,   600
To joys less innocent, as less refin'd,
Then genius danc'd a bacchanal, he crown'd
The brimming goblet, seiz'd the thyrsus, bound
His brows with ivy, rush'd into the field
Of wild imagination, and there reel'd   605
The victim of his own lascivious fires,
And dizzy with delight, profan'd the sacred wires.
   Anacreon, Horace, play'd in Greece and Rome
This Bedlam part; and, others nearer home.
When Cromwell fought for pow'r, and while he reign'd   610
The proud protector of the pow'r he gain'd,
Religion harsh, intolerant, austere,
Parent of manners like herself severe,
Drew a rough copy of the Christian face
Without the smile, the sweetness, or the grace;   615
The dark and sullen humour of the time
Judg'd ev'ry effort of the muse a crime;
Verse in the finest mould of fancy cast,
Was lumber in an age so void of taste:
But when the second Charles assum'd the sway,   620
And arts reviv'd beneath a softer day,

589 unmanacl'd] and unmanacl'd H   609 and] *written over illegible deleted word in H*
home.] home, *1782, corrected in Errata*   618 And verse with all the charms of Genius
grac'd, H

811875   K

Then like a bow long forc'd into a curve,
The mind releas'd from too constrain'd a nerve,
Flew to its first position with a spring
That made the vaulted roofs of pleasure ring.   625
His court, the dissolute and hateful school
Of wantonness, where vice was taught by rule,
Swarm'd with a scribbling herd as deep inlaid
With brutal lust as ever Circe made.
From these a long succession, in the rage   630
Of rank obscenity debauch'd their age,
Nor ceas'd, 'till ever anxious to redress
Th' abuses of her sacred charge, the press,
The muse instructed a well nurtur'd train
Of abler votaries to cleanse the stain,   635
And claim the palm for purity of song,
That lewdness had usurp'd and worn so long.
Then decent pleasantry and sterling sense
That neither gave nor would endure offence,
Whipp'd out of sight with satyr just and keen   640
The puppy pack that had defil'd the scene.
    In front of these came Addison. In him
Humour in holiday and sightly trim,
Sublimity and Attic taste combin'd,
To polish, furnish, and delight the mind.   645
Then Pope, as harmony itself exact,
In verse well disciplin'd, complete, compact,
Gave virtue and morality a grace
That quite eclipsing pleasure's painted face,
Levied a tax of wonder and applause,   650
Ev'n on the fools that trampl'd on their laws.
But he (his musical finesse was such,
So nice his ear, so delicate his touch)
Made poetry a mere mechanic art,
And ev'ry warbler has his tune by heart.   655
Nature imparting her satyric gift,
Her serious mirth, to Arbuthnot and Swift,
With droll sobriety they rais'd a smile

632 anxious] ready *H*   635 votaries to cleanse] Bards to cleanse away *H*   639 neither]
never *1782, corrected in Errata*   644 Attic] *H*; attic *1782*   656 satyric]
Sardonic *H*

At folly's cost, themselves unmov'd the while.
That constellation set, the world in vain 660
Must hope to look upon their like again.
    A. Are we then left—*B.* Not wholly in the dark,
Wit now and then, struck smartly, shows a spark,
Sufficient to redeem the modern race
From total night and absolute disgrace. 665
While servile trick and imitative knack
Confine the million in the beaten track,
Perhaps some courser who disdains the road,
Snuffs up the wind and flings himself abroad.
    Cotemporaries all surpass'd, see one, 670
Short his career, indeed, but ably run.
Churchill, himself unconscious of his pow'rs,
In penury consum'd his idle hours,
And like a scatter'd seed at random sown,
Was left to spring by vigor of his own. 675
Lifted at length by dignity of thought,
And dint of genius to an affluent lot,
He laid his head in luxury's soft lap,
And took too often there his easy nap.
If brighter beams than all he threw not forth, 680
'Twas negligence in him, not want of worth.
Surly and slovenly and bold and coarse,
Too proud for art, and trusting in mere force,
Spendthrift alike of money and of wit,
Always at speed and never drawing bit, 685
He struck the lyre in such a careless mood,
And so disdain'd the rules he understood,
The laurel seem'd to wait on his command,
He snatch'd it rudely from the muse's hand.
    Nature exerting an unwearied pow'r, 690
Forms, opens and gives scent to ev'ry flow'r,
Spreads the fresh verdure of the field, and leads
The dancing Naiads through the dewy meads,
She fills profuse ten thousand little throats
With music, modulating all their notes, 695
And charms the woodland scenes and wilds unknown,

---

659 *cropped in H*   666–9 *added later in H*   675 by vigor of his own.] unlook'd
for and alone, *H*

With artless airs and concerts of her own;
But seldom (as if fearful of expence)
Vouchsafes to man a poet's just pretence.
Fervency, freedom, fluency of thought,   700
Harmony, strength, words exquisitely sought,
Fancy that from the bow that spans the sky,
Brings colours dipt in heav'n that never die,
A soul exalted above earth, a mind
Skill'd in the characters that form mankind,   705
And as the sun in rising beauty dress'd,
Looks to the westward from the dappl'd east,
And marks, whatever clouds may interpose,
E'er yet his race begins, its glorious close,
An eye like his to catch the distant goal,   710
Or e'er the wheels of verse begin to roll,
Like his to shed illuminating rays
On ev'ry scene and subject it surveys,
Thus grac'd the man asserts a poet's name,
And the world chearfully admits the claim.   715
    Pity! Religion has so seldom found
A skilful guide into poetic ground,
The flow'rs would spring where'er she deign'd to stray,
And ev'ry muse attend her in her way.
Virtue indeed meets many a rhiming friend,   720
And many a compliment politely penn'd,
But unattir'd in that becoming vest
Religion weaves for her, and half undress'd,
Stands in the desart shiv'ring and forlorn,
A wint'ry figure, like a wither'd thorn.   725
The shelves are full, all other themes are sped,
Hackney'd and worn to the last flimsy thread,
Satyr has long since done his best, and curst
And loathsome ribaldry has done his worst,
Fancy has sported all her pow'rs away   730
In tales, in trifles, and in children's play,
And 'tis the sad complaint, and almost true,
Whate'er we write, we bring forth nothing new.
'Twere new indeed, to see a bard all fire,
Touch'd with a coal from heav'n assume the lyre,   735
And tell the world, still kindling as he sung,

With more than mortal music on his tongue,
That he who died below, and reigns above
Inspires the song, and that his name is love.
 For after all, if merely to beguile   740
By flowing numbers and flow'ry stile,
The tædium that the lazy rich endure,
Which now and then sweet poetry may cure,
Or if to see the name of idol self
Stamp'd on the well-bound quarto, grace the shelf,   745
To float a bubble on the breath of fame,
Prompt his endeavour, and engage his aim,
Debas'd to servile purposes of pride,
How are the powers of genius misapplied?
The gift whose office is the giver's praise,   750
To trace him in his word, his works, his ways,
Then spread the rich discov'ry, and invite
Mankind to share in the divine delight,
Distorted from its use and just design,
To make the pitiful possessor shine,   755
To purchase at the fool-frequented fair
Of vanity, a wreath for self to wear,
Is profanation of the basest kind,
Proof of a trifling and a worthless mind.
 A. Hail Sternhold then and Hopkins hail! *B.* Amen.   760
If flatt'ry, folly, lust employ the pen,
If acrimony, slander and abuse,
Give it a charge to blacken and traduce;
Though Butler's wit, Pope's numbers, Prior's ease,
With all that fancy can invent to please,   765
Adorn the polish'd periods as they fall,
One Madrigal of their's is worth them all.
 A. 'Twould thin the ranks of the poetic tribe,
To dash the pen through all that you proscribe.
 B. No matter—we could shift when they were not,   770
And should no doubt if they were all forgot.

THE PROGRESS OF ERROR

Si quid loquar audiendum.   HOR. LIB. 4. OD. 2

Sing muse (if such a theme, so dark, so long,
May find a muse to grace it with a song)
By what unseen and unsuspected arts
The serpent error twines round human hearts,
Tell where she lurks, beneath what flow'ry shades,   5
That not a glimpse of genuin light pervades,
The pois'nous, black, insinuating worm,
Successfully conceals her loathsome form.
Take, if ye can, ye careless and supine!
Counsel and caution from a voice like mine;   10
Truths that the theorist could never reach,
And observation taught me, I would teach.
   Not all whose eloquence the fancy fills,
Musical as the chime of tinkling rills,
Weak to perform, though mighty to pretend,   15
Can trace her mazy windings to their end,
Discern the fraud beneath the specious lure,
Prevent the danger, or prescribe the cure.
The clear harangue, and cold as it is clear,
Falls soporific on the listless ear,   20
Like quicksilver, the rhet'ric they display,
Shines as it runs, but grasp'd at slips away.
   Plac'd for his trial on this bustling stage,
From thoughtless youth to ruminating age,
Free in his will to chuse or to refuse,   25
Man may improve the crisis, or abuse.
Else, on the fatalist's unrighteous plan,
Say, to what bar amenable were man?

First version, 2–21 December 1780; revised and augmented in January and late March 1781.
COPY-TEXT: *1782*, pp. 41–72 (first printing). Collated: *H*, *P* (letter to Newton, 21 Jan. 1781, ll. 335–52 only).
Motto] Quisnam igitur sanus? qui non stultus—Sat 3. Lib 2 *H*

With nought in charge, he could betray no trust,
And if he fell, would fall because he must; 30
If love reward him, or if vengeance strike,
His recompence in both, unjust alike.
Divine authority within his breast
Brings every thought, word, action to the test,
Warns him or prompts, approves him or restrains, 35
As reason, or as passion, takes the reins.
Heav'n from above, and conscience from within,
Cry in his startled ear, abstain from sin.
The world around solicits his desire,
And kindles in his soul a treach'rous fire, 40
While all his purposes and steps to guard,
Peace follows virtue as its sure reward,
And pleasure brings as surely in her train,
Remorse and sorrow and vindictive pain.

    Man thus endued with an elective voice, 45
Must be supplied with objects of his choice.
Where'er he turns, enjoyment and delight,
Or present, or in prospect, meet his sight;
These open on the spot their honey'd store,
Those call him loudly to pursuit of more. 50
His unexhausted mine, the sordid vice
Avarice shows, and virtue is the price.
Here, various motives his ambition raise,
Pow'r, pomp, and splendor, and the thirst of praise;
There beauty woes him with expanded arms, 55
E'en Bacchanalian madness has its charms.

    Nor these alone, whose pleasures less refin'd,
Might well alarm the most unguarded mind,
Seek to supplant his unexperienced youth,
Or lead him devious from the path of truth, 60
Hourly allurements on his passions press,
Safe in themselves, but dang'rous in th' excess.

    Hark! how it floats upon the dewy air,
O what a dying, dying close was there!
'Tis harmony from yon sequester'd bow'r, 65
Sweet harmony that sooths the midnight hour;

36 takes] guides *H*   51 His] Her *H*   52 Avarice] Self Interest *H*   56 charms.
charms, *1782*

Long e'er the charioteer of day had run
His morning course, th' enchantment was begun,
And he shall gild yon mountain's height again,
E'er yet the pleasing toil becomes a pain.   70
    Is this the rugged path, the steep ascent
That virtue points to? Can a life thus spent
Lead to the bliss she promises the wise,
Detach the soul from earth, and speed her to the skies?
Ye devotees to your ador'd employ,   75
Enthusiasts, drunk with an unreal joy,
Love makes the music of the blest above,
Heav'ns harmony is universal love;
And earthly sounds, though sweet and well combin'd,
And lenient as soft opiates to the mind,   80
Leave vice and folly unsubdu'd behind.
    Grey dawn appears, the sportsman and his train
Speckle the bosom of the distant plain,
'Tis he, the Nimrod of the neighb'ring lairs,
Save that his scent is less acute than their's,   85
For persevering chace, and headlong leaps,
True beagle as the staunchest hound he keeps.
Charg'd with the folly of his life's mad scene,
He takes offence, and wonders what you mean;
The joy, the danger and the toil o'erpays,   90
'Tis exercise, and health and length of days,
Again impetuous to the field he flies,
Leaps ev'ry fence but one, there falls and dies;
Like a slain deer, the tumbril brings him home,
Unmiss'd but by his dogs and by his groom.   95
    Ye clergy, while your orbit is your place,
Lights of the world, and stars of human race—
But if eccentric ye forsake your sphere,
Prodigious, ominous, and view'd with fear.
The comets baneful influence is a dream,   100
Your's real, and pernicious in th' extreme.
What then—are appetites and lusts laid down,
With the same ease the man puts on his gown?
Will av'rice and concupiscence give place,

Charm'd by the sounds, your rev'rence, or your grace?   105
No. But his own engagement binds him fast,
Or if it does not, brands him to the last
What atheists call him, a designing knave,
A mere church juggler, hypocrite and slave.
Oh laugh, or mourn with me, the rueful jest,   110
A cassock'd huntsman, and a fiddling priest;
He from Italian songsters takes his cue,
Set Paul to music, he shall quote him too.
He takes the field, the master of the pack
Cries, well done Saint—and claps him on the back.   115
Is this the path of sanctity? Is this
To stand a way-mark in the road to bliss?
Himself a wand'rer from the narrow way,
His silly sheep, what wonder if they stray?
Go, cast your orders at your Bishop's feet,   120
Send your dishonour'd gown to Monmouth Street,
The sacred function, in your hands is made,
Sad sacrilege! No function but a trade.
   Occiduus is a pastor of renown,
When he has pray'd and preach'd the sabbath down,   125
With wire and catgut he concludes the day,
Quav'ring and semiquav'ring care away.
The full concerto swells upon your ear;
All elbows shake. Look in, and you would swear
The Babylonian tyrant with a nod   130
Had summon'd them to serve his golden God.
So well that thought th' employment seems to suit,
Psalt'ry and sackbut, dulcimer, and flute.
Oh fie! 'Tis evangelical and pure,
Observe each face, how sober and demure,   135
Extasy sets her stamp on ev'ry mien,
Chins fall'n, and not an eye-ball to be seen.
Still I insist, though music heretofore
Has charm'd me much, not ev'n Occiduus more,
Love, joy and peace make harmony, more meet   140
For sabbath evenings, and perhaps as sweet.

135 Psalt'ry] salt'ry *1782, corrected in Errata*   flute.] flute, *1782, corrected in Errata*
138–9]   Still I insist, if Music be no Crime,
                          Theirs is, however, sadly out of Time. *H*

Will not the sickliest sheep of ev'ry flock,
Resort to this example as a rock,
There stand and justify the foul abuse
Of sabbath hours, with plausible excuse?   145
If apostolic gravity be free
To play the fool on Sundays, why not we?
If he, the tinkling harpsichord regards
As inoffensive, what offence in cards?
Strike up the fiddles, let us all be gay,   150
Laymen have leave to dance, if parsons play.
    Oh Italy! Thy sabbaths will be soon
Our sabbaths, clos'd with mumm'ry and buffoon.
Preaching and pranks will share the motley scene,
Our's parcell'd out, as thine have ever been,   155
God's worship and the mountebank between.
What says the prophet? Let that day be blest
With holiness and consecrated rest.
Pastime and bus'ness both it should exclude,
And bar the door the moment they intrude,   160
Nobly distinguish'd above all the six,
By deeds in which the world must never mix.
Hear him again. He calls it a delight,
A day of luxury, observ'd aright,
When the glad soul is made heav'ns welcome guest,   165
Sits banquetting, and God provides the feast.
But triflers are engag'd and cannot come;
Their answer to the call is—*Not at home.*
    Oh the dear pleasures of the velvet plain,
The painted tablets, dealt and dealt again.   170
Cards with what rapture, and the polish'd die,
The yawning chasm of indolence supply!
Then to the dance, and make the sober moon
Witness of joys that shun the sight of noon.
Blame cynic, if you can, quadrille or ball,   175
The snug close party, or the splendid hall,
Where night down-stooping from her ebon throne,
Views constellations brighter than her own.
'Tis innocent, and harmless and refin'd,

151 if] when *H*   157] *indented in H*   162 must] should *H*

The balm of care, elysium of the mind.   180
Innocent! Oh if venerable time
Slain at the foot of pleasure, be no crime,
Then with his silver beard and magic wand,
Let Comus rise Archbishop of the land,
Let him your rubric and your feasts prescribe,   185
Grand metropolitan of all the tribe.
   Of manners rough, and coarse athletic cast,
The rank debauch suits Clodio's filthy taste.
Rufillus, exquisitely form'd by rule,
Not of the moral, but the dancing school,   190
Wonders at Clodio's follies, in a tone
As tragical, as others at his own.
He cannot drink five bottles, bilk the score,
Then kill a constable, and drink five more;
But he can draw a pattern, make a tart,   195
And has the ladies etiquette by heart.
Go fool, and arm in arm with Clodio, plead
Your cause, before a bar you little dread;
But know, the law that bids the drunkard die,
Is far too just to pass the trifler by.   200
Both baby featur'd and of infant size,
View'd from a distance, and with heedless eyes,
Folly and innocence are so alike,
The diff'rence, though essential, fails to strike.
Yet folly ever has a vacant stare,   205
A simp'ring count'nance, and a trifling air;
But innocence, sedate, serene, erect,
Delights us, by engaging our respect.
   Man, nature's guest by invitation sweet,
Receives from her, both appetite and treat,   210
But if he play the glutton and exceed,
His benefactress blushes at the deed.
For nature, nice, as lib'ral to dispense,
Made nothing but a brute the slave of sense.
Daniel ate pulse by choice, example rare!   215
Heav'n bless'd the youth, and made him fresh and fair.
Gorgonius sits abdominous and wan,

180 *first insertion in H ends here*   187 coarse] of *deleted H*   201] *indented in H*
205 vacant] Ideot *H*   206 simp'ring] vacant *H*

Like a fat squab upon a Chinese fan.
He snuffs far off th' anticipated joy,
Turtle and ven'son all his thoughts employ,   220
Prepares for meals, as jockeys take a sweat,
Oh nauseous! an emetic for a whet—
Will providence o'erlook the wasted good?
Temperance were no virtue if he cou'd.
    That pleasures, therefore, or what such we call,   225
Are hurtful, is a truth confess'd by all.
And some that seem to threaten virtue less,
Still hurtful, in th' abuse, or by th' excess.
    Is man then only for his torment plac'd,
The center of delights he may not taste?   230
Like fabled Tantalus condemn'd to hear
The precious stream still purling in his ear,
Lip-deep in what he longs for, and yet curst
With prohibition and perpetual thirst?
No, wrangler—destitute of shame and sense,   235
The precept that injoins him abstinence,
Forbids him none but the licentious joy,
Whose fruit, though fair, tempts only to destroy.
Remorse, the fatal egg by pleasure laid
In every bosom where her nest is made,   240
Hatch'd by the beams of truth denies him rest,
And proves a raging scorpion in his breast.
No pleasure? Are domestic comforts dead?
Are all the nameless sweets of friendship fled?
Has time worn out, or fashion put to shame   245
Good sense, good health, good conscience, and good fame?
All these belong to virtue, and all prove
That virtue has a title to your love.
Have you no touch of pity, that the poor
Stand starved at your inhospitable door?   250
Or if yourself too scantily supplied
Need help, let honest industry provide.
Earn, if you want, if you abound, impart,
These both are pleasures to the feeling heart.
No pleasure? Has some sickly eastern waste   255

223 good] Food H   224 cou'd] should H   243] indented in H   244 sweets
Joys deleted H

Sent us a wind to parch us at a blast?
Can British paradise no scenes afford
To please her sated and indiff'rent lord?
Are sweet philosophy's enjoyments run
Quite to the lees? And has religion none?   260
Brutes capable, should tell you 'tis a lye,
And judge you from the kennel and the sty.
Delights like these, ye sensual and profane,
Ye are bid, begg'd, besought to entertain;
Call'd to these crystal streams, do ye turn off   265
Obscene, to swill and swallow at a trough?
Envy the beast then, on whom heav'n bestows
Your pleasures, with no curses in the close.
   Pleasure admitted in undue degree,
Enslaves the will, nor leaves the judgment free.   270
'Tis not alone the grapes enticing juice,
Unnerves the moral pow'rs, and marrs their use,
Ambition, av'rice, and the lust of fame,
And woman, lovely woman, does the same.
The heart, surrender'd to the ruling pow'r   275
Of some ungovern'd passion ev'ry hour,
Finds by degrees, the truths that once bore sway,
And all their deep impression wear away.
So coin grows smooth, in traffic current pass'd,
'Till Cæsar's image is effac'd at last.   280
   The breach, though small at first, soon op'ning wide,
In rushes folly with a full moon tide.
Then welcome errors of whatever size,
To justify it by a thousand lies.
As creeping ivy clings to wood or stone,   285
And hides the ruin that it feeds upon,
So sophistry, cleaves close to, and protects
Sin's rotten trunk, concealing its defects.
Mortals whose pleasures are their only care,
First wish to be impos'd on, and then are.   290
And lest the fulsome artifice should fail,
Themselves will hide its coarseness with a veil.
Not more industrious are the just and true
To give to virtue what is virtue's due,

261, 262 you] ye H

The praise of wisdom, comeliness and worth,   295
And call her charms to public notice forth,
Than vice's mean and disingenuous race,
To hide the shocking features of her face.
Her form with dress and lotion they repair,
Then kiss their idol and pronounce her fair.   300
    The sacred implement I now employ
Might prove a mischief or at best a toy,
A trifle if it move but to amuse,
But if to wrong the judgment and abuse,
Worse than a poignard in the basest hand,   305
It stabs at once the morals of a land.
    Ye writers of what none with safety reads,
Footing it in the dance that fancy leads,
Ye novellists who marr what ye would mend,
Sniv'ling and driv'ling folly without end,   310
Whose corresponding misses fill the ream
With sentimental frippery and dream,
Caught in a delicate soft silken net
By some lewd Earl, or rake-hell Baronet;
Ye pimps, who under virtue's fair pretence,   315
Steal to the closet of young innocence,
And teach her unexperienc'd yet and green,
To scribble as you scribble at fifteen;
Who kindling a combustion of desire,
With some cold moral think to quench the fire,   320
Though all your engineering proves in vain,
The dribbling stream ne'er puts it out again;
Oh that a verse had pow'r, and could command
Far, far away, these flesh-flies of the land,
Who fasten without mercy on the fair,   325
And suck, and leave a craving maggot there.
Howe'er disguis'd th' inflammatory tale,
And covered with a fine-spun specious veil,
Such writers and such readers owe the gust
And relish of their pleasure all to lust.   330
    But the muse eagle-pinion'd has in view
A quarry more important still than you,

---

299 *second insertion in H begins here*   310 folly] Nonsense *H*   328 fine-spun
specious] specious fine-spun *H*   331–4 *follow* 352 *in H*

Down down the wind she swims and sails away,
Now stoops upon it and now grasps the prey.
    Petronius! all the muses weep for thee,   335
But ev'ry tear shall scald thy memory.
The graces too, while virtue at their shrine
Lay bleeding under that soft hand of thine,
Felt each a mortal stab in her own breast,
Abhorr'd the sacrifice, and curs'd the priest.   340
Thou polish'd and high finish'd foe to truth,
Gray beard corruptor of our list'ning youth,
To purge and skim away the filth of vice,
That so refin'd it might the more entice,
Then pour it on the morals of thy son   345
To taint *his* heart, was worthy of *thine own.*
Now while the poison all high life pervades,
Write if thou can'st one letter from the shades,
One, and one only, charg'd with deep regret,
That thy worst part, thy principles live yet;   350
One sad epistle thence, may cure mankind,
Of the plague spread by bundles left behind.
    'Tis granted, and no plainer truth appears,

---

335 Petronius!] Chesterfield! *P, H*   343 purge and skim away the filth] Simmer and
Scum off the Filth *P*; Purge and Scum the Fæculence *H*   353–434 *not in H, which
has instead the following lines*:

        Oh curst Thelyphthora, thy daring Page [see notes]
        The Shame and Scandal of a shameless Age,
        And He that wrote it, to discerning Eyes
        No Priest, but a mere Dervise in disguise,
        Was't not enough Lasciviousness unaw'd
        Like a fell Vulture spread his Wings abroad,
        With hideous Talons ev'ry Hour prepar'd
        To seize the Virgin least upon her Guard,
        But Marriage too that Heav'n invented Plan,
        Plac'd like a Barrier to the Lusts of Man,
        The Temple to which Chastity retires
        For Refuge from the Debauchee's base fires,
        Must be unbarr'd, and the Lock Pick'd by You,
        Laid open like a Brothel or a Stew?
        Is This a Blessing on the Church bestow'd?
        ('Tis what some Priests unblushing have avow'd)
        Why then the Candidates of Heav'n in Tears,
        What mean their lifted Hands and anxious Fears,
        Why Reigns Suspicion where once Peace prevail'd,
        Why has the Stream of Home born Comfort fail'd?

[Continued overleaf.

Our most important are our earliest years,
The mind impressible and soft, with ease   355
Imbibes and copies what she hears and sees,
And through life's labyrinth holds fast the clue
That education gives her, false or true.
Plants rais'd with tenderness are seldom strong,
Man's coltish disposition asks the thong,   360
And without discipline the fav'rite child,
Like a neglected forrester runs wild.
But we, as if good qualities would grow
Spontaneous, take but little pains to sow,
We give some latin and a smatch of greek,   365
Teach him to fence and figure twice a week,
And having done we think, the best we can,
Praise his proficiency and dub him man.

    From school to Cam or Isis, and thence home,
And thence with all convenient speed to Rome,   370
With rev'rend tutor clad in habit lay,
To teaze for cash and quarrel with all day,

Dispatch your Blessing to the lewd Levant,
One faithfull Wife is all we Christians want.
    One Woman, and One only, made for Man,
Shakes into Rubbish all the Labor'd Plan.
Had he, libidinous, a Wish express'd
For Two, would Heav'n have smil'd on his Request?
No. rather with Resentment waxing hot
Have dash'd him into Atoms on the Spot.
    Oh fall'n as low as ever Virtue fell,
From a Saint's Honor to the Sides of Hell,
Was it for This, and to be thus misled,
You rose a gaz'd at Wonder from the dead?
Was it for this, by no false Shame witheld,
You rais'd the Standard in the Christian Field,
Endur'd the Scoffing and illib'ral Sneer
Of Fools you pitied, while they shock'd your Ear?
You was a Soldier once of Worth approv'd,
Ay, ev'ry Inch his Soldier whom you Lov'd,
And do you quit the Cause you then held fast,
And Higgle for vile Appetite at last?
Take Hellebore, and Purge your sickly Brain,
And Burn your Book, and be yourself again.
The Muse your once blest Character reveres,
With her Reproof she mingles friendly Tears,
If she Probes deep, it is for your Releif,
Not half so much in Anger, as in Grief.

With memorandum-book for ev'ry town,
And ev'ry post, and where the chaise broke down:
His stock, a few French phrases got by heart,   375
With much to learn, but nothing to impart,
The youth obedient to his sire's commands,
Sets off a wand'rer into foreign lands:
Surpriz'd at all they meet, the goslin pair
With aukward gait, stretch'd neck, and silly stare,   380
Discover huge cathedrals built with stone,
And steeples tow'ring high much like our own,
But show peculiar light by many a grin
At Popish practices observ'd within.
    E'er long some bowing, smirking, smart Abbé   385
Remarks two loit'rers that have lost their way,
And being always primed with *politesse*
For men of their appearance and address,
With much compassion undertakes the task,
To tell them more than they have wit to ask.   390
Points to inscriptions wheresoe'er they tread,
Such as when legible were never read,
But being canker'd now, and half worn out,
Craze antiquarian brains with endless doubt:
Some headless hero or some Cæsar shows,   395
Defective only in his Roman nose;
Exhibits elevations, drawings, plans,
Models of Herculanean pots and pans,
And sells them medals, which if neither rare
Nor antient, will be so, preserv'd with care.   400
    Strange the recital! from whatever cause
His great improvement and new lights he draws,
The 'Squire once bashful is shame-fac'd no more,
But teems with pow'rs he never felt before:
Whether encreas'd momentum, and the force   405
With which from clime to clime he sped his course,
As axles sometimes kindle as they go,
Chaf'd him and brought dull nature to a glow;
Or whether clearer skies and softer air

373–4 replace the following, found in some copies on cancellandum leaf E6
            With memorandum-book to minute down
            The sev'ral posts, and where the chaise broke down:

That make Italian flow'rs so sweet and fair,   410
Fresh'ning his lazy spirits as he ran,
Unfolded genially and spread the man,
Returning he proclaims by many a grace,
By shrugs and strange contortions of his face,
How much a dunce that has been sent to roam,   415
Excels a dunce that has been kept at home.
   Accomplishments have taken virtue's place,
And wisdom falls before exterior grace;
We slight the precious kernel of the stone,
And toil to polish its rough coat alone.   420
A just deportment, manners grac'd with ease,
Elegant phrase, and figure form'd to please,
Are qualities that seem to comprehend
Whatever parents, guardians, schools intend;
Hence an unfurnish'd and a listless mind,   425
Though busy, trifling; empty, though refin'd;
Hence all that interferes, and dares to clash
With indolence and luxury, is trash;
While learning, once the man's exclusive pride,
Seems verging fast towards the female side.   430
   Learning itself receiv'd into a mind
By nature weak, or viciously inclin'd,
Serves but to lead philosophers astray
Where children would with ease discern the way.
And of all arts sagacious dupes invent   435
To cheat themselves and gain the world's assent
The worst is scripture warp'd from it's intent.
   The carriage bowls along and all are pleas'd
If Tom be sober, and the wheels well greas'd,
But if the rogue have gone a cup too far,   440
Left out his linch-pin or forgot his tar,
It suffers interruption and delay,
And meets with hindrance in the smoothest way.
When some hypothesis absurd and vain
Has fill'd with all its fumes a critic's brain,   445
The text that sorts not with his darling whim,
Though plain to others, is obscure to him.

435 And of all arts sagacious] Sure of all Artifices *H*   441 his linch-pin] the Linch
Pin *H*

The will made subject to a lawless force,
All is irregular, and out of course,
And judgment drunk, and bribed to lose his way,   450
Winks hard, and talks of darkness at noon day.
    A critic on the sacred book, should be
Candid and learn'd, dispassionate and free;
Free from the wayward bias bigots feel,
From fancy's influence, and intemp'rate zeal.   455
But above all (or let the wretch refrain,
Nor touch the page he cannot but profane)
Free from the domineering pow'r of lust,
A lewd interpreter is never just.
    How shall I speak thee, or thy pow'r address,   460
Thou God of our idolatry, the press?
By thee, religion, liberty and laws
Exert their influence, and advance their cause,
By thee, worse plagues than Pharaoh's land befel,
Diffus'd, make earth the vestibule of hell: 465
Thou fountain, at which drink the good and wise,
Thou ever-bubbling spring of endless lies,
Like Eden's dread probationary tree,
Knowledge of good and evil is from thee.
    No wild enthusiast ever yet could rest,   470
Till half mankind were like himself possess'd.
Philosophers, who darken and put out
Eternal truth by everlasting doubt,
Church quacks, with passions under no command,
Who fill the world with doctrines contraband,   475
Discov'rers of they know not what, confin'd
Within no bounds, the blind that lead the blind,
To streams of popular opinion drawn,
Deposit in those shallows, all their spawn.
The wriggling fry soon fill the creeks around,   480
Pois'ning the waters where their swarms abound;
Scorn'd by the nobler tenants of the flood,
Minnows and gudgeons gorge th' unwholesome food.
The propagated myriads spread so fast,

---

461 *second insertion in H ends here*   464 Pharaoh's] Phar'oh's *H*   467 ever-
bubbling spring] ever springing Source *H*   *between* 471 *and* 472 *are in H two deleted*
lines, identical with 492–3 *below*   483 th'unwholesome] the loathsome *H*

E'en Leuwenhoek himself would stand aghast,   485
Employ'd to calculate th' enormous sum,
And own his crab-computing pow'rs o'ercome.
Is this Hyperbole? The world well known,
Your sober thoughts will hardly find it one.
   Fresh confidence the speculatist takes   490
From ev'ry hare-brain'd proselyte he makes,
And therefore prints. Himself but half-deceiv'd,
'Till others have the soothing tale believ'd.
Hence comment after comment, spun as fine
As bloated spiders draw the flimsy line.   495
Hence the same word that bids our lusts obey,
Is misapplied to sanctify their sway.
If stubborn Greek refuse to be his friend,
Hebrew or Syriac shall be forc'd to bend;
If languages and copies all cry, No—   500
Somebody prov'd it centuries ago.
Like trout pursued, the critic in despair
Darts to the mud and finds his safety there.
Women, whom custom has forbid to fly
The scholar's pitch (the scholar best knows why)   505
With all the simple and unletter'd poor,
Admire his learning, and almost adore.
Whoever errs, the priest can ne'er be wrong,
With such fine words familiar to his tongue.
   Ye ladies! (for, indiff'rent in your cause,   510
I should deserve to forfeit all applause)
Whatever shocks, or gives the least offence
To virtue, delicacy, truth or sense,
(Try the criterion, 'tis a faithful guide)
Nor has, nor can have scripture on its side.   515
   None but an author knows an author's cares,
Or fancy's fondness for the child she bears.
Committed once into the public arms,
The baby seems to smile with added charms.

485 Leuwenhoek] Lewenhock *H*
496–7   Hence the same Word that Damns, severe but Just,
             The Letcher, is made Pander to his Lust. *H*
499 forc'd] ma *deleted H*
510–11   Ye Ladies! Hear me Preach without a Scoff,
           Ye Ladies! (for the Poor are too far off) *H*

Like something precious ventur'd far from shore,   520
'Tis valued for the dangers sake the more.
He views it with complacency supreme,
Solicits kind attention to his dream,
And daily more enamour'd of the cheat,
Kneels, and asks heav'n to bless the dear deceit.   525
So one, whose story serves at least to show
Men lov'd their own productions long ago,
Wooed an unfeeling statue for his wife,
Nor rested till the Gods had giv'n it life.
If some mere driv'ler suck the sugar'd fib,   530
One that still needs his leading string and bib,
And praise his genius, he is soon repaid
In praise applied to the same part, his head.
For 'tis a rule that holds for ever true,
Grant me discernment, and I grant it you.   535
    Patient of contradiction as a child,
Affable, humble, diffident and mild,
Such was Sir Isaac, and such Boyle and Locke,
Your blund'rer is as sturdy as a rock.
The creature is so sure to kick and bite,   540
A muleteer's the man to set him right.
First appetite enlists him truth's sworn foe,
Then obstinate self-will confirms him so.
    Tell him he wanders, that his error leads
To fatal ills, that though the path he treads   545
Be flow'ry, and he see no cause of fear,
Death and the pains of hell attend him there;
In vain; the slave of arrogance and pride,
He has no hearing on the prudent side.
His still refuted quirks he still repeats,   550
New rais'd objections with new quibbles meets,
'Till sinking in the quicksand he defends,
He dies disputing, and the contest ends;
But not the mischiefs: they still left behind,
Like thistle-seeds are sown by ev'ry wind.   555

526–8   So He, whose almost Breath-bestowing Art,
                Could all beside, to senseless Stone impart,
                Lov'd his own Work, and woo'd it for his Wife, *H*
540–1 *not in H*   548 slave] Dupe *H*

Thus men go wrong with an ingenious skill,
Bend the strait rule to their own crooked will,
And with a clear and shining lamp supplied,
First put it out, then take it for a guide.
Halting on crutches of unequal size,   560
One leg by truth supported, one by lies,
They sidle to the goal with aukward pace,
Secure of nothing, but to lose the race.
   Faults in the life breed errors in the brain,
And these, reciprocally, those again.   565
The mind and conduct mutually imprint
And stamp their image in each other's mint.
Each, sire and dam, of an infernal race,
Begetting and conceiving all that's base.
   None sends his arrow to the mark in view,   570
Whose hand is feeble, or his aim untrue.
For though e'er yet the shaft is on the wing,
Or when it first forsakes th' elastic string,
It err but little from th' intended line,
It falls at last, far wide of his design.   575
So he that seeks a mansion in the sky,
Must watch his purpose with a stedfast eye,
That prize belongs to none but the sincere,
The least obliquity is fatal here.
   With caution taste the sweet Circæan cup,   580
He that sips often, at last drinks it up.
Habits are soon assum'd, but when we strive
To strip them off, 'tis being flay'd alive.
Call'd to the temple of impure delight,
He that abstains, and he alone does right.   585
If a wish wander that way, call it home,
He cannot long be safe, whose wishes roam.
But if you pass the threshold, you are caught,
Die *then*, if pow'r Almighty save you not.
There hard'ning by degrees, 'till double steel'd,   590

556–9 *replace in H the following deleted lines*:
        Men would be sav'd, yet keep their Follies still,
        Their Maker's Pleasure, and their own fulfill.
        Aim at the Regions of Eternal Day,
        But Bargain for a Frolic by the Way.
562 goal] Mark *deleted H*   589 *then*] then *1782*; *see Commentary*

Take leave of nature's God, and God reveal'd,
Then laugh at all you trembl'd at before,
And joining the free-thinkers brutal roar,
Swallow the two grand nostrums they dispense,
That scripture lies, and blasphemy is sense: 595
If clemency revolted by abuse
Be damnable, then, damn'd without excuse.
   Some dream that they can silence when they will
The storm of passion, and say, *Peace, be still*;
But '*Thus far and no farther*,' when address'd   600
To the wild wave, or wilder human breast,
Implies authority that never can,
That never ought to be the lot of man.
   But muse forbear, long flights forebode a fall,
Strike on the deep-toned chord the sum of all.   605
   Hear the just law, the judgment of the skies!
He that hates truth shall be the dupe of lies.
And he that *will* be cheated to the last,
Delusions, strong as hell, shall bind him fast.
But if the wand'rer his mistake discern,   610
Judge his own ways, and sigh for a return,
Bewilder'd once, must he bewail his loss
For ever and for ever? No—the cross.
There and there only (though the deist rave,
And atheist, if earth bear so base a slave)   615
There and there only, is the pow'r to save.
There no delusive hope invites despair,
No mock'ry meets you, no deception there.
The spells and charms that blinded you before,
All vanish there, and fascinate no more.   620
   I am no preacher, let this hint suffice,
The cross once seen, is death to ev'ry vice:
Else he that hung there, suffer'd all his pain,
Bled, groan'd and agoniz'd, and died in vain.

        621 *not indented in* H

TRUTH

Pensentur trutinâ. HOR.

Man on the dubious waves of error toss'd,
His ship half founder'd and his compass lost,
Sees, far as human optics may command,
A sleeping fog, and fancies it dry land:
Spreads all his canvass, ev'ry sinew plies, 5
Pants for it, aims at it, enters it, and dies.
Then farewell all self-satisfying schemes,
His well-built systems, philosophic dreams,
Deceitful views of future bliss, farewell!
He reads his sentence at the flames of hell. 10
 Hard lot of man! to toil for the reward
Of virtue, and yet lose it—wherefore hard?
He that would win the race, must guide his horse
Obedient to the customs of the course,
Else, though unequall'd to the goal he flies, 15
A meaner than himself shall gain the prize.
Grace leads the right way, if you chuse the wrong,
Take it and perish, but restrain your tongue;
Charge not, with light sufficient and left free,
Your willful suicide on God's decree. 20
 Oh how unlike the complex works of man,
Heav'ns easy, artless, unincumber'd plan!
No meretricious graces to beguile,
No clust'ring ornaments to clog the pile,
From ostentation as from weakness free, 25
It stands like the cærulean arch we see,
Majestic in its own simplicity.

c. 21 December 1780–*c.* 21 January 1781.

COPY-TEXT: *1782*, pp. 73–102 (first printing). Collated: *H*

2 compass] Anchor *H*   3 Sees,] *H*; *no comma in 1782*   7 schemes] Dreams *H*
8 dreams] Schemes *H*   16 gain] claim *H*   17–20 *added later in H*
22 *severely cropped in H*

Inscrib'd above the portal, from afar
Conspicuous as the brightness of a star,
Legible only by the light they give,   30
Stand the soul-quick'ning words—BELIEVE AND LIVE.
Too many shock'd at what should charm them most,
Despise the plain direction and are lost.
Heav'n on such terms! they cry with proud disdain,
Incredible, impossible, and vain—   35
Rebel because 'tis easy to obey,
And scorn for its own sake the gracious way.
These are the sober, in whose cooler brains
Some thought of immortality remains;
The rest too busy or too gay, to wait   40
On the sad theme, their everlasting state,
Sport for a day and perish in a night,
The foam upon the waters not so light.
    Who judg'd the Pharisee? What odious cause
Expos'd him to the vengeance of the laws?   45
Had he seduc'd a virgin, wrong'd a friend,
Or stabb'd a man to serve some private end?
Was blasphemy his sin? Or did he stray
From the strict duties of the sacred day?
Sit long and late at the carousing board?   50
(Such were the sins with which he charg'd his Lord)
No—the man's morals were exact, what then?
'Twas his ambition to be seen of men;
His virtues were his pride; and that one vice
Made all his virtues gewgaws of no price;   55
He wore them as fine trappings for a show,
A praying, synagogue frequenting beau.
    The self-applauding bird, the peacock see—
Mark what a sumptuous Pharisee is he!
Meridian sun-beams tempt him to unfold   60
His radiant glories, azure, green, and gold;
He treads as if some solemn music near,
His measur'd step were govern'd by his ear,
And seems to say, ye meaner fowl, give place,
I am all splendor, dignity and grace.   65
    Not so the pheasant on his charms presumes,

63 were] was *H*

Though he too has a glory in his plumes.
He, christian like, retreats with modest mien,
To the close copse or far sequester'd green,
And shines without desiring to be seen.   70
The plea of works, as arrogant and vain,
Heav'n turns from with abhorrence and disdain;
Not more affronted by avow'd neglect,
Than by the mere dissemblers feign'd respect.
What is all righteousness that men devise,   75
What, but a sordid bargain for the skies?
But Christ as soon would abdicate his own,
As stoop from heav'n to sell the proud a throne.

His dwelling a recess in some rude rock,
Book, beads, and maple-dish his meagre stock,   80
In shirt of hair and weeds of canvass dress'd,
Girt with a bell-rope that the Pope has bless'd,
Adust with stripes told out for ev'ry crime,
And sore tormented long before his time,
His pray'r preferr'd to saints that cannot aid,   85
His praise postpon'd, and never to be paid,
See the sage hermit by mankind admir'd,
With all that bigotry adopts, inspir'd,
Wearing out life in his religious whim,
'Till his religious whimsy wears out him.   90
His works, his abstinence, his zeal allow'd,
You think him humble, God accounts him proud;
High in demand, though lowly in pretence,
Of all his conduct, this the genuine sense—
My penitential stripes, my streaming blood   95
Have purchas'd heav'n, and prove my title good.
Turn eastward now, and fancy shall apply
To your weak sight her telescopic eye.
The Bramin kindles on his own bare head
The sacred fire, self-torturing his trade,   100
His voluntary pains, severe and long,
Would give a barb'rous air to British song,

71 *indented in H*   72 disdain;] *semicolon supplied; punctuation cropped in H*   77 own]
Throne *H*   78] As Sell the confident Self Boaster, one. *H*   91 *indented in H*
92 God] Heav'n *H*
95–6   Behold! the Penitential Scars I bear
              Prove me a Saint, exclude me if you dare. *H.*

Nor grand inquisitor could worse invent,
Than he contrives to suffer, well content.
   Which is the saintlier worthy of the two?   105
Past all dispute, yon anchorite say you.
Your sentence and mine differ. What's a name?
I say the Bramin has the fairer claim.
If suff'rings scripture no where recommends,
Devis'd by self to answer selfish ends   110
Give saintship, then all Europe must agree,
Ten starvling hermits suffer less than he.
   The truth is (if the truth may suit your ear,
And prejudice have left a passage clear)
Pride has attain'd its most luxuriant growth,   115
And poison'd every virtue in them both.
Pride may be pamper'd while the flesh grows lean;
Humility may cloath an English Dean;
That grace was Cowper's—his confess'd by all—
Though plac'd in golden Durham's second stall.   120
Not all the plenty of a Bishop's board,
His palace, and his lacqueys, and, my Lord!
More nourish pride, that condescending vice,
Than abstinence, and beggary and lice.
It thrives in misery, and abundant grows   125
In misery fools upon themselves impose.
   But why before us Protestants produce
An Indian mystic or a French recluse?
Their sin is plain, but what have we to fear,
Reform'd and well instructed? You shall hear.   130
    Yon antient prude, whose wither'd features show
She might be young some forty years ago,
Her elbows pinion'd close upon her hips,
Her head erect, her fan upon her lips,
Her eye-brows arch'd, her eyes both gone astray   135
To watch yon am'rous couple in their play,
With boney and unkerchief'd neck defies
The rude inclemency of wintry skies,
And sails with lappet-head and mincing airs
Duely at clink of bell, to morning pray'rs.   140

108 *insertion begins here in H* (*see Commentary*)   130 Reform'd and well instructed?]
A Christian Generation? *H*

To thrift and parsimony much inclin'd,
She yet allows herself that boy behind;
The shiv'ring urchin, bending as he goes,
With slipshod heels, and dew drop at his nose,
His predecessors coat advanc'd to wear,   145
Which future pages are yet doom'd to share,
Carries her bible tuck'd beneath his arm,
And hides his hands to keep his fingers warm.
    She, half an angel in her own account,
Doubts not hereafter with the saints to mount,   150
Though not a grace appears on strictest search,
But that she fasts, and item, goes to church.
Conscious of age she recollects her youth,
And tells, not always with an eye to truth,
Who spann'd her waist, and who, where'er he came,   155
Scrawl'd upon glass Miss Bridget's lovely name,
Who stole her slipper, fill'd it with tokay,
And drank the little bumper ev'ry day.
Of temper as invenom'd as an asp,
Censorious, and her every word a wasp,   160
In faithful mem'ry she records the crimes
Or real, or fictitious, of the times,
Laughs at the reputations she has torn,
And holds them dangling at arms length in scorn.
    Such are the fruits of sanctimonious pride,   165
Of malice fed while flesh is mortified.
Take, Madam, the reward of all your pray'rs,
Where hermits and where Bramins meet with theirs,
Your portion is with them: nay, never frown,
But, if you please, some fathoms lower down.   170
    Artist attend—your brushes and your paint—
Produce them—take a chair—now draw a Saint.
Oh sorrowful and sad! the streaming tears
Channel her cheeks, a Niobe appears.
Is this a Saint? Throw tints and all away,   175
True piety is chearful as the day,
Will weep indeed and heave a pitying groan
For others woes, but smiles upon her own.

146 To which His Successor is certain Heir, *H*   149 *not indented in H*   165 *not
indented in H*   *following* 170] What Purpose has the King *deleted H (cf.* 179)

What purpose has the King of Saints in view?
Why falls the gospel like a gracious dew?   180
To call up plenty from the teeming earth,
Or curse the desart with a tenfold dearth?
Is it that Adam's offspring may be sav'd
From servile fear, or be the more enslav'd?
To loose the links that gall'd mankind before,   185
Or bind them faster on, and add still more?
The freeborn Christian has no chains to prove,
Or if a chain, the golden one of love;
No fear attends to quench his glowing fires,
What fear he feels his gratitude inspires.   190
Shall he for such deliv'rance freely wrought
Recompense ill? He trembles at the thought:
His masters int'rest and his own combin'd,
Prompt ev'ry movement of his heart and mind;
Thought, word, and deed, his liberty evince,   195
His freedom is the freedom of a Prince.
      Man's obligations infinite, of course
His life should prove that he perceives their force,
His utmost he can render is but small,
The principle and motive all in all.   200
You have two servants—Tom, an arch, sly rogue,
From top to toe the Geta now in vogue;
Genteel in figure, easy in address,
Moves without noise, and swift as an express,
Reports a message with a pleasing grace,   205
Expert in all the duties of his place:
Say, on what hinge does his obedience move?
Has he a world of gratitude and love?
No, not a spark—'tis all mere sharpers play;
He likes your house, your housemaid and your pay;   210
Reduce his wages, or get rid of her,
Tom quits you, with, your most obedient Sir—
      The dinner serv'd, Charles takes his usual stand,
Watches your eye, anticipates command,
Sighs if perhaps your appetite should fail,   215
And if he but suspects a frown, turns pale;
Consults all day your int'rest and your ease,

202 *indented in* H   213 *not indented in* H

Richly rewarded if he can but please,
And proud to make his firm attachment known,
To save your life would nobly risque his own.   220
Now, which stands highest in your serious thought?
Charles, without doubt, say you—and so he ought;
One act that from a thankful heart proceeds,
Excels ten thousand mercenary deeds.
   Thus heav'n approves as honest and sincere,   225
The work of gen'rous love and filial fear,
But with averted eyes th'omniscient judge,
Scorns the base hireling and the slavish drudge.
   Where dwell these matchless Saints? Old Curio cries—
Ev'n at your side, Sir, and before your eyes,   230
The favour'd few, th' enthusiasts you despise.
And pleas'd at heart because on holy ground,
Sometimes a canting hypocrite is found,
Reproach a people with his single fall,
And cast his filthy raiment at them all.   235
Attend—an apt similitude shall show,
Whence springs the conduct that offends you so.
   See where it smoaks along the sounding plain,
Blown all aslant, a driving dashing rain,
Peal upon peal redoubling all around,   240
Shakes it again and faster to the ground,
Now flashing wide, now glancing as in play,
Swift beyond thought the light'nings dart away;
Ere yet it came the traveller urg'd his steed,
And hurried, but with unsuccessful speed,   245
Now drench'd throughout, and hopeless of his case,
He drops the rein, and leaves him to his pace;
Suppose, unlook'd for in a scene so rude,
Long hid by interposing hill or wood,
Some mansion neat and elegantly dress'd,   250
By some kind hospitable heart possess'd,
Offer him warmth, security and rest;
Think with what pleasure, safe and at his ease,
He hears the tempest howling in the trees,

---

229 dwell] are *H*   232 pleas'd at heart because] because here and there *H*   233 Sometimes a canting] A Canting Rascal *H*   235 filthy] dirty *H*   236 similitude]
Comparison *H*   249 *insertion ends here in* *H*

What glowing thanks his lips and heart employ,   255
While danger past is turn'd to present joy.
So fares it with the sinner when he feels,
A growing dread of vengeance at his heels.
His conscience like a glassy lake before,
Lash'd into foaming waves begins to roar,   260
The law grown clamorous, though silent long,
Arraigns him, charges him with every wrong,
Asserts the rights of his offended Lord,
And death or restitution is the word;
The last impossible, he fears the first,   265
And having well deserv'd, expects the worst:
Then welcome refuge, and a peaceful home,
Oh for a shelter from the wrath to come!
Crush me ye rocks, ye falling mountains hide,
Or bury me in oceans angry tide—   270
The scrutiny of those all seeing eyes
I dare not—and you need not, God replies;
The remedy you want I freely give,
The book shall teach you, read, believe and live:
'Tis done—the raging storm is heard no more,   275
Mercy receives him on her peaceful shore,
And justice, guardian of the dread command,
Drops the red vengeance from his willing hand.
A soul redeem'd demands a life of praise,
Hence the complexion of his future days,   280
Hence a demeanor holy and unspeck'd,
And the world's hatred as its sure effect.
    Some lead a life unblameable and just,
Their own dear virtue, their unshaken trust.

255] The Favors he receives his Thoughts employ, *H*   256 While] And *H*
257 *indented in H*   sinner, when he feels *H*; *1782 punctuates* sinner when he feels,
258 heels. *H*; *1782 punctuates* heels,   262 Arraigns him, charges him] Charges him in
his Heart, *H*   265-6 *not in H*   266 worst:] *punctuation supplied*   272 God]
Heav'n *H*   277 dread] great *H*

ollowing 278

                You ask the Cause, and with a doubtfull Air;
                'Tis taught at Calvary, Go, Learn it There.
                                                        deleted H
279-82 *added later in H*   281 holy] blameless *H*
278-88   The Remedy is even at the Door;
              What Remedy?—a Penny to the Poor. *H*

They never sin—or if (as all offend)   285
Some trivial slips their daily walk attend,
The poor are near at hand, the charge is small,
A slight gratuity atones for all.
For though the Pope has lost his int'rest here,
And pardons are not sold as once they were,   290
No Papist more desirous to compound,
Than some grave sinners upon English ground:
That plea refuted, other quirks they seek,
Mercy is infinite and man is weak,
The future shall obliterate the past,   295
And heav'n no doubt shall be their home at last.
    Come then—a still, small whisper in your ear,
He has no hope that never had a fear;
And he that never doubted of his state,
He may perhaps—perhaps he may—too late.   300
    The path to bliss abounds with many a snare,
Learning is one, and wit, however rare:
The Frenchman first in literary fame,
(Mention him if you please—Voltaire? The same)
With spirit, genius, eloquence supplied,   305
Liv'd long, wrote much, laugh'd heartily and died:
The scripture was his jest-book, whence he drew
Bon môts to gall the Christian and the Jew;
An infidel in health, but what when sick?
Oh then, a text would touch him at the quick: 310
View him at Paris in his last career,
Surrounding throngs the demi-god revere,
Exalted on his pedestal of pride,
And fum'd with frankincense on ev'ry side,
He begs their flattery with his latest breath,   315
And smother'd in't at last, is prais'd to death.
    Yon cottager who weaves at her own door,
Pillow and bobbins all her little store,

following 316, *added later in H*

> Death draws a Curtain Man must not undraw,
> Behind it, are the Burnings of the Law.
> There, Blasphemy and Truth-reviling Wit
> Are paid for, in the Roarings of the Pit.

317 who] that *H*

Content though mean, and chearful, if not gay,
Shuffling her threads about the live-long day,   320
Just earns a scanty pittance, and at night
Lies down secure, her heart and pocket light;
She for her humble sphere by nature fit,
Has little understanding, and no wit,
Receives no praise, but (though her lot be such,   325
Toilsome and indigent) she renders much;
Just knows, and knows no more, her bible true,
A truth the brilliant Frenchman never knew,
And in that charter reads with sparkling eyes,
Her title to a treasure in the skies.   330
   Oh happy peasant! Oh unhappy bard!
His the mere tinsel, her's the rich reward;
He prais'd perhaps for ages yet to come,
She never heard of half a mile from home;
He lost in errors his vain heart prefers,   335
She safe in the simplicity of hers.
   Not many wise, rich, noble, or profound
In science, win one inch of heav'nly ground:
And is it not a mortifying thought
The poor should gain it, and the rich should not?   340
No—the voluptuaries, who ne'er forget
One pleasure lost, lose heav'n without regret;
Regret would rouse them and give birth to pray'r,
Pray'r would add faith, and faith would fix them there.
   Not that the Former of us all in this,   345
Or aught he does, is govern'd by caprice,
The supposition is replete with sin,
And bears the brand of blasphemy burnt in.
   Not so—the silver trumpet's heav'nly call,
Sounds for the poor, but sounds alike for all;   350
Kings are invited, and would kings obey,
No slaves on earth more welcome were than they;
But royalty, nobility, and state,
Are such a dead preponderating weight,
That endless bliss (how strange soe'er it seem)   355
In counterpoise, flies up and kicks the beam.

325 be] is *H*   326 Toilsome and indigent] So cast in Poverty *H*   330 treasure]
Mansion *deleted H*   341 voluptuaries] Voluptuous Tribe *H*   344 fix] place *H*

'Tis open and ye cannot enter—why?
Because ye will not, Conyers would reply—
And he says much that many may dispute
And cavil at with ease, but none refute.   360
Oh bless'd effect of penury and want,
The seed sown there, how vigorous is the plant!
No soil like poverty for growth divine,
As leanest land supplies the richest wine.
Earth gives too little, giving only bread,   365
To nourish pride or turn the weakest head:
To them, the sounding jargon of the schools,
Seems what it is, a cap and bells for fools:
The light they walk by, kindled from above,
Shows them the shortest way to life and love: 37c
They, strangers to the controversial field,
Where deists always foil'd, yet scorn to yield,
And never check'd by what impedes the wise,
Believe, rush forward, and possess the prize.

   Envy ye great the dull unletter'd small,   375
Ye have much cause for envy—but not all;
We boast some rich ones whom the gospel sways,
And one that wears a coronet and prays;
Like gleanings of an olive tree they show,
Here and there one upon the topmost bough.   380
   How readily upon the gospel plan,
That question has its answer—what is man?
Sinful and weak, in ev'ry sense a wretch,
An instrument whose chords upon the stretch
And strain'd to the last screw that he can bear,   385
Yield only discord in his maker's ear:
Once the blest residence of truth divine,
Glorious as Solyma's interior shrine,
Where in his own oracular abode,
Dwelt visibly the light-creating God;   390
But made long since like Babylon of old,
A den of mischiefs never to be told:
And she, once mistress of the realms around,
Now scatter'd wide and no where to be found,

358 Conyers] Newton *H*   359 many may dispute] many Dispute *H*   361 *indented in H*   366 nourish] cherish *H*   388] Archetype of Judaea's hallow'd Shrine, *H*

As soon shall rise and re-ascend the throne,   395
By native pow'r and energy her own,
As nature at her own peculiar cost,
Restore to man the glories he has lost.
Go bid the winter cease to chill the year,
Replace the wand'ring comet in his sphere,   400
Then boast (but wait for that unhop'd-for hour)
The self-restoring arm of human pow'r.
But what is man in his own proud esteem?
Hear him, himself the poet and the theme;
A monarch cloath'd with majesty and awe,   405
His mind his kingdom and his will his law,
Grace in his mien and glory in his eyes,
Supreme on earth and worthy of the skies,
Strength in his heart, dominion in his nod,
And, thunderbolts excepted, quite a God.   410
    So sings he, charm'd with his own mind and form,
The song magnificent, the theme a worm:
Himself so much the source of his delight,
His maker has no beauty in his sight:
See where he sits contemplative and fixt,   415
Pleasure and wonder in his features mixt,
His passions tam'd and all at his controul,
How perfect the composure of his soul!
Complacency has breath'd a gentle gale
O'er all his thoughts, and swell'd his easy sail: 420
His books well trimm'd and in the gayest stile,
Like regimented coxcombs rank and file,
Adorn his intellects as well as shelves,
And teach him notions splendid as themselves:
The bible only stands neglected there,   425
Though that of all most worthy of his care,
And like an infant, troublesome awake,
Is left to sleep for peace and quiet sake.
    What shall the man deserve of human kind,
Whose happy skill and industry combin'd,   430

399] Go, Shift the Seasons, and Reverse the Year, *H*   403 *indented in H*   407,
408 *in reverse order in H*   407 mien] Form *H*
411-12   So sings the Theorist his self-taught Praise,
                              And his own Worth with Extacy surveys. *H*

Shall prove (what argument could never yet)
The bible an imposture and a cheat?
The praises of the libertine profess'd,
The worst of men, and curses of the best.
Where should the living, weeping o'er his woes,   435
The dying, trembling at their awful close,
Where the betray'd, forsaken and oppress'd,
The thousands whom the world forbids to rest,
Where should they find (those comforts at an end
The scripture yields) or hope to find a friend?   440
Sorrow might muse herself to madness then,
And seeking exile from the sight of men,
Bury herself in solitude profound,
Grow frantic with her pangs and bite the ground.
Thus often unbelief grown sick of life,   445
Flies to the tempting pool or felon knife,
The jury meet, the coroner is short,
And lunacy the verdict of the court:
Reverse the sentence, let the truth be known,
Such lunacy is ignorance alone;   450
They knew not, what some bishops may not know,
That scripture is the only cure of woe:
That field of promise, how it flings abroad
Its odour o'er the Christian's thorny road;
The soul reposing on assur'd relief,   455
Feels herself happy amidst all her grief,
Forgets her labour as she toils along,
Weeps tears of joy, and bursts into a song.
    But the same word that like the polish'd share
Ploughs up the roots of a believer's care,   460
Kills too the flow'ry weeds where'er they grow,
That bind the sinner's Bacchanalian brow.
Of that unwelcome voice of heav'nly love,
Sad messenger of mercy from above,
How does it grate upon his thankless ear,   465
Crippling his pleasures with the cramp of fear!
His will and judgment at continual strife,
That civil war imbitters all his life;
In vain he points his pow'rs against the skies,

In vain he closes or averts his eyes,   470
Truth will intrude—she bids him yet beware—
And shakes the sceptic in the scorner's chair.
   Though various foes against the truth combine,
Pride above all opposes her design;
Pride, of a growth superior to the rest,   475
The subtlest serpent with the loftiest crest,
Swells at the thought, and kindling into rage,
Would hiss the cherub mercy from the stage.
   And is the soul indeed so lost, she cries,
Fall'n from her glory and too weak to rise,   480
Torpid and dull beneath a frozen zone,
Has she no spark that may be deem'd her own?
Grant her indebted to what zealots call
Grace undeserv'd, yet surely not for all—
Some beams of rectitude she yet displays,   485
Some love of virtue and some pow'r to praise,
Can lift herself above corporeal things,
And soaring on her own unborrow'd wings,
Possess herself of all that's good or true,
Assert the skies, and vindicate her due.   490
Past indiscretion is a venial crime,
And if the youth, unmellow'd yet by time,
Bore on his branch luxuriant then, and rude,
Fruits of a blighted size, austere and crude,
Maturer years shall happier stores produce,   495
And meliorate the well concocted juice.
Then conscious of her meritorious zeal,
To justice she may make her bold appeal,
And leave to mercy with a tranquil mind,
The worthless and unfruitful of mankind.   500
Hear then how mercy slighted and defied,
Retorts th' affront against the crown of pride.
   Perish the virtue, as it ought, abhorr'd,
And the fool with it that insults his Lord.
Th' atonement a Redeemer's love has wrought   505

---

470 closes or averts his] Shuts his unbenighted *H*   488 *cropped in H*
500 worthless] barren *H*   501 *indented in H*   503 as it ought,] worthless
and *H*

Is not for you, the righteous need it not.
Seest thou yon harlot wooing all she meets
The worn out nuisance of the public streets,
Herself from morn to night, from night to morn,
Her own abhorrence, and as much your scorn,   510
The gracious show'r, unlimited and free,
Shall fall on her, when heav'n denies it thee.
Of all that wisdom dictates, this the drift,
That man is dead in sin, and life a gift.
    Is virtue then, unless of christian growth,   515
Mere fallacy, or foolishness, or both,
Ten thousand sages lost in endless woe,
For ignorance of what they could not know?
That speech betrays at once a bigot's tongue,
Charge not a God with such outrageous wrong.   520
Truly not I—the partial light men have,
My creed persuades me, well employed may save,
While he that scorns the noon-day beam perverse,
Shall find the blessing, unimprov'd, a curse.
Let heathen worthies whose exalted mind,   525
Left sensuality and dross behind,
Possess for me their undisputed lot,
And take unenvied the reward they sought.
But still in virtue of a Savior's plea,
Not blind by choice, but destin'd not to see.   530
Their fortitude and wisdom were a flame
Celestial, though they knew not whence it came,
Deriv'd from the same source of light and grace
That guides the christian in his swifter race;
Their judge was conscience, and her rule their law,   535
That rule pursued with rev'rence and with awe,
Led them, however fault'ring, faint and slow,
From what they knew, to what they wish'd to know;
But let not him that shares a brighter day,
Traduce the splendor of a noon tide ray,   540

following 506

But mark me, when hereafter you appear
To plead your Merits in your Maker's Ear,
The Judge with all the Lightnings of his Eye
Shall Blast you,—Death shall be the Just Reply. *H*

515–46 *not in H*

Prefer the twilight of a darker time,
And deem his base stupidity no crime;
The wretch that slights the bounty of the skies,
And sinks while favour'd with the means to rise,
Shall find them rated at their full amount,   545
The good he scorn'd all carried to account.
 Marshalling all his terrors as he came,
Thunder and earthquake and devouring flame,
From Sinai's top Jehovah gave the law,
Life for obedience, death for ev'ry flaw.   550
When the great sov'reign would his will express,
He gives a perfect rule; what can he less?
And guards it with a sanction as severe
As vengeance can inflict, or sinners fear:
Else his own glorious rights he would disclaim,   555
And man might safely trifle with his name:
He bids him glow with unremitting love
To all on earth, and to himself above;
Condemns th' injurious deed, the sland'rous tongue,
The thought that meditates a brother's wrong;   560
Brings not alone, the more conspicuous part,
His conduct to the test, but tries his heart.
 Hark! universal nature shook and groan'd,
'Twas the last trumpet—see the judge enthron'd:
Rouse all your courage at your utmost need,   565
Now summon ev'ry virtue, stand and plead.
What, silent? Is your boasting heard no more?
That self-renouncing wisdom learn'd before,
Had shed immortal glories on your brow,
That all your virtues cannot purchase now.   570
 All joy to the believer! He can speak—
Trembling yet happy, confident yet meek.
 Since the dear hour that brought me to thy foot,
And cut up all my follies by the root,
I never trusted in an arm but thine,   575

547 his terrors as he came] its Terrors as it came *H*   549 Jehovah gave the] went
forth the fiery *H* 550] Denouncing Death on the minutest Flaw. *H*
558 all] Man *H*
568–9]   Oh had you been as diffident before,
    That Grace had shed a Glory on your Brow, *H*
575 an arm] a Name *H*

Nor hop'd, but in thy righteousness divine:
My pray'rs and alms, imperfect and defil'd,
Were but the feeble efforts of a child,
Howe'er perform'd, it was their brightest part,
That they proceeded from a grateful heart: 580
Cleans'd in thine own all-purifying blood,
Forgive their evil and accept their good;
I cast them at thy feet—my only plea
Is what it was, dependence upon thee;
While struggling in the vale of tears below,   585
That never fail'd, nor shall it fail me now.
    Angelic gratulations rend the skies,
Pride falls unpitied, never more to rise,
Humility is crown'd, and faith receives the prize.

    582 their] the *H*   589 and faith receives] the Christian gains *H*

EXPOSTULATION

Tantane, tam patiens, nullo certamine tolli
Dona sines?   VIRG.

Why weeps the muse for England? What appears
In England's case to move the muse to tears?
From side to side of her delightful isle,
Is she not cloath'd with a perpetual smile?
Can nature add a charm, or art confer   5
A new found luxury not seen in her?
Where under heav'n is pleasure more pursued,
Or where does cold reflection less intrude?
Her fields a rich expanse of wavy corn
Pour'd out from plenty's overflowing horn,   10
Ambrosial gardens in which art supplies
The fervor and the force of Indian skies,
Her peaceful shores, where busy commerce waits
To pour his golden tide through all her gates,
Whom fiery suns that scorch the russet spice   15
Of eastern groves, and oceans floor'd with ice
Forbid in vain to push his daring way
To darker climes, or climes of brighter day,
Whom the winds waft where'er the billows roll,
From the world's girdle to the frozen pole;   20
The chariots bounding in her wheel-worn streets,
Her vaults below where ev'ry vintage meets,
Her theatres, her revels, and her sports,
The scenes to which not youth alone resorts,
But age in spite of weakness and of pain   25
Still haunts, in hope to dream of youth again,
All speak her happy—let the muse look round
From East to West, no sorrow can be found,
Or only what in cottages confin'd,

Before 25 February–late March or early April 1781.
COPY-TEXT: *1782*, pp. 103–40 (first printing).
16 ice] ice; *1782*

Sighs unregarded to the passing wind;   30
Then wherefore weep for England, what appears
In England's case to move the muse to tears?
   The prophet wept for Israel, wish'd his eyes
Were fountains fed with infinite supplies;
For Israel dealt in robbery and wrong,   35
There were the scorner's and the sland'rer's tongue,
Oaths used as playthings or convenient tools,
As Int'rest biass'd knaves, or fashion fools,
Adult'ry neighing at his neighbour's door,
Oppression labouring hard to grind the poor,   40
The partial balance and deceitful weight,
The treach'rous smile, a mask for secret hate,
Hypocrisy, formality in pray'r,
And the dull service of the lip were there.
Her women insolent and self-caress'd,   45
By vanity's unwearied finger dress'd,
Forgot the blush that virgin fears impart
To modest cheeks, and borrowed one from art;
Were just such trifles without worth or use,
As silly pride and idleness produce,   50
Curl'd, scented, furbelow'd and flounc'd around,
With feet too delicate to touch the ground,
They stretch'd the neck, and roll'd the wanton eye,
And sigh'd for ev'ry fool that flutter'd by.
   He saw his people slaves to ev'ry lust,   55
Lewd, avaricious, arrogant, unjust,
He heard the wheels of an avenging God
Groan heavily along the distant road;
Saw Babylon set wide her two-leav'd brass
To let the military deluge pass;   60
Jerusalem a prey, her glory soil'd,
Her princes captive, and her treasures spoil'd;
Wept till all Israel heard his bitter cry,
Stamp'd with his foot and smote upon his thigh;
But wept and stamp'd and smote his thigh in vain,   65
Pleasure is deaf when told of future pain,
And sounds prophetic are too rough to suit
Ears long accustom'd to the pleasing lute;

59 two-leav'd] two leav'd *1782*

They scorn'd his inspiration and his theme,
Pronounc'd him frantic and his fears a dream,   70
With self-indulgence wing'd the fleeting hours,
Till the foe found them, and down fell the tow'rs.
   Long time Assyria bound them in her chain,
Till penitence had purg'd the public stain,
And Cyrus, with relenting pity mov'd,   75
Return'd them happy to the land they lov'd:
There, proof against prosperity, awhile
They stood the test of her ensnaring smile,
And had the grace in scenes of peace to show
The virtue they had learn'd in scenes of woe.   80
But man is frail and can but ill sustain
A long immunity from grief and pain,
And after all the joys that plenty leads,
With tip-toe step vice silently succeeds.
   When he that rul'd them with a shepherd's rod,   85
In form a man, in dignity a God,
Came not expected in that humble guise,
To sift, and search them with unerring eyes,
He found conceal'd beneath a fair outside,
The filth of rottenness and worm of pride,   90
Their piety a system of deceit,
Scripture employ'd to sanctify the cheat,
The pharisee the dupe of his own art,
Self-idolized and yet a knave at heart.
   When nations are to perish in their sins,   95
'Tis in the church the leprosy begins:
The priest whose office is, with zeal sincere
To watch the fountain, and preserve it clear,
Carelessly nods and sleeps upon the brink,
While others poison what the flock must drink;   100
Or waking at the call of lust alone,
Infuses lies and errors of his own:
His unsuspecting sheep believe it pure,
And tainted by the very means of cure,
Catch from each other a contagious spot,   105
The foul forerunner of a general rot:
Then truth is hush'd that heresy may preach,
And all is trash that reason cannot reach;

Then God's own image on the soul impress'd,
Becomes a mock'ry and a standing jest,   110
And faith, the root whence only can arise
The graces of a life that wins the skies,
Loses at once all value and esteem,
Pronounc'd by gray beards a pernicious dream:
Then ceremony leads her bigots forth,   115
Prepar'd to fight for shadows of no worth,
While truths on which eternal things depend,
Find not, or hardly find a single friend:
As soldiers watch the signal of command,
They learn to bow, to kneel, to sit, to stand,   120
Happy to fill religion's vacant place
With hollow form and gesture and grimace.
　　Such when the teacher of his church was there,
People and priest, the sons of Israel were,
Stiff in the letter, lax in the design   125
And import of their oracles divine,
Their learning legendary, false, absurd,
And yet exalted above God's own word,
They drew a curse from an intended good,
Puff'd up with gifts they never understood.   130
He judg'd them with as terrible a frown,
As if, not love, but wrath had brought him down,
Yet he was gentle as soft summer airs,
Had grace for other sins, but none for theirs.
Through all he spoke a noble plainness ran,   135
Rhet'ric is artifice, the work of man,
And tricks and turns that fancy may devise,
Are far too mean for him that rules the skies.
Th' astonish'd vulgar trembl'd while he tore
The mask from faces never seen before;   140
He stripp'd th' impostors in the noon-day sun,
Show'd that they follow'd all they seem'd to shun,
Their pray'rs made public, their excesses kept
As private as the chambers where they slept.
The temple and its holy rites profan'd   145
By mumm'ries he that dwelt in it disdain'd,
Uplifted hands that at convenient times
Could act extortion and the worst of crimes,

Wash'd with a neatness scrupulously nice,
And free from ev'ry taint but that of vice.   150
Judgment, however tardy, mends her pace
When obstinacy once has conquer'd grace.
They saw distemper heal'd, and life restor'd
In answer to the fiat of his word,
Confess'd the wonder, and with daring tongue,   155
Blasphem'd th' authority from which it sprung.
They knew by sure prognostics seen on high,
The future tone and temper of the sky,
But grave dissemblers, could not understand
That sin let loose speaks punishment at hand.   160
   Ask now of history's authentic page,
And call up evidence from ev'ry age,
Display with busy and laborious hand
The blessings of the most indebted land,
What nation will you find, whose annals prove   165
So rich an int'rest in almighty love?
Where dwell they now, where dwelt in antient day
A people planted, water'd, blest as they?
Let Egypt's plagues, and Canaan's woes proclaim
The favours pour'd upon the Jewish name;   170
Their freedom purchas'd for them, at the cost
Of all their hard oppressors valued most,
Their title to a country not their own,
Made sure by prodigies 'till then unknown,
For them, the state they left made waste and void,   175
For them, the states to which they went, destroy'd;
A cloud to measure out their march by day,
By night a fire to cheer the gloomy way,
That moving signal summoning, when best
Their host to move, and when it stay'd, to rest.   180
For them the rocks dissolv'd into a flood,
The dews condens'd into angelic food,
Their very garments sacred, old yet new,
And time forbid to touch them as he flew,
Streams swell'd above the bank, enjoin'd to stand,   185
While they pass'd through to their appointed land,
Their leader arm'd with meekness, zeal and love,
And grac'd with clear credentials from above,

Themselves secur'd beneath th' Almighty wing,
Their God their captain,* lawgiver, and king.   190
Crown'd with a thousand vict'ries, and at last
Lords of the conquer'd soil, there rooted fast,
In peace possessing what they won by war,
Their name far publish'd and rever'd as far;
Where will you find a race like theirs, endow'd   195
With all that man e'er wish'd, or Heav'n bestow'd?
    They and they only amongst all mankind
Receiv'd the transcript of th' eternal mind,
Were trusted with his own engraven laws,
And constituted guardians of his cause,   200
Theirs were the prophets, theirs the priestly call,
And theirs by birth the Saviour of us all.
In vain the nations that had seen them rise,
With fierce and envious yet admiring eyes,
Had sought to crush them, guarded as they were   205
By power divine, and skill that could not err,
Had they maintain'd allegiance firm and sure,
And kept the faith immaculate and pure,
Then the proud eagles of all-conqu'ring Rome
Had found one city not to be o'ercome,   210
And the twelve standards of the tribes unfurl'd
Had bid defiance to the warring world.
But grace abus'd brings forth the foulest deeds,
As richest soil the most luxuriant weeds;
Cur'd of the golden calves, their fathers' sin,   215
They set up self, that idol god within,
View'd a Deliv'rer with disdain and hate,
Who left them still a tributary state,
Seiz'd fast his hand, held out to set them free
From a worse yoke, and nail'd it to the tree;   220
There was the consummation and the crown,
The flow'r of Israel's infamy full blown;
Thence date their sad declension and their fall,
Their woes not yet repeal'd, thence date them all.
    Thus fell the best instructed in her day,   225

    * Vide Joshua v. 14.

_____

211 unfurl'd] unfurl'd: *1782*   215 calves, their fathers'] calves their fathers *1782*

And the most favor'd land, look where we may.
Philosophy indeed on Grecian eyes
Had pour'd the day, and clear'd the Roman skies;
In other climes perhaps creative art,
With pow'r surpassing theirs perform'd her part,   230
Might give more life to marble, or might fill
The glowing tablets with a juster skill,
Might shine in fable, and grace idle themes
With all th' embroid'ry of poetic dreams;
'Twas theirs alone to dive into the plan   235
That truth and mercy had reveal'd to man,
And while the world beside, that plan unknown,
Deified useless wood or senseless stone,
They breath'd in faith their well-directed pray'rs,
And the true God, the God of truth was theirs.   240
    Their glory faded, and their race dispers'd,
The last of nations now, though once the first;
They warn and teach the proudest, would they learn,
Keep wisdom or meet vengeance in your turn:
If we escap'd not, if Heav'n spar'd not us,   245
Peel'd, scatter'd, and exterminated thus;
If vice receiv'd her retribution due
When we were visited, what hope for you?
When God arises with an awful frown,
To punish lust, or pluck presumption down;   250
When gifts perverted or not duly priz'd,
Pleasure o'ervalued and his grace despis'd,
Provoke the vengeance of his righteous hand
To pour down wrath upon a thankless land,
He will be found impartially severe,   255
Too just to wink, or speak the guilty clear.
    Oh Israel, of all nations most undone!
Thy diadem displac'd, thy sceptre gone;
Thy temple, once thy glory, fall'n and ras'd,
And thou a worshipper e'en where thou mayst;   260
Thy services once holy without spot,
Mere shadows now, their antient pomp forgot;
Thy Levites once a consecrated host,
No longer Levites, and their lineage lost,
And thou thyself o'er ev'ry country sown,   265

With none on earth that thou canst call thine own;
Cry aloud thou that sittest in the dust,
Cry to the proud, the cruel and unjust,
Knock at the gates of nations, rouse their fears,
Say wrath is coming and the storm appears,   270
But raise the shrillest cry in British ears.
    What ails thee, restless as the waves that roar,
And fling their foam against thy chalky shore?
Mistress, at least while Providence shall please,
And trident-bearing queen of the wide seas—   275
Why, having kept good faith, and often shown
Friendship and truth to others, findst thou none?
Thou that hast set the persecuted free,
None interposes now to succour thee;
Countries indebted to thy pow'r, that shine   280
With light deriv'd from thee, would smother thine;
Thy very children watch for thy disgrace,
A lawless brood, and curse thee to thy face:
Thy rulers load thy credit year by year
With sums Peruvian mines could never clear,   285
As if like arches built with skilful hand,
The more 'twere press'd the firmer it would stand.
The cry in all thy ships is still the same,
Speed us away to battle and to fame,
Thy mariners explore the wild expanse,   290
Impatient to descry the flags of France,
But though they fight as thine have ever fought,
Return asham'd without the wreaths they sought:
Thy senate is a scene of civil jar,
Chaos of contrarieties at war,   295
Where sharp and solid, phlegmatic and light,
Discordant atoms meet, ferment and fight,
Where obstinacy takes his sturdy stand,
To disconcert what policy has plann'd,
Where policy is busied all night long   300
In setting right what faction has set wrong,
Where flails of oratory thresh the floor,
That yields them chaff and dust, and nothing more.
Thy rack'd inhabitants repine, complain,
Tax'd 'till the brow of labour sweats in vain,   305

War lays a burthen on the reeling state,
And peace does nothing to relieve the weight,
Successive loads succeeding broils impose,
And sighing millions prophecy the close.
  Is adverse providence when ponder'd well,   310
So dimly writ or difficult to spell,
Thou canst not read with readiness and ease,
Providence adverse in events like these?
Know then, that heav'nly wisdom on this ball
Creates, gives birth to, guides, consummates all: 315
That while laborious and quick-thoughted man
Snuffs up the praise of what he seems to plan;
He first conceives, then perfects his design,
As a mere instrument in hands divine:
Blind to the working of that secret pow'r   320
That balances the wings of ev'ry hour,
The busy trifler dreams himself alone,
Frames many a purpose, and God works his own.
States thrive or wither as moons wax and wane,
Ev'n as his will and his decrees ordain;   325
While honour, virtue, piety bear sway,
They flourish, and as these decline, decay.
In just resentment of his injur'd laws,
He pours contempt on them and on their cause,
Strikes the rough thread of error right athwart   330
The web of ev'ry scheme they have at heart,
Bids rottenness invade and bring to dust
The pillars of support in which they trust,
And do his errand of disgrace and shame
On the chief strength and glory of the frame.   335
None ever yet impeded what he wrought,
None bars him out from his most secret thought;
Darkness itself before his eye is light,
And Hell's close mischief naked in his sight.
  Stand now and judge thyself—hast thou incurr'd   340
His anger who can waste thee with a word,
Who poises and proportions sea and land,
Weighing them in the hollow of his hand,
And in whose awful sight all nations seem
As grasshoppers, as dust, a drop, a dream?   345

Hast thou (a sacrilege his soul abhors)
Claim'd all the glory of thy prosp'rous wars,
Proud of thy fleets and armies, stol'n the gem
Of his just praise to lavish it on them?
Hast thou not learn'd what thou art often told,   350
A truth still sacred, and believ'd of old,
That no success attends on spears and swords
Unblest, and that the battle is the Lord's?
That courage is his creature, and dismay
The post that at his bidding speeds away,   355
Ghastly in feature, and his stamm'ring tongue
With doleful rumor and sad presage hung,
To quell the valor of the stoutest heart,
And teach the combatant a woman's part?
That he bids thousands fly when none pursue,   360
Saves as he will by many or by few,
And claims for ever as his royal right
Th' event and sure decision of the fight.
    Hast thou, though suckl'd at fair freedom's breast,
Exported slav'ry to the conquer'd East,   365
Pull'd down the tyrants India serv'd with dread,
And rais'd thyself, a greater, in their stead,
Gone thither arm'd and hungry, returned full,
Fed from the richest veins of the Mogul,
A despot big with pow'r obtain'd by wealth,   370
And that obtain'd by rapine and by stealth?
With Asiatic vices stor'd thy mind,
But left their virtues and thine own behind,
And having truck'd thy soul, brought home the fee,
To tempt the poor to sell himself to thee?   375
    Hast thou by statute shov'd from its design
The Savior's feast, his own blest bread and wine,
And made the symbols of atoning grace
An office-key, a pick-lock to a place,
That infidels may prove their title good   380
By an oath dipp'd in sacramental blood?
A blot that will be still a blot, in spite
Of all that grave apologists may write,
And though a Bishop toil to cleanse the stain,
He wipes and scours the silver cup in vain.   385

And hast thou sworn on ev'ry slight pretence,
'Till perjuries are common as bad pence,
While thousands, careless of the damning sin,
Kiss the book's outside who ne'er look within?
    Hast thou, when heav'n has cloath'd thee with disgrace,   390
And long provok'd, repaid thee to thy face,
(For thou hast known eclipses, and endur'd
Dimness and anguish all thy beams obscur'd,
When sin has shed dishonour on thy brow,
And never of a sabler hue than now)   395
Hast thou with heart perverse and conscience sear'd,
Despising all rebuke, still persever'd,
And having chosen evil, scorn'd the voice
That cried repent—and gloried in thy choice?
Thy fastings, when calamity at last   400
Suggests th' expedient of an yearly fast,
What mean they? Canst thou dream there is a pow'r
In lighter diet at a later hour,
To charm to sleep the threat'nings of the skies,
And hide past folly from all-seeing eyes?   405

390–412 replace the following, found in some copies on the cancellandum leaf I6:

        Hast thou admitted with a blind, fond trust,
        The lie that burn'd thy father's bones to dust,
        That first adjudg'd them hereticks, then sent
        Their souls to Heav'n, and curs'd them as they went?
        The lie that Scripture strips of its disguise,
        And execrates above all other lies,
        The lie that claps a lock on mercy's plan,
        And gives the key to yon infirm old man,
        Who once insconc'd in apostolic chair
        Is deified, and sits omniscient there;
        The lie that knows no kindred, owns no friend
        But him that makes its progress his chief end,
        That having spilt much blood, makes that a boast,
        And canonizes him that sheds the most?
        Away with charity that sooths a lie,
        And thrusts the truth with scorn and anger by;
        Shame on the candour and the gracious smile
        Bestow'd on them that light the martyr's pile,
        While insolent disdain in frowns express'd,
        Attends the tenets that endur'd that test:
        Grant them the rights of men, and while they cease
        To vex the peace of others, grant them peace,
        But trusting bigots whose false zeal has made
        Treach'ry their duty, thou art self-betray'd.

The fast that wins deliv'rance, and suspends
The stroke that a vindictive God intends,
Is to renounce hypocrisy, to draw
Thy life upon the pattern of the law,
To war with pleasures idolized before,   410
To vanquish lust, and wear its yoke no more.
All fasting else, whate'er be the pretence,
Is wooing mercy by renew'd offence.
    Hast thou within thee sin that in old time
Brought fire from heav'n, the sex-abusing crime,   415
Whose horrid perpetration stamps disgrace
Baboons are free from, upon human race?
Think on the fruitful and well-water'd spot
That fed the flocks and herds of wealthy Lot,
Where Paradise seem'd still vouchsaf'd on earth,   420
Burning and scorch'd into perpetual dearth,
Or in his words who damn'd the base desire,
Suff'ring the vengeance of eternal fire:
Then nature injur'd, scandaliz'd, defil'd,
Unveil'd her blushing cheek, look'd on and smil'd,   425
Beheld with joy the lovely scene defac'd,
And prais'd the wrath that lay'd her beauties waste.
    Far be the thought from any verse of mine,
And farther still the form'd and fixt design,
To thrust the charge of deeds that I detest,   430
Against an innocent unconscious breast:
The man that dares traduce because he can
With safety to himself, is not a man:
An individual is a sacred mark,
Not to be pierc'd in play or in the dark,   435
But public censure speaks a public foe,
Unless a zeal for virtue guide the blow.
    The priestly brotherhood, devout, sincere,
From mean self-int'rest and ambition clear,
Their hope in Heav'n, servility their scorn,   440
Prompt to persuade, expostulate and warn,
Their wisdom pure, and giv'n them from above,
Their usefulness insur'd by zeal and love,
As meek as the man Moses, and withal
As bold as in Agrippa's presence, Paul,   445

Should fly the world's contaminating touch
Holy and unpolluted—are thine such?
Except a few with Eli's spirit blest,
Hophni and Phineas may describe the rest.
    Where shall a teacher look in days like these,   450
For ears and hearts that he can hope to please?
Look to the poor—the simple and the plain
Will hear perhaps thy salutary strain;
Humility is gentle, apt to learn,
Speak but the word, will listen and return: 455
Alas, not so! the poorest of the flock
Are proud, and set their faces as a rock,
Denied that earthly opulence they chuse,
God's better gift they scoff at and refuse.
The rich, the produce of a nobler stem,   460
Are more intelligent at least, try them:
Oh vain enquiry! they without remorse
Are altogether gone a devious course,
Where beck'ning pleasure leads them, wildly stray,
Have burst the bands and cast the yoke away.   465
    Now borne upon the wings of truth, sublime,
Review thy dim original and prime;
This island spot of unreclaim'd rude earth,
The cradle that receiv'd thee at thy birth,
Was rock'd by many a rough Norwegian blast,   470
And Danish howlings scar'd thee as they pass'd;
For thou wast born amid the din of arms,
And suck'd a breast that panted with alarms.
While yet thou wast a grov'ling puling chit,
Thy bones not fashion'd and thy joints not knit,   475
The Roman taught thy stubborn knee to bow,
Though twice a Cæsar could not bend thee now:
His victory was that of orient light,
When the sun's shafts disperse the gloom of night:
Thy language at this distant moment shows   480
How much the country to the conqu'ror owes,
Expressive, energetic and refin'd,
It sparkles with the gems he left behind:
He brought thy land a blessing when he came,
He found thee savage, and he left thee tame,   485

Taught thee to cloath thy pink'd and painted hide,
And grace thy figure with a soldier's pride,
He sow'd the seeds of order where he went,
Improv'd thee far beyond his own intent,
And while he rul'd thee by the sword alone,   490
Made thee at last a warrior like his own.
Religion if in heav'nly truths attir'd,
Needs only to be seen to be admir'd,
But thine as dark as witch'ries of the night,
Was form'd to harden hearts and shock the sight: 495
Thy Druids struck the well-strung harps they bore,
With fingers deeply dy'd in human gore,
And while the victim slowly bled to death,
Upon the tolling chords rung out his dying breath.
  Who brought the lamp that with awak'ning beams   500
Dispell'd thy gloom and broke away thy dreams,
Tradition, now decrepid and worn out,
Babbler of antient fables, leaves a doubt:
But still light reach'd thee; and those gods of thine
Woden and Thor, each tott'ring in his shrine,   505
Fell broken and defac'd at his own door,
As Dagon in Philistia long before.
But Rome with sorceries and magic wand,
Soon rais'd a cloud that darken'd ev'ry land,
And thine was smother'd in the stench and fog   510
Of Tiber's marshes and the papal bog:
Then priests with bulls and briefs and shaven crowns,
And griping fists and unrelenting frowns,
Legates and delegates with pow'rs from hell,
Though heav'nly in pretension, fleec'd thee well;   515
And to this hour to keep it fresh in mind,
Some twigs of that old scourge are left behind.*
Thy soldiery the pope's well-manag'd pack,
Were train'd beneath his lash and knew the smack,
And when he laid them on the scent of blood   520
Would hunt a Saracen through fire and flood.
Lavish of life to win an empty tomb,

* Which may be found at Doctors Commons.
___
520 blood] blood: *1782*

That prov'd a mint of wealth, a mine to Rome,
They left their bones beneath unfriendly skies,
His worthless absolution all the prize.   525
Thou wast the veriest slave in days of yore,
That ever dragg'd a chain or tugg'd an oar;
Thy monarchs arbitrary, fierce, unjust,
Themselves the slaves of bigotry or lust,
Disdain'd thy counsels, only in distress   530
Found thee a goodly spunge for pow'r to press.
Thy chiefs, the lords of many a petty fee,
Provok'd and harrass'd, in return plagu'd thee,
Call'd thee away from peaceable employ,
Domestic happiness and rural joy,   535
To waste thy life in arms, or lay it down
In causeless feuds and bick'rings of their own:
Thy parliaments ador'd on bended knees
The sov'reignty they were conven'd to please;
Whate'er was ask'd, too timid to resist,   540
Comply'd with, and were graciously dismiss'd:
And if some Spartan soul a doubt express'd
And blushing at the tameness of the rest,
Dar'd to suppose the subject had a choice,
He was a traitor by the gen'ral voice.   545
Oh slave! with pow'rs thou didst not dare exert,
Verse cannot stoop so low as thy desert,
It shakes the sides of splenetic disdain,
Thou self-entitled ruler of the main,
To trace thee to the date when yon fair sea   550
That clips thy shores, had no such charms for thee,
When other nations flew from coast to coast,
And thou hadst neither fleet nor flag to boast.
   Kneel now, and lay thy forehead in the dust,
Blush if thou canst; not petrified, thou must: 555
Act but an honest and a faithful part,
Compare what then thou wast, with what thou art,
And God's disposing providence confess'd,
Obduracy itself must yield the rest—
Then thou art bound to serve him, and to prove   560
Hour after hour thy gratitude and love.

555 canst;] canst, *1782*

Has he not hid thee and thy favour'd land
For ages safe beneath his shelt'ring hand,
Giv'n thee his blessing on the clearest proof,
Bid nations leagu'd against thee stand aloof,   565
And charg'd hostility and hate to roar
Where else they would, but not upon thy shore?
His pow'r secur'd thee when presumptuous Spain
Baptiz'd her fleet invincible in vain;
Her gloomy monarch, doubtful, and resign'd   570
To ev'ry pang that racks an anxious mind,
Ask'd of the waves that broke upon his coast,
What tidings? and the surge replied—all lost—
And when the Stuart leaning on the Scot,
Then too much fear'd and now too much forgot,   575
Pierc'd to the very center of thy realm,
And hop'd to seize his abdicated helm,
'Twas but to prove how quickly with a frown,
He that had rais'd thee could have pluck'd thee down.
Peculiar is the grace by thee possess'd,   580
Thy foes implacable, thy land at rest;
Thy thunders travel over earth and seas,
And all at home is pleasure, wealth and ease.
'Tis thus, extending his tempestuous arm,
Thy Maker fills the nations with alarm,   585
While his own Heav'n surveys the troubled scene,
And feels no change, unshaken and serene.
Freedom, in other lands scarce known to shine,
Pours out a flood of splendour upon thine;
Thou hast as bright an int'rest in her rays,   590
As ever Roman had in Rome's best days.
True freedom is, where no restraint is known
That scripture, justice, and good sense disown,
Where only vice and injury are tied,
And all from shore to shore is free beside.   595
Such freedom is—and Windsor's hoary tow'rs
Stood trembling at the boldness of thy pow'rs,
That won a nymph on that immortal plain,
Like her the fabled Phœbus woo'd in vain;
He found the laurel only—happier you,   600

595 beside.] beside, *1782*

Th' unfading laurel and the virgin too.*
   Now think, if pleasure have a thought to spare,
If God himself be not beneath her care;
If bus'ness, constant as the wheels of time,
Can pause one hour to read a serious rhime;   605
If the new mail thy merchants now receive,
Or expectation of the next give leave,
Oh think, if chargeable with deep arrears
For such indulgence gilding all thy years,
How much though long neglected, shining yet,   610
The beams of heav'nly truth have swell'd the debt.
When persecuting zeal made royal sport
With tortur'd innocence in Mary's court,
And Bonner, blithe as shepherd at a wake,
Enjoy'd the show, and danc'd about the stake;   615
The sacred book, its value understood,
Receiv'd the seal of martyrdom in blood.
Those holy men, so full of truth and grace,
Seem to reflection of a diff'rent race,
Meek, modest, venerable, wise, sincere,   620
In such a cause they could not dare to fear,
They could not purchase earth with such a prize,
Nor spare a life too short to reach the skies.
From them to thee convey'd along the tide
Their streaming hearts pour'd freely when they died,   625
Those truths which neither use nor years impair,
Invite thee, wooe thee, to the bliss they share.
What dotage will not vanity maintain,
What web too weak to catch a modern brain?
The moles and bats in full assembly find   630
On special search, the keen-ey'd eagle blind.
And did they dream, and art thou wiser now?
Prove it—if better, I submit and bow.
Wisdom and goodness are twin-born, one heart
Must hold both sisters, never seen apart.   635
   So then—as darkness overspread the deep,
Ere nature rose from her eternal sleep,

* Alluding to the grant of Magna Charta, which was extorted from king John by the Barons at Runnymede near Windsor.

624 tide] tide, *1782*

And this delightful earth and that fair sky
Leap'd out of nothing, call'd by the Most High,
By such a change thy darkness is made light,   640
Thy chaos order, and thy weakness, might,
And he whose pow'r mere nullity obeys,
Who found thee nothing, form'd thee for his praise.
To praise him is to serve him, and fulfil,
Doing and suff'ring, his unquestion'd will,   645
'Tis to believe what men inspir'd of old,
Faithful and faithfully inform'd, unfold;
Candid and just, with no false aim in view,
To take for truth what cannot but be true,
To learn in God's own school the Christian part,   650
And bind the task assign'd thee to thine heart:
Happy the man there seeking and there found,
Happy the nation where such men abound.
    How shall a verse impress thee? by what name
Shall I adjure thee not to court thy shame?   655
By theirs whose bright example unimpeach'd
Directs thee to that eminence they reach'd,
Heroes and worthies of days past, thy sires?
Or his, who touch'd their hearts with hallow'd fires?
Their names, alas! in vain reproach an age   660
Whom all the vanities they scorn'd, engage,
And his that seraphs tremble at, is hung
Disgracefully on ev'ry trifler's tongue,
Or serves the champion in forensic war,
To flourish and parade with at the bar.   665
Pleasure herself perhaps suggests a plea,
If int'rest move thee, to persuade ev'n thee:
By ev'ry charm that smiles upon her face,
By joys possess'd, and joys still held in chace,
If dear society be worth a thought,   670
And if the feast of freedom cloy thee not,
Reflect that these and all that seems thine own,
Held by the tenure of his will alone,
Like angels in the service of their Lord,
Remain with thee, or leave thee at his word;   675
That gratitude and temp'rance in our use
Of what he gives, unsparing and profuse,

Secure the favour and enhance the joy,
That thankless waste and wild abuse destroy.
  But above all reflect, how cheap soe'er   680
Those rights that millions envy thee, appear,
And though resolv'd to risk them, and swim down
The tide of pleasure, heedless of his frown,
That blessings truly sacred, and when giv'n
Mark'd with the signature and stamp of Heav'n,   685
The word of prophecy, those truths divine
Which make that Heav'n, if thou desire it, thine;
(Awful alternative! believ'd, belov'd,
Thy glory, and thy shame if unimprov'd,)
Are never long vouchsaf'd, if push'd aside   690
With cold disgust or philosophic pride,
And that judicially withdrawn, disgrace,
Error and darkness occupy their place.
  A world is up in arms, and thou, a spot
Not quickly found if negligently sought,   695
Thy soul as ample as thy bounds are small,
Endur'st the brunt, and dar'st defy them all:
And wilt thou join to this bold enterprize
A bolder still, a contest with the skies?
Remember, if he guard thee and secure,   700
Whoe'er assails thee, thy success is sure;
But if he leave thee, though the skill and pow'r
Of nations sworn to spoil thee and devour,
Were all collected in thy single arm,
And thou couldst laugh away the fear of harm,   705
That strength would fail, oppos'd against the push
And feeble onset of a pigmy rush.
  Say not (and if the thought of such defence
Should spring within thy bosom, drive it thence)
What nation amongst all my foes is free   710
From crimes as base as any charg'd on me?
Their measure fill'd—they too shall pay the debt
Which God, though long forborn, will not forget;
But know, that wrath divine, when most severe,
Makes justice still the guide of his career,   715
And will not punish in one mingled crowd,
Them without light, and thee without a cloud

Muse, hang this harp upon yon aged beech,
Still murm'ring with the solemn truths I teach,
And while, at intervals, a cold blast sings   720
Through the dry leaves, and pants upon the strings,
My soul shall sigh in secret, and lament
A nation scourg'd, yet tardy to repent.
I know the warning song is sung in vain,
That few will hear, and fewer heed the strain: 725
But if a sweeter voice, and one design'd
A blessing to my country and mankind,
Reclaim the wand'ring thousands, and bring home
A flock so scatter'd and so wont to roam,
Then place it once again between my knees,   730
The sound of truth will then be sure to please,
And truth alone, where'er my life be cast,
In scenes of plenty or the pining waste,
Shall be my chosen theme, my glory to the last.

HOPE

————doceas iter et sacra ostia pandas.

VIRG. EN. 6

Ask what is human life—the sage replies
With disappointment low'ring in his eyes,
A painful passage o'er a restless flood,
A vain pursuit of fugitive false good,
A scene of fancied bliss and heart-felt care,   5
Closing at last in darkness and despair.—
The poor, inur'd to drudgery and distress,
Act without aim, think little and feel less,
And no where but in feign'd Arcadian scenes,
Taste happiness, or know what pleasure means.   10
Riches are pass'd away from hand to hand,
As fortune, vice or folly may command;
As in a dance the pair that take the lead
Turn downward, and the lowest pair succeed,
So shifting and so various is the plan   15
By which Heav'n rules the mixt affairs of man,
Vicissitude wheels round the motley crowd,
The rich grow poor, the poor become purse-proud:
Bus'ness is labour, and man's weakness such,
Pleasure is labour too, and tires as much,   20
The very sense of it foregoes its use,
By repetition pall'd, by age obtuse.
Youth lost in dissipation, we deplore
Through life's sad remnant, what no sighs restore,
Our years, a fruitless race without a prize,   25
Too many, yet too few to make us wise.
    Dangling his cane about, and taking snuff,
Lothario cries, what philosophic stuff.
Oh querulous and weak! whose useless brain

Mid-May–mid-June 1781.

COPY-TEXT: *1782*, pp. 141–79 (first printing).

Once thought of nothing, and now thinks in vain,   30
Whose eye reverted weeps o'er all the past,
Whose prospect shows thee a disheartning waste,
Would age in thee resign his wintry reign,
And youth invigorate that frame again,
Renew'd desire would grace with other speech   35
Joys always priz'd, when plac'd within our reach.
    For lift thy palsied head, shake off the gloom
That overhangs the borders of thy tomb,
See nature gay as when she first began,
With smiles alluring her admirer, man,   40
She spreads the morning over eastern hills,
Earth glitters with the drops the night distils,
The sun obedient, at her call appears
To fling his glories o'er the robe she wears,
Banks cloath'd with flow'rs, groves fill'd with sprightly sounds, 45
The yellow tilth, green meads, rocks, rising grounds,
Streams edg'd with osiers, fatt'ning ev'ry field
Where'er they flow, now seen and now conceal'd,
From the blue rim where skies and mountains meet,
Down to the very turf beneath thy feet,   50
Ten thousand charms that only fools despise,
Or pride can look at with indiff'rent eyes,
All speak one language, all with one sweet voice
Cry to her universal realm, rejoice.
Man feels the spur of passions and desires,   55
And she gives largely more than he requires,
Not that, his hours devoted all to care,
Hollow-ey'd abstinence and lean despair,
The wretch may pine, while to his smell, taste, sight,
She holds a Paradise of rich delight,   60
But gently to rebuke his aukward fear,
To prove that what she gives, she gives sincere,
To banish hesitation, and proclaim
His happiness, her dear, her only aim.
'Tis grave philosophy's absurdest dream,   65
That Heav'n's intentions are not what they seem,
That only shadows are dispens'd below,
And earth has no reality but woe.

57 that,] that 1782

Thus things terrestrial wear a diff'rent hue,
As youth or age persuades, and neither true;   70
So Flora's wreath through colour'd chrystal seen,
The rose or lily appears blue or green,
But still th'imputed tints are those alone
The medium represents, and not their own.

    To rise at noon, sit slipshod and undress'd,   75
To read the news or fiddle as seems best,
'Till half the world comes rattling at his door,
To fill the dull vacuity 'till four,
And just when evening turns the blue vault grey,
To spend two hours in dressing for the day,   80
To make the sun a bauble without use,
Save for the fruits his heav'nly beams produce,
Quite to forget, or deem it worth no thought,
Who bids him shine, or if he shine or not,
Through mere necessity to close his eyes   85
Just when the larks and when the shepherds rise,
Is such a life, so tediously the same,
So void of all utility or aim,
That poor Jonquil, with almost ev'ry breath
Sighs for his exit, vulgarly call'd, death: 90
For he, with all his follies, has a mind
Not yet so blank, or fashionably blind,
But now and then perhaps a feeble ray
Of distant wisdom shoots across his way,
By which he reads, that life without a plan,   95
As useless as the moment it began,
Serves merely as a soil for discontent
To thrive in, an incumbrance, e'er half spent.
Oh weariness beyond what asses feel,
That tread the circuit of the cistern wheel,   100
A dull rotation never at a stay,
Yesterday's face twin image of to-day,
While conversation, an exhausted stock,
Grows drowsy as the clicking of a clock.
No need, he cries, of gravity stuff'd out   105
With academic dignity devout,
To read wise lectures, vanity the text;
Proclaim the remedy, ye learned, next,

For truth self-evident with pomp impress'd,
Is vanity surpassing all the rest.   110
   That remedy, not hid in deeps profound,
Yet seldom sought, where only to be found,
While passion turns aside from its due scope
Th' enquirer's aim, that remedy, is hope.
Life is his gift, from whom whate'er life needs,   115
And ev'ry good and perfect gift proceeds,
Bestow'd on man, like all that we partake,
Royally, freely, for his bounty sake.
Transient indeed, as is the fleeting hour,
And yet the seed of an immortal flow'r,   120
Design'd in honour of his endless love,
To fill with fragrance his abode above.
No trifle, howsoever short it seem,
And howsoever shadowy, no dream,
Its value, what no thought can ascertain,   125
Nor all an angel's eloquence explain.
   Men deal with life, as children with their play,
Who first misuse, then cast their toys away,
Live to no sober purpose, and contend
That their creator had no serious end.   130
When God and man stand opposite in view,
Man's disappointment must of course ensue.
The just Creator condescends to write
In beams of inextinguishable light,
His names of wisdom, goodness, pow'r and love,   135
On all that blooms below or shines above,
To catch the wand'ring notice of mankind,
And teach the world, if not perversely blind,
His gracious attributes, and prove the share
His offspring hold in his paternal care.   140
If led from earthly things to things divine,
His creature thwart not his august design,
Then praise is heard instead of reas'ning pride,
And captious cavil and complaint subside.
Nature employ'd in her allotted place,   145
Is hand-maid to the purposes of grace,
By good vouchsaf'd makes known superior good,
And bliss not seen by blessings understood.

That bliss reveal'd in scripture with a glow
Bright as the covenant-insuring bow,   150
Fires all his feelings with a noble scorn
Of sensual evil, and thus hope is born.
  Hope sets the stamp of vanity on all
That men have deem'd substantial since the fall,
Yet has the wond'rous virtue to educe   155
From emptiness itself a real use,
And while she takes as at a father's hand
What health and sober appetite demand,
From fading good derives with chymic art
That lasting happiness, a thankful heart.   160
Hope with uplifted foot set free from earth,
Pants for the place of her ethereal birth,
On steady wing sails through th' immense abyss,
Plucks amaranthin joys from bow'rs of bliss,
And crowns the soul while yet a mourner here,   165
With wreaths like those triumphant spirits wear.
Hope as an anchor firm and sure, holds fast
The Christian vessel, and defies the blast;
Hope! nothing else can nourish and secure
His new-born virtues, and preserve him pure;   170
Hope! let the wretch once conscious of the joy,
Whom now despairing agonies destroy,
Speak, for he can, and none so well as he,
What treasures center, what delights in thee.
Had he the gems, the spices, and the land   175
That boasts the treasure, all at his command,
The fragrant grove, th' inestimable mine,
Were light when weigh'd against one smile of thine.
  Though clasp'd and cradl'd in his nurse's arms,
He shine with all a cherub's artless charms,   180
Man is the genuine offspring of revolt,
Stubborn and sturdy, a wild ass's colt;
His passions, like the wat'ry stores that sleep
Beneath the smiling surface of the deep,
Wait but the lashes of a wintry storm,   185
To frown and roar, and shake his feeble form.

183 passions,] passions *1782*

From infancy through childhood's giddy maze,
Froward at school, and fretful in his plays,
The puny tyrant burns to subjugate
The free republic of the whip-gig state.   190
If one, his equal in athletic frame,
Or more provoking still, of nobler name,
Dares step across his arbitrary views,
An Iliad, only not in verse, ensues.
The little Greeks look trembling at the scales,   195
'Till the best tongue or heaviest hand prevails.
     Now see him launched into the world at large;
If priest, supinely droning o'er his charge,
Their fleece his pillow, and his weekly drawl,
Though short, too long, the price he pays for all;   200
If lawyer, loud whatever cause he plead,
But proudest of the worst, if that succeed.
Perhaps a grave physician, gath'ring fees,
Punctually paid for length'ning out disease,
No COTTON, whose humanity sheds rays   205
That make superior skill his second praise.
If arms engage him, he devotes to sport
His date of life, so likely to be short,
A soldier may be any thing, if brave,
So may a tradesman, if not quite a knave.   210
Such stuff the world is made of; and mankind
To passion, int'rest, pleasure, whim resign'd,
Insist on, as if each were his own pope,
Forgiveness, and the privilege of hope;
But conscience in some awful silent hour,   215
When captivating lusts have lost their pow'r,
Perhaps when sickness, or some fearful dream
Reminds him of religion, hated theme!
Starts from the down on which she lately slept,
And tells of laws despis'd, at least not kept;   220
Shows with a pointing finger and no noise,
A pale procession of past sinful joys,
All witnesses of blessings foully scorn'd,
And life abus'd—and not to be suborn'd.
Mark these, she says, these summoned from afar,   225
Begin their march to meet thee at the bar;

There find a Judge, inexorably just,
And perish there, as all presumption must.
  Peace be to those (such peace as earth can give)
Who live in pleasure, dead ev'n while they live,   230
Born capable indeed of heav'nly truth,
But down to latest age from earliest youth
Their mind a wilderness through want of care,
The plough of wisdom never ent'ring there.
Peace (if insensibility may claim   235
A right to the meek honours of her name)
To men of pedigree, their noble race
Emulous always of the nearest place
To any throne, except the throne of grace.
Let cottagers and unenlightened swains   240
Revere the laws they dream that heav'n ordains,
Resort on Sundays to the house of pray'r,
And ask, and fancy they find blessings there;
Themselves perhaps when weary they retreat
T' enjoy cool nature in a country seat,   245
T' exchange the center of a thousand trades,
For clumps and lawns and temples and cascades,
May now and then their velvet cushions take,
And seem to pray for good example sake;
Judging, in charity no doubt, the town   250
Pious enough, and having need of none.
Kind souls! to teach their tenantry to prize
What they themselves without remorse despise;
Nor hope have they nor fear of aught to come,
As well for them had prophecy been dumb;   255
They could have held the conduct they pursue,
Had Paul of Tarsus lived and died a Jew;
And truth propos'd to reas'ners wise as they,
Is a pearl cast—completely cast away.
  They die—Death lends them, pleas'd and as in sport,   260
All the grim honours of his ghastly court;
Far other paintings grace the chamber now,
Where late we saw the mimic landscape glow;
The busy heralds hang the sable scene
With mournful 'scutcheons and dim lamps between,   265
Proclaim their titles to the crowd around,

But they that wore them, move not at the sound;
The coronet placed idly at their head,
Adds nothing now to the degraded dead,
And ev'n the star that glitters on the bier,   270
Can only say, nobility lies here.
Peace to all such—'twere pity to offend
By useless censure whom we cannot mend,
Life without hope can close but in despair,
'Twas there we found them and must leave them there.   275
　　As when two pilgrims in a forest stray,
Both may be lost, yet each in his own way,
So fares it with the multitudes beguil'd
In vain opinion's waste and dang'rous wild;
Ten thousand rove the brakes and thorns among,   280
Some eastward, and some westward, and all wrong:
But here, alas! the fatal diff'rence lies,
Each man's belief is right in his own eyes;
And he that blames what they have blindly chose,
Incurs resentment for the love he shows.   285
　　Say botanist! within whose province fall
The cedar and the hyssop on the wall,
Of all that deck the lanes, the field, the bow'rs,
What parts the kindred tribes of weeds and flow'rs?
Sweet scent, or lovely form, or both combin'd,   290
Distinguish ev'ry cultivated kind,
The want of both denotes a meaner breed,
And Chloe from her garland picks the weed.
Thus hopes of every sort, whatever sect
Esteem them, sow them, rear them, and protect;   295
If wild in nature, and not duly found
Gethsemane! in thy dear, hallowed ground,
That cannot bear the blaze of scripture light,
Nor cheer the spirit, nor refresh the sight,
Nor animate the soul to Christian deeds,   300
Oh cast them from thee! are weeds, arrant weeds.
　　Ethelred's house, the center of six ways,
Diverging each from each, like equal rays,
Himself as bountiful as April rains,
Lord paramount of the surrounding plains,   305
Would give relief of bed and board to none,

But guests that sought it in th' appointed, ONE.
And they might enter at his open door,
Ev'n till his spacious hall would hold no more.
He sent a servant forth by ev'ry road,   310
To sound his horn and publish it abroad,
That all might mark, knight, menial, high and low,
An ord'nance it concern'd them much to know.
If after all, some headstrong, hardy lowt,
Would disobey, though sure to be shut out,   315
Could he with reason murmur at his case,
Himself sole author of his own disgrace?
No! the decree was just and without flaw,
And he that made, had right to make the law;
His sov'reign pow'r and pleasure unrestrain'd,   320
The wrong was his, who wrongfully complain'd.
    Yet half mankind maintain a churlish strife
With him, the donor of eternal life,
Because the deed by which his love confirms
The largess he bestows, prescribes the terms.   325
Compliance with his will your lot insures,
Accept it only, and the boon is yours;
And sure it is as kind to smile and give,
As with a frown to say, do this and live.
Love is not pedlars trump'ry, bought and sold,   330
He *will* give freely, or he *will* withold,
His soul abhors a mercenary thought,
And him as deeply who abhors it not;
He stipulates indeed, but merely this,
That man will freely take an unbought bliss,   335
Will trust him for a faithful gen'rous part,
Nor set a price upon a willing heart.
Of all the ways that seem to promise fair,
To place you where his saints his presence share,
This only can—for this plain cause, express'd   340
In terms as plain; himself has shut the rest.
But oh the strife, the bick'ring and debate,
The tidings of unpurchas'd heav'n create!
The flirted fan, the bridle and the toss,
All speakers, yet all language at a loss.   345
From stucco'd walls smart arguments rebound,

And beaus, adepts in ev'ry thing profound,
Die of disdain, or whistle off the sound.
Such is the clamor of rooks, daws, and kites,
Th' explosion of the levell'd tube excites,   350
Where mould'ring abbey-walls o'erhang the glade,
And oaks coëval spread a mournful shade.
The screaming nations hov'ring in mid air,
Loudly resent the stranger's freedom there,
And seem to warn him never to repeat   355
His bold intrusion on their dark retreat.
    Adieu, Vinoso cries, e'er yet he sips,
The purple bumper trembling at his lips,
Adieu to all morality! if grace
Make works a vain ingredient in the case.   360
The Christian hope is—waiter, draw the cork—
If I mistake not—blockhead! with a fork!
Without good works, whatever some may boast,
Mere folly and delusion—Sir, your toast.
My firm persuasion is, at least sometimes,   365
That heav'n will weigh man's virtues and his crimes,
With nice attention in a righteous scale,
And save or damn as these or those prevail.
I plant my foot upon this ground of trust,
And silence every fear with—God is just;   370
But if perchance on some dull drizzling day,
A thought intrude that says, or seems to say,
If thus th' important cause is to be tried,
Suppose the beam should dip on the wrong side,
I soon recover from these needless frights,   375
And God is merciful—sets all to rights.
Thus between justice, as my prime support,
And mercy fled to, as the last resort,
I glide and steal along with heav'n in view,
And—pardon me, the bottle stands with you.   380
I never will believe, the col'nel cries,
The sanguinary schemes that some devise,
Who make the good Creator, on their plan,
A being of less equity than man.
If appetite, or what divines call lust,   385
Which men comply with, e'en because they must,

Be punish'd with perdition, who is pure?
Then theirs, no doubt, as well as mine, is sure.
If sentence of eternal pain belong
To ev'ry sudden slip and transient wrong,   390
Then heav'n enjoins the fallible and frail,
An hopeless task, and damns them if they fail.
My creed (whatever some creed-makers mean
By Athanasian nonsense or Nicene)
My creed is, he is safe that does his best,   395
And death's a doom sufficient for the rest.
    Right, says an ensign, and for aught I see,
Your faith and mine substantially agree:
The best of ev'ry man's performance here,
Is to discharge the duties of his sphere.   400
A lawyer's dealing should be just and fair,
Honesty shines with great advantage there;
Fasting and pray'r sit well upon a priest,
A decent caution and reserve at least.
A soldier's best is courage in the field,   405
With nothing here that wants to be conceal'd,
Manly deportment, gallant, easy, gay,
An hand as lib'ral as the light of day;
The soldier thus endow'd, who never shrinks,
Nor closets up his thought what'er he thinks,   410
Who scorns to do an injury by stealth,
Must go to heav'n—and I must drink his health.
    Sir Smug! he cries (for lowest at the board,
Just made fifth chaplain of his patron lord,
His shoulders witnessing by many a shrug,   415
How much his feelings suffered, sat Sir Smug)
Your office is to winnow false from true,
Come, prophet, drink, and tell us what think you.
    Sighing and smiling as he takes his glass,
Which they that wooe preferment, rarely pass,   420
Fallible man, the church-bred youth replies,
Is still found fallible, however wise,
And differing judgments serve but to declare
That truth lies somewhere, if we knew but where.
Of all it ever was my lot to read   425
Of critics now alive or long since dead,

The book of all the world that charm'd me most
Was, well-a-day, the title-page was lost.
The writer well remarks, an heart that knows
To take with gratitude what heav'n bestows,   430
With prudence always ready at our call,
To guide our use of it, is all in all.
Doubtless it is—to which of my own store
I superadd a few essentials more;
But these, excuse the liberty I take,   435
I wave just now, for conversation sake.——
Spoke like an oracle, they all exclaim,
And add Right Rev'rend to Smug's honour'd name.

    And yet our lot is giv'n us in a land
Where busy arts are never at a stand,   440
Where science points her telescopic eye,
Familiar with the wonders of the sky,
Where bold enquiry diving out of sight,
Brings many a precious pearl of truth to light,
Where nought eludes the persevering quest,   445
That fashion, taste, or luxury suggest.
    But above all, in her own light array'd,
See mercy's grand apocalypse display'd!
The sacred book no longer suffers wrong,
Bound in the fetters of an unknown tongue,   450
But speaks with plainness art could never mend,
What simplest minds can soonest comprehend.
God gives the word, the preachers throng around,
Live from his lips, and spread the glorious sound:
That sound bespeaks salvation on her way,   455
The trumpet of a life-restoring day;
'Tis heard where England's eastern glory shines,
And in the gulphs of her Cornubian mines.
    And still it spreads. See Germany send forth
Her sons* to pour it on the farthest north: 460
Fir'd with a zeal peculiar, *they* defy
The rage and rigor of a polar sky,
And plant successfully sweet Sharon's rose,

---

* The Moravian missionaries in Greenland. Vide Krantz.

438 name.] name, *1782*

On icy plains and in eternal snows.
　　Oh blest within th' inclosure of your rocks,   465
Nor herds have ye to boast, nor bleating flocks,
No fertilizing streams your fields divide,
That show revers'd the villas on their side,
No groves have ye; no cheerful sound of bird,
Or voice of turtle in your land is heard,   470
Nor grateful eglantine regales the smell
Of those that walk at ev'ning where ye dwell—
But winter arm'd with terrors, here unknown,
Sits absolute on his unshaken throne,
Piles up his stores amid'st the frozen waste,   475
And bids the mountains he has built, stand fast,
Beckons the legions of his storms away
From happier scenes, to make your land a prey,
Proclaims the soil a conquest he has won,
And scorns to share it with the distant sun.   480
—Yet truth is yours, remote, unenvied isle,
And peace, the genuine offspring of her smile,
The pride of letter'd ignorance that binds
In chains of error, our accomplish'd minds,
That decks with all the splendor of the true   485
A false religion, is unknown to you.
Nature indeed vouchsafes for our delight
The sweet vicissitudes of day and night,
Soft airs and genial moisture, feed and cheer
Field, fruit and flow'r, and ev'ry creature here,   490
But brighter beams than his who fires the skies,
Have ris'n at length on your admiring eyes,
That shoot into your darkest caves the day
From which our nicer optics turn away.
　　Here see th' encouragement grace gives to vice,   495
The dire effect of mercy without price!
What were they?—what some fools are made by art
They were by nature, atheists, head and heart.
The gross idolatry blind heathens teach
Was too refin'd for them, beyond their reach;   500
Not ev'n the glorious sun, though men revere
The monarch most that seldom will appear,
And though his beams that quicken where they shine,

May claim some right to be esteem'd divine,
Not ev'n the sun, desirable as rare,   505
Could bend one knee, engage one vot'ry there;
They were what base credulity believes
True Christians are, dissemblers, drunkards, thieves.
The full-gorged savage at his nauseous feast
Spent half the darkness, and snor'd out the rest,   510
Was one, whom justice on an equal plan
Denouncing death upon the sins of man,
Might almost have indulg'd with an escape,
Chargeable only with an human shape.
    What are they now?—morality may spare   515
Her grave concern, her kind suspicions there.
The wretch that once sang wildly, danc'd and laugh'd,
And suck'd in dizzy madness with his draught,
Has wept a silent flood, revers'd his ways,
Is sober, meek, benevolent, and prays;   520
Feeds sparingly, communicates his store,
Abhors the craft he boasted of before,
And he that stole has learn'd to steal no more.
Well spake the prophet, let the desart sing,
Where sprang the thorn, the spiry fir shall spring,   525
And where unsightly and rank thistles grew,
Shall grow the myrtle and luxuriant yew.
    Go now, and with important tone demand
On what foundation virtue is to stand,
If self-exalting claims be turn'd adrift,   530
And grace be grace indeed, and life a gift;
The poor reclaim'd inhabitant, his eyes
Glist'ning at once with pity and surprise,
Amaz'd that shadows should obscure the sight
Of one whose birth was in a land of light,   535
Shall answer, Hope, sweet Hope, has set me free,
And made all pleasures else mere dross to me.
    These amidst scenes as waste as if denied
The common care that waits on all beside,
Wild as if nature there, void of all good,   540
Play'd only gambols in a frantic mood
(Yet charge not heav'nly skill with having plann'd

541 mood] mood; *1782*   542-3 (Yet . . . hand)] Yet . . . hand, *1782*

A play-thing world unworthy of his hand)
Can see his love, though secret evil lurks
In all we touch, stamp'd plainly on his works,   545
Deem life a blessing with its num'rous woes,
Nor spurn away a gift a God bestows.
   Hard task indeed, o'er arctic seas to roam!
Is hope exotic? grows it not at home?
Yes, but an object bright as orient morn,   550
May press the eye too closely to be borne,
A distant virtue we can all confess,
It hurts our pride and moves our envy less.
   Leuconomus (beneath well-sounding Greek
I slur a name a poet must not speak)   555
Stood pilloried on infamy's high stage,
And bore the pelting scorn of half an age,
The very butt of slander, and the blot
For ev'ry dart that malice ever shot.
The man that mentioned *him*, at once dismiss'd   560
All mercy from his lips, and sneer'd and hiss'd;
His crimes were such as Sodom never knew,
And perjury stood up to swear all true;
His aim was mischief, and his zeal pretence,
His speech rebellion against common sense,   565
A knave when tried on honesty's plain rule,
And when by that of reason, a mere fool,
The world's best comfort was, his doom was pass'd,
Die when he might, he must be damn'd at last.
   Now truth perform thine office, waft aside   570
The curtain drawn by prejudice and pride,
Reveal (the man is dead) to wond'ring eyes,
This more than monster in his proper guise.
   He lov'd the world that hated him: the tear
That dropped upon his Bible was sincere.   575
Assail'd by scandal and the tongue of strife,
His only answer was a blameless life,
And he that forged and he that threw the dart,
Had each a brother's interest in his heart.
Paul's love of Christ, and steadiness unbrib'd,   580
Were copied close in him, and well transcrib'd;
He followed Paul: his zeal a kindred flame,

His apostolic charity the same,
Like him cross'd chearfully tempestuous seas,
Forsaking country, kindred, friends, and ease;   585
Like him he labour'd, and like him, content
To bear it, suffer'd shame where'er he went.
    Blush calumny! and write upon his tomb,
If honest eulogy can spare thee room,
Thy deep repentance of thy thousand lies,   590
Which aim'd at him, have pierc'd th' offended skies,
And say, blot out my sin, confess'd, deplor'd,
Against thine image in thy saint, oh Lord!
    No blinder bigot, I maintain it still,
Than he that must have pleasure, come what will;   595
He laughs, whatever weapon truth may draw,
And deems her sharp artillery mere straw.
Scripture indeed is plain, but God and he
On scripture-ground, are sure to disagree;
Some wiser rule must teach him how to live,   600
Than that his Maker has seen fit to give,
Supple and flexible as Indian cane,
To take the bend his appetites ordain,
Contriv'd to suit frail nature's crazy case,
And reconcile his lusts with saving grace.   605
By this, with nice precision of design,
He draws upon life's map a zig-zag line,
That shows how far 'tis safe to follow sin,
And where his danger and God's wrath begin.
By this he forms, as pleas'd he sports along,   610
His well pois'd estimate of right and wrong,
And finds the modish manners of the day,
Though loose, as harmless as an infant's play.
    Build by whatever plan caprice decrees,
With what materials, on what ground you please,   615
Your hope shall stand unblam'd, perhaps admir'd,
If not that hope the scripture has requir'd:
The strange conceits, vain projects and wild dreams,
With which hypocrisy for ever teems,
(Though other follies strike the public eye,   620
And raise a laugh) pass unmolested by;
But if unblameable in word and thought,

A *man* arise, a man whom God has taught,
With all Elijah's dignity of tone,
And all the love of the beloved John,   625
To storm the citadels they build in air,
And smite th' untemper'd wall, 'tis death to spare.
To sweep away all refuges of lies,
And place, instead of quirks themselves devise,
LAMA SABACTHANI, before their eyes,   630
To prove that without Christ, all gain is loss,
All hope, despair, that stands not on his cross,
Except the few his God may have impress'd,
A tenfold frenzy seizes all the rest.
   Throughout mankind, the Christian kind at least,   635
There dwells a consciousness in ev'ry breast,
That folly ends where genuine hope begins,
And he that finds his heav'n must lose his sins:
Nature opposes with her utmost force,
This riving stroke, this ultimate divorce,   640
And while religion seems to be her view,
Hates with a deep sincerity, *the true*;
For this of all that ever influenced man,
Since Abel worshipp'd, or the world began,
This only spares no lust, admits no plea,   645
But makes him, if at all, completely free,
Sounds forth the signal, as she mounts her car,
Of an eternal, universal war,
Rejects all treaty, penetrates all wiles,
Scorns with the same indiff'rence frowns and smiles,   650
Drives through the realms of sin, where riot reels,
And grinds his crown beneath her burning wheels!
Hence all that is in man, pride, passion, art,
Pow'rs of the mind, and feelings of the heart,
Insensible of truth's almighty charms,   655
Starts at her first approach, and sounds to arms!
While bigotry with well-dissembled fears,
His eyes shut fast, his fingers in his ears,
Mighty to parry, and push by God's word
With senseless noise, his argument the sword,   660
Pretends a zeal for godliness and grace,
And spits abhorrence in the Christian's face.

Parent of hope, immortal truth, make known
Thy deathless wreaths, and triumphs all thine own:
The silent progress of thy pow'r is such,   665
Thy means so feeble, and despis'd so much,
That few believe the wonders thou hast wrought,
And none can teach them but whom thou hast taught.
Oh see me sworn to serve thee, and command
A painter's skill into a poet's hand,   670
That while I trembling trace a work divine,
Fancy may stand aloof from the design,
And light and shade and ev'ry stroke be thine.
    If ever thou hast felt another's pain,
If ever when he sigh'd, hast sigh'd again,   675
If ever on thine eye-lid stood the tear
That pity had engender'd, drop one here.
This man was happy—had the world's good word,
And with it ev'ry joy it can afford;
Friendship and love seem'd tenderly at strife,   680
Which most should sweeten his untroubl'd life;
Politely learn'd, and of a gentle race,
Good-breeding and good sense gave all a grace,
And whether at the toilette of the fair
He laugh'd and trifled, made him welcome there;   685
Or, if in masculine debate he shar'd,
Insur'd him mute attention and regard.
Alas how chang'd! expressive of his mind,
His eyes are sunk, arms folded, head reclind,
Those awful syllables, hell, death, and sin,   690
Though whisper'd, plainly tell what works within,
That conscience there performs her proper part,
And writes a doomsday sentence on his heart;
Forsaking, and forsaken of all friends,
He now perceives where earthly pleasure ends,   695
Hard task! for one who lately knew no care,
And harder still as learnt beneath despair:
His hours no longer pass unmark'd away,
A dark importance saddens every day,
He hears the notice of the clock, perplex'd,   700
And cries, perhaps eternity strikes next:
Sweet music is no longer music here,

And laughter sounds like madness in his ear,
His grief the world of all her pow'r disarms,
Wine has no taste, and beauty has no charms: 705
God's holy word, once trivial in his view,
Now by the voice of his experience, true,
Seems, as it is, the fountain whence alone
Must spring that hope he pants to make his own.
 Now let the bright reverse be known abroad,   710
Say, man's a worm, and pow'r belongs to God.
 As when a felon whom his country's laws
Have justly doom'd for some atrocious cause,
Expects in darkness and heart-chilling fears,
The shameful close of all his mispent years,   715
If chance, on heavy pinions slowly borne,
A tempest usher in the dreaded morn,
Upon his dungeon walls the lightnings play,
The thunder seems to summon him away,
The warder at the door his key applies,   720
Shoots back the bolt, and all his courage dies:
If then, just then, all thoughts of mercy lost,
When Hope, long ling'ring, at last yields the ghost,
The sound of pardon pierce his startled ear,
He drops at once his fetters and his fear,   725
A transport glows in all he looks and speaks,
And the first thankful tears bedew his cheeks.
Joy, far superior joy, that much outweighs
The comfort of a few poor added days,
Invades, possesses, and o'erwhelms the soul   730
Of him whom hope has with a touch made whole:
'Tis heav'n, all heav'n descending on the wings
Of the glad legions of the King of Kings;
'Tis more—'tis God diffus'd through ev'ry part,
'Tis God himself triumphant in his heart.   735
Oh welcome now, the sun's once hated light,
His noon-day beams were never half so bright,
Not kindred minds alone are call'd t' employ
Their hours, their days in list'ning to his joy,
Unconscious nature, all that he surveys,   740
Rocks, groves and streams must join him in his praise.

These are thy glorious works, eternal truth,
The scoff of wither'd age and beardless youth,
These move the censure and illib'ral grin
Of fools that hate thee and delight in sin: 745
But these shall last when night has quench'd the pole,
And heav'n is all departed as a scroll:
And when, as justice has long since decreed,
This earth shall blaze, and a new world succeed,
Then these thy glorious works, and they that share   750
That Hope which can alone exclude despair,
Shall live exempt from weakness and decay,
The brightest wonders of an endless day.
  Happy the bard, (if that fair name belong
To him that blends no fable with his song)   755
Whose lines uniting, by an honest art,
The faithful monitor's and poet's part,
Seek to delight, that they may mend mankind,
And while they captivate, inform the mind.
Still happier, if he till a thankful soil,   760
And fruit reward his honorable toil:
But happier far who comfort those that wait
To hear plain truth at Judah's hallow'd gate;
Their language simple as their manners meek,
No shining ornaments have they to seek,   765
Nor labour they, nor time nor talents waste
In sorting flowers to suit a fickle taste;
But while they speak the wisdom of the skies,
Which art can only darken and disguise,
Th' abundant harvest, recompence divine,   770
Repays their work—the gleaning only, mine.

CHARITY

Quâ nihil majus meliusve terris
Fata donavere, bonique divi,
Nec dabunt, quamvis redeant in aurum
Tempora priscum.
HOR. Lib. IV. Ode II

Fairest and foremost of the train that wait
On man's most dignified and happiest state,
Whether we name thee Charity or love,
Chief grace below, and all in all above,
Prosper (I press thee with a pow'rful plea)   5
A task I venture on, impell'd by thee:
Oh never seen but in thy blest effects,
Nor felt but in the soul that heav'n selects,
Who seeks to praise thee, and to make thee known
To other hearts, must have thee in his own.   10
Come, prompt me with benevolent desires,
Teach me to kindle at thy gentle fires,
And though disgrac'd and slighted, to redeem
A poet's name, by making thee the theme.
    God working ever on a social plan,   15
By various ties attaches man to man:
He made at first, though free and unconfin'd,
One man the common father of the kind,
That ev'ry tribe, though plac'd as he sees best,
Where seas or desarts part them from the rest,   20
Diff'ring in language, manners, or in face,
Might feel themselves allied to all the race.
When Cook—lamented, and with tears as just
As ever mingled with heroic dust,
Steer'd Britain's oak into a world unknown,   25
And in his country's glory sought his own,

Late June–12 July 1781.

COPY-TEXT: *1782*, pp. 180–211 (first printing).

Wherever he found man, to nature true,
The rights of man were sacred in his view:
He sooth'd with gifts and greeted with a smile
The simple native of the new-found isle,　　　　　　　30
He spurn'd the wretch that slighted or withstood
The tender argument of kindred blood,
Nor would endure that any should controul
His free-born brethren of the southern pole.
　　But though some nobler minds a law respect,　　35
That none shall with impunity neglect,
In baser souls unnumber'd evils meet,
To thwart its influence and its end defeat.
While Cook is loved for savage lives he saved,
See Cortez odious for a world enslaved!　　　　　　40
Where wast thou then sweet Charity, where then
Thou tutelary friend of helpless men?
Wast thou in Monkish cells and nunn'ries found,
Or building hospitals on English ground?
No—Mammon makes the world his legatee　　　　45
Through fear not love, and heav'n abhors the fee:
Wherever found (and all men need thy care)
Nor age nor infancy could find thee there.
The hand that slew 'till it could slay no more,
Was glued to the sword-hilt with Indian gore;　　50
Their prince as justly seated on his throne,
As vain imperial Philip on his own,
Trick'd out of all his royalty by art,
That stripp'd him bare, and broke his honest heart,
Died by the sentence of a shaven priest,　　　　　55
For scorning what they taught him to detest.
How dark the veil that intercepts the blaze
Of heav'ns mysterious purposes and ways;
God stood not, though he seem'd to stand aloof,
And at this hour the conqu'ror feels the proof.　　60
The wreath he won drew down an instant curse,
The fretting plague is in the public purse,
The canker'd spoil corrodes the pining state,
Starved by that indolence their mines create.
　　Oh could their antient Incas rise again,　　　65
How would they take up Israel's taunting strain!

Art thou too fall'n Iberia, do we see
The robber and the murth'rer weak as we?
Thou that hast wasted earth, and dared despise
Alike the wrath and mercy of the skies,   70
Thy pomp is in the grave, thy glory laid
Low in the pits thine avarice has made.
We come with joy from our eternal rest,
To see th' oppressor in his turn oppress'd.
Art thou the God the thunder of whose hand   75
Roll'd over all our desolated land,
Shook principalities and kingdoms down,
And made the mountains tremble at his frown?
The sword shall light upon thy boasted pow'rs,
And waste them, as thy sword has wasted ours.   80
'Tis thus Omnipotence his law fulfils,
And vengeance executes what justice wills.
    Again—the band of commerce was design'd
T' associate all the branches of mankind,
And if a boundless plenty be the robe,   85
Trade is the golden girdle of the globe;
Wise to promote whatever end he means,
God opens fruitful nature's various scenes,
Each climate needs what other climes produce,
And offers something to the gen'ral use;   90
No land but listens to the common call,
And in return receives supply from all;
This genial intercourse and mutual aid,
Cheers what were else an universal shade,
Calls nature from her ivy-mantled den,   95
And softens human rockwork into men.
Ingenious Art with her expressive face
Steps forth to fashion and refine the race,
Not only fills necessity's demand,
But overcharges her capacious hand;   100
Capricious taste itself can crave no more,
Than she supplies from her abounding store;
She strikes out all that luxury can ask,
And gains new vigour at her endless task.
Hers is the spacious arch, the shapely spire,   105
The painters pencil and the poets lyre;

From her the canvass borrows light and shade,
And verse more lasting, hues that never fade.
She guides the finger o'er the dancing keys,
Gives difficulty all the grace of ease,   110
And pours a torrent of sweet notes around,
Fast as the thirsting ear can drink the sound.
    These are the gifts of art, and art thrives most
Where commerce has enrich'd the busy coast:
He catches all improvements in his flight,   115
Spreads foreign wonders in his country's sight,
Imports what others have invented well,
And stirs his own to match them, or excel.
'Tis thus reciprocating each with each,
Alternately the nations learn and teach;   120
While Providence enjoins to ev'ry soul
An union with the vast terraqueous whole.
    Heav'n speed the canvass gallantly unfurl'd
To furnish and accommodate a world;
To give the Pole the produce of the sun,   125
And knit th' unsocial climates into one.—
Soft airs and gentle heavings of the wave
Impel the fleet whose errand is to save,
To succour wasted regions, and replace
The smile of opulence in sorrow's face.—   130
Let nothing adverse, nothing unforeseen,
Impede the bark that plows the deep serene,
Charg'd with a freight transcending in its worth
The gems of India, nature's rarest birth,
That flies like Gabriel on his Lord's commands,   135
An herald of God's love, to pagan lands.—
But ah! what wish can prosper, or what pray'r,
For merchants rich in cargoes of despair,
Who drive a loathsome traffic, gage and span,
And buy the muscles and the bones of man?   140
The tender ties of father, husband, friend,
All bonds of nature in that moment end,
And each endures while yet he draws his breath,
A stroke as fatal as the scythe of death.
The sable warrior, frantic with regret   145
Of her he loves, and never can forget,

Loses in tears the far receding shore,
But not the thought that they must meet no more;
Depriv'd of her and freedom at a blow,
What has he left that he can yet forego?   150
Yes, to deep sadness sullenly resign'd,
He feels his body's bondage in his mind,
Puts off his gen'rous nature, and to suit
His manners with his fate, puts on the brute.
    Oh most degrading of all ills that wait   155
On man, a mourner in his best estate!
All other sorrows virtue may endure,
And find submission more than half a cure;
Grief is itself a med'cine, and bestow'd
T' improve the fortitude that bears the load,   160
To teach the wand'rer, as his woes encrease,
The path of wisdom, all whose paths are peace.
But slav'ry!—virtue dreads it as her grave,
Patience itself is meanness in a slave:
Or if the will and sovereignty of God   165
Bid suffer it awhile, and kiss the rod,
Wait for the dawning of a brighter day,
And snap the chain the moment when you may.
Nature imprints upon whate'er we see
That has a heart and life in it, be free;   170
The beasts are chartered—neither age nor force
Can quell the love of freedom in a horse:
He breaks the cord that held him at the rack,
And conscious of an unincumber'd back,
Snuffs up the morning air, forgets the rein,   175
Loose fly his forelock and his ample mane,
Responsive to the distant neigh he neighs,
Nor stops, till overleaping all delays,
He finds the pasture where his fellows graze.
    Canst thou, and honour'd with a Christian name,   180
Buy what is woman-born, and feel no shame?
Trade in the blood of innocence, and plead
Expedience as a warrant for the deed?
So may the wolf whom famine has made bold
To quit the forest and invade the fold;   185
So may the ruffian who with ghostly glide,

Dagger in hand, steals close to your bed-side;
Not he, but his emergence forc'd the door,
He found it inconvenient to be poor.
Has God then giv'n its sweetness to the cane   190
Unless his laws be trampled on—in vain?
Built a brave world, which cannot yet subsist,
Unless his right to rule it be dismiss'd?
Impudent blasphemy! so folly pleads,
And av'rice being judge, with ease succeeds.   195
    But grant the plea, and let it stand for just,
That man make man his prey, because he *must*,
Still there is room for pity to abate
And sooth the sorrows of so sad a state.
A Briton knows, or if he knows it not,   200
The Scripture plac'd within his reach, he ought,
That souls have no discriminating hue,
Alike important in their Maker's view,
That none are free from blemish since the fall,
And love divine has paid one price for all.   205
The wretch that works and weeps without relief,
Has one that notices his silent grief,
He from whose hands alone all pow'r proceeds,
Ranks its abuse among the foulest deeds,
Considers *all* injustice with a frown,   210
But *marks* the man that treads his fellow down.
Begone, the whip and bell in that hard hand,
Are hateful ensigns of usurp'd command,
Not Mexico could purchase kings a claim
To scourge him, weariness his only blame.   215
Remember, heav'n has an avenging rod;
To smite the poor is treason against God.
    Trouble is grudgingly and hardly brook'd,
While life's sublimest joys are overlook'd.
We wander o'er a sun-burnt thirsty soil   220
Murm'ring and weary of our daily toil,
Forget t' enjoy the palm-tree's offer'd shade,
Or taste the fountain in the neighb'ring glade:
Else who would lose that had the pow'r t' improve
Th' occasion of transmuting fear to love?   225
Oh 'tis a godlike privilege to save,

And he that scorns it is himself a slave.—
Inform his mind, one flash of heav'nly day
Would heal his heart and melt his chains away;
'Beauty for ashes' is a gift indeed,   230
And slaves, by truth enlarg'd, are doubly freed:
Then would he say, submissive at thy feet,
While gratitude and love made service sweet,
My dear deliv'rer out of hopeless night,
Whose bounty bought me but to give me light,   235
I was a bondman on my native plain,
Sin forg'd, and ignorance made fast the chain;
Thy lips have shed instruction as the dew,
Taught me what path to shun, and what pursue;
Farewell my former joys! I sigh no more   240
For Africa's once lov'd, benighted shore,
Serving a benefactor I am free,
At my best home if not exiled from thee.
    Some men make gain a fountain, whence proceeds
A stream of lib'ral and heroic deeds,   245
The swell of pity, not to be confin'd
Within the scanty limits of the mind,
Disdains the bank, and throws the golden sands,
A rich deposit, on the bord'ring lands:
These have an ear for *his* paternal call,   250
Who makes some rich for the supply of all,
God's gift with pleasure in his praise employ,
And THORNTON is familiar with the joy.
    Oh could I worship aught beneath the skies,
That earth hath seen or fancy can devise,   255
Thine altar, sacred liberty, should stand,
Built by no mercenary vulgar hand,
With fragrant turf and flow'rs as wild and fair
As ever dress'd a bank or scented summer air.
Duely as ever on the mountain's height   260
The peep of morning shed a dawning light;
Again, when evening in her sober vest
Drew the grey curtain of the fading west,
My soul should yield thee willing thanks and praise
For the chief blessings of my fairest days: 265
But that were sacrilege—praise is not thine,

But his who gave thee and preserves thee mine:
Else I would say, and as I spake, bid fly
A captive bird into the boundless sky,
This triple realm adores thee—thou art come   270
From Sparta hither, and art here at home;
We feel thy force still active, at this hour
Enjoy immunity from priestly pow'r,
While conscience, happier than in antient years,
Owns no superior but the God she fears.   275
Propitious spirit! yet expunge a wrong
Thy rights have suffer'd, and our land, too long,
Teach mercy to ten thousand hearts that share
The fears and hopes of a commercial care;
Prisons expect the wicked, and were built   280
To bind the lawless and to punish guilt,
But shipwreck, earthquake, battle, fire and flood,
Are mighty mischiefs, not to be withstood,
And honest merit stands on slipp'ry ground,
Where covert guile and artifice abound: 285
Let just restraint for public peace design'd,
Chain up the wolves and tigers of mankind,
The foe of virtue has no claim to thee,
But let insolvent innocence go free.

    Patron, of else the most despised of men,   290
Accept the tribute of a stranger's pen;
Verse, like the laurel its immortal meed,
Should be the guerdon of a noble deed,
I may alarm thee, but I fear the shame
(Charity chosen as my theme and aim)   295
I must incur, forgetting HOWARD's name.
Blest with all wealth can give thee, to resign
Joys doubly sweet to feelings quick as thine,
To quit the bliss thy rural scenes bestow,
To seek a nobler amidst scenes of woe,   300
To traverse seas, range kingdoms, and bring home
Not the proud monuments of Greece or Rome,
But knowledge such as only dungeons teach,
And only sympathy like thine could reach;
That grief, sequester'd from the public stage,   305
Might smooth her feathers and enjoy her cage,

Speaks a divine ambition, and a zeal
The boldest patriot might be proud to feel.
Oh that the voice of clamor and debate,
That pleads for peace 'till it disturbs the state,   310
Were hush'd in favour of thy gen'rous plea,
The poor thy clients, and heaven's smile thy fee.
   Philosophy that does not dream or stray,
Walks arm in arm with nature all his way,
Compasses earth, dives into it, ascends   315
Whatever steep enquiry recommends,
Sees planetary wonders smoothly roll
Round other systems under her controll,
Drinks wisdom at the milky stream of light
That cheers the silent journey of the night,   320
And brings at his return a bosom charged,
With rich instruction, and a soul enlarged.
The treasured sweets of the capacious plan
That heav'n spreads wide before the view of man,
All prompt his pleased pursuit, and to pursue   325
Still prompt him, with a pleasure always new:
He too has a connecting pow'r, and draws
Man to the center of the common cause,
Aiding a dubious and deficient sight
With a new medium and a purer light.   330
All truth is precious if not all divine,
And what dilates the pow'rs must needs refine,
He reads the skies, and watching ev'ry change,
Provides the faculties an ampler range,
And wins mankind, as his attempts prevail,   335
A prouder station on the gen'ral scale.
But reason still unless divinely taught,
Whate'er she learns, learns nothing as she ought;
The lamp of revelation only, shows,
What human wisdom cannot but oppose,   340
That man in nature's richest mantle clad,
And graced with all philosophy can add,
Though fair without, and luminous within,
Is still the progeny and heir of sin.
Thus taught down falls the plumage of his pride,   345
He feels his need of an unerring guide,

And knows that falling he shall rise no more,
Unless the pow'r that bade him stand, restore.
This is indeed philosophy; this known,
Makes wisdom, worthy of the name, his own;   350
And without this, whatever he discuss,
Whether the space between the stars and us,
Whether he measure earth, compute the sea,
Weigh sunbeams, carve a fly, or spit a flea,
The solemn trifler with his boasted skill   355
Toils much, and is a solemn trifler still,
Blind was he born, and his misguided eyes
Grown dim in trifling studies, blind he dies.
Self-knowledge truly learn'd, of course implies
The rich possession of a nobler prize,   360
For self to self, and God to man reveal'd,
(Two themes to nature's eye for ever seal'd)
Are taught by rays that fly with equal pace
From the same center of enlight'ning grace.
Here stay thy foot, how copious and how clear   365
Th' o'erflowing well of Charity springs here!
Hark! 'tis the music of a thousand rills,
Some through the groves, some down the sloping hills,
Winding a secret or an open course,
And all supplied from an eternal source.   370
The ties of nature do but feebly bind,
And commerce partially reclaims mankind,
Philosophy without his heav'nly guide,
May blow up self-conceit and nourish pride,
But while his province is the reas'ning part,   375
Has still a veil of midnight on his heart:
'Tis truth divine exhibited on earth,
Gives Charity her being and her birth.
    Suppose (when thought is warm and fancy flows,
What will not argument sometimes suppose)   380
An isle possess'd by creatures of our kind,
Endued with reason, yet by nature blind.
Let supposition lend her aid once more,
And land some grave optician on the shore,
He claps his lens, if haply they may see,   385
Close to the part where vision ought to be,

But finds that though his tubes assist the sight,
They cannot give it, or make darkness light.
He reads wise lectures, and describes aloud
A sense they know not, to the wond'ring crowd,   390
He talks of light and the prismatic hues,
As men of depth in erudition use,
But all he gains for his harangue is—Well—
What monstrous lies some travellers will tell.

   The soul whose sight all-quick'ning grace renews,   395
Takes the resemblance of the good she views,
As di'monds stript of their opaque disguise,
Reflect the noon-day glory of the skies.
She speaks of him, her author, guardian, friend,
Whose love knew no beginning, knows no end,   400
In language warm as all that love inspires,
And in the glow of her intense desires
Pants to communicate her noble fires.
She sees a world stark blind to what employs
Her eager thought, and feeds her flowing joys,   405
Though wisdom hail them, heedless of her call,
Flies to save some, and feels a pang for all:
Herself as weak as her support is strong,
She feels that frailty she denied so long,
And from a knowledge of her own disease,   410
Learns to compassionate the sick she sees.
Here see, acquitted of all vain pretence,
The reign of genuine Charity commence;
Though scorn repay her sympathetic tears,
She still is kind, and still she perseveres;   415
The truth she loves, a sightless world blaspheme,
'Tis childish dotage, a delirious dream,
The danger they discern not, they deny,
Laugh at their only remedy, and die:
But still a soul thus touch'd, can never cease,   420
Whoever threatens war, to speak of peace,
Pure in her aim and in her temper mild,
Her wisdom seems the weakness of a child,
She makes excuses where she might condemn,
Reviled by those that hate her, prays for them;   425

420–1 cease, / Whoever threatens war,] cease / Whoever threatens war 1782

Suspicion lurks not in her artless breast,
The worst suggested, she believes the best;
Not soon provoked, however stung and teaz'd,
And if perhaps made angry, soon appeas'd,
She rather waves than will dispute her right,   430
And injur'd, makes forgiveness her delight.
   Such was the pourtrait an apostle drew,
The bright original was one he knew,
Heav'n held his hand, the likeness must be true.
   When one that holds communion with the skies,   435
Has filled his urn where these pure waters rise,
And once more mingles with us meaner things,
'Tis ev'n as if an angel shook his wings;
Immortal fragrance fills the circuit wide,
That tells us whence his treasures are supplied.   440
So when a ship well freighted with the stores
The sun matures on India's spicy shores,
Has dropt her anchor and her canvas furl'd,
In some safe haven of our western world,
'Twere vain enquiry to what port she went,   445
The gale informs us, laden with the scent.
   Some seek, when queazy conscience has its qualms,
To lull the painful malady with alms;
But charity not feign'd, intends alone
Another's good—theirs centers in their own;   450
And too short-lived to reach the realms of peace,
Must cease for ever when the poor shall cease.
Flavia, most tender of her own good name,
Is rather careless of a sister's fame,
Her superfluity the poor supplies,   455
But if she touch a character, it dies.
The seeming virtue weigh'd against the vice,
She deems all safe, for she has paid the price,
No charity but alms aught values she,
Except in porcelain on her mantle-tree.   460
How many deeds with which the world has rung,
From pride in league with ignorance have sprung?
But God o'erules all human follies still,
And bends the tough materials to his will.
A conflagration or a wintry flood,   465

Has left some hundreds without home or food,
Extravagance and av'rice shall subscribe,
While fame and self-complacence are the bribe.
The brief proclaim'd, it visits ev'ry pew,
But first the 'Squire's, a compliment but due: 470
With slow deliberation he unties
His glitt'ring purse, that envy of all eyes,
And while the clerk just puzzles out the psalm,
Slides guinea behind guinea in his palm,
'Till finding what he might have found before,   475
A smaller piece amidst the precious store,
Pinch'd close between his finger and his thumb,
He half exhibits, and then drops the sum;
Gold to be sure!—throughout the town 'tis told
How the good 'Squire gives never less than gold.   480
From motives such as his, though not the best,
Springs in due time supply for the distress'd,
Not less effectual than what love bestows,
Except that office clips it as it goes.

 But lest I seem to sin against a friend,   485
And wound the grace I mean to recommend,
(Though vice derided with a just design
Implies no trespass against love divine)
Once more I would adopt the graver stile,
A teacher should be sparing of his smile.   490

 Unless a love of virtue light the flame,
Satyr is more than those he brands, to blame,
He hides behind a magisterial air
His own offences, and strips others bare,
Affects indeed a most humane concern   495
That men if gently tutor'd will not learn,
That muleish folly not to be reclaim'd
By softer methods, must be made asham'd,
But (I might instance in St. Patrick's dean)
Too often rails to gratify his spleen.   500
Most sat'rists are indeed a public scourge,
Their mildest physic is a farrier's purge,
Their acrid temper turns as soon as stirr'd
The milk of their good purpose all to curd,
Their zeal begotten as their works rehearse,   505

By lean despair upon an empty purse;
The wild assassins start into the street,
Prepar'd to poignard whomsoe'er they meet;
No skill in swordsmanship however just,
Can be secure against a madman's thrust,   510
And even virtue so unfairly match'd,
Although immortal, may be prick'd or scratch'd.
When scandal has new minted an old lie,
Or tax'd invention for a fresh supply,
'Tis called a satyr, and the world appears   515
Gath'ring around it with erected ears;
A thousand names are toss'd into the crowd,
Some whisper'd softly, and some twang'd aloud,
Just as the sapience of an author's brain
Suggests it safe or dang'rous to be plain.   520
Strange! how the frequent interjected dash,
Quickens a market and helps off the trash,
Th' important letters that include the rest,
Serve as a key to those that are suppress'd,
Conjecture gripes the victims in his paw,   525
The world is charm'd, and Scrib. escapes the law.
So when the cold damp shades of night prevail,
Worms may be caught by either head or tail,
Forcibly drawn from many a close recess,
They meet with little pity, no redress;   530
Plung'd in the stream they lodge upon the mud,
Food for the famish'd rovers of the flood.
    All zeal for a reform that gives offence
To peace and charity, is mere pretence:
A bold remark, but which if well applied,   535
Would humble many a tow'ring poet's pride:
Perhaps the man was in a sportive fit,
And had no other play-place for his wit;
Perhaps enchanted with the love of fame,
He sought the jewel in his neighbour's shame;   540
Perhaps—whatever end he might pursue,
The cause of virtue could not be his view.
At ev'ry stroke wit flashes in our eyes,
The turns are quick, the polish'd points surprise,
But shine with cruel and tremendous charms,   545

That while they please possess us with alarms:
So have I seen, (and hasten'd to the sight
On all the wings of holiday delight)
Where stands that monument of antient pow'r,
Named with emphatic dignity, the tow'r,   550
Guns, halberts, swords and pistols, great and small,
In starry forms disposed upon the wall;
We wonder, as we gazing stand below,
That brass and steel should make so fine a show;
But though we praise th' exact designer's skill,   555
Account them implements of mischief still.
  No works shall find acceptance in that day
When all disguises shall be rent away,
That square not truly with the Scripture plan,
Nor spring from love to God, or love to man.   560
As he ordains things sordid in their birth
To be resolved into their parent earth,
And though the soul shall seek superior orbs,
Whate'er this world produces, it absorbs,
So self starts nothing but what tends apace   565
Home to the goal where it began the race.
Such as our motive is our aim must be,
If this be servile, that can ne'er be free;
If self employ us, whatsoe'er is wrought,
We glorify that self, not him we ought: 570
Such virtues had need prove their own reward,
The judge of all men owes them no regard.
True Charity, a plant divinely nurs'd,
Fed by the love from which it rose at first,
Thrives against hope and in the rudest scene,   575
Storms but enliven its unfading green;
Exub'rant is the shadow it supplies,
Its fruit on earth, its growth above the skies.
To look at him who form'd us and redeem'd,
So glorious now, though once so disesteem'd,   580
To see a God stretch forth his human hand,
T' uphold the boundless scenes of his command,
To recollect that in a form like ours,
He bruis'd beneath his feet th' infernal pow'rs,
Captivity led captive rose to claim   585

The wreath he won so dearly, in our name,
That thron'd above all height, he condescends
To call the few that trust in him his friends,
That in the heav'n of heav'ns, that space he deems
Too scanty for th' exertion of his beams,   590
And shines as if impatient to bestow
Life and a kingdom upon worms below;
That sight imparts a never-dying flame,
Though feeble in degree, in kind the same;
Like him, the soul thus kindled from above,   595
Spreads wide her arms of universal love,
And still enlarg'd as she receives the grace,
Includes creation in her close embrace.
Behold a Christian—and without the fires
The founder of that name alone inspires,   600
Though all accomplishments, all knowledge meet,
To make the shining prodigy complete,
Whoever boasts that name—behold a cheat.
    Were love in these the world's last doting years
As frequent, as the want of it appears,   605
The churches warm'd, they would no longer hold
Such frozen figures, stiff as they are cold;
Relenting forms would lose their pow'r or cease,
And ev'n the dipt and sprinkled, live in peace;
Each heart would quit its prison in the breast,   610
And flow in free communion with the rest.
The statesman skill'd in projects dark and deep,
Might burn his useless Machiavel, and sleep;
His budget often filled yet always poor,
Might swing at ease behind his study door,   615
No longer prey upon our annual rents,
Nor scare the nation with its big contents;
Disbanded legions freely might depart,
And slaying man would cease to be an art.
No learned disputants would take the field,   620
Sure not to conquer, and sure not to yield,
Both sides deceiv'd if rightly understood,
Pelting each other for the public good.
Did Charity prevail, the press would prove
A vehicle of virtue, truth and love,   625

And I might spare myself the pains to show
What few can learn, and all suppose they know.
   Thus have I sought to grace a serious lay
With many a wild indeed, but flow'ry spray,
In hopes to gain what else I must have lost,   630
Th' attention pleasure has so much engross'd.
But if unhappily deceiv'd I dream,
And prove too weak for so divine a theme,
Let Charity forgive me a mistake
That zeal not vanity has chanc'd to make,   635
And spare the poet for his subject sake.

CONVERSATION

Nam neque me tantum venientis sibilus austri,
Nec percussa juvant fluctû tam litora, nec quæ
Saxosas inter decurrunt flumina valles.
                                    VIRG. ECL. 5

Though nature weigh our talents, and dispense
To ev'ry man his modicum of sense,
And Conversation in its better part,
May be esteemed a gift and not an art,
Yet much depends, as in the tiller's toil,   5
On culture, and the sowing of the soil.
Words learn'd by rote, a parrot may rehearse,
But talking is not always to converse,
Not more distinct from harmony divine
The constant creaking of a country sign.   10
As alphabets in ivory employ
Hour after hour the yet unletter'd boy,
Sorting and puzzling with a deal of glee
Those seeds of science called his A B C ,
So language in the mouths of the adult,   15
Witness its insignificant result,
Too often proves an implement of play,
A toy to sport with, and pass time away.
Collect at evening what the day brought forth,
Compress the sum into its solid worth,   20
And if it weigh th' importance of a fly,
The scales are false or Algebra a lie.
Sacred interpreter of human thought,
How few respect or use thee as they ought!
But all shall give account of ev'ry wrong   25
Who dare dishonour or defile the tongue,

Mid-July–early August 1781.

COPY-TEXT: *1782*, pp. 212–57 (first printing).

Who prostitute it in the cause of vice,
Or sell their glory at a market-price,
Who vote for hire, or point it with lampoon,
The dear-bought placeman, and the cheap buffoon.   30
   There is a prurience in the speech of some,
Wrath stays him, or else God would strike them dumb;
His wise forbearance has their end in view,
They fill their measure and receive their due.
The heathen law-givers of antient days,   35
Names almost worthy of a Christian praise,
Would drive them forth from the resort of men,
And shut up ev'ry satyr in his den.
Oh come not ye near innocence and truth,
Ye worms that eat into the bud of youth!   40
Infectious as impure, your blighting pow'r
Taints in its rudiments the promised flow'r,
Its odour perish'd and its charming hue,
Thenceforth 'tis hateful for it smells of you.
Not ev'n the vigorous and headlong rage   45
Of adolescence or a firmer age,
Affords a plea allowable or just,
For making speech the pamperer of lust;
But when the breath of age commits the fault,
'Tis nauseous as the vapor of a vault.   50
So wither'd stumps disgrace the sylvan scene,
No longer fruitful and no longer green,
The sapless wood divested of the bark,
Grows fungous and takes fire at ev'ry spark.
   Oaths terminate, as Paul observes, all strife—   55
Some men have surely then a peaceful life,
Whatever subject occupy discourse,
The feats of Vestris or the naval force,
Asseveration blust'ring in your face
Makes contradiction such an hopeless case;   60
In ev'ry tale they tell, or false or true,
Well known, or such as no man ever knew,
They fix attention, heedless of your pain,
With oaths like rivets forced into the brain,
And ev'n when sober truth prevails throughout,   65
They swear it, 'till affirmance breeds a doubt.

A Persian, humble servant of the sun,
Who though devout yet bigotry had none,
Hearing a lawyer, grave in his address,
With adjurations ev'ry word impress,   70
Supposed the man a bishop, or at least,
God's name so much upon his lips, a priest,
Bowed at the close with all his graceful airs,
And begg'd an int'rest in his frequent pray'rs.
    Go quit the rank to which ye stood preferred,   75
Henceforth associate in one common herd,
Religion, virtue, reason, common sense
Pronounce your human form a false pretence,
A mere disguise in which a devil lurks,
Who yet betrays his secret by his works.   80
    Ye pow'rs who rule the tongue, if such there are,
And make colloquial happiness your care,
Preserve me from the thing I dread and hate,
A duel in the form of a debate:
The clash of arguments and jar of words   85
Worse than the mortal brunt of rival swords,
Decide no question with their tedious length,
For opposition gives opinion strength,
Divert the champions prodigal of breath,
And put the peaceably-disposed to death.   90
Oh thwart me not, Sir Soph. at ev'ry turn,
Nor carp at ev'ry flaw you may discern,
Though syllogisms hang not on my tongue,
I am not surely always in the wrong;
'Tis hard if all is false that I advance,   95
A fool must now and then be right, by chance.
Not that all freedom of dissent I blame,
No—there I grant the privilege I claim.
A disputable point is no man's ground,
Rove where you please, 'tis common all around,   100
Discourse may want an animated—No—
To brush the surface and to make it flow,
But still remember if you mean to please,
To press your point with modesty and ease.
The mark at which my juster aim I take,   105
Is contradiction for its own dear sake;

Set your opinion at whatever pitch,
Knots and impediments make something hitch,
Adopt his own, 'tis equally in vain,
Your thread of argument is snapt again;   110
The wrangler, rather than accord with you,
Will judge *himself* deceiv'd, and prove it too.
Vociferated logic kills me quite,
A noisy man is always in the right,
I twirl my thumbs, fall back into my chair,   115
Fix on the wainscot a distressful stare,
And when I hope his blunders are all out,
Reply discreetly—to be sure—no doubt.
    DUBIUS is such a scrupulous good man—
Yes—you may catch him tripping if you can.   120
He would not with a peremptory tone
Assert the nose upon his face his own;
With hesitation admirably slow,
He humbly hopes, presumes it may be so.
His evidence, if he were called by law,   125
To swear to some enormity he saw,
For want of prominence and just relief,
Would hang an honest man and save a thief.
Through constant dread of giving truth offence,
He ties up all his hearers in suspense,   130
Knows what he knows as if he knew it not,
What he remembers seems to have forgot,
His sole opinion, whatsoe'er befall,
Cent'ring at last in having none at all.
Yet though he teaze and baulk your list'ning ear,   135
He makes one useful point exceeding clear;
Howe'er ingenious on his darling theme,
A sceptic in philosophy may seem,
Reduced to practice, his beloved rule,
Would only prove him a consummate fool,   140
Useless in him alike both brain and speech,
Fate having placed all truth above his reach;
His ambiguities his total sum,
He might as well be blind and deaf and dumb.
    Where men of judgment creep and feel their way,   145
The Positive pronounce without dismay,

Their want of light and intellect supplied
By sparks absurdity strikes out of pride:
Without the means of knowing right from wrong,
They always are decisive, clear and strong;   150
Where others toil with philosophic force,
Their nimble nonsense takes a shorter course,
Flings at your head conviction in the lump,
And gains remote conclusions at a jump:
Their own defect invisible to them,   155
Seen in another they at once condemn,
And though self-idolized in ev'ry case,
Hate their own likeness in a brother's face.
The cause is plain and not to be denied,
The proud are always most provok'd by pride,   160
Few competitions but engender spite,
And those the most, where neither has a right.
    The point of honour has been deemed of use,
To teach good manners and to curb abuse;
Admit it true, the consequence is clear,   165
Our polished manners are a mask we wear,
And at the bottom, barb'rous still and rude,
We are restrained indeed, but not subdued;
The very remedy, however sure,
Springs from the mischief it intends to cure,   170
And savage in its principle appears,
Tried, as it should be, by the fruit it bears.
'Tis hard indeed if nothing will defend
Mankind from quarrels but their fatal end,
That now and then an hero must decease,   175
That the surviving world may live in peace.
Perhaps at last, close scrutiny may show
The practice dastardly and mean and low,
That men engage in it compelled by force,
And fear not courage is its proper source,   180
The fear of tyrant custom, and the fear
Lest fops should censure us, and fools should sneer;
At least to trample on our Maker's laws,
And hazard life, for any or no cause,
To rush into a fixt eternal state,   185
Out of the very flames of rage and hate,

Or send another shiv'ring to the bar
With all the guilt of such unnat'ral war,
Whatever use may urge or honour plead,
On reason's verdict is a madman's deed.   190
Am I to set my life upon a throw
Because a bear is rude and surly? No—
A moral, sensible and well-bred man
Will not affront me, and no other can.
Were I empow'rd to regulate the lists,   195
They should encounter with well-loaded fists,
A Trojan combat would be something new,
Let DARES beat ENTELLUS black and blue,
Then each might show to his admiring friends
In honourable bumps his rich amends,   200
And carry in contusions of his scull,
A satisfactory receipt in full.
    A story in which native humour reigns
Is often useful, always entertains,
A graver fact enlisted on your side,   205
May furnish illustration, well applied;
But sedentary weavers of long tales,
Give me the fidgets and my patience fails.
'Tis the most asinine employ on earth,
To hear them tell of parentage and birth,   210
And echo conversations dull and dry,
Embellished with, *he said*, and *so said I*.
At ev'ry interview their route the same,
The repetition makes attention lame,
We bustle up with unsuccessful speed,   215
And in the saddest part cry—droll indeed!
The path of narrative with care pursue,
Still making probability your clue,
On all the vestiges of truth attend,
And let *them* guide you to a decent end.   220
Of all ambitions man may entertain,
The worst that can invade a sickly brain,
Is that which angles hourly for surprize,
And baits its hook with prodigies and lies.
Credulous infancy or age as weak   225
Are fittest auditors for such to seek,

Who to please others will themselves disgrace,
Yet please not, but affront you to your face.
A great retailer of this curious ware,
Having unloaded and made many stare,   230
Can this be true? an arch observer cries—
Yes, rather moved, I saw it with these eyes.
Sir! I believe it on that ground alone,
I could not, had I seen it with my own.
A tale should be judicious, clear, succinct,   235
The language plain, and incidents well-link'd,
Tell not as new what ev'ry body knows,
And new or old, still hasten to a close,
There centring in a focus, round and neat,
Let all your rays of information meet: 240
What neither yields us profit or delight,
Is like a nurse's lullaby at night,
Guy Earl of Warwick and fair Eleanore,
Or giant-killing Jack would please me more.
    The pipe with solemn interposing puff,   245
Makes half a sentence at a time enough;
The dozing sages drop the drowsy strain,
Then pause, and puff—and speak, and pause again.
Such often like the tube they so admire,
Important trifles! have more smoke than fire.   250
Pernicious weed! whose scent the fair annoys
Unfriendly to society's chief joys,
Thy worst effect is banishing for hours
The sex whose presence civilizes ours:
Thou art indeed the drug a gard'ner wants,   255
To poison vermin that infest his plants,
But are we so to wit and beauty blind,
As to despise the glory of our kind,
And show the softest minds and fairest forms
As little mercy, as he, grubs and worms?   260
They dare not wait the riotous abuse,
Thy thirst-creating steams at length produce,
When wine has giv'n indecent language birth,
And forced the flood-gates of licentious mirth;
For sea-born Venus her attachment shows   265
Still to that element from which she rose,

And with a quiet which no fumes disturb,
Sips meek infusions of a milder herb.
   Th' emphatic speaker dearly loves t'oppose
In contact inconvenient, nose to nose,   270
As if the gnomon on his neighbour's phiz,
Touched with a magnet had attracted his.
His whisper'd theme, dilated and at large,
Proves after all a wind-gun's airy charge,
An extract of his diary—no more,   275
A tasteless journal of the day before.
He walked abroad, o'ertaken in the rain
Called on a friend, drank tea, stept home again,
Resumed his purpose, had a world of talk
With one he stumbled on, and lost his walk.   280
I interrupt him with a sudden bow,
Adieu dear Sir! lest you should lose it now.
   I cannot talk with civet in the room,
A fine puss-gentleman that's all perfume;
The sight's enough—no need to smell a beau—   285
Who thrusts his nose into a raree-show?
His odoriferous attempts to please,
Perhaps might prosper with a swarm of bees,
But we that make no honey though we sting,
Poets, are sometimes apt to mawl the thing.   290
'Tis wrong to bring into a mixt resort,
What makes some sick, and others *a-la-mort*,
An argument of cogence, we may say,
Why such an one should keep *himself* away.
   A graver coxcomb we may sometimes see,   295
Quite as absurd though not so light as he:
A shallow brain behind a serious mask,
An oracle within an empty cask,
The solemn fop; significant and budge;
A fool with judges, amongst fools a judge.   300
He says but little, and that little said
Owes all its weight, like loaded dice, to lead.
His wit invites you by his looks to come,
But when you knock it never is at home:
'Tis like a parcel sent you by the stage,   305
Some handsome present, as your hopes presage,

'Tis heavy, bulky, and bids fair to prove
An absent friend's fidelity and love,
But when unpack'd your disappointment groans
To find it stuff'd with brickbats, earth and stones.   310
    Some men employ their health, an ugly trick,
In making known how oft they have been sick,
And give us in recitals of disease
A doctor's trouble, but without the fees:
Relate how many weeks they kept their bed,   315
How an emetic or cathartic sped,
Nothing is slightly touched, much less forgot,
Nose, ears, and eyes seem present on the spot.
Now the distemper spite of draught or pill
Victorious seem'd, and now the doctor's skill;   320
And now—alas for unforeseen mishaps!
They put on a damp night-cap and relapse;
They thought they must have died they were so bad,
Their peevish hearers almost wish they had.
    Some fretful tempers wince at ev'ry touch,   325
You always do too little or too much:
You speak with life in hopes to entertain,
Your elevated voice goes through the brain;
You fall at once into a lower key,
That's worse—the drone-pipe of an humble bee.   330
The southern sash admits too strong a light,
You rise and drop the curtain—now its night.
He shakes with cold—you stir the fire and strive
To make a blaze—that's roasting him alive.
Serve him with ven'son and he chuses fish,   335
With soal—that's just the sort he would not wish,
He takes what he at first profess'd to loath,
And in due time feeds heartily on both;
Yet still o'erclouded with a constant frown,
He does not swallow but he gulps it down.   340
Your hope to please him, vain on ev'ry plan,
Himself should work that wonder if he can—
Alas! his efforts double his distress,
He likes yours little and his own still less,
Thus always teazing others, always teazed,   345

343 distress] disttess *1782*

His only pleasure is—to be displeas'd.
  I pity bashful men, who feel the pain
Of fancied scorn and undeserv'd disdain,
And bear the marks upon a blushing face
Of needless shame and self-imposed disgrace.   350
Our sensibilities are so acute,
The fear of being silent makes us mute.
We sometimes think we could a speech produce
Much to the purpose, if our tongues were loose,
But being tied, it dies upon the lip,   355
Faint as a chicken's note that has the pip:
Our wasted oil unprofitably burns
Like hidden lamps in old sepulchral urns.
Few Frenchmen of this evil have complained,
It seems as if we Britons were ordained   360
By way of wholesome curb upon our pride,
To fear each other, fearing none beside.
The cause perhaps enquiry may descry,
Self-searching with an introverted eye,
Concealed within an unsuspected part,   365
The vainest corner of our own vain heart:
For ever aiming at the world's esteem,
Our self-importance ruins its own scheme,
In other eyes our talents rarely shown,
Become at length so splendid in our own,   370
We dare not risque them into public view,
Lest they miscarry of what seems their due.
True modesty is a discerning grace,
And only blushes in the proper place,
But counterfeit is blind, and skulks through fear,   375
Where 'tis a shame to be ashamed t' appear;
Humility the parent of the first,
The last by vanity produced and nurst.
The circle formed we sit in silent state,
Like figures drawn upon a dial-plate,   380
Yes ma'am, and no ma'am, utter'd softly, show
Ev'ry five minutes how the minutes go;
Each individual suffering a constraint
Poetry may, but colours cannot paint,
As if in close committee on the sky,   385

Reports it hot or cold, or wet or dry;
And finds a changing clime, an happy source
Of wise reflection and well-timed discourse.
We next enquire, but softly and by stealth,
Like conservators of the public health,   390
Of epidemic throats if such there are,
And coughs and rheums and phtisic and catarrh.
That theme exhausted, a wide chasm ensues,
Filled up at last with interesting news,
Who danced with whom, and who are like to wed,   395
And who is hanged, and who is brought to bed,
But fear to call a more important cause,
As if 'twere treason against English laws.
The visit paid, with extasy we come
As from a seven years transportation, home,   400
And there resume an unembarrass'd brow,
Recov'ring what we lost we know not how,
The faculties that seem'd reduc'd to nought,
Expression and the privilege of thought.
    The reeking roaring hero of the chase,   405
I give him over as a desp'rate case.
Physicians write in hopes to work a cure,
Never, if honest ones, when death is sure;
And though the fox he follows may be tamed,
A mere fox-follower never is reclaimed.   410
Some farrier should prescribe his proper course,
Whose only fit companion is his horse,
Or if deserving of a better doom
The noble beast judge otherwise, his groom.
Yet ev'n the rogue that serves him, though he stand   415
To take his honour's orders cap in hand,
Prefers his fellow-grooms with much good sense,
Their skill a truth, his master's a pretence.
If neither horse nor groom affect the squire,
Where can at last his jockeyship retire?   420
Oh to the club, the scene of savage joys,
The school of coarse good fellowship and noise;
There in the sweet society of those
Whose friendship from his boyish years he chose,
Let him improve his talent if he can,   425

'Till none but beasts acknowledge him a man.
   Man's heart had been impenetrably sealed,
Like theirs that cleave the flood or graze the field,
Had not his Maker's all-bestowing hand
Giv'n him a soul and bade him understand.   430
The reas'oning pow'r vouchsafed of course inferred
The pow'r to cloath that reason with his word,
For all is perfect that God works on earth,
And he that gives conception, adds the birth.
If this be plain, 'tis plainly understood   435
What uses of his boon the Giver would.
The mind dispatched upon her busy toil
Should range where Providence has blest the soil,
Visiting ev'ry flow'r with labour meet,
And gathering all her treasures sweet by sweet,   440
She should imbue the tongue with what she sips,
And shed the balmy blessing on the lips,
That good diffused may more abundant grow,
And speech may praise the pow'r that bids it flow.
Will the sweet warbler of the live-long night   445
That fills the list'ning lover with delight,
Forget his harmony with rapture heard,
To learn the twitt'ring of a meaner bird,
Or make the parrot's mimickry his choice,
That odious libel on an human voice?   450
No—nature unsophisticate by man,
Starts not aside from her Creator's plan,
The melody that was at first design'd
To cheer the rude forefathers of mankind,
Is note for note deliver'd in our ears,   455
In the last scene of her six thousand years:
Yet Fashion, leader of a chatt'ring train,
Whom man for his own hurt permits to reign,
Who shifts and changes all things but his shape,
And would degrade her vot'ry to an ape,   460
The fruitful parent of abuse and wrong,
Holds an usurp'd dominion o'er his tongue:
There sits and prompts him with his own disgrace,
Prescribes the theme, the tone and the grimace,
And when accomplished in her wayward school,   465

Calls gentleman whom she has made a fool.
'Tis an unalterable fixt decree
That none could frame or ratify but she,
That heav'n and hell and righteousness and sin,
Snares in his path and foes that lurk within,   470
God and his attributes (a field of day
Where 'tis an angel's happiness to stray)
Fruits of his love and wonders of his might,
Be never named in ears esteemed polite.
That he who dares, when she forbids, be grave,   475
Shall stand proscribed, a madman or a knave,
A close designer not to be believed,
Or if excus'd that charge, at least deceived.
Oh folly worthy of the nurse's lap,
Give it the breast or stop its mouth with pap!   480
Is it incredible, or can it seem
A dream to any except those that dream,
That man should love his Maker, and *that* fire
Warming his heart should at his lips transpire?
Know then, and modestly let fall your eyes,   485
And vail your daring crest that braves the skies,
That air of insolence affronts your God,
You need his pardon, and provoke his rod,
Now, in a posture that becomes you more
Than that heroic strut assumed before,   490
Know, your arrears with ev'ry hour accrue,
For mercy shown while wrath is justly due.
The time is short, and there are souls on earth,
Though future pain may serve for present mirth,
Acquainted with the woes that fear or shame   495
By fashion taught, forbade them once to name,
And having felt the pangs you deem a jest,
Have prov'd them truths too big to be express'd:
Go seek on revelation's hallow'd ground,
Sure to succeed, the remedy they found,   500
Touch'd by that pow'r that you have dared to mock,
That makes seas stable and dissolves the rock,
Your heart shall yield a life-renewing stream,
That fools, as you have done, shall call a dream.
    It happened on a solemn even-tide,   505

Soon after He that was our surety died,
Two bosom-friends each pensively inclined,
The scene of all those sorrows left behind,
Sought their own village, busied as they went
In musings worthy of the great event: 510
They spake of him they loved, of him whose life
Though blameless, had incurred perpetual strife,
Whose deeds had left, in spite of hostile arts,
A deep memorial graven on their hearts:
The recollection like a vein of ore,   515
The farther traced enrich'd them still the more,
They thought him, and they justly thought him one
Sent to do more than he appear'd to have done,
T' exalt a people, and to place them high
Above all else, and wonder'd he should die.   520
E'er yet they brought their journey to an end,
A stranger joined them, courteous as a friend,
And asked them with a kind engaging air,
What their affliction was, and begged a share.
Informed, he gather'd up the broken thread,   525
And truth and wisdom gracing all he said,
Explained, illustrated and searched so well
The tender theme on which they chose to dwell,
That reaching home, the night, they said, is near,
We must not now be parted, sojourn here—   530
The new acquaintance soon became a guest,
And made so welcome at their simple feast,
He blessed the bread, but vanish'd at the word,
And left them both exclaiming, 'twas the Lord!
Did not our hearts feel all he deigned to say,   535
Did they not burn within us by the way?
   Now theirs was converse such as it behoves
Man to maintain, and such as God approves;
Their views indeed were indistinct and dim,
But yet successful being aimed at him.   540
Christ and his character their only scope,
Their object and their subject and their hope,
They felt what it became them much to feel,
And wanting him to loose the sacred seal,

521 E'er] E're *1782*

Found him as prompt as their desire was true,   545
To spread the new-born glories in their view.
Well—what are ages and the lapse of time
Matched against truths as lasting as sublime?
Can length of years on God himself exact,
Or make that fiction which was once a fact?   550
No—marble and recording brass decay,
And like the graver's mem'ry pass away;
The works of man inherit, as is just,
Their author's frailty and return to dust;
But truth divine for ever stands secure,   555
Its head as guarded as its base is sure,
Fixt in the rolling flood of endless years
The pillar of th' eternal plan appears,
The raving storm and dashing wave defies,
Built by that architect who built the skies.   560
Hearts may be found that harbour at this hour,
That love of Christ in all its quick'ning pow'r,
And lips unstained by folly or by strife,
Whose wisdom drawn from the deep well of life,
Tastes of its healthful origin, and flows   565
A Jordan for th' ablution of our woes.
Oh days of heav'n and nights of equal praise,
Serene and peaceful as those heav'nly days,
When souls drawn upward in communion sweet,
Enjoy the stillness of some close retreat,   570
Discourse as if released and safe at home,
Of dangers past and wonders yet to come,
And spread the sacred treasures of the breast
Upon the lap of covenanted rest.
   What always dreaming over heav'nly things,   575
Like angel-heads in stone with pigeon-wings?
Canting and whining out all day the word
And half the night? fanatic and absurd!
Mine be the friend less frequent in his pray'rs,
Who makes no bustle with his soul's affairs,   580
Whose wit can brighten up a wintry day,
And chase the splenetic dull hours away,
Content on earth in earthly things to shine,
Who waits for heav'n e'er he becomes divine,

Leaves saints t' enjoy those altitudes they teach,   585
And plucks the fruit plac'd more within his reach.
    Well spoken, Advocate of sin and shame,
Known by thy bleating, Ignorance thy name.
Is sparkling wit the world's exclusive right,
The fixt fee-simple of the vain and light?   590
Can hopes of heav'n, bright prospects of an hour
That comes to waft us out of sorrow's pow'r,
Obscure or quench a faculty that finds
Its happiest soil in the serenest minds?
Religion curbs indeed its wanton play,   595
And brings the trifler under rig'rous sway,
But gives it usefulness unknown before,
And purifying makes it shine the more.
A Christian's wit is inoffensive light,
A beam that aids but never grieves the sight,   600
Vig'rous in age as in the flush of youth,
'Tis always active on the side of truth,
Temp'rance and peace insure its healthful state,
And make it brightest at its latest date.
Oh I have seen (nor hope perhaps in vain   605
E'er life go down to see such sights again)
A vet'ran warrior in the Christian field,
Who never saw the sword he could not wield;
Grave without dullness, learned without pride,
Exact yet not precise, though meek, keen-eyed,   610
A man that would have foiled at their own play,
A dozen would-be's of the modern day:
Who when occasion justified its use,
Had wit as bright as ready, to produce,
Could fetch from records of an earlier age,   615
Or from philosophy's enlighten'd page
His rich materials, and regale your ear
With strains it was a privilege to hear;
Yet above all his luxury supreme,
And his chief glory was the gospel theme;   620
There he was copious as old Greece or Rome,
His happy eloquence seem'd there at home,
Ambitious, not to shine or to excel,

592 comes] come *1782, corrected in Errata*

But to treat justly what he lov'd so well.
  It moves me more perhaps than folly ought,   625
When some green heads as void of wit as thought,
Suppose *themselves* monopolists of sense,
And wiser men's ability pretence.
Though time will wear us, and we must grow old,
Such men are not forgot as soon as cold,   630
Their fragrant mem'ry will out last their tomb,
Embalmed for ever in its own perfume:
And to say truth, though in its early prime,
And when unstained with any grosser crime,
Youth has a sprightliness and fire to boast,   635
That in the valley of decline are lost,
And virtue with peculiar charms appears
Crown'd with the garland of life's blooming years;
Yet age by long experience well informed,
Well read, well temper'd, with religion warmed,   640
That fire abated which impells rash youth,
Proud of his speed, to overshoot the truth,
As time improves the grape's authentic juice,
Mellows and makes the speech more fit for use,
And claims a rev'rence in its short'ning day,   645
That 'tis an honour and a joy to pay.
The fruits of age, less fair, are yet more sound,
Than those a brighter season pours around,
And like the stores autumnal suns mature,
Through wintry rigours unimpaired endure.   650
  What is fanatic frenzy, scorned so much,
And dreaded more than a contagious touch?
I grant it dang'rous, and approve your fear,
That fire is catching if you draw too near,
But sage observers oft mistake the flame,   655
And give true piety that odious name.
To tremble (as the creature of an hour
Ought at the view of an almighty pow'r)
Before his presence, at whose awful throne
All tremble in all worlds, except our own,   660
To supplicate his mercy, love his ways,
And prize them above pleasure, wealth or praise,

642 speed,] speed *1782*

Though common sense allowed a casting voice,
And free from bias, must approve the choice,
Convicts a man fanatic in th' extreme,   665
And wild as madness in the world's esteem.
But that disease when soberly defin'd
Is the false fire of an o'erheated mind,
It views the truth with a distorted eye,
And either warps or lays it useless by,   670
'Tis narrow, selfish, arrogant, and draws
Its sordid nourishment from man's applause,
And while at heart sin unrelinquish'd lies,
Presumes itself chief fav'rite of the skies.
'Tis such a light as putrefaction breeds   675
In fly-blown flesh, whereon the maggot feeds,
Shines in the dark, but usher'd into day,
The stench remains, the lustre dies away.
    True bliss, if man may reach it, is composed
Of hearts in union mutually disclosed: 680
And, farewell else all hope of pure delight,
Those hearts should be reclaim'd, renew'd, upright.
Bad men, profaning friendship's hallow'd name,
Form, in its stead, a covenant of shame,
A dark confed'racy against the laws   685
Of virtue, and religion's glorious cause.
They build each other up with dreadful skill,
As bastions set point-blank against God's will,
Enlarge and fortify the dread redoubt,
Deeply resolv'd to shut a Saviour out,   690
Call legions up from hell to back the deed,
And curst with conquest, finally succeed:
But souls that carry on a blest exchange
Of joys they meet with in their heav'nly range,
And with a fearless confidence make known   695
The sorrows sympathy esteems its own,
Daily derive encreasing light and force
From such communion in their pleasant course,
Feel less the journey's roughness and its length,
Meet their opposers with united strength,   700
And one in heart, in int'rest and design,
Gird up each other to the race divine.

But Conversation, chuse what theme we may,
And chiefly when religion leads the way,
Should flow like waters after summer show'rs,   705
Not as if rais'd by mere mechanic pow'rs.
The Christian in whose soul, though now distress'd,
Lives the dear thought of joys he once possess'd,
When all his glowing language issued forth
With God's deep stamp upon its current worth,   710
Will speak without disguise, and must impart
Sad as it is, his undissembling heart,
Abhors constraint, and dares not feign a zeal,
Or seem to boast a fire he does not feel.
The song of Sion is a tasteless thing,   715
Unless when rising on a joyful wing
The soul can mix with the celestial bands,
And give the strain the compass it demands.
    Strange tidings these to tell a world who treat
All but their own experience as deceit!   720
Will they believe, though credulous enough
To swallow much upon much weaker proof,
That there are blest inhabitants of earth,
Partakers of a new æthereal birth,
Their hopes, desires and purposes estranged   725
From things terrestrial, and divinely changed,
Their very language of a kind that speaks
The soul's sure int'rest in the good she seeks,
Who deal with scripture, its importance felt,
As Tully with philosophy once dealt,   730
And in the silent watches of the night,
And through the scenes of toil-renewing light,
The social walk, or solitary ride,
Keep still the dear companion at their side?
No—shame upon a self-disgracing age,   735
God's work may serve an ape upon a stage,
With such a jest as fill'd with hellish glee
Certain invisibles as shrewd as he,
But veneration or respect finds none,
Save from the subjects of that work alone.   740
The world grown old, her deep discernment shows,
Claps spectacles on her sagacious nose,

Peruses closely the true Christian's face,
And finds it a mere mask of sly grimace,
Usurps God's office, lays his bosom bare,   745
And finds hypocrisy close-lurking there,
And serving God herself through mere constraint,
Concludes his unfeign'd love of him, a feint.
And yet God knows, look human nature through,
(And in due time the world shall know it too)   750
That since the flow'rs of Eden felt the blast,
That after man's defection laid all waste,
Sincerity towards th' heart-searching God,
Has made the new-born creature her abode,
Nor shall be found in unregen'rate souls,   755
Till the last fire burn all between the poles.
Sincerity! Why 'tis his only pride,
Weak and imperfect in all grace beside,
He knows that God demands his heart entire,
And gives him all his just demands require.   760
Without it, his pretensions were as vain,
As having it, he deems the world's disdain;
That great defect would cost him not alone
Man's favourable judgment, but his own,
His birthright shaken and no longer clear,   765
Than while his conduct proves his heart sincere.
Retort the charge, and let the world be told
She boasts a confidence she does not hold,
That conscious of her crimes, she feels instead,
A cold misgiving, and a killing dread,   770
That while in health, the ground of her support
Is madly to forget that life is short,
That sick, she trembles, knowing she must die,
Her hope presumption, and her faith a lie.
That while she doats and dreams that she believes,   775
She mocks her maker and herself deceives,
Her utmost reach, historical assent,
The doctrines warpt to what they never meant.
That truth itself is in her head as dull
And useless as a candle in a scull,   780
And all her love of God a groundless claim,
A trick upon the canvass, painted flame.

Tell her again, the sneer upon her face,
And all her censures of the work of grace,
Are insincere, meant only to conceal   785
A dread she would not, yet is forc'd to feel,
That in her heart the Christian she reveres,
And while she seems to scorn him, only fears.
    A poet does not work by square or line,
As smiths and joiners perfect a design,   790
At least we moderns, our attention less,
Beyond th' example of our sires, digress,
And claim a right to scamper and run wide,
Wherever chance, caprice, or fancy guide.
The world and I fortuitously met,   795
I ow'd a trifle and have paid the debt,
She did me wrong, I recompens'd the deed,
And having struck the balance, now proceed.
Perhaps, however, as some years have pass'd
Since she and I conversed together last,   800
And I have liv'd recluse in rural shades,
Which seldom a distinct report pervades,
Great changes and new manners have occurr'd,
And blest reforms that I have never heard,
And she may now be as discreet and wise,   805
As once absurd in all discerning eyes.
Sobriety perhaps may now be found,
Where once intoxication press'd the ground,
The subtle and injurious may be just,
And he grown chaste that was the slave of lust;   810
Arts once esteem'd may be with shame dismiss'd,
Charity may relax the miser's fist,
The gamester may have cast his cards away,
Forgot to curse and only kneel to pray.
It has indeed been told me (with what weight,   815
How credibly, 'tis hard for me to state)
That fables old that seem'd for ever mute,
Reviv'd, are hast'ning into fresh repute,
And gods and goddesses discarded long,
Like useless lumber or a stroller's song,   820
Are bringing into vogue their heathen train,
And Jupiter bids fair to rule again.

That certain feasts are instituted now,
Where Venus hears the lover's tender vow,
That all Olympus through the country roves,   825
To consecrate our few remaining groves,
And echo learns politely to repeat,
The praise of names for ages obsolete,
That having proved the weakness, it should seem,
Of revelation's ineffectual beam,   830
To bring the passions under sober sway,
And give the moral springs their proper play,
They mean to try what may at last be done
By stout substantial gods of wood and stone,
And whether Roman rites may not produce   835
The virtues of old Rome for English use.
May much success attend the pious plan,
May Mercury once more embellish man,
Grace him again with long forgotten arts,
Reclaim his taste and brighten up his parts,   840
Make him athletic as in days of old,
Learn'd at the bar, in the palæstra bold,
Divest the rougher sex of female airs,
And teach the softer not to copy theirs.
The change shall please, nor shall it matter aught   845
Who works the wonder if it be but wrought.
'Tis time, however, if the case stand thus,
For us plain folks and all who side with us,
To build our altar, confident and bold,
And say as stern Elijah said of old,   850
The strife now stands upon a fair award,
If Is'rael's Lord be God, then serve the Lord—
If he be silent, faith is all a whim,
Then Baal is the God and worship him.

   Digression is so much in modern use,   855
Thought is so rare, and fancy so profuse,
Some never seem so wide of their intent,
As when returning to the theme they meant.
As mendicants whose business is to roam,
Make ev'ry parish but their own, their home: 860
Though such continual zigzags in a book,
Such drunken reelings have an aukward look,

And I had rather creep to what is true,
Than rove and stagger with no mark in view,
Yet to consult a little, seem'd no crime,   865
The freakish humour of the present time.
But now, to gather up what seems dispers'd,
And touch the subject I design'd at first,
May prove, though much beside the rules of art,
Best for the public, and my wisest part.   870
And first let no man charge me that I mean
To cloath in fables every social scene,
And give good company a face severe
As if they met around a father's bier;
For tell some men that pleasure all their bent,   875
And laughter all their work, is life mispent,
Their wisdom bursts into this sage reply,
Then mirth is sin, and we should always cry.
To find the medium asks some share of wit,
And therefore 'tis a mark fools never hit.   880
But though life's valley be a vale of tears,
A brighter scene beyond that vale appears,
Whose glory with a light that never fades,
Shoots between scattered rocks and opening shades,
And while it shows the land the soul desires,   885
The language of the land she seeks, inspires.
Thus touched, the tongue receives a sacred cure
Of all that was absurd, profane, impure,
Held within modest bounds the tide of speech
Pursues the course that truth and nature teach,   890
No longer labours merely to produce
The pomp of sound, or tinkle without use,
Where'er it winds, the salutary stream
Sprightly and fresh, enriches ev'ry theme,
While all the happy man possess'd before,   895
The gift of nature or the classic store,
Is made subservient to the grand design
For which heav'n form'd the faculty divine.
So should an ideot while at large he strays,
Find the sweet lyre on which an artist plays,   900
With rash and aukward force the chords he shakes,
And grins with wonder at the jar he makes;

But let the wise and well-instructed hand,
Once take the shell beneath his just command,
In gentle sounds it seems as it complained   905
Of the rude injuries it late sustained,
'Till tun'd at length to some immortal song,
It sounds Jehovah's name, and pours his praise along.

RETIREMENT

——studiis florens ignobilis otî.

VIRG. GEOR. LIB. 4

Hackney'd in business, wearied at that oar
Which thousands once fast chain'd to, quit no more,
But which when life at ebb runs weak and low,
All wish, or seem to wish they could forego,
The statesman, lawyer, merchant, man of trade,   5
Pants for the refuge of some rural shade,
Where all his long anxieties forgot
Amid the charms of a sequester'd spot,
Or recollected only to gild o'er
And add a smile to what was sweet before,   10
He may possess the joys he thinks he sees,
Lay his old age upon the lap of ease,
Improve the remnant of his wasted span,
And having liv'd a trifler, die a man.
Thus conscience pleads her cause within the breast,   15
Though long rebell'd against, not yet suppress'd,
And calls a creature formed for God alone,
For heaven's high purposes and not his own,
Calls him away from selfish ends and aims,
From what debilitates and what inflames,   20
From cities humming with a restless crowd,
Sordid as active, ignorant as loud,
Whose highest praise is that they live in vain,
The dupes of pleasure, or the slaves of gain,
Where works of man are cluster'd close around,   25
And works of God are hardly to be found,
To regions where in spite of sin and woe,
Traces of Eden are still seen below,
Where mountain, river, forest, field and grove,

Late August–early October 1781.

COPY-TEXT: *1782*, pp. 258–98 (first printing).

Remind him of his Maker's pow'r and love.   30
'Tis well if look'd for at so late a day,
In the last scene of such a senseless play,
True wisdom will attend his feeble call,
And grace his action e'er the curtain fall.
Souls that have long despised their heav'nly birth,   35
Their wishes all impregnated with earth,
For threescore years employed with ceaseless care,
In catching smoke and feeding upon air,
Conversant only with the ways of men,
Rarely redeem the short remaining ten.   40
Invet'rate habits choak th' unfruitful heart,
Their fibres penetrate its tend'rest part,
And draining its nutritious pow'rs to feed
Their noxious growth, starve ev'ry better seed.

   Happy if full of days—but happier far   45
If e'er we yet discern life's evening star,
Sick of the service of a world that feeds
Its patient drudges with dry chaff and weeds,
We can escape from custom's ideot sway,
To serve the sov'reign we were born t' obey.   50
Then sweet to muse upon his skill display'd
(Infinite skill) in all that he has made!
To trace in nature's most minute design,
The signature and stamp of pow'r divine,
Contrivance intricate express'd with ease   55
Where unassisted sight no beauty sees,
The shapely limb and lubricated joint,
Within the small dimensions of a point,
Muscle and nerve miraculously spun,
His mighty work who speaks and it is done,   60
Th' invisible in things scarce seen reveal'd,
To whom an atom is an ample field.
To wonder at a thousand insect forms,
These hatch'd, and those resuscitated worms,
New life ordain'd and brighter scenes to share,   65
Once prone on earth, now buoyant upon air,
Whose shape would make them, had they bulk and size,
More hideous foes than fancy can devise,
With helmed heads and dragon scales adorn'd,

The mighty myriads, now securely scorn'd,   70
Would mock the majesty of man's high birth,
Despise his bulwarks and unpeople earth.
Then with a glance of fancy to survey,
Far as the faculty can stretch away,
Ten thousand rivers poured at his command   75
From urns that never fail through ev'ry land,
These like a deluge with impetuous force,
Those winding modestly a silent course,
The cloud-surmounting alps, the fruitful vales,
Seas on which ev'ry nation spreads her sails,   80
The sun, a world whence other worlds drink light,
The crescent moon, the diadem of night,
Stars countless, each in his appointed place,
Fast-anchor'd in the deep abyss of space—
At such a sight to catch the poet's flame,   85
And with a rapture like his own exclaim,
These are thy glorious works, thou source of good,
How dimly seen, how faintly understood!—
Thine, and upheld by thy paternal care,
This universal frame, thus wond'rous fair;   90
Thy pow'r divine and bounty beyond thought,
Ador'd and prais'd in all that thou hast wrought.
Absorbed in that immensity I see,
I shrink abased, and yet aspire to thee;
Instruct me, guide me to that heav'nly day,   95
Thy words, more clearly than thy works display,
That while thy truths my grosser thoughts refine,
I may resemble thee and call thee mine.
   Oh blest proficiency! surpassing all
That men erroneously their glory call,   100
The recompence that arts or arms can yield,
The bar, the senate or the tented field.
Compar'd with this sublimest life below,
Ye kings and rulers what have courts to show?
Thus studied, used and consecrated thus,   105
Whatever *is*, seems form'd indeed for us,
Not as the plaything of a froward child,
Fretful unless diverted and beguiled,
Much less to feed and fan the fatal fires

Of pride, ambition or impure desires,   110
But as a scale by which the soul ascends
From mighty means to more important ends,
Securely, though by steps but rarely trod,
Mounts from inferior beings up to God,
And sees by no fallacious light or dim,   115
Earth made for man, and man himself for him.
　　Not that I mean t' approve, or would inforce
A superstitious and monastic course:
Truth is not local, God alike pervades
And fills the world of traffic and the shades,   120
And may be fear'd amid the busiest scenes,
Or scorn'd where business never intervenes.
But 'tis not easy with a mind like ours,
Conscious of weakness in its noblest pow'rs,
And in a world where (other ills apart)   125
The roving eye misleads the careless heart,
To limit thought, by nature prone to stray
Wherever freakish fancy points the way,
To bid the pleadings of self-love be still,
Resign our own and seek our maker's will,   130
To spread the page of scripture, and compare
Our conduct with the laws engraven there,
To measure all that passes in the breast,
Faithfully, fairly, by that sacred test,
To dive into the secret deeps within,   135
To spare no passion and no fav'rite sin,
And search the themes important above all,
Ourselves and our recov'ry from our fall.
But leisure, silence, and a mind releas'd
From anxious thoughts how wealth may be encreas'd,   140
How to secure in some propitious hour,
The point of int'rest or the post of power,
A soul serene, and equally retired,
From objects too much dreaded or desired,
Safe from the clamours of perverse dispute,   145
At least are friendly to the great pursuit.
　　Op'ning the map of God's extensive plan,
We find a little isle, this life of man,
Eternity's unknown expanse appears

Circling around and limiting his years;   150
The busy race examine and explore
Each creek and cavern of the dang'rous shore,
With care collect what in their eyes excells,
Some, shining pebbles, and some, weeds and shells,
Thus laden dream that they are rich and great,   155
And happiest he that groans beneath his weight;
The waves o'ertake them in their serious play,
And ev'ry hour sweep multitudes away,
They shriek and sink, survivors start and weep,
Pursue their sport, and follow to the deep;   160
A few forsake the throng, with lifted eyes
Ask wealth of heav'n, and gain a real prize,
Truth, wisdom, grace, and peace like that above,
Seal'd with his signet whom they serve and love;
Scorn'd by the rest, with patient hope they wait   165
A kind release from their imperfect state,
And unregretted are soon snatch'd away
From scenes of sorrow into glorious day.
    Nor these alone prefer a life recluse,
Who seek retirement for its proper use,   170
The love of change that lives in ev'ry breast,
Genius, and temper, and desire of rest,
Discordant motives in one center meet,
And each inclines it's vot'ry to retreat.
Some minds by nature are averse to noise,   175
And hate the tumult half the world enjoys,
The lure of av'rice, or the pompous prize
That courts display before ambitious eyes,
The fruits that hang on pleasure's flow'ry stem,
Whate'er enchants them are no snares to them.   180
To them the deep recess of dusky groves,
Or forest where the deer securely roves,
The fall of waters and the song of birds,
And hills that echo to the distant herds,
Are luxuries excelling all the glare   185
The world can boast, and her chief fav'rites share.
With eager step and carelessly array'd,
For such a cause the poet seeks the shade,
From all he sees he catches new delight,

Pleas'd fancy claps her pinions at the sight,   190
The rising or the setting orb of day,
The clouds that flit, or slowly float away,
Nature in all the various shapes she wears,
Frowning in storms, or breathing gentle airs,
The snowy robe her wintry state assumes,   195
Her summer heats, her fruits, and her perfumes,
All, all alike transport the glowing bard,
Success in rhime his glory and reward.
Oh nature! whose Elysian scenes disclose
His bright perfections at whose word they rose,   200
Next to that pow'r who form'd thee and sustains,
Be thou the great inspirer of my strains.
Still as I touch the lyre, do thou expand
Thy genuine charms, and guide an artless hand,
That I may catch a fire but rarely known,   205
Give useful light though I should miss renown,
And poring on thy page, whose ev'ry line
Bears proof of an intelligence divine,
May feel an heart enrich'd by what it pays,
That builds its glory on its Maker's praise.   210
Woe to the man whose wit disclaims its use,
Glitt'ring in vain, or only to seduce,
Who studies nature with a wanton eye,
Admires the work, but slips the lesson by,
His hours of leisure and recess employs,   215
In drawing pictures of forbidden joys,
Retires to blazon his own worthless name,
Or shoot the careless with a surer aim.
   The lover too shuns business and alarms,
Tender idolator of absent charms.   220
Saints offer nothing in their warmest pray'rs,
That he devotes not with a zeal like theirs;
'Tis consecration of his heart, soul, time,
And every thought that wanders is a crime.
In sighs he worships his supremely fair,   225
And weeps a sad libation in despair,
Adores a creature, and devout in vain,
Wins in return an answer of disdain.
As woodbine weds the plants within her reach

Rough elm, or smooth-grain'd ash, or glossy beech,   230
In spiral rings ascends the trunk, and lays
Her golden tassels on the leafy sprays,
But does a mischief while she lends a grace,
Streight'ning its growth by such a strict embrace,
So love that clings around the noblest minds,   235
Forbids th' advancement of the soul he binds,
The suitor's air indeed he soon improves,
And forms it to the taste of her he loves,
Teaches his eyes a language, and no less
Refines his speech and fashions his address;   240
But farewell promises of happier fruits,
Manly designs, and learning's grave pursuits,
Girt with a chain he cannot wish to break,
His only bliss is sorrow for her sake,
Who will may pant for glory and excell,   245
Her smile his aim, all higher aims farewell!
Thyrsis, Alexis, or whatever name
May least offend against so pure a flame,
Though sage advice of friends the most sincere,
Sounds harshly in so delicate an ear,   250
And lovers of all creatures, tame or wild,
Can least brook management, however mild,
Yet let a poet (poetry disarms
The fiercest animals with magic charms)
Risque an intrusion on thy pensive mood,   255
And wooe and win thee to thy proper good.
Pastoral images and still retreats,
Umbrageous walks and solitary seats,
Sweet birds in concert with harmonious streams,
Soft airs, nocturnal vigils, and day-dreams,   260
Are all enchantments in a case like thine,
Conspire against thy peace with one design,
Sooth thee to make thee but a surer prey,
And feed the fire that wastes thy pow'rs away.
Up—God has formed thee with a wiser view,   265
Not to be led in chains, but to subdue,
Calls thee to cope with enemies, and first
Points out a conflict with thyself, the worst.
Woman indeed, a gift he would bestow

When he design'd a paradise below,   270
The richest earthly boon his hands afford,
Deserves to be belov'd, but not ador'd.
Post away swiftly to more active scenes,
Collect the scatter'd truths that study gleans,
Mix with the world, but with its wiser part,   275
No longer give an image all thine heart,
Its empire is not her's, nor is it thine,
'Tis God's just claim, prerogative divine.
   Virtuous and faithful HEBERDEN! whose skill
Attempts no task it cannot well fulfill,   280
Gives melancholy up to nature's care,
And sends the patient into purer air.
Look where he comes—in this embower'd alcove,
Stand close conceal'd, and see a statue move:
Lips busy, and eyes fixt, foot falling slow,   285
Arms hanging idly down, hands clasp'd below,
Interpret to the marking eye, distress,
Such as its symptoms can alone express.
That tongue is silent now, that silent tongue
Could argue once, could jest or join the song,   290
Could give advice, could censure or commend,
Or charm the sorrows of a drooping friend.
Renounced alike its office and its sport,
Its brisker and its graver strains fall short,
Both fail beneath a fever's secret sway,   295
And like a summer-brook are past away.
This is a sight for pity to peruse
'Till she resemble faintly what she views,
'Till sympathy contract a kindred pain,
Pierced with the woes that she laments in vain.   300
This of all maladies that man infest,
Claims most compassion and receives the least,
Job felt it when he groan'd beneath the rod,
And the barbed arrows of a frowning God,
And such emollients as his friends could spare,   305
Friends such as his for modern Jobs prepare.
Blest, (rather curst) with hearts that never feel,
Kept snug in caskets of close-hammer'd steel,
With mouths made only to grin wide and eat,

And minds that deem derided pain, a treat,   310
With limbs of British oak and nerves of wire,
And wit that puppet-prompters might inspire,
Their sov'reign nostrum is a clumsy joke,
On pangs inforc'd with God's severest stroke.
But with a soul that ever felt the sting   315
Of sorrow, sorrow is a sacred thing,
Not to molest, or irritate, or raise
A laugh at its expence, is slender praise;
He that has not usurp'd the name of man,
Does all, and deems too little, all he can,   320
T' assuage the throbbings of the fester'd part,
And staunch the bleedings of a broken heart;
'Tis not as heads that never ach suppose,
Forg'ry of fancy and a dream of woes,
Man is an harp whose chords elude the sight,   325
Each yielding harmony, disposed aright,
The screws revers'd (a task which if he please
God in a moment executes with ease)
Ten thousand thousand strings at once go loose,
Lost, 'till he tune them, all their pow'r and use.   330
Then neither heathy wilds, nor scenes as fair
As ever recompensed the peasant's care,
Nor soft declivities with tufted hills,
Nor view of waters turning busy mills,
Parks in which art preceptress nature weds,   335
Nor gardens interspers'd with flow'ry beds,
Nor gales that catch the scent of blooming groves,
And waft it to the mourner as he roves,
Can call up life into his faded eye,
That passes all he sees unheeded by: 340
No wounds like those a wounded spirit feels,
No cure for such, 'till God who makes them, heals.
And thou sad suff'rer under nameless ill,
That yields not to the touch of human skill,
Improve the kind occasion, understand   345
A father's frown, and kiss his chast'ning hand:
To thee the day-spring and the blaze of noon,
The purple evening and resplendent moon,
The stars that sprinkled o'er the vault of night

Seem drops descending in a show'r of light,   350
Shine not, or undesired and hated shine,
Seen through the medium of a cloud like thine:
Yet seek him, in his favour life is found,
All bliss beside, a shadow or a sound:
Then heav'n eclipsed so long, and this dull earth   355
Shall seem to start into a second birth,
Nature assuming a more lovely face,
Borrowing a beauty from the works of grace,
Shall be despised and overlook'd no more,
Shall fill thee with delights unfelt before,   360
Impart to things inanimate a voice,
And bid her mountains and her hills rejoice,
The sound shall run along the winding vales,
And thou enjoy an Eden e'er it fails.

   Ye groves (the statesman at his desk exclaims   365
Sick of a thousand disappointed aims)
My patrimonial treasure and my pride,
Beneath your shades your gray possessor hide,
Receive me languishing for that repose
The servant of the public never knows.   370
Ye saw me once (ah those regretted days
When boyish innocence was all my praise)
Hour after hour delightfully allot
To studies then familiar, since forgot,
And cultivate a taste for antient song,   375
Catching its ardour as I mused along;
Nor seldom, as propitious heav'n might send,
What once I valued and could boast, a friend,
Were witnesses how cordially I press'd
His undissembling virtue to my breast;   380
Receive me now, not uncorrupt as then,
Nor guiltless of corrupting other men,
But vers'd in arts that while they seem to stay
A falling empire, hasten its decay.
To the fair haven of my native home,   385
The wreck of what I was, fatigued I come,
For once I can approve the patriot's voice,
And make the course he recommends, my choice,
We meet at last in one sincere desire,

His wish and mine both prompt me to retire.   390
'Tis done—he steps into the welcome chaise,
Lolls at his ease behind four handsome bays,
That whirl away from bus'ness and debate,
The disincumber'd Atlas of the state.
Ask not the boy, who when the breeze of morn   395
First shakes the glitt'ring drops from ev'ry thorn,
Unfolds his flock, then under bank or bush
Sits linking cherry stones or platting rush,
How fair is freedom?—he was always free—
To carve his rustic name upon a tree,   400
To snare the mole, or with ill fashion'd hook
To draw th' incautious minnow from the brook,
Are life's prime pleasures in his simple view,
His flock the chief concern he ever knew:
She shines but little in his heedless eyes,   405
The good we never miss, we rarely prize.
But ask the noble drudge in state-affairs,
Escap'd from office and its constant cares,
What charms he sees in freedom's smile express'd,
In freedom lost so long, now repossess'd,   410
The tongue whose strains were cogent as commands,
Revered at home, and felt in foreign lands,
Shall own itself a stamm'rer in that cause,
Or plead its silence as its best applause.
He knows indeed that whether dress'd or rude,   415
Wild without art, or artfully subdued,
Nature in ev'ry form inspires delight,
But never mark'd her with so just a sight.
Her hedge row shrubs, a variegated store,
With woodbine and wild roses mantled o'er,   420
Green baulks and furrow'd lands, the stream that spreads
Its cooling vapour o'er the dewy meads,
Downs that almost escape th' enquiring eye,
That melt and fade into the distant skie,
Beauties he lately slighted as he pass'd,   425
Seem all created since he travell'd last.
Master of all th' enjoyments he design'd,
No rough annoyance rankling in his mind,
What early philosophic hours he keeps,

How regular his meals, how sound he sleeps!   430
Not sounder he that on the mainmast head,
While morning kindles with a windy red,
Begins a long look-out for distant land,
Nor quits till evening-watch his giddy stand,
Then swift descending with a seaman's haste,   435
Slips to his hammock, and forgets the blast.
He chuses company, but not the squire's,
Whose wit is rudeness, whose good breeding tires;
Nor yet the parson's, who would gladly come,
Obsequious when abroad, though proud at home,   440
Nor can he much affect the neighb'ring peer,
Whose toe of emulation treads too near,
But wisely seeks a more convenient friend,
With whom, dismissing forms, he may unbend,
A man whom marks of condescending grace   445
Teach, while they flatter him, his proper place,
Who comes when call'd, and at a word withdraws,
Speaks with reserve, and listens with applause,
Some plain mechanic, who without pretence
To birth or wit, nor gives nor takes offence,   450
On whom he rests well pleas'd his weary pow'rs,
And talks and laughs away his vacant hours.
The tide of life, swift always in its course,
May run in cities with a brisker force,
But no where with a current so serene,   455
Or half so clear as in the rural scene.
Yet how fallacious is all earthly bliss,
What obvious truths the wisest heads may miss;
Some pleasures live a month, and some a year,
But short the date of all we gather here,   460
Nor happiness is felt, except the true,
That does not charm the more for being new.
This observation, as it chanced, not made,
Or if the thought occurr'd, not duely weigh'd,
He sighs—for after all, by slow degrees,   465
The spot he loved has lost the pow'r to please;
To cross his ambling poney day by day,
Seems at the best, but dreaming life away,
The prospect, such as might enchant despair,

He views it not, or sees no beauty there,   470
With aching heart and discontented looks,
Returns at noon, to billiards or to books,
But feels while grasping at his faded joys,
A secret thirst of his renounced employs,
He chides the tardiness of every post,   475
Pants to be told of battles won or lost,
Blames his own indolence, observes, though late,
'Tis criminal to leave a sinking state,
Flies to the levee, and receiv'd with grace,
Kneels, kisses hands, and shines again in place.   480
   Suburban villas, highway-side retreats,
That dread th' encroachment of our growing streets,
Tight boxes, neatly sash'd, and in a blaze
With all a July sun's collected rays,
Delight the citizen, who gasping there   485
Breathes clouds of dust and calls it country air.
Oh sweet retirement, who would baulk the thought,
That could afford retirement, or could not?
'Tis such an easy walk, so smooth and strait,
The second milestone fronts the garden gate,   490
A step if fair, and if a show'r approach,
You find safe shelter in the next stage-coach.
There prison'd in a parlour snug and small,
Like bottled wasps upon a southern wall,
The man of bus'ness and his friends compress'd,   495
Forget their labours, and yet find no rest;
But still 'tis rural—trees are to be seen
From ev'ry window, and the fields are green,
Ducks paddle in the pond before the door,
And what could a remoter scene show more?   500
A sense of elegance we rarely find
The portion of a mean or vulgar mind,
And ignorance of better things, makes man
Who cannot much, rejoice in what he can;
And he that deems his leisure well bestow'd   505
In contemplations of a turnpike road,
Is occupied as well, employs his hours
As wisely, and as much improves his pow'rs,
As he that slumbers in pavilions graced

With all the charms of an accomplish'd taste.   510
Yet hence alas! Insolvencies, and hence
Th' unpitied victim of ill-judg'd expence,
From all his wearisome engagements freed,
Shakes hands with bus'ness, and retires indeed.
   Your prudent grand mammas, ye modern belles,   515
Content with Bristol, Bath, and Tunbridge-wells,
When health requir'd it would consent to roam,
Else more attach'd to pleasures found at home.
But now alike, gay widow, virgin, wife,
Ingenious to diversify dull life,   520
In coaches, chaises, caravans and hoys,
Fly to the coast for daily, nightly joys,
And all impatient of dry land, agree
With one consent to rush into the sea.—
Ocean exhibits, fathomless and broad,   525
Much of the pow'r and majesty of God.
He swathes about the swelling of the deep,
That shines and rests, as infants smile and sleep,
Vast as it is, it answers as it flows
The breathings of the lightest air that blows,   530
Curling and whit'ning over all the waste,
The rising waves obey th' increasing blast,
Abrupt and horrid as the tempest roars,
Thunder and flash upon the stedfast shores,
'Till he that rides the whirlwind, checks the rein,   535
Then, all the world of waters sleeps again.—
Nereids or Dryads, as the fashion leads,
Now in the floods, now panting in the meads,
Vot'ries of pleasure still, where'er she dwells,
Near barren rocks, in palaces or cells,   540
Oh grant a poet leave to recommend,
(A poet fond of nature and your friend)
Her slighted works to your admiring view,
Her works must needs excel, who fashion'd you.
Would ye, when rambling in your morning ride,   545
With some unmeaning coxcomb at your side,
Condemn the prattler for his idle pains,
To waste unheard the music of his strains,

515 mammas,] mammas *1782*

And deaf to all the impertinence of tongue,
That while it courts, affronts and does you wrong.   550
Mark well the finish'd plan without a fault,
The seas globose and huge, th' o'erarching vault,
Earth's millions daily fed, a world employ'd
In gath'ring plenty yet to be enjoy'd,
'Till gratitude grew vocal in the praise   555
Of God, beneficent in all his ways,
Grac'd with such wisdom how would beauty shine?
Ye want but that to seem indeed divine.
    Anticipated rents and bills unpaid,
Force many a shining youth into the shade,   560
Not to redeem his time but his estate,
And play the fool, but at a cheaper rate.
There hid in loath'd obscurity, remov'd
From pleasures left, but never more belov'd,
He just endures, and with a sickly spleen   565
Sighs o'er the beauties of the charming scene.
Nature indeed looks prettily in rhime,
Streams tinkle sweetly in poetic chime,
The warblings of the black-bird, clear and strong,
Are musical enough in Thomson's song,   570
And Cobham's groves and Windsor's green retreats,
When Pope describes them, have a thousand sweets,
He likes the country, but in truth must own,
Most likes it, when he studies it in town.
    Poor Jack—no matter who—for when I blame   575
I pity, and must therefore sink the name,
Liv'd in his saddle, lov'd the chace, the course,
And always, e'er he mounted, kiss'd his horse.
Th' estate his sires had own'd in antient years,
Was quickly distanc'd, match'd against a peer's.   580
Jack vanish'd, was regretted and forgot,
'Tis wild good-nature's never-failing lot.
At length, when all had long suppos'd him dead,
By cold submersion, razor, rope or lead,
My lord, alighting at his usual place,   585
The Crown, took notice of an ostler's face.
Jack knew his friend, but hop'd in that disguise

586 Crown] crown *1782*

He might escape the most observing eyes,
And whistling as if unconcern'd and gay,
Curried his nag and look'd another way.   590
Convinc'd at last upon a nearer view,
'Twas he, the same, the very Jack he knew,
O'erwhelm'd at once with wonder, grief and joy,
He press'd him much to quit his base employ,
His countenance, his purse, his heart, his hand,   595
Infl'ence and pow'r were all at his command.
Peers are not always gen'rous as well-bred,
But Granby was, meant truly what he said.
Jack bow'd and was oblig'd—confess'd 'twas strange
That so retir'd he should not wish a change,   600
But knew no medium between guzzling beer,
And his old stint, three thousand pounds a year.
Thus some retire to nourish hopeless woe,
Some seeking happiness not found below,
Some to comply with humour, and a mind   605
To social scenes by nature disinclin'd,
Some sway'd by fashion, some by deep disgust,
Some self-impoverish'd, and because they must,
But few that court Retirement, are aware
Of half the toils they must encounter there.   610
    Lucrative offices are seldom lost
For want of pow'rs proportion'd to the post:
Give ev'n a dunce th' employment he desires,
And he soon finds the talents it requires;
A business with an income at its heels,   615
Furnishes always oil for its own wheels.
But in his arduous enterprize to close
His active years with indolent repose,
He finds the labours of that state exceed
His utmost faculties, severe indeed.   620
'Tis easy to resign a toilsome place,
But not to manage leisure with a grace,
Absence of occupation is not rest,
A mind quite vacant is a mind distress'd.
The vet'ran steed excused his task at length,   625
In kind compassion of his failing strength,
And turn'd into the park or mead to graze,

Exempt from future service all his days,
There feels a pleasure perfect in its kind,
Ranges at liberty, and snuffs the wind.   630
But when his lord would quit the busy road,
To taste a joy like that he has bestow'd,
He proves, less happy than his favour'd brute,
A life of ease a difficult pursuit.
Thought, to the man that never thinks, may seem   635
As natural, as when asleep, to dream,
But reveries (for human minds will act)
Specious in show, impossible in fact,
Those flimsy webs that break as soon as wrought,
Attain not to the dignity of thought.   640
Nor yet the swarms that occupy the brain
Where dreams of dress, intrigue, and pleasure reign,
Nor such as useless conversation breeds,
Or lust engenders, and indulgence feeds.
Whence, and what are we? to what end ordain'd?   645
What means the drama by the world sustain'd?
Business or vain amusement, care or mirth,
Divide the frail inhabitants of earth,
Is duty a mere sport, or an employ?
Life an intrusted talent, or a toy?   650
Is there as reason, conscience, scripture say,
Cause to provide for a great future day,
When earth's assign'd duration at an end,
Man shall be summon'd and the dead attend?
The trumpet—will it sound? the curtain rise?   655
And show th' august tribunal of the skies,
Where no prevarication shall avail,
Where eloquence and artifice shall fail,
The pride of arrogant distinctions fall,
And conscience and our conduct judge us all?   660
Pardon me, ye that give the midnight oil,
To learned cares or philosophic toil,
Though I revere your honourable names,
Your useful labors and important aims,
And hold the world indebted to your aid,   665
Enrich'd with the discoveries ye have made,
Yet let me stand excused, if I esteem

A mind employ'd on so sublime a theme,
Pushing her bold enquiry to the date
And outline of the present transient state,   670
And after poising her advent'rous wings,
Settling at last upon eternal things,
Far more intelligent, and better taught
The strenuous use of profitable thought,
Than ye when happiest, and enlighten'd most,   675
And highest in renown, can justly boast.
   A mind unnerv'd, or indispos'd to bear
The weight of subjects worthiest of her care,
Whatever hopes a change of scene inspires,
Must change her nature, or in vain retires.   680
An idler is a watch that wants both hands,
As useless if it goes as when it stands.
Books therefore, not the scandal of the shelves,
In which lewd sensualists print out themselves,
Nor those in which the stage gives vice a blow,   685
With what success, let modern manners show,
Nor his, who for the bane of thousands born,
Built God a church and laugh'd his word to scorn,
Skilful alike to seem devout and just,
And stab religion with a sly side-thrust;   690
Nor those of learn'd philologists, who chase
A panting syllable through time and space,
Start it at home, and hunt it in the dark,
To Gaul, to Greece, and into Noah's ark;
But such as learning without false pretence,   695
The friend of truth, th' associate of sound sense,
And such as in the zeal of good design,
Strong judgment lab'ring in the scripture mine,
All such as manly and great souls produce,
Worthy to live, and of eternal use;   700
Behold in these what leisure hours demand,
Amusement and true knowledge hand in hand.
Luxury gives the mind a childish cast,
And while she polishes, perverts the taste,
Habits of close attention, thinking heads,   705
Become more rare as dissipation spreads,
'Till authors hear at length, one gen'ral cry,

Tickle and entertain us, or we die.
The loud demand from year to year the same,
Beggars invention and makes fancy lame,   710
'Till farce itself most mournfully jejune,
Calls for the kind assistance of a tune,
And novels (witness ev'ry month's review)
Belie their name and offer nothing new.
The mind relaxing into needfull sport,   715
Should turn to writers of an abler sort,
Whose wit well manag'd, and whose classic stile,
Give truth a lustre, and make wisdom smile.
　　Friends (for I cannot stint as some have done
Too rigid in my view, that name to one,   720
Though one, I grant it in th' gen'rous breast
Will stand advanc'd a step above the rest,
Flow'rs by that name promiscuously we call,
But one, the rose, the regent of them all)
Friends, not adopted with a school-boy's haste,   725
But chosen with a nice discerning taste,
Well-born, well-disciplin'd, who plac'd a-part
From vulgar minds, have honour much at heart,
And (tho' the world may think th' ingredients odd)
The love of virtue, and the fear of God!   730
Such friends prevent what else wou'd soon succeed,
A temper rustic as the life we lead,
And keep the polish of the manners clean,
As their's who bustle in the busiest scene.
For solitude, however some may rave,   735
Seeming a sanctuary, proves a grave,
A sepulchre in which the living lie,
Where all good qualities grow sick and die.
I praise the Frenchman,* his remark was shrew'd—
How sweet, how passing sweet is solitude!   740
But grant me still a friend in my retreat,
Whom I may whisper, solitude is sweet.
Yet neither these delights, nor aught beside
That appetite can ask, or wealth provide,
Can save us always from a tedious day,   745
Or shine the dullness of still life away;

* Bruyere.

Divine communion carefully enjoy'd,
Or sought with energy, must fill the void.
Oh sacred art, to which alone life owes
Its happiest seasons, and a peaceful close,   750
Scorn'd in a world, indebted to that scorn
For evils daily felt and hardly borne,
Not knowing thee, we reap with bleeding hands,
Flow'rs of rank odor upon thorny lands,
And while experience cautions us in vain,   755
Grasp seeming happiness, and find it pain.
Despondence, self-deserted in her grief,
Lost by abandoning her own relief,
Murmuring and ungrateful discontent,
That scorns afflictions mercifully meant,   760
Those humours tart as wines upon the fret,
Which idleness and weariness beget,
These and a thousand plagues that haunt the breast
Fond of the phantom of an earthly rest,
Divine communion chases as the day   765
Drives to their dens th' obedient beasts of prey.
See Judah's promised king, bereft of all,
Driv'n out an exile from the face of Saul,
To distant caves the lonely wand'rer flies,
To seek that peace a tyrant's frown denies.   770
Hear the sweet accents of his tuneful voice,
Hear him o'erwhelm'd with sorrow, yet rejoice,
No womanish or wailing grief has part,
No, not a moment, in his royal heart,
'Tis manly music, such as martyrs make,   775
Suff'ring with gladness for a Saviour's sake;
His soul exults, hope animates his lays,
The sense of mercy kindles into praise,
And wilds familiar with the lion's roar,
Ring with extatic sounds unheard before;   780
'Tis love like his that can alone defeat
The foes of man, or make a desart sweet.
   Religion does not censure or exclude
Unnumber'd pleasures harmlessly pursued.
To study culture, and with artful toil   785
To meliorate and tame the stubborn soil,

To give dissimilar yet fruitful lands
The grain or herb or plant that each demands,
To cherish virtue in an humble state,
And share the joys your bounty may create,   790
To mark the matchless workings of the pow'r
That shuts within its seed the future flow'r,
Bids these in elegance of form excell,
In colour these, and those delight the smell,
Sends nature forth, the daughter of the skies,   795
To dance on earth, and charm all human eyes;
To teach the canvass innocent deceit,
Or lay the landscape on the snowy sheet,
These, these are arts pursued without a crime,
That leave no stain upon the wing of time.   800
    Me poetry (or rather notes that aim
Feebly and vainly at poetic fame)
Employs, shut out from more important views,
Fast by the banks of the slow-winding Ouse,
Content, if thus sequester'd I may raise   805
A monitor's, though not a poet's praise,
And while I teach an art too little known,
To close life wisely, may not waste my own.

THE DOVES

Reas'ning at every step he treads,
   Man yet mistakes his way,
While meaner things whom instinct leads
   Are rarely known to stray.

One silent eve I wander'd late,   5
   And heard the voice of love,
The turtle thus address'd her mate,
   And sooth'd the list'ning dove.

Our mutual bond of faith and truth,
   No time shall disengage,   10
Those blessings of our early youth,
   Shall cheer our latest age.

While innocence without disguise,
   And constancy sincere,
Shall fill the circles of those eyes,   15
   And mine can read them there,

Those ills that wait on all below,
   Shall ne'er be felt by me,
Or gently felt, and only so,
   As being shared with thee.   20

About 26 May 1780.

COPY-TEXT: *1782*, pp. 299–301 (first printing). Collated: *A*, *P* (letter to Mrs. Newton [5 June 1780]), *H*.

Title] Antithelyphthora *A*, *P*
1–4]   Muse, Mark the much lamented Day,
                    When like a Tempest fear'd,
                Forth issuing on the Last of May,
                    Thelyphthora appear'd. *A*, *P*, *H*
5 One silent] That fatal *A*, *P*, *H*

When light'nings flash among the trees,
　　Or kites are hov'ring near,
I fear lest thee alone they seize,
　　And know no other fear.

'Tis then I feel myself a wife,   25
　　And press thy wedded side,
Resolv'd an union form'd for life,
　　Death never shall divide.

But oh! if fickle and unchaste
　　(Forgive a transient thought)   30
Thou couldst become unkind at last,
　　And scorn thy present lot,

No need of light'nings from on high,
　　Or kites with cruel beak,
Denied th' endearments of thine eye   35
　　This widow'd heart would break.

Thus sang the sweet sequester'd bird
　　Soft as the passing wind,
And I recorded what I heard,
　　A lesson for mankind.   40

A FABLE

A raven while with glossy breast,
Her new-laid eggs she fondly press'd,
And on her wicker-work high mounted
Her chickens prematurely counted,
(A fault philosophers might blame   5
If quite exempted from the same)
Enjoy'd at ease the genial day,
'Twas April as the bumkins say,
The legislature call'd it May.

24 know] feel *deleted* have *deleted A*　　　32 scorn thy present] weary of thy *deleted A*

9 May 1780.

copy-text: *1782*, pp. 302–3 (first printing). Collated: *A*, *H*.

But suddenly a wind as high   10
As ever swept a winter sky,
Shook the young leaves about her ears,
And fill'd her with a thousand fears,
Lest the rude blast should snap the bough,
And spread her golden hopes below.   15
But just at eve the blowing weather,
And all her fears were hush'd together:
And now, quoth poor unthinking Raph,
'Tis over, and the brood is safe;
(For ravens though as birds of omen,   20
They teach both conj'rers and old women
To tell us what is to befall,
Can't prophecy, themselves, at all.)
The morning came, when neighbour Hodge,
Who long had mark'd her airy lodge,   25
And destin'd all the treasure there
A gift to his expecting fair,
Climb'd like a squirrel to his dray,
And bore the worthless prize away.

MORAL

'Tis providence alone secures   30
In every change, both mine and your's.
Safety consists not in escape
From dangers of a frightful shape,
An earthquake may be bid to spare
The man that's strangled by a hair.   35
Fate steals along with silent tread,
Found oft'nest in what least we dread,
Frowns in the storm with angry brow,
But in the sunshine strikes the blow.

14–15] *A has*:   Lest the rude Blast that Threat'ned so,
                       And Rock'd her Cradle to and fro
                       Should split the Trunk, or Snap the Bough
                       Then fruitless all her Hopes to See,
                       A Pretty gaping Progeny:
in H these lines are deleted, and the present 14–15 *substituted, reading* Wind *for* blast
18 Raph] Ra'ph *A, H*   28 Climb'd] *A, H*; Clim'b *1782*   30 secures] insures
deleted A

A COMPARISON

The lapse of time and rivers is the same,
Both speed their journey with a restless stream,
The silent pace with which they steal away,
No wealth can bribe, no pray'rs persuade to stay,
Alike irrevocable both when past,   5
And a wide ocean swallows both at last.
Though each resemble each in ev'ry part,
A difference strikes at length the musing heart;
Streams never flow in vain; where streams abound,
How laughs the land with various plenty crown'd!   10
But time that should enrich the nobler mind,
Neglected, leaves a dreary waste behind.

ANOTHER

Addressed to a Young Lady

Sweet stream that winds through yonder glade,
Apt emblem of a virtuous maid—
Silent and chaste she steals along
Far from the world's gay busy throng,
With gentle yet prevailing force   5
Intent upon her destin'd course,
Graceful and useful all she does,
Blessing and blest where'er she goes,
Pure-bosom'd as that wat'ry glass,
And heav'n reflected in her face.   10

COPY-TEXT: *1782*, p. 304 (first printing). Collated: *H* (no variants).

April 1780.

COPY-TEXT: *1782*, pp. 304–5 (first printing). Collated: *H, U.*

Title] Another. *H*; *no title in U*   8 where'er] *H, U*; where're *1782*

VERSES, SUPPOSED TO BE WRITTEN BY ALEXANDER SELKIRK, DURING HIS SOLITARY ABODE IN THE ISLAND OF JUAN FERNANDEZ

I am monarch of all I survey,
　My right there is none to dispute,
From the center all round to the sea,
　I am lord of the fowl and the brute.
Oh solitude! where are the charms　　　　　　5
　That sages have seen in thy face?
Better dwell in the midst of alarms,
　Than reign in this horrible place.

I am out of humanity's reach,
　I must finish my journey alone,　　　　　　10
Never hear the sweet music of speech,
　I start at the sound of my own.
The beasts that roam over the plain,
　My form with indifference see,
They are so unacquainted with man,　　　　　15
　Their tameness is shocking to me.

Society, friendship, and love,
　Divinely bestow'd upon man,
Oh had I the wings of a dove,
　How soon wou'd I taste you again!　　　　　20
My sorrows I then might assuage
　In the ways of religion and truth,
Might learn from the wisdom of age,
　And be cheer'd by the sallies of youth.

Religion! what treasure untold　　　　　　　25
　Resides in that heav'nly word!
More precious than silver and gold,
　Or all that this earth can afford.

COPY-TEXT: *1782*, pp. 305–8 (first printing). Collated: *A*, *U* (copy in Mrs. Unwin's hand); *H*.

Title] Stanzas supposed to have been Written [to be written *U*] By Alexander Selkirk During his Abode in the Island of Juan Fernandez. *A*, *U*; Robinson Crusoe *H*
20 you] ye *A*, *U*, *H*　　　27 and] or *U*

But the sound of the church going bell
    These vallies and rocks never heard,   30
Ne'er sigh'd at the sound of a knell,
    Or smil'd when a sabbath appear'd.

Ye winds that have made me your sport,
    Convey to this desolate shore,
Some cordial endearing report   35
    Of a land I shall visit no more.
My friends do they now and then send
    A wish or a thought after me?
O tell me I yet have a friend,
    Though a friend I am never to see.   40

How fleet is a glance of the mind!
    Compar'd with the speed of its flight,
The tempest itself lags behind,
    And the swift winged arrows of light.
When I think of my own native land,   45
    In a moment I seem to be there;
But alas! recollection at hand
    Soon hurries me back to despair.

But the sea fowl is gone to her nest,
    The beast is laid down in his lair,   50
Ev'n here is a season of rest,
    And I to my cabbin repair.
There is mercy in ev'ry place,
    And mercy, encouraging thought!
Gives even affliction a grace,   55
    And reconciles man to his lot.

31 Ne'er] Never *A, U, H*
37–8   My Friends do they ever [never *U*] attend
                To the sad Recollection of Me,   *A, U; H at first as A, later*
deleted and the 1782 reading substituted
40 I am never to] that I never must *A, U, H*   41 fleet] Swift *deleted A*
45 own native land] Native Abode *A, U; so H at first, later deleted and the 1782 reading*
substituted
47–8   'Tis the Body, alas! with its Load,
                Still holds me a Prisoner here.   *A, U; so H at first, later*
deleted and the 1782 reading substituted
49 her] his *A, U*

ON THE PROMOTION OF EDWARD THURLOW, ESQ. TO THE LORD HIGH CHANCELLORSHIP OF ENGLAND

Round Thurlow's head in early youth,
    And in his sportive days,
Fair science pour'd the light of truth,
    And genius shed his rays.

See! with united wonder, cry'd   5
    Th' experienc'd and the sage,
Ambition in a boy supplied
    With all the skill of age.

Discernment, eloquence and grace,
    Proclaim him born to sway   10
The balance in th' highest place,
    And bear the palm away.

The praise bestow'd was just and wise,
    He sprang impetuous forth,
Secure of conquest where the prize   15
    Attends superior worth.

So the best courser on the plain
    E'er yet he starts is known,
And does but at the goal obtain
    What all had deem'd his own.   20

Early November 1779.

copy-text: *1782*, pp. 309–10 (first printing). Collated: *P, N* (letter to Joseph Hill, 14 Nov. 1779), *H*.

Title Lord High Chancellorship] Lord Chancellorship *P, N, H*   10 born to sway]
ev'ry Day *deleted P*   11 The balance in] Born to obtain *deleted P*   14 sprang]
sprung *P, N, H*

ODE TO PEACE

Come, peace of mind, delightful guest!
Return and make thy downy nest
    Once more in this sad heart:
Nor riches I, nor pow'r pursue,
Nor hold forbidden joys in view,   5
    We therefore need not part.

Where wilt thou dwell if not with me,
From av'rice and ambition free,
    And pleasures fatal wiles?
For whom alas! dost thou prepare   10
The sweets that I was wont to share,
    The banquet of thy smiles?

The great, the gay, shall they partake
The heav'n that thou alone canst make,
    And wilt thou quit the stream   15
That murmurs through the dewy mead,
The grove and the sequester'd shed,
    To be a guest with them?

For thee I panted, thee I priz'd,
For thee I gladly sacrific'd   20
    Whate'er I lov'd before,
And shall I see thee start away,
And helpless, hopeless, hear thee say—
    Farewell! we meet no more?

COPY-TEXT: *1782*, pp. 310–11 (first printing). Collated: *A, H*.

Title] *no title in A*   3 this sad] William's *A, H*   9 Whom nothing Base
beguiles? *A, H*   20 For] To *A, H*

HUMAN FRAILTY

Weak and irresolute is man;
   The purpose of to day,
Woven with pains into his plan,
   To morrow rends away.

The bow well bent and smart the spring,   5
   Vice seems already slain,
But passion rudely snaps the string,
   And it revives again.

Some foe to his upright intent
   Finds out his weaker part,   10
Virtue engages his assent,
   But pleasure wins his heart.

'Tis here the folly of the wise
   Through all his art we view,
And while his tongue the charge denies,   15
   His conscience owns it true.

Bound on a voyage of awful length
   And dangers little known,
A stranger to superior strength,
   Man vainly trusts his own.   20

But oars alone can ne'er prevail
   To reach the distant coast,
The breath of heav'n must swell the sail,
   Or all the toil is lost.

Before 2 December 1779.

COPY-TEXT: *1782*, pp. 311–13 (first printing). Collated: *U, H*.

17 voyage] Voy'ge *U*; Voy'age *H*   **21** alone can] alas could *U, H*

THE MODERN PATRIOT

Rebellion is my theme all day,
　　I only wish 'twould come
(As who knows but perhaps it may)
　　A little nearer home.

Yon roaring boys who rave and fight　　　　5
　　On t'other side the Atlantic,
I always held them in the right,
　　But most so, when most frantic.

When lawless mobs insult the court,
　　That man shall be my toast,　　　　　　10
If breaking windows be the sport
　　Who bravely breaks the most.

But oh! for him my fancy culls
　　The choicest flow'rs she bears,
Who constitutionally pulls　　　　　　　　15
　　Your house about your ears.

Such civil broils are my delight,
　　Tho' some folks can't endure 'em,
Who say the mob are mad outright,
　　And that a rope must cure 'em.　　　　　20

A rope! I wish we patriots had
　　Such strings for all who need 'em—
What! hang a man for going mad?
　　Then farewell British freedom.

June 1780 (?).

COPY-TEXT: *1782*, pp. 313–14 (first printing). Collated: *H*.
6 the Atlantic] th'Atlantic *H*　　　7 held] hold *H*

ON OBSERVING SOME NAMES OF LITTLE
NOTE RECORDED IN THE BIOGRAPHIA
BRITANNICA

Oh fond attempt to give a deathless lot,
To names ignoble, born to be forgot!
In vain recorded in historic page,
They court the notice of a future age,
Those twinkling tiney lustres of the land,   5
Drop one by one from Fame's neglecting hand,
Lethæan gulphs receive them as they fall,
And dark oblivion soon absorbs them all.
    So when a child, as playful children use,
Has burnt to tinder a stale last year's news,   10
The flame extinct, he views the roving fire,
There goes my lady, and there goes the 'squire,
There goes the parson, oh! illustrious spark,
And there, scarce less illustrious, goes the clerk.

REPORT
OF AN ADJUDGED CASE NOT TO BE FOUND
IN ANY OF THE BOOKS

Between Nose and Eyes a strange contest arose,
    The spectacles set them unhappily wrong;
The point in dispute was, as all the world knows,
    To which the said spectacles ought to belong.

Shortly before 3 September 1780.

COPY-TEXT: *1782*, pp. 314–15 (first printing). Collated: *U*.

Title] *no title in U*   1 attempt to] Attempt! to *U*   9 *not indented in U*

November (?) 1780.

COPY-TEXT: *1782*, pp. 315–17 (first printing). Collated: *U* (letter of 2 Dec. 1780), *P* (letter to Mrs. Newton, 17 Dec. 1780), *N* (letter to Joseph Hill, 27 Dec. 1780).

Title] Nose Plt Eyes Deft. Vid: Plowden. Folio 6000 *U*; *no title in P*; Nose Plt. Eyes Defts. *N*   1 a strange] once a *U*; a sad *N*   2 unhappily] Egregiously *U*

So the Tongue was the lawyer and argued the cause   5
    With a great deal of skill, and a wig full of learning,
While chief baron Ear sat to balance the laws,
    So fam'd for his talent in nicely discerning.

In behalf of the Nose, it will quickly appear,
    And your lordship he said, will undoubtedly find,   10
That the Nose has had spectacles always in wear,
    Which amounts to possession time out of mind.

Then holding the spectacles up to the court—
    Your lordship observes they are made with a straddle,
As wide as the ridge of the Nose is, in short,   15
    Design'd to sit close to it, just like a saddle.

Again would your lordship a moment suppose
    ('Tis a case that has happen'd and may be again)
That the visage or countenance had not a Nose,
    Pray who wou'd or who cou'd wear spectacles then?   20

On the whole it appears, and my argument shows
    With a reasoning the court will never condemn,
That the spectacles plainly were made for the Nose,
    And the Nose was as plainly intended for them.

Then shifting his side as a lawyer knows how,   25
    He pleaded again in behalf of the Eyes,
But what were his arguments few people know,
    For the court did not think they were equally wise.

So his lordship decreed with a grave solemn tone,
    Decisive and clear without one if or but—   30
That whenever the Nose put his spectacles on
    By day-light or candle-light—Eyes should be shut.

8 in] at *P, N*   19 countenance] Spectacles *deleted U*

ON THE BURNING OF LORD MANSFIELD'S LIBRARY, TOGETHER WITH HIS MSS. BY THE MOB, IN THE MONTH OF JUNE, 1780

So then—the Vandals of our isle,
　　Sworn foes to sense and law,
Have burnt to dust a nobler pile
　　Than ever Roman saw!

And MURRAY sighs o'er Pope and Swift,　　　　5
　　And many a treasure more,
The well-judg'd purchase and the gift
　　That grac'd his letter'd store.

Their pages mangl'd, burnt and torn,
　　The loss was *his alone*,　　　　　　　　　10
But ages yet to come shall mourn
　　The burning of *his own*.

ON THE SAME

When wit and genius meet their doom
　　In all devouring flame,
They tell us of the fate of Rome,
　　And bid us fear the same.

O'er MURRAY's loss the muses wept,　　　　　5
　　They felt the rude alarm,
Yet bless'd the guardian care that kept
　　His sacred head from harm.

22 June 1780.

COPY-TEXT: *1782*, p. 318 (first printing). Collated: *U, H*.

Title] On the Burning of Lord Mansfields Library together with his own MSS. *U*; On the Burning of Lord Mansfields Library together with his M.SS. by the Mob in June. 1780. *H*
2 to] of *U*　　　7 and] or *H*

Late June–early July 1780.

COPY-TEXT: *1782*, p. 319 (first printing). Collated: *H*.

There mem'ry, like the bee that's fed
From Flora's balmy store,   10
The quintessence of all he read
Had treasur'd up before.

The lawless herd with fury blind
Have done him cruel wrong,
The flow'rs are gone—but still we find   15
The honey on his tongue.

THE LOVE OF THE WORLD REPROVED;

OR,

HYPOCRISY DETECTED*

Thus says the prophet of the Turk,
Good mussulman abstain from pork;
There is a part in ev'ry swine,
No friend or follower of mine
May taste, whate'er his inclination,   5
On pain of excommunication.
Such Mahomet's mysterious charge,
And thus he left the point at large.
Had he the sinful part express'd
They might with safety eat the rest;   10
But for one piece they thought it hard
From the whole hog to be debarr'd,
And set their wit at work to find
What joint the prophet had in mind.

---

* It may be proper to inform the reader that this piece has already appeared in print, having found its way, though with some unnecessary additions by an unknown hand, into the Leeds Journal, without the author's privity.

---

15 gone] dead *H*

February or early March 1779.

COPY-TEXT: *1782*, pp. 320–2. Collated: *LM* (first printing, *Leeds Mercury*, 9 Nov. 1779), *A*, *H*.

Title] The Tale of the Mahometan Hog, Evincing the manifest Deception of the modern Christian World. *LM*; Almost a Christian. A Tale *A*; A Tale. *H*   *no footnote in LM, A, H*
2 abstain from] beware of *LM, deleted A*   4 friend or follower] Follower or Friend *LM, A, H*   9–14 *not in A, H*   13 And set their wit]So set their wits *LM*

Much controversy strait arose,   15
These chuse the back, the belly those;
By some 'tis confidently said
He meant not to forbid the head,
While others at that doctrine rail,
And piously prefer the tail.   20
Thus, conscience freed from ev'ry clog,
Mahometans eat up the hog.
    You laugh—'tis well—the tale apply'd
May make you laugh on t'other side.
Renounce the world, the preacher cries—   25
We do—a multitude replies.
While one as innocent regards
A snug and friendly game at cards;
And one, whatever you may say,
Can see no evil in a play;   30
Some love a concert or a race,
And others, shooting and the chase.
Revil'd and lov'd, renounc'd and follow'd,
Thus bit by bit the world is swallow'd;
Each thinks his neighbour makes too free,   35
Yet likes a slice as well as he,
With sophistry their sauce they sweeten,
'Till quite from tail to snout 'tis eaten.

THE LILY AND THE ROSE

The nymph must lose her female friend
    If more admir'd than she—
But where will fierce contention end
    If flow'rs can disagree?

Within the garden's peaceful scene
    Appear'd two lovely foes,

---

15 *not indented in A, H*   strait arose] therefore rose *LM*   19 While] Whilst *LM*
23 *not indented in A, H*   27 While] Whilst *LM*   32 and] or *LM*

? July 1780.

COPY-TEXT: *1782*, pp. 322–4 (first printing). Collated: *U, H*

Aspiring to the rank of queen,
  The lily and the rose.

The rose soon redden'd into rage,
  And swelling with disdain,   10
Appeal'd to many a poet's page
  To prove her right to reign.

The lily's height bespoke command,
  A fair imperial flow'r,
She seem'd design'd for Flora's hand,   15
  The sceptre of her pow'r.

This civil bick'ring and debate
  The goddess chanc'd to hear,
And flew to save, e'er yet too late,
  The pride of the parterre.   20

Your's is, she said, the nobler hue,
  And your's the statelier mien,
And 'till a third surpasses you,
  Let each be deem'd a queen.

Thus sooth'd and reconcil'd, each seeks   25
  The fairest British fair,
The seat of empire is her cheeks,
  They reign united there.

IDEM LATINE REDDITUM

Heu inimicitias quoties parit æmula forma,
  Quam raro pulchræ, pulchra placere potest?
Sed fines ultrà solitos discordia tendit,
  Cum flores ipsos bilis et ira movent.

17 This] The *U, H*

? July or early August 1780.

COPY-TEXT: *1782*, pp. 324–6 (first printing). Collated: *H.*

Title] Inter Lilium et Rosam Certamen (Quod Vide Suprá) Latine Redditum. *H*
1 parit] facit *H*

Hortus ubi dulces præbet tacitosque recessûs,   5
    Se rapit in partes gens animosa duas,
Hic sibi regales amaryllis candida cultûs,
    Illic purpureo vindicat ore rosa.

Ira rosam et meritis quæsita superbia tangunt,
    Multaque ferventi vix cohibenda sinû,   10
Dum sibi fautorum ciet undique nomina vatûm,
    Jusque suum, multo carmine fulta, probat.

Altior emicat illa, et celso vertice nutat,
    Ceu flores inter non habitura parem,
Fastiditque alios, et nata videtur in usûs   15
    Imperii, sceptrum, Flôra quod ipsa gerat.

Nec Dea non sensit civilis murmura rixæ,
    Cui curæ est pictas pandere ruris opes.
Deliciasque suas nunquam non prompta tueri,
    Dum licet et locus est, ut tueatur, adest.   20

Et tibi forma datur procerior omnibus, inquit,
    Et tibi, principibus qui solet esse, color,
Et donec vincat quædam formosior ambas,
    Et tibi reginæ nomen, et esto tibi.

His ubi sedatus furor est, petit utraque nympham   25
    Qualem inter Veneres Anglia sola parit,
Hanc penés imperium est, nihil optant amplius, hujus
Regnant in nitidis, et sine lite, genis.

THE NIGHTINGALE AND GLOW-WORM

A Nightingale that all day long
Had cheer'd the village with his song,
Nor yet at eve his note suspended,
Nor yet when even tide was ended,
Began to feel as well he might   5
The keen demands of appetite;
When looking eagerly around,
He spied far off upon the ground,
A something shining in the dark,
And knew the glow-worm by his spark,   10
So stooping down from hawthorn top,
He thought to put him in his crop;
The worm aware of his intent,
Harangu'd him thus right eloquent.

   Did you admire my lamp, quoth he,   15
As much as I your minstrelsy,
You would abhor to do me wrong,
As much as I to spoil your song,
For 'twas the self-same power divine,
Taught you to sing, and me to shine,   20
That you with music, I with light,
Might beautify and cheer the night.
The songster heard his short oration,
And warbling out his approbation,
Releas'd him as my story tells,   25
And found a supper somewhere else.

   Hence jarring sectaries may learn,
Their real int'rest to discern:
That brother should not war with brother,
And worry and devour each other,   30
But sing and shine by sweet consent,
'Till life's poor transient night is spent,

Late February 1780.

COPY-TEXT: *1782*, pp. 326–8 (first printing). Collated: *W*, *H*

Title and Glow-worm] and the Glow Worm *W*   7 looking eagerly] casting both his
Eyes *W*   8 spied] saw *W*, *H*   15 *not indented in W*   lamp] Tail *W*, *H*
22 beautify and cheer] Cheer and Beautify *W*, *H*

Respecting in each other's case
The gifts of nature and of grace.
   Those christians best deserve the name   35
Who studiously make peace their aim;
Peace, both the duty and the prize
Of him that creeps and him that flies.

VOTUM

O matutini rores, auræque salubres,
O nemora, et lætæ rivis felicibus herbæ,
Graminei colles, et amænæ in vallibus umbræ!
Fata modó dederint quas olim in rure paterno
Delicias, procul arte, procul formidine novi,   5
Quam vellem ignotus, quod mens mea semper avebat,
Ante larem proprium placidam expectare senectam,
Tum demùm exactis non infeliciter annis,
Sortiri tacitum lapidem, aut sub cespite condi!

ON A GOLDFINCH STARVED TO DEATH
IN HIS CAGE

Time was when I was free as air,
The thistles downy seed my fare,
   My drink the morning dew;
I perch'd at will on ev'ry spray,
My form genteel, my plumage gay,   5
   My strains for ever new.

But gawdy plumage, sprightly strain,
And form genteel were all in vain
   And of a transient date,

35 *not indented in* W, H   36 studiously] Study *to* W; Study [*and deleted*] *to* H

COPY-TEXT: *1782*, pp. 328–9 (first printing). Collated: H

4 modó dederint] iterum annuerent H   9 aut sub cespite condi!] *in* H, *written beneath* neque dicier, HIC EST. *which is not deleted*

Summer 1780

COPY-TEXT: *1782*, pp. 329–30 (first printing). Collated: H, U (no variants).

For caught and caged and starved to death,   10
In dying sighs my little breath
   Soon pass'd the wiry grate.

Thanks, gentle swain, for all my woes,
And thanks for this effectual close
   And cure of ev'ry ill!   15
More cruelty could none express,
And I, if you had shewn me less
   Had been your pris'ner still.

THE PINE APPLE AND THE BEE

The pine apples in triple row,
Were basking hot and all in blow,
A bee of most discerning taste
Perceiv'd the fragrance as he pass'd,
On eager wing the spoiler came,   5
And search'd for crannies in the frame,
Urg'd his attempt on ev'ry side,
To ev'ry pane his trunk applied,
But still in vain, the frame was tight
And only pervious to the light.   10
Thus having wasted half the day,
He trimmed his flight another way.
   Methinks, I said, in thee I find
The sin and madness of mankind;
To joys forbidden man aspires,   15
Consumes his soul with vain desires;
Folly the spring of his pursuit,
And disappointment all the fruit.
While Cynthio ogles as she passes
The nymph between two chariot glasses,   20

April–September 1779.

COPY-TEXT: *1782*, pp. 330–2 (first printing). Collated: *A, N* (letter to Joseph Hill, 2 Oct. 1779), *H*.

Title] Another on the same. *A, H*   7 Urg'd] Push'd *A, N*   9 still] all *A, N, H*
10 only pervious] pervious only *N, H*   13 *not indented in A, N*

She is the pine apple, and he
The silly unsuccessful bee.
The maid who views with pensive air
The show-glass fraught with glitt'ring ware,
Sees watches, bracelets, rings, and lockets,   25
But sighs at thought of empty pockets,
Like thine her appetite is keen,
But ah the cruel glass between!
  Our dear delights are often such,
Expos'd to view but not to touch;   30
The sight our foolish heart inflames,
We long for pine apples in frames,
With hopeless wish one looks and lingers,
One breaks the glass and cuts his fingers,
But they whom truth and wisdom lead,   35
Can gather honey from a weed.

HORACE. BOOK THE 2D. ODE THE 10TH

Receive, dear friend, the truths I teach,
So shalt thou live beyond the reach
  Of adverse fortunes pow'r;
Not always tempt the distant deep,
Nor always timorously creep   5
  Along the treach'rous shore.

He that holds fast the golden mean,
And lives contentedly between
  The little and the great,
Feels not the wants that pinch the poor,   10
Nor plagues that haunt the rich man's door,
  Imbitt'ring all his state.

The tallest pines feel most the pow'r
Of wintry blasts, the loftiest tow'r
  Comes heaviest to the ground,   15

29 *not indented in* H

COPY-TEXT: *1782*, pp. 332–4 (first printing). Collated: *C* (fragment, ll. 19–36 only); *H*

1 dear] my *H*   2 shalt thou] shall you *H*   7 He that holds fast] Whoe'er
pursues *H*

The bolts that spare the mountains side,
His cloud-capt eminence divide
    And spread the ruin round.

The well inform'd philosopher
Rejoices with an wholesome fear,   20
    And hopes in spite of pain;
If winter bellow from the north,
Soon the sweet spring comes dancing forth,
    And nature laughs again.

What if thine heav'n be overcast,   25
The dark appearance will not last,
    Expect a brighter sky;
The God that strings the silver bow,
Awakes sometimes the muses too,
    And lays his arrows by.   30

If hindrances obstruct thy way,
Thy magnanimity display,
    And let thy strength be seen,
But oh! if Fortune fill thy sail
With more than a propitious gale,   35
    Take half thy canvass in.

A REFLECTION ON THE FOREGOING ODE

And is this all? Can reason do no more
Than bid me shun the deep and dread the shore?
Sweet moralist! afloat on life's rough sea
The christian has an art unknown to thee;

20 an] a C, H   21 spite] Hours C, H   22 bellow] bellows C, H   25 thine]
your C, H   27 Expect] You'l see C, H
31–2   If Grief Assail your Aching Heart,
                        Your Magnanimity Exert, C, H
33 thy] your C, H   34 oh!]O, C, H   thy] your C, H   36 thy] your C, H

? 18 March–5 April 1781.

COPY-TEXT: 1782, pp. 334–5 (first printing).

He holds no parley with unmanly fears,   5
Where duty bids he confidently steers,
Faces a thousand dangers at her call,
And trusting in his God, surmounts them all.

TRANSLATIONS FROM VINCENT BOURNE
I. THE GLOW-WORM

Beneath the hedge, or near the stream,
  A worm is known to stray;
That shews by night a lucid beam,
  Which disappears by day.

Disputes have been and still prevail   5
  From whence his rays proceed;
Some give that honour to his tail,
  And others to his head.

But this is sure—the hand of might
  That kindles up the skies,   10
Gives *him* a modicum of light,
  Proportion'd to his size.

Perhaps indulgent nature meant
  By such a lamp bestow'd,
To bid the trav'ler, as he went,   15
  Be careful where he trod:

Nor crush a worm, whose useful light
  Might serve, however small,
To shew a stumbling stone by night,
  And save him from a fall.   20

Whate'er she meant, this truth divine
  Is legible and plain,
'Tis power almighty bids him shine,
  Nor bids him shine in vain.

COPY-TEXT: *1782*, pp. 335–7 (first printing).

Ye proud and wealthy, let this theme   25
Teach humbler thoughts to you,
Since such a reptile has its gem,
And boasts its splendour too.

2. THE JACK DAW

There is a bird who by his coat,
And by the hoarseness of his note,
    Might be suppos'd a crow;
A great frequenter of the church,
Where bishop-like he finds a perch,   5
    And dormitory too.

Above the steeple shines a plate,
That turns and turns, to indicate
    From what point blows the weather;
Look up—your brains begin to swim,   10
'Tis in the clouds—that pleases him,
    He chooses it the rather.

Fond of the speculative height,
Thither he wings his airy flight,
    And thence securely sees   15
The bustle and the raree-show
That occupy mankind below,
    Secure and at his ease.

You think no doubt he sits and muses
On future broken bones and bruises,   20
    If he should chance to fall;
No not a single thought like that
Employs his philosophic pate,
    Or troubles it at all.

He sees that this great roundabout   25
The world, with all its motley rout,
    Church, army, physic, law,

COPY-TEXT: *1782*, pp. 337–9 (first printing).

Its customs and its businesses
Are no concern at all of his,
    And says, what says he? Caw.   30

Thrice happy bird! I too have seen
Much of the vanities of men,
    And sick of having seen 'em,
Would chearfully these limbs resign
For such a pair of wings as thine,   35
    And such a head between 'em.

3. THE CRICKET

Little inmate, full of mirth,
Chirping on my kitchen hearth;
Wheresoe'er be thine abode,
Always harbinger of good,
Pay me for thy warm retreat,   5
With a song more soft and sweet,
In return thou shalt receive
Such a strain as I can give.

Thus thy praise shall be exprest,
Inoffensive, welcome guest!   10
While the rat is on the scout,
And the mouse with curious snout,
With what vermin else infest
Every dish and spoil the best;
Frisking thus before the fire,   15
Thou hast all thine heart's desire.

Though in voice and shape they be
Form'd as if akin to thee,
Thou surpassest, happier far,
Happiest grasshoppers that are,   20
Theirs is but a summer's song,
Thine endures the winter long,
Unimpair'd and shrill and clear,
Melody throughout the year.

COPY-TEXT: *1782*, pp. 339–41 (first printing).

Neither night nor dawn of day,   25
Puts a period to thy play,
Sing then—and extend thy span
Far beyond the date of man—
Wretched man, whose years are spent
In repining discontent;   30
Lives not, aged tho' he be,
Half a span compar'd with thee.

4. THE PARROT

In painted plumes superbly drest,
A native of the gorgeous east,
    By many a billow tost;
Poll gains at length the British shore,
Part of the captain's precious store,   5
    A present to his toast.

Belinda's maids are soon preferr'd
To teach him now and then a word,
    As Poll can master it;
But 'tis her own important charge   10
To qualify him more at large,
    And make him quite a wit.

Sweet Poll! his doating mistress cries,
Sweet Poll! the mimic bird replies,
    And calls aloud for sack,   15
She next instructs him in the kiss,
'Tis now a little one like Miss,
    And now a hearty smack.

At first he aims at what he hears
And listening close with both his ears,   20
    Just catches at the sound;
But soon articulates aloud,
Much to th' amusement of the crowd
    And stuns the neighbours round.

COPY-TEXT: *1782*, pp. 341–[3] (first printing).

A querulous old woman's voice   25
His humorous talent next employs,
   He scolds and gives the lie;
And now he sings, and now is sick,
Here Sally, Susan, come, come quick,
   Poor Poll is like to die.   30

Belinda and her bird! 'tis rare
To meet with such a well-match'd pair,
   The language and the tone,
Each character in every part
Sustain'd with so much grace and art,   35
   And both in unison.

When children first begin to spell
And stammer out a syllable,
   We think them tedious creatures;
But difficulties soon abate,   40
When birds are to be taught to prate,
   And women are the teachers.

THE SHRUBBERY

Written in a Time of Affliction

Oh happy shades! to me unblest,
   Friendly to peace, but not to me,
How ill the scene that offers rest,
   And heart that cannot rest, agree!

This glassy stream, that spreading pine,   5
   Those alders quiv'ring to the breeze,
Might sooth a soul less hurt than mine,
   And please, if any thing could please.

copy-text: *1782*, pp. 344–5 (first printing). Collated: *H*.

Title] The Spinny. *H*   3 ill] does *deleted H*   4 cannot rest,] Shuns it dis[agree]
deleted H

But fixt unalterable care
　Foregoes not what she feels within,　　　　　　　　　10
Shows the same sadness ev'ry where,
　And slights the season and the scene.

For all that pleas'd in wood or lawn,
　While peace possess'd these silent bow'rs,
Her animating smile withdrawn,　　　　　　　　　　15
　Has lost its beauties and its pow'rs.

The saint or moralist should tread
　This moss-grown alley, musing slow,
They seek like me the secret shade,
　But not like me, to nourish woe.　　　　　　　　　20

Me fruitful scenes and prospects waste,
　Alike admonish not to roam,
These tell me of enjoyments past,
　And those of sorrows yet to come.

THE WINTER NOSEGAY

What nature, alas! has denied
　To the delicate growth of our isle,
Art has in a measure supplied,
　And winter is deck'd with a smile.
See Mary what beauties I bring　　　　　　　　　　5
　From the shelter of that sunny shed,
Where the flow'rs have the charms of the spring,
　Though abroad they are frozen and dead.

'Tis a bow'r of Arcadian sweets,
　Where Flora is still in her prime,　　　　　　　　10

9 unalterable care] immoveable Despair *deleted H*　　　　11 Chain'd to inseparable Care
deleted H　　　　12 And] The *deleted H*　　　　14 peace possess'd these silent bow'rs]
Mercy ruled the Golden Hours *deleted H*　　　　15 smile] Beams *deleted H*　　　　24 sorrows yet] Miseries *deleted H*

Early November 1780.

COPY-TEXT: *1782*, pp. 346–7 (first printing). Collated: *H* (no variants).

A fortress to which she retreats,
   From the cruel assaults of the clime.
While earth wears a mantle of snow,
   These pinks are as fresh and as gay,
As the fairest and sweetest that blow,   15
   On the beautiful bosom of May.

See how they have safely surviv'd
   The frowns of a sky so severe,
Such Mary's true love that has liv'd
   Through many a turbulent year.   20
The charms of the late blowing rose,
   Seem grac'd with a livelier hue,
And the winter of sorrow best shows
   The truth of a friend, such as you.

MUTUAL FORBEARANCE, NECESSARY TO THE HAPPINESS OF THE MARRIED STATE

The lady thus address'd her spouse—
What a mere dungeon is this house,
By no means large enough, and was it,
Yet this dull room and that dark closet,
Those hangings with their worn out graces,   5
Long beards, long noses, and pale faces,
Are such an antiquated scene,
They overwhelm me with the spleen.
—Sir Humphry shooting in the dark,
Makes answer quite beside the mark.   10
No doubt, my dear, I bade him come,
Engag'd myself to be at home,
And shall expect him at the door
Precisely when the clock strikes four.

COPY-TEXT: *1782*, pp. 347–50 (first printing). Collated: *H, U*

Title] Patience Recommended to Wives that [Ladies who *U*] have Deaf Husbands. *H, U*
1 The Lady thus address'd] Thus says the Lady to *H*   2 How I detest this odious
House! *H, U*   3 By no means] It is not *H, U*   4 dull] low *H, U*   8 overwhelm]
almost kill *H, U*   11 bade] bid *H, U*

You are so deaf, the lady cried,   15
(And rais'd her voice and frown'd beside)
You are so sadly deaf, my dear,
What shall I do to make you hear?
Dismiss poor Harry, he replies,
Some people are more nice than wise,   20
For one slight trespass all this stir?
What if he did ride, whip and spur,
'Twas but a mile—your fav'rite horse
Will never look one hair the worse.
Well, I protest 'tis past all bearing—   25
Child! I am rather hard of hearing—
Yes, truly—one must scream and bawl,
I tell you you can't hear at all.
Then with a voice exceeding low,
No matter if you hear or no.   30
    Alas! and is domestic strife,
That sorest ill of human life,
A plague so little to be fear'd,
As to be wantonly incurr'd;
To gratify a fretful passion,   35
On ev'ry trivial provocation?
The kindest and the happiest pair,
Will find occasion to forbear,
And something ev'ry day they live
To pity, and perhaps, forgive.   40
But if infirmities that fall
In common to the lot of all,
A blemish, or a sense impair'd,
Are crimes so little to be spar'd,
Then farewel all that must create   45
The comfort of the wedded state,
Instead of harmony, 'tis jar
And tumult, and intestine war.
    The love that cheers life's latest stage,
Proof against sickness and old age,   50
Preserv'd by virtue from declension,

---

19 *indented in H, U*   poor Harry,] the Coachman? *U*   20 Some people are] You are
by far *H, U*   21 trespass] Blunder *H, U*   22–4 *not in H, U, which have* A
wiser man than He might Err.

Becomes not weary of attention,
But lives, when that exterior grace
Which first inspir'd the flame, decays.
'Tis gentle, delicate and kind,   55
To faults compassionate or blind,
And will with sympathy endure
Those evils it would gladly cure.
But angry, coarse, and harsh expression
Shows love to be a mere profession,   60
Proves that the heart is none of his,
Or soon expels him if it is.

TO THE REV. MR. NEWTON,
AN INVITATION INTO THE COUNTRY

The swallows in their torpid state,
    Compose their useless wing,
And bees in hives as idly wait
    The call of early spring.

The keenest frost that binds the stream,   5
    The wildest wind that blows,
Are neither felt nor fear'd by them,
    Secure of their repose.

But man all feeling and awake
    The gloomy scene surveys,   10
With present ills his heart must ach,
    And pant for brighter days.

Old winter halting o'er the mead,
    Bids me and Mary mourn,
But lovely spring peeps o'er his head,   15
    And whispers your return.

58 Those] The *H, U*   it would gladly] that it cannot *H*

Late 1780.

COPY TEXT: *1782*, pp. 351–2 (first printing). Collated: *H*.
Title] To the Same—An Invitation. *H*

Then April with her sister May,
  Shall chase him from the bow'rs,
And weave fresh garlands ev'ry day,
  To crown the smiling hours.   20

And if a tear that speaks regret
  Of happier times appear,
A glimpse of joy that we have met
  Shall shine, and dry the tear.

TRANSLATION OF PRIOR'S
CHLOE AND EUPHELIA

Mercator, vigiles oculos ut fallere possit,
  Nomine sub ficto trans mare mittit opes;
Lené sonat liquidumque meis Euphelia chordis,
  Sed solam exoptant te, mea vota, Chlöe.

Ad speculum ornabat nitidos Euphelia crines,   5
  Cum dixit mea lux, heus, cane, sume lyram.
Namque lyram juxtà positam cum carmine vidit,
  Suave quidem carmen dulcisonamque lyram.

Fila lyræ vocemque paro, suspiria surgunt,
  Et miscent numeris murmura mæsta meis,   10
Dumque tuæ memoro laudes, Euphelia, formæ,
  Tota anima intereá pendet ab ore Chlöes.

Subrubet illa pudore, et contrahit altera frontem,
  Me torquet mea mens conscia, psallo, tremo;
Atque Cupidineâ dixit Dea cincta coronâ,   15
  Heu! fallendi artem quam didicere parum.

---

24 *severely cropped in H*

About 1 May 1779.

COPY-TEXT: *1782*, pp. 353–4 (first printing). Collated: *U, H.*

Title] Translation of Prior's Poem beginning The Merchant to conceal his Treasure. *U, H*
8 lyram.] *U*; lyram, *1782*; *punctuation cropped in H*

BOADICEA,
AN ODE

When the British warrior queen,
  Bleeding from the Roman rods,
Sought with an indignant mien,
  Counsel of her country's gods,

Sage beneath a spreading oak   5
  Sat the Druid, hoary chief,
Ev'ry burning word he spoke,
  Full of rage and full of grief.

Princess! if our aged eyes
  Weep upon thy matchless wrongs,   10
'Tis because resentment ties
  All the terrors of our tongues.

Rome shall perish—write that word
  In the blood that she has spilt;
Perish hopeless and abhorr'd,   15
  Deep in ruin as in guilt.

Rome for empire far renown'd,
  Tramples on a thousand states,
Soon her pride shall kiss the ground—
  Hark! the Gaul is at her gates.   20

Other Romans shall arise,
  Heedless of a soldier's name,
Sounds, not arms, shall win the prize,
  Harmony the path to fame.

Then the progeny that springs   25
  From the forests of our land,
Arm'd with thunder, clad with wings,
  Shall a wider world command.

COPY-TEXT: *1782*, pp. 354–7 (first printing). Collated: *H*.
13 that] the *H*   24 the] their *H*

Regions Cæsar never knew,
   Thy posterity shall sway,   30
Where his eagles never flew,
   None invincible as they.

Such the bard's prophetic words,
   Pregnant with celestial fire,
Bending as he swept the chords   35
   Of his sweet but awful lyre.

She with all a monarch's pride,
   Felt them in her bosom glow,
Rush'd to battle, fought and died,
   Dying, hurl'd them at the foe.   40

Ruffians, pittiless as proud,
   Heav'n awards the vengeance due,
Empire is on us bestow'd,
   Shame and ruin wait for you.

HEROISM

There was a time when Ætna's silent fire
Slept unperceiv'd, the mountain yet entire,
When conscious of no danger from below,
She towr'd a cloud-capt pyramid of snow.
No thunders shook with deep intestine sound 5
The blooming groves that girdled her around,
Her unctuous olives and her purple vines,
(Unfelt the fury of those bursting mines)
The peasant's hopes, and not in vain, assur'd,
In peace upon her sloping sides matur'd. 10
When on a day, like that of the last doom,

33 bard's] bards *1782*

About midsummer, 1780.

COPY-TEXT: *1782*, pp. 357–62 (first printing). Collated: *H*.

Title] Heroism displayed. *H*   7, 8 *order reversed in H*   8 those bursting] her
bursting *H*

11–14   When on a day, foreknown and foreordain'd,
           Convulsive Throes her lab'ring Womb sustain'd,
           And teeming fast with a prodigious Birth,
           Shook the surrounding Seas and Solid Earth. *H*

A conflagration lab'ring in her womb,
She teem'd and heav'd with an infernal birth,
That shook the circling seas and solid earth.
Dark and voluminous the vapours rise,   15
And hang their horrors in the neighb'ring skies,
While through the stygian veil that blots the day,
In dazzling streaks the vivid light'nings play.
But oh! what muse, and in what pow'rs of song,
Can trace the torrent as it burns along?   20
Havock and devastation in the van,
It marches o'er the prostrate works of man,
Vines, olives, herbage, forests disappear,
And all the charms of a Sicilian year.

   Revolving seasons, fruitless as they pass,   25
See it an uninform'd and idle mass,
Without a soil t'invite the tiller's care,
Or blade that might redeem it from despair.
Yet time at length (what will not time atchieve?)
Cloaths it with earth, and bids the produce live,   30
Once more the spiry myrtle crowns the glade,
And ruminating flocks enjoy the shade.
Oh bliss precarious, and unsafe retreats,
Oh charming paradise of short liv'd sweets!
The self-same gale that wafts the fragrance round,   35
Brings to the distant ear a sullen sound,
Again the mountain feels th' imprison'd foe,
Again pours ruin on the vale below,
Ten thousand swains the wasted scene deplore,
That only future ages can restore.   40

   Ye monarchs, whom the lure of honour draws,
Who write in blood the merits of your cause,
Who strike the blow, then plead your own defence,
Glory your aim, but justice your pretence;
Behold in Ætna's emblematic fires   45
The mischiefs your ambitious pride inspires.

   Fast by the stream that bounds your just domain,
And tells you where ye have a right to reign,

17–18   Through the dun Air the vivid Lightnings Play,
          Shot from the Smoke that has Ecclips'd the Day.
25 *not indented in* H   39 wasted] dreary H   46 your] that H

A nation dwells, not envious of your throne,
Studious of peace, their neighbours and their own.   50
Ill-fated race! how deeply must they rue
Their only crime, vicinity to you!
The trumpet sounds, your legions swarm abroad,
Through the ripe harvest lies their destin'd road,
At ev'ry step beneath their feet they tread   55
The life of multitudes, a nation's bread;
Earth seems a garden in its loveliest dress
Before them, and behind a wilderness;
Famine and pestilence, her first-born son,
Attend to finish what the sword begun,   60
And ecchoing praises such as fiends might earn,
And folly pays, resound at your return.
A calm succeeds—but plenty with her train
Of heart-felt joys, succeeds not soon again,
And years of pining indigence must show   65
What scourges are the gods that rule below.
    Yet man, laborious man, by slow degrees,
(Such is his thirst of opulence and ease)
Plies all the sinews of industrious toil,
Gleans up the refuse of the general spoil,   70
Rebuilds the tow'rs that smok'd upon the plain,
And the sun gilds the shining spires again.
    Increasing commerce and reviving art
Renew the quarrel on the conqu'rors part,
And the sad lesson must be learn'd once more,   75
That wealth within is ruin at the door.
    What are ye monarchs, laurel'd heroes, say,
But Ætnas of the suff'ring world ye sway?
Sweet nature stripp'd of her embroider'd robe,
Deplores the wasted regions of her globe,   80
And stands a witness at truth's awful bar,
To prove you there, destroyers as ye are.
    Oh place me in some heav'n-protected isle,

59 and] [and *deleted*] with H   60 Attend] Attends H
61–2   And Praises such as Fiends from Hell might Earn
    With half your Pow'r, resound at your Return. H
78 Ætnas of the suff'ring] furious Ætnas in the H   79–82 *inserted later in* H
80 Delores] Mourning H   81 And stands] Stands up H   82 To prove you
there,] And Proves you [*illegible, deleted*] there H   83 *not indented in* H

Where peace and equity and freedom smile,
Where no Volcano pours his fiery flood,   85
No crested warrior dips his plume in blood,
Where pow'r secures what industry has won,
Where to succeed is not to be undone,
A land that distant tyrants hate in vain,
In Britain's isle, beneath a George's reign.   90

THE POET, THE OYSTER, AND SENSITIVE PLANT

An Oyster cast upon the shore
Was heard, though never heard before;
Complaining in a speech well worded,
And worthy thus to be recorded:
    Ah hapless wretch! condemned to dwell   5
For ever in my native shell,
Ordain'd to move when others please,
Not for my own content or ease,
But toss'd and buffeted about,
Now *in* the water, and now *out*.   10
'Twere better to be born a stone
Of ruder shape and feeling none,
Than with a tenderness like mine,
And sensibilities so fine;
I envy that unfeeling shrub,   15
Fast-rooted against ev'ry rub.
The plant he meant grew not far off,
And felt the sneer with scorn enough,
Was hurt, disgusted, mortified,
And with asperity replied.   20
    When, cry the botanists, and stare,
Did plants call'd sensitive grow there?
No matter when—a poet's muse is
To make them grow just where she chuses.
    You shapeless nothing in a dish,   25

COPY-TEXT: *1782*, pp. 362–5 (first printing). Collated: *H*.
Title and Sensitive] and the Sensitive *H*   6 For ever in my] A Pris'ner in [his *deleted*]
my *H*   16 Fast-rooted against] Insensible of *H*   21 When,] *H*; *no comma in 1782*

You that are but almost a fish,
I scorn your coarse insinuation,
And have most plentiful occasion
To wish myself the rock I view,
Or such another dolt as you.   30
For many a grave and learned clerk,
And many a gay unletter'd spark,
With curious touch examines me,
If I can feel as well as he;
And when I bend, retire and shrink,   35
Says, well—'tis more than one would think—
Thus life is spent, oh fie upon't!
In being touch'd, and crying, don't.
    A poet in his evening walk,
O'erheard and check'd this idle talk.   40
And your fine sense, he said, and yours,
Whatever evil it endures,
Deserves not, if so soon offended,
Much to be pitied or commended.
Disputes though short, are far too long,   45
Where both alike are in the wrong;
Your feelings in their full amount,
Are all upon your own account.
    You in your grotto-work inclos'd
Complain of being thus expos'd,   50
Yet nothing feel in that rough coat,
Save when the knife is at your throat,
Wherever driv'n by wind or tide,
Exempt from every ill beside.
    And as for you, my Lady Squeamish,   55
Who reckon ev'ry touch a blemish,
If all the plants that can be found
Embellishing the scene around,
Should droop and wither where they grow,
You would not feel at all, not you.   60
The noblest minds their virtue prove

28 most plentiful] I think, far more H
31–2   For ev'ry Bumkin far and near,
                        And many a Shrewd Philosopher, H
38 crying] Saying H

By pity, sympathy, and love,
These, these are feelings truly fine,
And prove their owner half divine.
    His censure reach'd them as he dealt it,   65
And each by shrinking shew'd he felt it.

TO THE REV. WILLIAM CAWTHORNE UNWIN

Unwin, I should but ill repay,
    The kindness of a friend,
Whose worth deserves as warm a lay
    As ever friendship penn'd,
Thy name omitted in a page,   5
That would reclaim a vicious age.

An union form'd, as mine with thee,
    Not rashly or in sport,
May be as fervent in degree,
    And faithful in its sort,   10
And may as rich in comfort prove,
As that of true fraternal love.

The bud inserted in the rind,
    The bud of peach or rose,
Adorns, though diff'ring in its kind,   15
    The stock whereon it grows
With flow'r as sweet or fruit as fair,
As if produc'd by nature there.

Not rich, I render what I may,
    I seize thy name in haste,   20
And place it in this first assay,
    Lest this should prove the last.
'Tis where it should be, in a plan
That holds in view the good of man.

64 prove] Speak *H*

18 March–late April 1781.

COPY-TEXT: *1782*, pp. 366–7 (first printing). Collated: *H, U*

Title William Cawthorne Unwin] W : C : Unwin *H*; William Unwin *U*   6 reclaim]
reform *deleted H*   17 or] and *deleted H*

The poet's lyre, to fix his fame,   25
Should be the poet's heart,
Affection lights a brighter flame
Than ever blaz'd by art.
No muses on these lines attend,
I sink the poet in the friend.   30

MISCELLANEOUS POEMS
1781

'METHINKS I SEE THEE DECENTLY ARRAY'D'

Methinks I see thee decently array'd
In long flour'd nightgown of stuff-damask made,
Thy cassock underneath it closely braced
With surcingle about thy mod'rate waist,
Thy morning wig grown tawny to the view   5
Though once a grizzle, and thy square toed shoe.
Thy day was, when the sacerdotal race
Esteem'd their proper habit no disgrace,
Or rather when the garb their order wears
Was not disgraced as now, by being theirs.   10
I speak of prigs—

VESTRIS

Poor Vestris! griev'd beyond all measure
At thought of having giv'n displeasure,
Although a Frenchman disconcerted,
And though light-heel'd, yet heavy-hearted,
Begs humbly to inform his friends   5
Next first of April, he intends
To take a Boat and row right down
To Cuckold's point from Richmond town,
And as he goes, alert and gay,
Leap all the Bridges in his way,   10
While Boat borne downward by the Tide
Shall catch him safe on t'other side.
   He hopes by this polite expedient
To prove himself their most Obedient
(Which shall be always his endeavour)   15
And jump into their former favour.

COPY-TEXT: *A*, whence first printed by A. Collyer, *Universal Review*, vii (1890), 292.

24–7 February 1781.

COPY-TEXT: *E* (John Johnson's hand). Collated: *U*, whence first printed by Southey, iv. 75–6.

Title] A Card *U*   2 At thought of having giv'n] To have incurr'd so much *U*
11 While] The *U*   by] with *U*   13 *not indented in U*   He hopes by this polite]
He humbly hopes by this *U*

TRANSLATION OF VERSES IN MEMORY OF
DR. LLOYD (I)

Th' old man, our aimable old man is gone—
Second in harmless pleasantry to none.
Ye, once his pupils, who with rev'rence just
View'd him, as all that were his pupils must,
Whether, his health yet firm, he gently strove   5
To rear and form you with a parent's love,
Or worn with Age, and pleas'd to be at large,
He came still mindfull of his former charge,
To smile on this glad circle ev'ry year,
And charm you with his humor, drop a tear.   10
Simplicity graced all his blameless life,
And he was kind, and gentle, hating strife.
Content was the best wealth he ever shared,
Though all men pay'd him love, and *One*, Reward.
Ye titles! we have here no need of you,   15
Go, give the Great ones their Eulogium due,
If Fortune more on others chose to shine,
'Twas not in Him to murmur or repine.
Placid Old Man! the turf upon thy breast,
May it lie lightly, sacred be thy rest,   20
Though living, thou hadst none thy fame to spread,
Nor ev'n a Stone to chronicle thee, dead.

TRANSLATION OF VERSES IN MEMORY OF
DR. LLOYD (II)

Our good old friend is gone, gone to his rest,
Whose social converse was, itself, a feast.

June or July 1781.

COPY-TEXT: *U*, whence first printed by Bruce, 1863, iii. 354–5.

Title] Translation of the Latin verses spoken in honor of the late Dr. Lloyd at the last Westminster Election. By W.C. who was two years under him while he was an Usher, and had afterwards the happiness of his Acquaintance.

COPY-TEXT: *E*, whence first printed by Hayley, 1803, ii. 387–8.

Title] The same in English. *E*; Verses, to the Memory of Dr. Lloyd, Spoken at the Westminster Election next after his decease. *1803 (following title of the Latin in E)*

Oh ye of riper age, who recollect
How once ye loved and eyed him with respect,
Both in the firmness of his better day,   5
While yet he ruled you with a father's sway,
And when, impair'd by time and glad to rest,
Yet still with looks in mild complacence dress'd,
He took his annual seat and mingled here
His sprightly vein with yours—now drop a tear.   10
In Morals blameless as in manners meek,
He knew no wish that he might blush to speak,
But, happy in whatever state below,
And richer than the rich in being so
Obtain'd the hearts of all, and such a meed   15
At length from One, as made him rich indeed.
Hence, then, ye titles, hence, not wanted here,
Go, garnish merit in a brighter sphere,
The brows of those, whose more exalted lot
He could congratulate, but envied not.   20
    Light lie the turf, good Senior! on thy breast,
And tranquil, as thy mind was, be thy rest!
Though, living, thou hadst more desert than fame,
And not a stone, now, chronicles thy name.

EPISTLE TO A LADY IN FRANCE

A PERSON OF GREAT PIETY AND MUCH AFFLICTED

Madam
    A stranger's purpose in these lays
Is to congratulate, and not to praise.
To give the Creature the Creator's due
Were guilt in me and an offence to you.
From man to man, or ev'n to woman paid   5
Praise is the medium of a knavish trade,

Summer 1781.

COPY-TEXT: S. Collated: U, W, E. First printed by Samuel Greatheed, *Theological Miscellany*, vi (1789), 332–4.

Title] *no title in* U; An Epistle to a Protestant Lady in France. By the Translator of the foregoing Pieces. W   3 the Creator's] her creator's U, W   4 guilt] Sin U, W
5 From] By U

A coin by craft for Folly's use design'd,
Spurious, and only current with the blind.
  The path of sorrow and that path alone
Leads to the land where sorrow is unknown,   10
No trav'ler ever reach'd that bless'd abode,
Who found not thorns and briars in his road.
The world may dance along the flow'ry plain
Cheer'd as they go by many a sprightly strain,
Where nature has her yielding mosses spread   15
With unshod feet, and yet unharm'd they tread,
Admonish'd, scorn the caution and the friend,
Bent all on pleasure, heedless of its end.
But He who knew what human hearts would prove,
How slow to learn the dictates of his love,   20
That, hard by nature and of stubborn will
A life of ease would make them harder still,
In pity to a chosen few design'd
To escape the common ruin of their kind,
Call'd for a cloud to darken all their years,   25
And said—Go spend them in the vale of tears.
Oh balmy gales of soul-reviving air,
Oh salutary streams that murmur there!
These flowing from the fount of Grace above,
Those breathed from lips of everlasting love!   30
The flinty soil indeed their feet annoys,
Chill blasts of trouble nip their springing joys,
An envious world will interpose its frown
To mar delights superior to its own,
And many a pang experienced still within   35
Reminds them of their hated inmate, Sin,
But ills of every shape and every name
Transform'd to blessings miss their cruel aim,
And ev'ry moment's calm that sooths the breast
Is giv'n in earnest of eternal rest.   40
  Ah be not sad, although thy lot be cast
Far from the flock and in a boundless waste,

12 Who] That *U*   15 yielding mosses] mossy velvet *U, W*   16 and yet
unharm'd they] they yet securely *U, W*   18 all on] upon *U, W*   23 a chosen
few] the sinners he *U, W*   24] To rescue from the ruins of mankind, *U, W*   To
escape] T'escape *E*   32 Chill blasts of trouble nip] And sudden sorrow nips *U, W*
42 boundless] distant *U, W*

No shepherds' tents within thy view appear,
But the Chief Shepherd, even there, is near,
Thy tender sorrows and thy plaintive strain   45
Flow in a foreign land, but not in vain,
Thy tears all issue from a source divine,
And ev'ry drop bespeaks a Saviour thine.
   So, once, in Gideon's fleece the dews were found,
And drought on all the drooping herbs around.   50

ON FRIENDSHIP

Amicitia, nisi inter bonos, esse non potest.
                                        Tully de Amicitia.

What Virtue can we name, or Grace,
But men unqualified and base
   Will boast it their possession?
Profusion apes the noble part
Of Liberality of heart,   5
   And Dullness of Discretion.

But, as the gem of richest cost
Is ever counterfeited most,
   So, always, Imitation
Employs the utmost skill she can   10
To counterfeit the Faithful man,
   The Friend of long duration.

---

44 Shepherd, even there, is] shepherd is for ever *U, W*   49 So, once,] 'Twas thus *U, W*

Originally composed early December 1781; revised version autumn 1782; final version before
summer 1791.

COPY-TEXT: *E*. Collated: *W, U, O* (ll. 1–177 only). First printed, from *W*, by Bull, 1801,
pp. 104–16.

Title] Friendship *W*   *Motto*] *not in W, U*   1 can we name, or] or what mental
W, U, O
7–12]   If ev'ry polish'd gem we find
                 Illuminating heart or mind,
                    Provoke to imitation,
                 No wonder friendship does the same,
                 That jewel of the [purest *W*] brightest flame,
                    Or rather constellation.   *W, U, O*

Some will pronounce me too severe—
But long experience speaks me clear;
   Therefore that censure scorning   15
I will proceed to mark the shelves
On which so many dash themselves,
   And give the Simple warning.

Youth, unadmonish'd by a guide,
Will trust to any fair outside—   20
   An errour soon corrected;
For who but learns with riper years,
That man, when smoothest he appears,
   Is most to be suspected?

But here again a danger lies,   25
Lest, thus deluded by our eyes
   And taking trash for treasure,
We should, when undeceived, conclude
Friendship, imaginary Good,
   A mere Utopian pleasure.   30

An acquisition, rather rare,
Is yet no subject of despair,
   Nor should it seem distressful
If either on forbidden ground,
Or where it was not to be found   35
   We sought it unsuccessful.

No Friendship will abide the test
That stands on sordid Interest
   And mean Self-love erected;

13–18

No knave but boldly will pretend
The requisites that form a friend,
   A real and a sound one,
Nor any fool he would deceive
But proves as ready to believe,
   And dream that he has found one.   *W, U, O*

19–20

Candid and generous and just,
Boys care but little whom they trust—   *W, U, O*

22 with] in *W*   26 thus deluded by] having misemploy'd *W, U, O*   27 taking]
taken *W, U, O*   28 should, when undeceived,] should unwarily *W, U, O*   29 imagi-
nary] a false ideal *W, U, O*   33 Nor is it wise complaining, *W, U, O*   36 it un-
successful] without attaining *W, U, O*   39 And] Or *W, U, O*

Nor such as may awhile subsist   40
'Twixt sensualist and sensualist
    For vicious ends connected.

Who hopes a Friend, should have a heart
Himself well furnish'd for the part,
    And ready on occasion   45
To show the Virtue that he seeks,
For 'tis an union that bespeaks
    A just reciprocation.

A fretful temper will divide
The closest knot that may be tied   50
    By ceaseless sharp corrosion,
A Temper passionate and fierce
May suddenly your joys disperse
    At one immense explosion.

In vain the Talkative unite   55
With hope of permanent delight—
    The secret just committed

41 'Twixt sensualist] Between the sot *W, U, O*
43–6]   Who seeks a friend, should come disposed
                         T'exhibit in full bloom disclosed
                             The graces and the beauties
                         That form the character he seeks;   *W, U, O*
48] Reciprocated duties.   *W*; A just exchange of duties.   *U*; A mutual share of duties.   *O*
between 49 *and* 50 *two stanzas are found in W, U, O:*
                         Reciprocation is implied,
                         And equal truth on either side,
                             And constantly supported;
                         'Tis senseless arrogance t'accuse
                         Another of sinister views,
                             Your own as much distorted.
Reciprocation] Mutual attention *W*   Your] Our *W*
                         But will sincerity suffice?
                         Its worth indeed transcends all price,
                             It must be made the basis,
                         But ev'ry virtue of the soul
                         Should constitute that charming whole,
                             All shining in their places.
Its worth indeed transcends] It is indeed above *W*; I grant it is above *U*   It must] And
must *W, U*   Should] Must *W, U*   that] the *W, U*
50 may] can *U*   51 By] With *U*   56 With hope] In hopes *W, U, O*

They drop through mere desire to prate,
Forgetting its important weight,
   And by themselves outwitted.   60

How bright soe'er the prospect seems,
All thoughts of Friendship are but dreams
   If Envy chance to creep in,
An envious man, if you succeed,
May prove a dang'rous foe indeed,   65
   But not a Friend worth keeping.

As Envy pines at good possess'd,
So, Jealousy looks forth distress'd
   On good that seems approaching,
And, if success his steps attend,   70
Discerns a rival in a Friend,
   And hates him for encroaching:

Hence Authors of illustrious name
(Unless belied by common fame)
   Are sadly prone to quarrel,   75
To deem the wit a friend displays
So much of loss to their own praise,
   And pluck each other's laurel.

A man renown'd for repartee
Will seldom scruple to make free   80
   With Friendship's finest feeling,
Will thrust a dagger at your breast,
And tell you 'twas a special jest,
   By way of balm for healing.

Beware of Tattlers, keep your ear   85
Close-stopt against the tales they bear,

58–9 *in reverse order in* W, U, O   61 soe'er] soere E   69 On] At O
70 success his steps] prosperity O   73 Hence] Thus O   77] A tax upon their
own just praise, W, U, O   83 tell you 'twas a special] say he wounded you in W, U, O
85–90   Whoever keeps an open ear
             For tattlers, will be sure to hear
               The trumpet of contention,
             Aspersion is the babbler's trade,
             To listen is to lend him aid,
               And rush into dissention. W, U, O

Fruits of their own invention;
The separation of chief friends
Is what their kindness most intends,
    Their sport is your dissention.   90

Friendship that wantonly admits
A joco-serious play of wits
    In brilliant altercation,
Is union such as indicates
(Like hand-in-hand Insurance plates)   95
    Danger of conflagration.

Some fickle creatures boast a soul
True as the needle to the pole,
    Yet shifting like the weather
The needle's constancy forego   100
For any novelty, and show
    Its variations rather.

Insensibility makes some
Unseasonably deaf and dumb

88 separation] seperation *E*
91–6]   A friendship that in frequent fits
                                   Of controversial rage, emitts
                                       The sparks of disputation,
                                   Like hand-in-hand [Insurance *W, U*] on office plates,
                                   Most unavoidably creates,
                                       The thought of conflagration. *W, U, O*
99–102   Their humour yet so various
                                   They manifest their whole life through
                                   The needle's variations too,
                                       Their love is so precarious. *W, U, O*
103–14] *these stanzas in reverse order in W*
103–5]   Some are so placid and serene
                                   (As Irish bogs are always green)
                                       They sleep secure from waking;   *W*

                                   [Some are so placid and serene *deleted*]
                                   As Irish bogs are always green,
                                   Some minds are sleepy and serene,
                                       Whose heart soe'er is aching   *U*

                                   As Irish bogs are always green,
                                   Some minds are placid and serene,
                                       Sleep without ever waking,   *O*

When most you need their pity; 105
'Tis waiting till the tears shall fall
From Gog and Magog in Guild Hall,
    Those play-things of the City.

The great and small but rarely meet
On terms of amity complete. 110
    Th'attempt would scarce be madder
Should any, from the bottom, hope
At one huge stride to reach the top
    Of an erected ladder.

Courtier and Patriot cannot mix 115
Their het'rogeneous politics
    Without an effervescence
Such as of salts with lemon-juice,
But which is rarely known t'induce,
    Like that, a coalescence. 120

Religion should extinguish strife
And make a calm of human life,
    But even those who differ
Only on topics left at large,
How fiercely will they meet and charge! 125
    No combatants are stiffer.

To prove alas! my main intent
Needs no great cost of argument,

106–8]   And are indeed a bog that bears
              Your unparticipated cares,
                  Unmoved and without quaking. *W, U, O*
111–14]   Plebeians must surrender
              And yield so much to noble folk,
              It is combining fire with smoke,
                  Obscurity with splendour. *W, U, O*
118 Such as] Like that *W, U, O*
119–20]   Which does not yet like that produce
                  A friendly coalescence. *W, U, O*
121 should] ought t' *U, O*   123 even those who] friends that chance to *W, U, O*
124 Only on topics] On points which God has *W*; On points that God has *U*; On points
however *O*   128 no great cost] no expence *W, U*; little cost *O*

No cutting and contriving;
Seeking a real friend we seem   130
T'adopt the chymists' golden dream,
　　With still less hope of thriving.

Then judge, or ere you chuse your man,
As circumspectly as you can,
　　And, having made election,   135
See that no disrespect of yours
Such as a friend but ill endures
　　Enfeeble his affection.

It is not timber, lead, and stone
An architect requires alone   140
　　To finish a great building;
The palace were but half complete
Could he by any chance forget
　　The carving and the gilding.

As similarity of mind   145
Or something not to be defined
　　First rivets our attention,
So, manners decent and polite,
The same we practis'd at first sight,
　　Must save it from declension.   150

129 No] Or *O*

between 132 *and* 133 *W*, *U*, *O* *have the following stanza*:
　　　　Sometimes the fault is all our own,
　　　　Some blemish [suddenly *U*] in due time made known
　　　　　　By trespass or omission,
　　　　Sometimes occasion brings to light
　　　　Our friend's defect long hid from sight,
　　　　　　And even from suspicion.

133 or ere you chuse] yourself, and prove *W*, *U*, *O*   136 See that no disrespect] Beware
no negligence *W*, *U*, *O*

between 138 *and* 139 *W*, *U*, *O* *have the following stanza*:
　　　　That secrets are a sacred trust,
　　　　That friends should be sincere and just,
　　　　　　That constancy [Sympathy *U*] befitts them,
　　　　Are observations on the case
　　　　That savour much of common place,
　　　　　　And all the world admitts them.

139 It is] But 'tis *W*, *U*   141 great] fine *W*, *U*   143 Could he by any chance]
If he could possibly *W*, *U*, *O*   145–56 *these stanzas in reverse order in W, O*
147 rivets] fixes *W*, *U*, *O*

The man who hails you Tom—or Jack—
And proves by thumping on your back
   His sense of your great merit,
Is such a friend that one had need
Be very much his friend indeed   155
   To pardon or to bear it.

Some friends make this their prudent plan—
'Say little, and hear all you can'
   Safe policy but hateful.
So barren sands imbibe the show'r,   160
But render neither fruit nor flow'r,
Unpleasant and ungrateful.

They whisper trivial things and small,
But, to communicate at all
   Things serious, deem improper;   165
Their fæculence and froth they show,
But keep their best contents below
   Just like a simm'ring copper.

These samples, for alas! at last
These are but samples and a taste   170
   Of evils yet unmention'd,
May prove the task a task indeed,
In which 'tis much if we succeed
   However well intention'd.

   Pursue the theme, and you shall find   175
   A disciplin'd and furnish'd mind

151 who] that *W, U, O*   152 thumping on] thumps upon *W, U, O*   153 His sense
of your great] How he esteems your *W*; How well he knows your *U, O*   157] Some
act upon [this prudent *W, U*] a cautious plan *W, U, O*
163–8]   The man I trust, if shy to me,
                 Shall find me as reserved as he,
                   No subterfuge or pleading
               [Shall *W*] Can win my confidence again
               I [will *W*] can by no means entertain
                   A spy on my proceeding. *W, U, O*
No subterfuge . . . entertain]
                 And deaf to all his pleading
                 I will withdraw my trust again
                 Determin'd not to entertain *U*
175 theme] search *W, U, O*   shall] will *W, U, O*   176] [Good sense *W*] Wisdom
and knowledge of mankind *W, U, O*

To be at least expedient,
And, after summing all the rest,
Religion ruling in the breast
   A principal Ingredient.   180

True Friendship has, in short, a grace
More than terrestrial in its face
   That proves it heav'n descended,
Man's love of woman not so pure,
Nor, when sincerest, so secure   185
   To last till life is ended.

A POETICAL EPISTLE TO LADY AUSTEN

DEC. 17, 1781

Dear Anna—Between friend and friend,
Prose answers every common end;
Serves, in a plain, and homely way,
T'express th'occurrence of the day;

178–*end*] *missing from* O
181–6 *in place of this stanza* W *has the following two stanzas*:

      The noblest Friendship ever known
      The Saviour's history makes known,
         Though some have turn'd and turn'd it,
      And whether being craz'd or blind,
      Or seeking with a bias'd mind,
         Have not, it seems, discern'd it.

      Oh Friendship! if my soul forego
      Thy dear delights while here below;
         To mortify and grieve me,
      May I myself at last appear
      Unworthy, base and insincere,
         Or may my friend deceive me!

181–2]   There is a sober serious grace,
                A Sanctity in Friendship's face, *U*
184 Man's] The *U*   Woman] Women *deleted U*
185 when sincerest] ev'n when truest *U*

17 December 1781.

COPY-TEXT: Hayley, 1803, i. 116–20 (first printing). Collated: *C* (copy in an unknown hand); *EM* (ll. 29–106 only, in the *Evangelical Magazine*, xi (1803), 174).

Title] *supplied from Johnson 1815*; A Letter from the late William Cowper Esqr. to a Lady: never before printed. Decbr. 17th. 1781 *C*; Extract of a Letter from the late William Cowper, Esq. to a Lady *EM*

Our health, the weather, and the news;   5
What walks we take, what books we chuse;
And all the floating thoughts, we find
Upon the surface of the mind.

But when a Poet takes the pen,
Far more alive than other men,   10
He feels a gentle tingling come
Down to his finger and his thumb,
Deriv'd from nature's noblest part,
The centre of a glowing heart!
And this is what the world, who knows   15
No flights, above the pitch of prose,
His more sublime vagaries slighting,
Denominates an itch for writing.
No wonder I, who scribble rhyme,
To catch the triflers of the time,   20
And tell them truths divine, and clear,
Which couch'd in prose, they will not hear;
Who labour hard to allure, and draw
The loiterers I never saw,
Should feel that itching, and that tingling,   25
With all my purpose intermingling,
To your intrinsic merit true,
When call'd to address myself to you.

Mysterious are his ways, whose power
Brings forth that unexpected hour,   30
When minds, that never met before,
Shall meet, unite, and part no more:
It is th'allotment of the skies,
The Hand of the Supremely Wise,
That guides and governs our affections,   35
And plans, and orders our connexions;
Directs us in our distant road,
And marks the bounds of our abode.
Thus we were settled when you found us,
Peasants and children all around us,   40

---

22 will] would *C*   37–8 *not in EM*   37 distant] destin'd *C*   39 we were
settled when] when we're settled where *C*; when we settled where *EM*

Not dreaming of so dear a friend,
Deep in the abyss of Silver-End.
Thus Martha, ev'n against her will,
Perch'd on the top of yonder hill;
And you, though you must needs prefer   45
The fairer scenes of sweet Sancerre,
Are come from distant Loire, to chuse
A cottage on the banks of Ouse.
This page of Providence, quite new,
And now just opening to our view,   50
Employs our present thoughts and pains,
To guess, and spell, what it contains:
But day by day, and year by year,
Will make the dark ænigma clear;
And furnish us perhaps at last,   55
Like other scenes already past,
With proof, that we, and our affairs
Are part of a Jehovah's cares:
For God unfolds, by slow degrees,
The purport of his deep decrees;   60
Sheds every hour a clearer light
In aid of our defective sight;
And spreads at length, before the soul,
A beautiful, and perfect whole,
Which busy man's inventive brain   65
Toils to anticipate in vain.

    Say Anna, had you never known
The beauties of a Rose full-blown,
Could you, tho' luminous your eye,
By looking on the bud, descry,   70
Or guess, with a prophetic power,
The future splendor of the flower?
Just so th'Omnipotent who turns
The system of a world's concerns,
From mere minutiæ can educe   75
Events of most important use;

---

49 *ndented C, EM*   50 to] on *C, EM*   52 guess, and spell] spell and guess *EM*
58 a] great C, *EM*,   68 beauties] beauty *EM*   74 a] the *C, EM*   75 educe]
adduce *C, EM*

And bid a dawning sky display
The blaze of a meridian day.
The works of man tend, one and all,
As needs they must, from great to small;   80
And vanity absorbs at length
The monuments of human strength.
But who can tell how vast the plan,
Which this day's incident began?
Too small perhaps the slight occasion   85
For our dim-sighted observation;
It pass'd unnotic'd, as the bird
That cleaves the yielding air unheard,
And yet may prove, when understood,
An harbinger of endless good.   90
   Not that I deem, or mean to call
Friendship a blessing cheap, or small;
But merely to remark, that ours,
Like some of nature's sweetest flowers,
Rose from a seed of tiny size,   95
That seem'd to promise no such prize:
A transient visit intervening,
And made almost without a meaning,
(Hardly the effect of inclination,
Much less of pleasing expectation!)   100
Produc'd a friendship, then begun,
That has cemented us in one;
And plac'd it in our power to prove,
By long fidelity and love,
That Solomon has wisely spoken;   105
'A three-fold cord is not soon broken.'

---

79 *indented EM*   86 dim-sighted] deminish'd *C*; diminish'd *EM*   87 as] like *C*,
EM   91 *not indented EM*   96 That] Which *EM*   101 then] thus *C, EM*

THE FLATTING-MILL

AN ILLUSTRATION

When a bar of pure silver or ingot of gold
Is sent to be flatted or wrought into length,
It is pass'd between cylinders often and roll'd
In an engine of utmost mechanical strength.

Thus tortur'd and squeez'd, at last it appears   5
Like a loose heap of ribbon, a glittering show,
Like music it tinkles and rings in your ears,
And warm'd by the pressure is all in a glow.

This process atchiev'd it is doom'd to sustain
The thump-after-thump of a gold-beater's mallet,   10
And at last is of service in sickness or pain
To cover a pill from a delicate palate.

Alas for the Poet! who dares undertake
To urge reformation of national ill—
His head and his heart are both likely to ache   15
With the double employment of mallet and mill.

If he wish to instruct he must learn to delight,
Smooth, ductile, and even his Fancy must flow,
Must tinkle and glitter like gold to the sight
And catch in its progress a sensible glow.   20

20 December 1781, later revised.

COPY-TEXT: *S*. Collated: *E*, *A*. First printed by Johnson, 1815.

Title] *the sub-title is not in A, 1815*   4 In an engine of utmost] By means of a mighty
deleted A   5 Thus tortur'd and squeez'd, at last it] The more it is mill'd it the brighter
deleted A   squeez'd] press'd *deleted A*   8 And] Grows *deleted A*   10 thump-
after-thump] thumps and the blows *A*   14 urge] press *A*
17–21 *first written in A*:

> His thoughts like the gold should be sterling and true,
> As ductile [and equal *deleted* as silver *deleted*] and
>   even his fancy should flow,
> Should jingle and tinkle, and shine to the view,
> And [all the way through should be all in a glow. *deleted*]
>   catch in its progress a sensible glow.

> [It must bear after all to be thump'd very fine *deleted*]
> After all he must beat it and thump it as fine

*these lines were then rewritten at the foot of the page in a form similar to S, but with these
variants*:   17 If he wish to instruct] Before he can teach   19 tinkle and glitter
like gold] jingle and tinkle, and shine   21 beat it as thin and] hammer and work it

After all he must beat it as thin and as fine
As the leaf that enfolds what an invalid swallows,
For Truth is unwelcome, however divine,
And unless you adorn it, a Nausea follows.

22 As] Like *deleted A*   24 you adorn] he adorn *E*; you disguise *A*

COMMENTARY

COMMENTARY

VERSES WRITTEN AT BATH, IN 1748

The punctuation in the second edition (1803) of Hayley's *Life of Cowper* is somewhat revised, but the changes are probably 'improvements' by Hayley.

Cowper may have known Joseph Mitchell's *The Shoe-Heel: A Rhapsody*, London, 1727 (Milford–Russell, p. 658), but his poem has almost nothing in common, beyond the title, with Mitchell's tedious effusion. The real affinity of these verses is with John Philips's *The Splendid Shilling*, especially in the treatment of 'low' matters (e.g. ll. 4–6).

l. 20. Cf. Pope, *Epistle to Dr. Arbuthnot*, l. 341.

A LETTER TO CHASE PRICE

Almost certainly this letter is Cowper's response to the news that his former schoolfellow Cyril Arthington had died. Arthington had been admitted to Westminster in 1745, aged fifteen, and had left in 1748 to go to University College, Oxford; he died on 28 May 1750. The reference to Oxford in the third of these poems suggests that Price, who was at this time an undergraduate at Christ Church, may have written from there.

'No, rather in the silent Tomb'

These lines derive in part from Cowley's Pindaric ode, 'Life', which begins:
We're ill by these *Grammarians* us'd;
We are abus'd by *Words*, grosly abus'd;
From the Maternal Tomb,
To the *Graves* fruitful *Womb*,
We call here *Life* . . .
(*Poems*, ed. A. R. Waller, Cambridge, 1905, pp. 209–11).

l. 7. Cf. Jer. 22: 10; Ezek. 24: 17.

l. 17. *We live to Dye, but dye to Live*. Adapted from Cowley's notes to 'Life', where he translates a passage from the lost *Phrixus* of Euripides (frag. 830): 'Who knows whether to *Live*, be not to *Dye*; and to *Dye* to *Live*?'

Mistress Clio. Here invoked simply as a representative Muse.

'Come Heavenly Muse'

l. 1. *Cowley*. Abraham Cowley (1618–67) was educated at Westminster School, and Cowper has just imitated his Pindaric manner. The 'Muse' whom he invokes at the beginning of his *Davideis* is Christ himself.

botch. 'To put together unsuitably, or unskilfully; to make up of unsuitable pieces' (Johnson).

'The Muses are Romantick Jades'

l. 7. *Thus sung old Horace.* Cf. *Epistles*, II. ii. 77.

'Curse, Curse'

ll. 1–2. In *T*, the first line reads 'Curse Curse the'; clearly a 'the', inserted over a caret before 'Verse' in the second line has been copied as part of the first line.

l. 11. *Wake.* The celebration of the feast-day of the patron saint of a church; an occasion of much rustic jollity.

l. 13. *Killbuck and Star.* Dogs' names, probably generic (the first suggests a staghound). As this passage suggests, bear-baiting remained popular if not fashionable well into the eighteenth century; it was not outlawed until 1835.

'WHY THOU SCURVY CURMUDGEON'

This has the air of an impromptu effusion, addressed to Chase Price while he and Walter Bagot were undergraduates at Christ Church, Oxford, in the early 1750s. Cowper's MS. may have been difficult to read because much corrected, or Price's copy may have been carelessly made; whatever the cause, this is the only poem in *T* which presents serious textual problems.

Failure to write letters seems to have been a common charge among these friends; see Cowper to Bagot, 12 Mar. 1749, and to Price, 1 Apr. 1752.

l. 3. *what mean you ?—have at ye !* This reading is conjectural. The words 'mean you' are added over a caret after 'what', which is followed in the line by 'hak e [?—here rendered *have*] at ye'.

l. 4. *Slubberdegullian.* 'A paltry, dirty, sorry wretch' (Johnson).

l. 6. *Watty.* Walter Bagot (1731–1806), close friend of Cowper and Price at Westminster School and for several years thereafter. See Ryskamp, esp. pp. 42, 177–81.

l. 10. *expose.* In the sense 'expose for sale'; *OED* records an example specifically referring to fish from 1771. The MS. reading 'expect' makes no sense.

l. 11. *Morn.* For MS. 'Morts'—another instance of Cowper's final -*n* being misread (cf. 'Written in a Fit of Illness, 1755', l. 17). The word 'Morts', 'harlots', was an easy misreading in this context.

l. 26. *Fame-besmearing Tiwey.* Apparently Tew, or Tyr, the Scandinavian god of war; the form 'Tiwey' seems to be derived from the genitive, *Tiwes*, as in OE. 'Tiwes-dæg'. His 'besmearing' of fame, rather than, say, bestowing it, fits the Billingsgate locale and the tone of travesty which prevails here.

l. 29. *Alecta.* One of the Furies, whose activities here referred to are described by Virgil, *Aeneid*, vii. 323–571. Her 'Trumpet' is the *cornu recurvum* of v. 513, and the 'smaller Bounds' are the encampment where the swains assembled on hearing its call.

TO MISS HALFORD, UPON HER STEALING A BOOK

Miss Halford has so far eluded further identification, but see notes on the next poem.

UPON MISS HALFORD, SINGING AND PLAYING UPON THE HARPSICORD

A letter from Lady Hesketh to Hayley, 1 Mar. 1802 (now in the Hyde Collection), contains the following passage: '. . . I shou'd intrude . . . to send you some Stanzas composed in very early youth by our dear friend, at the request of another who was greatly charm'd with the Lady, whom it cele-brates, and whom I knew; she sung and play'd well, but her extreme affec-tation disgusted *our Friend*, but as it had not the same effect on a *relation* of his who earnestly intreated him to celebrate her in Verse, he produced the following. . . .' The stanzas are now missing from the letter, but the descrip-tion fits this poem. Miss Halford was clearly a friend of Ashley Cowper's family. Perhaps Lady Hesketh's italics point to Theodora as the '*relation*' who asked for a poem.

ll. 1–4. Cf. Boileau, *L'Art poétique*, I. 37–8:

> Aimez donc la Raison. Que toujours vos écrits
> Empruntent d'elle seule et leur lustre et leur prix.

l. 5. *Cowley*. Presumably cited as the author of *The Mistress* (1647). However, the lady in question remains strictly anonymous, and the closest possible referents for ll. 5–6, 'The Innocent Ill' and 'Verses Lost upon a Wager', are rather remote. Prior (like Cowley an Old Westminster) addressed several poems to a Chloe, but none contains the images specified here. Cowper's reference is probably to love poets and their hyperboles in general.

'WHEREFORE DID I LEAVE THE FAIR'

The phraseology of this poem owes something to Prior's 'The Garland', in which 'The dappl'd Pink' and flowers 'in their Native Bed' appear (*Literary Works*, ed. Wright and Spears, 1971, I. 446–7).

l. 5. *Delia*. Not to be identified with Theodora Cowper, as the last stanza indicates.

ll. 19–24. The thought is obscure; roughly: 'Delia's kiss exceeded the beauty of these flowers even before they began to wilt, although before that happened they were as sweet as her smile.'

A CHARACTER

This poem was later adapted for presentation to Theadora, with the title 'Of Himself', q.v. This version suggests strongly that the 'Celia' of the previous poem was a real person, although that was almost certainly not her real name. The conclusion of this poem indicates that when it was written Cowper's love for her had passed, and it is tempting to read the two following pieces as evidence that love turned into something bordering on hostility. But the element of personal reference in those poems may be non-existent: the name 'Celia' had been used opprobriously by Swift and Prior, and was appropriate for any unpleasing representative of the sex, especially an imaginary one.

SONG ('No more shall hapless Celia's ears')

It is difficult to see here any possible reference to a young woman with whom Cowper had recently been in love, a conclusion confirmed by the poem's appearance in Theadora's collection.

TO C. P., ILL WITH THE RHEUMATISM

Chase Price was recovering from his illness when Cowper wrote to him on 1 April 1752, so this poem was probably composed before that date. The 'rheumatism' seems to have been of the kind then called 'acute'; that is, what is now commonly called rheumatic fever: inflammation and swelling of the joints, accompanied by high fever. It was often attributed to disordered humours (l. 4), and opium was a standard remedy (l. 22). Cowper has taken several hints from the opening lines of Pope's *The First Satire of the Second Book of Horace Imitated*.

l. 16. *Mead*. Richard Mead (1673–1754), a leading English physician in the first half of the eighteenth century, reputed to have earned between five and six thousand pounds a year. A man of wide-ranging scholarly interests, he was Pope's physician.

l. 20. *Probatum est*. 'It has been proved', i.e. shown to be effective, a phrase used by eighteenth-century physicians in prescriptions.

l. 22. *Blackmore*. Sir Richard Blackmore (1654–1729), author of *Prince Arthur* (1695), *Creation* (1712), and other epic poems; he was also a practising physician.

l. 23. *Garth*. Sir Samuel Garth (1661–1719), a physician who achieved literary fame with his satire *The Dispensary* (1699); a friend of Pope.

l. 32. *Torpedo-like*. The torpedo is the electric ray, 'a fish which . . . if touched even with a long stick, benumbs the hand that so touches it' (Johnson).

ll. 39–46. It is not certain whether Cowper later excerpted these lines for Theadora's collection, deeming them worth preserving apart from their original context; or whether he communicated the whole poem to her, and Croft deleted the rest of the poem as unworthy of publication.

IN A LETTER TO C. P. ESQUIRE

In his letter to Price of 1 April 1752 (*R*) Cowper explains that he composed these lines that morning, while walking in the fields before breakfast. He began, he says, by trying to devise a compliment to Price, and ended by praising his own judgement. He does not describe the result as an imitation of Shakespeare. Price's copy of *R* (*T*, p. 17), is headed 'To C:P'; there are no verbal variants.

Since the copy given to Theadora postdates that sent to Price, Croft's variants in ll. 7 and 9 are adopted into the present text.

'O! ASK NOT WHERE CONTENTMENT MAY ABIDE'

In his letter to Chase Price of 1 April 1752 Cowper introduces this poem (he does not call it a sonnet) as something 'said t'other Day'. It appears in Price's Commonplace Book (*T*, p. 17), presumably copied from that letter, headed 'A Sonnet / to C:P', and with two errors of transcription: 2 still] soft; 5 Mountain] Mountains. In form the poem is indeed an Italian sonnet with an additional final couplet.

l. 16. 'N:B: Pope says—An Honest Man's the Noblest Work of God' (Cowper's note). The reference is to *Essay on Man*, iv. 248.

'CUM TOT SUSTINEANT REGES ET TANTA, NEQUE ULLA'

These lines form part of a letter to 'Toby' (Chase Price), which is headed 'Great Berkhamstead I don't know when'. Wright dated it 1754, but it may well be earlier. All of the letter which followed these lines has been lost.

Translation

Since kings are responsible for so many and such great matters, and are not free, in any measure, to devote themselves to pleasures and delights; since the crown fastens varied sorrows to the head, and threats of wars oppress and harass; why do the people complain? Why do they mutter with a blind murmuring? Say, does he employ his heroic power madly, who, watchful, keeps guard thus, and so bears the burden of rule, lest the people be vexed in any way?

This [murmuring] is the offence of Satan, nor is there any more worthy of the devil, for this fault occurred first in Satan's breast. Give instead the rewards worthy of a man, and true love of the people will follow the benefits brought together for the people. Loving nations justly foster this [love], and guard it; it nurtures nations, loves, and guards them.

But you (if such there be) whoever would curse the awesome head of the prince, Hold! be silent; because fidelity to the king brings no rare reward, you madly suppose that the king you honour is unworthy; you honour yourself, which is the highest praise; it is enough for the free-born to have deserved foreign praise.

'MORTALS, AROUND YOUR DESTIN'D HEADS'

Lady Hesketh sent the copy in Theadora Cowper's hand to Hayley, apparently in November 1801, for use in the biography. It was accompanied by the copy of the translation from Bourne, 'On the Picture of a Sleeping Child'. (Hayley chose to print neither.) It is not clear why Theadora should have omitted the final stanza from her transcription.

'ANXIOUS AS SAD OFFENDERS ARE'

The position of this poem in *T*, immediately following poems addressed to Chase Price on 1 April 1752, when he was recovering from rheumatic fever, suggests that it may have been written to comfort him in his illness.

l. 17. *Nerve*. Sinew or tendon.

ll. 26–8. Cf. Matt. 11: 28.

AN APOLOGY FOR NOT SHOWING HER WHAT I HAD WROTE

Headed in Croft 'Cutfield, July, 1752'. The place is properly Catfield, in Norfolk, about fifteen miles north-west of Great Yarmouth, where Cowper's uncle, the Revd. Roger Donne, was Rector. Cowper had visited there frequently and happily as a boy (cf. Ryskamp, p. 7). It seems to have been during the summer visit of 1752 that he first fell in love with his cousin Theadora Cowper, to whom this poem is addressed, although he must often have seen her at her father's house in London.

'DELIA, TH' UNKINDEST GIRL ON EARTH'

Headed in Croft 'At the same place'; i.e. Catfield, in Norfolk, in the summer of 1752.

'THIS EVENING, DELIA, YOU AND I'

Headed in *T* 'Ibid' and in Croft 'At the same place'; i.e. Catfield, in the summer of 1752. Theadora told Hayley that this was the first poem that Cowper ever addressed to her (Ryskamp, p. 105 n.). The version that she first saw is represented by *T*, which is so early that Cowper had not yet adopted the poetical name of 'Delia' for his cousin. Croft's text represents a revised version, given to Theadora some time later. (On the relationship of *T* and Croft, see above, Introduction, pp. xxvi–xxvii.)

'IN A FOND HOUR MY DELIA SWORE'

Headed 'Ibid' in *T*, this is the last of the poems written at Catfield in 1752. It does not appear in Croft, either because Cowper did not include it in the collection which he prepared for Theadora, or, more probably, because Croft found the kiss and the embrace improper.

OF HIMSELF

This adaptation of the earlier 'A Character' is placed first in Croft, as if by way of introduction, but this appears to be accidental. It is here placed after the poems certainly written at Catfield in the summer of 1752.

'BID ADIEU, MY SAD HEART, BID ADIEU TO THY PEACE'

The copy in *T* is headed 'Berkhamstead/October 1752'. Theadora was presumably about to visit friends or relatives in Lancashire; Cowper would shortly have to return to London for the Michaelmas law term.

WRITTEN AFTER LEAVING HER AT NEW BARNS

Headed in Croft 'At Berkhamstead', and perhaps written in 1754, when Theadora stayed at New Barns with her father from July to October (Judith Madan to M. F. C. Cowper, 21 July 1754 (Hog MSS.)). New Barns, near St. Albans, was the seat of Lieutenant-Colonel Thomson (Ryskamp, p. 130). His friend Ashley Cowper had the use of his house while he was with his regiment.

l. 26. *sat*. Variant past tense of 'set', 'frequent in inferior writers of the second half of the 18th c.' (*OED*). Cf. also 'The Dog and the Water-Lily', l. 23.

ON HER ENDEAVOURING TO CONCEAL HER GRIEF
AT PARTING

l. 15. *prove*. 'Experience', 'suffer'.

THE SYMPTOMS OF LOVE

The three-line stanzas, unique in Cowper's verse, are modelled on Prior's 'Jinny the Just'.

ll.13–15. These lines do not appear in Croft, but they were certainly in Theadora's copy of the poem, for they appear in the version which Hayley copied into his *Vindication* from a transcript which Theadora had made for him (cf. Ryskamp, pp. 231–2). Presumably Croft or his advisers thought the stanza weak, and decided to omit it from the printed version.

AN ATTEMPT AT THE MANNER OF WALLER

In both *T* and Croft headed 'Drayton, March 1753'; probably Drayton in Norfolk, two miles north-west of Norwich, where one of the Donnes (Cowper's mother's family) may have had a home (Ryskamp, p. 64 n.).

A probable model is Waller's poem, 'To My Young Lady Lucy Sidney', which begins 'Why came I so untimely forth'.

HORTI AD FLORAM DEDICATIO. 1753

The 'nymph' of l. 20 is presumably Theadora, and the garden one which they visited together.

l. 5. *Flora*. The Roman goddess of gardens, married to the west wind (cf. l. 24).

l. 9. *Textili*. In an undated letter, probably of the 1780s, Cowper replies to queries about Greek and Latin composition sent him by a Mr. Collins. One of the Latin words which he mentions is *textilis*, 'which I know is found in one of Martial's best Epigrams'. He refers to VI. lxxx. 8: 'textilibus sertis'; modern editions read 'tonsilibus'.

ll. 19–20. The meaning intended is obscure, perhaps as a result of confusion between *affingere*, 'to fashion', and *affigere*, 'to affix'.

l. 24. *Favoni*. Favonius is another name for Zephyrus, the west wind.

Translation

THE DEDICATION OF THE GARDEN TO FLORA. 1753

O you, who watch over gardens consecrated to you (even when the fields are white with frost, or when the very Dog-star, being master of the heavens, scorches the glebe), Flora, crowned with a scented chaplet on your golden locks, preside over and protect my gardens, notwithstanding they are but poorly decked out. So that violets may not be wanting under the interlacing shade, rejoicing in the dew and rain, and that lilies may vie with the whiteness of fresh-fallen snows, grant that the swelling buds may spread out their opening bosoms to the sun, and drink in his rays and the genial showers, and not be consumed as the booty of snails. And do not at any time allow the stubborn satyrs to tear down my enclosures, while it pleases my nymph to weave at leisure a suitable garland. Equally I pray, O goddess, that wherever you bend your steps, no wind may blow on you, none blow unless the breath of gentle Zephyr.

WRITTEN IN A QUARREL

This may be referred to in the postscript of the letter to Chase Price of 21 February 1754, where Cowper speaks of a poem written during a 'difference' between himself and Theodora which has since been made up.

'HOPE, LIKE THE SHORT-LIVED RAY THAT GLEAMS AWHILE'

The title given this poem in *T*, 'Often expecting to meet her and disappointed', is hardly appropriate to the central concern of the piece: a permanent separation. Its tone suggests that it was composed about the time of the crisis in 1755.

1755

The initials 'R.S.S.' which head Croft's text (and appear in the title of the poem which follows) remained a mystery until Povey suggested that they represent the digits '1755', misread as letters (Milford–Russell, p. 659). This solution is confirmed by the content of this poem, which, balancing the claims of virtue and of money, clearly reflects the 1755 crisis in Cowper's relationship with Theodora.

WRITTEN IN A FIT OF ILLNESS. 1755

The letters 'R.S.S.' in Croft's text are a misreading of '1755'; see preceding.

l. 17. *Then* (for 'There', Croft). Final -*n* and final -*re* in Cowper's hand are easily confused.

'SEE WHERE THE THAMES, THE PUREST STREAM'

l. 14. *sucker*. i.e. 'succour', 'to shelter, protect'. *OED*, 'succour', 4, cites an apt quotation from Bunyan. 'Suckle' (Croft) is clearly an attempted emendation.

UPON A VENERABLE RIVAL

l. 19. *deviate into truth*. Cf. Dryden, *Mac Flecknoe*, l. 20.

ODE. SUPPOSED TO BE WRITTEN ON THE MARRIAGE OF A FRIEND

A difficult poem. The last three stanzas echo Cowper's other poems to Theodora written about the time their relationship was broken off (this is the last poem in Croft's collection), and they might plausibly be addressed by a bridegroom to his bride. But they are imperfectly linked to the opening stanzas, which are hardly appropriate to a friend's marriage—Orpheus and his lost Eurydice are not suited to an epithalamium. It may be that the title is a subterfuge, and that Cowper intended the poem as a covert assertion that he might yet recover his Eurydice from the shades of paternal disapproval. The reference in l. 35 to virtue as a 'vestal' (and therefore virgin) tends to support such an interpretation.

l. 4. *Hebrus*. A river in Thrace.

l. 5. *warbles*. Povey's conjecture is preferable to Southey's 'warblings', but the text may be irretrievably corrupt.

'HAPPY THE MAN WHOSE AMOROUS FLAME HAS FOUND'

l. 6. *Slacken*. 'Repress' (Johnson); 'moderate, make less intense' (*OED*)—but neither quotes a truly parallel usage.

A NEW BALLAD

Perhaps composed for the Nonsense Club.

Title. The use of 'garland' to mean a ballad, although not unique to Cowper, is very rare (it is not recorded in *OED*). See below, 'The Cock-Fighter's Garland' of 1789. 'The grey mare the better horse' is proverbial for a wife who rules her husband.

AN ODE ON READING MR. RICHARDSON'S HISTORY OF SIR CHARLES GRANDISON

This ode is a response to criticism of the religious tone of Richardson's novel, and in particular to a pamphlet, *Critical Remarks on Sir Charles Grandison, Clarissa and Pamela . . . By a Lover of Virtue*, published on 21 February 1754 (reprinted, Augustan Reprint Society, No. 21, 1950; cf. T. C. D. Eaves and B. D. Kimpel, *Samuel Richardson*, Oxford, 1971, pp. 407–9). Its author is a sceptic, a defender of 'sentimental unbelievers'—those who, like Socrates, Cicero, and Lord Bolingbroke, support the established religion as a social necessity while not believing its doctrines. He attacks Grandison as being an 'unnatural' character, for he is represented as being a good man, although (unlike Fielding's Mr. Allworthy) he has lived all his life 'in the world'; his character is therefore not 'poetically probable'. He is also represented as a Christian, 'and that too, in the strictest and most bigotted sense of the word; for he refuses the woman he loves, for a difference in religious principles. This . . . is likewise an inconsistency, for universal learning naturally leads to scepticism' (p. 20).

Richardson's authorship might be an open secret, but *Grandison* was published anonymously. The title and the last stanza of *Q*, the version that Cowper gave to Richardson, preserve this anonymity, whereas *T*, the version Cowper circulated to Chase Price, names Richardson in the title and in the last stanza, as does the later version given to Theadora and printed by Croft (in which the last stanza is recast). That is, Cowper gave to Richardson a version suitable for publication, and the most likely time for him to have done so is between the appearance of the pamphlet and the publication of the concluding volume of *Grandison* on 14 March 1754. He may have expected Richardson to preface his final instalment with testimonials; it would not have been out of character for him to do so. (On the MS. *Q*, and Cowper's acquaintance with Richardson, see C. A. Ryskamp, 'Samuel Richardson and William Cowper', *Library*, xix (1964), 234–8; T. C. D. Eaves and B. D. Kimpel, 'Cowper's "An Ode on Reading Mr. Richardson's 'History of Sir Charles Grandison'"', *Papers on Language and Literature*, ii (1966), 74–5.)

Cowper subsequently revised his ode; *T* represents an intermediate stage in this process (cf. esp. ll. 33–4). The final version was that presented to

Theodora, which is represented by *Croft* and by *X*, the copy in John Johnson's hand. This copy must derive from the copy made from Theodora's version, probably by Theodora herself, which Lady Hesketh sent to Hayley in April 1801. Johnson seems to have had some difficulty in reading his exemplar, since in four places alternative readings appear in *X*: l. 6: Croud/clod; l. 19: sword/hand; l. 25: these/such (deleted); l. 31: source/Cause. In view of this dubiety, it has seemed best to follow *Croft* for the text of the final stanza (while retaining the capitalization of *X*, for consistency with the rest of the poem); and elsewhere to adopt readings attested by both *Croft* and *X*, as witnesses to the revised text presented to Theodora.

In a letter to Hayley of 13 April 1801 (B.L. Add. MS. 30803A, fo. 122), Lady Hesketh urges him to publish these lines, because 'they will serve to rescue his Home from the *heavy* charge with which the Methodists have loaded it, of his being an Infidel! lost to all Sense of Piety and Virtue!—*'till he fell into their hands!*'

ll. 19–24. Richardson entered in *Q* the names of the characters alluded to; his annotations, with the passages in which the incidents occur, are as follows: ll. 19–20, 'Dr. Bartlett at Athens' (Volume II, Letter xxxvi); ll. 20–1 'Mansfields' (IV. ii); ll. 22–3, 'Emily' (IV. ix); l. 24, 'Sir Hargrave' (IV. xxxvi). He omitted to notice, as Eaves and Kimpel indicate, l. 23, Jeronymo (III. xx). This portion of *Q* is reproduced by Russell, Plate I (facing p. xxvi).

l. 35. *Resignation.* 'Submission without murmur to the will of God' (Johnson).

AN EPISTLE TO ROBERT LLOYD, ESQR. 1754

Robert Lloyd (1733–64) was the son of Pierson Lloyd, Under Master of Westminster School (see below, 'Verses to the Memory of Dr. Lloyd'). He was admitted to Westminster in 1740, and placed first among those elected to Trinity College, Cambridge, in 1751 (B.A., 1755; M.A., 1758). After a short and unhappy period as an usher at Westminster, he set out to earn a living by writing. He died in the Fleet, imprisoned for debt, on 15 December 1764. His association with Cowper is described by Ryskamp, esp. pp. 78–101.

Cowper's epistle was presumably written from London to Lloyd at Cambridge. It is a response to a verse epistle from Lloyd (ll. 25–30), which has not been preserved.

l. 3. *dear Mat Prior's easy jingle.* Prior, like Lloyd and Cowper, had been educated at Westminster School. He had written a number of works in octosyllabic couplets, one of them, *Alma: or, The Progress of the Mind* (1718), being among his most widely admired.

ll. 13–20. The 'banditti' may have been suggested by *Alma*, i. 84–9, where the Pope living quietly at Rome while his agents travel to and fro is offered as an image of the mind and its relation to the nerves as taught at Cambridge.

l. 32. *pitch-kettled*. 'A favourite phrase at the time when this Epistle was written, expressive of being puzzled, or what in the Spectator's time, would have been called *bamboozled*' (Hayley's note; he refers to *Tatler*, 230 (28 Sept. 1710)).

ll. 39–45. Cf. *Gammer Gurton's Needle*, I. v. Cowper probably read the play in volume I of Dodsley's *Select Collection of Old Plays* (1744), to which his father was a subscriber. He must here be writing from memory, since in the play Hodge is Gammer Gurton's servant, not her son, and it is the boy Cock who mistakes a straw for the lost needle. 'Grimalkin' (l. 44) is a generic name for an old cat; the cat in the play is called Gib.

ll. 49–60. Chasing butterflies was an activity commonly associated with virtuosi: cf. *Spectator*, 21 (24 Mar. 1711); Pope, *The Dunciad* (1743), iv. 421–36. Cowper seems to be recalling especially *Tatler*, 221 (7 Sept. 1710), in which a similar chase is described, and the phrase 'over hedge and ditch' occurs (ed. G. A. Aitken, 1899, iv. 134–5).

l. 52. *mews*. Probably to be understood as 'enclosed, i.e. narrow places', but this sense (perhaps created by the need for a rhyme) does not seem to be recorded elsewhere.

l. 59. *Culprit*. In the unusual sense of 'prisoner'; see *OED*.

ll. 67–8. On Prior's ease, see Cowper to William Unwin, 17 Jan. 1782.

l. 87. *chien sçavant*. A performing dog.

A LETTER IN VERSE TO JOSEPH HILL

Joseph Hill (1733–1811) came of a legal family and probably met Cowper in the late 1740s through the poet's uncle, Ashley Cowper, who was a trustee of Hill's father's will. He was to become Cowper's lifelong friend. (See Ryskamp, esp. pp. 79–82; W. Hooper, 'Cowper's "Sephus"', *N & Q*, 12 ser. v (1919), 258–9.)

The letter is dated from G[reat] Berk[hamsted], where Cowper was staying with his father, the Rector. It is addressed to Hill 'at No. 17 in Gloucester Street, Queen Square, London' (now Old Gloucester Street), close to Ashley Cowper's house in Southampton Row and a short walk from the Middle Temple, where Cowper had rooms and where his message would have to be delivered (cf. Ryskamp, pp. 64, 70–1).

l. 25. *your Dear Wife*. The allusion is obscure: Hill did not marry until 1771.

l. 30. *Laundress*. 'A caretaker of chambers in the Inns of Court' (*OED*).

THE SHADE OF HOMER: AN ODE

Antoine Houdar de la Motte (1672–1731) was a writer for the stage and champion of the Moderns. In 1714, undeterred by his ignorance of Greek, he published a verse 'translation' of the *Iliad* in twelve short books, based on the then recent rendering by Madame Dacier. The present ode is a poetical justification of the principles stated in his prefatory *Discours sur Homere*: 'j'ai suivi de l'Iliade, ce qui m'a paru devoir en être conservé, et j'ai pris la liberté de changer ce que j'y ai crû désagréable' (*Œuvres*, Paris, 1754, ii. 108).

The publication of la Motte's collected works in 1754 may have drawn Cowper's attention to this ode. It was about that time that he and his friend Alston began their study of Homer and of Pope's English translation (Ryskamp, pp. 50–1).

La Motte's ode is given in the Appendix, below.

l. 9. *Appion*. Apion, head of the Alexandrian school at the beginning of the Christian era, claimed to have conjured up the ghost of Homer to ascertain his birthplace, but he never revealed the result of this inquiry.

ON THE PICTURE OF A SLEEPING CHILD

A translation of 'In Statuam Sepulchralem Infantis Dormientis' (see Appendix for Latin text). Cowper substitutes a painting for Bourne's memorial sculpture.

Vincent Bourne (1695–1747) was educated at Westminster School and Cambridge, and served as an usher at Westminster School for twenty-seven years. His *Poematia, Latine partim reddita partim scripta* was first published in 1734. For Cowper's view of him as poet and as teacher, see his letter to Unwin, 23 May 1781.

l. 4. *spirits*. 'That which gives vigour or cheerfulness to the mind; the purest part of the body bordering, says *Sydenham*, on immateriality. In this meaning it is commonly written with the plural termination' (Johnson).

'DOOM'D, AS I AM, IN SOLITUDE TO WASTE'

Hayley introduces the poem as follows: 'The variety and depth of his sufferings, in early life, from extreme tenderness of heart, are very forcibly displayed in the following Verses, which formed part of a letter to one of his female relations, at the time they were composed [presumably Lady Hesketh]. The letter has perished; and the verses owe their preservation to the affectionate memory of the lady to whom they were addressed.'

l. 8. *Him*. 'Sir William Russel, the favourite friend of the young poet.' (Hayley's note.) He was the only son of Sir Francis Russell, Bt., of Chippenham, Cambridgeshire. He was admitted to Westminster School in February

1742/3, aged seven, and left in 1747, having succeeded his father as seventh Baronet in 1744. He pursued a military career (Ensign, 1st Foot Guards, 1751; Lieutenant and Captain, 1755), and was drowned whilst swimming in the Thames on 21 September 1757. It has always been assumed that these lines were composed shortly after Russell's death, but line 7 suggests that a longer interval may have elapsed.

TRANSLATIONS FROM THE SATIRES OF HORACE

A long-standing family friendship linked Cowper with William Duncombe (1690–1769) and his son John (1729–86). William Duncombe had for many years translated odes by Horace for his amusement, 'but without any intention of publishing them, till his son offered his assistance for completing the work; and undertook some of the Odes and Satires, all the Epodes, and the first book of Epistles' (A. Kippis, *Biographia Britannica*, v (1793), 508). John Duncombe enlisted the aid of friends to supplement his own and his father's endeavours, and of these Cowper was one.

In a letter to John Duncombe of 31 December 1757 Cowper speaks of a promise which he has not yet performed; he may possibly be referring to these translations. In any case, they were most probably composed after the publication of the first volume of 'Duncombe's Horace' (which contains the odes) in 1757.

Since the notes in *1759* were written by William Duncombe (Kippis, loc. cit.), they are omitted here.

THE FIFTH SATIRE OF THE FIRST BOOK

l. 30. *Bargemen*. From Appii Forum to Feronia the journey is made by canal boat.

l. 38. *Gears*. 'The traces by which horses or oxen draw' (Johnson).

THE NINTH SATIRE OF THE FIRST BOOK

Title. *Impertinent*. 'A trifler; a meddler; an intruder' (Johnson).

l. 46. *Gray or Mason*. Gray's *Odes* had been published in 1757, Mason's in 1756.

l. 51. *Beard*. John Beard (c. 1717–91), the English tenor for whom Handel composed the tenor parts in the *Messiah* and other oratorios.

l. 53. *Cooke*. Apparently a dancer (Christian name unknown) at Covent Garden, 1747–8, and at Drury Lane, 1749–54.

l. 75. *Rufus' Hall*. Westminster Hall, first built by William Rufus in 1099, and in Cowper's day the seat of the Court of Chancery.

l. 97. *Newcastle*. Thomas Pelham-Holles, Duke of Newcastle, Prime Minister 1754–6 and 1757–62. He was, like Horace's Maecenas, a patron of writers.

ll. 105–6. *by way/Of second Fiddle*. An earlier example of this expression than any recorded in *OED*.

l. 162. The Latin phrase *sub cultro*, here translated literally, means 'in extreme peril or distress'.

ADDRESSED TO MISS —— ON READING THE PRAYER FOR INDIFFERENCE

'The Prayer for Indifference' was written by Frances Greville, *née* Macartney, who married Fulke Greville, grandson of the fifth Lord Brooke, in 1748. It began to circulate in manuscript and then in newspapers and magazines in the late 1750s; it was first published in the *Edinburgh Chronicle*, 14–19 Apr. 1759 (I. A. Gordon, *Shenstone's Miscellany 1759–63*, Oxford, 1952, p. 139). John Johnson dated Cowper's response 1762 because he believed Mrs. Greville's poem was first published in that year; this date is probably too late.

Cowper's verses passed apparently unnoticed in a manuscript collection of poems by members of the Madan family until Mrs. Henry Cowper sent a copy to John Johnson in October 1813, when the supplementary volume of Cowper's poetry was first projected. Martin Madan's copy was entitled 'Addressed to Miss —— By W. C. of Olney on reading the Prayer for Indifference'; the designation 'of Olney' indicates that this copy must be some years later than the date of composition. Johnson told Hayley (17 Mar. 1814) that at first he had thought the poem was quite new to him; 'but I have frequently thought, within the last month or two, that Lady Hesketh *must* have repeated *detached* Stanzas to me at Weston, lamenting at the same time that she had forgot the rest, and could no where recover them' (Fitzwilliam Museum, Fairfax Murray Collection).

The structure of Cowper's poem is obscure. It offers a prayer for Miss ——'s use, a prayer for sympathy; there is commentary on that prayer (ll. 33–64, 69–84), and a concluding prayer for Miss ——. In this Cowper follows Mrs. Greville's example, for her prayer is addressed to Oberon, and leads to a prayer for Oberon. Her poem is conveniently available in the *Oxford Book of Eighteenth-Century Verse*, ed. D. Nichol Smith, Oxford, 1926, pp. 426–8.

Title. The date of Mrs. Greville's marriage renders it impossible that she should be the lady addressed, as Southey supposed.

l. 21. *Ob'ron*. Mrs. Greville's prayer is addressed to Oberon, who is called both 'fairy' and 'elf'. In some texts of her poem there are footnote references to *A Midsummer Night's Dream*, to which she alludes several times.

l. 67. *ethereal*. Here 'terrestrial' (the line means: 'as long as I live'). There may be a confused reminiscence of Akenside, *The Pleasures of Imagination* (1744), I. 41–2: 'there to breathe at large/Æthereal air' (cf. *OED*, s.v. *ethereal*, 3).

ll. 97–8. Cf. Gray, 'Ode on the Spring', ll. 1–4.

TRANSLATION OF FOUR CANTOS OF VOLTAIRE'S *LA HENRIADE*

This translation appeared as a part of the edition of Voltaire's works in English which was initiated in 1761, with Tobias Smollett as editor. He was assisted by Thomas Francklin, who was responsible for the volumes of poetry and drama, and it was probably through Francklin that the brothers John and William Cowper became involved in the project. Francklin (1721–84) was an Old Westminster who served as Regius Professor of Greek at Cambridge from 1750 to 1759. He is likely to have known John Cowper at Cambridge, and since it is recorded that he was 'sometime an Usher at the School', he may even have met William Cowper at Westminster in the 1740s. Whatever the nature of his acquaintance with the Cowpers, John Cowper was commissioned to translate the first eight cantos of the *Henriade*, and William undertook the fifth, sixth, seventh, and eighth. (The ninth was translated by Edward Burnaby Green, and the tenth by Cowper's friend, Robert Lloyd.) This division of the labour is reported in a review of *The Task* in the *Gentleman's Magazine*, lv, pt. ii (Dec. 1785), 986, almost certainly written by the old family friend of the Cowpers, John Duncombe. On reading the review, Cowper wrote to Lady Hesketh that the facts were correctly stated, and added that his brother had received twenty guineas for the first eight books (16 Jan. 1786). Joseph Hill recalled, forty years later, that both brothers had been 'very sick of their tasks'.

Despite the clear account given in the review, this translation was long believed lost, or at least unidentifiable, largely because Hayley became convinced that it had appeared in a magazine. For the story of the muddle and its resolution, see Ryskamp, pp. 232–6; also Russell, pp. 9–12.

Voltaire's *Henriade*, after surreptitious publication on the Continent as *La Ligue*, was first published under its present title in England in 1728, with a dedication to Queen Caroline. The hero is Henry de Bourbon, King of Navarre, later Henry IV of France. The main action of the poem begins as Henry of Navarre joins Henry III of France outside Paris, where the rebellious Catholic League and its leader, Mayenne, are besieged. Henry of Navarre is sent to England to seek help from Queen Elizabeth, to whom he recounts the story of the religious wars in France (cantos ii and iii). He then returns to France, just in time to save Henry III from defeat. Mayenne flies to Rome for aid. Discord returns from Rome when his mission concludes, and Paris is thrown into disorder as the factions of the League and the Parliament quarrel. Here begins canto v, the first translated by William Cowper. Henry III is assassinated, and Navarre becomes Henry IV. At the close of the eighth canto, Henry is barely victorious after heavy fighting. In the ninth, he falls under the amorous spell of Madame d'Estrées until the faithful Mornay reclaims him. Returned to his army (canto x), Henry renews the siege of Paris, which suffers a famine in consequence. Henry demonstrates his magnanimity by relieving the inhabitants; Heaven rewards his virtues; Truth descends to enlighten him; the war ends as the gates of Paris open to receive him.

Voltaire's epic was enormously popular throughout Europe (Frederick the Great wrote a glowing introduction to it), and was widely translated; there had been at least two complete versions in English before 1762. There is an excellent modern edition by O. R. Taylor, in Th. Besterman, ed., *Studies on Voltaire and the Eighteenth Century*, xxxviii–xl, Geneva, 1965. Voltaire's aims as an epic poet are lucidly summarized by I. O. Wade, *The Intellectual Development of Voltaire*, Princeton, 1969, pp. 93–109, 156–60.

The closeness of Cowper's translation may be gauged by a comparison of line numberings. The French figure is given first: canto v: 410 to 402; vi: 386 to 383; vii: 486 to 531; viii: 520 to 522. The disparity in canto vii is the result of a slightly looser rendering, especially of the vision of France under Louis XIV (ll. 386–441). The notes of the 1762 edition are translated, with many omissions, from the 'Notes de l'Editeur', i.e. Voltaire, which accompany the French text. The Arguments to the cantos are likewise taken, with minor alterations, from the French.

vii. ll. 69–70. Cf. Pope, *The Universal Prayer*, ll. 1–4. Voltaire has: 'C'est cet Etre infini qu'on sert et qu'on ignore:/Sous les noms differens le monde entier l'adore' (73–4).

viii. ll. 183–6. These are quoted from ll. 287–8 and 290–1 of Addison's *The Campaign* (1705). The passage was a famous one; cf. Johnson's discussion of it, *Lives of the English Poets*, ed. G. B. Hill, Oxford, 1905, ii. 129–31. Voltaire has:

> Ou tel que du vrai Dieu les Ministres terribles,
> Ces puissances des Cieux, ces êtres impassibles,
> Environnés des vents, des foudres, des éclairs,
> D'un front inaltérable ébranlent l'univers. (185–8)

A SONG OF MERCY AND JUDGMENT

Mrs. Collyer believed that this song 'could only belong to the time immediately after the recovery in 1764' (*Universal Review*, vii (1890), 278).

Povey believed that 'thy list'ning Saints' (l. 76) referred to the Unwins, and dated the poem 1765–7 accordingly. But on 3 April 1767 Cowper wrote to his cousin Maria F. C. Cowper that he could not relate his story to the Unwins—no doubt because Morley Unwin was not one of the 'saints'. It is more likely that the 'Song' was composed after his removal to Olney in the autumn of 1767. On 10 August of that year, when Morley Unwin was dead and the move impending, he wrote to his aunt, Mrs. Madan: 'I want to be with the Lord's People, having great Need of quickening Intercourse and the Communion of his Saints.' To the same correspondent, on 24 March 1770, he wrote of his recently deceased brother: 'He has left me to sing of Mercy and Judgment.'

The text of *A* extends over three pages; Cowper wrote out the alternating refrain in full after the first two stanzas on each page.

'TO JESUS, THE CROWN OF MY HOPE'

This is probably the beginning of a hymn which Cowper never completed, and should be dated accordingly about 1771. The copyist(s) of *Y* and *1816*, which omit the third stanza, may have interpreted marks on Cowper's lost manuscript as a cancellation of these lines. The variants in ll. 5 and 15 may likewise reflect alternative readings in the author's draft. For an account of the lost manuscript, see above, Introduction, p. xxviii.

The collation attempts to record all readings which derive immediately or ultimately from independent sightings of the manuscript (although *Y* and *1816* may have a common source). The first printing—in the *Baptist Magazine* only a month or two after Sam Roberts discovered the manuscript —is not collated because its source is unknown. Povey surmises that the poem was submitted by the Revd. John Sutcliff, the Baptist minister of Olney from 1775 to 1814. Sutcliff is named by Thomas Taylor as the source of the very similar text which Taylor printed in *1833*.

In many editions the four stanzas given here are followed by a spurious continuation of four more, perhaps the work of Priscilla Gurney, to whose *Hymns Selected from Various Authors*, Norwich, 1818, pp. 242–3, they have been traced (see Russell, pp. 27–8).

OLNEY HYMNS

The arrangement of *Olney Hymns*, 1779, is Newton's; his subject headings are not preserved in this text. In Book I, *On Select Passages of Scripture*, the references appear at the head of each hymn. In Book II, *On Occasional Subjects*, the relevant subjects are as follows: i. Seasons. Before annual [New Year] sermons: nos. 22–4; Christmas: no. 25; ii. Ordinances. On opening a place for social prayer: no. 26; Sacramental hymns: nos. 27, 28; Prayer: no. 29;

Scripture: no. 30; iii. Providences. Funeral hymns: no. 31. In Book III, *On the Rise, Progress, Changes, and Comforts of the Spiritual Life*, thus: Seeking, pleading, hoping: nos. 32, 34; Conflict: nos. 35–45; Comfort, nos. 46–53; Dedication and surrender: nos. 54–7; Cautions: nos. 58–64; Praise: nos. 65–67.

For a discussion of the canonical problem and its solution by Kenneth Povey, see below, under no. 33.

Hymn 1: 'Oh for a closer walk with God'

At the end of 1767 Mrs. Unwin was seriously ill, and Cowper feared she might be taken from him. In the letter of 10 December 1767 to Mrs. Madan (his aunt, the former Judith Cowper) he gives this account of the composition: 'I began to compose them [these lines] Yesterday Morning before Daybreak, but fell asleep at the End of the two first Lines, when I awaked again the third and fourth were whisper'd to my Heart in a way which I have often experienced.'

Always one of Cowper's most popular hymns, this was reprinted several times from Conyers's 1772 *Collection*. First by Augustus Montague Toplady, *Psalms and Hymns for Public and Private Worship*, 1776, p. 141, under the title 'Self-Examination' and with alterations of Conyers's text; thence by William Taylor and Herbert Jones, *A Collection of Psalms and Hymns*, 1777, pp. 93–4 (entitled 'The Complaint'). It appeared also in the *Gospel Magazine*, iv (Dec. 1777), between pp. 560 and 561 (untitled; engraved with music). The copy in the Maitland–Madan Commonplace Book, p. 89, is taken from the letter of 10 December 1767 and has no independent authority.

That letter shows that this was not conceived as a hymn on a select passage of Scripture.

l. 2. *Frame*. 'Natural or habitual disposition, temper, turn of thought, etc.' (*OED*).

ll. 3–4. Cf. Ps. 119: 105.

ll. 13–14. Cf. Gen. 8: 8–12; Matt. 3: 16.

Hymn 2: 'The saints should never be dismay'd'

ll. 6–8. Many later editions continue God's speech to the end of l. 8—an error, as reference to the passage in Genesis shows.

ll. 23–4. Quoted by Newton, in the form 'The promise may be long deferr'd,/ But never comes too late', in Letter I to Mrs. P——, (May 1774), *Cardiphonia*, 1781, ii. 113. The variants may reflect merely a lapse of memory on Newton's part; however, it is possible that they represent an earlier version. L. 21 may originally have read 'Wait for his seasonable word', later altered to avoid the repetition from the previous stanza.

Hymn 4: 'By whom was David taught'

Conyers's title is 'Divine strength in human weakness'.

ll. 1–6. Cf. I Sam. 17: 38–54.

Hymn 5: 'Jesus, whose blood so freely stream'd'

Most later editions read 'Jehovah-Shalom' in the title, to accord with the verse of Judges cited. Newton may, however, have had in mind Heb. 7: 2.

Hymn 6: 'Ere God had built the mountains'

The paraphrase from Proverbs ends at l. 16.

ll. 25–8. Cf. 1 Pet. 2: 23–4.

l. 31. Cf. Rev. 14: 2.

l. 32. Cf. Matt. 9: 13.

Hymn 7: 'God gives his mercies to be spent'

This hymn is referred to Ecclesiastes, but not to a specific text.

l. 24. Cf. Deut. 33: 27.

Hymn 8: 'I will praise thee ev'ry day'

l. 20. Cf. Joel 3: 17.

Hymn 9: 'The Lord will happiness divine'

l. 15. Cf. Ps. 40: 13.

Hymn 10: 'Hear what God the Lord hath spoken'

It is uncertain whether the readings of *1779* represent revisions by Newton, or misreadings of his transcription; however, since they include one undoubted error, it has seemed best to incorporate all the variants found in M. F. C. Cowper's Commonplace Book.

l. 5. *Thorns of heart-felt tribulation.* 'Themes' (*1779*) is wrong; the reference is to Hos. 2: 6. The mistake was put right in the third edition (1783), but reappears in the fourth (1787) and many subsequent editions.

Hymn 15: 'There is a fountain fill'd with blood'

Untitled in Conyers's *Collection*.

ll. 5–6. Cf. Luke 23: 39–43.

Hymn 18: 'Hark, my soul! it is the Lord'

Its appearance in 1768 in the *Collection of Psalms and Hymns Extracted from Various Authors* edited by T. Maxfield, Assistant Chaplain to the Countess of Huntingdon, indicates that this is one of Cowper's earlier hymns. It may well antedate his association with Newton. It was later printed in the *Gospel Magazine*, vi. 370 (Aug. 1771), signed 'Omega'; and by R. Conyers, *A Collection of Psalms and Hymns*, 1772, pp. 57-8, entitled 'The Voice of Christ'.

Hymn 22: 'Bestow, dear Lord, upon our youth'

Nos. 22-4 appear under the general heading, 'Hymns before annual Sermons to young people, on new-years' evenings'. The New Year was a season which Newton observed specially both in Olney and later in London, as many references in his letters indicate. It is noteworthy that 31 of the 42 hymns relating to 'Seasons' in Book II are referred to the beginning or the end of the year, although this is not a 'season' recognized by the Church's calendar, as Russell points out (*Bibliography*, p. 16).

Hymn 23: 'Sin has undone our wretched race'

l. 24. Cf. Amos 4: 12.

Hymn 25: 'My song shall bless the Lord of all'

The title joins Old and New Testaments, and may be roughly translated 'The Eternal-the Lord will save'.

l. 9. Cf. Luke 2: 16.

ll. 11-12. Cf. Gen. 1.

l. 16. Cf. Isa. 7: 14.

Hymn 26: 'Jesus, where'er thy people meet'

Written for the opening, early in April 1769, of the Great Room for prayer meetings. This Room, 'a noble place, with a parlour behind it', was part of the Great House, a mansion belonging to the Earl of Dartmouth and conveniently located close to the Olney church. The House was unoccupied, and a smaller room had hitherto been used for prayer meetings; now the Earl had given his permission for the use of the larger space. The Great Room held about 130 people, and accommodated the more populous meetings on Tuesday and Sunday evenings. The opening was planned for Tuesday, 4 April 1769, but may have been postponed for a week (*Letters by the Reverend John Newton*, ed. Josiah Bull, 1869, p. 65).

l. 16. Identical with Milton, *Il Penseroso*, l. 166 (Bailey).

Hymn 27: 'This is the feast of heav'nly wine'

l. 3. Cf. John 15: 1.

Hymn 29: 'What various hind'rances we meet'

l. 2. The question mark instead of exclamation at the end of this line, as at no. 48, l. 2, suggests that the compositor of *1779* had trouble in distinguishing these symbols in Newton's handwriting.

l. 6. Cf. Gen. 28: 10–19.

l. 24. Cf. Ps. 66: 16.

Hymn 31: 'His Master taken from his Head'

ll. 1–4. Cf. 2 Kgs. 2: 12.

ll. 9–10. Cf. 1 Cor. 3: 4–6; 2 Tim. 4: 7.

Hymn 32: 'My former hopes are fled'

l. 3–4. Cf. Eph. 2: 1, 5; Col. 2: 13.

l. 7. Cf. Rom. 3: 20.

l. 12. Cf. Matt. 3: 7.

Hymn 33: 'Breathe from the gentle South, O Lord'

This hymn was written by John Newton. In the Preface to *Olney Hymns*, Newton explains that he has distinguished Cowper's compositions by prefixing to each the letter 'C'. Unfortunately, one of his own was so marked in the first edition. Cowper mentions this twice in letters to Thomas Park (20 July 1792, 5 Jan. 1793), but he did not have the book to hand and could not specify the error. The identification of the interloper has been made more difficult by the inconsistencies of marking in later editions of *Olney Hymns*, and by the assertions of Hayley and John Johnson, apparently following a mis-statement by Greatheed in his memorial sermon (*A Practical Improvement of the Divine Counsel*, Newport Pagnell, 1800, p. 15) that Cowper had written sixty-eight of the *Hymns*. The problem was solved by Kenneth Povey, who observed that in the second edition the 'C' was removed from the headings of the first ten hymns of Book III so marked in the first edition (8, 10, 13, 15–20, 23), while in the third edition it was restored to all but no. 10, which in subsequent editions is consistently ascribed to Newton. He deduced that the printer of the second edition had misunderstood an instruction to delete the 'C' from the heading of no. 10, and therefore that this hymn was composed by Newton. This conclusion is confirmed by stylistic considerations; see *Poetical Works*, rev. Russell, 1967, p. 681.

Hymn 34: 'To those who know the Lord I speak'

ll. 3–4. Cf. Isa. 61: 10.

l. 5. Cf. Isa. 53: 3.

Hymn 35: 'God moves in a mysterious way'

The date rests on the authority of Greatheed, who says in his memorial sermon: 'Our departed friend conceived some presentiment of this sad reverse [the collapse of January 1773] as it drew near; and during a solitary walk in the fields, he composed a hymn, which is so appropriate to our subject, and so expressive of the faith and hope which he retained so long as he possessed himself . . .' (*A Practical Improvement of the Divine Counsel*, Newport Pagnell, 1800, p. 18, followed by the hymn).

The copy in the Maitland–Madan Commonplace Book is headed: 'Hymn by Mr. William Cowper of Olney, sent me, by the Reverend Mr. Newton. February 18, 1773.' While the reading 'Beneath' in l. 15 is unsupported elsewhere and almost certainly an error of transcription, the fact that this dated early copy and the undated copy in M. F. C. Cowper's Commonplace Book agree in l. 20 against all the printed texts from 1774 onward suggests that Newton revised this line to give it a less striking form for publication.

Newton's 1774 text was reprinted by R. Conyers, *A Collection of Psalms and Hymns*, rev. ed., 1774, pp. 258–9. The hymn's appearance in the *Gospel Magazine, or Treasury of Divine Knowledge* in July of that year (i. 307), signed 'J. W.', is probably the result of circulation in manuscript, since it exhibits a corrupt reading, 'never-fading', in l. 6. A text closely resembling Newton's 1774 text, but entitled 'Providence', was printed by Augustus Montague Toplady, *Psalms and Hymns for Public and Private Worship*, 1776, p. 131, and thence reprinted by William Taylor and Herbert Jones, *A Collection of Psalms and Hymns*, 1777, p. 142.

A text resembling *O*, but reading 'everlasting' in l. 6, appears under the title 'On Providence' in the anonymously edited *Collection of Hymns for Public Worship*, York, 1774, p. 133.

Title. Alludes to 2 Pet. 1: 19, and John 1: 5.

ll. 13–16. Quoted by Newton, without attribution, in Letter VI to Mrs. ——, dated '1772', in *Cardiphonia* (1781), ii. 276. This quotation further confirms the reading 'Behind' in l. 15. In the passage immediately preceding, Newton cites John 13: 7, a reference to which is given at l. 21 of this hymn in *Olney Hymns*.

Hymn 36: ''Tis my happiness below'

This hymn appears in *O* immediately following no. 35, and headed: 'By the Same. 1773.' In *C* it is headed: 'Hymn by Mr. W. C. of Olney. 1773.' The dates should of course be taken as dates of transcription, not of composition. It seems likely that both these copies derive ultimately from a common source, but in the absence of any indication of provenance it has seemed best to choose *1779* for copy-text.

According to Julian's *Dictionary of Hymnology*, 1907, p. 1178, this hymn appeared about 1774 in a collection of hymns published for the use of the chapel of the Countess of Huntingdon's Connection in Bath, but no copy of that edition has been located (see Russell, p. 17).

Hymn 37: 'O how I love thy holy word'

l. 24. Cf. Heb. 4: 9.

Hymn 38: 'The billows swell, the winds are high'

ll. 1–8. Cf. Mark 4: 37–9.

Hymn 39: 'God of my life, to thee I call'

l. 7. Cf. John 10: 9.
ll. 11–12. Cf. Isa. 45: 19.

Hymn 40: 'My soul is sad and much dismay'd'

Wright says that this hymn was inspired by lectures of Newton's on *Pilgrim's Progress* (*Life of Cowper*, 1892, p. 199). Newton was lecturing on *Pilgrim's Progress* at a meeting at the Great House on 1 December 1772, little more than a month before Cowper relapsed into insanity (Josiah Bull, *John Newton*, 1868, p. 183). The reference to Apollyon does seem to point to Bunyan rather than to the Book of Revelation, but the connection of the hymn with Newton's lecture remains uncertain. The anguished tone of the hymn, although consistent with what is known of Cowper's state of mind late in 1772, is not a reliable guide to the date of composition.

Title. Cf. Ps. 23: 4.
l. 3. *Apollyon*. Cf. Rev. 9: 11.
l. 5. Cf. Rev. 20: 10, etc.
l. 15. Cf. Heb. 4: 12.

Hymn 41: 'When darkness long has veil'd my mind'

l. 11. Cf. 1 John 4: 8; Mal. 3: 6.
l. 12. Cf. Jas. 1: 17.

Hymn 42: 'The Saviour hides his face!'

ll. 7–8. Cf. Ps. 42: 1.

Hymn 43: 'Dear Lord accept a sinful heart'

Newton's text was reprinted by R. Conyers, *A Collection of Psalms and Hymns*, new ed., 1774, pp. 256–7.

Hymn 44: 'Lord, who hast suffer'd all for me'

l. 7. Cf. Exod. 3: 2.

l. 8. Cf. Eccles. 7: 6.

ll. 13–16. Cf. Josh. 7: 21.

ll. 17–18. Cf. Matt. 26: 67; 27: 29.

Hymn 45: 'O Lord, my best desire fulfill'

l. 8. Cf. Isa. 25: 8.

l. 20. Cf. Job 4: 19.

Hymn 46: 'How blest thy creature is, O God'

In the Maitland–Madan Commonplace Book this and the next hymn appear following the end of Cowper's account of his conversion (i.e. the *Memoir*, here joined with his narrative of his brother's conversion as *Adelphæ*). They are preceded by this note:

N.B. I have added two Hymns, which I compos'd *at St. Albans*, not for the composition, but because they are specimens of my first Christian thoughts, being written very shortly after my conversion, and I am glad to present them, because I cannot read them over now, without feeling *that joy of heart*, which the Lord gave me, *fresh'ning as it were*, upon my mind, at the perusal of them. (*O*, p. 86.)

A note on p. 112 shows that the hymns were copied in September 1772 from Newton's transcript of Cowper's narratives. They are headed 'Hymn I' and 'Hymn II'. In both, each line begins with quotation marks, which are omitted in the present text.

Title. Cf. Rev. 21: 5.

l. 4. Cf. Luke 1: 78.

ll. 7–8. Cf. Mal. 4: 2.

l. 9. Cf. Isa. 35: 7 (noted in *1779*).

l. 17. *golden/Silver* (*O*). The reading of *O* was perhaps suggested by the next line, which might be taken to refer to the moon.

l. 20. *Goal.* Here in the rare sense of the starting-point of a race (cf. *OED*), although in the case of the sun this is of course the end also. Cf. *Charity*, ll. 555–6.

Hymn 47: 'Far from the World, O Lord I flee'

See preceding note. Greatheed, in his funeral sermon (*A Practical Improvement of the Divine Counsel*, Newport Pagnell, 1800, pp. 13–14) says that Cowper wrote no. 46 shortly after his conversion experience, and this hymn 'when entering on his retirement'—i.e. his retirement to Huntingdon in

1765. But Greatheed may have inferred this order of composition from the hymns, and may indeed have been influenced by the title given this hymn in *1779*. Since he does not claim Cowper's authority explicitly at this point, his testimony should perhaps be received with caution.

ll. 19–20. The changes in these lines may have been made to forestall any charges of unseemly eroticism in addresses to Christ.

Hymn 48: 'To tell the Saviour all my wants'

The reference to 'former friends' in l. 17 suggests that this, like the two preceding hymns, may have been written soon after Cowper's conversion.

Hymn 49: 'Sometimes a light surprizes'

ll. 3–4. Cf. Mal. 4: 2.

ll. 7–8. Cf. 2 Sam. 23: 4.

Hymn 52: 'I was a groveling creature once'

ll. 9–12. Cf. Deut. 34: 1–4.

ll. 19–20. Cf. 1 Cor. 10: 12.

Hymn 53: 'When Hagar found the Bottle spent'

Newton may well be responsible for the revisions found in the *1779* text. The alteration of l. 3 obviates the objection (noted by Povey) that in Genesis 21 the angel does not, strictly speaking, guide Hagar to the well. The new l. 19 is simpler, and points the lesson of the hymn more clearly, thus making it more apt for public use.

Three scripture references are provided in *1779*: l. 1, Gen. 21: 19; l. 5, 1 Kgs. 17: 14; l. 12, Isa. 33: 16.

Hymn 54: 'I thirst, but not as once I did'

ll. 11–12. Cf. Isa. 55: 13.

Hymn 56: 'Sin enslav'd me many years'

While the conversion described here is a conventional one in its outline, the second stanza gives sufficient detail to suggest that this hymn is genuinely autobiographical. It may be an early composition.

Hymn 58: 'The new-born child of gospel-grace'

ll. 15–16. The early editions all open the speech in l. 15, making nonsense of the passage.

Hymn 60: 'The Lord receives his highest praise'

l. 6. *the precepts' holy light.* That is, the Ten Commandments, in allusion to Prov. 6: 23.

Hymn 61: 'Too many Lord, abuse thy grace'

The change of title somewhat softens the application of this hymn, reflecting perhaps Newton's desire, expressed in the Preface to *Olney Hymns*, to avoid religious discord.

Hymn 62: 'What thousands never knew the road!'

l. 1. Cf. Matt. 7: 14.

l. 12. Cf. Gen. 3: 18.

Hymn 64: 'Grace, triumphant in the throne'

ll. 15–16. Cf. Rev. 6: 16.

'TALES ET NOSTRI VIGUISSENT, JESUS, AMORES' and 'CÆSA EST NOSTRA COLUMBA, ET NOSTRO CRIMINE, CUJUS'

Both these poems are written in Cowper's hand on the verso of the title-page of a copy of John Gill, *An Exposition of the Book of Solomon's Song, Commonly Called Canticles*, 2nd ed., 1751. The first is dated precisely, and it is probable that the second was likewise written early in 1774.

On the back of the frontispiece portrait of Gill is written, in Cowper's hand: 'Given by Wm Cowper to his dear Friend and Brother in Christ, John Newton.' There is no date, but the expression 'Brother in Christ' places the inscription before Cowper's crisis of January 1773. Cowper had access to this souvenir of happier days when he was being cared for at the Vicarage, from April 1773 to May 1774.

In his introduction to the two lines printed in the *Monthly Magazine*, Dyer reports 'a circumstance mentioned by a person of a poetical genius, of St. John's [College, Cambridge], who, when at college, used to visit Mr. Newton, of Olney, at whose house the ingenious and amiable Mr. Cowper then resided; it was, that in some of his most melancholy moments, he used to write lines affectingly descriptive of his own unhappy state'. Reprinting the lines in his *Privileges of the University of Cambridge*, ii, 1824, 3rd arabic pagination, p. 111, Dyer identified his informant as the Revd. Brian Bury Collins (?1752–?1807), who was a sizar of St. John's College from 1771 to 1775, and who had strong Methodist sympathies. Dyer's text begins: 'Caesa Amor meus est', and reads 'posthinc potero' in l. 2; these are probably memorial variants.

The Cowper Museum copy of Gill's *Exposition* was bought at the Newton sale by a Mr. John Poynder, and was passed down in the Poynder family until it was presented to the Museum in 1930 by F. C. Poynder. John Poynder, in a long note on the front flyleaf, offers literal translations of the Latin. Slightly revised, they read thus:

I. Such also, O Jesus, would our loves have flourished, had not your right hand deserted its own work. Now I have enemies as numerous as there are gods and men; alas! what a sacrificial offering, by how great a death, do I fall.

II. My dove is slain, and by my own crime; ah! under whose, under whose wings shall I henceforth take shelter? There is no escape. Never will thunderbolts charged with such destructive fury strike so accursed a wretch.

Both refer to the subject of Gill's book, the Song of Solomon. The first line of the second poem refers specifically to 6: 9. 'Monstrum' means literally 'a portent, a prodigy, something against the course of nature'.

'HATRED AND VENGEANCE, MY ETERNAL PORTION'

This poem has traditionally been assigned to 1763, on the basis of a guess in a footnote in the Cox edition of Cowper's *Memoirs* (1816, p. 61), which Southey converted into a downright statement of fact (i. 141). Povey, however, has established 1774 as the likely date of composition by both internal and external evidence: (1) the belief underlying the poem—that his case is unique—is one that Cowper came to hold after the crisis of 1773, and not before; (2) this belief also appears in the Latin verses Cowper wrote in Gill's *Exposition* (see above), the first quatrain of which is dated 8 Feb. 1774; (3) the poem was written on the same sheet of paper as 'Heu quam remotus', dated 31 Dec. 1774. For a general account of that lost manuscript, see above, Introduction, p. xxviii.

Bruce (iii. 340) notes 'a curious similarity between these dreadful sapphics and a poem by Francis Davison upon the passion of Christ, commencing, 'Hatred Eternal! Furious revenging!'' The poem is not by Davison, but anonymous; the resemblance is at best superficial (cf. H. E. Rollins, ed., *A Poetical Rhapsody 1602–1621*, Cambridge, Mass., 1931, i. 198).

l. 15. *Fall'n, and | I'm call'd*. It would be easy to misread Cowper's capital F as I'; the reverse error would be very difficult. 'Fated' (*1835*) is speciously attractive but an obvious emendation (cf. l. 19 n.). Southey suggested 'in anguish' for 'if vanquish'd', which is mere tampering, but the sense of the passage is difficult: Cowper seems to say that *if* vanquished he *will* receive the punishment that he *is* (l. 19) now receiving. But we should not expect Cowper's logic to be impeccable in a poem like this.

l. 16. *Abiram*. One of those who rebelled with Korah against the authority of Moses and Aaron; see Numbers 16. (The name is spelt 'Abiron' in the Vulgate and the Douai Bible, which probably accounts for the spelling 'Abyron' in *G*, copied by the Roman Catholic Courtenay.) Verse 30 is particularly relevant: 'But if the Lord make a new thing, and the earth open her mouth, and swallow them up, with all that appertain unto them, and they go down quick into the pit; then ye shall understand that these men have provoked the Lord.'

l. 19. *fed with judgments*. From Ezekiel 34: 16. The reading of *1835*, 'judgment', is probably an emendation made by someone who recalled this passage; Southey, who did not, stigmatized 'fed' as corrupt.

'HEU QUAM REMOTUS VESCOR AB OMNIBUS'

In connection with the date, 'die ultimo 1774', it may be noted that the New Year, although not a holy day of the Church of England, was an occasion to which Newton attached considerable significance. *Olney Hymns*, for instance, contains six hymns for the New Year, twenty-three for Newton's New Year sermons to young people, and two for 'the close of the year' (Book II. i–xxix, xli, xlii). It is therefore not surprising that Cowper should look back on his situation at the end of December.

The manuscript in Cowper's hand, now lost, in which this poem was found is described above in the Introduction, p. xxviii.

The poem is somewhat cryptic, and hard to translate; the following is rather free:

Alas, how remote I live from all whose company I used to enjoy under the paternal roof; how I am forgotten, I who have quitted that once joyful region, that home, those companions.

And above all, you are a cause of lamentation to me, you, dearer than light or limbs, you who are mine in the nuptial bond—I forsook you, left you shivering under the stroke.

But my father did not beget me to be unfeeling, nor did a lioness in a cave filled with thorn-bushes rear me at her breast to be footloose; but this my fate willed.

And, just as the waves of the sea are moved, while I was vexed by a thousand fears, I was compelled into the jaws of Avernus, I perished completely in the black river.

l. 5. The reference is to Theadora Cowper.

l. 16. *amne*. The Styx.

THE CANTAB.

A translation of Vincent Bourne's 'Eques Academicus' (see Appendix II).

On 13 July 1777 Cowper asked Joseph Hill, through whom he was borrowing books from a circulating library, to send him 'Vincent Bourne's Latin Poems the last Edition'; he returned the volume about 23 October. However, this request does not necessarily mean that he did not then possess a copy of Bourne's poems, and therefore that his translations must have been made during the period indicated. The specified 'last Edition' was the greatly augmented quarto of 1772, which the owner of an earlier edition might well wish to consult. Cowper is known to have possessed at one time or another two of the earlier editions: his copy of the 1750 edition, signed and dated 'June 5, 1758', is now in the Clark Library, Los Angeles; a copy of the 1743 edition was in his library when he died (Sir G. Keynes, 'The Library of William Cowper', *Trans. Cambridge Bibl. Soc.* iii, pt. 1 (1960), 47, 54). Whether or not he had a copy of his own, his interest in Bourne in 1777 suggests that this, and the four other translations published in 1782, may have been made at that time.

Neither university is named in Bourne's original, but the title seems to be a jesting allusion to the fact that Unwin, like Bourne himself, was a Cambridge man.

ON THE TRIAL OF ADMIRAL KEPPEL

The MS. (Ash, fo. 5, same sheet as 'The Pine Apple and the Bee') is annotated by John Johnson 'about the end of the year 1778'; in fact, like the closely related poem which follows, it cannot have been composed before mid-February 1779. Both comment on events surrounding the trial by court martial on capital charges of negligence of Admiral Keppel (1725–86), and his honourable acquittal.

On 27 July the Channel fleet under Keppel engaged inconclusively with a superior French fleet, which retired to Brest. There was dissatisfaction with this result, culminating in a public accusation that Sir Hugh Palliser (1723–96), Vice-Admiral of the Blue, had ignored Keppel's orders to take his place in line. Palliser responded with a signed letter in the *Morning Post* laying all the blame on Keppel. After stormy debates in the House of Commons, of which both were members, Palliser, demanded, and the Admiralty granted, that Keppel be court-martialled. Great public sympathy was shown for Keppel both before and during the trial, which ran from 7 January to 11 February 1779, because he was seen as the innocent victim of a corrupt Admiralty and an unpopular administration; the fleet fired congratulatory salutes on his acquittal, and London was illuminated in his honour. See T. Keppel, *Life of Augustus Viscount Keppel*, London, 1842, ii. 75–187.

AN ADDRESS TO THE MOB
ON OCCASION OF THE LATE RIOT AT THE
HOUSE OF SIR HUGH PALLISER

The MS. *A* is annotated by John Johnson 'about the end of the year 1778', but this is impossible, since the event which gave rise to the poem occurred on the night of 11 February 1779, when the London mob, celebrating Keppel's acquittal, broke into Palliser's house in Pall Mall and burned his furniture in St. James's Square, later burning him in effigy on Tower Hill (T. Keppel, *Life of Augustus Viscount Keppel*, ii. 190–1).

ll. 15–18 probably refer, not to any remark made at Palliser's subsequent court martial (as Bailey's note implies), but to the comment made by Keppel during his court martial, on his official report of the action of 27 July: 'It commends Sir Hugh Palliser. It does what I meant to do. I meant to commend his bravery, or what appeared to me as such, in the engagement' (Keppel, ii. 153).

TRANSLATION OF THE 16TH. ODE OF
THE 2D. BOOK OF HORACE

Cowper's translation, as it stands in *H*, is a stanza-for-stanza, if not a line-for-line version of Horace's ode. The eighth stanza was probably omitted from *M* (presumably the earlier manuscript) on account of the difficulty of handling the mythological names in an English version; the solution was to express the point in general rather than specific terms—the only instance in which Cowper manifestly deserts his original (see notes below).

l. 10. *a Consul's Guard*. In Horace, 'consularis . . . lictor'.

ll. 29–30. Horace cites two examples from mythology:

> abstulit clarum cita mors Achillem,
> longa Tithonum minuit senectus . . . .

l. 35. *the best Purple Tyre affords*. 'African purple' in Horace.

ll. 36–40. Cowper's emphasis differs from Horace's: 'the Sparing One ['Parca', i.e. Fate], properly so called, has given me a little country place and the light breath of Greek song and to scorn the envious crowd.'

A TALE, FOUNDED ON A FACT, WHICH
HAPPENED IN JANUARY, 1779

The date of composition is uncertain, but must lie between that of the events described and the inscription of *H* in the summer of 1780.

The text presents difficulties. *1803* differs considerably from *H*. While some of the divergencies might be explained as examples of editorial inter-ference by Hayley (e.g., 'improvements' in ll. 32, 33; ll. 43–5 omitted as being unduly pietistic), it yet seems unlikely that Hayley based his text on *H*, to which he certainly had access. This impression is confirmed by the fact that in four instances *1803*, *C*, *AM*, *SR* all agree on a reading, against *H*. We deduce that Cowper revised the poem after it was inscribed in *H*, and that the other texts derive from that revision. But these four texts differ from each other, and it is hard to reconstruct the lost archetype. It is clear that circulation in manuscript may account for variants in *AM* and *SR*, and we know from other evidence that Hayley felt free to alter and omit; that Mrs. Cowper was an inaccurate copyist, reducing *C*'s credibility; that the type-setting of the *Arminian Magazine* was exceedingly careless. Since *C* and *1803* are the texts most likely to have been copied from an exemplar in Cowper's hand, we have displaced the readings of *H* only when *C* and *1803* agree with each other against *H*. In l. 44 we follow *C*, *AM*, *SR* against *H*; here there is no *1803* either to confirm (cf. l. 14) or to deny (cf. l. 36) the reading shared by these three. There is too some theological basis for preferring 'Gain'd' to 'Seiz'd' (see note).

The *AM* text is headed 'Dawgreen, near Wakefield, Feb. 28, 1781'. This provides a *terminus ante quem* for the revision of the poem, and also suggests a source for this text. For Dawgreen, as Povey points out, is a hamlet in the parish of Dewsbury, the vicar of which was the Revd. Matthew Powley, Mrs. Unwin's son-in-law. He is unlikely to have submitted the poem to the *Arminian Magazine* himself, but it is highly likely that the poem circulated in manuscript in his parish, and thus found its way into the Methodist publication.

It is not known when or how Cowper heard the story on which this poem is based. The story is given with the poem by Wills in *SR*, and both were reprinted in a number of pamphlets against cock-fighting; see Russell, pp. 147–9. The alleged incident took place near Leeds; the name of the short-lived convert is not recorded, but the 'Fellow Lab'rer' of l. 14 was called Robert Hazlem.

l. 17. *had taken Place*. In a sense now obsolete, 'had weight or influence'. The narrative in this central section is far from clear, largely because of Cowper's carelessness with pronouns: 'His' (l. 19) and 'He' (l. 23) refer to the protagonist.

l. 43. *the Race allotted him to Run*. Cf. Heb. 12: 1: 'the race that is set before us'.

l. 44. *Just Enter'd in the Lists he Gain'd* [*Seized H*] *the Crown*. The textual prob-lem here seems to arise out of some confusion of thought. The athletic metaphor of the previous line apparently betrayed Cowper into setting his hero in a place of contest, not against the world, but against other potential martyrs; this impropriety is softened by the reading 'Gain'd'. Cf. the revision, in the same direction, in 'Truth', l. 589: from 'the Christian gains the prize' to 'and faith receives the prize'. 'On the list' (*SR*) is a good emendation, 'list' (sing.) being the starting-point of a race.

THE BEE AND THE PINE APPLE

Cowper wrote to William Unwin on 3 December 1778 that he had been given 'Six Fruiting Pines' by the gardener at Mr. Wrighte's home, Gayhurst House (located one mile beyond Weston Underwood on the Newport Pagnell road). These ought to have been flowering in their frame in the following April, when apricots and peaches would also have been in bloom (P. Miller, *Gardeners Kalendar*, 4th ed., London, 1737, pp. 96, 119). 'The Bee and the Pine Apple' was therefore presumably written sometime during the five months or so before Cowper sent his other, and probably later, treatment of the same subject to Joseph Hill on 2 October 1779 (see 'The Pine Apple and the Bee').

The text in *H* is verbally identical with *A*, but it is clearly a fair copy; the punctuation has been revised, to the advantage of the sense, and such abbreviated forms as '&' and 'y̆' are written out in full. The title of *A* is retained here to prevent confusion.

ΕΠΙΝΙΚΙΟΝ

There is no external evidence as to date of composition, but in content and in spirit this seems to belong with the patriotic poems of the autumn of 1779.

ΕΠΙΝΙΚΙΟΝ. The title means 'victory song'; Cowper was no doubt familiar with the word as applied to the victory songs of Pindar.

l. 3. *Her Eastern Empire*. Pondicherry, the last French foothold in India, capitulated on 16 October 1778. In the West Indies, France lost St. Lucia to the British late in 1778—but took St. Vincent the following year.

TO SIR JOSHUA REYNOLDS

The copy in *U* (fos. 90–1) is bound in between Cowper's letters to Unwin of 26 November and 15 December 1781; to the poem is prefixed the following, in Cowper's hand:

In a time of so much national Distress, when War with one Country seems to beget War with another by a kind of necessary and unavoidable procreation, it is fit that somebody beside the Laureat, should now and then sing [her *deleted*] poor Britannia a Song of Encouragement, and as far at least as a few Verses can do it, endeavor to cheer her Spirits. His Muse is known to be an Hireling, and gains the less respect to what she produces upon that account. Mine is a Volunteer, disinterested and free, her Word therefore may be taken especially when she proposes to prophecy, which is a serious Business and not to be trifled with. You are welcome to make what Use you please of the following. It is a year old, but the public Affairs give it even a greater propriety now than it had when it was first composed.

This is neither dated nor signed, but above is written in Unwin's hand:

March 19. The following came to my hand above a Year ago—which is needful to be remembered.—I wish Mr. Cowper did not dwell so much on England's Glory—which for the present I doubt is a Non-Entity.

Povey notes that the poem with its preface has the appearance of being prepared for submission to a newspaper or magazine; Unwin had merely to direct the MS. to an editor. He seems not to have done so.

The copy in *H*, inscribed in the summer of 1780, lacks the two lines which refer to Holland; Britain declared war on the Dutch on 20 December 1780, accusing them of treaty-violations in trading with the Americans (*Annual Register*, xxiii, for 1780, 376–9). This event was clearly the occasion for the preparation of *U*. Unwin therefore wrote his note on 19 March 1782. If the poem was 'a year old' in December 1780, it was originally composed late in 1779, a dating which is confirmed by Cowper's references to this and 'A Present for the Queen of France' in his letters to Hill and Newton of 2 and 4 December 1781, where he says that they were written two or three years before.

Cowper may well have seen Reynolds's early works before he left London in 1763, but there is little in the poem to suggest that it is addressed to Reynolds for any other reason than that, as President of the Royal Academy, he was the official representative of British art. The poem is, in fact, akin to the 'instructions to a painter' poems of the Restoration period; the picture it suggests, in so far as it would be paintable, is a political cartoon.

l. 10. *the Muse.* None of the Muses is responsible for painting; their 'special Mandate' is that of a committee acting *ultra vires*.

l. 13. *Tintz (H).* This formation of the plural with the letter -z is unique in Cowper's MSS. He may have felt the word to be foreign, or he may have wished to call attention to it as a technical term. Lord Chesterfield used a final -z in French words where we should expect -s, as, *succez, bontez* (*The Letters of Philip Dormer Stanhope*, ed. B. Dobrée, 1932, i. xxiv).

l. 20. *a paper kite.* Cowper describes a kite of the 'pear' type, still familiar as a children's toy. The words 'Blaze like a Meteor' (l. 22) suggest that he may have had in mind the use of kites in firework displays; possibly he recalled the episode of Sidrophel's astronomical theorizing over a boy's kite in Butler's *Hudibras*, II. iii. 413 ff. Kite-flying is apposite here because of Franklin's famous experiment with a kite in a thunderstorm (reported by Joseph Priestley, *The History and Present State of Electricity*, London, 1767, pp. 180–1), which gave rise to the inscription on the French medallion struck in his honour in 1778: 'Eripuit coelo fulmen, sceptrumque tyrannis.' See C. Hart, *Kites: An Historical Survey*, London, 1967, pp. 73–80, 84–5.

A PRESENT FOR THE QUEEN OF FRANCE

Cowper's letters to Hill and Newton of 2 and 4 December 1781 indicate that this poem was composed about the same time as 'To Sir Joshua Reynolds', both inspired by the unsuccessful attempts of the French admiral, d'Estaing, to recapture St. Lucia (December 1778) and Savannah (October 1779).

The copy in *H* is the only manuscript known. On first seeing it, Hayley wrote to Lady Hesketh (28 July 1802): 'the Poem on the Queens of England & France I would not print upon any account—as it appears to me utterly unworthy of our dear Bard' (B.L. Add. MS. 30803B, fo. 60).

l. 10. We have not been able to trace the presentation of the watch.

l. 30. *Great and Good.* This phrase, also in 'To Sir Joshua Reynolds', l. 26, is taken from the letter dated 17 July 1778 from Henry Laurens, President of Congress, to the royal commissioners who offered tentative peace terms in the summer of 1778: 'Nothing but an earnest desire to spare the further effusion of human blood could have induced them [the Congress] to read a paper, containing expressions so disrespectful to his Most Christian Majesty, the great and good ally of these states' (quoted in *Gentleman's Magazine*, xlviii (1778), 366–7).

ON THE VICTORY GAINED BY SIR GEORGE RODNEY

On 16 January 1780, at night in a storm off Cape St. Vincent, an English fleet under Admiral Sir George Brydges Rodney (1719–92) defeated a squadron of the Spanish navy and thus relieved Gibraltar. Letters from Rodney confirming this success reached London on 28 February (*Gentleman's Magazine*, l (1780), 145–7), and on the following two days thanks were voted to him, first by the Commons and then by the Lords. In addition, the opposition wanted Rodney to be appointed to some lucrative post, since his financial embarrassments were notorious. 'The post of Lieutenant General of the Marines, which had been instituted as a reward for extraordinary merit and service, and which had unusually continued vacant ever since the resignation of Sir Hugh Palliser [a year before; see above, 'An Address to the Mob'], was the immediate object which the opposition had in view, in favour of Sir George Rodney; but this was mentioned only as matter of conversation, or proposal to the ministers, as they would not seem to prescribe to the crown by any specification' (*Annual Register*, xxiii, for 1780,

123). Cowper in his title, though not in his poem, seems to have taken the opposition's wish for the sovereign's deed.

l. 2. *The Trojan Hero*. Aeneas—but he plucked the Golden Bough above ground, before his descent into the Underworld, and not in Tartarus itself (*Aeneid*, vi. 201–11). The allusion is to the badge of the Royal Marines, a globe surrounded by a laurel wreath.

A SIMILE TRANSLATED FROM *PARADISE LOST*

The date of composition is not certain, but the passage in Cowper's letter to Unwin of 8 June 1780 which introduces the 'Simile' indicates that it is being sent in return for two Latin inscriptions which Unwin had sent to Cowper; it may therefore have been written shortly before that date. Hayley, printing from the letter to Unwin, omitted the fourth line, perhaps, as Milford suggested, because Cowper wrote 'Nimbosumque' instead of the correct 'Nimbosusque'. This mutilated version was frequently reprinted. The simile is found in *Paradise Lost*, ii. 488–95; the letter of 8 June suggests that he translated it from memory.

IN SEDITIONEM HORRENDAM

The Gordon Riots took place during the first week of June 1780. On the 18th of that month, Cowper wrote to William Unwin that as soon as he read in the paper the surmise that the Riots had been engineered by the French, he wrote Latin verses on the subject; that these verses were intended to mortify the French rather than comfort the English, and will therefore fail of their purpose, for he has no means of communicating them to the French; if Unwin thinks them insufficiently harsh, he is to burn them. Unwin did not take the hint that he should publish them.

There appear to have been numerous rumours that the Riots were instigated by French, Spanish, or American agents, but the probable stimulus of Cowper's poem is a handbill which was distributed in London on 8 June:

NO FRENCH RIOTERS. This is to give notice that it now appears, that the horrible riots which have been committed in this city, have been promoted by French money, and to call upon all honest men to stand forth against rioters, who, under the cloak of religion, are wantonly destroying our property, and endeavouring to overset our happy constitution. If the *French* are suffered, by these means, to prevail, Popery will certainly be introduced, which we have no reason to fear from a *British* Parliament. (*Political Magazine*, i (1780), 443.)

THE SAME IN ENGLISH

Hayley did not print this from *H* in *1803*, so it was first published as a part of the letter to Unwin of 11 July 1780, in which Cowper acknowledges receipt of several translations of 'In Seditionem Horrendam' and now furnishes his own. This, he stipulates, is not to be published. *U* is here chosen as copy-text since it probably postdates *H*, which is dated 'June 1780'.

TRANSLATION OF AN EPITAPH FOR
WILLIAM NORTHCOT

Sent to William Unwin as part of the letter of 2 July 1780 (manuscript now lost), together with revised versions of Unwin's memorial inscription and his Latin verses. According to the inscription, William Northcot died, aged ten, on 7 April 1780; he was the only son of William and Mary Northcot, presumably parishioners of Unwin's. The Latin verses are given in the letter as follows (the last line is by Cowper):

> Care, vale! Sed non æternùm, care, valeto!
>   Namque iterùm tecum, sim modò dignus, ero.
> Tum nihil amplexus poterit divellere nostros,
>   Nec tu marcesces, nec lacrymabor ego.

EPIGRAMMA CELEBRATISSIMUM JOHANNIS DRYDEN

Sent in a letter to William Unwin on 11 July 1780; the passage which introduces it suggests that it was then a recent composition. Cowper remarks on the difficulty of translating Dryden's English, which he says is equal in 'closeness' to the most compact Latin. Dryden's epigram, which begins 'Three *Poets*, in three distant *Ages* born', was widely admired; see 'Hibernicus', 'Dryden's Epigram on Milton', *N & Q*, clxxiii (1937), 149-50.

A RIDDLE

In his letter to William Unwin of 18 June 1780 Cowper announces that he has 'lately' composed a riddle, but is too fatigued to transcribe it immediately. He sent it to Unwin as part of the letter of 27 July 1780, and to Newton, with apologies for its frivolity, on 31 July 1780. Hayley's omission of the last two lines, when he published the riddle as part of the letter to Newton, was undoubtedly on the ground of their impropriety.

The answer, 'a kiss', was given in verses signed 'J. T.' in the *Gentleman's Magazine*, lxxvi (1806), 1224.

l. 3. *Fau'lt*. The apostrophe indicates that the *l* of 'Fault' should not be pronounced, for the sake of the rhyme.

l. 5. *extra'ordinary*. The apostrophe indicates that the *a* and the *o* are to be run together into one syllable, for the sake of the metre.

TO MR. NEWTON ON HIS RETURN FROM RAMSGATE

This poem appears as part of a letter from Cowper to Newton of 13 October 1780, which is a reply to one sent by Newton on 11 October. In his letter Newton describes his visit to Ramsgate: 'I had one delightful morning at the North foreland, when I stood on the top of the light house & contemplated my old acquaintance the Sea.' The ex-slave-trader explains that the smoothness of the sea seemed to tempt him to return to it, but he recalled its deceitfulness, and would not trust it again. He then wrote the following verses:

> Thus on a height, in safety I survey,
> That wide, deceitful storm-vex'd sea, the World.
> How often there the thoughtless and the gay,
> Are lost: on rocks and on each other hurl'd.
> Kindled by thee, dear Lord, thus may I shine
> Timely to warn them of each dang'rous shelf,
> Rememb'ring well their perils once were mine,
> I fear for them, tho' now secure myself.

The original of Cowper's letter of 13 October 1780 is lost; in the copy which does survive, the text of the poem has no substantive variants from *H*, although it is untitled. The copy in a letter from Hayley to Lady Hesketh of 28 July 1802 is, as the context indicates, his transcription of *H* (B.L. Add. MS. 30803B, fo. 60). In the 1812 edition of Hayley's *Life*, 'of' (l. 1) is wrongly emended to 'have'; this reading was taken over into *1815*, and thence found its way into most nineteenth-century editions before Benham's.

Newton's brief holiday in Ramsgate was in the company of his patron, John Thornton (J. Bull, *John Newton*, 1868, p. 251). For Cowper's visits to Ramsgate, and his feelings about the place, see his letters to Unwin, (early) July and 17 July 1779, and to Mrs. Newton, 5 Oct. 1780; also Ryskamp, pp. 130–4.

l. 13. *Sea of Troubles.* Cf. *Hamlet*, III. i. 59.

THE YEARLY DISTRESS, OR, TYTHING TIME AT STOCK

The MS. *U* was sent through the mail, and is postmarked 30 OC[tober]. Povey reasoned that the year must be 1780, because of the reference, in the undated letter to Unwin which begins: 'You are sometimes indebted' to 'that Tragi-Comical Ditty for which you thank me'. This letter must have been written in the first half of November 1780, for it refers to the *Monthly Review* for October of that year as a recent publication. Povey's conclusion is confirmed by Newton's correspondence with Cowper; on 29 November 1780 Newton wrote that he had recently seen Unwin, who had told him of something that would enhance his collection of Cowperiana, 'a copy of verses you sent him for his consolation when he was perplex'd about parish business'; on 2 December Cowper replied that if Newton thought 'any thing so local as the Tything Time Ditty' worth having, he would send it.

There is some evidence that the poem had not taken its final form when it was inscribed in *H*: the deletion in l. 22, the later insertion of ll. 45–8, and some now illegible erasures in the penultimate stanza. There is no doubt that *U* is the final version of the poem.

On 7 September 1783 Cowper wrote Unwin that he had seen 'the Tything Time in the General Evening, but my Royal George in Latin I have not yet seen'. He referred almost certainly to the 4–6 September issue of the *General Evening Post*, since the poem does not appear in any other issue published during August or September, but that issue cannot be found. It is probable that the *General Evening Post* reprinted this poem from the *Public Advertiser* of 22 August. For that publication Unwin was undoubtedly responsible; the same newspaper published the 'Royal George in Latin' on 23 August 1780.

The location of the action is identified as 'Stock in Essex' in the title first in *1800*.

Some notion of the kind of event which Unwin dreaded every year may be gathered from the diary of his contemporary, the Revd. James Woodforde of Weston Longueville in Norfolk, as this for 1783: 'Dec. 2 . . . This being my Tithe Audit Day, the following People attended, and paid me every thing that was due. [A list of 25 names]—They all dined, spent the Afternoon and Evening till 10. o'clock, and then they all went to their respective homes, it being my desire that they would not stay after 10 o'clock. I gave them for Dinner a Leg of Mutton boiled, and Capers, some Salt Fish, plenty of Plumb Puddings and a Couple of boiled Rabbitts, with a fine large Surloin of Beef rosted. Plenty of Wine, Punch, and strong Beer after Dinner till 10 o'clock. We had this Year a very agreeable meeting here, and were very agreeable— no grumbling whatever.' (*The Diary of a Country Parson*, ed. J. Beresford, London, 1924–31, ii. 107–8.)

l. 1. Povey notes a resemblance to the first line of Air XII of Act I of Gay's *Beggar's Opera*: 'Oh, ponder well! be not severe'; sung to the air 'Now ponder well, ye parents dear'.

l. 65. *Boobies*. Although 'Boobies' and 'Loobies' are close in meaning, the former seems more appropriate in this context, since, according to *OED*, the latter is a word more often applied to boys than to grown mean, and these are bald-pated farmers.

TO MISS CREUZÉ ON HER BIRTHDAY

This is found in an undated letter from Cowper to William Unwin. Povey assigns the letter to November 1780, because in it Cowper mentions the *Monthly Review* for October 1780 as a recent publication, and because he also refers to the collecting of tythes (see notes to 'The Yearly Distress', above).

The Creuzés were friends of Unwin's, who stayed with them from time to time, as Cowper's correspondence indicates; his letter of 2 December 1780 is directed to Unwin 'at Mr. Crewzé's / Laytonstone / Essex'. Stella was perhaps the daughter of the 'Fra. Creuze, Esq; Leightonstone, Essex' who subscribed for a fine-paper copy of Cowper's *Homer*.

It appears that Unwin had asked for a poetical compliment which he might present to Miss Creuzé, for Cowper says in his letter: 'I have endeavour'd to comply with your Request, though I am not good at Writing upon a Given Subject.' And following the poem: 'If you like it, use it—if not, you know the Remedy. It is serious yet Epigrammatic, like a Bishop at a Ball.'

POEMS AGAINST MADAN'S THELYPHTHORA, *1780*

On 27 February 1780 Cowper informed William Unwin that 'a certain Kinsman of your humble Servant's has written a Tract, now in the Press, to prove Polygamy a Divine Institution. A plurality of Wives is intended, but not of Husbands.' The kinsman was Cowper's cousin, the Reverend Martin Madan (1725–90), and the book was his *Thelyphthora, or, A Treatise on Female Ruin*, published by Dodsley on 31 May 1780.

Martin Madan was Chaplain of the Lock Hospital, which had been established in 1747 'for the cure of females suffering from disorders contracted by a vicious course of life'. He was therefore in a position to see at first hand the social consequences of the sexual *mores* of the age. Too often a girl suffered the fate so dreaded by Richardson's Pamela: seduced and then cast off, she drifted down the social scale, became a street-walker and at last a hospital case—if she was lucky. Madan's cure was the reverse of conventional. He argues that copulation is by divine ordinance the act which makes a marriage, and that therefore the man who takes a girl's virginity must regard her, economically at least, as his wife, and as such entitled to a competence for life. Madan objects particularly to the Marriage Act of 1753, which laid down uniform conditions for a valid marriage: where the ceremony must be performed, by whom conducted, by whom witnessed, how registered. By this legislation, says Madan, 'we have reduced the most solemn of all ties to a sort of *civil institution*, the most sacred of all obligations to a mere *civil contract*; and where the *latter* can be avoided, the *former* is as *totally* vacated, as if it had never been.' He continues:

By God's express command from *Mount Sinai*, where the laws concerning *moral good and evil*, were eternally and unalterably fixed, no man could *take* a virgin and then *abandon* her. He shall surely endow her to be his wife. Exod. xxii. 16. And again Deut. xxii. 29. She shall be his wife; BECAUSE HE HAS HUMBLED HER, he may not put her away all his days. (i. 9–10.)

In the months before the book appeared, numerous appeals were made to Madan to suppress it. He refused to do so, and his opponents had to answer him in print. This was not easy, for Madan had been trained as a lawyer, and makes his case well. There were, accordingly, many attacks on the book and its author which were merely abusive, among which must be reckoned *Antithelyphthora*. Indeed, Cowper's knowledge of the book when he wrote the poem was entirely second-hand, though he did later read part of the second volume (to Newton, 23 Apr. 1781).

Cowper wrote several short poems against *Thelyphthora* in the course of spring and summer 1780; these are here brought together with *Antithelyphthora*. See also 'The Progress of Error'. This aspect of Cowper's career is studied by L. Hartley, 'Cowper and the Polygamous Parson', *Modern Language Quarterly*, xvi (1955), 137–41.

LOVE ABUSED. THE THOUGHT SUGGESTED BY *THELYPHTHORA*

This poem cannot be closely dated, but its position in *H* (p. 1) suggests composition before the beginning of June. The *H* text certainly predates that in *U* (fo. 40), which forms part of a letter dated 27 July 1780.

EPIGRAM ON *THELYPHTHORA*

Cowper first heard of Madan's *Thelyphthora* before 6 February 1780, when he thanked Newton for an advance copy of the title-page. This 'Epigram' was the second poem to be inscribed in *H* (p. 3), and was probably composed before the beginning of June 1780.

'IF JOHN MARRIES MARY . . .'

It is difficult to date this epigram. No manuscript is known to survive, although it is clear that Cowper sent a copy of it to Newton some weeks or more probably months before 25 November 1780, when Newton wrote: 'I saw your—If John marries Mary in one of the News-papers, but I had no hand in sending it there.' Cowper replied on 27 November that Newton was the only person to whom he had ever sent or showed a copy of this 'Bagatelle', nor had Cowper repeated it to anybody except Mrs. Unwin. 'The Inference is fair and easy, that you have some Friend who has a good Memory.'

Johnson prints the poem in his note to this passage in *Private Correspondence*, where he misdates Cowper's letter 27 November 1781. He gives no indication of his source. The newspaper printing to which Newton refers has not been traced; almost certainly it was from this that the *GM* text was taken. While *GM*'s title can scarcely be authentic—Cowper never read volume I of the *Thelyphthora*, in which the chapter on polygamy appears (To Newton, 23 Apr. 1781)—the variants in the third line just possibly may be Cowperian, and are therefore recorded.

According to John Johnson, the poem was printed [from *GM*?] in *Elegant Extracts in Verse*, but we have not been able to discover in which of the many editions of that famous anthology it appears.

ANTITHELYPHTHORA

We cannot be certain when Cowper began work on *Antithelyphthora*, but since the action of the poem is an allegory of the appearance of an article in the *Monthly Review* for October 1780, published at the end of that month, it cannot have been earlier than the beginning of November.

The date of completion can be established, but some of the evidence is missing. We have Cowper's letter to Newton of 27 November, but there must have been one written a day or two earlier which has been lost. On 25 November Newton sent to Cowper for his approval a letter intended for the Revd. Thomas Haweis; in his covering letter he mentions having seen 'If John Marries Mary' in a newspaper. Cowper's reply of 27 November, of which only the first part has been preserved, refers to that epigram, and also speaks of 'my Poem lately mentioned', clearly another work. Newton began a letter to Cowper on 28 November; on that day he wrote: 'The sooner you send the 192 verses the better.' On the following day he added that he had received Cowper's approval of his draft letter to Haweis, i.e. the letter of 27 November. It is clear that Cowper must have written to Newton on 25 or 26 November to announce that he had produced a 192-line poem.

The text of the poem as it was first inscribed in *H* runs not to 192 lines, however, but to 200 (misnumbered 199 by Cowper). This is *Antithelyphthora* as it was on 27 November, for in his letter to Newton of that date Cowper wrote: 'Mrs. Unwin having suggested the Hint, I have added just as many Lines to my Poem lately mentioned, as to make up the whole Number 200. I had no intention to write a round Sum, but it has happened so. She thought there was a fair Opportunity to give the Bishops a Slap, and as it would not have been civil to have denied a Lady so reasonable a Request, I have just made the Powder fly out of their Wigs a little.' Of the eight lines added, then, four are 129–32; probably ll. 119–22 are the other four, since they darken the offence of the bishops, and are the only lines in the vicinity which could be removed as a unit without damaging the narrative.

On 2 December Cowper sent to Newton a copy of the poem, which, he says, 'has made a Shoot or two since I wrote last, and had I kept it longer by me, would probably have continued growing to the last'. The 'shoots' are the present ll. 125–8 and 133–4; significantly, lines which amplify the matter added at Mrs. Unwin's behest. These lines are added on the blank p. [112] of *H*, establishing that the text of *H* was originally inscribed before they were composed. It was indeed probably inscribed on the 26th since the eight lines suggested by Mrs. Unwin form part of the original text of *H*; also, while in his letter of the 27th Cowper gives the number of lines correctly as 200, in *H* itself they are misnumbered 199; the error presumably predates the correct figure.

Four further lines occurred to Cowper for insertion in a second impression of *Anti-Thelyphthora*, and these he communicated to Newton on 21 December 1780. There was no second impression, and so these lines (175–8) are here printed in their proper place for the first time.

Newton's remarks of 28 November 1780 indicate by implication what must have been said in Cowper's lost letter: 'My bookseller Jo— Johnson says that Secret-keeping respecting Authorship is one branch of the Mystery of their business. He has promised to keep mine—for it is as much mine as yours. *You* will be quite out of the reach of suspicion—nor would I have it known for something that I am the Editor. He engages to preserve the most exact and profound silence on this head. There is no fear of your being brought into expence for so small a publication upon so popular a subject, and fabricated by *you* [as an old friend of Newton's?]. But I have stipulated that according to the sale and success of the Poem, he shall make the unknown Author the fullest compensation that an honest Bookseller can possibly afford.' Cowper having supplied the poem, Johnson proceeded smartly with the publication, doubtless because of its topicality. On 22 December Newton reported that it was almost ready for publication, and on the 30th he promised to send two or three copies by the hand of an Olney resident then visiting London, since the book was ready. It was to be advertised 'on Monday', that is, on 1 January 1781.

The suspicion voiced in Cowper's letter to Newton of 2 December 1780 proved to be justified: the printer did take liberties with the copy. On 30 December Newton apologized for the fact that somebody had changed one word; which word, unfortunately, he did not specify. Cowper, it is clear, did not read proof—that was Newton's duty as 'Editor'—and *H* is accordingly chosen here as copy-text.

There is no record of Cowper's having received any payment from Joseph Johnson for *Anti-Thelyphthora*. After his death it was carefully suppressed by the family, and later apparently forgotten, so that while the references in letters to Newton would have brought it to light eventually, it was only by chance that Southey discovered its existence and was able to include it in the *Works* (Russell, p. 36).

Motto. 'Ah, wretched man, in what a Charybdis [deadly whirlpool] are you labouring' (Horace, *Odes*, I. xxvii. 18–19: 'laboras' is the reading commonly found in eighteenth-century texts). Horace is addressing a young man who loves disastrously, and the next line is relevant: 'O lad, worthy of a better flame!'

l. 1. *Airy del Castro*. Martin Madan, author of *Thelyphthora*. See the reference to an 'Air-built Castle' in the letter to Newton of 19 November 1780 (which Cowper misdated 1781). Cf. Johnson's definition of 'airy': 'Without reality; without any steady foundation in truth or nature; vain; trifling.'

l. 6. *Hypothesis*. 'A supposition; a system formed upon some principle not proved' (Johnson).

l. 32. *wanton*. Here in Johnson's sense 3: 'Frolicksome; gay; sportive; airy.'

ll. 40–5. The characteristic philosophical tenet of Berkeley, who wrote in his *Treatise Concerning the Principles of Human Knowledge* (1710): 'For as to what is said of the absolute existence of unthinking things without any reference to their being perceived, that seems perfectly unintelligible. Their *esse* is *percipi*, nor is it possible that they should have any existence, out of the minds or thinking things which perceive them' (*Works*, Dublin, 1784, i. 24).

ll. 46–51. In his *Sacred Theory of the Earth* (first published in Latin in 1681, later translated and enlarged) Thomas Burnet advanced the 'hypothesis' (as he himself calls it) that the Earth was before the Flood smooth and ovoid; that the Flood was caused by the Providential collapse of a part of the outer crust, which released the waters confined within; and that when the waters receded, the surface of the Earth assumed the lineaments with which we are familiar (Part I, chapters v and vi). For a full account of Burnet's theory, and the controversy it provoked, see M. H. Nicolson, *Mountain Gloom and Mountain Glory*, Ithaca, N.Y., 1959, pp. 184–270.

l. 52. *Dædalus*. The fabulous artificer of Crete, who made wings to which feathers were attached with wax; his son Icarus flew too close to the sun, and fell into the sea when the wax melted.

l. 53. *Wildgoose*. 'Wild, fantastic, very foolish or risky' (*OED*, citing this passage).

l. 71. The first part of Badcock's review appeared in the October number of the *Monthly Review* (lxiii (1780), 273–87); the second part, which Cowper had not seen when he wrote this, in the November number (pp. 321–39). *Thelyphthora* had been published on 31 May.

l. 83. *Philyrea*. The mock privet, usually now spelt 'phillyrea'.

l. 84. *old Chaucer's merry Page*. As Pope's 'Imitation' suggests, Chaucer was often regarded as a merely bawdy poet; cf. C. F. E. Spurgeon, *Five Hundred Years of Chaucer Criticism and Allusion*, Cambridge, 1925, I. 401, 402, 407, 411, 421, 423, for comparable references to him in the years 1731–80.

l. 107. *Circassians*. In Cowper's day the Circassians were deemed 'chiefly remarkable for the beauty of their children, the seraglios of Turky and Persia being usually supplied with boys and young virgins from this and the neighbouring country of Georgia' (*Encyclopaedia Britannica*, Edinburgh, 1768).

l. 122. 'When a knight was degraded, his spurs were chopp'd off' (note in *1781*).

l. 125. *the Sabine youth*. Cf. Livy, I. ix–x.

l. 129. *the Mitred few*. The bishops. For Mrs. Unwin's urging Cowper to add these lines, see head-note above.

l. 136. *Sir Marmadan*, 'Monthly Review for October' (note in *1781*). The champion is associated with the moon since the moon-goddess is the chaste and fair Diana. The author of the review was Samuel Badcock (1747–88), a dissenting minister. He was a man of considerable learning who at one time attracted the attention of Joseph Priestley. He wrote widely for periodicals, and was most highly esteemed as a reviewer for the Monthly Review.

ll. 175–8. On the composition and inclusion of these lines, see head-note above. Madan had based his argument on close (and, so Cowper believed, perverse) interpretation of Old Testament texts, fortified by quotations in Hebrew.

l. 200. *Phineas-like*. Properly Phinehas, the grandson of Aaron; the story is told in Numbers 25. The Israelites had begun 'to commit whoredom with the daughters of Moab', and were visited with a plague in consequence. Seeing an Israelite take a Moabitish woman into his tent, Phinehas 'rose up from among the congregation, and took a javelin in his hand; And he went after the man of Israel into the tent, and thrust both of them through, and the woman through her belly. So the plague was stayed from the children of Israel' (7–8). This act was endowed with exemplary significance; cf. Ecclus. 45: 23–4.

l. 204. *conscious*. 'Inwardly sensible of wrong-doing' (*OED*).

POEMS BY WILLIAM COWPER, OF THE INNER TEMPLE, ESQ.

Title-page. Cf. Virgil, *Aeneid*, viii. 22–5.

The French quotation is from chapter xi, 'De la Vérité', of *La Jouissance de Soi-Même* (1758), by Louis-Antoine de Caraccioli (1721–1803). Little is known of Caraccioli's life; he was a copious writer on moral and religious subjects who in later life produced several unreliable historical works. See Cowper's letters to Newton on this title-page (7 Nov. 1781); on his proposal to translate *La Jouissance* (Feb. 1784 and 8 Mar. 1784); on Lady Austen's gift to him of *La Jouissance* and another book by Caraccioli (19 Mar. 1784).

TABLE TALK

The third of the 'moral satires' to be written, 'Table Talk' is first mentioned in Cowper's letter to Newton of 4 February 1781; it was then recently completed. Cowper believed that this poem would be popular on account of its references to current events, and consequently placed it first in the volume, before 'The Progress of Error' and 'Truth', the first and second of the satires. (See also his letter to Newton, 22 Oct. 1781.)

In contrast to its two predecessors, 'Table Talk' was not extensively revised after being written out in *H*; Cowper's alterations and additions are relatively insignificant, save in one place: the deletion of the original ll. 13–30, and the substitution of the present ll. 13–28. This was done in response to a protest by Newton, who appears to have thought the original lines too jocular in tone. Writing to him on 5 March 1781, Cowper explains that he intended these lines as a 'Catch', to tempt the reader to continue. Newton renewed his objection, and on 18 March Cowper sent him the new lines, at the same time stating, rather plaintively, his dislike of political themes in his verse.

Some light is thrown on Cowper's intentions in this poem by his choice of title. Johnson defines 'tabletalk' as 'Conversation at meals or entertainments; table discourse', and cites Atterbury: 'No fair adversary would urge loose tabletalk in controversy, and build serious inferences upon what was spoken but in jest.' The poem seems to owe something of its general conception to Churchill's *The Conference*, which is cast in the form of 'table talk' and debates the responsibilities of the poet, albeit in a very different vein (cf. l. 670 n.).

Motto. Horace, *Epistles*, I. xiii. 6–7: 'If by chance the heavy burden of my poem should chafe you, throw it away.'

l. 6. *laurel that the very light'ning spares.* It has been erroneously believed since classical times that lightning never strikes the laurel.

l. 72. *Nor judge by statute a believer's hope.* The reference here is uncertain; it is probably to the Catholic Relief Act of 1778 (18 Geo. III, c. 60) and to the Act of 1779 'for the further relief of Protestant dissenting ministers and schoolmasters' (19 Geo. III, c. 44). Spiller, however, suggests that Cowper has in mind here the Test Act, and cites 'Expostulation', ll. 376 ff., which certainly refer to that statute, but what Cowper says of it there is hardly reconcilable with this passage. In any case, the Test Act was not enacted in the reign of George III.

l. 84. *charge you with a bribe.* This had been the fate of Samuel Johnson on the publication of his pro-administration pamphlets of the 1770s; see notes to ll. 110, 143 below.

ll. 93–100. Editors have searched in vain for this story in the works of

Francisco Gomez de Quevedo y Villegas (1580–1645). Cowper was pre-sumably recalling the sixth and seventh of Quevedo's *Visions* (familiar to the eighteenth century in the translation of Sir Roger L'Estrange), which are set in Hell, but the anecdote seems to be his own invention. There are many monarchs in Quevedo's Hell.

ll. 105, 106. *Alfred's name . . . the Sixth Edward's.* The reign of Alfred was proverbially 'golden' (see Johnson's *London*, l. 248). Edward VI, who died before his sixteenth birthday, seems an odd companion in this context, but is no doubt mentioned on account of his zeal for the reformed religion.

l. 110. *His quit-rent ode, his pepper-corn of praise.* A quit-rent (purely nominal rent) might be as little as a peppercorn; the reference is to the odes customarily provided by eighteenth-century poets laureate for New Year's Day and royal birthdays. The association of ideas seems to have been current: cf. Matthew Green, *The Spleen*, ll. 656–7: 'the feather'd throng, / Who pay their quit-rents with a song'; and Thomas Moore, *Life of R. B. Sheridan*, London, 1825, i, 151, quotes from an unpublished attack on Johnson's *Taxation No Tyranny* of 1775: 'Such pamphlets will be as trifling and insincere as the venal quit-rent of a birth-day ode.'

l. 115. *free from censure, over-aw'd by fear.* Elliptical for: '(all) censure, which is overawed by fear.' H has no comma after 'censure', but this would permit the interpretation: 'that censure (only) which has been overawed.'

l. 143. *a band call'd patriot*, i.e. opponents of the administration. Cf. Johnson's pamphlet, *The Patriot*, 1774: 'those who, by deceiving the credulous with fictitious mischiefs, overbearing the weak by audacity of falsehood, by appealing to the judgement of ignorance, and flattering the vanity of mean-ness, by slandering honesty and insulting dignity, have gathered round them whatever the kingdom can supply of base, and gross, and profligate; and *raised by merit to this bad eminence*, arrogate to themselves the name of PATRIOTS' (*Works*, 1787, x. 92). For the use of the term in a positive sense, see below, ll. 335 ff., and J. S. Watson, *The Reign of George III, 1760–1815*, Oxford, 1960, pp. 63–5.

l. 152. *th'unwash'd artificer.* Spiller cites Shakespeare, *King John*, iv. ii. 201: 'another lean, unwash'd artificer.' The context is similar.

l. 178. *contrive the payment.* That is, of the National Debt, which is regarded as remote from the proper scope of poetry and from the concern of individual poets, who are proverbially poor.

l. 182. *Not Brindley nor Bridgewater.* James Brindley (1716–72) was trained originally as a mechanical engineer, but in 1759 he turned his attention to canal-building, at the suggestion of Francis Egerton, third Duke of Bridgewater (1736–1803). Brindley designed numerous canals, including the Grand Trunk Canal, with Bridgewater's support.

l. 183. *the course of Helicon.* Helicon is not a river but a mountain in Boeotia sacred to the Muses where are found the springs of Hippocrene and Aganippe.

l. 201 ff. The influence of climate on national physique and national character was a topic often aired in the eighteenth century. The classic formulation is that of Montesquieu, in Book XIV of *De L'Esprit des Lois* (1750), which may be reflected in this passage.

l. 237. *frisk.* 'A frolick; a fit of wanton gaiety' (Johnson).

l. 241. *feasting on an onion and a crust.* Perhaps in allusion to the figure (actually an exiled Highlander) in the foreground of Hogarth's famous picture, *The Gate of Calais.*

l. 259. *Britain's charter'd land.* Cf. 'Expostulation', ll. 596 ff.

l. 273. *Free to prove all things and hold fast the best.* Cf. I Thess. 5: 21.

l. 309. *Olympic speed.* Horse- and chariot-races were of course the most important events of the ancient Olympic games.

ll. 310–28. The London magistrates were weak and ineffective in dealing with the Gordon Riots, which convulsed London at the beginning of June 1780. Among the outrages which followed the 'No Popery' demonstrations of Lord George Gordon and his Protestant Association were the release of the Newgate prisoners and burning of the Prison, together with many other arson attempts (see below, 'On the Burning of Lord Mansfield's Library'). After more than a week of rioting, order was restored by the arrival of regular troops (l. 317). Lines 320–1 probably refer to the disturbances at the Houses of Parliament at the start of the riots. Cf. l. 447.

l. 339. *when Chatham died.* William Pitt, first Earl of Chatham (1708–78), who had 'saved' England in the Seven Years War (ll. 367, 386). On 7 April 1778 he came to the House of Lords to express publicly his continued opposition to the granting of immediate independence to the American colonies. As he rose to speak for the second time he suffered a stroke, and the debate was adjourned. He died on 11 May.

l. 349. *a Paul or Tully.* St. Paul is probably associated with Cicero not so much as a preacher as a forensic orator (Acts 24, 26); cf. 'Expostulation', l. 445. Cowper must have known Hogarth's painting, *Paul before Felix*, executed for Lincoln's Inn in 1750.

l. 360. *Gideon earn'd a victory not his own.* See Judg. 6.

l. 361. *subserviency.* 'Instrumental fitness or use' (Johnson).

l. 384. *Th'inestimable estimate of Brown.* John Brown (1715–66), a clergyman, published his *Estimate of the Manners and Principles of the Times* in 1757. It reached an eighth edition in the following year. 'We are rolling to the Brink of a Precipice that must destroy us. . . . the Character of the Manners of our

Times . . . on a fair Examination, will probably appear to be that of a *"vain, luxurious,* and *selfish* EFFEMINACY"' (2nd ed., 1757, pp. 15, 29). The book appears to have impressed Cowper considerably. Brown, who had written against Shaftesbury (*Essays on the Characteristics,* 1751) under Warburton's aegis, and enjoyed the patronage of Lord Hardwicke, apparently became slightly deranged, and cut his throat on 23 September 1766.

l. 417. *lett.* This now obsolete spelling is found in *H.*

l. 458. *Obduracy takes place.* In the obsolete sense of 'takes effect'.

l. 476. *shock.* 'Concussion; external violence' (Johnson).

l. 487. *ev'ry feeling line. OED,* citing this passage, glosses 'line': 'A "cord" in the body.' This is probably right, but the passage is strongly affected by Pope, *Essay on Man,* i. 217–18:

> The Spider's touch, how exquisitely fine,
> Feels at each thread, and lives along the line . . . .

ll. 500–1. *the graceful name | Of prophet and of poet.* The Latin word *vates,* 'seer', was used in its other sense, 'poet', by several Augustan authors.

l. 503. *ev'ry hallow'd druid was a bard.* This belief appears to have arisen from the remark of Caesar (*Gallic War,* vi. 14) that instruction in the druidic schools was by the learning of many verses—he does not mention bards as such. (Other classical writers tend to distinguish between bards and druids.) Cowper's view was in accord with current opinion, as for example that of the acute Joseph Ritson (d. 1803): 'The Celts, or Gauls, had, among them, poets, that sung melodious songs, whom they called *bards,* who, to their musical instruments, not unlike harps or lyres, chanted forth the praises of some, and the dispraises of others. Those who either, of their own accord, were induced to follow the profession of a druid, or were sent by their parents and relations, were taught to repeat a great number of verses by heart. These druids, or poets . . .' (*Memoirs of the Celts or Gauls,* London, 1827, 196).

l. 507. *To set a distich upon six and five.* To compose Latin elegiac couplets, consisting of a hexameter followed by a pentameter.

l. 509. *And makes his pupils proud with silver-pence.* See notes to 'Translation of Prior's Chloe and Euphelia', below. Such rewards for good composition were still given in Southey's day, 1788–92 (*Life of Cowper,* i. 16).

l. 527. *the two figures at St. Dunstan's.* The church of St. Dunstan's-in-the-West, Fleet Street, was demolished and rebuilt, 1829–31. Benham quotes Northouck's *History of London,* 1773: 'The dial of the clock projects over the street at the extremity of a beam; and over it by a kind of whimsical conceit, calculated only for the amusement of countrymen and children, is an Ionic porch, containing the figures of two savages, carved and painted, as big as life, which with knotted clubs alternately strike the hours and quarters on two bells hung between them.'

l. 537. *fumbles.* 'To puzzle; to strain in perplexity' (Johnson).

l. 547. *push-pin.* A children's game, often cited contemptuously as a means of wasting time.

l. 553. *pounce.* To seize with the pounces, or talons.

ll. 556–9. This passage is modelled on Dryden's epigram on Milton, which Cowper had Latinized in 1780—see above. The 'Mantuan swan' is Virgil.

l. 566. *Halcyons.* Kingfishers.

l. 583. *paddock.* The spelling 'paddoc' is almost certainly a misprint, for *OED* does not record such a variant; in any case, it is not Cowper's spelling.

ll. 608–9. Anacreon is noted for his celebration in verse of wine and pleasure; Horace is named presumably on account of his appreciation of young women and old vintages—Cowper may have forgotten that he also supplied the motto for this poem. 'Bedlam' seems a harsh way to say 'foolish', but the usage is justifiable in law; cf. R. Burn, *Ecclesiastical Law*, 5th ed., 1788, s.v. 'Wills': 'He that is overcome with drink, during the time of his drunkenness, is compared to a madman . . .'.

ll. 610–11. This passage is clearly influenced by Pope's *Epistle to Augustus*, ll. 139–281, especially 215–20 (on Addison).

ll. 670–89. Charles Churchill was born in 1732, and educated at Westminster School, where he was a contemporary of Cowper. Unsuccessful as clergyman and teacher, he was driven by poverty to write. His brief but popular and lucrative career as a satirical poet was cut short when he died in France in 1764. He was associated with the group of Old Westminsters known as the Geniuses, particularly with Robert Lloyd. In an undated letter to Unwin (probably of March 1780) Cowper gives an extended appreciation of Churchill's poetry. On Cowper's personal acquaintance with Churchill, see Ryskamp, pp. 90–4.

l. 735. *Touch'd with a coal from heav'n.* Cf. Isa. 6: 5–8.

l. 760. Thomas Sternhold (d. 1549), M.P. for Plymouth, and John Hopkins (d. 1570), a clergyman, versified the Psalms. The complete Psalter (to which others contributed) first appeared in 1562, and was hundreds of times reprinted until enthusiasm for it waned about 1830. Despite its continued popularity (twenty-five editions in the years 1771–80), 'Sternhold and Hopkins' was widely regarded as pedestrian, fit for simple souls; see Pope, *Epistle to Augustus*, ll. 229–40, and Cowper's essay on country churches, *The Connoisseur*, no. 134, 19 Aug. 1756.

764. For Cowper's youthful reading of Butler, Pope, and Prior, see Ryskamp, pp. 57–9.

THE PROGRESS OF ERROR

It is unlikely that Cowper began composing 'The Progress of Error' before 2 December 1780, when he dispatched *Antithelyphthora* to Newton; on 21 December he wrote to Newton: 'It will not be long perhaps before you will receive a poem of much greater length than the Knightly one, it is called the *Progress of Error.*' Study of the manuscript in *H* and of the correspondence with Newton reveals that the poem consisted, in late December, of only 468 lines; that the version which reached Newton about the third week of January 1781 was about 100 lines longer; and that the version which appeared in *1782*, 624 lines long, was the end-product of further substantial revision which took place towards the end of March 1781.

When Cowper inscribed the first version in *H*, presumably in late December 1780, he numbered the lines to a total of 468, averaging 29 lines to a page. Subsequently, probably about a month later, in order to augment the poem, he tore out several leaves and substituted others, but he neither cancelled nor revised the original numbering, so that the extent and to some degree the nature of the additions can be determined.

The original version with Cowper's numbering runs to l. 76 at the foot of p. 123, and takes up again with l. 164 at the top of p. 129; thus, 87 lines have been removed, which must have occupied three leaves. In their place two leaves of different paper stock have been inserted, inscribed recto and verso by Cowper in a somewhat cramped and hurried hand. Page totals for pp. 125, [126], 127, and [128] are 27, 32, 31, and 14 lines respectively, making a grand total of 104 lines; there has been a net addition of 17 lines. Since this is considerably less than the average number of lines to a page, a mere insertion of this length would require the removal of two leaves at most; therefore Cowper must have revised this section of the poem extensively, and it is scarcely possible to differentiate between what has been added and what was already in the original version.

From l. 164 at the top of p. 129, the original version with its numbering continues without interruption to l. 280 at the foot of p. 135; it resumes with l. 310 at the top of p. 141. It is clear that one leaf (containing the original ll. 281–309) has been removed and two leaves inserted, again inscribed by Cowper in a comparatively cramped and hurried hand, though this time somewhat improved after he mended his pen half-way down p. 137. Page totals for pp. 137, [138], 139, and [140] are 32, 32, 30, and 33 lines respectively, making a grand total of 127 lines, representing a net addition to the poem of 98 lines.

Two lines at the top of p. 137 complete a paragraph; similarly, two lines at the foot of p. [140] begin the paragraph which continues on p. 141. Presumably these lines (299–300 and 460–1 of the final version) survive from the original version; there are then 25 lines to be accounted for from the original version. It is likely that these are the lines on p. [140] which begin 'Sure of all Artifices Dupes invent' and continue with what survives almost unchanged

as ll. 436–59 of the final text. This passage would follow naturally after
l. 300, 'Dupes' picking up the idea of men willingly self-deceived by folly.

It seems to have occurred to Cowper, however, to discuss *Thelyphthora* in
a wider context, treating it less as an example of human folly than as an
example, the crowning example, of the misuse of the power of the written
word. Hence the new material begins with the attack on the novelists,
which was followed, in the version sent to Newton in mid-January 1781, by
the four lines on the eagle-pinioned Muse (i.e. ll. 308–34 of the final version),
which led straight into an extended attack on *Thelyphthora* and Martin
Madan—46 lines of it, followed by the 25 lines of milder criticism discussed
above. Then on 21 January 1781 Cowper wrote to Newton that since he had
sent the poem he had added 18 lines on Lord Chesterfield, which should be
inserted after the address to the novelists. This is where it appears in *H*,
indicating that the present pp. 137–[140] were inscribed and inserted into
H after the Chesterfield passage had been composed, probably in the second
half of January 1781. (It may be noted here that the inserted pages were
inscribed before they were inserted; the left-hand margins of pp. 137 and 139
were so narrow that the first words are all but obscured by the binding.)

In his letter to Newton of 5 March 1781 Cowper assents to Joseph
Johnson's request that his name be given in the projected volume of poems,
on condition that the authorship of *Anti-Thelyphthora* never be revealed, and
that 'The Progress of Error' be returned so that he might cancel 'the passage
relating to Thelyphthora; for though in that passage I have neither belied
my own Judgment nor slandered the Author, yet on account of Relationship
and for reasons I need not suggest to you, I should not chuse to make a public
Attack upon his performance'. Cowper is here especially concerned to
expunge everthing which might be taken as personally and particularly
applicable to Martin Madan, and he asks Newton to recommend appropriate
deletions to him. He promises 'to supply the hiatus with something that may
make Amends for the Loss, either in the same place or in some other part of
the Poem'. The resulting work of deletion and substitution, apparently not
begun when he wrote to Newton on 18 March, was done before 8 April,
when the revised text was sent to London. The 46-line attack on *Thelyphthora*
was removed, and in its place stood the present ll. 353–434, 82 lines in place
of 46. The new material was integrated into the existing text by a reworking
of 'Sure of all Artifices Dupes invent' into the present l. 435.

A further alteration required a cancel. On 7 July 1781, Cowper called to
Newton's attention a flaw at ll. 373–4, where the rhyme-word of each line
was the same: 'to minute down / . . . and where the Chaise broke down';
he provides an improved couplet which had come to him suddenly the
previous night:

> With memorandum book for ev'ry town
> And ev'ry Inn, and where the Chaise broke down.

It is not clear whether he expects Newton to have the correction made, or is merely telling of it. At all events, the change was not made, for on 17 February 1782 Cowper had to ask Joseph Johnson to correct this one last error: 'I did not omit to send the alteration either to you or to Mr. Newton, but it has been forgot.' Apparently what he had sent to Johnson differed from what he had sent to Newton, since l. 374 of the cancel has 'post' not 'Inn'.

Hayley records: 'I was informed by Mrs. Unwin that she strongly solicited her friend to devote his thoughts to Poetry, of considerable extent, on his recovery from his very long fit of mental dejection, suggesting to him, at the same time, the first subject of his Song, "The Progress of Error!" [sic] . . .' (*Life of Cowper*, 1803, i. 106). While this statement telescopes the sequence of events, tactfully omitting all mention of *Anti-Thelyphthora*, there is no reason to doubt its truth. On the title 'The Progress of Error', see J. D. Baird, 'Cowper's Concept of Truth', in R. Runte, ed., *Studies in Eighteenth Century Culture VII*, Madison, Wisconsin, 1978, pp. 367–73.

Motto. From Horace, *Odes*, IV. ii. 45: 'If I say anything worth hearing.' The motto in *H* is from Horace, *Satires*, iii. 158: 'Who then is in his right mind? He who is not foolish.'

l. 4. *The serpent error.* This image probably owes something to Spenser's Error, whose 'vomit full of bookes and papers was' (*The Faerie Queene*, I. i. xx).

ll. 13–22. A strongly Evangelical attack on clergy who have not seen the light.

l. 84. *Nimrod.* The character is almost certainly a composite one, but Thomas Wright believed that Cowper 'had in his eye the Rev. Mr. Pomfret, rector of the neighbouring village of Emberton' (*Life of William Cowper*, 1892, p. 267). The name 'Nimrod' acquires a particularly sarcastic force when applied to a 'hunting parson'; cf. Genesis 10: 9.

l. 94. *tumbril.* Any lumbering rural cart, but specifically a dung-cart.

l. 121. *Monmouth Street.* This street, now obliterated by Shaftesbury Avenue, was notorious throughout the eighteenth century for its second-hand clothing stores.

l. 124. *Occiduus.* Traditionally taken as a punning reference to Charles Wesley (1707–88); *occiduus* being Latin for 'western'. However, there is no evidence that Wesley ever sponsored or even countenanced Sunday concerts; he did not play the fiddle (l. 126); he was vigorously opposed to such places as Ranelagh and Vauxhall, and so would never have given the advice ascribed to Occiduus in Cowper's letter to Newton, 9 September 1781 (T. Jackson, *The Life of Charles Wesley, M.A.*, 1841, ii. 371–6). Jackson suggests that Martin Madan is intended: he played the fiddle; he was 'evangelical', i.e. Calvinist (l. 134), as Wesley was not; and he was 'western' inasmuch as he was Chaplain of the Lock Hospital, then situated near Hyde Park, in the

West End of London. This identification is tempting, but wants solid confirming evidence, not forthcoming. In any case, Cowper may have attacked Wesley on a basis of false information.

l. 148. *the tinkling harpsichord.* The letter to Newton of 9 September 1781 shows that instrumental music was particularly objectionable because it lacked words which might direct the mind to God; it therefore counted as a sensual pleasure.

ll. 157–66. This passage is based on Isa. 58: 13–14. The prophet there emphasizes that pleasure is to be foregone on the sabbath, whereas the O.T. writers usually demand rest from labour; but the passage suits Cowper's purpose all the better in consequence.

l. 169. *the velvet plain.* The same phrase, used of a card-table, is found in Pope, *The Rape of the Lock*, iii. 44.

l. 184. *Comus.* Milton's masque gave Cowper several hints for the treatment of his theme. For the 'silver beard', cf. the epithet 'greybeard' applied to Lord Chesterfield (l. 342).

l. 188. *Clodio.* A name of dubious reputation, evoking the Clodia who was Catullus's Lesbia, and her brother Publius Clodius, 'remarkable for his licentiousness, avarice, and ambition' (Lemprière).

l. 189. *Rufillus.* Cf. Horace, *Satires*, I, ii. 27: 'pastillos Rufillus olet, Gargonius hircum' ('Rufillus smells of aromatic lozenges, Gargonius of goat').

l. 215. *Daniel ate pulse.* Cf. Dan. 1: 8–16.

l. 217. *Gorgonius.* The name comes from Horace; see l. 189n. above. Modern editors follow Bentley, whose edition of Horace appeared in 1711, in spelling the name 'Gargonius', but 'Gorgonius' is found in many eighteenth-century editions, and this was probably the form known to Cowper in his school-text.

ll. 259–60. This passage may owe something to Milton's *Comus*, ll. 476–80.

l. 335. *Petronius.* The courtier, politician, and author of Nero's time, described as 'elegantiae arbiter' by Tacitus (*Annals* xvi. 18), who committed suicide in A.D. 66. This is a particularly apt classical parallel for Philip Dormer Stanhope, 4th Earl of Chesterfield (1694–1773), who was all of these things—and whose book, like Petronius's, could be stigmatized as wicked. After Chesterfield's death, Mrs. Eugenia Stanhope, the widow of his natural son, published (under the supervision of the Stanhope family) *Letters Written by the Earl of Chesterfield to His Son, Philip Stanhope* (1774). The book was widely read. Cowper's is one of several hostile judgements. Cowper's father probably knew Chesterfield when both were undergraduates at Cambridge; almost certainly he was the 'Jack Cowper' whose enslavement to a 'nymph' is recorded in Chesterfield's letter to the Hon. George Berkeley, 25 June O.S. [1713] (*Letters*, ed. Bonamy Dobrée, 6 vols., 1932, ii. 9).

l. 360. *Man's coltish disposition.* Cf. Job 11: 12.

l. 362. *forrester.* 'A bird or beast of the forest; *spec.* one of the rough ponies bred in the New Forest' (*OED*, citing this passage).

l. 441. *Left out his linch-pin or forgot his tar.* The linch-pin held the wheel on the axle; the tar (i.e. pine tar) was used as a lubricant.

l. 485. *Leuwenhoek.* Anthony van Leeuwenhoek (1632–1723), of Delft, a microscopist who contributed many papers to the *Philosophical Transactions* of the Royal Society. Cowper's knowledge of his work was probably gleaned from Henry Baker's widely read popularization, based largely on Leeuwenhoek's papers, *The Microscope Made Easy* (1742; many later editions). Cowper borrowed this book in 1777 (letters to Hill, 13 July and 23 Oct.). Leeuwenhoek did make some observations of the circulation of the blood in crabs (Baker, 1743 ed., pp. 128–9), but he does not seem to have computed their numbers. The marine context suggests that Cowper may have had in mind Leeuwenhoek's estimate of the reproductive powers of the codfish, in which he claimed that the milt of a single male codfish 'contained more living *Animalcules,* than there are People alive upon the Face of the whole Earth at one and the same Time'; the argument, in which the word 'computes' is used, is reported in full by Baker (pp. 155–6). Leeuwenhoek also computed the reproductive capacity of the louse, in connection with which the crab-louse is mentioned (Baker, pp. 181–2); some recollection of this passage may have led Cowper to write 'crab' instead of 'cod'.

l. 526. *So one.* Pygmalion.

l. 538. *Sir Isaac, and such Boyle and Locke.* Sir Isaac Newton (1642–1727); the Hon. Robert Boyle (1627–91), proponent of 'Boyle's law' and founder of the Lectures for the defence of Christianity; John Locke (1632–1704).

l. 580. *Circæan Cup.* In the *Odyssey,* Book x, Circe's drugs turn her guests into beasts. The spelling, not uncommon in the eighteenth century, is an example of the confusion of *e* and *æ.*

l. 589. *Die then, if pow'r Almighty save you not.* The italicization of 'then', though not observed by earlier editors, was clearly intended by Cowper, who wrote as follows to Joseph Johnson on 6 August 1781: 'Die *then*— / The word Italicized to direct the Emphasis, the objection to that line I suppose must vanish. At least I can see none. The Sentiment I take to be unquestionably true. I confess the two lines that close the period are two of my favorites, they may possibly at first sight, seem chargeable with some harshness of Expression, but that harshness is rather to be ascribed to the truth they convey, than to the terms in which it is conceived. Every body knows that a final rejection of the Gospel, must terminate in destruction. The words *damnable* and damned may be vehement indeed, but they are no more than adequate to the case, nor would any other words that I can think of do justice to the Idea they intend. That Vehemence is indeed the very circumstance that gives them a peculiar propriety in the place they occupy, they bring up the rear of a whole clause of admonitions and cautions, and therefore cannot make too forcible an Impression. They are the lead at the end of the bludgeon.'

l. 599. '*Peace, be still.*' Cf. Mark 4: 39.

l. 600. '*Thus far and no farther.*' Adapted from Job 38: 11.

TRUTH

This poem was being planned, if not yet being written, on 21 December 1780, when Cowper wrote to Newton that 'The Progress of Error' 'will be succeeded by another, in due time, the length of which is not at present determined, called *Truth*'. Exactly a month later, on 21 January 1781, he told Newton that he shrank from the thought of transcribing 'Truth', 'which is already longer than its Elder Brother, and is yet to be lengthen'd by the addition of perhaps 20 Lines, perhaps more'. But Cowper's attention was already engaged by 'Table Talk', and although he informed Newton on 4 February that 'Truth' was long since finished, no transcript of it was sent to London until Cowper submitted to Newton the complete copy of his projected volume, on 8 April 1781.

Cowper augmented 'Truth' considerably after first entering it in his book. The original version, with line-numbering by Cowper, runs to 472 lines, just four lines longer than the original version of 'The Progress of Error'. Then—and this may be the prospective addition mentioned on 21 January 1781—he decided to insert the description of the prude and other matter, and removed from the book two leaves which contained the original ll. 105–60. Two new leaves were inserted, inscribed recto and verso in a somewhat hurried hand; the punctuation is so light as to be in places inadequate. The new material consisted of the following lines of the printed poem; 127–170 (the prude, with linking passages before and after); 197–237 (the contrasted servants, and the retort to Curio). That these are the added paragraphs is established beyond doubt by the fact that Cowper, who always liked to know how many lines he had composed, numbered the new lines as he added them, in order to keep his grand total up to date. This total, after four lines were added a little further on (ll. 279–82 in the printed version), stood at 561 lines.

The next addition—and this is more probably than the preceding the addition mentioned on 21 January 1781—was a 32-line passage on the virtuous pagans, and an attack on deism (ll. 515–46 of the printed version). Cowper did not follow his earlier practice of tearing out pages and rewriting extensively in order to introduce new material; these lines do not appear in

H. But Cowper none the less calculated the total number of lines (593), since the last of the four lines (which were not published in *1782*) added after l. 316 is numbered 597. The final addition was ll. 17–20 of the printed version, the last of which is numbered in *H* 601.

The omissions which reduced the printed version to a total of 589 lines were probably decided on as Cowper transcribed the poem for the press in March 1781.

Believing that 'Truth' 'is *so* true that it can hardly fail of giving offence to an unenlighten'd Reader', that is, one who did not subscribe to evangelical tenets, Cowper suggested to Newton on 8 April 1781 that he might write an explanatory preface to the poem, 'in Order to obviate in some measure those prejudices that will naturally erect their bristles against it'. Newton did not write such a preface to the poem, but he subsequently accepted Cowper's alternative suggestion, and wrote a preface to the whole volume.

Motto. The reference is to Horace, *Epistles*, II. i. 28–30: 'si . . . Romani pensantur eadem scriptores trutina'; 'if the Roman writers are weighed in the same scale.' By truncating the quotation and changing the verb from indicative to subjunctive, so that the motto means 'let them be weighed in the scale', Cowper has abandoned the Horatian context and introduced biblical overtones; cf. Dan. 5: 27.

l. 4. *a sleeping fog*. Cf. Cowper to Newton, 19 Nov. 1780, speaking of Martin Madan: 'Sanguin and Confident as he has been his Mortification will be extreme, when he finds that what he took for Terra firma, was a mere Vapour hanging in the Horizon, in Pursuit of which he has Run his Vessel upon Shoals that must prove fatal to her.'

l. 31. BELIEVE AND LIVE. Cf. John 6: 47; 1 Tim. 1: 16.

ll. 48–50. For the accusations, cf. Mark 2: 7; Luke 6: 2; Luke 15: 2.

ll. 53–7. Cf. Luke 18: 10–14.

l. 83. *Adust*. 'Burnt up; hot as with fire, scorched' (Johnson).

l. 119. *Cowper's*. Spencer Cowper (1713–74), second son of the first Earl Cowper, was educated at Westminster School and Exeter College, Oxford. He was Dean of Durham from 1746 until his death, Durham being then the richest see in England. His was the 'second stall' because the Bishop's was the first.

l. 124. *lice*. 'No man living abhorrs a louse more than I do, but Hermits are notoriously infested with those vermin; it is even a part of their supposed meritorious mortification to encourage the breed. The fact being true becomes an important feature in the face of that folly I mean to expose, and having occasion to mention the loathsome Animal I cannot, I think, do better than call him by his loathsome name. It is a false delicacy that is offended by the mention of any thing that God has seen fit to create, where the laws of modesty are not violated, and therefore we will not mind it' (Cowper to Joseph Johnson, 6 Aug. 1781).

l. 131. *Yon antient prude.* Cowper here describes Hogarth's print, *Morning*, first of the *Times of the Day* series published in 1738. Since he mentions only one amorous couple (136), while there are two in the print, he may have been writing from memory, but his account is both vivid and accurate. On this passage, and the imaginary painting which follows (171–8), see R. W. Desai, 'William Cowper and the Visual Arts', *BNYPL* lxxii. 360–2.

l. 139. *lappet-head.* A lady's cap with lappets, or streamers, attached.

l. 156. *Miss Bridget's lovely name.* The name is borrowed from Squire All-worthy's sister, who, according to Fielding, is the lady portrayed in Hogarth's *Morning* (*Tom Jones*, I. xi). In her conversation, however, Cowper's prude more strongly resembles Mrs. Western, who dwelt on her conquests and her cruelty for half-an-hour and more (ibid. XVII. iv).

l. 202. *Geta.* The name of a slave in two plays by Terence, *Adelphi* and *Phormio.* The Geta of the latter has a much larger and more significant part; Cowper may have seen this play performed at Westminster in 1743 (J. Sargeaunt, *Annals of Westminster School*, 1898, p. 270).

l. 229. *Curio.* This name appears to be used without reference to any pre-vious proprietor; it perhaps indicates the character of the questioner, whose curiosity is tinged with unedifying scepticism.

l. 297. *a still, small whisper.* Cf. 1 Kgs. 19: 12.

ll. 311–16. Voltaire (1694–1778) arrived in Paris, after an absence of twenty-seven years, on 10 February 1778. Cowper probably read the reports of his enthusiastic reception which were published in the *Gentleman's Magazine* in March, April, and May of that year (xlviii. 109–10; 149–52; 213–14); his death on 30 May was reported in June (ibid. 286). There is a Gallophobe pun in 'frankincense' (314).

l. 318. *Pillow and bobbins.* Instruments of lace-making; Olney was a centre of that craft.

l. 356. *flies up and kicks the beam.* Cf. *Paradise Lost*, iv. 1004.

l. 358. *Conyers.* The Revd. Richard Conyers, educated at Jesus College, Cambridge, prominent Evangelical divine, was vicar of Helmsley, Yorkshire, 1756–76; through the patronage of John Thornton, with whom he was con-nected by marriage, he became vicar of St. Paul's, Deptford, 1775–86. He died on 23 April 1786, aged 62. (See L. E. Elliot-Binns, *The Early Evangelicals*, 1953, pp. 309–11.) Conyers became acquainted with Mrs. Unwin through her son William, whom he met at Cambridge in the early 1760s. It was Conyers who urged John Newton to call on Cowper and the recently widowed Mrs. Unwin at Huntingdon in 1767, a visit which led to their removal to

Olney. The substitution of Conyers's name for Newton's (which appears in *H*), whether made by Cowper or by Newton himself, was therefore not inappropriate.

l. 364. *richest*. 'Of choice or superior quality' (*OED*, citing this passage).

l. 378. *one that wears a coronet and prays*. William Legge (1731–1801), 2nd Earl of Dartmouth. He was educated with Cowper at Westminster School, and then at Trinity College, Oxford. He succeeded to the title in 1750. He served in the ministry of his old friend Lord North from 1772 to 1782. He was noted for his personal piety, and was an intimate friend of the Countess of Huntingdon. He nominated John Newton to the curacy of Olney, and was the recipient of letters from Newton which were published as *Cardiphonia* (1781).

l. 382. *what is man?* Cf. Ps. 8: 4.

l. 388. *Solyma*. The second part of the Greek name for Jerusalem; cf. Pope, *Messiah*, l. 1.

ll. 445–9. One found to have committed suicide was buried in the highway with a stake through his body; all his goods and chattels were forfeit to the king. Blackstone's comment is relevant: 'A *felo de se* therefore is he that deliberately puts an end to his own existence, or commits any unlawful malicious act, the consequence of which is his own death. . . . The party must be of years of discretion, and in his senses, else it is no crime. But this excuse ought not to be strained to that length, to which our coroner's juries are apt to carry it, *viz.* that the very act of suicide is an evidence of insanity . . .' (*Commentaries*, Oxford, 1768–9, iv. 189 (Bk. IV, c. 14)).

l. 451. *what some bishops may not know*. Cf. the attack on the bishops in *Antithelyphthora*, ll. 129–32 and note.

l. 472. *the scorner's chair*. Cf. Ps. 1: 1: 'the seat of the scornful'.

l. 476. *The subtlest serpent with the loftiest crest*. Cf. *Paradise Lost*, x. 528–32.

ll. 507–12. Cf. Luke 7: 36–50; also Matt. 21: 31.

EXPOSTULATION

Composition began before 25 February 1781, when Cowper sent Newton an account of the poem and complained of a lack of facility in writing. On 18 March, however, he was writing 'with tolerable ease' and, he believed, 'with more Emphasis and Energy than in either [*sic*] of the others'. The poem was finished before 8 April, when Cowper sent to Newton the complete copy (as then planned) for his volume.

Cowper read the proofs of 'Expostulation' in September 1781. Two months later he became uneasy about ll. 389–412, a sharp attack on Popery, and about 20 November, probably in a letter now lost, he consulted Newton about them. Newton agreed that the passage should be changed, and in his reply of 27 November, Cowper rejoices that he will not be accused 'of Bigotry, or a design to make a certain denomination of Christians odious, at the hazard of the public peace' (a glance at the Gordon Riots). The same day he asked Joseph Johnson if there was time to make the substitution; on 4 December he sent the requisite twenty-four lines of fresh material to Newton. A cancel was required; on 17 February 1782 Cowper wrote to Johnson that he had not seen proof—probably he never did. Some copies were published with the cancellandum leaf I6 (see Russell, pp. 50–2).

No manuscript of 'Expostulation' is known to survive, and it may be that Cowper, having run out of space in his book (*H*), did not bother to make a copy for his own reference. Certainly this poem seems less carefully composed than its predecessors: there are many minor obscurities, it is not always clear who or what is being apostrophized, and the argument is in places incoherent. The punctuation gives little help.

It is clear from his letter to Newton of 17 December 1781 and from 'Table Talk', l. 384, that Cowper was deeply impressed by John Brown's *Estimate of the Manners and Principles of the Times*, and its relation to the public events of the years surrounding its publication in 1757. Cowper saw a parallel in 1781 with the events of the earlier period, and 'Expostulation' may be seen as a religious reworking of Brown's theme. (The *Estimate* is a secular tract.)

There is another kind of model which Cowper probably had in mind. Sermons preached on such occasions as 30 January (Martyrdom of Charles I) and 5 November (Gunpowder Plot) not infrequently suggested parallels between the history of Israel and that of modern England. There was no question in Cowper's time of identifying the English with the Israelites as God's chosen people, as had been done in the mid-seventeenth century, but there was more than mere historical analogy to underlie comparisons. The new basis for the parallel is well expounded in a sermon which Cowper might possibly have heard, or later read, preached on 29 May 1746 at St. Margaret's, Westminster, by John Tunstall, Chaplain to the Archbishop of Canterbury. God, he says, had an explicit covenant with the Jewish people which illuminates the tacit covenant he has with all the peoples of the earth. The foundation of the explicit covenant was the ten commandments. 'Now these commandments, comprizing the main principles and duties of piety to God and of righteousness to men, are by nature *the words of the covenant* between God and all mankind. So deep is their foundation in our natural constitution and essential relations to God and each other; so bright is their evidence to undepraved reason, that we are not obliged to observe them because we have given an express consent for that purpose either to God or man, but we ought universally to consent about them because we are originally obliged to observe them.' (*A Sermon Preached before the Honourable House of Commons*, 1746, pp. 4–5. See below, l. 198n.)

There is a sermon by South, preached 5 November 1670, which develops at length a parallel which resembles Cowper's both in tone and in a number of details (*Sermons Preached upon Several Occasions*, Oxford, 1823, iv. 79–101). Whether or not Cowper recalled it, it indicates that 'Expostulation' belongs to a well-established Anglican homiletic tradition.

Motto. From Virgil, *Aeneid*, v. 390–1: 'Will you so tamely allow such great gifts to be taken away without a fight?'

l. 15. *the russet spice*. Cinnamon.

ll. 24–6. Cf. Pope, *Of the Characters of Women*, ll. 241–2.

ll. 28–30. On the poverty of the Olney lace-makers, familiar to Cowper, see his letter to Hill, 8 July 1780.

ll. 33–4. *wish'd his eyes | Were fountains*. Cf. Jer. 9: 1.

l. 39. *Adult'ry neighing at his neighbour's door*. Cf. Jer. 5: 8.

l. 53. *They stretch'd the neck, and roll'd the wanton eye*. Cf. Isa. 3: 16.

ll. 57–8. Perhaps a reminiscence of Jer. 47: 3.

l. 59. *Saw Babylon set wide her two-leav'd brass*. Bruce cites Herodotus i. 179 on the bronze or brass gates of Babylon, but Cowper was more probably recalling Isa. 45: 1–2.

ll. 73 ff. Cf. Ezra 1.

l. 89. *beneath a fair outside*. Cf. Matt. 23: 27.

l. 106. *a general rot*. Cowper seems here to confuse leprosy and sheep-rot. The cause of sheep-rot was not certainly known, but usually ascribed to rain and wet pastures. Sheep-rot was not thought to be contagious, nor was pure water supposed a cure. Cowper seems to have in mind the story of Naaman (2 Kgs. 5), who was cured of leprosy by bathing in the river Jordan.

ll. 145–6. Cf. Matt. 21: 12–13.

l. 149. Cf. Mark 7: 3–4.

ll. 155–6. Cf. Luke 11: 14–20.

ll. 157–60. Cf. Matt. 16: 2–3.

ll. 177–8. Cf. Exod. 13: 21.

ll. 179–80. Cf. Exod. 40: 34–7.

l. 181. Cf. Num. 20: 7–11.

l. 182. Cf. Exod. 16: 14–15.

l. 183. *old yet new*. Cf. Deut. 8: 4.

l. 185. *Streams swell'd above the bank*. Cf. Josh. 3: 13–16; 4: 18: 'the waters of Jordan returned unto their place, and flowed over all his banks, as they did before' (Cowper's recollection was faulty).

l. 188. Cf. Deut. 34: 9; Josh. 1.

l. 198. *the transcript of th'eternal mind.* Robert South, in his sermon on Matt. 5: 44, preached 29 May 1670, calls the law of Moses 'a true and perfect transcript of the said moral law'; he had earlier said that the matter of the Commandments (except the fourth) 'is of natural moral right, and by consequence carries with it a necessary and eternal obligation' (*Sermons*, Oxford, 1823, ii. 296, 294).

l. 199. *engraven laws.* Cf. Exod. 31: 18.

ll. 201–2. Cf. Rom. 9: 4–5.

ll. 209–10. Jerusalem was captured by Pompey in 63 B.C.

l. 215. *Cur'd of the golden calves.* 'The Expression has a figurative boldness in it which appears to me poetical' (to Joseph Johnson, 16 Sept. 1781). In reference to the calf made by Aaron, Exod. 32, and to Jeroboam's two calves of gold, 1 Kgs. 12: 28.

ll. 229 ff. As Bailey notes, an adaptation of Virgil, *Aeneid*, vi. 847 ff., thus translated by Dryden:

> Let others better mold the running Mass
> Of Mettals, and inform the breathing Brass;
> And soften into Flesh a Marble Face:
> Plead better at the Bar; describe the Skies,
> And when the Stars descend, and when they rise.
> But, *Rome*, 'tis thine alone, with awful sway,
> To rule Mankind; and make the World obey . . . (vi. 1168–74)

l. 246. *Peel'd.* Plundered; cf. Isa. 18: 2.

l. 259. *ras'd.* By the Romans under Titus, A.D. 80.

l. 267. *Cry aloud.* 'Though the verse has rather an unusual run, I chose to begin it in that manner for the sake of Animation, and am not able to alter it without flattening its Energy quite away' (to Joseph Johnson, 16 Sept. 1781).

l. 284. *load thy credit.* 'The National Debt was nearly doubled during the American War. In 1775 it was £124,000,000; in 1783, £238,000,000' (Benham). For Cowper's continuing concern with this issue, see his letter to Hill, 9 Dec. 1781.

ll. 288–93. There had been a number of naval engagements with the French during the preceding two years, but none had proved decisive.

ll. 294–303. The allusion is general, but there may be specific reference to the opposition attempts to remove Lord North in the spring of 1780 (Dunning's motion, etc.).

l. 305. The Land Tax stood at four shillings throughout the war, and in the parliamentary session of 1780 (for example) additional duties were levied on wines and vinegar, salt, malt, low wines and spirits, tobacco, starch, and hair powder.

l. 313. *Providence adverse.* 'The reduplication of those words [cf. l. 310] was a point I rather labor'd for the sake of Emphasis, and the transposition of them strikes me as artfull and as having a agreeable Effect upon the Ear' (to Joseph Johnson, 16 Sept. 1781).

l. 326. *honour, virtue, piety.* These are the three 'principles' which Brown in his *Estimate* (cf. 'Table Talk', l. 348n.) sees as tending to 'counterwork the *selfish Passions . . .* the Principle of *Religion,* the Principle of *Honour,* and the Principle of *public Spirit*' (2nd ed., 1757, Pt. II, sec. vi, p. 53).

l. 338. *Darkness itself before his eye is light.* Cf. Ps. 139: 12.

l. 339. *Hell's close mischief naked in his sight.* Cf. Job. 26: 6.

ll. 342–5. Cf. Isa. 40: 12–17, 22.

ll. 346–53. Cowper may here be recalling a passage from the end of a discussion of the prayers used on general fast days in the *Gentleman's Magazine* for December 1780 (xl. 564): 'At the commencement of the present hostilities did we not often hear some very hyperbolical, nay even presumptuous epithets uttered? Was it not without reserve, and without palliation, declared, that the British parliament was omnipotent, and that the forces sent to reduce the revolted Americans to an unconditional submission to its laws were invincible? "What God," says the pious and learned President of Magdalen College, "has joined together, it is the error of the times to put asunder; to think only of our fleets and armies, and to forget our faith and practice."'

ll. 352–3. Cf. 1 Sam. 17: 47.

l. 359. *a woman's part.* Cf. Isa. 19: 16.

l. 360. *when none pursue.* Cf. Lev. 26: 17.

l. 361. *by many or by few.* Cf. 1 Sam. 14: 6.

ll. 364 ff. For similar sentiments on the British role in India, see Cowper's letter to Lady Hesketh, 16 Feb. 1788.

l. 374. *truck'd.* Exchanged; usually with the implication, as here, that something valuable has been given for something worthless. The following line is obscure, but perhaps refers to the high prices charged for places in the East India Company's service.

ll. 376–81. The Test Act of 1672 required municipal officials, military officers, and office-holders under the Crown to take the oaths of supremacy and obedience, to abjure the doctrine of transubstantiation, and to take communion according to the order of the Church of England. These requirements were adjusted from time to time, e.g. by the Relief Act of 1778 (cf.

'Table Talk', l. 72n.), but the use of the communion as a 'test' was not dropped until 1828 (9 Geo. IV, c. 17).

l. 384. *a Bishop*. William Warburton (1698–1779), Bishop of Gloucester from 1760. In 1736 he published *The Alliance between Church and State: or, The Necessity and Equity of an Established Religion and a Test Law Demonstrated*. In fact, Warburton shows no awareness that the cup was stained: his theory is that the state and the largest sect form an alliance whereby the state protects the Church, which on its part lends moral stability to the state; he asks the reader 'to have this always in mind, that the true end for which Religion is established is, not to provide for the true Faith, but for Civil Utility, as the key to open to him the whole mystery of this Controversy' (4th ed., 1766, p. 347).

l. 386. *sworn on ev'ry slight pretence*. Cf. Blackstone, *Commentaries*, IV, chap. 10, sect. 16: 'it is much to be questioned how far any magistrate is justifiable in taking a voluntary *affidavit* in any extrajudicial matter, as is now too frequent upon every petty occasion: since it is more than possible, that by such idle oaths a man may frequently *in foro conscientiae* incur the guilt, and at the same time evade the temporal penalties, of perjury' (Oxford, 1769, p. 137).

ll. 389–412. These lines were substituted by means of a cancel; see head-note.

l. 401. *an yearly fast*. During the American War, as during previous wars in Cowper's lifetime, days of 'public fast and humiliation' were appointed by royal proclamation, approximately once a year, usually in February; church services were held, with specially appointed prayers (see l. 346n.). The 1776 proclamation is addressed to the people 'as they tender the favour of Almighty God, and would avoid his wrath and indignation' (*Gentleman's Magazine*, xlvi. 505).

ll. 406–13. Cf. Isa. 58: 3–7.

l. 420. Cf. Gen. 13: 10.

l. 421. Cf. Gen. 19: 24–5.

l. 422. Cf. Jude 7.

l. 444. *As meek as the man Moses*. Cf. Num. 12: 3.

l. 445. Cf. Acts 26.

ll. 448–9. Eli was the worthy priest, teacher of Samuel; Hophni and Phine[h]as were his wicked sons: cf. 1 Sam. 2: 12.

l. 465. Cf. Ps. 2: 3.

l. 466. *borne upon the wings of truth, sublime*. Perhaps a reminiscence of *Paradise Lost*, vii. 421.

ll. 468–507. Benham and others have remarked on the inaccuracy of Cowper's history in this passage: (1) if ll. 470–1 are a reference to the Vikings, they misrepresent chronology; (2) the Latin element in modern English owes very little indeed to the Roman occupation (see next note); (3) the major eighteenth-century historians agree that the Britons were less rather than more able to defend themselves at the end of that occupation than they had been at the beginning of it; (4) Woden and Thor were deities of the Saxons, not of the Britons—but it is not certain that Cowper means to ascribe them to the Britons. These errors, with the possible exception of the second, appear to be Cowper's own; we have not been able to trace them to any history book.

ll. 480–3. There is a possible source for this curious statement in William Robertson's *History of Scotland during the Reigns of Queen Mary and of King James VI*, first published in 1759. Cowper may possibly have misremembered Robertson's assertion (controversial at the time) that the Romans' 'long residence in the island had polished, in some degree, the rude inhabitants, and the Britons were indebted to their intercourse with the Romans, for the art of writing, and the use of numbers, without which it is impossible long to preserve the memory of past events' (16th ed., 1802, i. 203). While Cowper had certainly read Robertson's *History of America* (cf. 'Charity', l. 40n.), it is not clear that he knew the other work; the context of his refusal of 'Robertson' (unspecified) in his letter to Unwin of 22 June 1780 might suggest that he did.

ll. 496–9. Probably based ultimately on the lurid account of Diodorus Siculus, v. 31. Cf. 'Table Talk', l. 503n.

ll. 504–7. Cf. 1 Sam. 5: 4.

l. 517. Doctors' Commons, in the south-west corner of St. Paul's Church-yard, was both a college for doctors of civil law and the seat of the ecclesiastical courts of the Archbishop of Canterbury, together with the Consistory Court of the Bishop of London and the High Court of Admiralty. Cowper has in mind the Court of Faculties and Dispensations in particular, and probably reflects an opinion common among practitioners in the lay courts; Blackstone writes of 'such ecclesiastical courts, as have only what is called a *voluntary* and not a *contentious* jurisdiction; which are merely concerned in doing or selling what no one opposes, and which keep an open office for that purpose (as granting dispensations, licences, faculties, and other remnants of the papal extortions)' (*Commentaries*, iii, Oxford, 1768, p. 66).

l. 519. *smack.* The crack of the whip, not its impact ('slap' and similar senses date from the nineteenth century).

ll. 550–3. Benham is probably right to see an allusion to the reign of Charles II, when the Dutch fleet sailed into the Medway (1667).

ll. 570–3. This anecdote is Cowper's own invention.

l. 574. *the Stuart.* Charles Edward, the Young Pretender (1720–88). He reached

Derby at the head of his Highland forces on 4 December 1745, and began his retreat two days later.

l. 577. *helm.* 'The station of government' (Johnson).

l. 599. *her.* The nymph Daphne, pursued by Apollo, was turned into a laurel, symbolic here of victory and peace. Cowper's account of Runnymede (three miles downstream from Windsor) recalls Denham's in *Cooper's Hill*, ll. 325–6:

> Faire liberty pursu'd, and meant a Prey
> To lawless power, here turn'd, and stood at bay.

l. 614. *Bonner, blithe as shepherd at a wake.* Edmund Bonner (1500?–1569), Bishop of London, depicted by Foxe as a sadistic prosecutor of heretics. *wake*: 'the local annual festival of an English (now chiefly rural) parish, observed . . . as an occasion for making holiday' (*OED*).

l. 623. *Nor spare a life too short to reach the skies.* I.e. no martyr for the Protestant cause was too young to be granted his reward in heaven.

ll. 624–5. Understand 'the tide which their hearts poured'.

l. 643. *form'd thee for his praise.* Cf. Isa. 43: 21.

l. 651. *bind the task assign'd thee to thine heart.* Cf. Prov. 6: 21.

l. 659. *his, who touch'd their hearts.* Cf. 1 Sam. 10: 26.

l. 664. *the champion in forensic war.* As Spiller notes, a reference to Thomas Erskine (1750–1823), who defended Lord George Gordon at his trial for high treason on 5–6 February 1781. In the course of his famous speech, 'he exclaimed with peculiar bitterness, that if a man could bring a paper signed from the best of principles, from the purest motives of humanity, and adduce it as a proof of guilt, to convict the person acting from such excellent principles to death, By God, he must be an assassin. . . . he repeated, *I say, by God, that man is a ruffian*, who shall, after this, presume to build upon such honest, artless conduct, as an evidence of guilt' (*Political Magazine*, ii (Feb. 1781), 105, 106).

l. 694. Britain in 1781 was at war with the Americans, France, Spain, and Holland, and had no allies.

l. 718. *hang this harp upon yon aged beech.* Cf. Ps. 137: 2: 'We hanged our harps upon the willows'; the beech-tree comes from the beginning of Virgil's *Eclogues*.

HOPE

A tear in the manuscript of Cowper's letter to Newton, 13 May 1781, has removed the end of a sentence which begins: 'I have lately begun a Poem, which if ever [. . .]'. This is probably a reference to 'Hope', which is mentioned as 'lately enter'd upon' in Cowper's letter to Unwin of 23 May. A month later, on 24 June, he wrote, again to Unwin, that the delay in publication of his planned volume had enabled him to add 'Hope' to its contents.

No manuscript copy of the poem is known to survive.

Motto. Virgil, *Aeneid*, vi. 109: '. . . do you teach the way, and throw open the sacred portals!'

l. 28. *Lothario.* The name of the notorious rake, seducer of the heroine in Rowe's *The Fair Penitent*, 1703. No direct application need be supposed here, but it should be noted that Charles Churchill had used the name in the course of an extended attack on the Earl of Sandwich in *The Candidate*, 1764, ll. 307–414. This identification is recalled in an anonymous poem, 'A Short Essay on Charles Churchill', published (where Cowper must surely have seen it) in the *Gentleman's Magazine* for September 1780:

> . . . Yet all unruffled in his air,
> Lothario lolls on easy chair;
> And hums a tune, and twirls his seal,
> Contemplating the public weal . . . (l. 433).

l. 46. *tilth.* 'The result or produce of tillage; crop, harvest' (*OED*, citing this passage).

ll. 57–61. Obscure; the sense is: 'not so that, his hours being devoted . . . the wretch may pine, while . . . but so as to rebuke gently . . .'.

l. 71. *colour'd chrystal.* Perhaps a reference to a type of Claude[-Lorraine] glass, tinted so as to impart to the landscape seen through it the gradation of tones typical of Claude's paintings.

l. 75. *slipshod.* Wearing slippers on the feet.

l. 76. *fiddle.* Although the absolute use would be exceptional, it is tempting to take a hint from Johnson and gloss 'to trifle', i.e. to waste time in trivial employments. But a passage in Charles Churchill's *Gotham* (i. 139–42) indicates that 'playing the fiddle' is indeed meant:

> All, from the Fiddle (on which ev'ry Fool,
> The pert Son of dull Sire, discharg'd from School,
> Serves an apprenticeship in College ease,
> And rises thro' the *Gamut* to degrees) . . .

l. 77. *rattling at his door.* The greater the prestige of a caller, the louder was the footman's knock; a special 'London knock' was cultivated for the purpose. See Fielding, *Tom Jones*, XIII. iv.

l. 89. JONQUIL. This name for a very precious young man may have been suggested by Lady Winchilsea, 'The Spleen', ll. 40–1:

> Now the *Jonquille* o'ercomes the feeble Brain;
> We faint beneath the Aromatick Pain . . .

l. 116. *ev'ry good and perfect gift proceeds.* Cf. Jas. 1: 17.

l. 126. Perhaps a reference to *Paradise Lost*, vii. 112–14.

l. 150. *the covenant-insuring bow.* Cf. Gen. 9: 8–17.

l. 159. *chymic.* Here 'alchemical' in an approving sense; from something transitory is derived lasting happiness.

l. 164. *Plucks amaranthin joys from bow'rs of bliss.* Cf. *Paradise Lost*, xi. 77–80, and for the wreaths, ibid. iii. 352–61.

l. 167. *Hope as an anchor firm and sure.* Cf. Heb. 6: 19.

ll. 181–2. Cf. Job. 11: 12; also Ps. 78: 8.

l. 190. *whip-gig.* A 'gig' is something that whirls around, here a whipping-top.

l. 198. *supinely.* Indolently, inertly.

l. 199. *Their fleece his pillow.* The 'fleece' is presumably what the clergyman has shorn from his flock in the way of tithes, etc., though the usage seems otherwise unexampled. The 'pillow' is both figurative and real, the cushion in the pulpit, as shown, for example, in Hogarth's engraving, *The Sleeping Congregation* (which Cowper may be recalling). 'Drawl' ('to utter any thing in a slow driveling way'—Johnson) seems to be almost a technical term for public, especially ecclesiastical declamation; cf. *The Task*, i. 95: 'The tedious rector drawling o'er his head'; also Pope, *The Dunciad* (1743), ii. 387–90.

l. 205. COTTON. Nathaniel Cotton (1705–88) studied under Boerhaave, and settled at St. Albans about 1740, where he remained for the rest of his life. The friend of Edward Young, he achieved some fame as a poet, being a contributor to Dodsley's *Collection* and the author of *Visions in Verse* (1751). He was well known as a physician specializing in mental illness. Cowper spent eighteen months in his 'Collegium Insanorum' at St. Albans (1763–5), and his advice was sought by Newton during the crisis of 1773–4. Cowper was particularly grateful to Cotton for encouraging him in the Evangelical way: see his letter to Lady Hesketh, 4 July 1765, and Ryskamp, pp. 160–2, 261.

l. 230. *Who live in pleasure, dead ev'n while they live.* Cf. 1 Tim. 5: 6.

ll. 250–1. Johnson and Boswell discussed the contrast in religious observance between the town (London) and the country on Good Friday, 14 April 1775; Johnson said that Good Friday 'was, upon the whole, very well observed even in London'.

l. 265. *mournful 'scutcheons.* These are not the hatchment, a single, specially constructed funeral escutcheon hung outside the house of the deceased, but escutcheons with which the coffin would be decorated in the funeral procession—eight were used for the funeral of Lord Chatham in 1778, for instance. Cf. Johnson, *Rambler*, 73 (27 Nov. 1750): 'I dreamed every night of escutcheons and white gloves'; also Gray, 'A Long Story', l. 6.

l. 276. *pilgrims.* Travellers of any kind.

l. 283. *Each man's belief is right in his own eyes.* Cf. Judg. 21: 25.

l. 287. *The cedar and the hyssop on the wall.* Cf. 1 Kgs. 4: 33.

l. 298. *That* of course is governed by 'hopes' (294)—but Cowper seems to have forgotten his conditional clause.

l. 302. *Ethelred's house.* There is no connection with any of the historical Ethelreds, and the choice of name is a mystery. The anecdote derives from Matt. 22: 1–14.

l. 381. *the col'nel.* The modern pronunciation, although recorded by Sheridan in 1780, was not universal at that time, and the apostrophe is intended to forestall a trisyllable (see *OED*). Johnson says: 'it is now generally sounded with only two distinct syllables, *col'nel.*'

l. 397. *ensign.* The standard-bearer of a regiment, usually of the lowest commissioned rank, equivalent to the modern second lieutenant.

l. 402. *there.* Cf. Cowper's letter to Joseph Johnson, 20 October 1781: 'I acknowledge with pleasure the accuracy of your remark on the two lines you have scored in the first page of the inclosed sheet, but though the word *there* in its critical and proper use is undoubtedly an adverb denoting locality, yet I cannot but think that in the familiar strain of poetical colloquy, (especially if the gay careless air of the speaker in the present instance be considered) a less exact application of it may be allowed.—We say in common speech— you was scrupulous on that Occasion; *there* I think you was wrong—meaning, in that part of your conduct. I do not know indeed that I should hesitate to give it that sense if I were writing prose for the press instead of Verse, or on any other occasion whatsoever.'

l. 415. *many a shrug.* 'A motion of the shoulders usually expressing dislike or aversion' (Johnson). Cf. Mr. Darcy, who could listen to the pompous inanities of Sir William Lucas 'with very decent composure. If he did shrug his shoulders, it was not till Sir William was out of sight' (*Pride and Prejudice*, III. xviii *ad fin.*).

l. 416. *Sir Smug. OED* cites this passage under 'sir', sense 3: 'Used fancifully, or as a mock title'; but the relevant sense may be no. 5: 'Used (as a rendering of L. *dominus*), with the surname of the person, to designate a Bachelor of Arts in some Universities' (certainly current in Cowper's day). 'Smug' is probably used in Johnson's sense: 'Nice; spruce; dressed with affectation of niceness, but without affectation.' (Cf. Cowper's *Odyssey*, xv. 403–4: 'sleek their heads, / And smug their countenances'.) The opprobrious modern sense should not be assumed. The young parson has just been placed on the first rung of the ladder which may lead him to a bishopric (ll. 414, 438).

l. 458. *her Cornubian mines.* As Benham suggested, a reference to Wesley's success in preaching to the Cornish miners.

l. 460. The book mentioned in Cowper's note is David Crantz, *The History of Greenland: containing a description of the country, and its inhabitants: and particu-*

larly, a relation of the Mission, carried on for above these thirty years by the Unitas Fratrum . . . Translated from the High-Dutch, 1767. This moving account portrays the natives as greedy, brutal, deceitful, crafty, cruel, and given to noisy dancing and riotous revels, but not, as Cowper asserts (508), drunkards. Drunkenness was so common around Olney that perhaps the characteristic was transferred to the Greenlanders. (See, for example, the letter to Newton, 25 Aug. 1781.)

l. 463. *sweet Sharon's rose.* Cf. S. of S. 2: 1.

ll. 469–72. Cf. S. of S. 2: 11–12.

l. 509. Understand 'the full-gorged savage who at his nauseous feast'.

ll. 524–7. Cf. Isa. 35: 1; 55: 13.

ll. 540–5. An awkward passage, which even changed punctuation cannot much help. The words 'though secret evil lurks / In all we touch' is a second parenthetical statement. The root of the problem is the contradictory views of nature which Cowper tries to combine.

l. 554. *Leuconomus.* From Greek *leuko-*, 'white', and *nomos,* 'place of pasturage'. George Whitefield (1714–70), son of the proprietor of the Bell Inn at Gloucester, was educated at Pembroke College, Oxford, where he encountered the Wesleys. In 1741, already famous as a preacher on both sides of the Atlantic, Whitefield broke with John Wesley over the issue of 'free grace'. Cowper's admiration is partly that of a fellow-Calvinist. Whitefield was widely attacked throughout his career, but Cowper seems to have particularly in mind the production of Samuel Foote's *The Minor* in 1760. Mr. Squintum (Whitefield had a squint) does not appear on stage, but is shown to be a hypocrite and a cheat of the most squalid kind. Foote apparently borrowed the idea from Joseph Reed's *The Register Office* (written 1759); in turn Israel Pottinger wrote a sequel, *The Methodist* (1761; never produced), in which Mr. Squintum is a character. Considerable controversy surrounded *The Minor,* no doubt well known to Cowper at the time, since Martin Madan wrote a pamphlet, 'A Letter to David Garrick, Esq., occasioned by the intended representation of the "Minor" at the Theatre Royal in Drury Lane' (1760).

l. 625. *the beloved John.* Cf. John 13: 23.

l. 627. Cf. Ezek. 13: 10–16, esp. 15.

l. 630. LAMA SABACTHANI. Properly 'Sabachthani'; cf. Matt. 27: 46.

l. 644. *Since Abel worshipp'd.* Cf. Genesis 4. Cain's murder of Abel is the first instance of seeming religion hating the true. The words 'or the world began' are puzzling, since Cowper seems to be talking about postlapsarian, fallen human nature; but perhaps he intends merely to affirm that '*the true*' has always existed.

l. 646. Cf. John 9: 32.

ll. 716–19. Bailey notes the ambiguity of syntax, and, supposing the apodosis to begin at 'The thunder', places a semicolon after 'away'. The apodosis begins at 'Upon', and 'chance' (716) is an adverb.

l. 742. *These are thy glorious works.* Echoed from *Paradise Lost*, v. 153.

l. 746. *when night has quench'd the pole.* 'Pole' here means 'the sky, the heavens', as in Blake's 'A Poison Tree', l. 14: 'When the night had veil'd the pole'; however, there may also be a reminiscence of *Othello*, ii. i. 15: 'And quench the Guards of th'ever-fixed pole [star].'

l. 747. *heav'n is all departed as a scroll.* Cf. Rev. 6: 14.

l. 749. Cf. 2 Pet. 3: 10–13.

l. 764. *Judah's hallow'd gate.* Cf. Jer. 7: 2.

CHARITY

It is often said that this poem was written in two weeks, but it is difficult to ascertain the termini precisely. The first datable reference is in a letter to Newton of 7 July 1781: 'I have advanced so far in Charity, that I have ventured to give Johnson Notice of it, and his Option whether he will print it now or hereafter. I rather wish he may chuse the present time, because it will be a proper Sequel to Hope, and because I am willing to think it will embellish the Collection.' Cowper adds that he expects to send the completed poem on the following Friday, that is, on the 13th. It is a safe assumption that the poem was begun before the end of June. No manuscript copy is known to survive.

On 22 July 1781 Cowper wrote to Newton: 'taking it for granted that the new marriage bill would pass, I took occasion in the address to liberty to celebrate the joyfull Æra, but in doing so afforded another proof that poets are not always prophets, for the House of Lords have thrown it out. I am however provided with four lines to fill up the gap, which I suppose it will be time enough to insert, when the copy is sent down.' Wright (*The Correspondence of William Cowper*, 1904, i. 331n.) locates the address to liberty in 'Table Talk', i.e. ll. 260–335, but this cannot be correct, for Cowper had already seen proof of that passage. He must therefore be referring to ll. 254–89 of 'Charity'. The only readily detachable four lines here are ll. 272–5, on the familiar topic of 'priestly power'.

The 'new marriage bill' was that of Charles James Fox, designed to make radical amendments in Lord Hardwicke's Marriage Act of 1753. Lord Chancellor Thurlow was opposed to the discussion of a bill 'which peremptorily declared the Marriage Act to be pregnant with inconvenience'. On 12 July he carried the House with him, and the bill was lost. Thus Cowper could not have known of the bill's fate when he dispatched a copy of the poem to Newton on the 13th. The contents of the cancelled four lines is unknown.

Motto. From Horace, *Odes*, IV. ii. 37–40: 'than which [i.e. charity] nothing greater or better have the fates and good gods given to the world, nor will they give, even though the times should return to the Golden Age.' In the original the passage begins with the word 'quo', referring to Caesar; Cowper requires the feminine pronoun to refer to *caritas*.

l. 23. *Cook*. Captain James Cook, born 1728, was killed by natives on the island of Hawaii on 14 February 1779. News of his death took almost a year to reach London. It is recorded in the *Gentleman's Magazine* for January 1780, where it is said that Cook 'as a voyager, was almost singular, that he never knowingly injured, but always studied to benefit the savages whom he visited' (l. 44). Cowper had read Cook's account of his second voyage, *A Voyage towards the South Pole* [cf. l. 34] *and Round the World*, on its first appearance in 1777 (letters to Hill, 13 July and 28 Oct. 1777). For a less favourable view of Cook, see the letter to Newton, 9 Oct. 1784.

l. 40. *Cortez*. The name is spelt 'Cortes' in Cowper's source, William Robertson's *History of America* (1777), which he mentions in his letter to Hill, 1 Mar. 1778.

l. 41. *then*. That is, about 1520; a decade before the dissolution of the religious houses in England.

ll. 51–6. Every editor of Cowper knows who imprisoned Montezuma, and who strangled Atahualpa; but Cowper himself confuses them. Lines 51–4 apply to the Mexican Montezuma, who was tricked into giving himself into the custody of Cortez, and died in despair at having betrayed his people. Lines 55–6 apply to Atahualpa, last of the Incas of Peru, whose death-warrant was signed by the same Friar Valverde who then persuaded him to embrace the Christian faith in order that he might be strangled rather than burned.

l. 52. *vain imperial Philip*. 'Philip, possessing that spirit of unceasing assiduity, which often characterizes the ambition of men of moderate talents, entertained such an high opinion of his own resources, that he thought nothing too arduous for him to undertake' (Robertson, 4th ed., 1783, iii. 311). The conquests of Mexico and Peru took place during the reign of Charles V, and not of his son Philip II. Cowper has been accused of supposing that Philip was, like his father, Holy Roman Emperor, but the charge is ill-founded, for he seems to understand 'imperial' as 'royal; possessing royalty', as Johnson defines it.

ll. 61–4. Cf. Robertson: '. . . when opulence pours in suddenly, and with too full a stream, it overturns all sober plans of industry, and brings along with it a taste for what is wild and extravagant, and daring in business or in action' (iii. 310). The language of ll. 62–3 suggests a covert reference to syphilis: 'By communicating it to their conquerors they have . . . amply avenged their own wrongs' (ii. 75).

ll. 67, 71. Cf. Isa. 14: 10–11.

l. 82. Cf. Deut. 32: 35, Ps. 149: 7–9.

ll. 83–130. The general tenor of this passage recalls Thomson's account of Industry in *The Seasons*, 'Autumn', ll. 43–150.

l. 135. Cf. Luke 1: 19, 26.

l. 139. *gage and span*. Both verbs mean 'to measure'; the first, to measure the diameter, the second, to measure the circumference (cf. 'Truth', l. 155).

l. 162. *all whose paths are peace*. Cf. Prov. 3: 12.

l. 188. *emergence*. 'Pressing necessity. A sense not proper' (Johnson, citing Addison).

l. 192. *brave*. 'Excellent; noble; it is an indeterminate word, used to express the superabundance of any valuable quality, in men or things' (Johnson).

ll. 202–3. Despite Cowper's assurance, it is not easy to find an apposite proof-text; one might cite, for example, 1 Tim. 2: 4.

l. 204. Cf. 1 Cor. 15: 22.

l. 205. Cf. 1 Cor. 7: 23.

l. 217. Cf. Prov. 14: 31.

l. 230. '*Beauty for ashes*'. Cf. Isa. 61: 3.

l. 253. John Thornton (1720–90) inherited a fortune from his father, and was at the time of his death reputed one of the greatest merchants of Europe (*Gentleman's Magazine*, lx. 1056). He was well known for his liberality to the poor, and for his support of the Evangelical clergy (he presented Newton to the rectory of St. Mary Woolnoth in 1779). See head-note to *Olney Hymns*, and Cowper's memorial poem of November 1790.

l. 271. *From Sparta hither*. For a relevant account of Spartan virtues, see Thomson's *Liberty*, ii. 109–34; Collins in his 'Ode to Liberty' names Sparta first in the sequence of free states.

ll. 272–5. Probably the four lines which replace a comment on Fox's marriage bill—see head-note.

ll. 276–89. In reference to Lord Beauchamp's bill for the relief of debtors, which was debated in the Commons during the first half of 1780, but was never acted upon—at least in part because the Gordon Riots supervened.

l. 296. John Howard (1726–90) began his career as a prison-reformer when he became High Sheriff of Bedfordshire in 1773 and discovered abuses in the county gaols. He began the tours of prisons which led to the publication in 1777 of *The State of the Prisons in England and Wales . . . and an Account of Some Foreign Prisons*, expanded in 1780. He died at Kherson in the Crimea, where he was inspecting military hospitals (see Cowper to John Bacon, 7 Sept. 1790). Here, and in the preceding passage, Cowper shows knowledge of Burke's speech to the electors of Bristol before the 1780 election. In this speech, which was printed at the time, Burke first defends his support of Beauchamp's bill (see previous note), and then speaks of Howard: 'He has visited all Europe,—not to survey the sumptuousness of palaces, or the stateliness of temples; not to make accurate measurements of the remains of ancient grandeur, nor to form a scale of the curiosity of modern art; not to collect medals, or collate manuscripts:—but to dive into the depths of dungeons; to plunge into the infections of hospitals; to survey the mansions of sorrow and pain; to take the gage and dimensions of misery, depression and contempt; to remember the forgotten, to attend the neglected, to visit the forsaken, and to compare and collate all the distresses of all men in all countries. His plan is original; and it is as full of genius as it is of humanity. It was a voyage of discovery; a circumnavigation of charity' (*Works*, 1803, iii. 380–1).

ll. 317–22. Influenced perhaps by reminiscence of Addison's *Spectator*, 465 (23 Aug. 1712), which includes the ode, 'The spacious firmament on high'.

ll. 335–6. Cf. *Paradise Lost*, v. 508–12.

ll. 347–8. Cf. Amos 5: 2.

ll. 352–4. There is no reason to suppose that Cowper had particular experiments in mind. Line 354 is certainly slightly satirical, but to attempt to weigh a sunbeam (I have found no record of such an attempt) might not have seemed completely absurd to adherents of the corpuscular theory of light, still widely current in Cowper's day.

l. 376. *a veil of midnight on his heart*. Cf. 2 Cor. 3: 15.

l. 432. *the pourtrait*. Cf. 1 Cor. 13.

ll. 438–9. Cf. *Paradise Lost*, v. 285–7.

l. 446. Cf. *Paradise Lost*, iv. 156–9.

l. 460. *mantle-tree*. Mantelpiece.

l. 469. *The brief*. 'A letter patent issued by the sovereign as Head of the Church, licensing a collection in the churches throughout England for a specified object of charity' (*OED*). Briefs appear to have been used in Cowper's time mostly to raise money for the building of churches.

l. 470. *the 'Squire's*. See Cowper's account of the prestige and power of the rural squire at church, in *Connoisseur*, 134, 19 Aug. 1756.

l. 484. *office clips it*. A writer signing himself 'Regulator' gives the following figures for a brief to raise funds to build a church in Essex: total collected, £420. 7s.; from which had to be deducted £324. 12s. 4d., made up thus: 9,908 briefs at 6d. per parish, £247. 14s.; additional salary for London, £5; to clerks, £1. 1s.; patent, fees, etc., £70. 17s. 4d. The parish received less than one-quarter of the amount collected. There were reports that a parish in Buckinghamshire had incurred a net loss (*Gentleman's Magazine*, xlviii (1778), 124). It is not surprising that church briefs became obsolete in the nineteenth century.

l. 499. *St. Patrick's dean.* Jonathan Swift, Dean of St. Patrick's Cathedral, Dublin.

l. 526. *Scrib.* A scornful abbreviation of 'scribler' (cf. Pope, *Epistle to Arbuthnot*, ll. 89–94), and, as Spiller suggests, perhaps a glance at the Scriblerus Club.

l. 536. *a tow'ring poet's pride.* Cf. Pope, *Epilogue to the Satires*, ii. 208–9:

> Yes, I am proud; I must be proud to see
> Men not afraid of God, afraid of me . . .

ll. 547–51. As a schoolboy at Westminster; see Ryskamp, p. 28.

l. 584. *He bruis'd beneath his feet th' infernal pow'rs.* Cf. Rom. 16: 20.

l. 587. *thron'd above all height, he condescends.* Cf. *Paradise Lost*, iii. 58.

l. 588. Cf. John 15: 14–15.

l. 608. *Relenting forms.* 'Relenting' in the obsolete sense of 'melting' as well as in the usual figurative sense; 'forms' are the outward forms of church practice and order.

l. 609. *the dipt and sprinkled.* The Baptists and other Christians. Cowper probably has in mind such instances as the experience of John Newton, who had sought to join a Baptist congregation at Liverpool in 1755. He did not do so because they denied full communion to any who had not been baptized by immersion, even though they had been previously baptized by aspersion, and Newton did not see the necessity for a second baptism (J. Bull, *John Newton*, 1868, p. 78).

l. 613. *his useless Machiavel.* That is, his handbook of cynical statecraft would be irrelevant.

l. 614. *budget.* Here in the original sense, still current in Cowper's day, of a bag or wallet, although the modern sense—a statement of the national accounts, and proposed taxation—dominates the lines that follow.

l. 616. *rents.* Revenues generally, income.

l. 617. Swollen, excessive (cf. 'Expostulation', ll. 304–9). There is also a suggestion of the common eighteenth-century sense, 'pregnant'; the sight of a swollen budget-bag is threatening.

l. 624. *the press*. Not just periodical publications or daily newspapers, but all printing (cf. 'The Progress of Error', ll. 301–30).

CONVERSATION

The date of composition (mid-July to early August 1781) is established by Cowper's letters to Newton, 22 July 1781, and to Joseph Johnson, 6 Aug. 1781. Cowper at first intended the poem for the opening of a second volume of verse.

No manuscript copy of the poem is known to survive.

Motto. Virgil, *Eclogues*, v. 82–4: 'For the whisper of the rising south wind does not rejoice me so much [as the shepherd's song], nor shores lashed by the wave, nor rivers which flow down among rocky dells.'

l. 22. *Algebra.* Here signifying arithmetic, or mathematics in general.

ll. 25–6. Cf. Matt. 12: 36–7.

l. 30. *placeman.* The holder of or aspirant to a 'place', usually an office in the gift of the administration, which appoints such persons as will serve political or interested motives.

ll. 35–8. Perhaps an allusion to Plato's exclusion of poets from his ideal state.

l. 39. Cf. 'Retirement', ll. 765–6n.

l. 55. *as Paul observes.* Cf. Heb. 6: 16.

l. 58. *Vestris.* Probably Auguste Vestris (1760–1842), the dancer; see 'Vestris'.

ll. 67–74. The lawyer is presumably Erskine (cf. 'Expostulation', l. 664n.). The use of the Zoroastrian Persian as *ingénu* was probably suggested by Montesquieu's *Lettres persanes*, but this anecdote is not found there.

l. 91. *Sir Soph.* The 'Sir' is contemptuous, and particularly cutting since it was the regular appellation of a bachelor of arts (cf. 'Hope', l. 416n.). 'Soph', abbreviated from 'sophister', was the common term for a second- or third-year undergraduate at Cambridge, one preparing for the academic exercises known as acts and opponencies; that is, public disputation, often on philosophical topics. Cf. D. A. Winstanley, *Unreformed Cambridge*, Cambridge, 1935, pp. 41–7.

l. 163. *The point of honour.* The obligation of a gentleman to seek satisfaction, customarily by a duel, for an injury or insult.

l. 198. *Let* DARES *beat* ENTELLUS *black and blue.* The boxing match between these warriors, in which Entellus is the victor, is described by Virgil, *Aeneid*, v. 362–484.

ll. 243–4. Guy, Earl of Warwick, is the hero of a medieval tale popular into the nineteenth century in chapbook form, as were accounts of Jack the

Giant-killer—both are mentioned by Fielding, *Joseph Andrews*, I. i. 'Fair Eleanor' is the heroine of the ballad 'Lord Thomas and Fair Ellinor' which according to Wheatley was still current in broadsides in the mid-nineteenth century; see T. Percy, *Reliques of Ancient English Poetry*, ed. H. B. Wheatley, 1910, III. 82–5. (The name appears in various forms, in some versions as 'Annet'.)

ll. 245–68. Cowper excuses Newton from this censure in his letter of 18 September 1781, and refers to Isaac Hawkins Browne's skit, 'A Pipe of Tobacco', which touches on a number of the same topics while praising tobacco. See also 'An Epistle to the Rev. William Bull' (June 1782).

l. 250. *trifles*. The emendation 'triflers' has been widely accepted, but it is not necessary; 'trifle' is used here in the now obsolete transferred sense, 'a worthless person, a trifler' (*OED*).

ll. 253–4. It was not proper to 'fumigate the ladies'; cf. Browne, 'A Pipe of Tobacco', IV:

> Ladies, when pipes are brought, affect to swoon;
> They love no smoke, except the smoke of town . . .

ll. 255–6. 'But for destroying insects on fruit-trees, there is an invention called Fumigating Bellows, having a tube or pipe to fix on occasionally, in which is burned tobacco; and by working the bellows, the smoak of the tobacco will issue forth in a full stream, and kill the insects' (T. Maw *et al.*, *Every Man His Own Gardener*, 11th ed., London, 1787, p. 189).

ll. 261–4. Smoking, like drinking, was commonly indulged in after dinner; cf. Browne, 'A Pipe of Tobacco', III:

> But chief, when *Bacchus wont with thee to join*
> *In genial strife*, and orthodoxal ale,
> *Stream life and joy into the Muses' bowl.*

l. 271. A reminiscence of *Spectator*, 617, 8 Nov. 1714: '*Tom Tyler's* Phiz is something damaged by the Fall of a Rocket, which hath almost spoiled the Gnomon of his Countenance.'

l. 274. *a wind-gun's airy charge*. Cf. Pope, *Dunciad* (1743), I. 181–2.

l. 283. *civet*. A perfume derived from the civet-cat; hence the nonce coinage, 'puss-gentleman'.

l. 286. *a raree-show*. 'A show carried in a box' (Johnson); a peep-show. The term is depreciatory.

l. 292. *a-la-mort*. Originally 'mortally sick', but here probably 'dejected, dispirited'.

l. 299. *budge*. 'Solemn in demeanour, important-looking, pompous, stiff, formal' (*OED*).

l. 356. *the pip*. A disease of poultry, in which their mouths and throats are choked.

ll. 357–8. It was believed that the Romans had invented lamps which, shut up in tombs, burned perpetually until the moment the tombs were opened. Cf. Pope, *Elegy to the Memory of an Unfortunate Lady*, ll. 19–20.

l. 391. *epidemic throats*. *OED* defines 'epidemic' here as a nonce use: 'affected with an epidemic'.

l. 392. 'Rheums' are colds in the head; 'phthisic' is properly consumption, but here probably means any severe affection of the throat or lungs.

l. 421. *the club*. Not a building, but periodical gatherings of like-minded people, usually held in a tavern.

l. 425. *Let him improve his talent*. Cf. Matt. 25: 14–30.

ll. 441–2. Cf. S. of S. 4: 11.

l. 456. *the last scene of her six thousand years*. In reference to the ancient prophecy that the world would last two thousand years before the Law, two thousand under the Law, and two thousand under the Messiah.

l. 470. *Snares in his path*. Cf. Prov. 22: 5.

l. 474. *never named in ears esteemed polite*. Cf. Pope, *Epistle to Burlington*, l. 150: 'Who never mentions Hell to ears polite.'

l. 502. Cf. Matt. 8: 27; Num. 20: 11.

ll. 505–36. A paraphrase of Luke 24: 13–32; for testimony to the power of that passage, see the letter to Lady Hesketh, 1 Aug. 1765.

l. 527. *searched*. Here in the special sense derived from John 5: 39: 'drew out the significance of'.

l. 544. *wanting him to loose the sacred seal*. Cf. Rev. 5: 2.

l. 549. *on God himself exact*. For the usage 'exact on/upon', cf. Ps. 89: 22.

l. 558. *The pillar of th'eternal plan*. Cf. 1 Tim. 3: 15. This passage is generally inspired by the parable of the house built upon a rock, Matt. 7: 24–7.

ll. 564–6. Cf. John 4: 14. The Jordan is named in reference to Christ's baptism.

l. 588. *Known by thy bleating*. Perhaps in reference to the tell-tale bleating which betrayed Saul's wilful disobedience to the Lord's command, 1 Sam. 15: 14.

l. 590. *The fixt fee-simple*. The undisputed property.

ll. 605–24. The identity of the 'vet'ran warrior' remains a mystery. Most commentators suggest John Newton, but ll. 613–18 would hardly be true of him. Milford–Russell suggests Dr. John Nicoll (1683–1765), Head Master of Westminster from 1733 to 1753, presumably because Cowper commends him in the *Memoir* for the pains he took to prepare the boys for confirmation. It may be that Cowper had no single person in mind; that this is an idealized and perhaps composite portrait. He is not generally reluctant in these poems to name those he desires to praise.

l. 730. *As Tully with philosophy.* The relevant passage in *De Senectute*, 2 is thus translated by Melmoth: 'Can we sufficiently then express our sense of the obligations we owe to Philosophy, who thus instructs her disciples how to pass through every successive period of human life, with equal satisfaction and complacency?' (London, 1777, p. 4.)

l. 731. *the silent watches of the night.* Cf. Ps. 63: 6.

l. 736. *an ape upon a stage.* That is, Foote's mimicry of Whitefield; cf. 'Hope', ll. 556 ff. and note.

l. 751. *the flow'rs of Eden felt the blast.* Cf. *Paradise Lost*, xii. 633–6.

l.756. Cf. 2 Pet. 3: 7, 10.

l. 777. *historical assent.* That is, assent to the truth of the Gospels as historical documents merely; in contrast to a 'lively faith'. Cowper is attacking the Latitudinarian views of such as Tillotson, who claims that just as we believe in the existence and deeds of Alexander the Great and Julius Caesar on the basis of historical records, so, 'if we have the doctrine and history of the gospel, and all the evidences of our Saviour's divine authority, conveyed down to us, in as credible a manner, as any of these ancient matters of fact are, which mankind do most firmly believe, then we have sufficient ground to be assured of it' (*Sermons*, 1757, xii. 72). Whitefield, preaching on Whit Sunday 1739, illustrates Cowper's response: 'many now read the Life, Sufferings, Death and Resurrection of Jesus Christ, in the same Manner as learned Men read *Caesar's Commentaries*, or *the Conquests of* Alexander. As Things rather intended to afford Matter for Speculation, than to be acted over again in and by us' (reprinted 1789, p. 3).

ll. 817 ff. Benham sees here a reference to the activities of Sir Francis Dashwood and his friends at Medmenham Abbey, especially to the notorious portrait of Dashwood in the garb of a friar adoring the Venus de Medici. Such an allusion is possible, but Benham perhaps underestimates the ironic nature of this passage.

l. 842. *palæstra.* Wrestling school.

l. 850. Cf. 1 Kgs. 18: 21.

l. 883. *glory with a light that never fades.* Cf. 1 Pet. 5: 4.

RETIREMENT

The dating is established by Cowper's letters to Unwin, 25 Aug. 1781, in which he describes at some length his ideas and aims in this poem, and to Newton, 14 Oct. 1781, in which he announces the dispatch of a fair copy.

The inability to proceed with the composition mentioned in the letter to Unwin can have been only a temporary check.

No manuscript copy of the poem is known to survive.

Motto. From Virgil, *Georgics,* IV. 564 (substituting 'florens' for 'florentem'): 'flourishing in the pursuits of sequestered ease.'

ll. 25–6. A commonplace; cf. Addison, *Spectator*, 465, 23 Aug. 1712: 'In our Retirements every thing disposes us to be serious. In Courts and Cities we are entertained with the Works of Men, in the Country with those of God' (the whole of this essay is relevant); cf. also *The Task*, i. 749.

l. 32. *the last scene*. Cf. 'Conversation', l. 456n.

ll. 51–72. For Cowper's interest in microscopy, cf. 'The Progress of Error', l. 485n.

ll. 87–92. Cf. *Paradise Lost*, v. 153–9.

l. 164. *Seal'd with his signet whom they serve*. Cf. Rev. 7: 3; also 9: 4.

l. 177. *pompous*. 'Splendid; magnificent; grand' (Johnson).

l. 218. *shoot the careless*. That is, lure the unwary into sin.

l. 247. *Thyrsis, Alexis*. Thyrsis is the unsuccessful competitor in a singing match in Virgil's *Eclogue* vii; Alexis is the fair but cruel youth addressed in *Eclogue* ii.

ll. 279 ff. William Heberden (1710–1801), the famous physician, teacher, and medical researcher. Cowper in his *Memoir* relates that he consulted Heberden shortly before his breakdown in 1763, but in vain. After his suicide attempt he feared an apoplexy, and sent for a physician (whom he does not name), who reassured him and urged him to go into the country. M. J. Quinlan, in his edition of the *Memoir* (*Proceedings of the American Philosophical Society*, xcvii (1953), 375), points out that this was very probably Heberden again.

l. 365. *the statesman*. This word did not have its modern commendatory sense. Johnson defines: 'A politician; one versed in the arts of government', and 'One employed in public affairs'.

l. 421. *baulks*. Strips of unploughed land separating or enclosing ploughed areas.

l. 444. *dismissing forms*. Laying aside the observance of social distinctions.

l. 453. *The tide of life*. This phrase, and the rest of this sentence, may have been suggested by Horace, who, in a poem which treats of retirement, speaks of 'the waves and tempests of the town' (*Epistles*, II. ii. 85).

l. 487. *baulk*. Refuse to entertain.

l. 494. Bottles of sugar-water were hung on fruit-trees to distract and trap marauding wasps.

l. 521. *caravans and hoys*. Caravans were covered wagons in which servants might be required to travel (cf. *Connoisseur*, 25, 18 July 1754); hoys were large boats used to transport people or goods in coastal traffic.

l. 552. *globose*. Spherical, here 'surrounding the globe'; perhaps influenced by *Paradise Lost*, v. 752–4.

l. 561. *Not to redeem his time*. Cf. Eph. 5: 16.

ll. 569–70. Cf. *The Seasons*, 'Spring', ll. 604, 708–9.

ll. 571–2. Pope names the famous gardens at Stowe in a passage setting forth the ideals of landscape gardening in his *Epistle to Burlington*, ll. 57–70, but he does not describe them. (Cowper's library does not appear to have included Pope's English poems.) The other reference is of course to *Windsor Forest*.

ll. 575–602. Cowper speaks of 'Jack' as if he were a real person, but if so his identity remains a secret. The story may be Cowper's invention; or, more probably, a reworking of part of the popular mythology surrounding Granby. John Manners, Marquis of Granby (1721–70), achieved fame and vast popularity as a dashing military commander during the Seven Years War; i.e. during Cowper's last seven years in London. He was noted for his convivial habits and reckless generosity. His name is connected with several inns and taverns in and around London, but none apparently called the Crown, which was in any case a common name for hostelries.

l. 650. *an intrusted talent*. Cf. Matt. 25: 14–30.

ll. 651–4. Cf. 2 Pet. 3: 10–14.

l. 655. Cf. 1 Cor. 15: 52.

l. 688. *Built God a Church*. The church built by Voltaire at Ferney has for a motto the words *Deo Erexit Voltaire*.

ll. 691–4. Probably, as Spiller suggests, a reference to Horne's *Letter to Mr. Dunning* (1778), a book which might have had additional interest for Cowper if he recalled that Horne, later and better known as Horne Tooke, had attended Westminster School briefly during Cowper's time there.

l. 739. *the Frenchman*. Not, as Cowper's note claims, La Bruyère, but rather, as H. G. Wright pointed out (*MLR* xl (1945), 129–30), Jean-Louis Guez de Balzac, in the first of his *Entretiens* (1657): 'La solitude est certainement vne belle chose; Mais il y a plaisir d'auoir quelqu'vn qui sçache respondre, à qui on puisse dire de temps en temps, que c'est vne belle chose!' (ed. B. Beugnot, Paris, 1972, i. 52). Cowper's misattribution may be explained by facts given in Beugnot's note on this passage: Balzac's sentiment was reproduced almost exactly in Brillon's *Theophraste moderne* (1699), and in this appearance was criticized in Vigneul-Marville's *Sentimens critiques sur les caractères de M. de La Bruyère* (1701), either of which Cowper may have read.

l. 761. *wines upon the fret*. Wines in the stage of secondary fermentation.

ll. 765–6. Cf. Job 37: 8.

ll. 767 ff. Cf. 1 Sam. 19 ff.

ll. 785–800. The harmless pleasures mentioned here were all, at one time or another, Cowper's.

THE DOVES

The letter to Mrs. Newton in which the poem appears is not dated by Cowper, but it is endorsed with the date 5 June 1780. If this is correct, 'The Doves' must have been written about 26 May, since Cowper says in the letter that it is 'about 10 Days old'. The present first stanza was probably composed in March 1781, when Cowper prepared the shorter poems for publication; the purpose of the substitution is of course to eliminate direct reference to Madan's book. The letter explains that the two doves represent Mr. and Mrs. Newton.

A FABLE

In his letter to Newton of 10 May 1780 Cowper introduces his fable by telling how the previous day he had seen (in Mrs. Aspray's neighbouring orchard) a raven's nest threatened with destruction in a storm 'and versified the following thoughts on the occasion'. There is no mention of 'neighbour Hodge' in the letter, the original of which has unfortunately been lost.

A COMPARISON

Its position in *H* provides the *terminus ante quem* of early June 1780, but ther are no other indications as to the date or occasion of this poem.

l. 10. *How laughs the land with various plenty crown'd!* Cf. Dryden, 'Of the Pythagorean Philosophy', translated from Ovid, *Metamorphoses*, xv, l. 304: 'Then laughs the childish Year with Flourets crown'd'; also, *The Task*, vi. 765–6: 'The fruitful field / Laughs with abundance'.

ANOTHER. ADDRESSED TO A YOUNG LADY

Introduced in the letter to Unwin of 8 June 1780 as 'An English Versification of a Thought that popp'd into my Head about 2 Months since', i.e. in April 1780. It is not clear whether the sub-title added in *1782* is to be taken literally or not; in the letter to Unwin, Cowper says that the compliment is as applicable to Unwin's wife as to his yet unmarried sister-in-law.

VERSES, SUPPOSED TO BE WRITTEN BY
ALEXANDER SELKIRK

Cowper probably copied these 'Verses' into *H* about the middle of June 1780; there is no other evidence as to their date. The copy in *U*, which Mrs. Unwin wrote in 4-line stanzas, is collated because its two variants from *A* may have had Cowper's at least temporary approval—as the variant in the title seems to have done, for it was adopted in *1782*. Title apart, *H* as originally inscribed had only one substantive variant from *A* (l. 49). The major revisions in the fifth and seventh stanzas probably date from March 1781, when Cowper was preparing a selection of his shorter pieces for the printer. The three further alterations (ll. 20, 31, 40) which are not recorded in *H* may have been made in proof.

This poem was popular, and often reprinted; in at least one instance, as the genuine production of Selkirk himself (*Scots Magazine*, xlix (1787), 528).

ON THE PROMOTION OF EDWARD THURLOW, ESQ.

Sending this to Hill in the letter of 14 November 1779, Cowper says: 'Your Approbation of my last Heliconian Present, encourages me to send you another. I wrote it indeed on purpose for you.' The present was 'The Pine Apple and the Bee', sent to Hill on 2 October; these lines were probably written early in November.

Edward Thurlow (1731–1806) became friends with Cowper in 1751, when both were studying law under the aegis of Mr. Chapman, and their association continued until Cowper's departure from London in 1763. It is far from certain that 'th'experienc'd and the sage' of those years foresaw a great future for the young Thurlow—he had been sent down from Cambridge for idleness and insubordination; nor can many have perceived grace in a man notorious for his brutal manners. He became Lord High Chancellor and Baron Thurlow of Ashfield, Sussex, on 3 June 1778 (see Cowper to Hill, 6 June 1778), and was removed at Fox's behest on formation of the Fox–North coalition, 9 April 1783; he resumed the office when Pitt became Premier, 23 December 1783, and was forced to resign finally on 15 June 1792. (On Cowper's association with him, see Ryskamp, pp. 60–3, and authorities there cited.) It was appropriate that Cowper should write such a poem for Hill, since it was he who had long ago introduced the two men, and Thurlow, on becoming Chancellor, had appointed Hill Secretary of Lunatics (W. Hooper, 'Cowper's "Sephus"', *N & Q*, 12th ser. v (1919), 258). For a later, less favourable, account of Thurlow, see 'The Valediction', ll. 7–26.

ODE TO PEACE

Often dated 1773, on no better authority than that of J. S. Memes, who assigned these verses to 'the commencement of Cowper's second attack of mental indisposition' (*Poems*, 1846 ed., p. 348). But this is just a guess. The original reading of l. 3, 'William's heart', indicates that the poem is indeed a personal utterance, but it is a prayer for the *return* of peace, and might have been written at any time subsequent to 1773. The fact that it appears in *H*, which contains no poem known to have been written before 1779, further suggests that it was composed in the late 1770s.

ll. 15–17. The stream is presumably the Ouse, but the grove and the shed are more difficult to identify. Cowper uses the word 'shed' only once elsewhere in his verse, in 'The Winter Nosegay', l. 6, where he refers to his greenhouse. If the greenhouse is meant here, then the 'grove' must be Mrs. Aspray's neighbouring orchard (cf. 'A Fable', above).

HUMAN FRAILTY

There is no clear indication of the date of composition, but the context in which this poem appears in *U*, in the letter to Unwin of 2 December 1779, is generally congruous in sentiment, suggesting that it was then a recent composition.

l. 5. *spring*. 'A recoil or rebound of something after being bent or forced out of its normal position or form' (*O.E.D.*)

THE MODERN PATRIOT

On 27 February 1780 Cowper wrote to William Unwin: 'When I wrote last I was a little inclined to send you a copy of Verses entitled the Modern Patriot, but was not quite pleased with a Line or two which I found it difficult to mend, therefore did not. At Night I read Mr Burke's Speech in the newspaper, and was so well pleased with his Proposals for a Reformation, and with the Temper in which he made them, that I began to think better of his Cause and burnt my Verses.' These verses, then, were *almost* sent with the letter to Unwin of 13 February, which is concerned with the reform agitation being pressed by the parliamentary Opposition. In that letter Cowper mentions specifically Sir George Savile, who presented the famous Yorkshire petition to the Commons on 8 February (see *London Magazine*, xlix (1780), 45, 122–3, for the petition and Savile's speech). The reference to Burke's 'Cause' suggests that the verses were directed against the Opposition, seen as hotheads of Savile's stamp; Burke's speech was that delivered on 11 February, when he presented his 'Plan for the Better Security of the

Independence of Parliament' (*Works*, London, 1803, iii. 229–352). The question is whether any of the February poem survives in the present one of the same title, which, as Povey noted, appears to have been written after the Gordon Riots in June 1780, a dating consistent with its position in *H*. The second and fourth stanzas would be applicable to the Opposition at large, but fit Lord George Gordon equally well; the question is really unanswerable. For a more detailed treatment of Gordon as a madman, see below, 'Cum Ratione Insanire'.

ON OBSERVING SOME NAMES OF LITTLE NOTE

On 3 September 1780 Cowper wrote to William Unwin that he thought he would read no more of the first volume of the *Biographia Britannica*. His criticism in verse was suggested, he says, by the observation that divines who had written nothing but a long-forgotten controversial pamphlet might well have been omitted—an observation which lends additional point to the final couplet.

The work referred to is *Biographia Britannica: or, The Lives of the Most Eminent Persons who have flourished in Great Britain and Ireland, from the earliest ages, to the present times . . .*, 2nd edn., edited by Andrew Kippis (1725–95), an eminent Nonconformist scholar and preacher. Only five volumes were published (1778–93); the work is prolix, and Cowper was not alone in his complaint: see Boswell, *Life of Johnson*, Oxford, 1934–64, iii. 174 and n. 3.

REPORT OF AN ADJUDGED CASE

Introducing this gentle satire in his letter to Hill of 27 December 1780, Cowper says it was written 'before the Sun had taken leave of our Hemisphere', which ought to mean 'before the autumnal equinox' but probably means 'before the winter solstice', an interpretation made the more likely by the fact that Cowper copied these lines three times in December 1780 (see textual headnote). The "Report" was probably composed late in November.

Vid: Plowden. Folio 6000 (U). The famous *Commentaries ou Reportes de Edmunde Plowden*, 1578–88; anonymous English translation, 1761. Plowden's foliation runs only to 567.

l. 7. *chief baron Ear*. The Chief Baron presided over the Court of Exchequer, which though originally a court concerned only with the king's revenues, was in Cowper's day divided into a court of common law and a court of equity. The letter to Hill indicates that Cowper envisaged this case as an action at common law. Such actions were brought in the Exchequer Court by means of a legal fiction, grounded on a writ of *quo minus*, 'in which the plaintiff suggests that he is the king's farmer or debtor, and that the defendant hath done him the injury or damage complained of; *quo minus sufficiens existit,* by which he is the less able, to pay the king his debt or rent' (Sir William Blackstone, *Commentaries on the Laws of England,* Oxford, 1765–8, iii. 45).

l. 12. *possession time out of mind.* Although spectacles are of course personal property, they appear to be treated rather as real property in Tongue's argument. Blackstone defines a complete title to 'lands, tenements, and hereditaments' as consisting in a union of the right of possession (the spectacles are made for the nose, ll. 13–16) with the right of property (no one else could be entitled to the spectacles, ll. 17–20); 'and when to this double right the actual possession [l. 11] is also united, . . . then, and then only, is the title completely legal' (*Commentaries,* ii. 199). The phrase 'time out of mind', which at first meant the first year of the reign of Richard I, had by the eighteenth century come to mean in practice twenty years. In his letter to Mrs. Newton of 17 December 1780, Cowper says that the quarrel of nose and eyes broke out while 'Mrs. Unwin sat Knitting with her Spectacles on', but it is not clear whether Mrs. Unwin had then worn her glasses for twenty years.

l. 32. *Eyes should be shut.* 'Possession does not necessarily imply use or enjoyment' (W. J. Byrne, *A Dictionary of English Law,* 1923, s.v. 'Possession').

ON THE BURNING OF LORD MANSFIELD'S LIBRARY

Described as composed that morning in Cowper's letter to Unwin of 22 June 1780; he adds: 'you may print the Lines if you Judge them Worth it.' Unwin seems not to have published them.

On the fifth night of the Gordon Riots, Tuesday, 6 June 1780, the mob attacked the Bloomsbury Square house of William Murray, first Earl of Mansfield (1705–93), Lord Chief Justice from 1756 to 1788. The rioters looted the house, burned its contents on the street, and then set fire to the building itself. 'The destruction of Lord Mansfield's papers may be considered as a public loss: a great number of manuscript volumes of notes, and other professional papers, collected with unremitted assiduity, and written with his own hand, being burnt. One of them was a large quarto, on the distinct Privileges of both Houses of Parliament' (*London Magazine,* xlix (June 1780), 287). 'His Lordship's loss is estimated as £30,000. His valuable library cost him £10,000. In it were some of the most choice and scarcest manuscripts ever in the possession of any individual. His valuable collection of pictures shared the same fate. All his Lordship's note books, in his own hand, to the number of 200, were consumed. This is an irreparable loss to the gentlemen of the bar; as they contained the experience of near half a century' (*Political Magazine,* i (June 1780), 436). For the circumstances of the attack, see J. Holliday, *The*

Life of William late Earl of Mansfield, 1797, pp. 408–12; and John, Lord Campbell, *The Lives of the Chief Justices of England,* 1849, ii. 522–5, where it is stated that several of Mansfield's books had been annotated by Pope, Bolingbroke, and other friends of his youth, and that all his correspondence with such figures was likewise destroyed.

ON THE SAME

On 11 July 1780 Cowper wrote to William Unwin that he would not 'Enter into a Critical Examen of the two Pieces upon Lord Mansfield's Loss', which implies that the second such piece had reached Unwin several days before, at least.

ll. 7–8. Mansfield refused to leave his house in Bloomsbury Square until the very last moment, and barely escaped with his wife to his country home, Caen Wood in Highgate, whither some of the rioters attempted, but in vain, to follow him.

ll. 15–16. *but still we find | The honey on his tongue.* Probably a reference to Mansfield's speech in the House of Lords on 19 June 1780, on the laws relating to riots, at the beginning of which he said: 'My Lords, I shall not deliver my opinions from books: God knows I have none' (*Political Magazine,* i (June 1780), 451).

THE LOVE OF THE WORLD REPROVED

Southey (viii. 323) prints the following excerpt from a letter from Newton to John Thornton, 13 March 1779: 'you may perhaps remember the tale of the Mahometan Hog, which I once sent to Mrs. Thornton; Mr. Cowper lately versified it, and I reserve the other side to transmit you a copy. He did it in about an hour; it gives a proof that his faculties are no ways hurt by his long illness, and likewise that the taste and turn of his mind are still the same. The six lines included in brackets are an addition of mine.' (The original of this letter has dropped out of sight.)

The six lines by Newton are ll. 9–14 in the present text; Newton seems not to have communicated them to Cowper in March 1779, for they are found neither in *A* nor in *H,* and in his letter to Newton of 31 December 1781 Cowper writes that he has received proof as far as the middle of the 'Mahometan Hog' (i.e. to the end of sig. X), but 'your lines which when we had the pleasure of seeing you here, you said you would furnish him with, are not inserted in it.' Newton must have furnished his six lines directly to Joseph Johnson, and p. 320 was reset. The footnote is clearly Newton's work also.

The poem may have been contributed to the *Leeds Mercury* (not 'Journal') by Matthew Powley, whose parish of Dewsbury lies not far from Leeds; certainly it is there introduced by what Povey calls a 'heavily sectarian' letter signed 'Plain and Literal Sense'. It is collated here because it may record some of Cowper's first thoughts. The text in the *Gentleman's Magazine*, l (Sept. 1780), 435–6, is a reprint of *LM*, with the title abridged.

l. 2. *abstain from*. This alteration in the text of *A* is in Mrs. Unwin's hand.

l. 12. *the whole hog*. 'Has the well known American expression of "*going the whole hog*" originated from this story?' (Southey, loc. cit.). *OED* is ambiguous on the point, but cites this passage and no other. The expression was widely current in the 1830s in the vocabulary of Jacksonian politics, but the earliest occurrence in the U.S.A. so far located is in a non-political context (1827). Those interested may consult: R. H. Thornton, *An American Glossary*, Philadelphia, 1912, pp. 368–9; J. A. Weingarten, *An American Dictionary of Slang*, New York, 1954, p. 379; M. M. Mathews, *A Dictionary of Americanisms*, Chicago, 1951, p. 1869. Southey's question remains open.

THE LILY AND THE ROSE

It is a notable feature of *H* that whereas most of the poems which form pairs appear together, 'The Lily and the Rose' and its Latin translation are separated by five quite unrelated pieces. The most obvious reason why this might be so is that the Latin was composed some time after the English, by which time other poems had taken their places in the book. Since pp. 1–89 of *H* were inscribed in the summer and autumn of 1780, it is to that period that we must look for evidence bearing upon this hypothesis.

The copy *U* is found in an undated fragment of a letter to William Unwin. Wright printed it twice in the *Correspondence*, at i. 420–1 and iii. 88–9. Povey, in his 'Notes for a Bibliography of Cowper's Letters', *RES* vii (1931), 185, rightly urged the deletion of the second appearance, but made no comment on the first, which appears for no perceptible reason at the end of 1781 in Wright's chronological sequence. This fragment begins: 'As I Promised you Verse if you would send me a Frank, I am not willing to return the Cover without some . . .' We are to look therefore for such a promise; we find one in the letter of 6 August 1780: 'When you can send me some Franks, I can send you some Verses.' The next letter to Unwin in the dated series belongs to 3 September, suggesting a gap in the series, and it is not franked.

The fragment continues, after the text of the poem: 'I must refer you to those unaccountable Gaddings and Caprices of the Human Mind, for the Cause of this Production; for in general, I believe, there is no Man who has less to do with the Ladies' Cheeks than I have. I suppose it would be best to antedate it, and to imagine that it was written 20 years ago, for my Mind was never more in a trifling Butterfly Trim than when I composed it, even in the earliest Follies of my Life. And what is worse than All this, I have Trans-lated it into Latin—but that, some other time.' This is written as if both poem and translation were fairly recent. If we date the fragment approxi-mately mid-August, this would place composition of the English version early in July, say, the Latin at the end of that month or early in August, datings consistent with the placing of the poems in *H*.

Cowper here draws together two traditional and related topics: flowers and ladies, and red versus white in ladies' cheeks. R. Colie, *My Ecchoing Song*, Princeton, 1970, pp. 158–9, gives numerous references, starting with the Song of Solomon 2: 1. Two eighteenth-century examples probably known to Cowper are: (1) from an anonymous prologue to Terence's *Adelphœ* included in the 1772 edition of Bourne's *Miscellaneous Poems*: 'Hair thinly scattered on my cheek there grows, / Where bloom'd the lily once, where blush'd the rose.' (2) from the opening of Edward Moore's fable, ' The Nightingale and Glow-worm' (1744; discussed further below): 'The prudent nymph, whose cheeks disclose / The lily and the blushing rose . . .'.

THE NIGHTINGALE AND GLOW-WORM

A copy of this fable was sent to Unwin with the letter of 27 February 1780, but the poem became separated from the letter. The copy here collated as *W* may be that sent to Unwin; certainly it is the earliest of the three versions now known, as the variant readings indicate.

The poem is introduced as follows in the letter to Unwin: 'My Whishing Wit has produced the following, the subject of which is more important than the manner in which I have treated it seems to imply. I only premise that in a Philosophical Tract in the Register, I found it asserted that the glow-worm is the Nightingale's proper food.' The first sentence suggests that the poem was then a recent composition. The 'Register' must be the *Annual Register*, which has a section devoted to philosophical essays, but the search for the piece Cowper read has so far proved vain. Perhaps he read it somewhere else. In any case, the belief that nightingales fed on glow-worms was widespread at the time, and persisted into the nineteenth century. Cf. a poem which Cowper may have unconsciously recalled in writing his, Edward Moore's 'The Nightingale and Glow-worm', from his *Fables* (1744), in which a glow-worm, priding herself on her glow, is noticed by a nightingale which tells her, before consuming her, that ''tis thy beauty brings thy fate . . . Beauty wrecks whom she adorns'.

VOTUM

This may be translated:

A PRAYER

O morning dews, and healthful airs, O groves, and herbage rejoicing in the happy streams, grassy hills, and pleasant shady places in the valleys! If only the fates might give those pleasures which, once, on the paternal estate, I, unknown, far from artifice, far from dread, did so greatly desire, what my soul always craved: to wait for a peaceful old age before my own household god, then at last, the years not unhappily completed, to be allotted the silent tombstone, or to be laid beneath the sod!

ON A GOLDFINCH STARVED TO DEATH IN HIS CAGE

In his letter to William Unwin of 9 November 1780 Cowper remarks of this poem: 'I wrote the following last Summer. The Tragical Occasion of it really happen'd at the next House to ours' (probably in the home of Dick Coleman, Cowper's protégé).

THE PINE APPLE AND THE BEE

For notes on the probable date of composition, and on Cowper's cultivation of pineapples, see above, 'The Bee and the Pine Apple', p. 496.

The occasion of Cowper's sending a copy of this fable to Joseph Hill was his reading in a newspaper that the Jamaica fleet was arriving: 'I hope it imports some Pine Apple Plants for Me.'

Title. A and *H* have 'Another on the same' because in both this poem immediately follows 'The Bee and the Pine Apple' (which is called 'The Pine Apple and the Bee' in *H*); presumably this poem was the later-written of the two.

l. 8. *his trunk.* The bee's proboscis; the usage in reference to insects is rare, and now obsolete (*OED*).

HORACE. BOOK THE 2ND. ODE THE 10TH

The fragment *C* occupies the recto of a piece of paper, approximately 6″ by 4″, on the verso of which is written the first eleven lines of Cowper's translation of *Odes*, I. ix. A pencil inscription records that this was given to 'L. C.' by Lady Throckmorton as a specimen of Cowper's handwriting, 11 October 1827. The other half of the original sheet has been lost.

If allowance be made for the exigencies of rhyme and metre, Cowper's translation is quite close to the original.

l. 28. *The God.* Apollo, who is named in Horace's poem.

A REFLECTION ON THE FOREGOING ODE

Since this is not found either in *H* or in *C*, it is likely that it was composed when Cowper was preparing a selection of his shorter poems for *1782*.

TRANSLATIONS FROM VINCENT BOURNE

These four poems, 'The Glow-worm', 'The Jack Daw', 'The Cricket', and 'The Parrot', are translations of Bourne's 'Cicindela', 'Cornicula', 'Ad Grillum. Anacreonticum', and 'Simile Agit in Simile' respectively. For the Latin texts, see Appendix II.

These translations may date from 1777 (for discussion, see above, 'The Cantab.'). Whatever their date, they certainly made some time before 6 August 1780, when Cowper asked Unwin to return them to him. Unwin did not comply, for when Cowper broke the news to him that he planned to publish a volume of poems, on 1 May 1781, he added a postscript: 'I shall be glad of my translations from V. Bourne in your next frank.' Unwin responded to this second request; on 10 May Cowper wrote to him: 'there are two wanting of my translations of Bourne, of which the Glow-worm is one. Perhaps you never had it.' The letter to Newton of 13 May 1781 indicates that Unwin had sent three poems, presumably 'The Jack Daw', 'The Cricket', and 'The Parrot', but neither 'The Glow-worm' nor 'The Cantab.'.

There were other copies besides those in Unwin's possession. On 25 April 1781, before opening negotiations with Unwin, Cowper wrote to Newton that he wished to add to the projected volume 'those copies I translated from Vincent Bourne, but having no transcript of them myself, I must beg you to take the trouble either to send them hither, or to get them written out for me'. Newton, however, proposed sending his copies direct to Joseph Johnson; on 13 May Cowper hoped he had not yet done this, since he wanted to revise the last two stanzas of 'The Cricket': 'One of them was disgraced by a false rhime, and the other was too long by two lines.'

No manuscript of any of the four translations published in *1782* is known to have survived.

2. THE JACK DAW

On 31 January 1782 Cowper wrote as follows to Joseph Johnson, cueing his remarks to p. 338 of the proofs of *1782*, i.e. to ll. 13–30 of this poem: 'Though perhaps the exactest rhimes may not be required in these lighter pieces, I yet chuse to be as regular in this particular as I can, and have there-fore displaced half a Stanza for the sake of introducing better.' Which half-stanza he displaced is unknown.

For comments on the problems of translating from Bourne's Latin, with special reference to this poem, see the letter to Unwin, 23 May 1781.

THE SHRUBBERY,
WRITTEN IN A TIME OF AFFLICTION

This is often dated 1773, but this is a mere guess by Memes, who opines: 'Composed soon after the lines "To Peace"' (i.e. 'Ode to Peace', q.v.). The phrase 'written in a time of affliction', which no doubt gave Memes his cue, was added for publication; it is therefore to be regarded as an explanation to the reader of the occasion of such a poem, rather than as an autobiographical statement. In any case, Cowper was never wholly free of 'affliction' after the crisis of 1773. The fact that the poem is found in *H* suggests that it was composed in 1779 or 1780; since it is there followed by two poems known to have been written in the autumn of 1780, it may have been composed as late as October of that year.

Cowper's revisions in *H* are unusually extensive and interesting, but even more interesting is the change of title. The original title, 'The Spinny', confirms Wright's identification of the place referred to: 'Bounded on one side by the Ho-Brook is a long narrow plantation called, locally, the First Spinnie, but better known to readers of Cowper as the Shrubbery' (*Life of Cowper*, 1892, pp. 357–8). Cowper and Newton had prayed for each other there, and it undoubtedly had poignant associations for Cowper; see his letter to Newton, 9 July 1785.

The word 'spinn[e]y', meaning a copse or clump of trees, whether natural or deliberately planted, is well exemplified from Elizabethan times; *OED*'s earliest citation of 'shrubbery', on the other hand, dates from 1748—in a letter from Lady Luxborough to William Shenstone, a notable 'improver'. In changing the title of his poem, Cowper was not only eliminating a local reference; he was also emphasizing the irony of a modern pleasance which evokes only misery.

THE WINTER NOSEGAY

This poem has generally been regarded as one of the earliest-written in the 1782 volume, and Milford assigned it conjecturally to 1777, perhaps because Cowper's first reference to his greenhouse is found in the letter to Joseph Hill of 5 January 1777. It now appears, however, that this was in fact one of the latest of the shorter poems in the 1782 collection. In his letter to Cowper of 15 November 1780 John Newton thanks him for a copy of 'The Winter Nosegay'. This had probably been sent to him with the letter of 11 November, in which Cowper remarks that he has been much occupied in his garden; unfortunately, that letter is known only through a late (post-1812) and incomplete copy. The poem's position in *H* is consistent with the dating implied by these letters.

Povey notes that this may be the poem addressed to Mrs. Unwin to which

Cowper refers in his letter to Mrs. King of 12 March 1790 as having given him particular pleasure in the writing.

MUTUAL FORBEARANCE
NECESSARY TO THE HAPPINESS OF THE MARRIED STATE

This poem was certainly inscribed in *H* in November 1780, but it cannot be inferred that it was composed at that time. The copy in *U* is found in the 'appendix' of undated poetical manuscripts.

It is interesting that Cowper did not record in *H* any of the numerous revisions which appear in *1782*; they may have been made in proof.

l. 5. *hangings.* That such decorations were not very uncommon may be gathered from Johnson's *Idler*, no. 13, which satirizes undue attention to needlework in female education.

TO THE REV. MR. NEWTON
AN INVITATION INTO THE COUNTRY

Newton's letters to Cowper of October and November 1780 contain numerous references to a hoped-for spring visit to Olney, and it is natural to suppose that this poem was composed towards the end of that year. It was inscribed in *H* some time in January 1781. Newton came to Olney in June 1781 (J. Bull, *John Newton*, London, 1868, p. 255), his first visit to the area since his removal to London in January 1780.

Title. In *H* this poem follows 'To Mr. Newton on His Return from Ramsgate', hence the abridged title.

l. 1. *The swallows in their torpid state.* Cowper here accepts (perhaps for poetical effect only) the hypothesis that swallows hibernate rather than migrate; probably also the belief that they hibernate under water, concealed in the mud of streams (cf. l. 5). Both these theories were held at the time; see Daines Barrington's essay 'On the Torpidity of the Swallow Tribe, when they disappear', in his *Miscellanies*, London, 1781, pp. 225–44. As Gilbert White's references to the topic in *The Natural History of Selborne* show, even so careful an observer as he could be persuaded (by Barrington) to entertain the torpidity theory. A good survey of the debate is to be found in the *Encyclopaedia Britannica*, 3rd edn., Edinburgh, 1797, s.v. 'Swallow'.

l. 14. *me and Mary.* It is interesting that Cowper, who was at first so reluctant to allow his name to appear on the title-page of his book, should have included such a reference as this to himself and Mrs. Unwin. The Mary of 'The Winter Nosegay' might be a poetical artifice, but in a poem addressed to a well-known clergyman direct identification could hardly be avoided.

TRANSLATION OF PRIOR'S CHLOE AND EUPHELIA

Between the title and the poem in *U* Cowper inserts the following note: Not having the Poem, and not having seen it these 20 years, I had much ado to recollect it, which has obliged me to tear off the first Copy, and write another.' At the foot of the page stands the date 1 May 1779. It is probable that this is the concluding portion of the undated fragment which begins 'You are my Mahogany Box' and which ends with the following passage; he has been day-dreaming, imagining various successes that were not his at Westminster: '. . . I was a School Boy in high Favor with the Master, receivd a Silver Groat for my Exercise, and had the Pleasure of seeing it sent from Form to Form for the Admiration of all who were able to understand it. Do you wish to see this highly applauded Performance? It follows on the other side.' At this point (the foot of fo. 131ᵛ) the fragment ends. The binder of the Unwin MSS. has followed it with Cowper's first version of Vincent's verses on Dr. Lloyd (q.v.), no doubt because of the obvious connection with Westminster School, but this cannot be right, since Cowper is presenting verses which would have made an acceptable school exercise thirty years before. A translation from Prior would have been acceptable; there are three of them in Bourne's *Poematia*.

The poem translated is 'An Ode'; see *The Literary Works of Matthew Prior*, ed. H. B. Wright and M. K. Spears, Oxford, 1959, i. 259. Despite his 'much ado to recollect it', Cowper provides a fairly close translation; perhaps as a result of confused recollection, he has reorganized the second stanza, which in the original runs:

> My softest Verse, my darling Lyre
> Upon Euphelia's Toylet lay;
> When Cloe noted her Desire,
> That I should sing, that I should play.

(Prior spells 'Cloe' throughout.)

BOADICEA. AN ODE

The only certain evidence as to date is the *terminus ante quem* of January 1781, when the poem was inscribed in *H*. Modern editors have accepted the speculation of Memes: 'This spirit-stirring ode was suggested by the reading of Hume's history, during the winter of 1780.' Cowper refers to Hume's *History* in his letter to Unwin of 8 May 1780: 'I am now reading, and have read 3 Volumes of, Hume's History, one of which is engrossed entirely by that Subject'—i.e. the rebellion against Charles I, which Cowper goes on to discuss at some length. He most likely knew Hume's *History* in an eight-volume edition, of which four were issued between 1763 and 1778, and there is therefore no certainty that he ever read the beginning of it. In any case, the content of the ode is largely imaginary, and bears no relation to Hume's account of Boadicea.

The main inspiration of Cowper's ode is clearly Gray's *The Bard*. The action is similar, save that here it is the monarch and not the prophet who rushes to death. In both, a British bard foretells the ruin of the immediate oppressor, and foresees national glory in the remote future; in Cowper's treatment, however, the theme of *translatio imperii* is central to the Druid's message. There is an interesting analogue, 'The Mexican Prophecy. An Ode' in octosyllabic couplets, by John Scott of Amwell, in which a demon in the form of the idol Tlcatlepuca foretells the triumph of the *conquistadores*; this was not published until 1782.

l. 2. *Bleeding from the Roman rods*. This detail is found in Tacitus, *Annals*, XIV. xxi; it is not given by Hume, who says only that Boadicea 'had been treated in the most ignominious manner by the Roman tribunes' (*The History of England . . . to the Accession of Henry VII*, London, 1762, i. 6).

l. 6. *the Druid*. None of the classical sources speaks of Boadicea seeking counsel in this way, but all explain that she seized the opportunity to revolt in A.D. 59 when the Roman commander and most of his forces were destroying the Druids' headquarters in Anglesey.

ll. 21–2. Possibly influenced by Cassius Dio, *Roman History*, lxii. 6, where Boadicea refers to Nero 'who, though in name a man, is in fact a woman, as is proved by his singing, lyre-playing and beautification of his person' (trans. E. Cary, Loeb Classical Library, 1924–7, viii. 93). There may also be a contemporary allusion, to the popularity of Italian singers in London in the eighteenth century.

l. 39. *Rush'd to battle, fought and died*. The obvious interpretation is that Boadicea died in battle, but Cowper may be equivocating in order to maintain the heroic tone. Hume, loc. cit., following Tacitus, *Annals*, XIV. xxxvii, says: 'Boadicea herself, rather than fall into the hands of the enraged victor, put an end to her own life by poison.' Dio says (lxii. 12) that after her defeat in battle she 'fell sick and died' (ibid., pp. 104–5).

HEROISM

On 21 December 1780 Cowper sent to John Newton 'a long thought in verse for your perusal. It was produced about last midsummer, but I never could prevail with myself, till now, to transcribe it.' That this 'long thought' was 'Heroism' is confirmed by Newton's reply, dated 22 December, in which he says: 'have receiv'd yours with Mt. Ætna.' The poem's position in *H* is consistent with the date of composition given by Cowper.

It appears from Cowper's letter to Joseph Johnson of early December 1781 (with which was enclosed 'Friendship', q.v.) that he had originally intended

'Heroism' to stand at the beginning of the shorter poems; now he would prefer it at the end: 'but if the press has gone forward and begun *Ætna*, it is of no great importance; otherwise I should prefer this arrangement, as we shall then begin and end with a compliment to the King—who, (poor man) may at this time be glad of such a tribute.'

Writing to Newton on 17 December 1781, Cowper wonders whether he may be charged, in relation to ll. 3–4, 'with an unphilosophical error in supposing that Ætna was once unconscious of intestine fires and as lofty as at present, before the commencement of the eruptions'. Should he write an 'apologetical note' to avoid appearing a dunce in the eyes of review-readers? 'I say a note, because an alteration of the piece is impracticable, at least without cutting off its head and setting on a new one, a task I should not readily undertake, because the lines which must in that case be thrown out, are some of the most poetical in the performance.' Fortunately, Newton found neither note nor alteration needful; see Cowper's letter to him, 13 January 1782.

The variants from the text of *H* which appear in *1782* are not recorded in *H*; it is not clear whether Cowper made these changes while preparing copy for the printer, or in proof.

After more than three months of rumblings and earthquakes, Mount Etna erupted violently on 18 May 1780; further eruptions followed for about six weeks (*Annual Register*, xxiii, for 1780, 91–2). It should be noted that volcanoes were a matter of some interest in 1780, since Sir William Hamilton's account of the 1779 eruption of Vesuvius was published in the *Philosophical Transactions of the Royal Society*, lxx, pt. i, 42–84, and subsequently abstracted or excerpted in a number of periodicals, e.g. *Gentleman's Magazine*, l (1780), 476–7; *London Magazine*, xlix (1780), 469–76, with a reproduction (facing p. 463) of the engraving which accompanies Hamilton's account in *Phil. Trans.* (facing p. 84).

ll. 17–18. It was widely believed that volcanic eruptions were accompanied by lightning; Hamilton speaks of 'electrical fire', but lightning-flashes are shown in the engraving.

THE POET, THE OYSTER, AND SENSITIVE PLANT

This poem was inscribed in *H* in November 1780, but there is no indication of when it was composed.

l. 49. *grotto-work*. The dominant sense of 'grotto' here is not 'cave' but 'structure of shells'; cf. Evelyn's *Diary*, 27 February 1644: 'the Mons Parnassus, which consists of a Grotto or shell house erected on the summit of the hill' (ed. E. S. de Beer, Oxford, 1955, II. 108), and other citations in *OED*.

l. 55. *Lady Squeamish*. There are characters of this name in Wycherley's

The Country Wife and Otway's *Friendship in Fashion*, but Cowper is not referring to these. Johnson's definition of 'squeamish' is apt: 'Nice; fastidious; easily disgusted; having the stomach easily turned; being apt to take offence without much reason. It is used always in dislike either real or ironical.'

TO THE REV. WILLIAM CAWTHORNE UNWIN

This poem forms part of an undated fragment of a letter to Unwin. This was perhaps written as a supplement to the letter to Unwin of 10 May 1781, since it deals with the same matter, Unwin's pique at having been kept in the dark about the impending publication. Cowper sends this poem as a proof of his warm regard, and he assures Unwin that it is not a response to his remonstrance, but a tribute composed earlier and already in the publisher's hands. If this statement is true, the poem was probably composed between 18 March 1781, when Cowper first seriously considered including some of his short poems in his volume, and the last days of April, when he prepared a selection for publication. Such termini are consistent with the poem's position as the last item in *H*.

ll. 13–16. The procedure described is inoculating, and the terms 'rind' and 'stock' are correct; e.g. 'make an horizontal Cut across the Rind of the Stock' (P. Miller, *Gardeners Dictionary*, 3rd edn., London, 1737, s.v. 'Inoculating, *or* Budding'). Apparently the method was less common for roses than for peaches (ibid., s.v. 'Rosa').

'METHINKS I SEE THEE DECENTLY ARRAY'D'

This fragment is written on the recto of a bill-head of James Nickolls, an Olney lace manufacturer; at the foot, written apparently with another pen, are the words: 'After rain I fancy it will write very well.' (The page is reproduced in facsimile in the *Universal Review*, vii (1890), 270.) On the verso of the sheet is a draft of 'The Flatting Mill'. These lines seem to be the beginning of a passage intended for one of the satires of *1782* which came to nothing, and should therefore be dated some time in 1781.

The clergy were giving up the use of distinctive clerical dress for everyday wear during Cowper's lifetime. The process was complete by Jane Austen's time; cf. Mary Crawford's remark: 'Luckily there is no distinction of dress now-a-days to tell tales'—that is, Edmund Bertram can pass for a layman in company (*Mansfield Park*, II. xii).

l. 6. *a grizzle*. A grey wig, especially the kind usually worn by clergymen; see quotations in *OED*.

l. 11. *prigs*. Presumably Cowper was going on to describe those who have laid clerical dress aside; Johnson defines a prig as 'a pert, conceited, saucy, pragmatical little fellow'.

VESTRIS

This piece must have been inspired by a newspaper account, and written on or a day or two before 27 February 1781, when Cowper sent it to Unwin in a letter. It concludes a paragraph of sombre reflection on the incident. Unwin is empowered to send it to the 'Poets Corner', but no early printing is known. The revised version in E was inscribed in the autumn of 1790.

On 22 February 1781 a large audience crowded into the King's Theatre, Haymarket, to see the French dancer Vestris. 'When the curtain was drawn up, the stage appeared to be half full of spectators; at which the galleries in particular seemed to be so offended, that they would not suffer the opera to go on. . . . it was the resolution of the gallery that the performance [which was for Vestris's benefit] should not proceed until the stage was cleared.— The repeated efforts of Mr. Whitworth's eloquence, united with profound bows of Mons. Vestris, gained gradually on the audience; and at half past nine the business was compromised, and the opera was suffered to go on' (*Morning Herald*, Sat., 24 Feb. 1781).

The Vestris referred to here and in the poem is Auguste (1760–1842), famous for his lively and athletic style of dancing. His father, Gaetano Vestris (1729–1808), who retired in this same year, also participated in the Haymarket performance; the *Morning Herald* contrasts his 'grace and majesty' with the 'elegant activity' of his son. 'The feats of Vestris' are mentioned in 'Conversation', l. 58.

The original title, 'A Card', obviously means 'an eccentric or odd character, a droll'; this sense is barely recognized by *OED*, and first there exemplified from Dickens, 1836 (s.v. Card, *sb.*², 2. c.).

l. 8. *Cuckold's point*. A spot on the Surrey bank of the Thames in Rotherhithe, then marked by a pair of horns mounted on a pole. By starting from Richmond, Vestris would have to vault all of the seven bridges then crossing the Thames in and around London: Richmond, Kew, Putney, Battersea, Westminster, Blackfriars, and London Bridge.

TRANSLATION OF VERSES IN MEMORY OF
DR. LLOYD (I)

It is difficult to date this first translation precisely. The manuscript has been bound together with a letter-fragment belonging to 1 May 1779 (see above, 'Translation of Prior's Chloe and Euphelia'): in fact, it belongs with the undated letter to Unwin generally assigned to *c.* 1 July 1781, which begins: 'I thought it a tribute due to my old friend, who deserved that what has been learnedly spoken of him in Latin, should be spoken of him in plain English also, to translate the pretty and elegant Exercise you sent me. If you chuse to do so, you may send my Attempt to the printer, for though the Scissars have passed through the line, I can spell out his request for a Version' (B.L. Add. MS. 24155, fo. 12). This suggests that Unwin had sent Cowper a newspaper clipping, but the periodical in question has not been traced, nor is this version known to have been printed in any periodical. Other references in the letter make it possible that it was written at the end of July rather than at the beginning of that month.

Pierson Lloyd (1704?–5 January 1781) was educated at Westminster School and Trinity College, Cambridge. He was an usher at Westminster School for more than twenty years, and Under Master from 1749 until his retirement in 1771; he also held numerous ecclesiastical appointments and was awarded a Lambeth D.D. in 1771. He was the father of Cowper's close friend of his London years, Robert Lloyd. The Latin verses were written by his successor both as usher and as Under Master, William Vincent (1739–1815), later a famous Head Master. They were recited in Hall at the annual Election of scholars to Christ Church, Oxford, and Trinity, Cambridge, which took place in the week following Rogation Sunday. The dates in 1781 were 21 to 23 May. (See J. Sargeaunt, *Annals of Westminster School*, London, 1898, pp. 26–32, and Ryskamp, pp. 21–2.) The text of Vincent's verses given in the Appendix below is that which Cowper wrote out in *E*, which derives presumably from the text Unwin sent him.

l. 1. *aimable*. Cowper's characteristic spelling of this word, which may reflect his pronunciation, is here preserved, although it is not recognized as an alternative spelling in *OED*.

TRANSLATION OF VERSES IN MEMORY OF DR. LLOYD (II)

The date of this second version is unknown, but it cannot have been composed later than the summer of 1791, when it was inscribed in *E*.

The following note precedes Vincent's Latin verses in *E*: 'I make no apology for the introduction of the following lines, though I have never learned who wrote them. Their elegance will sufficiently recommend them to persons of classical taste and erudition, and I shall be happy if the English version that they have received from me, be found not to dishonour them. Affection for the memory of the worthy man whom they celebrate, alone prompted me to this endeavour.' The Latin verses follow, and then Cowper's translation. Hayley reverses the order, and transfers the title and footnote from the Latin to the English version, in *1803*.

l. 16. *One*. In *E*, Cowper has a footnote referring to the footnote to '*Unius*'

(l. 16), which reads: 'He was usher and under-master of Westminster near fifty years, and retired from his occupation when he was near seventy, with a handsome pension from the King.' Cowper's source for this information was perhaps the newspaper cutting that Unwin had sent him.

EPISTLE TO A LADY IN FRANCE

This poem cannot have been written earlier than the first week of July 1781, when Cowper became acquainted with Lady Austen. He subsequently revised it before John Johnson copied it into the Entry Book, i.e. between 1782 and 1790. The earliest extant manuscript is *U*, where the poem forms part of the letter of 15 December 1781, and is introduced thus: 'I send you on the other side some lines I addressed last summer to a Lady in France; a particular friend of Lady Austen, a person much afflicted, but of great piety, and patience—a Protestant.—they are not for publication and therefore I send them.' The copy in *W* was inscribed less than a year later, in the autumn of 1782. The first printing, in the *Theological Miscellany*, was as part of a series of letters exchanged by Lady Austen and Mme Billacoys contributed by Greatheed; the text is plainly corrupt (e.g. 'solitary' for 'salutary', l. 28).

The 'Lady' of the title was Mme Billacoys, formerly Jane Saunders, who accompanied Lady Austen as her waiting-woman when Sir Robert Austen and his wife took up residence at Sancerre, near Bourges, in 1763. She attracted the attention of a local worthy, and the following year, aged 26, she was married to Cyprien Billacoys, aged 60. At the time of her marriage she became a Roman Catholic, apparently as a formality. During a subsequent visit to England, Lady Austen adopted Evangelical tenets, which on her return she shared with Mme Billacoys, of whom Greatheed writes: 'She needed every consolation of religion, for she found her husbands temper very violent; and his eldest Son by a former Marriage, alarmed by the appearance of a young family, prosecuted his father to obtain his Mother's Dowry, according to the Coutumes de Paris. Her sensibility to the principles of Religion was however accompanied with horror at her adoption of Popery, to which she had never attended except by her husband's compulsion.' (See K. Povey, 'Cowper and Lady Austen', *RES* x (1934), 419–21, for these and further details.)

l. 2. *congratulate*. 'To rejoice in participation' (Johnson).

l. 49. *Gideon's fleece*. See Judg. 6: 36–8; and, for another reference to that passage, 'To a Young Friend on His Arriving at Cambridge Wet', below.

l. 50. *herbs*. Incorrectly emended to 'flocks' by Hayley, who must have misread 'herbs' as 'herds', which he recognized as the wrong noun of multitude for sheep. The word is quite clearly written in *E*, and Hayley may have been misled by an inaccurate transcript.

ON FRIENDSHIP

In a letter of 4 December 1781, Cowper informed Newton that he was at work on a poem in stanzas; when he next wrote to Newton, on 17 December, he revealed that it was on the subject of friendship, and that, having finished it, he had sent it direct to Joseph Johnson, in the hope that it might stand at the head of the shorter pieces in the 1782 volume. Johnson, however, did not approve of the poem, and on 31 December Cowper wrote again to Newton, accepting Johnson's decision, and adding: 'if I should live to write again, I may possibly take up that subject a second time, and cloath it in a different dress, it abounds with excellent matter, and much more than I could find room for in 2 or 3 pages.'

The first version of 'On Friendship', written and rejected in December 1781, has disappeared, and we can only guess how much of it survives in the existing manuscripts. But Cowper did not forget his half-promise to revise his poem, and the four manuscripts now known testify to his difficulties with it. The earliest is *W*, dating from the end of October 1782, when it was presented to the Revd. William Bull; for discussion, see notes to the translations from Madame Guyon. Then on 30 November 1782 Cowper promised William Unwin a copy of this poem; it is reasonable to suppose that the undated manuscript *U* was written shortly after this date. The manuscript *O* is unfortunately incomplete—the last page has been lost—and its dating is necessarily uncertain, but the general tenor of its variants suggests that it postdates *U*. The final version, *E*, is the result of a radical revision. It was inscribed in the Entry Book in the summer of 1791, but the work of revision may have been done long before; the apparent indication of a *terminus ante quem* turns out to be unhelpful (see note to l. 107).

Bailey (p. 700) denies that the 'Variations' printed by Hayley in *1803* are the variants from *E* found in Bull, *1801*. I believe he is mistaken. Bull printed from *W*, with five notable errors: 'prove' (17); 'dream' and 'had' (18); 'discussion' (90); 'deviation' (100). The first two and the last of these errors appear in the 'Variations' of *1803*, thus confirming the natural interpretation of Hayley's words (i. 210); viz., that these 'Variations' are the variants found in Bull, *1801*. The two *1801* readings that do not appear among the 'Variations' are both impossible readings, and Hayley emended them: 'had' correctly to 'has', 'discussion' incorrectly to 'contention' (with 'invention' for 'contention' three lines earlier). Hayley omitted minor variants, so 'a needle' (98) does not appear.

Motto. From Cicero, *De Amicitia*, xviii. 65: 'Ita fit verum illud, quod initio dixi, amicitiam nisi inter bonos esse non posse.' 'Thus it becomes true, as I said at the beginning, that friendship cannot exist except among good men.'

l. 95. *hand-in-hand Insurance plates.* Metal plates were affixed to buildings in order to identify property insured by a particular company, for the guidance of company-operated fire brigades. Cowper refers to the well-known symbol of the Hand-in-Hand company. See A. E. Bulau, *Footprints of Assurance*, New York, 1953, pp. 127 ff.

l. 107. *Gog and Magog*. Cowper has a note in *E*: 'This was written before the removal of them.' We can find no evidence that these famous wooden figures were moved between the time of their installation in the Guildhall in 1708 and their relocation in 1815. See William Hone, *Ancient Mysteries Described, Especially the English Miracle Plays*, 1823, p. 256: 'Until the last reparation of Guildhall, in 1815, the present giants stood with the old clock and a balcony of iron-work between them, over the stairs leading from the Hall to the Courts of Law and the Council Chamber.' After this 'reparation', the giants were placed on pillars flanking the west window, on the opposite side of the Hall; see Hone's protest, *The Every-Day Book and Table Book*, n.d., i. 1454 (under date 9 November).

A POETICAL EPISTLE TO LADY AUSTEN

No authoritative manuscript of this poem is known to exist. The relationship between Hayley's version and the slightly different ones offered by *C* and *EM* remains obscure. Since Greatheed contributed to the same (Apr. 1803) number of the *Evangelical Magazine* that contains *EM* the first of two articles on Cowper (see Russell, p. 262), it is reasonable to suppose that he supplied the copy for *EM*, particularly in view of his interest in Lady Austen (see K. Povey, 'Cowper and Lady Austen', *RES* x (1934), 417–27). The omission of the first twenty-nine lines as insufficiently edifying for evangelical readers would be natural enough. *C* shares so many readings with *EM* that they must have had a common source, probably in Greatheed's papers; perhaps *C* was copied for a friend of Greatheed's who wanted the entire poem rather than the truncated version. Hayley's complete version had indeed already appeared (before 10 January 1803; Russell, p. 251), but it is clear from his articles that Greatheed did not suppose that many readers of the *Evangelical Magazine* would see the *Life of Cowper*. Dubious though *C*'s authority may be, its readings are interesting enough to merit recording; 'destin'd' (l. 37) may even be right.

l. 42. *Silver-End*. Both *C* and *EM* have a note: 'The place where Mr. C [Cowper *EM*] then resided.' Silver End is the name of the south-east corner of the Olney market-square, where Cowper's house was, and whence the road runs to the village of Clifton Reynes, where Lady Austen had been staying with her sister. Silver End had 'low' associations, and the name is used by Cowper in a derogatory sense; see below, 'To My Dearest Cousin, on Her Removal of Us from Silver End to Weston'.

l. 46. *Sancerre*. *C* has a note: 'The lady had recently returned from France';

the same note is appended to 'Loire' in the next line in *EM*. See above, 'Epistle to a Lady in France'.

l. 106. Cf. Eccles. 4: 12: 'And if one prevail against him, two shall withstand him; and a three-fold cord is not quickly broken.'

THE FLATTING MILL

Cowper sent Newton a copy of this poem, presumably in a version close to the final state of *A*, on 21 December 1781, as 'a few lines on a thought which struck me yesterday. . . . I should think they might occupy the place of an Introduction [to the forthcoming *Poems*], and shall call them by that name, if I did not judge the name I have given them necessary for the information of the reader. A flatting Mill is not met with in every street . . . it happened to me however to spend much of my time in one when I was a boy, when I frequently amused myself with watching the operation I describe.' Newton, however (or Joseph Johnson), thought the poem merely repeated the point made in the epigraph from Caraccioli already chosen for the title-page, and in his letter to Newton of 31 December Cowper accepted this verdict, though not without some protest.

The metaphor of the gilding of distasteful pills seems to have appealed to Cowper, for he also uses it at some length in his letter to Newton of 3 May 1780.

The gilding of pills was introduced by Avicenna in the tenth century, and fell into disuse early in the nineteenth, with the introduction of machine-made pills (C. H. LaWall, *The Curious Lore of Drugs and Medicines*, Garden City, N.Y., 1927, pp. 107, 504). John Quincy, in his *Complete English Dispensatory* (12th edn., London, 1742), arguing against the quasi-magical values ascribed to gold, defines its justifiable use in pharmacy thus: 'to beautify some Medicines to the Eye; and guard the Palate against the Nauseousness of some others which are made into Pills' (p. 250). See also Garth's *Dispensary*, ll. 13–14.

APPENDICES

APPENDIX I

Newton's Preface to Poems, *1782*

The idea of a Preface was first suggested by Cowper in a letter to Newton of 8 April 1781. Cowper fears that an 'unenlighten'd Reader' would be offended by 'Truth', and suggests that Newton should write an explanatory preface to that poem, designed to obviate prejudices. Alternatively, he adds, Newton might care to write a preface for the whole volume. Newton chose the latter, but he does not seem to have hurried: Cowper returned a draft to him on 18 September, and on 22 October wrote urging Newton to name 'Conversation' along with 'Table Talk' in his reference to the lighter pieces. Newton did not make the alteration. Then in February 1782 Joseph Johnson decided that while Newton's preface might 'recommend the volume to the Religious, it would disgust the profane, and that there is in reality no need of any preface at all'. He asked for, and got, Cowper's permission to negotiate with Newton for its cancellation (to William Unwin, 24 Feb. 1782).

Some copies of *1782* exist with the Preface included; it may be that Newton agreed with Johnson that the Preface should be left out of most copies but bound up with a few, which could be presented to friends. The copy inscribed by Cowper to the Revd. William Bull (a close friend of Newton's) has the Preface; the one he gave to Lord Dartmouth (Newton's patron, but Cowper's former schoolfellow) has not. Since many copies with the Preface also have the cancellanda (sigs. E6, I6), it seems that the binders had already started work before Johnson had his last-minute misgivings.

The Preface was included in the fifth edition of Cowper's *Poems* (1793) and in subsequent editions (Russell, pp. 42–3).

When an Author, by appearing in print, requests an audience of the Public, and is upon the point of speaking for himself, whoever presumes to step before him with a preface, and to say, 'Nay, but hear me first,' should have something worthy of attention to offer, or he will be justly deemed officious and impertinent. The judicious reader has probably, upon other occasions, been before hand with me in this reflection: and I am not very willing it should now be applied to me, however I may seem to expose myself to the danger of it. But the thought of having my own name perpetuated in connection with the name in the title page, is so pleasing and flattering to the feelings of my heart, that I am content to risk something for the gratification.

This Preface is not designed to commend the Poems to which it is prefixed. My testimony would be insufficient for those who are not qualified to judge properly for themselves, and unnecessary to those who are. Besides, the reasons which render it improper and unseemly for a man to celebrate his own performances, or those of his nearest relatives, will have some influence in suppressing much of what he might otherwise wish to say in favour of a *friend*, when that friend is indeed an *alter idem*, and excites almost the same emotions of sensibility and affection as he feels for himself.

It is very probable these Poems may come into the hands of some persons, in whom the sight of the Author's name will awaken a recollection of incidents and scenes which, through length of time, they had almost forgotten. They will be reminded of *one*, who was once the companion of their chosen hours, and who set out with them in early life, in the paths which lead to literary honours, to influence and affluence, with equal prospects of success. But he was suddenly and powerfully withdrawn from those pursuits, and he left them without regret; yet not till he had sufficient opportunity of counting the cost, and of knowing the value of what he gave up. If happiness could have been found in classical attainments, in an elegant taste, in the exertions of wit, fancy, and genius, and in the esteem and converse of such persons as in these respects were most congenial with himself, he would have been happy. But he was not—He wondered (as thousands in a similar situation still do) that he should continue dissatisfied, with all the means apparently conducive to satisfaction, within his reach—But in due time, the cause of his disappointment was discovered to him—He had lived without God in the world. In a memorable hour, the wisdom which is from above visited his heart. Then he felt himself a wanderer, and then he found a guide. Upon this change of views, a change of plan and conduct followed of course. When he saw the *busy* and the *gay* world in its true light, he left it with as little reluctance as a prisoner, when called to liberty, leaves his dungeon. Not that he became a Cynic or an Ascetic—A heart filled with love to God, will assuredly breathe benevolence to men. But the turn of his temper inclining him to rural life, he indulged it, and the providence of God evidently preparing his way and marking out his retreat, he retired into the country. By these steps the good hand of God, unknown to me, was providing for me one of the principal blessings of my life; a friend and a counsellor, in whose company for almost seven years, though we were seldom seven successive

waking hours separated, I always found new pleasure. A friend, who
was not only a comfort to myself, but a blessing to the affectionate
poor people, among whom I then lived.

Some time after inclination had thus removed him from the hurry
and bustle of life, he was still more secluded by a long indisposition,
and my pleasure was succeeded by a proportionable degree of anxiety
and concern. But a hope, that the God whom he served would support him under his affliction, and at length vouchsafe him a happy
deliverance, never forsook me. The desirable crisis, I trust, is now
nearly approaching. The dawn, the presage of returning day, is
already arrived. He is again enabled to resume his pen, and some of
the first fruits of his recovery are here presented to the public. In his
principal subjects, the same acumen which distinguished him in the
early period of life, is happily employed in illustrating and enforcing
the truths of which he received such deep and unalterable impressions in his maturer years. His satire, if it may be called so, is benevolent, (like the operations of the skilful and humane surgeon who
wounds only to heal) dictated by a just regard for the honour of God,
an indignant grief excited by the profligacy of the age, and a tender
compassion for the souls of men.

His favourite topics are least insisted on in the piece entitled
Table Talk; which therefore, with some regard to the prevailing
taste, and that those who are governed by it may not be discouraged
at the very threshold from proceeding farther, is placed first. In most
of the larger Poems which follow, his leading design is more explicitly avowed and pursued. He aims to communicate his own percep-
tions of the truth, beauty, and influence of the religion of the Bible.
—A religion which, however discredited by the misconduct of many
who have not renounced the christian name, proves itself, when
rightly understood, and cordially embraced, to be the grand *desi-
deratum*, which alone can relieve the mind of man from painful and
unavoidable anxieties, inspire it with stable peace and solid hope, and
furnish those motives and prospects, which, in the present state of
things, are absolutely necessary to produce a conduct worthy of a
rational creature, distinguished by a vastness of capacity, which no
assemblage of earthly good can satisfy, and by a principle and pre-
intimation of immortality.

At a time when hypothesis and conjecture in philosophy are so
justly exploded, and little is considered as deserving the name of
knowledge, which will not stand the test of experiment, the very

use of the term *experimental* in religious concernments, is by too many unhappily rejected with disgust. But we well know, that they who affect to despise the inward feelings which religious persons speak of, and to treat them as enthusiasm and folly, have inward feelings of their own, which, though they would, they cannot suppress. We have been too long in the secret ourselves to account the proud, the ambitious, or the voluptuous, happy. We must lose the remembrance of what we once were, before we can believe, that a man is satisfied with himself, merely because he endeavours to appear so. A smile upon the face is often but a mask worn occasionally and in company, to prevent, if possible, a suspicion of what at the same time is passing in the heart. We know that there are people, who seldom smile when they are alone, who therefore are glad to hide themselves in a throng from the violence of their own reflections; and who, while by their looks and their language they wish to persuade us they are happy, would be glad to change conditions with a dog. But in defiance of all their efforts, they continue to think, forebode, and tremble. This we know, for it has been our own state, and therefore we know how to commiserate it in others—From this state the Bible relieved us—When we were led to read it with attention, we found *ourselves* described.—We learnt the causes of our inquietude—we were directed to a method of relief—we tried, and we were not disappointed.

Deus nobis hæc otia fecit.

We are now certain that the gospel of Christ is the power of God unto salvation, to every one that believeth. It has reconciled us to God, and to ourselves, to our duty, and our situation. It is the balm and cordial of the present life, and a sovereign antidote against the fear of death.

Sed hactenus hæc. Some smaller pieces upon less important subjects close the volume. Not one of them I believe was written with a view to publication, but I was unwilling they should be omitted.

Charles Square, Hoxton,
   February 18, 1782.
JOHN NEWTON.

APPENDIX II

Poems Translated by Cowper

Some of the poems which Cowper translated are now hard to find outside the largest libraries. Texts of these are given below.

Antoine Houdar de la Motte

L'OMBRE D'HOMERE: ODE

Homere, l'honneur du Permesse,
Toi, qui par de sublimes airs
Assuras aux Dieux de la Gréce
L'immortalité de tes Vers;
Parois, sors du Royaume sombre,   5
Et dérobe un moment ton Ombre
A la foule avide des morts;
Céde à l'innocente magie
De la poëtique énergie,
Et des graces de mes accords.   10

    Oui, ma Muse aujourd'hui t'évoque;
Non pas que nouvel Appion,
Je brûle de sçavoir l'époque
Du débris fameux d'Ilion.
Non, pour sçavoir si ton génie   15
Fut Citoyen de Mæonie,
Ou de l'Isle heureuse d'Yo;
Tu peux d'un éternel silence
Voiler ton obscure naissance,
Echappée aux yeux de Clio.   20

    Un désir plus noble m'anime,
Et sans en craindre le danger,
Je veux forcer ton chant sublime
D'animer un lut étranger.
Je veux sous un nouveau langage   25
Rajeunir ton antique ouvrage,

Viens toi-même, viens m'exciter;
Secondes, régles mon yvresse,
Et si ta gloire t'intéresse,
Dis-moi comme il faut t'imiter.   30

 Effet surprenant de ma Lyre!
Divin Homere, je te vois;
Tu sors brillant du sombre Empire;
J'écoute, imposes-moi tes loix.
Loin cette aveugle obéissance,   35
Dit-il, pour m'imiter, commence
A bannir ces respects outrés;
Sur mes pas qu'un beau feu te guide,
Je réprouve l'esprit timide,
Dont mes Vers sont idolâtrés.   40

 Homme, j'eus l'humaine foiblesse;
Un Encens superstitieux,
Au lieu de m'honorer, me blesse;
Choisis, tout n'est pas précieux.
Prends mes hardiesses sensées,   45
Et du fond vif de mes pensées,
Songe toujours à t'appuyer;
Du reste je te rends le maître;
A quelque prix que ce puisse être,
Sauve moi l'affront d'ennuyer.   50

 Mon siécle eut des Dieux trop bizarres,
Des Héros d'orgueil infectés;
Des Rois indignement avares;
Défauts autrefois respectés.
Adoucis tout avec prudence;   55
Que de l'exacte bienséance
Ton ouvrage soit revêtu;
Respectes le goût de ton âge,
Qui, sans la suivre davantage,
Connoît pourtant mieux la vertu.   60

 Ne bornes pas la ressemblance
A des traits stériles et secs;
Rends ce nombre, cette cadence
Dont jadis je charmai les Grecs.

Sois fidéle au style héroïque,   65
Au grand sens, au tour pathétique,
Enfans d'un travail assidu.
Qu'en ce choix la raison t'éclaire,
Je plaisois, si tu ne sçais plaire,
Crois que tu ne m'as pas rendu.   70

    Ose imaginer que la Parque,
Démentant ses sévères loix,
Permet a la fatale barque
De me remettre aux bords François:
Dans leur sobre et modeste langue,   75
Crois que plus d'une harangue
J'abrégerois mes longs combats;
Mes Héros dignes de leur gloire,
Impatiens de la victoire,
Vaincroient, et ne se loueroient pas.   80

    Du faux merveilleux de la Fable
Mes Vers se seroient garantis,
Et j'y tiendrois au vrai-semblable
Les Dieux mêmes assujettis.
De Vulcain la main trop sçavante,   85
Par une gravure mouvante,
N'orneroit pas un bouclier;
D'Achille, par une autre image,
Il animeroit le courage,
Et sçauroit le justifier.   90

    Tu m'entends; Pluton me rappelle;
L'Ombre disparoît a ces mots.
Enflammés d'une ardeur nouvelle,
Peignons les Dieux et les Héros.
Je vois au sein de la Nature,   95
L'idée invariable et sûre,
De l'utile beau, du parfait.
Homere m'a laissé la Muse,
Et si mon orgueil ne m'abuse,
Je vais faire ce qu'il eût fait.   100

          Œuvres, Paris, 1754, i (I), 153–8.

POEMS BY VINCENT BOURNE

IN STATUAM SEPULCHRALEM INFANTIS DORMIENTIS

INFANS venuste, qui sacros dulces agens
   In hoc sopores marmore,
Placidissimâ quiete compôstus jaces,
   Et inscius culpæ et metûs,
Somno fruaris, docta quam dedit manus   5
   Sculptoris; et somno simul,
Quem nescit Artifex vel Ars effingere,
   Fruaris Innocentiæ.

Poematia, London, 1732, p. 137.

EQUES ACADEMICUS

CALCARI instruitur Juvenis; geminove vel uno,
   Haud multùm, aut ocreis cujus, et unde, refert;
Fors fortasse suo, fortasse aliunde, flagello;
   Quantulacunque suî, pars tamen ipse suî.
Sic rite armatus, quinis (et fortè minoris)   5
   Conductum solidis scandere gestit equum.
Lætus et impavidus, quà fert fortuna (volantem
   Cernite) quadrupedem pungit, et urget iter.
Admisso cursu, per rura, per oppida, fertur:
   Adlatrant catuli, multaque ridet anus.   10
Jamque ferox plagis, erectâ ad verbera dextrâ,
   Calce cruentato lassat utrumque latus.
Impete sed tanto vixdum confecerit ille
   Millia propositæ sexve, novemve, viæ;
Viribus absumptis, fessusque labore, caballus   15
   Sternit in immundum seque equitemque lutum.
Vectus iter peraget curru plaustrove viator?
   Proh pudor et facinus! cogitur ire pedes.
Si, nec inexpertum, seniorem junior audis,
   Quæ sint exiguæ commoda disce moræ.   20
Quam tibi præcipio, brevis est, sed regula certa:
   Ocyùs ut possis pergere, lentus eas.

Miscellaneous Poems, London, 1772, pp. 180–1.

CICINDELA

Sub sepe exiguum est, nec rarò in margine ripæ,
    Reptile, quod lucet nocte, dieque latet,
Vermis habet speciem, sed habet de lumine nomen;
    At priscâ à famâ non liquet, unde micet.
Plerique à caudâ credunt procedere lumen;   5
    Nec desunt, credunt qui rutilare caput.
Nam superas stellas quæ nox accendit, et illi
    Parcam eadem lucem dat, moduloque parem.
Forsitan hoc prudens voluit natura caveri,
    Ne pede quis duro reptile contereret: 10
Exiguam, in tenebris ne gressum offenderet ullus,
    Prætendi voluit forsitan illa facem.
Sive usum hunc natura parens, seu maluit illum,
    Haud frustra accensa est lux, radiique dati.
Ponite vos fastus, humiles nec spernite, magni;   15
    Quando habet et minimum reptile, quod niteat.
        Miscellaneous Poems, London, 1772, p. 234.

CORNICULA

Nigras inter aves avis est, quæ plurima turres,
    Antiquas ædes, celsaque fana colit.
Nil tam sublime est, quod non audace volatu,
    Aeriis spernens inferiora, petit.
Quo nemo ascendat, cui non vertigo cerebrum   5
    Corripiat, certè hunc seligit illa locum.
Quo vix à terrâ tu suspicis absque tremore,
    Illa metûs expers incolumisque sedet.
Lamina delubri supra fastigia, ventus
    Quâ cœli spiret de regione, docet;   10
Hanc ea præ reliquis mavult, secura perîcli,
    Nec curat, nedum cogitat, unde cadat.
Res inde humanas, sed summa per otia, spectat,
    Et nihil ad sese, quas videt, esse videt.
Concursus spectat, plateâque negotia in omni,   15
    Omnia pro nugis at sapienter habet.

Clamores, quos infra audit, si forsitan audit,
  Pro rebus nihili negligit, et crocitat.
Ille tibi invideat, felix cornicula, pennas,
  Qui sic humanis rebus abesse velit.   20
        Miscellaneous Poems, London, 1772, p. 228.

AD GRILLUM, ANACREONTICUM

O qui meæ culinæ
Argutulus choraules,
Et hospes es canorus,
Quacunque commoreris,
Felicitatis omen;   5
Jucundiore cantu
Siquando me salutes,
Et ipse te rependam,
Et ipse, quâ valebo,
Remunerabo musâ.   10

Dicêris innocensque
Et gratus inquilinus;
Nec victitans rapinis,
Ut sorices voraces,
Muresve curiosi,   15
Furumque delicatum
Vulgus domesticorum,
Sed tutus in camini
Recessibus, quiete
Contentus et calore.   20

Beatior cicadâ,
Quæ te referre formâ,
Quæ voce te videtur;
Et saltitans per herbas,
Unius, haud secundæ,   25
Æstatis est chorista:
Tu carmen integratum
Reponis ad Decembrem,
Lætus per universum
Incontinenter annum.   30

Te nulla lux relinquit,
Te nulla nox revisit,
Non musicæ vacantem,
Cursive non solutum:
Quin amplies canendo,   35
Quin amplies fruendo,
Ætatulam, vel omni,
Quam nos homunciones
Absumimus querendo,
Ætate longiorem.   40

Miscellaneous Poems, London, 1772, pp. 151–2.

SIMILE AGIT IN SIMILE

Cristatus, pictisque ad Thaida psittacus alis,
   Missus ab Eoo munus amante venit.
Ancillis mandat primam formare loquelam,
   Archididascaliæ dat sibi Thais opus.
Psittace, ait Thais, fingitque sonantia molle   5
   Basia, quæ docilis molle refingit avis.
Jam captat, jam dimidiat tyrunculus; et jam
   Integrat auditos articulatque sonos.
Psittace mi pulcher pulchelle, hera dicit alumno;
   Psittace mi pulcher, reddit alumnus heræ.   10
Jamque canit, ridet, deciesque aegrotat in horâ,
   Et vocat ancillas nomine quamque suo.
Multaque scurratur mendax, et multa jocatur,
   Et lepido populum detinet augurio.
Nunc tremulum illudit fratrem, qui suspicit, et pol!   15
   Carnalis, quisquis te docet, inquit, homo est:
Argutæ nunc stridet anûs argutulus instar;
   Respicit, et Nebulo es, quisquis es, inquit anus.
Quando fuit melior tyro, meliorve magistra!
   Quando duo ingeniis tam coiere pares!   20
Ardua discenti nulla est, res nulla docenti
   Ardua; cùm doceat fœmina, discat avis.

Miscellaneous Poems, London, 1772, pp. 166–7.

William Vincent

VERSES IN MEMORY OF DR. LLOYD

Abiit senex! periit senex amabilis!
  Quo non fuit jucundior.
Lugete vos, ætas quibus maturior
  Senem colendum præstitit,
Seu quando, viribus valentioribus   5
  Firmoque fretus pectore
Florentiori vos juventute excolens
  Curâ fovebat patriâ,
Seu quando fractus, jamque donatus rude,
  Vultu sed usque blandulo,   10
Miscere gaudebat suas facetias
  His annuis leporibus.
Vixit probus, purâque simplex indole,
  Blandisque comis moribus,
Et dives æquâ mente—charus omnibus,   15
  Unius auctus munere.
Ite tituli! meritis beatioribus
  Aptate laudes debitas!
Nec invidebat ille, si quibus favens
  Fortuna plus arriserat.   20
Placide senex! levi quiescas cespite,
  Etsi superbum nec vivo tibi
Decus sit inditum, nec mortuo
  Lapis notatus nomine.

E, pp. 114–15.

APPENDIX III

Poems, 1748–1782, sometimes attributed to Cowper

A REFLECTION ON THE YEAR 1720

Fifty-two lines, beginning 'The Clouds grew big, the thunder roll'd on high'. Published in *The Student, or the Oxford Monthly Miscellany*, i (1750), 34–5. Printed as 'possibly Cowper's' by Ryskamp, pp. 226–8, on account of the imagery of sea, storm, and castaway, and the signature 'W.C.'. However, it is hard to see why Cowper, aged 18, should have written such a poem, and his connection with the periodical remains doubtful. One of the initiators of *The Student* was Bonnell Thornton; Povey suggests that 'W.C.' may have been William Cowper of the Park (1722–69), who was a contemporary of Thornton's at Westminster and at Oxford. Cf. Russell, pp. 1–2.

ON A JACOBITE PARSON AND POET

Twenty-eight lines, beginning 'Thy Duty is a Steady thing'. Found in Chase Price's Commonplace Book (*T*), and printed by Ryskamp, *BC*, pp. 477–8. While Cowper may have written political poems of this kind, nothing in this specimen suggests his hand. The parson is called 'Joseph', and the song may have been aimed at the Revd. Joseph Trapp (1679–1747), whose epitaph appears a few pages earlier in the Commonplace Book. Trapp was reputed to write songs of a Jacobitical tendency (cf. *Huntington Library Quarterly*, xxxix (1976), 318). If Trapp was the target, this poem was probably written before Cowper began versifying.

OHE, JAM SATIS EST

Six lines, beginning 'Sic Genitor Crebo Confossi vulnere nati'. Found in Chase Price's Commonplace Book (*T*), and printed by Ryskamp, *BC*, p. 478. The lines are signed 'Cowper'. However, in *T* they follow and are clearly associated with the epitaph composed by Robert Freind, Head Master of Westminster School 1711–33, for the monument in Westminster Abbey to the Hon. Philip Carteret (1692–1711). They are probably the work of the Revd. John Cowper, the poet's father, who was Carteret's contemporary at Westminster.

TO PEACE

Twenty-eight lines, beginning 'Come lovely gentle peace of Mind'. Published in the *Gentleman's Magazine*, xxviii (1758), 329; reprinted in part as possibly Cowper's by Ryskamp, pp. 111–12. The subject and its treatment are thoroughly conventional, and the external evidence for the attribution is too slight. Cf. Russell, pp. 5–6.

EPITAPH ON GENERAL WOLFE

Eight lines, beginning 'Whilst George in sorrow bows his laurell'd head'. Printed by Ryskamp, pp. 229–31, as possibly Cowper's. The manuscript reported in a sale catalogue as being in Cowper's hand now appears to be in Lady Hesketh's hand. The author of the epitaph was almost certainly the Revd. George Lewis, Vicar of Westerham, Kent, where Wolfe's memorial stands. Cf. Russell, pp. 8–9.

AN ODE SECUNDUM ARTEM

Seventy-two lines, beginning 'Shall I begin with *Ah*, or *Oh*?' Published in the *St. James's Magazine*, iii (1763), 187–9; attributed to Cowper by Southey and included in many later editions; in Milford pp. 288–9. Certainly the work of Robert Lloyd, as Bailey demonstrates (p. 666).

A THUNDER STORM

Eighty-six lines, beginning 'The Sky begins to lower and thick'ning Clouds'. First printed by Thomas Wright, *The Life of William Cowper*, 1892, pp. 177–9; in Milford, pp. 626–8. Bailey makes short work of Wright's attribution (p. 664).

THE WAITING SOUL

Twenty-four lines, beginning 'Breathe from the gentle South, O Lord'. See under *Olney Hymns*, no. 33.

PSALM 114th

Thirty-six lines, beginning 'When Israel by Jehovah call'd'. Found in the Madan family scrap-book (now Bodleian MS. eng. poet. c. 51) and first printed by [F. Madan], *New Poems by William Cowper*, 1931, pp. 13–15; in Milford, pp. 675–6. The version is headed in the scrapbook 'by Willm Cowper Esq.', but is in fact by Dean Spencer Madan (1713–74); it may possibly have been revised by Cowper. Cf. K. Povey, *Trans. Durham and Northumberland Architectural and Archaeological Soc.* xi (1958), 38.

INDEX OF TITLES

An asterisk indicates an alternative title.

INDEX OF FIRST LINES

An asterisk indicates a variant first line.

INDEX OF NAMES

This is a selective index of names of persons (and a few persons not named but clearly identifiable) appearing in the poetry. It is not an index to the Commentary.